Björn Wiemer, Barbara Sonnenhauser (Eds.)
Clausal Complementation in South Slavic

Trends in Linguistics Studies and Monographs

Editors
Chiara Gianollo
Daniël Van Olmen

Editorial Board
Walter Bisang
Tine Breban
Volker Gast
Hans Henrich Hock
Karen Lahousse
Natalia Levshina
Caterina Mauri
Heiko Narrog
Salvador Pons
Niina Ning Zhang
Amir Zeldes

Editor responsible for this volume
Daniël Van Olmen

Volume 361

Clausal Complementation in South Slavic

Edited by
Björn Wiemer, Barbara Sonnenhauser

DE GRUYTER
MOUTON

ISBN 978-3-11-126729-6
e-ISBN (PDF) 978-3-11-072585-8
e-ISBN (EPUB) 978-3-11-072593-3

Library of Congress Control Number: 2021941369

Bibliographic information published by the Deutsche Nationalbibliothek
The Deutsche Nationalbibliothek lists this publication in the Deutsche Nationalbibliografie;
detailed bibliographic data are available on the Internet at http://dnb.dnb.de.

© 2023 Walter de Gruyter GmbH, Berlin/Boston
This volume is text- and page-identical with the hardback published in 2022.
Typesetting: Integra Software Services Pvt. Ltd.
Printing and binding: CPI books GmbH, Leck

www.degruyter.com

Preface

This volume presents a collection of articles that share a focus on South Slavic languages and clausal complementation. They offer insights on this topic from various perspectives, taking up issues relevant not only for specialists of (South) Slavic languages, but also for the broader linguistic community interested in clause combining, areal linguistics, language contact, diachronic syntax and/or corpus linguistics. In their entirety, the studies assembled here cover the entire linguistic geography of South Slavic, including exclave varieties in Italy as well as contact with non-Slavic languages such as Albanian and Hungarian.

The volume arose from the workshop "Variation in space and time: clausal complementation in South Slavic," which was funded by the Swiss National Science Foundation and organized by the editors on March 17–19, 2016, at the University of Zurich. Most of the contributors to this volume were also participants in that workshop. We thank every author for their continued motivation to contribute to this joint endeavor, which, as we hope, will help establish directions for the study of clause combining, in particular of clausal complementation, in Slavic languages in a modern framework. We are also obliged to an anonymous reviewer who provided thoroughgoing and valuable comments on every article and to Giulia Morra for her assistance in creating the index. Moreover, we thank the publishing house De Gruyter and, in particular, the editors in charge of the TiLSM series for taking our volume on board.

Björn Wiemer & Barbara Sonnenhauser (Mainz / Zurich),
April 2021

Contents

Preface —— V

Chapter I: **Introduction**

Barbara Sonnenhauser and Björn Wiemer
Clausal complementation in South Slavic: Introduction —— 3

Chapter II: **Complementation structures**

Björn Wiemer
A general template of clausal complementation and its application to South Slavic: theoretical premises, typological background, empirical issues —— 29

Alexander Letuchiy
Clausal complements of certain nominalizations in Bulgarian: Relevant parameters —— 160

Iliyana Krapova
Complementizers and particles inside and outside of the left periphery: The case of Bulgarian revisited —— 211

Liljana Mitkovska and Eleni Bužarovska
Clausal complementation of visual perception verbs in Balkan Slavic —— 270

Chapter III: **Complementation in space**

Marc L. Greenberg
Antemurale innovationis: Clausal complementation in the Slovene Mura River (Prekmurje) dialect and its Balkan parallels —— 317

Walter Breu
Complementisers in language contact. The influence of Italian *che* on South Slavic and Albanian in Molise and beyond —— 342

Chapter IV: **Complementation in time**

Hanne Martine Eckhoff
The history of Slavonic clausal complementation: A corpus view —— 387

Jasmina Grković-Major
The development of emotion predicate complements in Serbian —— 415

Barbara Sonnenhauser
Slovene *naj*: An (emerging) clausal complementiser? —— 442

Author Bio Notes —— 477

Language index —— 481

Subject index —— 483

Chapter I: **Introduction**

Barbara Sonnenhauser and Björn Wiemer
Clausal complementation in South Slavic: Introduction

1 South Slavic as a test case for variation

The South Slavic area forms part of different zones of convergence and divergence, with intersecting isoglosses reflecting multiple language contacts: Bulgarian, Macedonian and East Serbian dialects belong to the so-called Balkan League (the *Balkan Sprachbund*, including also Albanian, Greek, and Rumanian), while Slovene has been related to a Central European Linguistic Area, which includes also Slovak, Czech, German, and Hungarian (cf. Newerkla 2007, Kurzová 2019); in-between we have the varieties of the Serbian-Croatian (mainly Štokavian) dialect continuum which are in many respects transitional. Whereas the *Sprachbund* notion is troublesome,[1] and will therefore be avoided, the complicated overlap of isogloss bundles testifies to a complex layering of intersecting dialectal clines and convergence with non-related contact languages. This situation is probably best characterized as a contact superposition zone (Koptjevskaja-Tamm and Wälchli 2001), which implies an intersection of convergence zones resulting from multiple overlaps of different continua (or smaller clusters).

Given their dialectal differentiation and the multitude of contact situations, the South Slavic languages are a particularly interesting test case for the analysis and systematization of linguistic diversity encountered within one language subfamily. One case in point is the variability in the patterns of clausal complementation. On the basis of exemplary studies, this volume gives insights into the systematicity of this variability from different theoretical, empirical and methodological points of view.[2]

---

[1] Cf. Nau (2012), Wiemer (2019a; 2021: 282) for critical discussions of 'linguistic areas' (with further references), Dedio, Ranacher, and Widmer (2019) for a methodological approach of how to gain evidence for linguistic areas. This approach has been applied to the Balkans – with a specific focus on Romance (within and outside the Balkans) – in Widmer, Dedio, and Sonnenhauser (2021).
[2] The basic ideas that are discussed in the papers gathered in this volume were first presented at the workshop "Variation in space and time: clausal complementation in South Slavic" (University

Barbara Sonnenhauser, University of Zurich, Switzerland, Slavisches Seminar, Plattenstrasse 43, CH-8032, Zürich, e-mail: barbara.sonnenhauser@uzh.ch
Björn Wiemer, Johannes-Gutenberg-Universität (Mainz, Germany), Institut für Slavistik, Turkologie und zirkumbaltische Studien (ISTziB), Jakob-Welder-Weg 18, 55099, Mainz, e-mail: wiemerb@uni-mainz.de

https://doi.org/10.1515/9783110725858-001

The highly complex and diverse linguistic picture of South Slavic brings with it two challenges for a description of clausal complementation: 1) capturing the variation on a systematic, empirical basis that allows for meaningful comparisons (see § 2), 2) assessing the potential causes that might have been contributing to this multifaceted picture (see § 3).

2 Patterns of clausal complementation

Clausal complementation is represented by "biclausal syntactic constructions in which the predicate of one clause "entails reference to another proposition or state of affairs" (Cristofaro 2003: 95), expressed in a second clause" (Schmidtke-Bode 2014: 7). This is certainly one of the shortest definitions given in the literature on clausal complementation. It contains some notions which are neither self-explaining nor unproblematic. For instance, the opposition between bi- and monoclausal units is anything but clear-cut (and probably forms a continuum) and no less dependent on theoretical premises than the distinction between states of affairs (SoAs) and propositions. Moreover, speaking of 'entailment of reference' has its syntactic corollary in the distinction of 'governed by' (argument) vs. 'supplementary' (adjunct), which is equally fuzzy.

In any case, and independent of discussions about categories, clausal complementation (CC) is a particularly complex phenomenon, since it consists of many components whose interaction is, to a large extent, still poorly understood. The main components to be considered for a comprehensive understanding of this interaction are captured by the template in Figure 1.

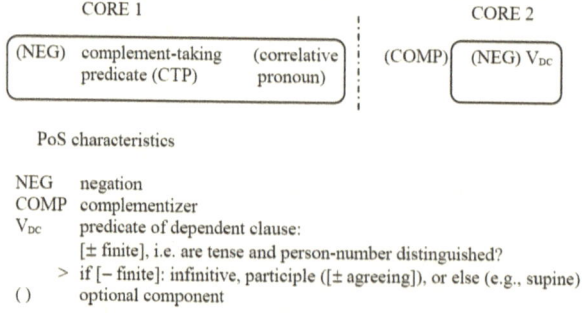

PoS characteristics

NEG   negation
COMP   complementizer
V_{DC} predicate of dependent clause:
        [± finite], i.e. are tense and person-number distinguished?
    >   if [– finite]: infinitive, participle ([± agreeing]), or else (e.g., supine)
( )   optional component

Figure 1: Maximum template of clausal complementation.

---

of Zurich, March 2016), funded by the Swiss National Science Foundation SNSF (grant number IZ32Z0_166419/1) and the University of Zurich *Hochschulstiftung* foundation.

This general template and the parameters included allow for a systematic, empirically based investigation of the structural conditions as well as the development and changes of CC as observed in the contemporary and historic varieties of South Slavic. It builds on the assumption that there are some necessary (or definitorial) properties, which correspond to Schmidtke-Bode's definition quoted above, and some additional properties which are typical, but not necessary, or which are necessary only under specific conditions or for specific phenomena. Thus, the template also includes properties which have been neglected in research, such as the PoS-characteristics of the complement-taking predicate. Moreover, it accounts for the often pivotal role of complementizers in indicating meaning differences that correlate with meaning alternations of complement-taking predicates, while simultaneously complementizers cannot be claimed to be a necessary component of clausal complementation. These considerations do not only make zero complementizers a questionable notion, but they leave space for the study of emergent complementizers and their variation (together with other complementizing structures) along a gradient from emergence to entrenchment. This template is elaborated and commented on systematically in Wiemer (this volume).

The internal diversity of CC has grown as a consequence of the stepwise replacement of infinitives by finite structures, with the diachronic stages of this process becoming manifest in the areal differentiation of contemporary South Slavic. The areal continuum stretches from the southeast (= Balkan Slavic), where the infinitive has disappeared as a form,[3] via the Štokavian (Serbian-Croatian) dialect continuum, where the infinitive as a form still exists, but the preferences for choosing infinitival or finite complements (plus an additional connective) differs (and the conditions are still poorly understood), up to the northwestern (Kajkavian) corner, i.e. mainly Slovene, where non-finite complements – including the supine – are still better attested than in the rest of South Slavic. This areal continuum corresponds to the diachronic direction of infinitive loss, which started in the southeast (cf. Joseph 1983; 2019). In general, the basic morphosyntactic isoglosses across South Slavic run on a southeast – northwest axis, although the hotbeds and directions of spread differ.[4] This is indicative of a more intricate

---

[3] Even if some Bulgarian varieties still show remnants of an abridged infinitive, this form is attested only in complex predicates, but not in clausal complementation proper (Wiemer, this volume: § 2.3.2).

[4] South Slavic dialect continua reflecting inner-Slavic development have been established on the basis of phonological and morphological isoglosses smoothly running in parallel (e.g., Ivić 1958: 32). It would be intriguing to establish whether these accepted isogloss bundles at any degree correspond to clines and the development of properties that are related to clausal complementation. Since infinitives and *da*-clauses play a prominent role in clausal complementation,

overlap between the regions for which particular areal features have been discussed at least since Sandfeld (1926), and internal South Slavic dialect continua, which started forming since, by the end of the 6th century AD, Slavic-speaking population settled on the Balkans and reached the Adriatic coast up to the southeastern branches of the Alps (cf. Holzer 2014: 1122); see further § 3.

In turn, the different degrees at which the infinitive has retreated (from change of preferences in favor of finite clauses to entire loss) are probably only the most prominent part of a general retreat of non-finite verb forms. Admittedly, Slavic languages have never frequently employed participles in clausal complementation; likewise, the supine, which is anyway preserved only in Slovene (apart from Lower Sorbian in the North Slavic area), is by its very function rather restricted to purpose clauses after verbs of directed movement.

Taken together, these considerations give an illustration why South Slavic is highly relevant for the complex question of how to differentiate the effects of language contact from those of family-internal developments, i.e. shared ancestry (cf. Widmer, Dedio, and Sonnenhauser 2021), and of universal tendencies; see further § 3.

Another well-known process which has led to an increase of internal differentiation in CC is the loss of irrealis restrictions of the central and most versatile connective element, namely *da*, in the western part of South Slavic. In areal terms, the preservation of the original irrealis function of *da* appears to be complementary to infinitive loss, as Balkan Slavic is not only most conservative in retaining the irrealis function of *da*, but also more innovative than the western part of South Slavic in establishing *da* as an ubiquitous connective on practically all levels of constituency (cf. Wiemer 2018: 295–306, Sonnenhauser and Widmer 2020). This enormous spread has been concomitant to the restructuring of strict rules of clitic placement typical for all South Slavic languages. However, only in Balkan Slavic has *da* consistently been integrated into verb-oriented clusters of proclitics, by which it has participated in the partial morphologization of clitics (Spencer and Luís 2012: 59–65, 124–126, 153–157). Remarkably, one may even assume that by this very process the evolution of *da* as a complementizer has been precluded (cf. Wiemer, this volume: § 2.2.3, for a justification). By contrast, in the middle part of South Slavic (the Štokavian area) *da* shows a split of distributional patterns concerning not only its behavior as a clitic (vs. clause-initial connective),

---

it is plausible to assume that some such correlation should exist. However, in view of the lack of reliable data required for a sensible diachronic interpretation of contemporary isoglosses and clines such an endeavor would not be an easy task. Apart from that, there are a lot of understudied phenomena related to clausal complementation which until now have not made it into focal topics of research in South Slavic (or Balkan linguistics).

but also constraints (vs. their lack) on admissible TAM forms. In Slovene, in turn, even these constraints appear to be loosened (Wiemer, this volume: § 2.2.3, for a comprehensive treatment). In contrast to the rather "unidirectional" areal cline, it is less clear where the loss of irrealis restrictions of *da* began; the most probable "candidates" are the northwestern end (early Slovene, Kajkavian) and the Adriatic coast (Čakavian); cf. Grković-Major (2004; 2020) and Greenberg (this volume). In either case, language contact (with German, Vulgar Latin or Italian, respectively) can be assumed to have been a catalyst of this process.

Apart from these most prominent examples, an increase of internal South Slavic differentiation has ensued from other phenomena. The replacement of the old subjunctive (or conditional), based on *bi* (< Common Slavic *byti* 'be'), by *da*-constructions and their interaction with the complex tense-aspect system in Balkan Slavic has yielded new preferred manners of expressing hypothetical or otherwise irreal situations (e.g., the Macedonian future/expectative marker *ќe* in combination with the imperfect) that are encountered in all kinds of complex sentences. This contrasts with the continued interaction of the old conditional marker with clause-initial connectives in the northwestern corner of South Slavic (compare *da+bi* in Slovene), which reminds us of North Slavic (Topolińska 2003). Another phenomenon to be considered is the different distribution and spread of specialized factive complementizers, i.e. of complementizers which introduce logically presupposed propositions (compare *što* in Serbian-Croatian and Macedonian). Such complementizers are intimately connected to causal conjunctions, both in their individual histories (Grković-Major, this volume) and in micro-areal patterns due to language contact (Breu, this volume), although not all causal connectives, while evolving into complementizers, keep a factivity requirement; for instance, Bulg. *če* most probably originated from a causal connective (Sonnenhauser 2015: 46), but it is now predominantly used as neutral (or default) complementizer. Furthermore, even though they have remained one of the most understudied domains in complementation in South Slavic, contrasts of factual vs. non-factual complements[5] after predicates with propositional complements (i.e. those related to knowledge or belief, or related to speech acts) are particularly interesting, since patterns vary not only between most closely related languages (e.g., Bulgarian and Macedonian), but also for the means chosen and the

---

[5] This contrast deals with the strength of epistemic support (for propositional complements) and the distinction between SoA (= non-factual, e.g. purpose or embedded deontic clauses) and propositional complements (as objects of epistemic assessment). Factuality must not be confused with factivity; the latter is here taken to refer only to complements with logically presupposed propositional content (e.g., *He regrets / doesn't regret that P*, P is presupposed). For clarification cf. Wiemer (this volume: § 2.2.2).

verbs (or other predicative units) that allow for a meaningful choice of clausal connectives. For instance, while Bulgarian and Macedonian basically share a possibility to distinguish between strong and weak epistemic support for the content of propositional complements, namely by choosing *da* (weak support) vs. Bulg. *če*/Mac. *deka* (strong support), the particular complement-taking predicates (CTPs) which favor (or disfavor) *da* in case of weak support can differ. In addition, one has to consider the relation of these connectives to Mac. *kako*/Bulg. *kak*, which can introduce either SoA or propositional complements, and the impact of negation. Negation generally weakens epistemic support for those CTPs which otherwise indicate strong support. Since complements are entailed by CTPs (see above), changes in the degree of epistemic support also have an impact on the assessment of the content of propositional complements of belief-related CTPs. This explains phenomena known as negative concord or NEG-raising (e.g., *She believes that P* vs. *She doesn't believe that P* ≅ *She believes that not-P*).[6] As a rule, differences of complementizer choice between languages (or varieties on a lower taxonomical level) become seizable not just by contrasting singular examples, but as a stochastic tendency (whose functional underpinnings need to be explained). This is shown by Mitkovska and Bužarovska's (this volume) analysis of variation among complements of verbs of visual perception, with their extensions into epistemic uses, in Macedonian and Bulgarian. Therefore, usage-based accounts (usually with corpus data) are indispensable to grasp differences that exist even between closely related languages (or varieties). They are also indispensable for "empirical checks" of assumptions made, for instance, in formal semantics, such as Giannakidou and Mari's (2016) proposal of (non)veridicality in the assertion or presupposition of the CTP to influence the choice of subjunctive or indicative complements and the different parametrization even among closely related languages. This, of course, is true not only for marking epistemic distance, but also in all concerns whenever variation matters. Such data-driven approaches in turn require a reasonable amount of data – which is still a challenge for South Slavic varieties – edited in a maximally theory-neutral way such that diatopic and diachronic comparison becomes possible (cf. Eckhoff, this volume).

From an areal point of view, the certainly most salient (though still little known) division in the choice of clause connectives for marking propositional complements against which the speaker distances themselves is Sln. *naj* (< *nehati 'let') in relation to its cognate *neka* in the remainder of South Slavic (and *n(i)ech* in West Slavic).

---

[6] Cf. Wiemer (this volume: § 2.1, § 2.2.4). For analogous findings in North Slavic cf. Dobrushina (2012, Russian), Wiemer (2015, Polish), Hansen, Letuchiy, and Błaszczyk (2016, Russian, Polish). For a general discussion cf. Kehayov and Boye (2016: 818–824).

While Sln. *naj* shows properties of an emerging complementizer which suspends propositional content (Sonnenhauser, this volume), its South Slavic cognates can hardly be treated as complementizers, although they also are used in contexts with suspended propositions. Moreover, the epistemic functions of these complementizers are probably diachronically secondary, as, in all likelihood, they derive from uses in directive speech acts, in deontic contexts and in purpose clauses. Therefore, a comparative analysis of Sln. *naj* and its South (and West) Slavic cognates promises to reveal reliable insights into the developmental paths from causative verbs ('let, allow', etc.) to clausal connectives, up to complementizers, and their diachronic relation to auxiliaries. This comparison should be extended to other causative constructions, among them those based on *da* + present indicative (on which see above).

The relation between clausal connectives and auxiliaries brings us to the question of how clausal complementation relates to mood marking, in particular where both meet (see below). By a similar token, the investigation of *naj* and its cognates vis-à-vis the diachronic development of *da* as an ubiquitous connective of clauses and within complex predicates would probably yield insights allowing for more reliable generalizations concerning the relation between epistemic distancing, on the one hand, and directive speech acts and deontic modality, on the other. In the case of both *da* and *naj*, as indicated above, their employment to mark suspended propositions (epistemic distancing, weak epistemic support or indirect evidentiality) obviously only followed on more original employment in more "interactive" contexts of speech (and these more original usage types are still encountered frequently). This looks like another instance of subjectification (as introduced by Traugott 1989 and subsequent work); however, the tight entrenchment with syntax experienced by *da* and *naj* on different levels of constituency (and with different ranges of variability) as well as their obviously complementary areal distribution and different age provide us with an ideal starting point for the study of repeated similar (though not identical) developmental paths in the confines of one language subfamily. Moreover, *da* and *naj* show that, although uses in propositional complements appear to have emerged only at later stages, this development did not preclude their employment as complementizers, i.e. in tighter structures of clause combining. That is, we observe syntactic tightening in parallel to widening of semantic scope (from directive, or goal-directed, speech acts to subjective judgments regarding propositional content). This is remarkable inasmuch as widening of semantic scope is concomitant to, or even implied by, the Traugottian notion of subjectification, while simultaneously it seems to be unfavorable for the tightening of syntactic scope. This seeming contradiction has been the reason why the scope criterion has been neglected in grammaticalization research, to an extent that it recently has been excluded from an attempt at quantifying effects of change associated with grammaticalization in Bisang et al.

(2020). Obviously, there still is a principled point to be made for the relationship between syntactic and semantic scope (and associated changes), for which the study of clausal complementation can provide fruitful theoretical insights, and we find a particularly rich empirical basis for this kind of study in South Slavic.

However one may decide on the chronology and probable connections between the issues mentioned so far, we recognize that South Slavic, in particular its eastern part, supplies a playground for research in the relation between clausal complementation and non-indicative mood, provided the latter is conceived of as a clause-level distinction (not as a distinction of verbal morphology). Simultaneously, this issue is but a manifestation of a broader phenomenon characteristic especially of Balkan Slavic, namely the rise of a systematic architecture of periphrastic verb forms, based on the *l*-participle[7] and various auxiliary elements (of which *da* is but one). These periphrastic forms have been bones of contention when it comes to delimiting from each other morphology and syntax. On the one hand, these forms can be shown to take part in the formation of complex paradigms; as such they are usually presented in standard grammars and handbooks on Balkan Slavic verb morphology, but see also analyses with a more far-reaching theoretical appeal as the one in Spencer (2003). On the other hand, since these complex forms are used productively and the composition of their parts (auxiliary elements + lexical verb) is to a large degree compositional, claims to treat them as part of syntax cannot be dismissed *a priori*; cf. Spencer and Popova (2015: 214–227) and Sims and Joseph (2019) for elaborate discussion. Again, whatever side one may take, the architecture of the morphology – syntax interface of South Slavic, in particular Balkan Slavic, languages is extraordinarily rich in "objects" to be considered with scrutiny, also for the relevant diachronic facts, and valuable for crosslinguistic comparison. Morever, these objects intersect with phenomena belonging to clausal complementation, namely with those that demonstrate a tighter conceptual connection (or even dependence) between the involved predicative nuclei (as on the high-integration end of semantic integration scales; cf. Wiemer, this volume: § 2.1).

The selected examples discussed in this section surely show that South Slavic is extraordinarily rich in internally differentiated patterns of CC. Obviously, a thorough and methodologically well-considered examination of the different patterns, both in terms of structure and usage, can cast light on many issues that have been hotly debated in more general research on CC beyond this particular subgroup of languages (see § 5).

---

[7] The *l*-participle originally marked the lexical verb in the periphrastic perfect (including the pluperfect and the future perfect). It still is used in this way for periphrastic tense forms, but only in Balkan Slavic has it preserved its original perfect functions, while in the remainder (again along a southeast – northwest cline) we observe a shift from perfect to general past. For the general background cf. Meermann and Sonnenhauser (2016), Arkadie vand Wiemer (2020).

3 Common heritage, areality, universal tendencies

Since here we are emphasizing the internal differentiation of South Slavic languages and already have pointed at some diachronic tendencies applying to this subfamily in general or to some part of it, we can hardly avoid raising the issue of what has caused the changes leading to this differentiation. Concomitantly, one may ask how these changes, and the variation behind them, can be systematicized and which methods and tools should be employed to approach them.

The first issue, about factors and mechanisms of change, practically amounts to an equilibration of factors that favor (or impede) change and convergence between genealogically unrelated languages. Such an equilibration can be conceived of as methodological triangulation, inasmuch as three groups of factors and angles have been separated in areal typology and related disciplines, namely: (i) provenance from common ancestor languages, (ii) areal neighborhood (usually leading to language contact), and (iii) general cognitive and communicative principles, which have been considered responsible for Greenbergian markedness relations (Croft 2009) and which are often referred to as 'universal tendencies' (Heine and Kuteva 2005). Triangulation in this sense has been suggested and, to some extent, elaborated on in Wiemer, Seržant, and Erker (2014) and Wiemer (2019a), with respect to clausal complementation in Wiemer (2018).[8]

A major problem with triangulating phenomena related to CC arises from the fact that inner-South Slavic synchronic clines and isoglosses often cannot be interpreted diachronically in a straightforward manner. That is, it is particularly difficult to put particular phenomena in chronogical order, all the more as usually these phenomena are gradable (in terms of spread on a diatopic or diastractic axis, in terms of variation with concurrent patterns, and probably in other regards). Moreover, change, as a rule, starts from minor or covert patterns, so that it is desirable to estimate increase in frequency and loss of constraints. Furthermore, we would like to know whether the spread of particular phenomena relates to non-linguistic factors, such as socio-cultural circumstances, e.g. more remarkable migration waves. In addition, we have to assess the likelihood that changes might not have occurred spontaneously, i.e. without some more remarkable "external" trigger, exactly because variation with minor patterns may always be assumed to exist. This applies in particular to spontaneous discourse in non-standardized varieties. For instance, consider the prominent example of the infinitive and its

---

8 Ranacher et al. (2021) propose a Bayesian clustering algorithm to detect geographic contact areas in language data in the presence of inheritance and universal preference as confounding effects. One of their case studies is the Balkans.

gradual replacement by finite structures, especially in complementation and other subordinate clauses: in order to assess the role of contact (against "internally" motivated change) we, strictly speaking, need to know how widespread finite structures have been prior to their spread in disfavor of the infinitive in the speech communities under consideration; and we need to know more about the overall distribution of these concurrent patterns of clause structures in a much larger, surrounding area.

This said, i.e. apart from the aforementioned three "angles", we must not neglect the impact exerted by meta-linguistic factors. Such factors usually become more palpable not in a diatopic, but in a diastratic or diaphasic dimension (in Coseriu's 1988 terms). They surface particularly in standardisation, accompanied by the influence of grammar writing following prestigious models. Prescriptive efforts aiming at differentiation at the expenses of variation or decisions motivated by considerations of language policy may have led to a differentiation on the level of the standard languages that is not necessarily observed for the spoken (urban and dialectal) varieties. In the Balkan Slavic context, this can be seen, e.g., on the discussions concerning the usage of the 'long' and 'short' article for masculine singular nouns (Fielder 2019). Another relevant factor is the dialectal basis chosen for the standard language. Consider, for instance, the Slovene relative pronoun *kdor*, which appears in the contemporary standard language as specialised marker for free relative clauses, but is unknown in the eastern dialects (Sonnenhauser 2019). This consideration makes the investigation of non-standard and historical data an even more urgent requirement. To our knowledge, clausal complementation has so far hardly been studied from this angle in South Slavic.

Meta-linguistic factors often have to do with dialect levelling under the influence of some roof variety, but also more fundamentally with speech habits guided by the awareness of implicit norms.[9] More particularly, linguistic behavior can be tailored to the communicative needs of multilingual (or "multivarietal") speaker communities which are highly heterogeneous as for individual speakers' competence in the particular languages involved in multilateral contact. Such situations create particular communicative pressure to make one's intention clear. On this background, Topolińska (2008 [1994]) even ventured a hypothesis according to which some of the so-called Balkanisms are more or less direct outcomes of communicative requirements posed by intensive multilateral contact. According to this hypothesis, these conditions favored the rise of means which enable speakers to ease disambiguation of reference or to mark the reality status

---

9 Cf. Wiemer (2021) for a survey of motives leading to structural convergence and research seeking to disclose these motives.

of denoted events. It concerns, first of all, such prominent Balkanisms like the definite article, clitic doubling and the evidential extensions of the perfect, but – provided such a hypothesis can be tested – one may well add choices of complementation devices triggered by realis vs. irrealis contrasts (see § 2). Convergence as for means that are sensitive to such functionally motivated choices never arise out of the blue; instead they must have existed at least as minor choices in an "inventory" of variants for the expression of particular communicative means, before they started being preferred for one reason or other. This reason can be the largest common denominator in a multilingual speech community, but the other two angles mentioned above (genealogical heritage and general tendencies) should not be dismissed. In fact, these different motives can work in conspiracy, so that it is often difficult or impossible to disentangle them.

The situation on the Balkans is additionally complicated by the fact that, despite Ottoman Turkic hegemony for many centuries, none of the "autochthonous" Balkan languages dominated over the others. There was, thus, no process of creolization (in contrast to so-called New Englishes; cf. Trudgill 2006, Ziegeler 2017). Rather, what we observe amounts to metatypy, i.e. "the wholesale restructuring of a language's semantic and syntactic structures as a result of language contact" (Heine and Kuteva 2005: 180).[10] Metatypy leads to isomorphism, which favors intertranslatability (cf. Gołąb 1990, Lindstedt 2000, among many others). It relies on the calquing of grammatical contrasts (PAT-borrowing) and often involves massive loan translations (including polysemy copying), but no re-lexification or MAT-borrowing.[11] However, below the surface, substantial differences in detail may appear concerning the extent to which these general structures apply and the specific morphosyntactic means employed, relating, among others, to specific language-internal conditions or different starting points of converging developments (Sonnenhauser and Widmer 2020, Joseph 2001). As concerns South Slavic in its entirety, the history of its varieties abounds in changes of political and economic authorities and of concomitant borders of states, or other administrative units. This brought about changes in non-Slavic and Slavic roof varieties, sometimes cutting across "indigenous" territories in the South Slavic dialect continuum. A good example in case is the Torlak variety, which was divided by the political boundaries established at the end of the 19th century and has since then been under the influence of different standard languages (Balkan Slavic Bulgarian/Macedonian and West South Slavic Serbian); cf. Vuković (2000; 2021). Such

---

10 The term was originally coined by Ross (1996; 2007, among other publications) to characterize complex contact situations (and their results) in New Guinea.
11 On the distinction between PAT- and MAT-borrowing cf. Matras (2007) and Sakel (2007). Polysemy copying in South Slavic clausal complementation is analyzed by Breu (this volume).

an administrative-political "to and fro" also conditioned a rather late onset of standardization processes.

Thus, enormous structural diversity has been caused to a large degree by changing ethnographic and political circumstances during the last 1,500 years, which have left traces on formal and functional differentiation in patterns and the variability of CC in South Slavic languages. This differentiation has remained understudied, since, except for Balkanisms and the "*da*-split" caused by loss of irrealis features beyond Balkan Slavic (see § 2), phenomena related to CC have been treated rather promiscuously and unsystematically, if not for particular languages, so at least on a general South Slavic background, let alone in comparison to North Slavic. For instance, only recently have phenomena related to the "*da*-split" been considered another Balkanism by Topolińska (1997) and Ammann and van der Auwera (2004). As explained above, this split provides a neat illustration of how Balkan features intersect with the South Slavic dialect continuum (reflected in the standard languages), but it also shows the need for scrutiny in its diachronic assessment, not only on a South Slavic, but a general Slavic backdrop (cf. Wiemer 2017: 325–330; 2018: 293–306; 2019b: 120–127). To sum up, broader typological comparisons have been drawn only with respect to features considered Balkanisms. Apart from that, so far no serious attempts have been undertaken in triangulating the motives of change and the resulting differentiation on a diatopic, diastratic and a diaphasic level, and to relate them to meta-linguistic factors.

We thereby have come to the issue of systematisation. The high diversity of structures relevant for CC in South Slavic has remained a weak point in research, and this unsatisfying state of the arts is accompanied by problems in data collection and processing, predominantly in corpora. It is in general very difficult to find a sufficiently unified methodology and to apply a reasonably defined set of comparable categorial distinctions. One promising approach is a strictly decompositional one, as applied in Šimko (2020) for the development of definiteness marking in 17th to 19th century Damaskini texts. This point also raises the question of how corpora should be annotated (Eckhoff, this volume).

4 The contributions to this volume

The contributions to this volume cover the entire South Slavic territory. Most contributions focus on particular aspects of complementation, a large part deals with the contemporary standard languages Slovene, Serbian, Bulgarian, and Macedonian, while others focus on older stages and/or non-standard varieties and the impact of language contact, primarily with non-Slavic languages. They all present in-depth studies and thus contribute to an overarching collective aim, which consists in a comprehensive picture of the patterns of CC on which South Slavic languages profile against a wider typological background, but also diverge internally if we look closer at details in the contemporary stage and in diachronic development. We thus hope to set some standards in methodological approaches to the empirical investigation of CC not only in South Slavic, but also beyond this subfamily. The general goals to be envisaged can be divided into the following three issues:

(a) Determining the components and parameters which distinguish different patterns of CC and characterize their particular components. This implies a critical evaluation and treatment of notions involved in the analysis of CC.
(b) Elaborating on the factors which have led to particular CC patterns in sub-areas of South Slavic and which thus have been contributing to the complex picture of clausal complementation in this subfamily.
(c) Problems that need to be met when it comes to the classification of data on the basis of corpora and other resources.

The individual papers assembled in this volume make profound contributions to many of these issues by examining different parts of the template given in Figure 1. By taking this template as a common point of reference, the articles help establish a structured inventory of forms and functions of CC in South Slavic from a diachronic and diatopic perspective. The papers complement each other in their sources of data, which is partially explained by their different focus on diachronic or contemporary varieties, and on language contact or on accounts of single languages.

Apart from this introduction, the volume is divided into three parts whose contributions primarily focus, respectively, on the typology and parameters of CC structures (Part II), on the dispersion of CC patterns in geographical space (Part III), and on the dispersion of CC patterns in diachrony or in earlier stages (Part IV).

Part II starts with the article by **Björn Wiemer**. It is meant to set the stage for a comprehensive treatment of clausal complementation in South Slavic. It develops a general template for CC constructions reproduced above as Figure 1 and distinguishes its separate components. Since capturing CC implies a couple of notions which are complex themselves, these notions are surveyed first, before the different components of the template are assessed one after another on the basis of South Slavic material. Although the focus here is on the contemporary stage, some "excurses" into diachrony are inevitable, in particular as concerns the infinitive and other non-finite forms and the spread of *da*-constructions. As for the latter, some considerable part of the survey deals with the relation between complementation devices indicating a non-factual (= irrealis) status of the complements and non-indicative mood (in particular the so-called 'analytical subjunctives'). The analysis includes a critical assessment of the state of the arts in this domain for South Slavic. It shows why clause-initial connectives and verb-oriented proclitics (united under the label of 'complementation devices')[12] fulfil a central role in CC especially in South Slavic and why, consequently, their differentiated treatment is of particular importance. This includes special attention to emergent patterns and the issue why some such patterns make it into entrenched structures (of the respective language), while others do not. Apart from metatheoretical discussion, the comprehensive data-driven step-by-step analysis of the components of the CC template is meant as a proposal of how to provide a consistent and systematic analysis of CC, for which the empirical situation in modern South Slavic is only a convenient starting point, but which might be applied further in broader cross-linguistic comparison.

Alexander Letuchiy presents a corpus-based case study of complement clauses with nominal attachment sites in Bulgarian. The central question behind this study is why the distribution of clausal complements with nominal heads differs from the distribution of the same type of complements after cognate verbs. Letuchiy considers a variety of syntactic and semantic factors, both in the complement and the complement-taking predicate. He observes that Grimshaw's (1990) traditional account of action nouns based on syntactic and actional classes of verbs is insufficient to explain the encountered distributional biases in Bulgarian corpus data. His main conclusion is that, among a battery of heterogeneous factors, the main parameter appears to be the opposition of situation proper vs. occurrence, which is close to, but not identical with the distinction between state of affairs (SoA) and proposition (which has been pronounced, first and foremost, in Boye and Kehayov 2016). This parameter also closely interacts with the known parameter of actional classes, but differences in semantic role relations prove important as well. In general, Letuchiy's analysis strongly supports the claim for multifactorial approaches to explaining different (dis)preferences and types of clausal complements with verbal vs. nominal attachment sites.

Iliyana Krapova analyzes the Bulgarian declarative complementizer *če* 'that' and the interrogative complementizers *dali* and *li* 'if/whether'. She argues in favor of a Split CP approach, according to which the left periphery of embedded clauses (in particular of complement clauses) can provide slots for more than a single complementizer (C position). She thereby develops arguments of Rizzi (1997, and subsequent publications) in favor of an ordering hierarchy of

---

[12] The term is here adopted from Boye and Kehayov (2016).

complementizers within the same clause. In particular, Krapova finds evidence for a stable ordering of *dali/li* (COMP1) preceding *če* (COMP2); for the former she proposes an additional projection (VeridP) which takes the latter (FinP) into its scope. She argues that such an account is more suitable for explaining both this order and the interpretation of the involved connectives in view of some yet badly understood interaction between complementizers and Topic or Focus phrases. Concomitantly, Krapova discusses evidence in support of regarding *da* as a "modal particle" situated lower in the constituency tree and, thus, in a functional domain closer to the predicate of the dependent clause.

Liljana Mitkovska and **Eleni Bužarovska** inquire into the variation of complementation patterns for the basic verbs of visual perception in contemporary Standard Macedonian and Standard Bulgarian (Mac. *gleda/vidi*, Bulg. *gledam, viždam/vidja*). For this purpose they submit large representative samples to an in-depth analysis. Following Dik and Hengeveld (1991), the authors propose a threefold division capturing the relation between visual perception and knowledge states: immediate perception, mental perception triggered by visual experience (called 'primary mental perception'), and knowledge obtained by inference from direct physical evidence (called 'secondary mental perception'). These semantic distinctions are mapped onto the employment of Mac. *kako, deka, da* and Bulg. *kak, če, da* as complementation devices. The authors find that, in general, the threefold semantic division matches with the opposition between *kak(o)* and *deka/če*, but they also disclose a broader distribution for Mac. *kako* (vs. *deka*) in comparison to Bulg. *kak* (vs. *če*). This is interpreted as indicative of primary mental perception occupying an intermediary position between the two other conceptual configurations, but also as evidence that in Bulgarian the opposition between immediate and mental perception tends to be blurred. As for *da*, the data shows that in both languages this marker is used consistently not only after negated verbs of visual perception, but also in certain expressive contexts. However, unlike in Bulgarian, where *da* is frequently employed for immediate perception, in Macedonian its occurrence is restricted to mental perception.

The two contributions of Part III are united by their focus on locally restricted non-standard varieties and the impact of contact, mainly with non-Slavic varieties. Based on diverse textual sources and grammars available for different periods, **Marc L. Greenberg** investigates the evolution of the opposition between *da* and *ka* used as complementizers in Prekmurje Slovene, a non-standard variety of Slovene at the northern periphery of South Slavic which for a long time has been, and partially still is, under Hungarian rule. What strikes the eye is that, by the early 20th century, in Prekmurje Slovene *da* was used as an irrealis connective (vs. *ka* for realis contexts), which set it apart from the rest of western South Slavic (including the remaining Slovene varieties) and brought it close to Balkan

Slavic. More specifically, "there are at least two distinctions operating with the *ka:da* contrast, one opposing real vs. irreal and another opposing description vs. emotion/evaluation"; this very much resembles the situation in contemporary Bulgarian (see above). Nonetheless, the author concludes that the origin of the irrealis feature of *da* in Prekmurje Slovene must have been independent from Balkan Slavic, first of all because the loss of irrealis function for *da* must have reached the northern periphery of South Slavic already by the 11th century. Moreover, the later opposition between *da+bi* (IRR+conditional) vs. *ka* broke down in the second half of the 20th century in favor of *ka*, which thereby became the default complementizer. Given the fact that the remainder of Slovene has generalized *da* as default complementizer, the question arises why Prekmurje Slovene went another way, even if contact with central Slovene had not been interrupted. The author suggests that linguistic identity, i.e. the desire to distinguish it from Standard Slovene, may have affected the choice among alternatives in usage.

The contribution by **Walter Breu** presents a consistent analysis of complementizers and complementation structures in South Slavic (Molise Slavic, Resian) and Albanian (Italo-Albanian) minority dialects in Italy. It thus has a dedicated focus on recent and ongoing language contact outside the "indigenous" South Slavic and Albanian territory, with a due account of the diachronic backdrop; it thereby makes a pronounced contribution to methodological triangulation (see § 3). The main body of data derives from personal fieldwork, but data from other sources are accounted for as well, first of all since the author provides a systematic comparison with Standard Croatian (and other varieties of the BCMS-group), Standard Slovene, Standard Albanian and Italian (standard and dialects). Clausal complementation is analysed in connection with relative and causal clauses (and the interrogative pronoun 'what'), as these are well-attested sources of complement clauses. In particular, the Italian connective *che* functions in all of these domains. The author shows this connective to have been the basis of different cases of PAT-borrowing, or of polysemy copying, in the aforementioned minority languages, although in every single variety this process has yielded slightly different results. Moreover, Molise Slavic and Resian have PAT-borrowed the Italian pattern of opposing factual and non-factual (more precisely: intentional) complements. Only in Molise have the Slavic and Albanian varieties MAT-borrowed It. *che*, however with different functional range. The consistent comparison of diverse replica varieties and their Italian model varieties brings to light also some implicational relationships. For instance, if the relativizer is borrowed, it also functions as a complementizer, but not vice versa.

Part IV unites articles with a focus on historical varieties and/or diachronic change. **Hanne Eckhoff** makes a corpus-driven contribution to the study of changes in dominant complementation patterns in Old Church Slavonic (OCS, a South Slavic variety) compared to the earliest attested stages of East Slavic and of Middle Russian. Simultaneously, she contributes to an assessment of the explanatory potential of electronic diachronic corpora and of methodological pitfalls hidden in probably any kind of syntactically annotated corpus. The corpora used belong to the PROIEL and TOROT treebanks (see https://proiel.github.io/, Haug and Jøhndal 2008, Eckhoff and Berdicevskis 2015). The author addresses the problem of ambiguous dependency relations: how can clausal complementation be identified if the syntactic relation between a clause-initial connective and a preceding predicative expression (as a potential complement-taking predicate) and a verb in its own clause is not clear? A particular case in point is OCS *jako*, among other units which can be variably classified as "particle", interrogative pronoun, adverb, or else. Eckhoff performs two case studies. The first is carried out on texts belonging to the canonical body of OCS, for which interannotator agreement and retrievability are shown to work well, provided one knows how to make use of annotation conventions. The second examines the history of East Slavic *čьto* 'what, which, that' and illustrates how one can tackle with a clause-combining element in the course of diachronic change.

Jasmina Grković-Major provides a comprehensive survey of complementation patterns of emotion predicates in the history of Serbian, with a particular concern for disentangling internal and external factors of change. She thereby makes a dedicated contribution to methodological triangulation (see § 3). Her considerations are embedded into the broader issue of how transitivity and configurationality got on shape in ancient stages of Indo-European languages and how the continued strengthening of configurational syntax became manifest in the history of Serbian (on a general Slavic background). Special attention is paid to complements of factive predicates, since there is a tight conceptual relation between presupposed propositions and their emotional evaluation, together with a link to causality. This explains the prominent role of causal conjunctions as sources of factive complementizers (e.g., Serb. *jer(e)*, *što*). Concomitantly, the author emphasizes the significance of different waves of innovation which overlapped in the Serbian territory and which led to its transitional properties between typical Balkan features (*da*-clauses as non-factual complements) and innovations which spread from the west and southwest (a factive – non-factive split in the complementizer system), together with a continued spread of realis uses of *da*-clauses at the expense of *što*-clauses (as specialized markers of factivity).

Barbara Sonnenhauser's study on Sln. *naj* is devoted to a chapter in the most recent history of Slovene. The highly versatile element *naj* can function as an auxiliary in complex predicates denoting hortative or permissive speech acts, and also as a propositional particle marking epistemic distance and reportive evidentiality. In addition, it may function as a subordinative conjunction introducing purpose clauses, and it has been analysed as behaving like an emergent complementizer. Based both on systematic corpus queries and a perusal of contemporary and historical grammars of Slovene, Sonnenhauser traces the flexible semantic and syntactic behaviour of *naj* in order to eventually assess the degrees to which *naj* displays functions that can be considered typical of complementizers. Thereby, the paper also touches upon the question as to how such functions can be identified without ready-made categorical notions and distinctions that are in themselves problematic (see § 2). It proposes to start from the most general function complementizer-like elements assume, i.e. the marking of a particular element or structure as part of a larger syntactic unit, and decomposes it into smaller-scale features. The latter include an element's potential of building up hierarchical predicational structures, its ability to fill in a valency slot of a verbal or nominal structure, and its not being available as a target of agreement. While an elaboration of this proposal remains a task for the future, the results of the empirical analysis suggest that, while sharing its functional origin with its cognates in other South Slavic (and in West Slavic) languages, *naj* has advanced considerably further toward becoming a clausal subordinator (see § 2). In this way, the paper contributes to uncovering in more detail the variety of strategies of clausal complementation encountered in the South Slavic languages and the diversity in the underlying diachronic processes.

5 Relevance beyond Slavic

As suggested by our state-of-the-arts report and the survey of contributions, this volume not only provides insights for Slavic linguistics, but also contributes in at least three respects to more general debates in linguistics: (i) formal and functional aspects of clause linkage, (ii) factors involved in language change and areal clustering, and (iii) questions related to data processing.

(i) Clause linkage

One very general problem underlying theoretical approaches to the diversity of South Slavic CC, which is shared by virtually all types of analysis, consists in the fact that CC is not only a multifaceted phenomenon (Kehayov and Boye 2016), but in addition a still not very well-defined notion. As a consequence, research on CC makes use of diverse concepts and covers quite different structures, forms and functions. Among the main issues to be clarified are the semantic and syntactic features of CTPs, the morphosyntactic status and provenance of complementizers, the relation between matrix and dependent clause, the morphosyntactic shape of clausal complements, and the properties of the predicate in the dependent clause. These questions are closely related to the delimitation of complementation structures from other types of clause linkage (such as relative or adverbial clauses) and more integrated structures (such as control and raising structures, or complex predicates). Such issues are primarily addressed in Wiemer (this volume) in connection with a general template of clausal complementation, which is also meant as a basis of crosslinguistic comparison.

(ii) Language change
The synchronic variation found among complementation structures is the result of manifold diachronic processes. As far as we can judge from the earliest written sources, the development started off from a restricted set of explicit connectives between clauses, and neither these nor distinctions of mood or finite – non-finite contrasts mapped onto more clear-cut functional distinctions along a coordination (or juxtaposition) – subordination cline; in particular, the status of clause connectives concerning this cline was diffuse. An increase in the formal inventory and the functional possibilities can be observed as the written documents get more and more diversified in terms of linguistic varieties and in terms of functional styles, with the emergence of vernacular patterns in written media playing an important role. One case in point is the employment of *če* alongside *kako* in 17th–18th century Balkan Slavic texts, which can be related to the development of literary styles (Sonnenhauser 2015). Similarly, emerging norms spreading with influential and widespread media might suggest a diachronic development that actually is a genre-based diffusion and stabilization of one specific option (cf. Sonnenhauser 2019 for the Slovene relative pronoun *kdor*). Therefore, in addition to triangulation (see § 3) an evaluation of the paths of development has to take into account standard and non-standard data and consider the possible impact of genres, registers and styles. For all these aspects, different kinds of contact scenarios need to be considered: inner-Slavic and areal, oral and literary contact as well as contact mediated by translation. Sketching this interaction of internal development, external contact and meta-linguistic influences is a challenge not only for an analysis of the formal and functional development of CC patterns, but for accounts of language change in general.

(iii) Corpus linguistics
The diversity encountered among complementation structures and the frequent polyfunctionality (or heterosemy) of complementizers is a challenge for the collection of data and their processing in corpora, in particular as concerns the annotation of (potential) complementizers and complement taking predicates, and the mapping of form and function (cf. Haug and Eckhoff 2011 and Eckhoff, this volume, for a discussion of Old Church Slavonic and early East Slavic). The development of a compatible format for approaching the data and the application of tools adequate for the investigation of CC tie up with current debates in

corpus linguistics, in particular on annotation schemas for non-standard and transitional varieties (cf., e.g., Vuković 2021 for Torlak, Vuković et al. 2019 for the development of an annotation scheme encompassing diachronic and diatopic transitional Balkan and South Slavic varieties) as well as in typology, in particular as concerns the status of linguistic categories as comparative or language-specific concepts (cf. Haspelmath 2010; 2015).

(iv) Additional topics

Including papers that discuss the degrees of clause integration and the position of the clause linking elements in the syntactic structure from a synchronic and diachronic point of view, this volume also contributes to topics in general syntactic theory such as cyclical change (van Gelderen 2009; cf. Sonnenhauser, this volume) or the structure of the left periphery and the CP domain (Rizzi 1997) and its relation to semantics, information structure and discourse (as depicted in the cartographic approach, e.g., by Shlonsky 2010); cf. Krapova (this volume). To the extent that contributions in this volume also discuss the semantics of CTPs and its impact on the choice of complementation formats, first of all on variation among connectives, the topics raised also relate to lexical typology, which is concerned with the interrelation of lexicon and grammar within a particular lexical field (cf. Koptjevskaja-Tamm 2012); cf. Mitkovska and Bužarovska (this volume), also Wiemer (this volume: § 2.1). From a diachronic perspective, here also belongs the development of complementizer functions exhibited by function words (compare all kinds of loosely defined particles) and other lexical elements such as adverbs, pronouns and other *wh*-elements.

References

Ammann, Andreas & Johan van der Auwera. 2004. Complementizer-headed main clauses for volitional moods in the languages of south-eastern Europe. In Olga Mišeska Tomić (ed.), *Balkan Syntax and Semantics*, 293–314. Amsterdam & Philadelphia: Benjamins.

Arkadiev, Peter & Björn Wiemer. 2020. Perfects in Baltic and Slavic. In Robert Crellin & Thomas Jügel (eds.), *Perfects in Indo-European Languages and Beyond*, 124–214. Amsterdam & Philadelphia: Benjamins.

Bisang, Walter, Andrej Malchukov & the Mainz Grammaticalization Project team (Iris Rieder, Linlin Sun, Marvin Martiny, Svenja Lueli). 2020. Position paper: Universal and areal patterns in grammaticalization. In Walter Bisang & Andrej Malchukov (eds.), *Grammaticalization Scenarios: Cross-linguistic Variation and Universal Tendencies. Vol. 1: Grammaticlization Scenarios from Europe and Asia*, 1–87. Berlin & Boston: De Gruyter Mouton.

Boye, Kasper & Petar Kehayov (eds.). 2016. *Complementizer Semantics in European Languages*. Berlin & Boston: De Gruyter Mouton.

Coseriu, Eugenio. 1988. Die Begriffe "Dialekt", "Niveau" und "Sprachstil" und der eigentliche Sinn der Dialektologie. In J. Albrecht (ed.), *Energeia und Ergon (Sprachliche Variation – Sprachgeschichte – Sprachtypologie). Studia in honorem Eugenio Coseriu*, vol. 1, 15–43. Tübingen: Narr.

Cristofaro, Sonia. 2003. *Subordination*. Oxford: Oxford University Press.

Croft, William. 2009. *Typology and Universals*. 2nd ed. Cambridge: Cambridge University Press.

Dedio, Stefan, Peter Ranacher & Paul Widmer. 2019. Evidence for Britain and Ireland as a linguistic area. *Language* 95 (3). 498–522.

Dik, Simon & Kees Hengeveld. 1991. The hierarchical structure of the clause and the typology of perception verb complements. *Linguistics* 29. 231–259.

Eckhoff, Hanne Martine & Aleksandrs Berdicevskis. 2015. Linguistics vs. digital editions: The Tromsø Old Russian and OCS Treebank. *Scripta & e-Scripta* 14–15. 9–25.

Fielder, Grace E. 2019. The semiotics of ideology: the definite article rule in Bulgarian. *Balkanistica* 32 (2). 45–70.

Gast, Volker & Holger Diessel. 2012. The typology of clause linkage: status quo, challenges, prospects. In Volker Gast & Holger Diessel (eds.), *Clause Linkage in Cross-Linguistic Perspective (Data-Driven Approaches to Cross-Clausal Syntax)*, 1–36. Berlin & Boston: De Gruyter Mouton.

Giannakidou, Anastasia & Alda Mari. 2016. Mixed (non)veridicality and mood choice with emotive verbs. *Chicago Linguistics Society* 51. 181–196. (available at: https://jeannicod.ccsd.cnrs.fr/ijn_01181251, accessed April 28, 2012).

Gołąb, Zbigniew. 1990. The ethnic background and internal linguistic mechanism of the so-called Balkanization of Macedonian. *Balkanistica* 10. 13–19.

Grimshaw, Jane. 1990. *Argument Structure*. Cambridge, MA: MIT Press.

Grković-Major [Grković-Mejdžor], Jasmina. 2004. Razvoj hipotaktičkog *da* u starosrpskom jeziku [Development of the hypotactic *da* in Old Serbian]. *Zbornik Matice srpske za filologiju i lingvistiku* 47 (1–2). 185–203.

Grković-Major, Jasmina. 2020. *Da*-clauses (connectives). In Marc L. Greenberg (ed.), *Encyclopedia of Slavic Languages and Linguistics online*. Brill: Leiden. (available at https://referenceworks.brillonline.com/browse/encyclopedia-of-slavic-languages-and-linguistics-online).

Hansen, Björn, Alexander Letuchiy & Izabela Błaszczyk. 2016. Complementizers in Slavonic (Russian, Polish, and Bulgarian). In Kasper Boye & Petar Kehayov (eds.), *Complementizer Semantics in European Languages*, 175–223. Berlin & Boston: De Gruyter Mouton.

Haspelmath, Martin. 2010. Comparative concepts and descriptive categories in cross-linguistic studies. *Language* 86 (3). 663–687.

Haspelmath, Martin. 2015. Descriptive scales versus comparative scales. In Ina Bornkessel-Schlesewsky, Andrej L. Malchukov & Marc D. Richards (eds.), *Scales and Hierarchies (A Cross-Disciplinary Perspective)*, 45–58. Berlin & Boston: De Gruyter Mouton.

Haug, Dag T. T. & Marius L. Jøhndal. 2008. Creating a Parallel Treebank of the Old Indo-European Bible Translations. In Caroline Sporleder & Kiril Ribarov (eds.), *Proceedings of the Second Workshop on Language Technology for Cultural Heritage Data (LaTeCH 2008)*, 27–34. (available at: https://proiel.github.io/)

Haug, Dag & Hanne Eckhoff. 2011. *The PROIEL corpus as a source to Old Church Slavic: a practical introduction* (Presentation available at: http://www.hf.uio.no/ifikk/english/research/projects/proiel/Activities/proiel/publications/corpus_intro.pdf, accessed March 11, 2016)

Heine, Bernd & Tania Kuteva. 2005. *Language Contact and Grammatical Change*. Cambridge: Cambridge University Press.

Holzer, Georg. 2014. Vorhistorische Periode. In Tilman Berger, Karl Gutschmidt, Sebastian Kempgen & Peter Kosta (eds.), *Slavische Sprachen (Ein internationales Handbuch zu ihrer Struktur, ihrer Geschichte und ihrer Erforschung)*, 2. Halbband; Reihe HSK, 1117–1131. Berlin & Boston: De Gruyter Mouton.

Ivić, Pavle. 1958. *Die serbokroatischen Dialekte. Ihre Struktur und Entwicklung. Erster Band: Allgemeines und die štokavische Dialektgruppe*. 's Gravenhage: Mouton.

Joseph, Brian D. 1983. *The Synchrony and Diachrony of the Balkan Infinitive: A study in Areal, General, and Historical Linguistics*. Cambridge: Cambridge University Press.

Joseph, Brian D. 2001. Is Balkan comparative syntax possible? In Maria Luisa Rivero & Angela Ralli (eds.), *Comparative Syntax of Balkan Languages*, 17–43. Oxford: Oxford University Press.

Joseph, Brian D. 2019. Balkan infinitive loss, event structure and switch reference. *Balkanistica* 32 (2). 137–153.

Kehayov, P. & K. Boye. 2016. Complementizer semantics in European languages: Overview and generalizations. In Kasper Boye & Petar Kehayov (eds.), *Complementizer Semantics in European Languages*, 809–878. Berlin & Boston: De Gryuter Mouton.

Koptjevskaja-Tamm, Maria 2012. New directions in lexical typology. *Linguistics* 50 (3). 373–394.

Koptjevskaja-Tamm, Maria & Bernhard Wälchli. 2001. The Circum-Baltic languages: An areal-typological approach. In Östen Dahl & Maria Koptjevskaja-Tamm (eds.), *The Circum-Baltic Languages. Typology and Contact*, vol. 2, 615–750. Amsterdam & Philadelphia: Benjamins.

Kurzová, Helena. 2019. Defining the Central European convergence area. In Andrii Danylenko & Motoki Nomachi (eds.), *Slavic on the Language Map of Europe: Historical and Areal-Typological Dimensions*, 261–289. Berlin, Boston: De Gruyter Mouton.

Lindstedt, Jouko. 2000. Linguistic Balkanization: contact-induced change by mutual reinforcement. In Dicky Gilbers, John Nerbonne & Jos Schaeken (eds.), *Languages in Contact*, 231–246. Amsterdam & Atlanta: Rodopi.

Matras, Yaron. 2007. The borrowability of grammatical categories. In Yaron Matras & Jeanette Sakel (eds.), *Grammatical Borrowing in Cross-Linguistic Perspective*, 31–74. Berlin & New York: Mouton de Gruyter.

Meermann, Anastasia & Barbara Sonnenhauser. 2016. Das Perfekt im Serbischen zwischen slavischer und balkanslavischer Entwicklung. In Alena Bazhutkina & Barbara Sonnenhauser (eds.), *Linguistische Beiträge zur Slavistik. XXII. JungslavistInnen-Treffen in München, 12. bis 14. September 2013*, 83–110. Munich: Sagner.

Nau, Nicole. 2012. Modality in an areal context: The case of a Latgalian dialect. In Björn Wiemer, Bernhard Wälchli & Björn Hansen (eds.), *Grammatical Replication and Borrowability in Language Contact*, 465–508. Berlin, Boston: De Gruyter Mouton.

Newerkla, Stefan. 2007. Areály jazykového kontaktu ve střední Evropě a německo-český mikroareál ve východním Rakousku [Areas of language contact in central Europe and the German-Czech micro-area in eastern Austria]. *Slovo a slovesnost* 68. 271–286.

Ranacher, Peter, Nico Neureiter, Rik van Gijn, Barbara Sonnenhauser, Anastasia Escher, Robert Weibel, Pieter Muysken and Balthasar Bickel. 2021. Contact-tracing in cultural evolution: a Bayesian mixture model to detect geographic areas of language contact. *Journal of the Royal Society Interface* (forthcoming).

Rizzi, Luigi. 1997. The fine structure of the left periphery. In Liliane Haegeman (ed.), *Elements of Grammar*, 281–337. Dordrecht: Kluwer.

Ross, Malcolm D. 1996. Contact-induced change and the comparative method: Cases from Papua New Guinea. In Mark Durie & Malcolm D. Ross (eds.), *The Comparative Method Reviewed*, 180–217. New York & Oxford: Oxford University Press.

Ross, Malcolm. 2007. Calquing and metatypy. *Journal of Language Contact* 1. 116–143.

Sakel, Jeanette. 2007. Types of loans: Matter and pattern. In Yaron Matras & Jeanette Sakel (eds.), *Grammatical Borrowing in Cross-Linguistic Perspective*, 15–30. Berlin & New York: Mouton de Gruyter.

Sandfeld, Kristian. 1926. *Balkanfilologien. En oversigt over dens resultater og problemer*. København: Bianco Lunos. [French translation 1968: *Linguistique balkanique. Problèmes et résultats*. Paris: Klincksieck.]

Schmidtke-Bode, Karsten. 2014. *Complement Clauses and Complementation Systems: A Cross-Linguistic Study of Grammatical Organization*. Jena (unpubl. PhD thesis).

Shlonsky, U. 2010. The cartographic enterprise in syntax. *Language and Linguistics Compass* 4 (6). 417–429.

Šimko, Ivan. 2020. Definiteness markers in the *Life of St Petka*. *Zeitschrift für Slawistik* 65 (2). 272–307.

Sims, Andrea D. & Brian D. Joseph. 2019. Morphology versus syntax in the Balkan verbal complex. In Iliyana Krapova & Brian D. Joseph (eds.), *Balkan Syntax and (Universal) Principles of Grammar*, 99–150. Berlin & Boston: De Gruyter Mouton.

Sonnenhauser, Barbara. 2015. Functionalising syntactic variance: declarative complementation with *kako* and *če* in 17th to 19th century Balkan Slavic. *Wiener slavistisches Jahrbuch (Neue Folge)* 3. 41–72.

Sonnenhauser, Barbara. 2019. Interrogative, indefinite, relative *kdo(r)*. Why Slovene is (not so) different. *Zeitschrift für Slavische Philologie* 75 (1). 151–181.

Sonnenhauser, Barbara & Paul Widmer. 2020. Indeed, nothing lost in the Balkans. Assessing morphosyntactic convergence in an areal context. *Balkanistica* 33. 103–131.

Spencer, Andrew. 2003. Periphrastic paradigms in Bulgarian. In Uwe Junghanns (ed.), *Syntactic Structures and Morphological Information*, 249–282. Berlin & New York: Mouton de Gruyter.

Spencer, Andrew & Ana R. Luís. 2012. *Clitics. An Introduction*. Cambridge: Cambridge University Press.

Spencer, Andrew & Gergana Popova. 2015. Periphrasis and inflection. In Matthew Baerman (ed.), *The Oxford Handbook of Inflection*, 197–230. Oxford: Oxford University Press.

Topolińska, Zuzanna 1997. The opposition [+/- factive] and its main exponents in Macedonian. *Lětopis* 44 (1). 57–66.

Topolińska, Zuzanna. 2003. Means for grammatical accommodation of finite clauses: Slovenian between South and West Slavic. *Sprachtypologie und Universalienforschung* 56 (3). 306–322.

Topolińska, Zuzanna. 2008. Factivity as a Grammatical Category in Balkan Slavic and Balkan Romance. In Zuzanna Topolińska: *Z Polski do Macedonii. Studia językoznawcze, tom I: Problemy predykacji*, 173–184. Kraków: Lexis. [Reprinted from *Slavia Meridionalis* I (1994). 105–121.]

Traugott, Elizabeth Closs. 1989. On the rise of epistemic meanings in English: an example of subjectification in semantic change. *Language* 65 (1). 31–55.

Trudgill, Peter. 2006. *New-Dialect Formation (The Inevitability of Colonial Englishes)*. Edinburgh: Edinburgh University Press.

van Gelderen, Elly. 2009. Renewal in the left periphery: economy and the complementizer layer, *Transactions of the Philological Society* 107 (2). 131–195.

Vuković, Teodora. 2020. Torlak. In Marc L. Greenberg (ed.), *Encyclopedia of Slavic Languages and Linguistics online*. Brill: Leiden. (available at: https://referenceworks.brillonline.com/browse/encyclopedia-of-slavic-languages-and-linguistics-online)

Vuković, Teodora. 2021. Representing variation in a spoken corpus of an endangered dialect. The case of Torlak. *Language Resources and Evaluation* 55 (1). 1–26. (available at: https://link.springer.com/article/10.1007/s10579-020-09522-4)

Vuković, Teodora, Nora Muheim, Olivier-Andreas Winistörfer, Anastasia Makarova, Ivan Šimko & Sanja Bradjan. 2019. Corpora and processing tools for non-standard contemporary and diachronic Balkan Slavic. *The 12th International Conference on Recent Advances in Natural Language Processing (RANLP 2019), Varna, Bulgaria, 2 September 2019–4 September 2019*, 62–68.

Widmer, Paul, Stefan Dedio & Barbara Sonnenhauser. 2021. Convergence by shared ancestry in Romance. *Journal of Language Contact* 14. 53–71.

Wiemer, Björn. 2015. Meždu nakloneniem i fossilizaciej: O mnogolikoj sud'be klitiki *by* [Between mood and fossilization: on the multi-facetted fate of the clitic *by*]. In Ljudmila Popović, Dojčil Vojvodić & Motoki Nomachi (eds.), *U prostoru lingvističke slavistike (Zbornik naučnih radova povodom 65 godina života akademika Predraga Pipera)*, 189–224. Belgrade: Univerzitet u Beogradu.

Wiemer, Björn. 2017. Main clause infinitival predicates and their equivalents in Slavic: Why they are not instances of insubordination. In Łukasz Jędrzejowski & Ulrike Demske (eds.), *Infinitives at the Syntax-Semantics Interface: A Diachronic Perspective*, 265–338. Berlin & Boston: De Gruyter Mouton.

Wiemer, Björn. 2018. On triangulation in the domain of clause linkage and propositional marking. In Björn Hansen, Jasmina Grković-Major & Barbara Sonnenhauser (eds.), *Diachronic Slavonic Syntax: The Interplay between Internal Development, Language Contact and Metalinguistic Factors*, 285–338. Berlin & Boston: De Gruyter Mouton.

Wiemer, B. 2019a. "Matrëška" and areal clusters involving varieties of Slavic. On methodology and data treatment. In Andrii Danylenko & Motoki Nomachi (eds.), *Slavic on the Language Map of Europe*, 21–61. Berlin & Boston: De Gruyter Mouton.

Wiemer, Björn. 2019b. On illusory insubordination and semi-insubordination in Slavic: Independent infinitives, clause-initial particles and predicatives put to the test. In Karin Beijering, Gunther Kaltenböck & María Sol Sansiñena (eds.), *Insubordination. Theoretical and Empirical issues*, 107–166. Amsterdam & Philadelphia: Benjamins.

Wiemer, Björn. 2021. Convergence. In Evangelia Adamou & Yaron Matras (eds.), *The Routledge Handbook on Language Contact*, 276–299. London: Routledge.

Wiemer, Björn, Il'ja Seržant & Aksana Erker. 2014. Convergence in the Baltic-Slavic contact zone (Triangulation approach). In Juliane Besters-Dilger, Cynthia Dermarkar, Stefan Pfänder & Achim Rabus (eds.), *Congruence in Contact-induced Language Change (Language Families, Typological Resemblance, and Perceived Similarity)*, 15–42. Berlin & New York: De Gruyter.

Ziegeler, Debra. 2017. Historical replication in contact grammaticalization. In Daniël Van Olmen, Hubert Cuyckens & Lobke Ghesquière (eds.), *Aspects of Grammaticalization. (Inter)Subjectification and Directionality*, 311–352. Berlin & Boston: De Gruyter Mouton.

Chapter II: **Complementation structures**

Björn Wiemer
A general template of clausal complementation and its application to South Slavic: theoretical premises, typological background, empirical issues

Abstract: The article starts with a definition of clausal complementation as "biclausal syntactic constructions in which the predicate of one clause 'entails reference to another proposition or state of affairs' (Cristofaro 2003: 95), expressed in a second clause" (Schmidtke Bode 2014: 7). Key notions, and problems with their application, are discussed and a maximum template of clausal complementation is presented. This provides a systematic grid for a comprehensive treatment of relevant phenomena in contemporary South Slavic languages. Furthermore, this grid serves as a point of departure for systematic comparison not only within South Slavic (in both syn- and diachrony), but also on a typological backdrop. The main body of the article is devoted to a survey of facts, phenomena and approaches to particular components of this template, with a focus on complementation markers and their relation to mood. The article ends with an attempt at giving a typological profile of South Slavic languages in domains relevant for clausal complementation and points out research desiderata.

Keywords: clausal complementation, clitics, complementizers, (non-)factuality, Semantic Integration Hierarchy, realis-irrealis distinctions, South Slavic

Acknowledgments: This article would not have been possible in its current form without countless discussions over, and supplies of, data with which I was presented, first of all, by Mladen Uhlik (Slovene) as well as by Eleni Bužarovska and Liljana Mitkovska (Macedonian), Jasmina Grković-Major (Serbian), and Iliyana Krapova (Bulgarian). I furthermore profited from the competence of Veronika Kampf and Teodora Radeva-Bork (Bulgarian), and of Mirjana Mirić, Ljudmila Popović, Stefan Savić, Tomislav Sočanac and Teodora Vuković (Croatian, Serbian). It goes without saying that none of these colleagues has to be blamed for any kind of shortcomings, which are my exclusive responsibility.

Björn Wiemer, Johannes-Gutenberg-Universität (Mainz, Germany), Institut für Slavistik, Turkologie und zirkumbaltische Studien (ISTziB), Jakob-Welder-Weg 18, D-55099 Mainz, e-mail: wiemerb@uni-mainz.de

https://doi.org/10.1515/9783110725858-002

1 Introduction

Clausal complementation is represented by "biclausal syntactic constructions in which the predicate of one clause 'entails reference to another proposition or state of affairs' (Cristofaro 2003: 95), expressed in a second clause" (Schmidtke-Bode 2014: 7). In order to delimit the field and in order to present a maximum template of clausal complementation, I will follow this definition. This template generalizes over particular instances, it can serve as the basis of comparison of constructions within a given language and for cross-linguistic purposes. Although it can be used for synchronic as well as diachronic matters. Here, I will restrict myself mainly to the contemporary stage with some account of more recent diachrony. The template will be developed in this section, afterwards, its components will be applied to a survey of relevant phenomena in contemporary South Slavic languages (§ 2). After this main part, I will discuss some problematic issues (§ 3). The focus is not on areality as such, although some rather obvious areal features will be dealt with, and the survey is mainly restricted to standard varieties. Hopefully, a systematic account of the features implied by the template and the notional distinctions behind them will supply a more unified schema for describing the "space of variation" in usage-based synchronic and diachronic studies on the areal (diatopic), diastratic and diaphasic patterns of variation and change in South Slavic as well as other languages. As far as possible, typological background will be provided in all sections. The final section (§ 4) gives a summary used for conclusions and an outlook.

Before presenting the template, some comments on the definition cited above seem appropriate. First, it implies that a construction be biclausal and that the unit which is interpreted as an argument of some predicate have the format of a clause; compare the probably shortest definition of clausal complementation as "predication manifested in argument slots" (Horie and Comrie 2000: 1). In typological literature, 'clause' is usually captured as a unit which houses the predicate and its (core) arguments; in addition, it can include adjuncts, i.e., NPs or PPs which are not arguments of the predicate (cf. Van Valin 2005). Schmidtke-Bode (2014: 27) cites Kroeger (2005: 32), who considers a clause "the smallest grammatical unit that can express a proposition", or a "grammatical unit which expresses a single predicate and its arguments" (2005: 53). Thus, a clause which, in its entirety, is an argument of a higher-order predicate (a.k.a. matrix predicate) must itself contain a predicate-argument structure that can be interpreted independently from the matrix clause; in addition, it can, though need not, code a proposition (for this term see below), but it does not have independent illocutionary force (cf. Ransom 1986: 3 *et passim*). The latter condition is a general one for subordination (Lehmann 1988: § 3.1.2, Cristofaro 2003: 18 *et passim*); for our purposes it is important since it excludes quotation from complementation (as well as parentheticals, see below). The higher-order predicate (in the matrix clause) is customarily called 'complement-taking predicate' (henceforth CTP). Since the distinction between mono- and biclausal sentences is fuzzy, the notion of 'embedded predicate' may be employed as an umbrella term to unite clausal complementation proper (biclausal structures), monoclausal structures with complex predicates (e.g. with phasal verbs or modal auxiliaries)[1] and fuzzy cases in-between.

The term '(clausal) complementation' shall here be restricted to biclausal constructions. This restriction rules out raising (as in *John seems to be troubling himself with raising*), which yields monoclausal structures (vs biclausal structures as in *It seems that John is troubling himself with raising*). This restriction renders nominalizations problematic, which will be addressed in § 3.3. At the moment suffice it to point out one property which nominalizations usually do not share with verbal predicates. While the latter, as a rule, can be used as self-standing predicates in isolated utterances after thetic questions ('What happened?'), their nominalizations cannot;[2] compare (1):

(1) a. *The committee members took decisions on all issues.*
 b. *Dear committee members, please take decisions!*
 c. *A: Alright, so what? B:* ??*Decisions.* (vs *We have taken our decisions.*)

This property does not imply that all utterances contain propositions (e.g., (1b) does not), but (almost) all utterances contain an illocution, even if (as in B's reply in (1c)) it cannot be "decoded", since *decisions* somehow lacks anchorage in space and time. Thus, having the status of a predicate of an isolated utterance (or of an utterance in a dialogic turn) and having illocutionary force are different things. Even non-clausal units can "count as full and complete contributions to the discourse" (Hengeveld and Mackenzie 2008: 5), but not all non-clausal units can be used as predicative units. Obviously, this depends on whether, in an answer to a thetic question (see A's turn in (1c)), the nominalization bears features of tense and whether, and how, arguments of the underlying verb root or stem are realized (see § 3.3). Thus, even if, under certain conditions, action nouns may count as a marginal type of clausal complementation, they do not have independent temporal reference.

---

1 See from a generative perspective Tomić (2012: 234).
2 In Russian linguistics this property has usually been called *predikativnost'* 'predicativity': a grammatical property (or complex of properties) which distinguishes clauses from other syntactic constituents (Testelec 2001: 229–234).

Second, Schmidtke-Bode's definition quoted above requires that the dependent clause be an <u>argument</u> of a higher-order predicate in a matrix clause.[3] The definition is similar if dependent clauses are conceived of "in terms of their respective pragmatic-syntactic functions: A complement clause functions as a referential unit, expressing an argument of the matrix clause predicate;[4] (...) an adverbial clause functions as a modifier of the main predicate of the matrix clause" (van Lier 2009: 67). As mentioned above, the predicate of the matrix clause is the complement-taking predicate (CTP).

Third, for clausal complementation in the strict sense, the clause which "entails reference to another proposition or state of affairs" (see above) must be embedded into a larger structure which looks as in [1] (here and in the following, square brackets indicate scope):

[1] [complement sentence   ]
    [matrix clause [complement clause]]

In line with Schmidtke-Bode (2014), I will call this larger structure 'complement sentence'. Such sentences capture only part of what Deutscher (2000) terms the Functional Domain of Complementation. This domain comprises various ways of how clauses may be combined with each other and of how different states of affairs (or propositions; see below) can be inserted into one another. Thus, all three sentences (2a)–(2c) denote the same relationship between two situations (i.e., reference to another state of affairs), although they code it differently:

(2) a. *I can't understand [John's immediate refusal of*   (rather) monoclausal
       the offer].
    b. *I can't understand [that John refused the offer*   biclausal, subordinate
       immediately].
    c. *John refused the offer immediately, and I can't*   biclausal, coordinate
       understand it.

Only (2b) jointly fulfils two conditions: (i) the predicate-argument structure **refuse** (*John, offer*) is embedded as a syntactic constituent under a higher predicate (**understand** (1SG, PROP)), and (ii) this constituent has the format of a clause. In (2a), by contrast, the predicate-argument structure **refuse** (*John, offer*) is not

---

[3] Compare terms like 'sentential argument', which can be considered synonyms of 'clausal complement'.
[4] Similarly in Croft (2000: 88).

expressed as a clause (at least this status is questionable); consequently, the entire sentence is monoclausal. In turn, (2c) is biclausal, however the predicate-argument structure **refuse** (*John, offer*) is not embedded, but treated as a propositional (or factive) antecedent of a pronoun (*it*) in the other clause. The gradient nature of noun phrases (NPs) in relation to clauses will be dealt with in § 3.3.

As pointed out by Schmidtke-Bode (2014: 7–9), Noonan's (2007) classical definition[5] as well as Cristofaro's (2003: 47) definition of subordination as "a cognitive situation corresponding to the non-assertion of one of the linked SoAs", are based on semantic terms. For this reason, they are often not suitable to discriminate between embedded biclausal structures and their functional equivalents, and this is undesirable in cross-linguistic comparison (cf. already Lehmann 1988) and the study of diachronic change. In particular, differentiation becomes more difficult when comparing closely related languages. We are interested in the ways these languages diverge or converge in diachronic and areal terms (or in relation to any other parameter of variation). In this respect, one should follow Dixon (1995, 2006), who distinguishes between clausal complementation proper and complementation strategies (see § 3.1). Both add up to complementation patterns and complementation systems. Dixon's definition of complement clauses *sensu stricto* requires that they function as syntactic arguments within a higher clause (see [1]) and that they have the internal structure of a clause. The latter means that arguments of complement clauses are coded in a way that is maximally similar to their coding in independent main clauses.[6] In other words: if deranking occurs, it should be minimal. This is a gradable property, but the more the internal structure of the clause resembles a noun phrase, the more it will be considered a complementation strategy, not clausal complementation proper (see § 3.3; cf. also Schmidtke-Bode 2014: 31–32).

Moreover, Dixon inquires into the relation between complement clauses and CTPs. This leads to implicational hierarchies as they might now be investigated in (certain branches of) lexical typology. Namely, Dixon (2006: 15) predicts that "in every language that has complement clauses [based on the other criteria; BW], they function as a core argument (...) for verbs with meanings such as 'see', 'know', 'believe', and 'like' (insofar as the language has such verbs); and also for 'tell' if there is an indirect speech construction, and for 'want' if (...) realized as a lexical verb". We will return to these implicational relations in § 2.1.

---

[5] Complementation is "the syntactic situation that arises when a notional sentence or predication is an argument of a predicate" (Noonan 2007: 52).

[6] "(...) its arguments, if not omitted by a grammatical rule specifically associated with the complement clause in question, should be marked in the same way as in main clauses, and have much the same grammatical properties" (Dixon 2006: 15).

Fourth, Schmidtke-Bode's definition specifies that there is reference to another proposition or state of affairs. There has been quite some discussion of these notions in typological literature over the last 2–3 decades, and there is a time-honoured discussion of these notions in analytical (language) philosophy. The essence of this discussion has been summarized in Boye (2010, 2012: §§ 4–5).[7] Boye's findings and suggestions largely build on Lyons' (1977) distinction between second- and third-order entities. A wealth of linguistic facts requires a distinction of mere descriptions of situations (including their participants and internal temporal make-up) and the anchoring of such situations in some specific temporal and spatial localization. States of affairs (SoAs) amount just to descriptions of situations (i.e. predicate-argument structures plus possible modifying adjuncts) which do not yet have reference, whereas propositions assign reference to SoAs, i.e. they are anchored to some specific time interval and spatial coordinates. This is why SoAs can be extended in time (i.e., they have some aspectual properties) and they "feed" propositions; the latter, in turn, have reference, with the effect that one can ask for whether they are true or not. In other words: only propositions are the target of judgments specified in space and time, as are epistemic judgments ('probably', 'likely', 'doubtful', etc.) and the evidential background (information source) of an utterance. Above that, propositions supply the basis of moral or other evaluative judgments ('good – bad', 'fortunately – unfortunately'), which underlie factive predicates (see § 2.2.2). Therefore, these three classes of modifiers – epistemic, evidential, evaluational (a.k.a. validational) – are varieties of propositional modifiers, regardless of their morphosyntactic format (clitic, word, phrase, clause). Consequently, complement clauses can be subdivided by the criterion of whether they code an SoA or a proposition, although this division is not without problems.

Moreover, since units with very different morphosyntactic formats can function as propositional modifiers, predicative units able to serve as CTPs of clausal complements containing propositions can themselves turn into comments on these propositions. This radically changes the syntactic and communicative asymmetry between the two clauses; see the following figure:

---

[7] Cf. also Cristofaro (2003: 109–111), Schmidtke-Bode (2014: 34).

	CORE 1	CORE 2
(3)	Albert thought	(that) you are such a scoundrel.
(4)	It's a shame	(that) we are late.
	potential CTP	potential complement clause

Figure 1: Asymmetry relations between adjacent clauses / cores.

In each example, each core expresses a proposition, although in (3) Core 1 may be assumed to be more in need of an additional argument slot filled by Core 2 than this is the case in (4), since Core 1 in (3) can hardly stand by itself, at least it is communicatively insufficient.[8] However, in communicative terms, Core 1 of both (3) and (4) can be treated rather as a comment on Core 2, regardless of syntactic dependency, i.e., irrespective of whether Core 2 is an argument of the predicate in Core 1 (then we get complementation) or not. Communicative asymmetry can be tested: only the foregrounded (= asserted) parts can become the target of a focusing operation, e.g. of a question, or they can be negated. Thus, for instance, in

(3) a. *Albert thought you are such a scoundrel.*
   Do you agree? / Aren't you aware of that?

the target of the question is ambiguous (out of further context): does it refer to 'Albert thought P', or to 'you are such a scoundrel'? (The same applies for (4).) Such a question targets the core which is foregrounded in communicative terms. If Core 1 is backgrounded, its status as matrix clause, and of the whole construction as a complementation sentence, remains shaky, unless there is an additional linking element (*that*) introducing Core 2 and thereby marking it as a dependent clause. If this element is amiss, Core 1 can become a parenthetical expression commenting on Core 2, and the whole construction is monoclausal. Since communicative back- vs foreground[9] is flexible and independent from syntactic analysis, and there may be a lack of explicit linking elements, discussions of zero complementizers often become problematic, particularly if Core 2 contains a proposition (see § 3.4).

The term 'proposition' has often been employed in a lax way, also by authors with a heavy impact on our understanding of clausal complementation. See, for instance, Ransom (1986) or Lehmann (1988), who understand a proposition as

---

8 Cf. Schmidtke-Bode (2014: 22–26) on criteria and diagnostics of the argumenthood of clauses.
9 This corresponds to discursively primary vs secondary use in Boye and Harder (2007, 2012).

"the semantic correlate of a (possibly desentencialized) clause" (1988: § 1). See furthermore Dixon (2006), for whom a "complement clause will always describe a proposition. This can be a fact, an activity or a potential state" (2006: 15). However, in the sense defined above, activities and potential states do not by themselves represent propositions. Consider some more traditional linguistic descriptions, such as the Russian Academy Grammar (Švedova 1980), which distinguish clause types by "sentence mood" and illocutions (e.g., Russ. *On rabotaet / rabotal / budet rabotat' / rabotal by* 'He works / worked / will work / would work' and *Rabotal by on! / Pust' on rabotaet! / Rabotaj!* 'If only he worked! / May he work! / Work!') united into paradigms whose members are said to share the same proposition (equivalent to Bally's 1950 'dictum') and are said to differ only in terms of their 'modus' (cf. Testelec 2001: 241–242). Here, 'proposition' refers to what may be paraphrased as 'common (or underlying) semantic description of a situation (= SoA), void (or regardless) of illocutionary force' (cf. also Gegovski 2014, Topolinjska 2014: 218). In the following, such sloppy usage of the term 'proposition' will be avoided. Note furthermore that a definition of complement clauses as referential units (see van Lier's definition quoted above) is tantamount to saying that these units are <u>able to</u> acquire referential status (in some world or other), but it does not imply that these units in a particular utterance are really anchored in the space and time of some world.

These premises provided, I want to propose a general template which determines the role and place of distinct units that may be involved in clausal complementation, as well as how they may interact with each other. The template indicates slots in a (theoretically possible) maximum construction. It should help identify and compare components of diverse constructions and is meant to be a grid, or checklist, not only for crosslinguistic comparison, but also for diatopic, diastratic and diaphasic variation on a smaller scale, namely within the South Slavic languages, including an account of their diachronic dimension. The template should therefore comply with two requirements which, in analogy to Van Valin's (2005: 3) general considerations regarding theories of clause structure, can be formulated as follows:

[2] General considerations for a theory of clausal complementation:
    (a) A theory of clausal complementation should capture all of the universal features of clauses without imposing features on languages in which there is no evidence for these features.
    (b) A theory should represent comparable structures in different languages in comparable ways.

The remainder of this article provides a comprehensive account of Figure 2, illustrated and examined for each component on South Slavic material, with a focus on complementation markers (see § 2.2). The account implies a critical assessment of certain key notions used in research on clausal complementation and related fields, to point out consequences for the analysis of relevant phenomena in South Slavic.

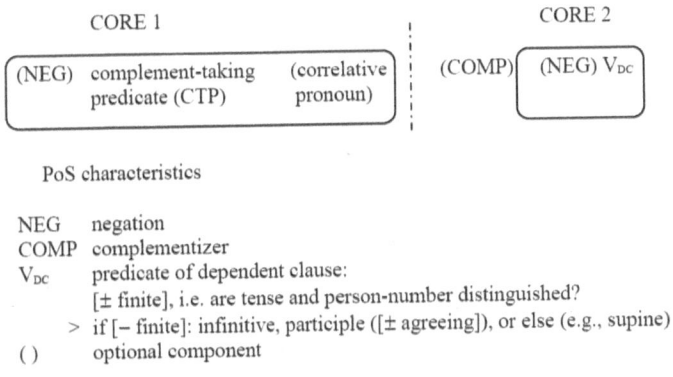

PoS characteristics

NEG   negation
COMP   complementizer
V$_{DC}$ predicate of dependent clause:
       [± finite], i.e. are tense and person-number distinguished?
       > if [– finite]: infinitive, participle ([± agreeing]), or else (e.g., supine)
( )   optional component

Figure 2: Maximum template of clausal complementation.

It should be added that contrasting meanings between different types of clausal complementation cannot always be associated with just one component of such a general template. Although I will be eager to pinpoint minimal pair conditions related to just one distinct element of complementation, there are many cases in which meaning contrasts arise from (or are signalled by) an interplay between different parts of the entire construction. This has been argued for convincingly and elegantly already by Ransom (1986).

Two further remarks concerning terminology are necessary. First, 'Balkan Slavic' refers to the (south)eastern part of South Slavic, i.e., Bulgarian, Macedonian and the eastern Serbian Torlak dialects. Second, to avoid clumsy circumscriptions, I will use '(clause) connective' or 'complementation marker' (see § 2.2) as an umbrella term for all kinds of clause-linking devices, comprising not only doubtless complementizers and disputable cases like *da* (see § 2.2.3), but also WH-words regardless of whether they have eventually turned into full-fledged complementizers or not. If the status of a connective in an example is left unspecified, I will use the gloss CON. For *da* I will alternatively use IRR (= irrealis marker).

2 The components of the maximum template of clausal complementation

This main part of the article discusses the components of the maximum template in Figure 2.

2.1 Semantics of the complement-taking predicate

Complement-taking predicates (CTPs) are chosen from a restricted set of verbs (and other predicative units). According to Dixon (2006: 8–14), they are recruited from cross-linguistically recurrent semantic classes. Presumably, units belonging to these classes share some meaning potential with notional distinctions made by clausal complements, and this is why CTPs determine the (range of) choices of connectives, as they set the stage for semantically admissible, or required, complementation markers in the dependent clause. The mirror image of these selection restrictions of CTPs is that new complementizers establish themselves via an expansion across CTPs with which they are compatible. Naturally, such an expansion corresponds to a loss of specific semantic features that characterize a complementizer while it is emerging. A particularly good case to demonstrate this is the spread of *da* as a complementizer in Serbian-Croatian (cf. Grković-Major, this volume, and see § 2.2.3 below). Analogous considerations apply to paradigmatic forms of the dependent predicate, although the inventory of TAM-forms to choose from in South Slavic is very restricted. We may thus say that CTPs and complementation markers are in harmony with each other. First of all, many CTPs determine whether the clausal complement contains a proposition or an SoA (Kehayov and Boye 2016b: 811–813), and this neatly correlates with hierarchies of semantic integration (see below). In case there is a choice, we may speak of meaning alternation in the (potential) CTP[10] to which complementation markers adapt. Of course, this ability to adapt implies that complementation markers have a meaning potential of their own (see § 2.2).

---

[10] Some authors (e.g., Anand and Hacquard 2013) have argued for a multicomponent analysis of predicates such as *hope*, claiming that they contain a doxastic component, which triggers 'indicative' selection, and a bouletic component, which triggers 'subjunctive' selection (cf. also Smirnova 2012); see examples (10a) and (10b) below. Here, I will not engage in questions of how meaning alternations of potential CTPs should be analyzed and whether they are best captured by the notion of polysemy, monosemy or homonymy.

Consider, for instance, contemporary Bulgarian. Verbs like *zaplašvam* 'threat' can take complements with either *če* or *da* (although the latter option seems to be rare with this verb); see (5) and (6). The same applies to the commissive verb *obeštavam* 'promise' (see 7 and 8, both are from children's letters to Santa Claus).

Bulgarian
(5) *Neizvesten   zaplašva,   če   šte   vzrivi*
    unknown-(M.SG)   threaten[IPFV].PRS-(3SG)   COMP   FUT   blast[PFV].PRS-(3SG)
    mosta na metroto v Kiev.
    'The unknown man threatens **that** he will blast the metro bridge in Kiev.'
    (https://www.haskovo.net/news/478736/neizvesten-zaplashva-che-shte-vzrivi-mosta-na-metroto-v-kiev)

(6) *Moskva zaplašva   da   otreže*
    PN   threaten[IPFV].PRS-(3SG)   CON   cut_off[PFV].PRS-(3SG)
    dostăpa na Ukrajna do ruskite pazari.
    'Moscow threatens **that** it will cut off Ukraine's access to the Russian markets.'
    (https://www.investor.bg/centralna-i-iztochna-evropa/335/a/moskva-zaplashva-da-otreje-dostypa-na-ukraina-do-ruskite-pazari--180547/)

(7) *Obeštava-m,   če   šte   băd-a*
    promise[IPFV].PRS-1SG   COMP   FUT   be.FUT-1SG
    naj-poslušnoto dete v Bălgarija.
    'I promise **that** I will be the most obedient child in Bulgaria.'
    (https://nova.bg/news/view/2019/12/24/272772...)

(8) *Tazi godina ne bjax poslušen,*
    no obeštava-m   da   băd-a   prez sledvaštata.
    but promise[IPFV].PRS-1SG CON   be.FUT-1SG
    'This year I haven't been obedient, but I promise **that** I will be during the next year.' (https://nova.bg/news/view/2019/12/20/272415/...)
    (All exapmples accessed on 01/24/2020.)

A similar case can be made for imagination and pretence verbs, compare (9):

(9) *Predstavja-m   si,   če / da   săm*
    imagine[IPFV].PRS-1SG   REFL.DAT   COMP / CON   AUX.PRS.1SG
    na morskija   brjag.
    on sea(ADJ).DEF.SG.M   shore[M]-(SG)
    'I am imagining myself being at the seaside.' (V. Kampf, p.c.)

Especially for these verbs, it is difficult to pin down factors that influence the choice of *če* vs *da*: is it the degree of control of the CTP-subject over the "announced" (resp. imagined or pretended) event, or is it rather epistemic commitment, or yet another factor? Weak vs strong degree of epistemic support is known to influence complementizer choice (and the choice of form in the dependent predicate). Compare the observation that those cognitive verbs (a.k.a. verbs of epistemic attitude) which otherwise imply strong or neutral support take an irrealis-complementizer if they are negated (see § 2.2.4.1). Clearly, the aforementioned questions can hardly be answered to any satisfactory degree prior to a thorough usage-based multivariate analysis, ideally applied to every single CTP.

Other instances of variable complementizer choice conditioned by meaning variation in the CTP are

- the distinction between factive and non-factive uses of emotion predicates, be they verbal (e.g., Serb. *stideti se* 'be ashamed'; cf. Grković-Major, this volume) or nominal (e.g., Mac. *dobro* 'good', see § 2.4). On factivity see § 2.2.2.
- the distinction between knowledge/belief-based and intention/volition-based use of cognitive verbs like Bulg. *mislja* 'think' (see 10a and 10b); the former is associated with epistemic (and doxastic), the latter with deontic (and bouletic) modality.
- the distinction between description of events and description of manner (see 11 and 12 and § 2.2.5).

Bulgarian

(10) a. *Mislj-a,* ***če*** *reši-x vsički zadači*
    think[IPFV]-PRS.1SG COMP solve[PFV]-AOR.1SG all task.PL
    na testa.
    on test.DEF
    'I think I (have) solved all tasks from the test.'

b. *Mislj-a* ***da*** *izlezn-a malko na văzdux.*
    think[IPFV]-PRS.1SG CON go_out[PFV]-PRS.1SG a_bit on air
    'I think I'll go a little bit out into fresh air.' (V. Kampf, p.c.)

Croatian

(11) *Kroz san je čuo* ***da / kako*** *ga netko*
    through sleep AUX.PRS.3SG heard COMP 3M.ACC somebody
    zov-e.
    call[IPFV].PRS-3SG
    'Through his sleep he heard that somebody called him / . . .somebody calling him.'
    (from Mihaljević 2009: 320)

Bulgarian
(12) Čuva-m **da / kak / če** bi-e časovnik.
hear[IPFV].PRS-1SG CON / COMP beat[IPFV]-PRS.3SG clock
'I (can) hear the clock beating.' (V. Kampf, p.c.)

The latter two types of variation have been studied in other Slavic languages (cf. Dobrushina 2012 on Russian) and beyond (e.g., Boye and Kehayov (eds.) 2016). For more detailed considerations concerning these phenomena see § 2.2.4.1. From a diachronic perspective, variation often leads to shifts in the choice of connectives, and thus to shifts in their range of functions. Well-known cases from South Slavic are the replacement of *jako* (*ěko*) by *kako* (and by *če* in Bulgarian) and the loss of irrealis restrictions for *da* outside of Balkan Slavic (see §§ 2.2.3–4).

Dixon's (2006) notion of CTPs also includes complex predicates and is thus wider than the one used here, but it maps well onto Semantic Integration Hierarchies as they have been proposed since Givón (1980). Recent elaborate versions have been presented in the context of Role & Reference Grammar (e.g., Van Valin 2005: 208–209) and by Cristofaro (2003: 122), from where Table 1 is reproduced:

Table 1: Complement-taking predicates and semantic integration.

semantic integration:	no semantic integration:
Semantic Integration Hierarchy	
phasals > modals > manipulatives1 ('make') > manipulatives2 ('order'), desideratives, perception	knowledge*, propositional attitude, utterance**

* This includes inferential and reportive uses of perception CTPs (e.g., *I see that he has left; I hear that you passed the exam*).
** Relates to illocutionary and behavioral aspects of speech (as with quotatives).

The Semantic Integration Hierarchy (SIH) can partially be read as an implicational hierarchy (Cristofaro 2003: 122–131). It describes a continuum in the semantic relation between predicative units: are we dealing with facets of a single situation or with two independent events? The highest integration in this sense is located in the left upper corner (phasals and modals), the loosest integration is found in the right half. The SIH also correlates with a distinction between same-subject and different-subject contructions: the tightest connections (phasals, modals) are only of the same-subject type, while different-subject constructions become more and more possible the further we move toward loose integration.[11] It is fur-

---

[11] This type of gradient corresponds most clearly to Dixon's (2006) classification of CTPs.

thermore easy to integrate Noonan's (2007) distinction between independent and dependent time reference: dependent time reference applies to all complement types on the SIH's left. Crucially, this hierarchy demonstrates an iconic association between the semantic relation (loose – tight) and the tightness of the syntactic relation between the involved predicative units. First of all, this concerns argument structure (is it shared or not?), and this maps onto the issue of whether we are dealing with mono- or biclausal structures.

The split between the left and the right half practically coincides with the distinction between SoA and propositional complements. Among the domains on the left side we have to distinguish between SoA-complements (in the lower part) and complex predicates (in the upper part). In contrast to SoA-complements (basically, manipulatives2 and desideratives), phasals and modals do not have argument structures of their own. Therefore, these are here excluded from clausal complementation, whereas control constructions are included; they belong to the middle part of the SIH's left half.

The distinction between monoclausal constructions and biclausal constructions is not clear-cut, but the SIH allows to pinpoint the zone of transition between both. The critical point is certainly the 'manipulatives1' category, which denotes direct (or factitive) causation and, thus, belongs to analytical causatives (compare *She makes me believe in astrology*).[12] These constructions are critical for clausal complementation, since it is not self-evident that the complex event denoted jointly by two verbs can be treated as biclausal; the "predicate of effect" is causally dependent on some action of a subject which belongs to the "predicate of causation" (Kemmer and Verhagen 1994: 117). However, direct causation (manipulatives1) can be distinguished from CTPs lower on the SIH by the fact that the caused event is normally conceived of as realized (hence the name 'factitive'), it can therefore easily be conceived of as a single event.

These considerations are connected to empirical questions: (i) are different kinds of causation (direct-indirect = manipulative1-manipulative2, factitive-permissive-curative, etc.) distinguished by auxiliary verbs, and (ii) how freely analytical causatives are used with different kinds of lexical verbs? In this regard, our knowledge is still very limited, but generally, analytical causatives have been recognized as more weakly developed in the Eastern part of Slavic; in particular, this concerns factitives (cf. von Waldenfels 2015). Bulgarian seems to deviate from this areal pattern in terms of the general token frequency of analytical causatives,

---

12 So-called resultatives, a kind of secondary predicates also belong here; compare *She drives me crazy* or *Bob wiped the table clean*. However, these are almost inexistent in Slavic languages (cf. Holvoet 2008: 131–132) and need not concern us further.

but not with respect to factives (cf. Levshina 2015: 495–496, 509–510). Regardless, direct causation with Bulg. *karam, nakarvam* 'drive' (+ lexical verb) is at least a well-attested option (cf. Levshina 2015: 504). It would be premature to draw any comparisons to other South Slavic languages since, to my knowledge, analytical causatives have remained a research gap and are, thus, a domain that urgently requires empirical research.

Another critical area on the SIH is complements of perception verbs. Situated at the border to CTPs with propositional complements, their own clausal complements are better characterized as SoAs inasmuch as they cannot be modified by sentential adverbs (or other propositional modifiers); cf. Boye (2010, 2012). Probably, the borderline character of complements of perception CTPs arises because direct perception refers to real events. However, such processes are just described as unfolding in the immediate experience of an observer. Propositions do not just refer to unfolding processes, they imply statements (or questions) which involve judgments. With regard to situations (= SoAs), propositions are located on a metalevel (see § 1). Consequently, one cannot refer to (and evaluate) events as long as they are simply described as occurring in some world from the perspective of some conscious subject. An empirically more interesting question is the tight relation of perception to characterization of manner. This relation manifests itself in a close connection of complementizers that can mark manner and clausal complements of perception predicates (see § 2.2.5).

In sum, both the SIH and Dixon's (2006) verb classification allow for predictions concerning the selection of complementation markers and the range of forms of the dependent predicate. In Slavic linguistics, predictions of such correlations were tested for Russian by Dobrushina (2012), but they belong among the big desiderata for South Slavic clausal complementation.

2.2 Complementizers

In a most theory-neutral way, complementizers can be defined as heads of clausal arguments which are not themselves constituents of the clauses which they head. They are signs that explicitly mark the argument relation to a superordinate (= matrix) predicate.[13] Any such definitions bear the problem that they presuppose

---

[13] X'-approaches assumed that complementizers are heads of S'-constituents, but that they can also occur in main clauses (e.g., Rudin 1986, in particular pp. 72–78; also Tiševa 2001a: 168). Given our definition, the latter is excluded. The question to be asked is thus under which conditions a connective gets complementizer status, not whether it also occurs in main clauses. In Minimalism it is assumed that complementizers head CP-constituents.

categorial distinctions which usually require great scrutiny and may be not unproblematic, at least from an analytical, data-driven point of view (compare the argument – adjunct distinction). This is one reason why complementizers shall be conceived of here as a gradient category (or concept); this implies that we will be dealing with core and (probably many more) peripheral representatives. Fuzzy edges of this category can be gleaned when the criteria which complementizers are considered to fulfil only apply partially (cf. Sonnenhauser, this volume, for a similar position).

Most complementizers (at least in European languages) occur clause-initially, a property which they share with conjunctions (= adverbial subordinators) and WH-words, which introduce embedded partial questions. Joseph (2016: 272) assumes that in head-initial (= right-branching) languages (as those on the Balkans) complementizers sharply delimit clause boundaries, at least typically so, but he also admits that complementizers are a gradient concept. In fact, Joseph's additional condition (delimitation of a clause boundary) would leave us with very few (if any) "real" complementizers, for instance, in Bulgarian. Here, we observe that units commonly regarded as complementizers can be pushed to the second position, if they are marked for some communicative purpose, e.g., if an NP is topicalized (13). The same applies to relativizers like *deto* (14), e.g., if focalized (cf. Krapova, this volume, for a detailed generative account):

Bulgarian
(13) *Kaza-x,* $_{TOPIC}$[*knig-i-te*] ***če*** Ivan *trjabva*
 say[PFV]-AOR.1SG book-PL-DEF.PL COMP PN AUX.NEC
 da gi dones-e.
 CON 3PL.ACC bring[PFV].PRS-3SG
 'I said **that**, $_{TOPIC}$[as for the books], Ivan should bring them.'

(14) $_{TOPIC}$[*Knig-i-te*], $_{FOCUS}$[*na dete-to*] ***deto*** Ivan *e*
 book-PL-DEF.PL of child-DEF.SG COMP PN AUX.PRS.3SG
 kupi-l.
 buy[PFV]-LPT-(SG.M)
 '$_{TOPIC}$[As for the books], it is $_{FOCUS}$[for the child] **that** Ivan bought them.'
 (adapted from Rudin 1986: 47; cf. also Tiševa 2001b)

The same applies to Mac. *deka*, at least in the spoken language (cf. Mitkovska and Bužarovska, this volume: § 4.1, for discussion).

The onset of this phenomenon seems to reach back at least into the 18th century. Cf. Sonnenhauser (2015: 58–65), who proposes subject-to-object-raising as an alternative explanation. If we accept such an analysis, the claim that complementizers mark off clause boundaries could be maintained. However, a neat (re-)definition of the relation between the units of syntactic and information structure is required, and such an analysis does not explain why non-subjects can be "raised" as well (see ex. 13 and 14).

Since Bresnan (1970), it has often been assumed that there can be only one complementizer per clause and that it cannot be preceded by prepositions; these properties distinguish complementizers from WH-words and relative pronouns (Rudin 1986: 51–53). Alternatively, some researchers consider complementizers to be incompatible with each other in one clause;[14] this strict replacement condition mirrors the tendency of complementizers to organize into loose paradigms, but it also excludes the notion of double complementizers (see § 3.5). More recent generative approaches, starting with Rizzi (1997), assume that more than one complementizer is possible in a clause; they are not assigned to one fixed position, but are arranged in a CP-area (cf. Krapova, this volume, for details and references).

An approach to complementizers as a gradient concept harmonizes with the distinction between canonical complementizers (i.e. core members of the category) and complementation markers (Joseph 2016; Kehayov and Boye 2016b). Complementation markers can be defined as "all means (including in principle word order and intonation) of identifying [clausal] complements"; then canonical complementizers "serve to identify balanced (in the sense of Stassen 1985) complements" (Kehayov and Boye 2016b: 810). Since in Balkan Slavic the infinitive has become almost inexistent and in the remainder of South Slavic complementizers with infinitival (or other non-finite) predicates have been marginalized (see § 2.3.2), this issue is relevant from a diachronic perspective. Nevertheless, in general, we can follow Kehayov and Boye (2016b) in establishing subset relations (from left to right) between

[3]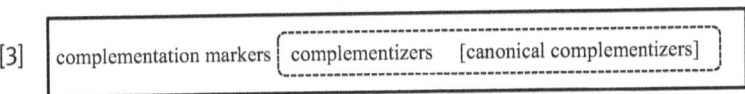

As concerns the morphosyntactic format, Noonan (2007: 55) characterizes complementizers as

[4] "a word, particle, clitic or affix, one of whose functions it is to identify the entity as a complement".

---

14 For a description in terms of Government and Binding cf. Rudin (1986: 41–43).

This vague definition does not restrict the format of the units in question on an unbound – bound morpheme (or word – affix) cline. By contrast, Kehayov and Boye (2016a: 1) seem to imply that complementizers are words ("conjunctions that have the function of identifying clauses as complements"). In South Slavic, units that can be undisputably regarded as complementizers equally undisputably have word status; those which are disputed complementizers behave like clitics, or even as clitics acquiring properties of affixes.[15] This issue is intimately connected with the question of 'analytic (subjunctive) mood' (see § 2.2.3).

These topics will surface in the subsequent overview, which is mainly based on contrasts of functional distinctions crucial for a typology of complementizers (and, more broadly, complementation markers) and their distribution in South Slavic. In general, we can still confirm Ransom's (1986: 2) dictum that complementizer contrasts have been investigated much less systematically than mood contrasts. Partially, this may be because the former have often been subsumed under the latter, but also because complementizers show a broader and more fine-grained gamut of functional distinctions than do moods. After more than 30 years of scholarly dispute, this opinion does not seem to have lost its validity, in particular for South Slavic.

2.2.1 Formulation of the task

Most (not all) complementizers (and associated complementation markers) have concomitant functions which bear on modal and/or illocutionary values of the clauses they head.[16] Looking for contrasts in the choice of complementation markers implies that we distinguish restrictions in the distribution of each of them, but also ask whether, in the first place, there is a choice between two (or more) items and, if there is such a choice, which aspects in the relation between the CTP and its complement are highlighted.[17]

---

[15] Some generative approaches regard complementizers as bound morphemes (e.g., Roberts and Roussou 2003: 22–23).

[16] Cf. Hansen, Letuchiy, and Błaszczyk (2016: 203–204) on Russian, Polish and Bulgarian, from a more comprehensive perspective cf. Boye, van Lier, and Theilgaard Brink (2015), Kehayov and Boye (2016b).

[17] Instances with a meaningful choice of complementation markers can be compared to Differential Argument Marking (a notion applying to clause level). This comparison accounts for the broader analogy between the distinction of syntactically vs semantically motivated case marking and complementizers with and without additional functions (beyond the syntactic function of marking a clause as a complement of a matrix predicate).

2.2.2 Factivity vs factuality

In the literature on clausal complementation, and on clause semantics in general, the term 'factive' is used in at least two different, largely incommensurable senses. '(Non-)factive' and the less widespread term '(non-)factual' are often used synonymously. Since this creates confusion and is, thus, detrimental for a comprehensive typology of phenomena related to complementation, I will first clarify the distinction itself and make a terminological proposal (§ 2.2.2.1), before I will comment on the related term 'veridicality' (§ 2.2.2.2) and dwell upon the relation between factivity (in its narrow sense) and causality (§ 2.2.2.3).

2.2.2.1 Factivity ≠ factuality

Basically, the notion 'factive/factivity' has been employed in two senses.[18] In one sense it was introduced in the logically oriented tradition by Kiparsky and Kiparsky (1970) to mean propositions that are presupposed as true (and which do not admit any alternatives); in other words: a factive proposition is excluded from the scope of negation, i.e. it remains true even if the embedding predicate is negated (see ex. 15a and 15b). Accordingly, factive predicates have clausal complements containing such a proposition. Typical examples are complements of verbs like *regret* and *complain*; all other kinds of CTPs with propositional complements are simply non-factive.[19] Among factive CTPs we also find many non-verbal predicates denoting emotional states or moral judgments (on the axis 'good – bad' or 'appropriate – inappropriate') as, for instance, *Sally was sad / happy / excited / surprised that P*. Factive predicates also occur with non-clausal arguments (e.g., *The commission welcomed her initiative*; *Their punctual arrival relieved everybody*), in which case the nominal complement (*her initiative*, *their punctual arrival*) represents a condensed proposition (something like *She took the initiative (to do S)*; *They arrived on time*). There are also factive sentential adverbs (e.g. *(un)fortunately, deplorably, luckily*), i.e., adverbs which have scope over presupposed propositions. Importantly, the presupposed status of P normally

---

[18] Cf. Wiemer (2017: 273–275), where however the relation to (non-)assertiveness was not shown very clearly and different terminological choices were made.

[19] In fact, the notion of (non-)factivity is not a binary one, but allows for gradations (cf. Karttunen 1973, Hooper and Thompson 1973, Abusch 2010, Simons 2013, among many others). We may say that core members of factive predicates operate as strong presupposition triggers, while peripheral members are more flexible in that their presupposition may be cancelled under certain environments. The same distinction applies to complementizers (see the comments at the bottom of Table 2 and Krapova, Sočanac, and Wiemer, forthcoming-a).

implies that it represents given information and thus remains in the communicative background; the focus rests on the factive CTP or adverb, respectively.

The other sense in which 'factivity' has come to be employed is much less specific, in fact, it comprises a mixed bag. On the one hand, it refers to the distinction of whether some subject (the grammatical subject or the speaker) judges a proposition as true or not, or downtones this judgment. This distinction is equivalent to (degrees of) epistemic support as investigated, e.g., in Boye (2010, 2012). Importantly, epistemic support operates on propositions; however, these are not presupposed, but represent the focus of the message, and the epistemic agent does not exclude alternative propositions to hold true (i.e., that s/he might be wrong). Compare (15a)–(15b), in which the complement clause contains a presupposed proposition, and (16a)–(16b), in which the complement clause contains a proposition that is the target of the epistemic judgment denoted by the CTP; negation of the CTP (see 16b) bears on the truth-value in the complement:

(15) a. *Alice complains that Adam doesn't like her.*
     b. *Alice does not complain that Adam doesn't like her.*

(16) a. *Alice thinks / believes / is sure that Adam doesn't like her.*
     b. *Alice doubts / doesn't think (believe) / isn't sure that Adam doesn't like her.*

On the other hand, the unspecific use of 'factivity' includes clauses (or their CTPs) that do not contain any proposition, but SoAs. Complements of volitional predicates like *wish, want, desire* belong to this category, but also of predicates denoting manipulative speech acts like *order, ask* (= *request*), *insist* (see the bottom line in Figure 3). These are related to deontic (or bouletic), but not to epistemic modality. The broad usage of the term '(non-)factive' practically coincides with '(ir)realis'-distinctions as discussed in the typological literature (for recent surveys cf. Mauri and Sansò 2012, 2016; also Nikolaeva 2016: 80–84); see Figure 3. Most briefly, 'irrealis' is a general characteristic of all clauses that do not predicate over a situation with an episodic referential anchoring. Importantly, lack of anchorage usually corresponds to a world with a modal background (deontic, epistemic, or other), but specific reference is denied or suspended; the latter happens with modifiers or CTPs indicating weak epistemic support, but also in conditionals and with habituals. In the literature on South Slavic clausal complementation, this distinction is practically equal with the opposition of 'indicative' vs '(analytic) subjunctive', which has usually been treated under the label of '(non-)assertiveness'.

It is easy to see that this very broad use of '(non-)factivity' is not only vague, as it comprises very different domains of modality (or of irrealis meanings), but also that it contradicts the specific use of 'factive' which is tied to logically presupposed propositions. The only domain where both usages of 'factive' overlap is clauses containing a proposition (which may be suspended),[20] but in the broad usage of the term clauses housing a proposition only form a subclass, while in its narrow usage containing a (non-suspended) proposition is a necessary premise. Moreover, only in the narrow sense 'factive' strictly correlates with backgrounded parts of communicative structure, and this fact has been noticed as important for phenomena related to clausal complementation. Namely, only factive (= presupposed) complements combine realis features with non-assertiveness: some proposition is only presupposed, but not asserted, as true. This explains why, for instance, in most Romance languages such complements trigger the morphological subjunctive,[21] while in Slavic they are coded with the indicative. This observation was captured by Noonan (2007) when he compared (ir)realis and (non-)assertive as associated, but independent dimensions. See Figure 3, which takes up Noonan's comparison. (Non-)assertiveness is understood in terms of communicative structure, and the only domain where it does not overlap with the (ir)realis distinction is factive (= backgrounded, presupposed) complements.

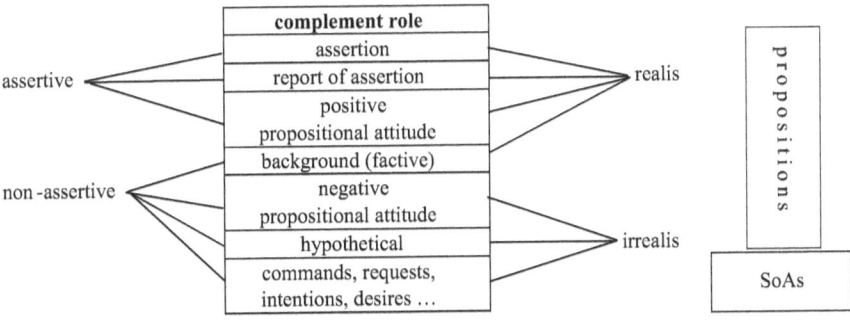

Figure 3: Assertiveness vs (ir)realis-distinctions (following Noonan 2007).

The distinction between propositions and SoAs was added. Crucially, all complement types but those in the last line (denoting commands, desires, etc.) contain propositions, although the non-assertive ones downtone the propositional content, either because it is backgrounded (as with factive complements in the narrow sense), or because epistemic support is weakened or suspended (for suspension of

---

[20] Consequently, the extensional intersection of 'factive' complement clauses in either reading belongs to the section with weak semantic integration (in terms of the SIH) and with undisputably biclausal structure.
[21] Cf. Marques (2009). Remarkably, an exception is Rumanian (2009: 180).

assertiveness see § 2.2.2, § 2.2.3.1). As shown above, the broad usage of 'non-factive' does not discriminate between propositions and SoAs.

In order to avoid undesirable vagueness and misunderstandings connected to the term 'factive/factivity', I suggest employing it only in the specific, narrow sense (after Kiparsky and Kiparsky 1970) and to unite the remainder of the other (still different) senses under the term '(non-)factual / (non-)factuality'. This terminological "regulation" may, at first sight, be a bit unusual (given the indiscriminate usage in much of the literature on South Slavic),[22] but it provides a clear-cut and brief distinction which is vital for the semantics of complementation techniques, not only in a broader cross-linguistic perspective, but particularly in the internal diversity of South Slavic (see below). Moreover, in practice, the term '(non-)factual(ity)' has already become customary to mark exactly this broader domain of clause semantics among linguists of different convictions and specializing on various languages.[23] Henceforth, this terminological distinction will be abided by strictly.[24] In South Slavic (non-)factuality and factivity intersect, and this intersection becomes tangible when we compare the usage domains of the basic complementation markers, especially in Balkan Slavic.

+factual complementizers tend to be the default (or standard) complementizers, inasmuch as no particular epistemic commitment is marked, i.e., strong epistemic support is conventionally implied. This seems to be the reason why this type of complementizer has ousted, or is ousting, the narrowly factive one in contemporary standard Serbian-Croatian (Grković-Major, this volume). Thus, *žao* 'be sorry' can take either *što* or *da*, both in the affirmative (17a) and with negation (17b):

---

[22] Cf. Topolińska (2003; 2006; 2008a; 2008b), Laskova (2009: 169), Lindstedt (2010), Gegovski (2014: 104), Joseph (2016), among many others.

[23] For instance, by Krapova (2001), Mirić (2018: 203) with respect to South Slavic and, for other languages, by Narrog (2005, 2009), Cornillie and Pietrandrea (2012), Rentzsch (2015). Compare also Diewald (1999), who uses Germ. *faktisch* (= factual) with respect to modal auxiliaries, and the general practice in the contributions to Nuyts and Van der Auwera (2016) and Aikhenvald (2018).

[24] Unfortunately, Kehayov and Boye (2016b: 825–828 and passim) put it the other way around: they use 'factual' for complementation markers and clausal complements with presupposed content but keep 'factive' (in the classical sense adopted here) only for CTPs, without motivating this decision. This follows Boye (2012), where 'factive' is used synonymously to denote 'full epistemic support', thus in the sense of 'factual' as proposed here.

Serbian-Croatian

(17) a. Žao   mi   je   **da / što**   je   Ivan
        pity   1SG.DAT   AUX.PRS.3SG   COMP   AUX.PRS.3SG   PN
        otiša-o.
        go_away[PFV]-PST-(SG.M)
        'I am sorry that / that$_{FACT}$ Ivan left.'

   b. Nije   mi   žao   **da / što**   je   Ivan
      NEG_AUX.PRS.3SG   1SG.DAT   pity   COMP   AUX.PRS.3SG   PN
      otiša-o.
      go_away[PFV]-PST-(SG.M)
      'I am not sorry that / that$_{FACT}$ Ivan left.'

The restriction of *što* to factive complements can be seen with CTPs of cognitive attitude implying neutral or strong epistemic support (+factual), where *što* is excluded:[25]

(18) a. Misli-m,   da / *što   je   Ivan
        think[IPFV].PRS-1SG   COMP   AUX.PRS.3SG   PN[M]-NOM
        doša-o.
        come[PFV]-PST-(SG.M)
        'I think that Ivan has come.'

   b. Ne   misli-m,   da / *što   je
      NEG   think[IPFV].PRS-1SG   COMP   AUX.PRS.3SG
      Ivan   doša-o.
      PN[M]-NOM   come[PFV]-PST-(SG.M)
      'I don't think that Ivan has come.'

The development may also go into the opposite direction, from a factive (and causal) one toward the standard complementizer. This is what probably happened to Bulg. *če*, which can be used with factive CTPs instead of *deto*, as shown in (19a) and (19b):

Bulgarian

(19) a. Radva-m   se   **če / deto**   Ivan   dojd-e.
        glad[IPFV].PRS-1SG   REFL   COMP   PN   come[PFV]-AOR.3SG
        'I'm glad that / that$_{FACT}$ Ivan came.'

---

[25] In these sentences, *što* could be interpreted only as a causal connective ('I think **why** has Ivan come'), which reflects its diachronic provenance (cf. Grković-Major, this volume).

b. *Ne   radva-m   se   če / deto   Ivan   dojd-e.*
   NEG   glad[IPFV].PRS-1SG   REFL   COMP   PN   come[PFV]-AOR.3SG
   'I'm not glad that / that_FACT Ivan came.'

However, only *če* is appropriate, and *deto* excluded, with non-factive CTPs. Compare (10a), repeated here slightly amended (10a'), with its negated equivalent in (10a"):

(10) a'. *Mislj-a,   če / *deto   reši-x   vsički   zadači*
         think[IPFV].PRS-1SG   COMP   solve[PFV]-AOR.1SG   all   task.PL
         na test-a.
         on test-DEF
         (No ne săm săvsem siguren.)
         'I think **that** I (have) solved all tasks from the test. (But I'm not entirely sure.)'

     a". *Ne   mislj-a,   če / *deto   reši-x   vsički*
         NEG   think[IPFV].PRS-1SG   COMP   solve[PFV]-AOR.1SG   all
         zadači   na test-a.
         task.PL on test-DEF
         'I don't **that** think I (have) solved all tasks from the test.'

Although the distribution in the Balkan Slavic languages is not actually complementary, their data seem to present the clearest "sharework" between (i) strictly factive (Bulg. *deto*, Mac. *što*), (ii) epistemically neutral (+factual) (Bulg. *če*, Mac. *deka, oti*)[26], and (iii) non-factual (Bulg./Mac. *da*) complementation markers in South Slavic. The non-factual connectives conflate propositional and SoA-complements, while +factual and factive complementizers always (and trivially) introduce propositional complements. These properties are summarized in the following table.

Table 2: Factive and (non-)factual complementation markers in South Slavic.

	strictly factive	factual (epistemically neutral)	non-factual
Bulgarian	deto	če	da
Macedonian	što	deka, oti (dial., among other dialectal units)	da

---

26 *Oti* is an old borrowing from Greek and now dialectally restricted. Since I am unaware of any functional difference between *oti* and *deka* (or of related research), I will not deal with *oti* further and just assume that what can be said about *deka* also applies to *oti*.

Table 2 (continued)

	strictly factive	factual (epistemically neutral)	non-factual
Serbian-Croatian	što	da (≈ da_1 in § 2.2.3)	da (≈ da_2 in § 2.2.3)
Slovene	—	da	da, naj (see § 2.2.4.2)
	presupposed proposition cannot be cancelled	presupposed proposition can be cancelled	no presupposed proposition
	complements necessarily propositional		propositional or SoA complements

The following examples illustrate that one and the same CTP can acquire different properties along the factive/factual divide (or otherwise: that it is flexible with respect to these properties) and that these properties influence the choice of the complementation marker:

Bulgarian
(20) a. *Pomn-iš   li **deto** s   Marija se*
       remember[IPFV]-PRS.2SG Q COMP with PN REFL
       sreštna-xte   na pazar-a?
       meet[PFV]-AOR.2PL on market-DEF
       'Do you remember **that** with Maria you met at the market?'
       *Ne   pomn-iš   li **deto***
       NEG remember[IPFV]-PRS.2SG Q COMP
       s Marija se sreštnaxte na pazara?
       "Don't you remember **that** with Maria you met at the market?' → factive
   b. *Pomnj-a,   **če** Marija njakoga pee-še*
       remember[IPFV]-PRS.1SG COMP PN ever sing[IPFV]-IMPF.3SG
       (No može i da greša.)
       'I remember **that** Maria at a time used to sing.
       (But I may be mistaken.)'   → factual
   c. *Az   ne   pomnj-a,   **če** Marija*
       1SG.NOM NEG remember[IPFV]-PRS.1SG COMP PN
       e   pee-l-a   njakoga,
       AUX.PRS.3SG sing[IPFV]-LPT-SG.F ever
       no ti može i da si prav.
       'I don't remember **that** Maria sometimes used to sing, but you may as
       well be right.'   → factual

(20) d. *Ne   pomnj-a   Marija **da**   e*
       NEG   remember[IPFV]-PRS.1SG   PN   CON AUX.PRS.3SG
       pee-l-a   njakoga.
       sing[IPFV]-LPT-SG.F   ever
       'I do not remember Maria to have sung ever.'   → non-factual
                                                           (weak epistemic support)

It is intriguing that the factive complementizer *deto* can be used with semi-factive verbs (i.e. cognitive verbs like *pomnja* 'remember', *razbiram* 'understand'; see f. 28) in yes/no-questions (see 20a), but only to a restricted extent in assertions. For instance, *deto* could not replace *če* in (20b) and (20c), but conversely *če* could be used as a substitute for *deto* in (20a) causing hardly any change in meaning. These issues seem to require an item-by-item analysis of pertinent CTPs (similarly to what was postulated in § 2.1). This applies to Macedonian, too, where the distribution of *što* (factive) vs *deka* (+factual) slightly differs from the Bulgarian pattern.[27]

While Slovene seems to lack a specific factive complementizer, Serbian employs *što* for this purpose, although it still has "a fuzzy, transitional status between an adverbial and a complement clause" (see § 2.2.2.3). However, syntactic differentiation occurred between *što* and *zato što*: "in present-day Serbian *zato što* (...) introduces causal clauses, the cause of an emotion, being its object at the same time, is expressed by the shorter form *što*" (Grković-Major, this volume: § 3.4).

In general, factive complementizers fill out a small niche and are often pushed by +factual complementizers, provided these have not themselves turned into +factual complementizers (like Bulg. *če*). The distinction between epistemically neutral and factive clausal complements creates one of the "neuralgic spots" in South Slavic indicative of areal differentiation and its diachronic background. First of all, the chronological relation between different processes needs clarification. Moreover, the areal differentiation does not coincide with the traditional divide into eastern (= Balkan) and western South Slavic: on the one hand, in Bulgarian a factive complementizer has become the default complementizer (*če*) and can itself replace another (more recent?) factive complementizer (*deto*), while in Serbian-Croatian and Macedonian the (probably) oldest factive complementizer (*što*) can be replaced by a (younger?) +factual complementizer (Mac. *deka*, Serb.-Cr. *da*). On the other hand, Macedonian shares the restriction of *da* to the irrealis domain with Bulgarian (see § 2.2.3), but a tendency toward using

---

[27] I am particularly obliged to Iliyana Krapova and Eleni Bužarovska for insightful discussions. Cf. also Krapova, Sočanac, and Wiemer (forthcoming-a).

kako 'how' for propositional complements with other than perception CTPs with Serbian-Croation (see § 2.2.5). Slovene appears to be "unaffected" by such processes. Altogether the different functional intersections of these complementation markers are indicative of shifts in their paradigmatic relations (i.e., replacement conditions), whose intricacies can probably be disclosed only in an item-by-item analysis of CTPs (including negation, mood marking and narrative embedding, which can lead to clashes of attitude holders).

2.2.2.2 Veridicality

Veridicality is another term not used unanimously, even among formal semanticists and generativists, who have been applying it in the first place. In one approach, a predicate is to be considered veridical iff it logically entails the truth of its complement ($Vp \vDash p$), otherwise the predicate is non-veridical. Compare (21) and (22), # marks an infelicitous continuation:

Serbian-Croatian
(21) *Marija zna / shvaća da je Ivan oženjen (#ali to nije istina).*
 'Marija knows / understands that Ivan is married (but it's not true).'

(22) *Marija misli / vjeruje da je Ivan oženjen (ali to nije istina).*
 'Marija thinks / believes that Ivan is married (but it's not true).'

This narrow definition of veridicality is based on a classical understanding of entailment, which ties up the judgment about truth to the speaker of the utterance; it does not allow for a switch of this judgment from the speaker to another epistemic agent (a.k.a. attitude holder), typically the grammatical subject of the matrix clause (for this approach cf. Egrè (2008)).

An alternative approach has been proposed by Giannakidou (1998; 2009 etc.). Her definition of veridicality allows for switches between epistemic agents, with the consequence that truth entailments are relativized to the epistemic model of some individual x ($x \ Vp \rightarrow p$, according to x) who is not necessarily the speaker. Consequently, both (21) and (22) would be considered veridical, and there practically can be only two cases of non-veridical statements: (i) statements in which a proposition is not supported by any individual's epistemic model; this includes cases in which propositions are suspended (as in conditional clauses or the future), (ii) statements with embedded clauses that do not contain any proposition, such as embedded directive illocutions (after CTPs like *demand, urge, request*) or of volitional predicates (*want* etc.). We easily see that Giannakidou's looser notion of entailment practically equals truth inference, or epistemic commitment. Thereby this treatment makes veridicality identical to factuality, as defined in § 2.2.2.1 (cf. Krapova, Sočanac, and Wiemer, forthcoming-b, for a concise overview of the relevant notions and approaches).

Giannakidou's approach has become very popular among specialists in South Slavic; cf., for instance, Todorović (2015: 52), and Krapova (this volume), but also Smirnova (2012), who modified Giannakidou's approach in that it is strength of epistemic support (either of P or of non-P) which decides about (non-)veridicality. By capturing veridicality (and thus factuality) in terms of epistemic (or doxastic) models, Giannakidou's and Smirnova's approaches resemble Kratzer's quantificational approach to modal semantics based on conversational backgrounds (Kratzer 1981; 2012 etc.). However, the notion of veridicality adds nothing to the principled difference between factivity and factuality made in § 2.2.2.1. Any predicate of epistemic (or doxastic) attitude, i.e., any predicate implying a propositional complement, allows for factual or non-factual usage (respectively for strong, neutral or weak epistemic support), and usually such predicates allow for a switch of epistemic agent (a problem, though, being *know* and *be aware (of)* and their translational equivalents). For this reason, I refrain from using the notion of veridicality; introducing it would rather enhance the risk of creating confusion in light of the different treatments of veridicality.

2.2.2.3 Factivity and causality

Factive complementizers are tightly connected to causality, both in diachronic and synchronic terms; this applies to Bulg. *če*, to Mac. *deka* and to *što* in Macedonian and Serbian-Croatian. Thus, it is no accident that, for instance, Bulg. *če* can be found as an adverbial subordinator of reason clauses (see 23), and in many cases, *če*-clauses as complements of factive CTPs simultaneously convey a causal meaning (see 24). By the same token, the complementizer contrast in the Croatian examples (25a) and (25b) shows that factive *što* implies an explanation for the state of the subject (*bojao se* 'he was afraid'). With emotive factive predicates the syntactic function of complementing can hardly be disentangled from reason (causal relations).[28]

---

[28] Of course, in addition to emotive predicates, another prominent group of factive predicates is related to knowledge ('cognitive' factive predicates), such as '(come to) know', 'realize', 'understand', 'remember', 'forget'. For these predicates no relation to cause and reason is obvious. However, although cognitive factives do not seem to create the same sort of problems for a distinction between adjunct and complement clauses as do (sometimes) emotive factives (see above), cognitive factives have been shown to sometimes lose their factive properties, i.e., under certain conditions (e.g., in conditionals) their complements do not code presupposed propositions (Karttunen 1971). On an average, they behave rather like "soft" presupposition triggers,

Bulgarian

(23) Trăgn-i   sega,   **če**   šte   stan-e   kăsno!
    depart[PFV]-IMP.SG now   CON   FUT   become[PFV]-PRS.3SG   late
    'Go now, **because** it will be late!'
    (from Tomić 2006: 458)

(24) Radva-m   se,   **če**   me   razbira-š.
    be_glad[IPFV]-PRS.1SG   REFL   COMP   1SG.ACC   understand-PRS.2SG
    'I am glad **that** you understand me.'

Croatian

(25) a. Boja-o   se   **da**   nije
       fear[IPFV]-PST-(SG.M)   REFL   COMP   NEG.AUX.PRS.3SG
       nauči-o   lekcij-u
       learn[PFV]-PST-(SG.M)   lesson-ACC
       'He was afraid **that** he might not have learnt his homework.'
                                           → possible fact (not verified)

   b. Boja-o   se   **što**   nije
       fear[IPFV]-PST-(SG.M)   REFL   COMP   NEG.AUX.PRS.3SG
       nauči-o   lekcij-u
       learn[PFV]-PST-(SG.M)   lesson-ACC
       'He was afraid **that** (= because) he had not learnt his homework.'
                                           → fact taken for granted

   (from Mønnesland 1972: 153; my translations)

To explain this tight correlation and the diachronic provenance of factive complementizers from causal connectives, we have to realize that factivity is tightly connected to emotional or ethical judgments ('good – bad') about states. These judgments presuppose the propositions which are their "objects", because these propositions are employed to motivate the judgment (respectively the state it refers to); these propositions then can easily figure both as reason for the judgment about the state and as its proper "content". Therefore, it is almost impossible to separate targets of emotional or moral judgment from factivity, and the conceptual link between both is causality.

On the one hand, this tight connection precludes decisions as to whether it is factivity or causality which determines the semantics of the relevant comple-

---

while emotive predicates are more reliable, and thus "hard" presupposition triggers (cf. Krapova, Sočanac, and Wiemer, forthcoming-a).

mentizers (cf. Breu, this volume, and Grković-Major, this volume, for discussion). On the other hand, this raises the question as to what are the criteria to decide whether or not some causal connective also introduces a clausal argument to some higher predicate. Obviously, these criteria depend on the semantics of suitable predicates, which leads us back to the general problems in dealing with the grey zone between (clear) arguments and (clear) adjuncts. In addition, the problem with emotive predicates seems to be that, since they imply reason as their "content", virtually any causal connective is compatible and could be used to introduce a clausal complement. Frequency of occurrence with emotive predicates may thus be a crucial factor raising the expectability of some particular causal connective among others. Another factor may be more subtle meaning distinctions which manifest themselves not with clausal, but with NP- or PP-arguments of emotive predicates; the distribution of the latter may then correlate with the (im)possibility of, or (dis)preference for, some causal connective as factive complementizer. For instance, Bulg. *deto* can be used as a factive complementizer only after emotive predicates which otherwise combine with prepositional phrases (PPs) headed by *za* (e.g., *radvam se / žal mi, deto* P 'I'm glad / sorry that P', analogous to *radvam se / žal mi za* NP); by contrast, emotive predicates which take PPs headed by *ot* only allow for factive complements introduced by *če* (e.g., *boja se / strax me e, če / *deto* P 'I'm afraid / frightened that P', analogous to *boja se / strax me e ot* NP); cf. Krapova (2010: 1265–1269).

Since this area has remained understudied, in the following I will mention only those factive complementizers which have been qualified as such by some specialist or other (see the synopsis in § 2.2.8).

2.2.3 *da*: complementizer vs mood marker

The literature on the status and usage types of South Slavic *da* is legion, hence it is not possible to provide even a remotely comprehensive survey of this discussion. The central point to be considered is the relation of complementizers to mood distinctions, i.e., to the discussion of *da* as a marker of '(analytical) subjunctive', which has been a permanent topic of Balkan and South Slavic linguistics.[29] Practically

---

[29] Surveys on this discussion can be found in Feleško (1974), Kramer (1986: 20–64), Georgievski (2009), Tomić (2012), Gegovski (2014) for Macedonian, by Genadieva-Mustafčieva (1970: § 2), Petrova-Schick (1973), Rudin (1986: 54–57), Tiševa (2001a: 168–171), Viktorova (2009), Smirnova (2012), Ivanova (2014: 107–113), Pitsch (2020: 229–230) for Bulgarian, by Todorović (2015: 39–59) for Serbian/Croatian. Cf. also Mitkovska and Bužarovska (this volume: § 2.3) and Grković-Major (forthcoming).

every textbook or survey on the grammar of Balkan languages deals with analytical mood, for which in Balkan Slavic *da* is the main player.[30]

The intense and long-standing interest in the functions and the status of *da* can be explained by its ubiquity in South Slavic, conditioned by its central and versatile role not only in clause-combining, but also in the formation of complex predicates (Wiemer 2014a; 2017: 300–305, 325–330; 2018: 299–303) and of complex clause connectives, that is all along the SIH (see Table 1). The following Serbian example provides a good impression of this role. It shows the employment of *da* as [a] complementizer, [b] connective within complex predicates, [c] adverbial subordinator (= conjunction; here: of a purpose clause):

Serbian
(26) *Marija   misli*   [a] *da sam   rek-l-a*
     PN.NOM think[IPFV].PRS-(3SG)   AUX.PRS.1SG say[PFV]-PST-SG.F
     [a] *da   ću*   [b] *da   napiše-m   knjig-u*
            FUT.1SG   write[PFV].PRS-1SG   book-ACC
     [c] *da   postane-m   slavn-a.*
                     become[PFV].PRS-1SG   famous-NOM.SG.F
     'Mary thinks **that** I said **that** I will write a book **in order to** become famous.' (from Todorović 2015: 25)

In function [b] an infinitive (*ću napisati* or even *napisati=ću*) instead of the *da*-construction could have been used Serbian-Croatian. In Balkan Slavic the *da*-construction is now the only option, since the infinitive as morphological form of the verb has practically been lost. Compare complements of object-control verbs as in

Macedonian
(27) *Nareduva-m   Marija da   dojd-e   vednaš.*
     order[IPFV].PRS-1SG   PN   CON come[PFV].PRS-3SG   immediately
     'I order Maria to come immediately.' (lit. . . . *Maria that (she) comes*. . .)

This functional equivalence has been a reason why clauses headed by *da* have often been compared to infinitival complements, and in these clauses, *da* has been considered a kind of auxiliary (similar to Engl. *to* + infinitive), in particular by generativists (cf. Krapova 2001; Nikolaeva 2013: 102). *Da*-clauses have also been regarded as a replacement of the infinitive from a diachronic point of

---

[30] Cf. Feleszko (1979), Kramer (1992), Tomić (2006), Lindstedt (2010), Friedman (2011), Joseph (2016), Mirić (2018), among others.

view, although the diachronic relation between different stages of the infinitive loss and the expansion of *da*-constructions still requires some further clarification of details (cf. Grickat 1975; Asenova 2002; Jačeva-Ulčar 2014: 162). A process concomitant to *da*'s expansion over clause and predicate types is its semantic change: *da* has been known as a marker of irrealis meanings ever since its oldest attestations. *Da* has preserved this property in Balkan Slavic, but it has lost it in the western part of South Slavic. This correlates with two facts: first, in Balkan Slavic *da* has become a verb-oriented proclitic (see ex. 27 and § 2.2.3.4); second, in general *da* cannot co-occur with other clitics related to irrealis functions, like the future marker or *bi* of the Common Slavic conditional. In the western part of South Slavic, *da* practically does not have any clitic properties; instead, it itself can serve as host of enclitics, as such it can be used together with future clitics (as in the Serbian example above: *da ću* 'that I will') and the inherited conditional marker (*bi* + *l*-participle) as in ex. 28 below (see further § 2.2.3.3). These phenomena are evidently related. As it seems, the onset of semantic change just mentioned occurred very early, at least in the northwestern periphery of the South Slavic territory (cf. Greenberg, this volume and Grković-Major 2020; this volume), but many details of this process are still unknown. In contemporary South Slavic, we observe a clear-cut split between an eastern group (= Balkan Slavic) and the remainder in the western part. To which extent, and for which properties, an areal transition (e.g., in the eastern Serbian dialects) can be captured, is one of the unanswered questions in usage-based research; the same applies to diatopic, diastratic and diaphasic variation between infinitival and *da*-clauses in the western part as well as changes in the combinability of *da* with the *bi*-conditional inherited from Common Slavic particularly in the western half of South Slavic (see below).

An important pacesetter of the discussion concerning *da* was Gołąb (1954, 1964a), although his observations were partially based on archaic uses (concerning the conditional; see below). Following him as well as Ivić (1970), many researchers dealing with Serbian-Croatian have argued for two distinct (homonymous) units with the shape *da*: da_1 – a complementizer, and da_2 – a mood marker. Crucially, both operate on clause level. Gołąb himself argued in favor of two different morphemes *da* (which he assumed to reflect different diachronic provenance). One *da* (= da_1) is a complementizer (a "conjunction" introducing a "subordinate objective clause"), the other (= da_2) a "modal adverbial particle" (Gołąb 1964a: 8). Regardless of terminology, the difference becomes clear with one of Gołąb's Serbian examples (Gołąb 1964a: 8):

Serbian

(28) *Zahteva-o   sam   od   nj-ih*
      demand[PFV]-PST-(SG.M) AUX.PRS.1SG   from   3-GEN.PL
      da *mi   dad-u   hiljad-u   dinar-a*
              1SG.DAT   give[PFV].PRS-3PL   thousand-ACC   dinar-GEN.PL
      da *mog-u* || **da** *bi-h*   *moga-o*   *putova-ti*
              can.PRS-1SG   COND-1SG   can-PST-(SG.M)   travel[IPFV]-INF
      u   Italij-u.
      in   Italy-ACC
      'I required from them **that** they give me one thousand dinars **so that** I could go to Italy.'

The first occurrence of *da* (= *da₁*) introduces a clausal complement of the transitive verb *zahtevati* 'demand', whereas the second occurrence (= *da₂*) adds an adverbial clause, i.e., a clause not required by the valency frame of any predicate. Note that in this second occurrence *da* freely combines with the conditional marker *bi* (+ *l*-participle). This difference, based on the argument – adjunct distinction, led Gołąb to claim that *da₂* is part of a mood paradigm, although on its face value, *da* is just a clause-initial particle which in either case codes an event as irreal (potential, hypothetic, counterfactual) with respect to the given reference interval (e.g., the past interval set by *zahtevao sam* 'I demanded').

Simultaneously, Gołąb pointed out another distinction, which applies even if we restrict ourselves to clausal complementation. If the *da*-clause occurs in combination with the present tense of an imperfective (ipfv.) verb, it can be ambiguous (out of context) as in (29a): the *da*-clause may relate either to real events (see (i)) or it may encode an event which is intended, recommended or in some other way irreal (see (ii)), however this second interpretation might require more contextual support. The situation changes if the predicate of the *da*-clause is a perfective (pfv.) verb in the present tense, as in (30a). In this case, only the irrealis-reading is available.

(29) a. *Ja   sam   mu   govori-o   nekoliko*
         1SG.NOM   AUX.PRS.1SG   3.DAT.M   say[IPFV]-PST-(SG.M) several
         put-a   da   nje-gova   dec-a
         time-GEN.PL   POSS-NOM.PL   children-NOM
         igraj-u   u   naš-oj   bašt-i.
         play[IPFV].PRS-3PL   in   our-LOC.SG.F   garden[F]-LOC.SG
     (i)   'I told him several times **that** his children <u>play</u> in our garden.'
     (ii) 'I told him several times **that** his children <u>should play</u> in our garden.'

(30) a. *Meni   moj-a star-a majk-a   govori*
      1SG.DAT   (my old mother)-NOM.SG.F   say[IPFV].PRS-(3SG)
      da   <u>*urani-m*</u>   *svak-o jutr-o   na vod-u.*
      get_up_early[PFV].PRS-1SG (every morning)-ACC on water-ACC
      'My old mother says me **that** every morning <u>I should get up</u> to fetch water.'

Examples like these illustrate that, in Serbian (and Croatian, Slovene), *da*-clauses with pfv. verbs in the present tense restrict the interpretation to the irrealis-domain, whereas *da*-clauses with ipfv. verbs in the present tense (and other tense-aspect forms) can be used to denote real events. Note that these considerations rest entirely on distributional properties of *da* with finite verb forms in their clause – i.e., it is not *da* alone which encodes a modality or mood distinction – and that unambiguous irrealis-readings are conditioned by the combination of *da* with present tense forms of pfv. verbs. Moreover, Gołąb shows that the realis vs irrealis-reading of the *da*-clause depends on the CTP. The mirror image of this is that, in Serbian (Croatian), present tense uses with irrealis-readings cannot freely be exchanged for other tense-aspect forms. This fact was the reason why, since Ivić (1970), Serbian and Croatian linguists distinguish *nemobilan prezent* (for irrealis readings) from *mobilan prezent* (see § 2.2.3.1). Gołąb (1964a: 9–10 et passim) argues that his observations justify contrasting *da* + pfv. present as a 'modal particle' (= da_2) against *da* + [*bi* + *l*-participle] as a 'subordinating conjunction' (= da_1).[31]

Therefore, Gołąb actually merged the complement – adjunct distinction with a distinction between subordinator and 'modal particle', with the latter being part of 'analytical mood', mostly with a function from the domain of volition (optative, permissive, etc.). He suggested that da_2 participates in a new verbal paradigm which, in diachronic terms, came to supplant the older conditional inherited from Common Slavic. Many linguists followed this line of argumentation, at least implicitly (cf. the survey in Todorović 2015: 39–45, most of the authors mentioned in fnn. 29–30, and Topolińska's work).

In fact, the *bi*-conditional has withdrawn from clausal complements of directive CTPs (see below). This does not apply to speech acts in general, as in Serbian-Croatian the *bi*-conditional can be encountered in reported speech with CTPs denoting declarative speech acts; compare (31):

---

[31] Cf. also Browne (1986: 50–62). For a summary on Gołąb's (1964a) and Ivić's (1970) insights concerning Serbian cf. Todorović (2015: 39–45).

Serbian
(31) *Saopšti-l-a*   mi   je   da   bi
     inform[PFV]-PST-SG.F   1SG.DAT   AUX.PRS.3SG   COMP   COND
     doš-l-a   / da   bi   An-a   *doš-l-a.*
     come[PFV]-PST-SG.F   COMP   COND   PN-NOM   come[PFV]-PST-SG.F
     'She$_i$ informed me that she$_j$ / Ana$_k$ would come.'
     (J. Grković-Major, p.c.)

The same applies to Slovene. The conditional has been ousted with directive CTPs in Serbian-Croatian, and in Slovene it now can at best occur with recommendations, as in (32):

Slovene
(32) *Reke-l*   sem   mu,   da   bi
     say[PFV]-PST-(SG.M)   AUX.PRS.1SG   3.DAT.M   COMP   COND
     napisa-l-i   *poročil-o.*
     write[PFV]-PST-SG.F   report-ACC
     'I said to him that they might write the report.'
     (from Uhlik and Žele 2018b: 215)

Recommendations (or suggestions) are a kind of attenuated directives. This fits well into the general picture that in western South Slavic the conditional has a hedging function, as it "softens" the illocutionary force and thus makes it more polite. In this function, it often co-occurs with modal auxiliaries (compare Engl. *could, might* or Germ. *würde* or *Konjunktiv I*). This function is no prerogative of complement clauses, as it occurs in adjuncts (see the purpose clause in ex. 28 above) and main clauses as well.

Topolińska (2003: 318–319) argues that Slovene *da + bi* (+ *l*-participle) is used somewhat more often than in Serbian-Croatian (while in Balkan Slavic this combination has practically disappeared). This would give us a clear areal cline, with Slovene showing most similarity to North Slavic clause linkage patterns, whose most fundamental opposition builds on a distinction between complementizers with and without univerbalized *by* (compare Pol. *że/by*, Russ. *čto/by*, etc. as specialized complementizers). Topolińska remarks that, in this respect, Slovene occupies an intermediate position between South and North Slavic and that South Slavic specifics of *da*-clauses are "becoming less frequent" in Slovene. It is not clear whether this covertly diachronic assumption is to be understood as a recent change in the preference for patterns of clause combining: has *da + bi* as means of irrealis marking in clause combining become (again) more prominent than it used to be after *da* + pfv. present tense had "conquered" this domain?

Or has the domain of *da + bi* never been that much restricted as in the rest of more recent South Slavic? Clearly, this question needs special investigation, also in view of a probably high degree of variation between dialects and on a diastratic and diaphasic level.

The ousting of the *bi*-conditional after directive CTPs seems to be recent: Gołąb (1964a: 9–10) used Serbian data from the late 19th century. They demonstrate that, at that time, the *bi*-conditional could still be employed in embedded directive speech acts (see the obsolete interpretations of 29b and 30b marked with †), while now the same structure can only be interpreted with lowered degree of assertiveness connected to other types of speech acts, e.g., a wish (see (iii) for 29b), or with suspended propositions, e.g., with habitual meaning, which weakens the degree of support by the attitude holder (see (ii) for 30b, where the attitude holder is the grammatical subject of the matrix clause):

(29) b. *Ja sam mu govorio nekoliko puta **da bi** njegova deca igrala u našoj bašti.*
~~(i) 'I told him several times **that** his children play in our garden.'~~
† (ii) 'I told him several times **that** his children should play in our garden.'
(iii) 'I told him several times **that** his children would like to play in our garden.'

(30) b. *Meni moja stara majka govori **da** bih uranila svako jutro na vodu.*
† (i) 'My old mother says me **that** every morning I should get up to fetch water.'
(ii) 'My old mother tells me **that** I used to get up every morning to fetch water.'

Meanwhile the use of the *bi*-conditional after directive CTPs has become obsolete: it has gone in standard Serbian-Croatian and is considered highly unusual in Slovene (M. Uhlik, p.c.). Its function to mark irreal clausal complements has almost entirely been taken over by the combination *da* + pfv. present. Note that this change is not dependent on subordination, as it applies to main clauses as well.[32] Basically the same holds for Slovene, with *naj* as another "competitor" in this field (see § 2.2.4.2). In Balkan Slavic the use of the *bi*-conditional has become heavily restricted in almost all environments,[33] while in western South Slavic

---

[32] For a survey on Serbian cf. Piper (1998) and Popović (2018). In Slovene, no past habitual reading is available (M. Uhlik, p.c.). For some survey on *bi* in Slovene cf. Topolińska (2003).
[33] It is not used for past habitual, but also has now only restricted use in conditional, purpose or other adverbial clauses. It is more frequent in main clauses, where it has found a niche in optative use (often in petrified expressions and together with *da*; see ex. 37). For surveys cf. Kramer

it can be used for politeness in direct and embedded requests and embedded declarative speech acts (see above).

In general, the following motifs have been inciting discussions about the grammatical status of *da*:
(a) *da*'s function as marker of irrealis functions, or of suspended assertiveness (in Balkan Slavic).
(b) restrictions on TAM forms in *da*-clauses.
(c) *da*'s paradigmatic relation to canonical complementizers (and WH-words).
(d) *da*'s behavior as a clitic (mainly in Balkan Slavic).

These motifs should be considered against the syntagmatic and paradigmatic distribution of *da* (vs other clause-initial 'particles') in each particular language variety. Let us assess them briefly. The question whether we are dealing with one or more *da*s (and whether we are assuming homonymy, polysemy or whatever kind of functional alternation) turns out to be tangential for these considerations.

2.2.3.1 Suspended assertiveness and dependent clauses

A major reason why *da* is regarded as marker of analytical subjunctive resides in the (often tacit) assumption that subjunctives primarily or exclusively occur in subordinate clauses; in fact, subjunctives are often defined in this way. In turn, subordinate clauses are often compared to infinitival clauses, i.e., to clauses with reduced (morphological) finiteness (no tense or agreement marking), and in many usage types *da*-clauses are equivalent to infinitive-clauses. However, tense and agreement marking only superficially indicate distinctions of main vs dependent clauses; conceptually, finiteness is an epiphenomenon (or symptom) of assertiveness (or assertativity, cf. Evans 2007). Following Nikolaeva (2013: 113), "[a]n assertive utterance makes a statement about a certain time span by identifying a point on the time line in which the respective proposition is true. Canonically finite clauses are temporally independent and assert a proposition located in the past, present, or future with respect to the moment of speech." Assertiveness is lowered, or suspended, if the speaker refrains from, or weakens, their epistemic commitment to the proposition, or relegates its assessment to another attitude holder. This happens in reportive evidentiality, but it may also happen in clausal complements of verbs marking representative speech acts (i.e., in reported speech) or epistemic attitudes (for a partial survey cf. Padučeva 2005).

(1986: 104–129), Labroska (2018), Mitkovska (2018) on Macedonian, Ivanova (2018) on Bulgarian, and Gołąb (1964b), Tomić (2006) in general. On the grammatical distribution of *bi* and Balkan Slavic mood distinctions carried by WANT-based irrealis-marking cf. Belyavski-Frank (2003).

Other types of utterances do not contain any proposition at all (see § 2.2.2.1). Lack or suspension of assertiveness are equivalent to irrealis meanings, and this is what *da*-clauses indicate, at least in Old Church Slavonic and Balkan Slavic (cf. Ivanova 2014: 130 for Bulgarian); in the western part of South Slavic this feature hinges on choice of tense and aspect (see § 2.2.3.2).

However, suspension, lack or lowering of assertiveness is no exclusive feature of dependent clauses. Among non-assertive speech acts we find imperatives, hortatives, optatives, deliberative questions, and exclamations. All of them are typically expressed by self-standing *da*-clauses, which is only a consequence of the fact that they convey independent illocutions.[34] Thus, the term 'analytical subjunctive' can be taken to simply mean an agglomeration of subordinate clauses with suspended (or lowered) assertiveness; these are often coded by clauses containing *da*, either as their initial head or as a verb-oriented proclitic (see § 2.2.3.4).

2.2.3.2 Restrictions on the choice of tense-aspect forms

In the typological literature declarative main clauses have usually been employed as a gauge against which subjunctive clauses are figured out. That is, subjunctives have been characterized by sets of markers that either differ from the forms used in declarative main clauses, or that are only subsets of forms which are freely available in declarative main clauses (Cristofaro 2003: 58; Nikolaeva 2013; see § 2.3). This, again, mainly applies to markers associated with finiteness, i.e., tense and person-number agreement.

In South Slavic, there are no specific sets of verb forms used exclusively in dependent (complement or adverbial) clauses, but *da*-clauses considered to represent an 'analytical subjunctive' allow only for a reduced array of TAM-forms in comparison to main declarative clauses. As for tense-aspect, some combinations are strongly preferred in *da*-clauses, others are excluded, unless for specific interpretations. In Balkan Slavic, it is only present tense forms of pfv. verbs which are really restricted to the scope of *da* or, alternatively, to other 'modal' clitics, namely the clitic which marks the future (Mac. *ḱe*, Bulg. *šte*). Inasmuch as these clitics cannot occur under the scope of *da*, we may say that *da*-clauses do not allow for future tense. They can however themselves occur in the scope of Mac. *ḱe* / Bulg. *šte* in epistemic or evidential use (cf., for instance, Sims and Joseph 2019: 111, 121, with further references), although very specific circumstances must apply, and these uses seem to have become obsolete (see below).

---

34 Assertiveness should not be confused with illocutionary force. Lack of an independent illocution has been considered the hallmark of subordination, i.e., also of complementation (vs juxtaposition, e.g. quotation), in its entirety.

In general, aorist and imperfect are used in assertive contexts (e.g., in narration), and this is why Friedman (2000; 2004, etc.) dubs them 'confirmative'. However, in Macedonian the aorist can, although very rarely, occur in a *da*-clause, but only provided this clause itself falls under the scope of some propositional (epistemic or evidential) operator, e.g. Mac. *mora* 'must' (see 33); cf. Wiemer (2014a: 141–142). As for the imperfect, we find some attestations of it in the scope of *da* in some older Macedonian dialects (mainly the western ones) to express an evidential (inferential or reportive) meaning anchored to a reference point anterior to the speech interval (see 34). A reportive meaning was also possible with *da* + *l*-participle (= perfect) in the scope of *ḱe* (see 35).

Macedonian
(33) *Mora* **da** *zarabotij-a*   *mnogu* *pari.*
      must   earn[PFV]-AOR.3SG much   money
      'They must / probably have earned a lot of money.'

(34) †*Ḱe* **da** *dojd-eše.*
      FUT   come[PFV]-IMPF.3SG
      'S/he would have come. / S/he probably came.'

(35) †*Ḱe* **da** *ima-l-e*   *dojde-no*   *ovde* *porano.*
      FUT   have-LPT-PL   come[PFV]-PP_INDECL here   earlier
      '(As reported) they seem to have come here before.'
      (from Tomić 2006: 445; 2012: 393; her translations)

Examples like (34) and (35) now sound archaic. More generally, combinations *ḱe* + *da* have been replaced by *kako da* (L. Mitkovska, p.c.), on which see § 2.2.5. This may be taken as indicative that the combination *mora* + *da* is turning into a complex unit that functions as a propositional modifier, and that *ḱe* + *da* was on the same way before this combination died out. By the same token, (33)–(35) would not represent *da*-clauses proper. All these propositional operators are indeclinable; in diachronic terms, they have arisen as petrified PRS.3SG-forms of verbs (e.g., *morati* 'must', *xotěti* 'will'), so that reanalysis of dependency relations becomes an issue, and in Macedonian, this process appears to be more advanced than in Bulgarian (see § 3.6).

The same possibly holds true for *da*-clauses which, at least superficially, occur in the scope of invariant *bi* (see 36). This is exactly the opposite of the order *da* + *bi*-conditional, which is well-attested in the western part of South Slavic (see above). Tomić (2012: 392–393) claims structures as in (36) to be "restricted to western Macedonia":

Macedonian (dialectal, colloquial ?)
(36) *Jas   bi   da   dojd-am.*
     1SG.NOM COND IRR come[PFV]-PRS.1SG
     'I would like to come.'

Such a claim is questionable (cf. a detailed account of western Macedonian in Labroska 2018). Instead, *da*-clauses in the scope of *bi* nowadays appear to be "popular among young (and some not very young) people in Skopje, as well as among some politicians", and Serbian might be considered as the source of this spread (L. Mitkovska, p.c.).

Regardless of the domain of spread and its source, it may be asked whether this structure is to be analyzed as (36a, suggested by Tomić) or rather as (36b):

(36) a. *jas bi [da dojdam]*
     b. *jas [bi da [dojdam]]*

(36a) interprets *da* + V$_{fin}$ as a complement of *bi*, in analogy to what was assumed for (33)–(35), with the difference that in (36) there is a subject that triggers person-number agreement in the finite verb. (36b), by contrast, implies that *bi* and *da* have fused into a complex irrealis marker in which *bi*'s requirement to combine with the *l*-participle has been suppressed by *da*; following this analysis we would no longer be dealing with a biclausal construction. However, (36b) would go "against the grain" for all we know about Balkan Slavic (namely, the retreat of structures embedded under *bi*), whereas support for (36a) comes from native speaker judgments due to which it is natural to segment (36) with a pause between *bi* and *da* (L. Mitkovska, p.c.).

Under this more justifiable analysis *bi* continues to behave as an enclitic, and this seems to be the case, too, with examples adduced from older dialectal speech in which *bi* is preceded by *ako* 'if' or another *da* (noted by Tomić 2006: 439, 2012: 393); in both cases we observe the lack of a subject:

Macedonian (western dialects, now obsolete)
(37) *Ako   bi   da   mu   potrebv-et   pari...*
     if   COND IRR 3.DAT.M need[PFV].PRS-3SG   money
     'If he happens to need money...'

(38) *Da   bi   da   pukne-š!*
     IRR COND IRR burst[PFV].PRS-2SG
     'May you burst!' (lit. 'that would that you burst')

Tomić does not mention that these examples are really archaic, and they were probably not very common even at the time they were recorded. Thus, already Hausman (1956: 22) suggested that they represented combinations of *bi* (from the old conditional) with new Balkan forms (based on *da*), which arose during a period of competition. Combinations with *bi* can thus be regarded as lexicalized remnants of an older conditional, and this would explain "why we have so different and haphazard groupings" (L. Mitkovska, p.c., to whom I am particularly obliged for these insights).

Turning now to the western part of South Slavic, the situation is much simpler as far as aorist and imperfect are rarely used (in Serbian-Croatian) or have vanished altogether (in Slovene), so that the former *l*-perfect came to be used as a general past in all cases (Slovene) or predominantly so (Serbian-Croatian). The distribution of non-past forms remains interesting, since the present tense of pfv. verbs tends toward the same contexts of suspended or lacking assertiveness as in Balkan Slavic (see § 2.2.3). The issue to which extent this tendency is stronger in Serbian-Croatian than in Slovene remains open for further usage-based research: neither in Slovene nor in Serbian-Croatian do pfv. verbs in the present tense depend on *da* (or other irrealis markers), and in either language they are encountered in independent clauses, e.g., in the narrative present or (as for Serbian-Croatian) in descriptions of habitual sequences. Only the latter relate to irrealis functions, due to a lack a specific reference interval.

Concomitantly, one has to ask at which degree pfv. present tense functionally overlaps with the uses of the *bi*-conditional, which has established itself in the reportive domain (for non-directive CTPs) and strengthened its employment for politeness reasons (see § 2.2.3); it does not compete with *da* + pfv. present in either of these domains. Nevertheless, there may be competition between *da* + pfv. present and the *bi*-conditional for habitual contexts in Serbian-Croatian as well as for purpose (and maybe some more adverbial) clauses (also in Slovene). Another issue entirely understudied (at least in usage-based terms) is the relation of *da* + pfv. present and the future (marked by inflected *ću*... in Serbian-Croatian, *bom*... in Slovene): the future combines with *da* if it is used as a clausal subordinator (complement and purpose clauses), but not in complex predicates. In main clauses it only rarely occurs in optative use, but even then, it sounds archaic. The combination with the future clitic can thus be considered a reliable sign of subordination (Grković-Major, this volume: § 2.2).

2.2.3.3 Paradigmatic relation to canonical complementizers

As for Balkan Slavic, a main argument against considering *da* a complementizer is its behavior as a verb-oriented proclitic (see § 2.2.2.4). This behavior is strict notwithstanding the fact that *da* often stands in a paradigmatic relationship with undisputable complementizers. Compare (39–40):

Bulgarian
(39) *Kazva-t* ***če*** *deca-ta pej-at.*
say[IPFV].PRS-3PL COMP children-DEF.PL sing[IPFV].PRS-3PL
'They say **that** the children are singing.'

(40) a. *Iska-m deca-ta* ***da*** *pej-at.*
want[IPFV].PRS-1SG children-DEF.PL CON sing[IPFV].PRS-3PL

(40) b. **Iskam **da** decata pejat.*
'I want the children to sing.' (lit. '... **that** the children sing.')
(from Rudin 1986: 59)

(40b) shows that *da* cannot occur in the same linear position relative to the verb of its clause as can *če*. Concomitantly, the fact that the subject argument (*decata*) of this clause is separated from the verb (*pejat*) by *da*, is not caused by marked information structure, as there is no other option available. Even with unmarked topics *da* is never separated from the (lexical) verb unless by other clitics. This clearly differs from the behavior of complementizers, which typically occupy clause-initial position and can themselves function as host of 2P-clitics. They can also be separated from them, e.g., by object NPs in marked topic position, but these NPs need not precede the complementizer. Compare ex. (12) and (13) in § 2.2 with the following one:

Bulgarian
(41) *T-oj kaza,* ***če*** knig-a-ta *săm*
3-NOM.SG.M say[PFV].AOR-(3SG) COMP book[F]-SG-DEF.SG.F AUX.PRS.1SG
mu ja bi-l da-l.
3.M.DAT 3.F.ACC AUX-LPT-(SG.M) give[PFV]-LPT-(SG.M)
'He said **that**, as for the book, I'd have given it to him.'
(from Kosta and Zimmerling 2014: 460)

In addition, *da* co-occurs with complementizers, such as Bulg. *dali* 'if' (42), with Bulg. *če* as a causal, final or consecutive conjunction, or interpreted as a complement of cataphoric pronouns (43),[35] as well as with Bulg. *deto* introducing relative clauses and WH-words introducing embedded questions (44) and (45):[36]

Bulgarian
(42) Ne   znaj-a,   **dali** da   otid-a.
     NEG   know[IPFV]-PRS.1SG   Q   IRR go_away[PFV]-PRS.1SG
     'I don't know **whether** to go.'

(43) Žen-a-ta   sedna   tak-a,   **če**
     woman[F]-SG-DEF.SG.F   sit_down[PFV].AOR-(3SG)   such-NOM.SG.F   COMP
     da   me   vižda.
     IRR   1SG.ACC   see.PRS.3SG
     'The woman sat so **that** she could see me / **in order to** see me.'

(44) Ima-m   edn-a knig-a,   **deto** da   ja   četa.
     have.PRS-1SG   (one book)-SG.F   COMP   IRR   3SG.F.ACC   read[IPFV].PRS-1SG
     'I have a book to read.' (more lit. '... that I can read')

(45) Čudja   se   **kogo**   da   pita-m.
     wonder[IPFV].PRS-1SG   REFL   who-ACC   IRR   ask[IPFV].PRS-1SG
     'I wonder **who** to ask.'
     (from Rudin 1986: 60–61; see also Tomić 2006: 468–471)

In all these cases, *da* simply marks a situation as irreal: either it is not anchored to some specific reference time (see 43 and 44), or the occurrence of some specific situation is not asserted for some other reason (see 42, 45). The more specific function of the preceding connective is compatible with this general function of *da*.

Analogous remarks apply to Macedonian (Tomić 2006: 433–435). For instance, *da* may be preceded by *kako* 'how':

---

[35] On correlative pronouns see § 2.5. Sometimes *če da* occurs directly after an indefinite and referentially unspecific NP, e.g., *Ne săm žena, če da plača* 'I am not a woman to cry / who would cry' (from Tomić 2006: 459). Superficially, this makes *če* resemble a relativizer. However, the clause introduced by *če* scopes over a predication made about an unspecific referent, and *da* is sensitive to the fact that this correlates with a non-realized situation (SoA). The same type of predication over a situation with an unspecific referent can be observed for Serb.-Cr. *da*, with the difference that it has lost irrealis restrictions and functions as default complementizer. Compare *Tražim ženu da se uda za mene* 'I'm looking for a woman to marry me / who would marry me' (by courtesy of M. Uhlik).
[36] Cf. Krapova (this volume). Similar observations apply to Modern Greek *na* (vs *oti* and *pu*). Cf. Philippaki-Warburton (1994), who also disqualifies *na* as a complementizer because it cliticizes to the verb. This reasoning is adopted by Todorović (2015: 52).

Macedonian

(46) *Uča-m* **kako da** *pišuva-m so penkalo.*
 learn[IPFV].PRS-1SG how IRR write[IPFV].PRS-1SG with pen
 'I'm learning **how** to write with a pen.'

Here the manner-connective *kako* 'how' introduces a clause which does not code a proposition, since *pišuvam so penkalo* refers to a non-realized ability. Tomić (2006: 433–435) comments that in (46) *kako* may be omitted, but this is possible only if the CTP itself implies manner (see § 3.5). Thus, *da* and *kako* are not redundant, but they are compatible in SoA-complements.

Outside of Balkan Slavic, *da* behaves like a verbal proclitic only in complex predicates, i.e., for connections with a high degree of semantic integration. This is where it can follow the future marker in Serbian-Croatian:

(47) *Ja ću da kuva-m ručak.*
 1SG.NOM FUT.1SG IRR cook[IPFV].PRS-1SG lunch-(ACC)
 'I will cook lunch.'
 (from Todorović 2015: 17, 72)

Contrary to its behavior in complex predicates, when Serb.-Cr. or Sln. *da* is employed in biclausal constructions (as complementizer or conjunction), it does not behave like a clitic at all. Instead, it occupies the first position in the clause and can function as a host for enclitics; various constituents can interfere between *da* and the verb. Compare (48–50):

Serbian

(48) *Zna-m da Jovan dolazi sutra.*
 know[IPFV].PRS-1SG COMP PN-(NOM) come[IPFV].PRS-(3SG) tomorrow
 'I know that Jovan comes tomorrow.'
 (from Todorović 2015: 28)

Croatian

(49) *Vidje-l-a se težnj-a da se u*
 see-PST-SG.F REFL intention[F]-NOM.SG COMP REFL in
 t-om genre-u otkrij-u nov-i put-ovi.
 (this genre)-LOC.SG.M discover[PFV].PRS-3PL (new path)-NOM.PL
 'The intention to discover new paths in that genre was evident.'
 (lit. '(it) was seen the intention that ...')
 (from Mihaljević 2009: 341)

Slovene
(50) Reke-l   mi   je,   da   jutri
     say[PFV]-PST-(SG.M) 1SG.DAT AUX.PRS.3SG COMP tomorrow
     pride.
     come[PFV].PRS-3SG
     'He told me that he (would) come tomorrow.'
     (from Uhlik and Žele 2018b: 215)

Above, we already noted that *da* can be followed by the conditional marker *bi* (+ *l*-participle) or the future marker (cf. also Todorović 2015: 93–95). In terms of linear sequence, this yields a mirror image to *da*'s behavior in complex predicates. It is this complementary behavior as clitic-host vs verb-oriented proclitic which contributed to the assumption that we are dealing with two different *da*-units, a complementizer (*da*₁) and a subjunctive marker (*da*₂); see § 2.2.3.

2.2.3.4 Clitic behavior

As was mentioned above, in contemporary Macedonian and Bulgarian, *da* consistently occurs immediately before the lexical verb. It may be separated from this verb only by other clitics, e.g., by negation and pronominal or auxiliary clitics:

Bulgarian
(51) Da ne bi **da**   **si**   **se**   otkaza-l?
               CON   AUX.PRS.2SG REFL   refuse[PFV]-LPT-(SG.M)
     'Have you really refused? / You haven't really refused, have you?'

Macedonian
(52) Treba **da** **ja**   plati-me   kazn-a-ta,   neli?
     need   CON 3.F.ACC   pay[IPFV]-PRS.1PL   fine[F]-SG-DEF.SG.F   PTC
     'We have to pay the fine, right?'

(53) **Da** **ne** **si**   **mu**   **go**   da-l-a   poveče!
     CON   NEG   AUX.PRS.2SG   3.M.DAT 3.M.ACC   give[PFV]-LPT-SG.F   more
     'Don't give it to him any more, or else!'
     (from Bužarovska and Mitkovska 2017: § 1; and Spencer and Luís 2012: 125)

This applies not only to independent clauses (as in 51–53), but also to embedded structures, i.e., to clausal complementation, adverbial subordination and in complex predicates.³⁷ As for the latter, see Bulgarian, where *da* participates in the suppletive formation of the negated future anterior (*šte* vs *njama da* + *l*-participle; 54a and 54b), and optionally in the unnegated future (55):³⁸

Bulgarian
(54) a. *Az   šte   săm   mu   go   da-l.*
         1SG.NOM FUT AUX.PRS.1SG 3.DAT.M 3.M.ACC give[PFV]-LPT-(SG.M)
         'I will have given it to him.'
     b. *Az   njama   da   săm   mu   go*
         1SG.NOM BE.NEG CON AUX.PRS.1SG 3.M.DAT 3.M.ACC
         da-l.
         give[PFV]-LPT-(SG.M)
         'I won't have given it to him.'
         (from Spencer and Luís 2012: 125)

(55) *Šte   (da) piša*³⁹
      FUT   CON   write[IPFV].TR_INF
      'I will write' (Asenova 2002: 210)

All this indicates that Balkan Slavic *da* has been moving down a morphologization cline (free word > clitic > affix): *da* (together with pronominal clitics) has lost promiscuous attachment, which is a typical property of clitics, and this brings these morphemes closer to affixes (Spencer and Luís 2013).⁴⁰ This process became possible because 2P-clitic clusters consistently occurred immediately before the finite verb, so that they were reanalyzed as verbal proclitics. One of the consequences of this process of tightening is the rise of agreement marking of object-NPs by the doubling of pronominal clitics. This effect is named after A. Tobler and A. Mussafia, who described it for Romance languages in the 19th century (Spencer and Luís 2012: 63–64). Alternatively, *da* was able to develop 2P-property in some contexts, e.g., after prosodically independent words, while it retained its ability to serve as hosts for enclitics. This is what we observe in Serbian-Croatian and Slovene (see § 2.2.3.3).

---

37 Cf. Halpern (1996), Dimitrova-Vulchanova (1999), Hauge (1999 [1976]), Franks (2008), for Bulgarian, Wiemer (2014a), Sims and Joseph (2019: 123) for Macedonian, with further references.
38 The case is analogous for the 'have'-future (*imam+da*); cf. Asenova (2002: 206).
39 *Piša* is a truncated infinitive (see § 2.3.2). In the Southeast Serbian Timok dialects *da* tends to be optional after the future marker (which likewise tends to be uninflected) as well (Mirić 2018).
40 On the dual nature of these clitics cf. Kosta and Zimmerling (2014: 462–463); cf. also Sims and Joseph (2019: 123–126).

Therefore, the South Slavic languages differ exactly with respect to the consequences of the Tobler-Mussafia effect: Macedonian and Bulgarian have developed proclitic clusters and *da* is integrated to them consistently, regardless of the main or embedded status of the predicate-argument structure.[41] If *da* occurs clause-initially, only the verb-oriented proclitic cluster can separate it from the lexical verb. Outside of Balkan Slavic, *da* can host other clitics, but it can also be separated from the (finite) verb by full NPs. Moreover, contrary to Balkan Slavic, Serbian-Croatian pronominal clitics, which relationally belong to an embedded verb can be moved before *da*, and even before the embedding predicate, i.e., they can undergo clitic climbing, at least as a marginal option; compare (56) and (57) from Jurkiewicz-Rohrbacher, Hansen, and Kolaković (2017),[42] cf. also Stjepanović (2004) and Kolaković, Jurkiewicz-Rohrbacher, and Hansen (2019).

(56) [...] *poče-o$_1$*   ***im$_2$***   *je*   *da*
         start[PFV]-PST-(SG.M)   3.DAT.PL   AUX.PRS.3SG   CON
         govori$_1$ *o*   *dolask-u*   *ov-e grup-e*
         say[IPFV].PRS-(3SG)   about   arrival-LOC   (this group)-GEN.SG
         'he began to speak to them about the arrival of this group'

(57) [...] *i*   *poče-l-o$_1$*   ***mi$_2$***   *je*
         and   start[PFV]-PST-SG.N   1SG.DAT   AUX.PRS.3SG
         da   *se$_2$*   *vrti$_2$*   *u*   *glav-i.*
         CON   REFL   rotate[IPFV].PRS-(3SG)   in   head-LOC
         'and I started to feel dizzy.'

The marginal status of clitic climbing produces an array of disparate acceptability judgments by native speakers. However, even though infrequent, within South Slavic clitic climbing has been observed only for Serbian-Croatian, and even there it is possible only for raising verbs (modals and phasal verbs) and CTPs with subject control (e.g., *nastojati* 'strive', *usp(ij)eti* 'succeed'); it has not

---

[41] Macedonian has gone slightly further than Bulgarian: not only do Macedonian pronominal clitics proclitically attach to the verb (except for imperatives and gerunds), but, contrary to their Bulgarian cognates, they can even occupy clause-initial position (e.g., *Mi go dade Vera včera* 'Vera gave it to me yesterday'); cf. Spencer and Luís (2012: 65). However, *da* can occur clause-initially (as part of the cluster) in both Macedonian and Bulgarian.
[42] The authors also show that clitic climbing may occur if the complement-embedding predicate is in the future or compound past (which themselves take a clitic auxiliary). This disproves claims raised by Todorović (2015).

been attested with object-control CTPs (e.g., *dozvoliti* 'allow', *zamoliti* 'ask'), nor with predicates showing lower degrees of semantic integration with their clausal complement. That is, clitic climbing appears to be possible only for enclitic pronouns out of *da*-complements which exhibit a high degree of integration with the embedding predicate (as do structures with embedded infinitives). They have not been attested with unequivocally biclausal structures, unless subject-control is involved. We can thus say that *da* used as a complementizer almost always (subject control being an exception) blocks clitic climbing, or conversely: that clitic climbing occurs only (marginally) with embedded structures for which an alternative realization with the infinitive is possible (and then clitic climbing is obligatory).

These observations allow to infer that clitic clusters and clitic climbing do not correlate and that both phenomena are but weakly related to clausal complementation: neither is *da* affected by clitic climbing (in Serbian-Croatian), nor does the inclusion of *da* into verb-oriented clusters of proclitics tell us anything about the subordinated (i.e. syntactically dependent) status of the clause in which it occurs (in Balkan Slavic).

2.2.3.5 Balkan Slavic *da* with realized events

The fact that, in Balkan Slavic, *da* has been integrated into proclitic clusters and serves as a connective in complex predicates explains an otherwise peculiar phenomenon: in connections close to the high-integration end of the SIH *da* is used as the only possible connective, even if the entire complex refers to realized (i.e., factual) events. This is the case particularly with implicative (58) and some factive verbs (59) in Bulgarian; equivalent examples for Macedonian can be found as well:

Bulgarian

(58) *"Liteks"* **uspja** *da vzem-e* Karadžinov.
 PN manage[PFV].AOR-(3SG) CON take[PFV].PRS-3SG PN
 '"Liteks" **managed to arrest** Karadžinov.'

(59) *Novovremc-i* **ne** *zabravi-xa da publikuva-t*
 contemporary-PL NEG forget[PFV].AOR-3PL CON publish.PRS-3PL
 imot-i-te si v internet.
 property-PL-DEF.PL REFL.DAT in internet
 'Contemporaries **did not forget to publish** their properties on the internet.'
 (from Ivanova 2014: 130)

Time adverbials demonstrate clause-union properties of such sentences. See (60), in which *utre* 'tomorrow' has wide scope over the whole sentence, despite its linear position:

(60) Šte zabravj-a da kupj-a luk <u>utre.</u>
FUT forget[PFV].PRS-1SG CON buy[PFV].PRS-1SG onion tomorrow
'I will forget to buy onions <u>tomorrow</u>.'
(from Krapova 2001: 118)

2.2.3.6 Between mono- and biclausality

Balkan Slavic *da*-complements after desideratives are difficult to classify as mono- or biclausal, since their properties are sometimes incommensurable in this respect. On the one hand, we find that complements after Bulg. *ne iskam* 'not want' license their polarity items as if they were part of a monoclausal structure. Compare an example from Hansen, Letuchiy, and Błaszczyk (2016: 214):

(61) Ne iska-m tova da svărši nikoga.
NEG want[IPFV].PRS-1SG this CON end[PFV].PRS-(3SG) never
'I don't want this to end (ever).'

As the authors point out, the negative-polarity item *nikoga* is licensed by the negation in the main clause (this may be qualified as NEG-raising). Its polar equivalent *njakoga* 'ever' is possible as well, at least for some speakers. The same variability we observe in Macedonian (L. Mitkovska, p.c.), and even colloquial Serbian allows for either item (*Ne želim da se ovo* **nikada / ikada** *završi* as translation of ex. 61; J. Grković-Major, p.c.).

On the other hand, when Bulg. *iskam* 'want' is combined with a clausal argument, the highest-ranking (= most agent-like) individual argument of this clause is more likely to be coded like its subject (62a) and not like an object (62b) of *iskam* (cf. also Lindstedt 2010: 416):

Bulgarian
(62) a. Iska-m t-oj da pe-e.
  want[IPFV]-PRS.1SG 3-SG.M.NOM CON sing[IPFV]-PRS.3SG
 b. ?Iska-m go da pe-e.
  want[IPFV]-PRS.1SG 3SG.M.ACC CON sing[IPFV]-PRS.3SG
  'I want him to sing.' (lit. '... that he sings.')
  (from Rudin 1986: 69–70)

For full NPs this tendency appears to be even stronger, since when they follow *iskam*, they are always treated as subjects. This differs from the pattern with perceptual CTPs, which would have a NP, or pronoun, marked as an object (see § 2.2.5).

While the problems just discussed concerned complements with a rather high degree of semantic integration, similar clause-union phenomena can be observed in Bulgarian with CTPs at the low-integration end of the SIH as well. They have to do with the weakening of epistemic support (see more in § 2.2.4.1) after suitable CTPs, for instance if an assumption is expressed:

(63) V   tj-ax   zlato-to   se   predpolaga   da
     in   3-LOC.PL   gold[N]-DEF.N   REFL   assume[IPFV].PRS-(3SG)   CON
     e   59 ton-a.
     be.PRS.3SG   ton-COUNT
     'In them, it is supposed, there are 59 tons of gold.', or:
     'In them 59 tons of gold are supposed (to be).'
     (from Hansen, Letuchiy, and Błaszczyk 2016: 213)

Apart from weak epistemic support (favoring *da*), such examples are remarkable since most of the content of the complement, namely the local adjunct and the argument NP (*zlatoto* 'gold.DEF'), finds itself before the CTP. This looks like raising, but it may also be qualified simply as marked topicalization, which, in turn, appears to be only part of a larger picture. Namely, in Bulgarian we also encounter WH-fronting, i.e., in a construction with marked focus, in which an argument of a purpose clause, by becoming the target of narrow focus, occurs outside of its clause (in linear terms); compare an example from Letuchiy (this volume: § 2.3), also for more discussion:

(64) Kakvo   si   došă-l   da   kupi-š
     what   AUX.PRS.2SG   come-LPT-(SG.M)   CON   buy[PFV]-PRS.2SG
     'What is it that you came (in order) to buy?'
     (more literally: 'What did you come (in order) to buy?')

Such constructions would be ungrammatical in other Slavic languages (like Russian, Polish), but also in English and German, which otherwise tolerate various bridging constructions (that resemble ex. 64). See further in § 3.6.

2.2.3.7 Summary on the *da*-issue

To some extent, the question of whether *da* is a complementizer or a marker of analytical subjunctive (or whatever kind of mood) depends on one's definition of these notions; at any rate, it depends on how we envisage the relation between morphosyntax and clause semantics. If, with Noonan (2007: 55), we define complementizers as "a word, particle, clitic or affix, one of whose functions it is to identify the entity as a complement", nothing prevents us from regarding verbal clitics (or even affixes) as complementizers, provided "their" clause can be identified as an argument of some higher predicate. But without restricting the notion 'complementizer' by morphosyntactic formats this notion inevitably overlaps with the traditional notion of 'subjunctive' understood as a morphological category marked on the verb by sets of endings (cf. Bybee, Perkins, and Pagliuca 1994: 213, Thieroff 2010: 2, among others). In South Slavic, *da* can be treated either way if subjunctive (or mood in general) is treated as a clausal category marked by some morpheme that somehow interacts with the predicate in its clause, and maybe also from their CTPs. This is the practice in Gołąb (1964a), in Topolińska (2003 etc.), among many others, but also in generative literature. In Balkan Slavic, this interaction becomes particularly obvious, since *da* has turned into a proclitic strictly oriented toward the verbal predicate of its clause and thereby acquiring affix-like properties. In the remainder of South Slavic *da* has developed rather in the opposite direction (or preserved its inherited morphotactic behavior), inasmuch as it firmly occurs in clause-initial position, regardless of the distance to the finite verb, so that purported mood distinctions solely result from co-occurrence restrictions with tense-aspect forms (compare Ivić's *nemobilan prezent* in Serbian-Croatian). It is therefore only natural to assume that mood distinctions are just calculated (or follow) from distributional restrictions of tense-aspect forms (maybe additionally from CTPs) and not (or not mainly) from the choice of clause-initial connectives. This applies all the more when these connectives are followed by markers of acknowledged older moods (like *da* + [*bi*+*l*-form] in western South Slavic), but this holds true for independent clauses as well. That is, the assumed 'subjunctive – indicative' distinction does not hinge on subordination (or on complementation in particular), and whether complementation takes place (and clause-initial *da* can be considered a complementizer) has to be decided on the basis of independent criteria, such as change of person-deictic anchorage and lack of independent illocutionary force (see § 2.2.4.2).

Concomitantly, a prominent split between Balkan Slavic and the remainder of South Slavic is *da*'s retention of an irrealis-function in the former and loss of realis – irrealis discrimination in the latter. On the backdrop of this loss, outside of Balkan Slavic, the restrictions in the choice of tense-aspect forms could gain in prominence, since their weight as a reliable signal of lowered assertiveness has increased. Thus, in semantic terms, the innovation occurs in the western half of South Slavic, while Balkan Slavic is innovative in pulling *da* down a morphologization cline.

These two opposite directions of conservative vs innovative properties of *da* are summarized in the following figure:

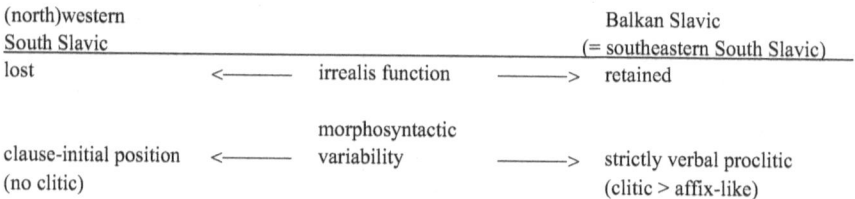

Figure 4: Changes of *da* in South Slavic.

In sum, as concerns syntactic scope, both complementizers and mood are clausal categories. If we drop morphosyntactic conditions, classifications of complementizers and of moods will practically coincide for embedded clauses, and a preference for the one or the other nomenclature becomes a question of personal taste. The low degree of morphological boundedness exhibited by *da* even as a verbal proclitic, on the one hand, and the restrictions on TAM forms for *da* with irrealis functions, on the other, have been the major causes of long-lasting disputes concerning its status.

2.2.4 +/- factual distinctions

If we accept the distinction between [± factual] and [± factive] (see § 2.2.2) and put aside factive complements, complementation markers which code [± factual] contrasts also support basic splits, or clines, between the southeastern (= Balkan) and the northwestern part of South Slavic. This split becomes evident if we distinguish two types of contrasts: (i) [– factual] *da* vs some [+ factual] complementation marker, and (ii) *da* neutral with respect to factuality vs some [– factual] complementation marker. The former contrast is typical of Balkan Slavic, the latter can be found in the northwestern corner of South Slavic, i.e., Slovene. Importantly, this coarse areal division applies to clausal complementation, not necessarily to other uses of the respective morphemes (e.g., as conjunctions or analytical mood markers). The next two subsections are concerned with these contrasts.

2.2.4.1 [– factual] *da* vs [+ factual] complementation marker

In Bulgarian, the alternation between *če* and *da* is, as a rule, meaningful, mainly, because some CTPs allow to choose either of them. Here, again, some researchers refer to 'dual mood choice' (e.g., Krapova, Sočanac, and Wiemer, forthcoming-b: § 2). The point is that *če* indicates propositions which the relevant epistemic agent (speaker or matrix-clause subject) regards as true; this contrasts with two uses of *da*, which either signals weak epistemic support (or denial) for a proposition, or it marks lack of a proposition. The epistemic [± factual] contrast applies to CTPs of cognitive attitude, typically under negation (see 65), the proposition – SoA contrast applies to perception verbs (see 66):[43]

Bulgarian
(65) a. *Ivan ne vjarva če Marija e*
    PN NEG believe[IPFV].PRS-(3SG) COMP PN[F] be.PRS.3SG
    bremenn-a.
    pregnant-F.SG
    'Ivan does not believe **that** Mary is pregnant.' (= believes that not P)
   b. *Ivan ne vjarva Marija da e*
    PN NEG believe[IPFV].PRS-(3SG) PN[F] CON be.PRS.3SG
    bremenn-a.
    pregnant-F.SG
    'Ivan does not believe Mary **to be** pregnant.' (= does not believe that P)
    (from Krapova, Sočanac, and Wiemer, forthcoming-b)

(66) a. *Ne čuva-š li če pe-e gor-a-ta?*
    NEG feel[IPFV].PRS-2SG Q COMP sing[IPFV]-PRS.3SG forest[F]-SG-DEF.SG.F
    'Don't you hear that the forest is singing?'
   b. *Ne čuva-š li da pe-e gor-a-ta?*
    NEG feel[IPFV].PRS-2SG Q CON sing[IPFV]-PRS.3SG forest[F]-SG-DEF.SG.F
    'Don't you hear the forest sing?'
    (from Tomić 2006: 467)

Stronger epistemic support indicated by *če*, as in (65a), tends to be equivalent with the negation of the proposition in the complement (*Ivan vjarva če Marija ne e bremenna* 'Ivan believes **that** Marija is not pregnant'). This phenomenon has been described as NEG-raising (cf. Siegel 2009, among others).

This applies to Slovene as well, where we can encounter uses of *da* with the *bi*-conditional that weaken epistemic support. This happens if CTPs of cognitive attitudes (see 67), but sometimes also CTPs referring to perception (see 68), occur under negation:

---

[43] Cf. Rudin (1986: 58, 71) for Bulgarian, Tomić (2006: 459) for Macedonian. On Bulgarian perception verbs cf. Tomić (2006: 466–468).

Slovene

(67) *Yellenova ne misli, da bi velik padec*
PN NEG think[IPFV].PRS-(3SG) COMP COND (large fall[M])-NOM.SG
vrednost-i delnic bistveno vpliva-l
value-GEN share-(GEN.PL) significantly influence[IPFV]-PST-(M.SG)
na gospodarsk-o rast.
on (economic growth)-ACC
'Yellenova doesn't think that a large drop in the value of the shares would significantly affect economic growth.'
(by courtesy of M. Uhlik)

(68) *Ni-sem ga še vide-l,*
NEG-AUX.PRS.1SG 3M.ACC yet see[IPFV]-PST-(SG.M)
da bi se smeja-l.
COMP COND REFL laugh[IPFV]-PST-(SG.M)
'I haven't yet seen him laughing.' (lit. 'that he would have laughed')
(from Uhlik and Žele 2018b: 228)

However, this usage of the conditional seems to be less widespread than in equivalent structures, for instance, in Russian (Uhlik and Žele 2018b: 226), and it is likewise unusual in Serbian-Croatian (see further in § 2.3.3).

As for Bulg. *če* vs *da*, in certain cases, it is hard or impossible to formulate the functional contrast. See already § 2.1 on 'threat' and 'promise'; other cases in point are complement clauses of Bulg. *nadjavam se* 'hope' if they relate to events that are supposed to have happened prior to the reference interval:

(69) a. *Nadjava-m se **če** Petăr e*
hope[IPFV]-PRS.1SG REFL COMP PN[M] AUX.PRS.3SG
zamina-l.
leave[PFV]-LPT-(SG.M)
b. *Nadjava-m se Petăr **da** e*
hope[IPFV]-PRS.1SG REFL PN[M] CON AUX.PRS.3SG
zamina-l.
leave[PFV]-LPT-(SG.M)
'I hope **that** Peter has left.'

The contrast appears to be clearer if the event is presented as posterior to the reference interval:

(70) a. Ivan   se   nadjava,   če   šte   spečeli-š.
        PN   REFL   hope[IPFV]-(PRS.3SG)   COMP   FUT   be_late-PRS.2SG
    b. Ivan   se   nadjava   da   spečeli-š.
        PN   REFL   hope[IPFV]-(PRS.3SG)   CON   be_late-PRS.2SG
        'Ivan hopes **that** you will win.'

While (70a) highlights an epistemic component of prediction, (70b) highlights the volitional (or bouletic) component inherent to the semantics of *nadjavam se* 'hope'. It is easy to suppress the volitional component with anterior reference (as in 69b), since it does not make much sense. A slightly different way of making the distinction between *če* and *da* palpable is to say that *če* marks "speaker's commitment to the truth and the factual status of the embedded proposition", while *da* expresses "speaker's belief in the possible realization of the embedded event" (Krapova 1998: 88) or "the lack of commitment and the existence of doubts on part of the speaker for *da*" (Petkova-Schick 1973: 277, referred to by Sonnenhauser 2015: 66). For an analysis of this type of variation with CTPs denoting hope and belief in Macedonian cf. Bužarovska and Mitkovska (2014; 2015). They found that especially with 'believe' (Bulg. *vjarva* / Mac. *veruva*), *da*-clauses are more frequent than in Macedonian.

According to Ivanova and Gradinarova (2015: 259), the (ir)realis-distinction of *če* vs *da* can also bear on the referential and the syntactic status of the complement-taking expression. Thus, in (70a) the noun in the matrix clause is marked with a definite article and thus used referentially; it is implied that the addressee owns a house and, thus, *če* is used. By contrast, in (71b) the same noun does not have an article and can be qualified as the predicate, which is modified by the *da*-clause because nothing is implied about the existence of a house:

(71) a Ščasti-e-**to**   e,   če / *da   ima-š
        luck[N]-SG-DEF.SG.N   be.PRS.3SG   COMP / CON   have[IPFV].PRS-2SG
        svoj   dom.
        REFL_POSS   house
        'It is your luck that you (do) have your house.'
    b. Ščasti-e   e,   *če / da   ima-š   svoj
        luck[N]-SG   be.PRS.3SG   COMP / CON   have[IPFV].PRS-2SG   REFL_POSS
        dom.
        house
        'It is luck to have a (= one's own) house.'

In fact, *če* in (71a) marks a factive complement, and therefore the predicative noun is definite (for predicative nouns as CTPs see also § 3.1). Again, the same applies to Macedonian.

In conclusion, if complementation markers show an (ir)realis contrast, the irrealis member can be chosen to emphasize weak epistemic support. For *da*, this phenomenon demonstrates a more recent extension from the domain of volition and deontic modality into knowledge/belief-related complements (i.e., into epistemic and doxastic modality).[44]

2.2.4.2 [± factual] *da* vs [– factual] complementation marker

Since outside of Balkan Slavic, *da* no longer discriminates between factual and non-factual complements (see § 2.2.3), *da* is "available" for other semantic contrasts in that part of South Slavic. Given that *da* has become the epistemically neutral complementizer, contrasts occur with units that can have complementizer function and that simultaneously mark non-factuality. The prime candidate for this function is *neka* resp. Sln. *naj*. These cognate units continue a petrified 3SG.PRS.IND-form of the verb **nexati* 'let, release' (compare etymological equivalents in all West Slavic languages and adjacent East Slavic).[45] For all cognates I will use NEKA as a general label, i.e., when no particular language needs to be specified.

NEKA is primarily employed in complex predicates; it combines with present-tense indicative forms of lexical verbs (predominantly in third, rarely in first, hardly ever in second person)[46] to mark meanings from the permissive (hortative, jussive) or optative domain. For this reason, NEKA figures in discussions of analytic moods in all these languages, and it shows a large functional overlap with *da* in adverbial subordination (e.g., in concessive and conditional clauses at least in Bulgarian and Serbian-Croatian); cf. Kramer (1986: 65–75) for a survey on South Slavic, Čakărova (2008) for a survey on Bulgarian, also Topolińska (2003; 2008b) and the relevant contributions to Rothstein and Thieroff (eds., 2010). Like *da* in conservative South Slavic, NEKA can be considered an irrealis marker with a "career" that started in the domain of directive speech acts

---

44 Since *da* is chosen also with complements after epistemic CTPs coding weak epistemic support, a proposal to regard *da* as a complementizer with narrower semantic scope (i.e., with scope over SoAs, not propositions) does not seem adequate (see Petar Kehayov referred to in Joseph 2016: 273, f. 19).

45 According to Szucsich (2010: 399), NEKA derives from the negated form of Srb. *hajati* 'care' (resp. its cognates); cf. also Čakărova (2008: 115), Sonnenhauser (this volume: § 4.1). If this assumption is correct it relates to an even earlier time (compare with the etymology presented in Uhlik 2018: 404 and in Snoj 2016, *sub verbum*).

46 According to Kramer (1986: 68, 73), Mac. NEKA has, on rare occasions, been attested with imperfect forms of the lexical verb, namely in counterfactual conditionals and loosely subordinated unfulfillable directives. Čakărova (2008: 121) provides statistical figures of the distribution over grammatical persons in Bulgarian.

and deontic modality. In addition, it can be regarded as an at least emergent complementizer mainly outside of Balkan Slavic, i.e., in those South Slavic languages in which *da* has not developed into a verb-oriented proclitic. Only in Macedonian, NEKA can be considered a strictly verbal proclitic (Kramer 1986: 65), while in Bulgarian and Serbian-Croatian it behaves like a full-fledged word unit occurring predominantly clause-initially; the same applies to Sln. *naj* (cf. Sonnenhauser, this volume, for details).

As for Balkan Slavic, Topolińska (2008b: 208) considers examples like the following one to show clausal complementation:

Macedonian
(72)   *Kaž-i   mu   neka   dojd-e.*
        say[PFV]-IMP.SG 3M.DAT   come[PFV]-PRS.3SG
   (i) 'Tell him may he come!'   direct speech
>? (ii) 'Tell him that he (may) come!'   complementation

However, in such instances the directive speech act introduced by *neka* can be treated as direct speech; *neka dojde* (with third-person addressee) can occur as an independent sentence, so that (72) would represent a juxtaposition (see (i)). It is difficult, or even impossible, to prove that *neka dojde* occurs as a clausal complement to *kaži* 'say!' (see (ii)), because even under this condition, no indexical shift would occur: the third-person form after *neka* would not shift to second-person, since person deixis would be oriented toward the speaker of (72), not to his immediate addressee (*mu* 'him'). Knowledge about the prosodic structure would be helpful, but as they stand, such examples are only weakly indicative of embedding. Topolińska (2008b: 208) remarks that such examples are not mentioned in those parts of grammars that deal with subordination; the same applies to Bulgarian, also with respect to *neka da*.

The situation is not much different for Serbian. Topolińska (2008b: 208) adduces examples from the Academy dictionary, in one of them we find a switch of person deixis indicative of indirect (i.e. embedded) speech:

Serbian
(73) [...] *majk-a   mi   reč-e,   **neka** mu*
           mother[F]-NOM.SG 1SG.DAT say[PFV]-AOR.3SG   3M.DAT
     skoči-m   na leđa ...
     jump[PFV].PRS-1SG
     'my mother told me to jump on his back' (lit. '... **may** I jump on his back')

Likewise, the recent Serbian academy syntax does not mention *neka* explicitly as a complementizer, and it appears in only one example:

(74) *Ali, Nano, baš se doktor Mirko juče zabrinuo,*
    *i   kaza-o   mi   **neka** dođ-e   i*
    and say[PFV]-PST-(SG.M) 1SG.DAT   come[PFV].PRS-3SG also
    taj za srce.
    DEM.NOM.SG.M
    'But, Nana, Dr Mirko was very concerned yesterday, and he told me **that** the one for the heart **should** come.' (lit. '... he told me **may** the one for the heart come.') (from Alanović 2018: 168)

One wonders how widespread this use is: whether NEKA occurs in linear sequences only after speech act verbs or also after other predicates able to take the form of a CTPs, so that NEKA has a better chance of becoming a complementizer. The few known contexts in which NEKA can be analyzed in this manner are colloquial. The question of its spread has thus a diastratic as well as a diatopic dimension.

The situation changes considerably with Sln. *naj*, which is much more advanced on its way toward a complementizer.[47] Like its cognates in other Slavic languages, the original use of *naj* as a petrified form of a lexical verb (probably 'let') was a hortative or permissive marker in complex predicates. Starting from directive speech acts it gradually expanded into complex sentences, until it could be interpreted as a complementizer. Sonnenhauser (this volume: § 4.4) presents a well-considered scenario of how *naj* became established in complementation, and Holvoet and Konickaja (2011) have elaborated on a plausible pathway based on interpretive (or echoic) deontics, which ends up with the employment of *naj* as an epistemic or reportive marker both in main and dependent clauses. In main clauses, this function needs support from the conditional (*bi* + *l*-participle), as in (75); cf. Holvoet and Konickaja (2011: 12), Uhlik (2018: 411):

(75) *Šol-a   **naj** **bi**   zače-l-a   delova-ti*
    school[F]-NOM.SG   COND begin[PFV]-PST-SG.F work[IPFV]-INF
    že   t-o jesen.
    already (this autumn)-ACC
    'Reportedly, school has started work this autumn already.'

---

[47] I am very much indebted to Mladen Uhlik for a discussion of all facts and details (both judgments and corpus data) pertaining to the subsequent analysis. The usual disclaimers apply.

As a potential complementizer, *naj* must occur clause-initially, its reportive function is then harmonic with the speech act denoted by the (possible) matrix predicate; in this sense, as a complementizer *naj* does not have an independent reportive function:

(76) *Reke-l   sem   j-im,   **naj** pridej-o*
     say[PFV]-PST-(SG.M) AUX.PRS.1SG 3-DAT.PL   come[PFV].PRS-3PL
     pozneje.
     later
  (i) 'I said to them$_i$ that they$_i$ should come later.'
  (ii) 'I said to them$_i$ (that) they$_k$ should come later.' ('. . . May they$_k$ come later!')

(77) *Popoldne   je   šef   končno ukaza-l,*
     afternoon   AUX.PRS.3SG   boss-(NOM.SG) finally order[PFV]-PST-(SG.M)
     naj *me   pokličej-o   k   nj-emu.*
             1SG.ACC   call[PFV].PRS-3PL to 3-DAT.SG.M
     'In the afternoon the boss finally ordered that they call me to (come to) him.' ('. . . May they call me')
     (from Uhlik 2018: 412)

(78) *V Vatikanu se je vrgla pred noge papežu Piju IX.*
     *in   ga   prosi-l-a,   **naj** nj-o   in   njen-ega*
     and   3.ACC.M   ask[IPFV]-PST-F.SG   3-ACC.SG.F   and POSS-ACC.SG.M
     mož-a   zaščiti . . .
     husband-ACC   defend[PFV].PRS-(3SG)
     'At the Vatican she threw herself down before the feet of pope Pius IX and implored him to safeguard her and her husband. . .'
     (from Topolińska 2003: 313)

It is not always evident that such clauses represent indirect speech (i.e., complementation), instead of juxtaposed direct speech (i.e., quotes). This can be stated only if the person-deictic expressions in the utterance are oriented toward the actual, not to the reported speech act. However, in the original hortative use *naj* + present tense (i.e., direct speech) is restricted to the third person, it does not occur with second person (Topolińska 2003); if, then, in both the *naj*-clause and the preceding clause (= potential matrix clause) the relevant expressions refer to third persons, reported speech (= complementation) cannot be clearly stated, unless the preceding clause also contains a third person expression with a coreferential participant in the clause conveying the reported speech event. Another clear clue of reported speech is the presence of a first or second person expression in the *naj*-clause.

For instance, in (76) the speaker relates his own speech act which was directed not to the addressee of the actual speech event, but to a third party (*jim* 'they.DAT'). In the reading (i), i.e., if the elliptic 3PL-subject of the *naj*-clause (*pridejo* '(they) come') is coreferential with that third party (= the addressee of the reported speech act), a switch of person deixis is obvious. Otherwise, i.e., if no coreference applies (see (ii)), (76) need not be interpreted as complementation, since, under this condition, the *naj*-clause corresponds to the original directive illocution. In contrast, in (77) we cannot rely on anaphoric relations, but *me* 'me' after *naj* means the speaker of the actual speech report, and only *šef* 'boss' remains the issuer of the original speech act. In (78), again, *njo* 'her' and *njenega moža* 'her husband' point back anaphorically to the woman in the grammatical subject of the preceding clause, who can be established as the issuer of the request. Therefore, (77) and (78) represent complementation, not juxtaposed direct speech.

Reading (i) of (76) is comparable to examples with purpose or consecutive clauses, i.e., adverbial subordination; see (79):

(79) *Pojd-i   k   sestr-i,   **naj** ti   zašij-e   srajc-o.*
     go[PFV]-IMP.SG to sister-DAT   2SG.DAT sew[PFV].PRS-3SG shirt-ACC
     'Go to your sister, **may** she stitch up the shirt for you.'
     ⊃ '… **so that** she can/will stitch up the shirt for you.'
     (from Topolińska 2003: 315; translation adapted)

Here we see a consecutive implicature following from a sequence of directive speech acts. Hence, *naj* has also been qualified as an adverbial subordinator.[48] The distinction between adverbial and argument clauses headed by *naj* becomes obvious by paying attention to distributional facts: although *naj* can in principle be combined with the future (Topolińska 2003: 320, Uhlik 2018) and this seems to be nothing unusual for adverbial subordinate clauses, (e.g., with concessive function), *naj* + future is very unusual and hardly attested in corpus data for clausal complements.

---

48 Cf. Topolińska (2003). As indicative of adverbial subordination we may regard the use of another than the third person, e.g. *Naj sem*.1SG *se še tako trudil, mi*.1.DAT *ni uspelo* 'Although I tried very hard, I didn't succeed' (more lit. 'May I have tried very hard, I didn't succeed'); by courtesy of M. Uhlik.

As a complementizer *naj* is thus restricted to CTPs which denote directive speech acts. Although embedded clauses headed by *naj* as in (76)–(78) do not have an independent illocution (or at least this proves impossible to test), they preserve a hortative (or permissive) connotation. On the one hand, this is what makes *naj* a non-factual complementizer (in contrast to *da*). On the other hand, the original hortative function (oriented toward a third person) carries over into complementation, and this causes another paradigmatic contrast between *naj* and *da*: *naj* cannot be used as a complementizer in reported speech if the matrix clause includes speaker and addressee of the actual (= reporting) speech act. Compare (76) with (80):

(80) Ukaza-l sem ti, da pride-š
 order[PFV]-PST-(SG.M) AUX.PRS.1SG 2SG.DAT COMP come[PFV].PRS-2SG
 jutri.
 tomorrow
 'I asked you **that** you come tomorrow (> to come tomorrow).'

Compare also (81):

(81) a. Reke-l mi je, naj prinese-m
  say[PFV]-PST-(SG.M) 1SG.DAT AUX.PRS.3SG bring[PFV].PRS-1SG
  piv-o.
  beer-ACC
 b. Reke-l si mi, da prinese-m
  say[PFV]-PST-(SG.M) AUX.PRS.2SG 1SG.DAT COMP bring[PFV].PRS-1SG
  piv-o.
  beer-ACC
  'You told me that I should bring the beer.'

That is, not only is person deixis adapted to the perspective of the reporting subject, but complementizer choice is sensitive to presence/absence of the participants of the actual speech act. In this contrast, *naj* continues to indicate an indirect transmission of directive illocutions, whereas *da* implies direct issuing (Uhlik 2018: 412). For both markers this distinction is reinterpreted under conditions of embedding, which presupposes syntactic tightening with suitable CTPs. Their (almost) complementary distribution befits the fact that *naj* in embedding is a newcomer, while *da* has been functioning as a complementizer for a much longer time. Admittedly, this contrast is not absolutely "watertight"; compare (81c), in which the aforementioned contrast is neutralized (at least in the colloquial standard; M. Uhlik, p.c.):

(81) c. Rek-l-i   so   ti,   **naj / da** prinese-š
       say[PFV]-PST-PL AUX.PRS.3PL   2SG.DAT   COMP   bring[PFV].PRS-2SG
       piv-o.
       beer-ACC
       'They told you **that** you should bring the beer.'

In the corpus one can find realizations of either type. At present one can only guess what explains the observed situation. First of all, *naj* and *da* are distributed complementarily for directive illocutions in direct speech: *naj* occurs with third person, *da* with second person (*Naj / *Da prinese pivo!* 'May s/he bring beer!' vs *Da / *Naj prineseš pivo!* 'Bring beer!'). This observation does not hold as neatly for the imperative. Both *da* and *naj* can occasionally be found with the imperative, but for *da* such occurrences seem to be restricted to clauses that follow after verbs of speech (Uhlik and Žele 2018b: 215), and *naj* in this position is judged as hardly acceptable:

(81) d. Rek-l-i   so   ti,   da / ?naj   prines-i
       say[PFV]-PST-PL AUX.PRS.3PL   2SG.DAT   COMP   bring[PFV]-IMP.SG
       piv-o.
       beer-ACC
       'They told you that you bring the beer.' (lit. '... (You) bring the beer!')

Conversely, in direct speech *da* + imperative appears to be strongly avoided; *naj* is attested, though it is rare (Sonnenhauser, this volume: § 2.1). In light of this, one wonders how (80d) has to be analyzed: if *da* is considered a complementizer, the remaining part (*prinesi privo!*) would be a quote. Alternatively, *da* + imperative might be considered a grammatical collocation that tends to occur only under embedding, but such an assumption seems unusual. In these cases, usage-based investigations might help by first clarifying how the empirical distribution really looks like. However, there should be clear criteria for delimiting reported and direct speech (which in this case might coincide with the distinction between complementation and mood marking).

Moreover, although *naj* operates under a considerably higher number of restrictions than *da* does, it betrays a characteristic of well-established subordinators and of embedding, namely: a *naj*-clause can be inserted within its matrix clause. This applies for both verbal (82) and nominal attachment sites (83):

(82) *Reke-l   sem   mu,   naj   odda*
       say[PFV]-PST-(SG.M) AUX.PRS.1SG 3M.DAT   submit[PFV].PRS-(3SG)
       seminarsko nalogo, že prejšnji teden.
       'I said to him [**that** he should submit his seminar work] already last week.'

(83) *Obvestil-o,*   ***naj***   *se*   *čim prej*   *oglasi-mo,*
    message[N]-NOM.SG   REFL   the_quicker   announce[PFV].PRS-1PL
    je bilo objavljeno na oglasni deski.
    'The message [**that** we should show up as quickly as possible] appeared at the bulletin board.'

Admittedly, these examples are constructed, authentic natural examples are hard to find. Another hallmark of embedding – preposing of *naj*-clauses before potential matrix clauses – has not been attested and can be considered even more unusual (M. Uhlik, p.c.).

All in all, *naj* is much younger than *da*, and its provenance has been more restricted from the start. This shows up in token frequency and embeddability under *da* as well (see Sonnenhauser, this volume, for a comparison). Additional usage-based research should establish the conditions on the distribution of both markers in detail, including dialectal and diachronic data.

2.2.5 Perception

Viberg (1983) introduced a tripartite classification of perception verbs: 'Experience' verbs (non-agentive, e.g., 'see', 'hear'), 'Activity' verbs (agentive, e.g., 'watch', 'listen'), and 'Copulative' verbs (non-agentive, e.g., 'seem'). Experiencer verbs can be taken broadly to include lexemes such as 'find', 'recognize', 'find out', 'spot' (cf. Georgievski 2009: 71 for Macedonian, Grković-Major 2018a: 344 for Old Serbian). The two groups of non-agentive verbs are lexical converses of each other: Experiencer verbs code the animate perceiver as nominative subject (syntactic pivot) and follow a canonical transitive pattern (NOM-ACC), while Copulative verbs code the stimulus as nominative subject and the perceiver as a dative (DAT-NOM), if the perceiver is coded at all. Only the latter form 'impersonal' predicates (i.e., clauses without canonical subjects), for which the clausal complement occupies the subject slot (see 84). 'Activity' verbs (not to be confounded with Vendler's actionality class) pattern syntactically like experience verbs.[49]

In addition to lexical converses ('see, hear, feel' vs 'seem, appear') Experiencer verbs can also be "converted" into Copulative verbs by derivation with the reflexive clitic *se* (e.g., Mac. *se vidi* 'is seen' > 'can be seen / is visible'). Only verbs with the coding pattern of Copulatives allow for a specialized 'as if'-complementizer

---

[49] For more details on these groups cf. Moiseeva (1998), for the difference between Experiencer and Activity verbs cf. Mitkovska and Bužarovska (this volume).

like Mac. *kako da* 'as if' (Bužarovska 2006), e.g., with *čini se* and *izgleda* 'appear, look (like)' (see 84) or the reflexive converses of 'see' and 'hear' (see 85). Often, there is a choice between *kako da* and the default complementizer (*deka*), this choice usually implies different degrees of epistemic support (see § 2.2.4.1).

Macedonian

(84) *Izgleda*
    a. *kako da leta.*
                  fly[IPFV].PRS-(3SG)
    b. *kako da poleta.*
                  fly[PFV].AOR-(3SG)
    c. *kako da ḱe poleta.*
                  fly[PFV].PRS-(3SG)

'It appears as if s/he (a) is flying / (b) flew off / (c) will fly.'

(85) *Mi se vide / slušna* **kako da**
    1SG.DAT REFL see[PFV].AOR-(3SG) hear[PFV].AOR-(3SG) as_if
vrne.
rain[IPFV].PRS-(3SG)
'It seemed to me **as if** it was raining.'

The converse relationship is also crucial for meaning syncretisms of perception verbs: the Copulative CTPs (DAT-NOM pattern) tend toward similative meanings ('as if, as though'), whereas the first two groups (NOM-ACC pattern) often combine perception with manner ('how'). On the other hand, both Experience and Copulative verbs (but not Activity verbs) are employed in marking indirect evidentiality (more precisely: inferential meanings) as they are prone to shifting into cognition. In fact, perception and cognition verbs often intersect in their secondary uses, which is reflected in complementizer choice; cf. Gnjatović and Matasović (2010: 94–95) on Croatian, Mitkovska and Bužarovska (this volume) on Balkan Slavic, and Wiemer and Kampf (2011: 64–66) on Bulgarian units with the similative markers *kato* and *sjakaš* (*kato če (li)*, *sjakaš (če)*, *kato da*, *sjakaš da*), for which it remains to be clarified whether they represent transparent combinations with other complementation markers (*da, li, če*) or holistic units. Compare *Izgležda,* **kato če (li) / sjakaš (če)** *e pijan* 'It seems **as if** he is/were drunk'. An analogous remark applies to Sln. *kot da* (see 86).

Other verbs which can have 'as if'-complements denote behavior (incl. pretence), see (86)–(88), and verbs denoting unspecifically 'feel', as in (89):

Slovene
(86) *Vede   se, **kot da**   ve vse*
 behave[IPFV].PRS-(3SG) REFL like COMP know[IPFV].PRS-(3SG)
 */**kot   da**   bi   vede-l-a   vse.*
 like COMP COND-(3SG) know[IPFV]- LF-SG.F everything
 'She behaves **as if** she knows everything.'

Bulgarian
(87) *Tj-a   se   dărži   (taka), **sjakaš***
 3-SG.F REFL behave[IPFV]-(PRS.3SG) such   as_if
 zna-e   vsičko.
 know[IPFV]-PRS.3SG everything
 'She behaves **as if** she knows everything.'

Macedonian
(88) *Se   odnesuva   **kako da** bi-l-a   vo Amerika.*
 REFL behave[IPFV].PRS-(3SG) as_if   be-LPT-SG.F In America
 'She behaves **as if** she had been to America.'

(89) *Vsušnost se   čuvstvuva-te   **kako da** ḱe se*
 actually REFL feel[IPFV].PRS-2PL as_if   FUT REFL
 razboli-te.
 get_sick[PFV].PRS-2PL
 'Actually you feel like you get sick.'

Evidently, the link between perception and behavior is similative meaning; however, comparison (similative) and manner are often difficult to tell apart.

The similative reading of Copulative verbs shows no constraints on tense-aspect forms (see 84–89). The fact that 'confirmative' tenses like the aorist (see 83b) as well as the future marker *ḱe* (see 84c, 89) can occur after *kako da* shows that *da* has become an integral part of a complex connective which is no longer transparent semantically. Curiously, *kako da* can nonetheless be split, e.g., by adverbs or non-clitic pronouns, so that *da* preserves its position as a verbal proclitic. This applies both to a subjectless CTP (90a) and to a CTP agreeing with the subject in the complement (90b); (91) has an elliptical subject:

(90) a. *Izgleda   **kako** t-ie da ḱe poleta-at.*
  seem[IPFV].PRS-(3SG) as   3-PL if FUT fly[PFV].PRS-3PL
  'It seems **that** they are about to fly.'

b. *Izgleda-at* **kako** <u>sega</u> **da** *ḱe poleta-at.*
seem[IPFV].PRS-3PL as now if FUT fly[PFV].PRS-3PL
'They look **like** they are <u>now</u> about to fly.'

(91) *Se odnesuva* **kako** <u>ništo</u> **da** *ne zna-e.*
REFL behave[IPFV].PRS-(3SG) as nothing if NEG know[IPFV]-PRS.3SG
'She behaves **as if** she does not know <u>anything</u>.'

The same applies to *kako da* used as an independent particle (e.g., ***Kako*** <u>*tie / sega*</u> ***da*** *ḱe poletaat* 'Apparently they are about to fly'); for the relation between both syntactic uses see § 3.6. Other South Slavic languages have 'as if'-connectives, but they seem to be employed rather as particles or restricted to adverbial subordination (Wiemer 2018: 311–313). However, Croat. *kao* can be used as a "similative complementizer" in combination with either *da* or *što*:

(92) a. *Ov-i avion-i izgledaj-u* **kao da** *će*
DEM-NOM.PL airplane-NOM.PL look-PRS.3PL like COMP FUT.3PL
upravo poletje-ti.
just fly[PFV]-INF
'These airplanes look **as if** they are about to fly off.'
(T. Sočanac, p.c.)
b. *On se kreć-e po t-im krug-ov-ima*
3SG.M.NOM REFL rotate[IPFV]-PRS.3SG on DEM-LOC.PL circle-PL-LOC
kao što *rib-a pliva u mor-u.*
like COMP fish-NOM.SG swim[IPFV]-(PRS.3SG) in sea-LOC
'On moves around in these circles **as** a fish swims in the sea.'
(St. Savić, p.c.)

This combinability suggests that *kao da* and *kao što* are not lexicalized complex complementizers, but semantically transparent combinations in which *kao* scopes over the clausal units headed by either *da* or *što* (see § 3.5).

If we now turn to manner readings of perception verbs, future readings are not logical. Whenever manner is involved Mac. *kako* competes with *da* paradigmatically, but they do not combine to *kako da*.[50] The employment of the manner complementizer *kako* has been considered to be favored in particular by verbs imply-

---

50 Slavic languages usually do not follow rules of *consecutio temporum*, i.e., ipfv. present tense is used as a default irrespective of the tense-aspect form of the CTP. Only rarely can we find other forms in the complement (e.g., the imperfect in Macedonian; Georgievski 2009: 71–72). For some discussion cf. Mitkovska and Bužarovska (this volume: § 3.1, § 4.2).

ing an active involvement (i.e., Viberg's Activity verbs), at least in Serbian-Croatian (Mønnesland 1972: 150).

As concerns syntax, perception verbs are prone to ambiguities which become the locus of reanalysis. Copulative verbs show behavior which leads to the rise of epistemic particles and superficially resembles subject-to-subject raising (see § 3.6). The structure becomes ambiguous with Experiencer verbs, when they mark immediate perception and the object-NP naming the observed object (or person) occurs before the complementation marker. This phenomenon has been discussed in connection with subject-to-object raising; compare (93):

Macedonian (dialectal)
(93) <u>Go</u>   vide   <u>Denk-a</u>   **kako** se   niša
     3M.ACC   see.AOR-(3SG)   PN-ACC   how   REFL   sway[IPFV].PRS-(3SG)
     nadolu od kaj tretata kota.
     'He saw <u>Denko</u> swaying down from the third point' ('... **as** he was swaying down...')

In such cases *kako* (or whatever connective) might also be interpreted as a relativizer or as a subordinator introducing a temporal adjunct ('while'); cf. Mitkovska and Bužarovska (this volume: § 4.1). The applies to Mac. *kade* and *kaj*, mentioned by Georgievski (2009: 72–73) as equivalents of *kako* (see 90), although they are dialectal and less frequent. Another such unit marginally used as a complementizer might be Croat. *gdje* (see 95), which is mentioned in Mihaljević (2009) with this function, but rejected by other native speakers:

Macedonian (dialectal)
(94) *se opulil Marko ot Isarot*
     i   ja   vide-l   <u>sestra</u>   <u>si</u>   **kaj**   raboti
     and   3.F.ACC   see-LPT-(SG.M)   sister   REFL.DAT   how   work[IPFV].PRS-(3SG)
     so argati.
     'Marc looked up from the fortress and saw <u>his sister</u> work**ing** with the labourers.'

Croatian
(95) *Primijeti-o*   *je*   *čovjek-a,*   **gdje**   *trči*
     notice[PFV]-PST-(SG.M)   AUX.PRS.3SG   man-ACC   where   run[IPFV].PRS-(3SG)
     spram automobil-a.
     toward car-GEN
     'He noticed a man running toward the car.' ('... **that** he / **how** he / **who** was running...')
     (from Mihaljević 2009: 343)

The relativizer reading frequently arises since coreference of the subject-NP in the complement (Core 2) and the object-NP in the matrix clause (Core 1) is usually not marked by pronouns (pro drop). The relative clause or temporal adjunct interpretation becomes less plausible when the complement codes an irreal (e.g., an undesirable) situation and, correspondingly, the CTP is negated; compare (96):

Bulgarian
(96) Da   ne   săm   te   ču-l   vtori păt
     NEG   AUX.PRS.1SG 2SG.ACC   hear[IPFV]-LPT-(3SG) second_time
     da prikazva-š   taka!
     CON   talk[IPFV].PRS-2SG   such
     'That I won't hear you talking like that a second time!'
     (from Ivanova 2018: 66)

As can be seen from examples like (93) and (94), the connection between the matrix and the *da*-clause can be made tighter by cataphoric clitic doubling: the pronominal clitic in the accusative anticipates the "dropped" subject of the *da*-clause or, as in the dialectal example (93), the full NP marked with accusative who behaves like the object of the matrix predicate. Pitsch (2020: 237), following Smirnova (2012), draws attention that Bulgarian perception verbs may also be followed by *da*-clauses which include an initial pronoun in the nominative. Thus, apart from structures like *Viždam* (ja_i.ACC.F) [*Marija$_i$ da zatvarja prozoreca*] 'I see Maria closing the window', one may also encounter structures like *Viždam* [*tja*.NOM.F / *Marija da idva*] 'I see she / Maria is coming'. Notably, a sentence like the latter "is felicitous in a context where the perceiver sees a woman approaching, but is not entirely sure that it really is Maria" (Pitsch 2020: 237). We may add that this observation agrees with the lack of clitic doubling: the identity of the referent is not provided, which lowers referentiality.

In general, the meaning alternation between observation/perception and cognition correlates with the choice of the complementation marker: the standard complementizer (Mac. *deka*, Bulg. *če*, western South Slavic *da*) is chosen if the complement does not mark direct perception, but refers to a cognitive act (inference) or to hearsay (Georgievski 2009: 73 for Macedonian), but it never seems excluded from a perception reading either. In this respect *da* seems vaguer than an alternative HOW-marker (cf. Uhlik and Žele 2018b: 222–223, 226–227 for Slovene, Grković-Major, this volume, for Serbian). Moreover, Mitkovska and Bužarovska (this volume) demonstrate that the correlation between the choice of the complementation marker and the contrast between perception and cognitive processes is more consistent in Macedonian (*kako* vs *da*) than in Bulgarian (*kak* vs *da*), since in Bulg. *da* is encroaching into the "territory" of immediate perception.[51] A similar point has been made by Mihaljević (2009: 320–322) for Croatian. However, the opposite phenomenon of *kako* occurring as a complementizer with other than perception predicates has been observed for Serbian as well (see below).

Complementizer contrasts that distinguish between direct perception and inferences based on perception are related to evidentiality, and they have been described for many languages (cf. Aikhenvald 2004: 121–122; Kehayov and Boye 2016b). In Bulgarian, apart from some more special units (based on *kato* and *sjakaš*; see above), such contrasts have commonly been shown to apply among *če*, *da* and *kak*. They are illustrated with the following examples from Petkova-Schick (1973: 279):

Bulgarian
(97) a. Starec-ăt   vidja,   **če**   Elka sliza
        old_man.SG-DEF.SG.M see.AOR-(3SG) COMP   PN   go_down-(PRS.3SG)
        bărzo po pătja.
        'The old man saw **that** Elka quickly comes down the road.'
     b. Starec-ăt   vidja   Elka **da**   sliza
        old_man.SG-DEF.SG.M see.AOR-(3SG) PN   CON   go_down-(PRS.3SG)
        bărzo po pătj-a.
        'The old man saw Elka quickly **coming** down the road.'
     c. Starec-ăt   vidja   **kak**   Elka sliza
        old_man.SG-DEF.SG.M see.AOR-(3SG) how   PN   go_down-(PRS.3SG)
        bărzo po pătj-a.
        'The old man saw **how** Elka quickly comes down the road.'

The difference between *da* and *kak* (after CTPs of perception) is much more difficult to pinpoint, as both imply that the time of the denoted situation overlaps with the observer interval. Compare (98–99):

---

[51] Cf. also Tomić (2006: 430), who regards Macedonian as more restrictive when it comes to the employment of epistemically marked connectives (instead of the default complementizer) after perception verbs. She contrasts Macedonian not only to Bulgarian, but also to Greek and Albanian. In areal terms this appears unusual, since Macedonian is, as it were, in the middle of these languages. One should therefore ask whether this characterization is valid for different local varieties, in particular in Southwestern Macedonia (and adjacent parts).

Bulgarian

(98) I   go   vidja-x   **kak** guzno   se   obărna   nastrana.
    and 3M.ACC see.AOR-1SG how   guilty.ADV   REFL   turn[PFV].AOR-(3SG)
    'And I saw him **how** he turned away like a hangdog.'

(99) T-oj   vidja   Borislav **da** stoi
    3-SG.M   see.PRS-(3SG)   PN   CON   stand[IPFV].PRS-(3SG)
    izpraven do vratata na kabineta mu.
    'He saw Borislav standing up to the door of his office.'
    (from Ivanova and Gradinarova 2015: 261)

We may assume that this is just a context type for which *da* and *kak* cooccured during their evolution into complementation devices: complements of perception CTPs basically code SoAs, and they are in a middle position of the SIH. These conditions supply the soil for both an irrealis marker (like Balkan Slavic *da*) and for a complementizer specialized for manner (like *kak*). Such an overlap can also create differences between closely related languages. Thus, in Macedonian the use of *da* is more restricted than in Bulgarian, e.g., in contexts of direct perception and without negation; correspondingly, in equivalents of (97b) Mac. *da* is avoided or even unacceptable (for details cf. Mitkovska and Bužarovska, this volume). An analogous point applies to the relation between Croat. *gdje* and *kako*, but here *gdje* anyway appears to be much more marginal as a complementizer; cf. Mihaljević (2009: 320–321), who discusses idiolectal variation.

A closer connection between the epistemically neutral (= standard) complementizer and *kako* can also be observed in Standard Serbian, where *kako* is attested with propositional complements, e.g., in factual clauses after CTPs of speech or cognition (100), but also after the commissive CTP *obećati* 'promise' (101); the latter, strictly speaking, entails a suspended proposition (Petrović 2003: 38–41):

Serbian

(100) *Prethodno   su   američk-i medij-i   javi-l-i*
     earlier   AUX.PRS.3PL   (American media)-NOM.PL   report[PFV]-PST-PL
     kako je   Kolenović   ubijen
     how   be.PRS.3SG   PN[M]   killed-(SG.M)
     posle svađe opisane kao žučna rasprava o bivšoj Jugoslaviji. (Politika)
     'Earlier, US media reported **that** (how?) Kolenović was killed after an altercation described as gall discussion on the former Yugoslavia.'

(101) Marsalis je obeća-o **kako** ne-će
 PN[M] AUX.PRS.3SG promise[PFV]-PST-(SG.M) how NEG-FUT.3SG
 poštova-ti
 respect[IPFV]-INF
 američki običaj poučnih obraćanja publici između kompozicija.
 'Marsalis promised not to respect (= **that** he would not respect) the American custom of instructive addressing to the public in-between composition.'
 (from Alanović 2018: 175–176)

The non-factual flair becomes evident in light of the elements following CTPs denoting cognitive attitudes of weak epistemic support (or even doubt; see 102). The same effect arises if the speaker does not share the viewpoint of another attitude holder mentioned in the context (see 103):

(102) britansk-a vlad-a najzad potvrdi-l-a da
 (British government)-NOM.SG.F finally confirm[PFV]-PST-SG.F COMP
 sumnja **kako** je reč
 doubt[IPFV]-(PRS.3SG) how be.PRS.3SG speech-(NOM.SG)
 o Krojcfeld-Jakobovoj bolesti.
 'The British government has finally confirmed that it doubted **that** it was the Kreutzfeldt-Jakob disease.' (Politika)

(103) A nađe se i danas gadova
 koj-i bi nas hte-l-i uveri-ti
 REL-NOM.PL COND-(3PL) 1PL.ACC want[IPFV]-PST-PL convince[PFV]-INF
 kako zločin u Jasenovc-u ni-je
 how crime[M]-(NOM.SG.) in PN-LOC NEG-AUX.PRS.3SG
 bi-o tako strašan.
 be-PST-(SG.M) such terrible-(NOM.SG.M)
 'Even today there are bastards who want to convince us **that** the crime in Jasenovac was not so terrible.' (Politika)
 (from Alanović 2018: 177)

Note that the Macedonian cognate does not signal weak epistemic support (see 93). Presumably, Serbian *kako* serves this purpose because *da* does not mark irrealis anymore and the paradigmatic relation between complementation markers after CTPs with propositional complements has diverged. This topic requires more research.

Sln. *kako* is restricted to the domain of perception (and to manner), no extension into the domain of knowledge/belief-related CTPs has been observed

(M. Uhlik, p.c.; and Uhlik and Žele 2018b: 215). If perception verbs are negated and shift into the epistemic (or evidential) domain, complements in the conditional are well-attested, but the complementizer is *da*, not *kako* (Uhlik and Žele 2018b: 220–221); see § 2.2.3 and the next example (see also 86):

Slovene
(104) *Ni-sem   sliša-l,   da   bi   danes*
      NEG-AUX.PRS.1SG hear-PST-(SG.M)   COMP   COND-(3SG)   today
      v Rusij-i   obstaja-l
      in Russia-LOC   exist[IPFV]-PST-(SG.M)
      kakršen koli sistem množičnega preverjanja (...).
      'I haven't heard **that** there would exist any mass check system today in Russia (...).'

2.2.6 Apprehension

Apart from Mac. *kako da* 'as if', Balkan Slavic has morphologically complex connectives which can serve as complementizers of complements denoting apprehension (compare Engl. *lest*): Mac. *da ne* (< *da* + NEG), Bulg. *da ne bi* (< *da* + NEG + COND). Due to the specific semantics, which involves the negation of wish ('if only not / may not') and some epistemic component ('P might have happened / might happen'), both connectives can serve this function only when they follow CTPs denoting fear or similar states. Furthermore, they can introduce main clauses, in which they have a much wider range of uses (including miratives and deliberative questions). Yet, whereas Mac. *da ne* can indicate apprehension also in main clauses, Bulg. *da ne bi* cannot. The latter also requires another *da* to introduce the modified clause (see 105), which relates to the usual tense-aspect constraints known for *da* in Balkan Slavic (see § 2.2.3). Mac. *da ne*, in turn, displays these restrictions only in complementizer use, but not in main clauses. Consequently, in complement clauses, these connectives can never be followed by a verb in the aorist, imperfect or future, but only by the present (106) or a perfect (105).

Bulgarian
(105) *Strax   me   e   da ne bi   da   ne   e*
      fear   1SG.ACC be.PRS.3SG   lest   CON   NEG   AUX.PRS.3SG
      doš-l-a.
      arrive[PFV]-LPT-SG.F
      'I fear **that** she **might** not have come.'

Macedonian
(106) Tina   molče-še,   isplaše-n-a   da   ne
      PN   be_quiet[IPFV]-IMPF.3SG   fraighten[PFV]-PP-SG.F   IRR   NEG
      ima   i   taa   takov virus.
      have[IPFV].PRS.3SG also   3F.NOM   such_virus-ACC.SG
      'Tina kept quiet, fearing **that** she **might** have the same virus.'
      (from Mitkovska, Bužarovska, and Ivanova 2017: 67)

Note that negation in this complex connective is not transparent and can never be stressed; Mac. *da ne* can be immediately followed by sentence negation. For comprehensive analyses cf. Ivanova (2014b) and Mitkovska, Bužarovska, and Ivanova (2017).

In western South Slavic, there are no specialized complementation markers of apprehension, and the form of predicates in complement clauses of 'fear'-verbs are not restricted to particular tense forms or mood forms. The negation in *da ne* is transparent and optional, which is probably connected to the loss of an irrealis-function of *da*, and particularly in Slovene, infinitival complements are encountered as well; cf. Uhlik and Žele (2017: 98–103), from where these examples are cited:

Slovene
(107) a. *Boji-m   se,   da   (ne)   bi   pozabi-l*
         fear[IPFV].PRS-1SG REFL   COMP   NEG   COND(-3SG)   forget[PFV]-LF-(SG.M)
         denarnic-o.
         purse-ACC
         'I fear that I might / will forget my purse.'
      b. *Boji-m   se   pozabi-ti   denarnic-o.*
         fear[IPFV].PRS-1SG REFL   forget[PFV]-INF   purse-ACC
         'I fear to forget my purse.'

The lack of restrictions and the transparent character of *da (ne)* might explain why outside of Balkan Slavic, no specialized 'apprehensional complementizers' have emerged (Wiemer, forthcoming).

2.2.7 Embedded interrogative clauses

Yes/no-interrogative clauses are usually embedded by a specialized complementizer, e.g., Bulg./Mac. *dali*, Serb.-Croat. *li*, Sln. *ali*, *če*. Such IF-units, widespread in other languages as well, are called 'uncertainty complementizers' by

Kehayov and Boye (2016b: 818–822). Importantly, they differ from epistemic contrasts (irrealis-complementation markers vs epistemically neutral = standard complementizers) discussed in § 2.2.4. The latter ones do not show a diachronic relation to conditional or polar interrogative markers, they are not restricted to epistemic modality (and thus to propositional complements), and when used for epistemic contrasts they mark other sorts of distance than just ignorance (as do IF-complementizers).

Bulg./Mac. enclitic *li* sometimes superficially resembles full-fledged complementizers. This occurs when it scopes over the entire clause (as would *dali*); compare (108):

Bulgarian

(108) a. *Pita-xa   me   **dali**   e   kupi-l*
         ask-AOR.3PL   1SG.ACC   Q   AUX.PRS.3SG   buy[PFV]-LPT-(SG.M)
         vestnik-a.
         newspaper-DEF

   b. *Pita-xa   me   kupi-l   **li**   e*
      ask-AOR.3PL   1SG.ACC   buy[PFV]-LPT-(SG.M)   Q   AUX.PRS.3SG
      vestnik-a.
      newspaper-DEF
      'They asked me **whether** he bought the newspaper.'

However, this is only a side effect; *li*'s behavior markedly differs from that of *dali*. It is not *per se* placed in adjacency to the lexical verb (in the same way as is *da*), but it is a real enclitic occurring just after any focused element or even larger constituents (Tiševa 2008; Krapova, this volume; as for Macedonian cf. Tomić 2012: 228, 412–414; and Sims and Joseph 2019: 123–125). If classified as a 2P-enclitic, the domains of cliticization turn out to be extremely variable. Thus, *li* is used to indicate just any marked focus (109) and (110), a question as such (111) and (112), or it marks deliberative or echo-questions (113). In the latter two cases, it serves as an illocutionary (not a propositional) operator and can co-occur with *dali* (see 111); consequently, it then takes *dali* into its scope:

Bulgarian
(109) *Vie **li** namerixte kăštata?*
      'Was it you who found the house?'

(110) *Koj **li** e vzel knigata?*
      'Who(ever) could have taken the book?'

(111) *Znaeš* **li** *dali e v kăšti?*
'Do you know if s/he is at home?'

(112) *Da se vărne* **li** *dovečera?*
'Should s/he come back tonight?'

(113) A: *Da xodim s tramvaj.*
B: *Da xodim s tramvaj* **li**?
'A: Let's go by tram. B: You (really) want to go by tram?'
(from Rudin 1986: 64–67)

Moreover, *dali* is more frequently found attaching to nominals and it can be combined with a wider range of CTPs than *li*. For instance, *dali* can be used after *bespokoja se* 'worry' (Hansen, Letuchiy, and Błaszczyk 2016: 217). This makes *dali* suitable as a complementizer in apprehensional contexts, too (see § 2.2.6).

2.2.8 Synopsis on complementation markers

The following table presents a synopsis of the main complementation markers employed in South Slavic standard languages. It can only provide a rough impression, but does not do justice to various intersections, e.g., if some marker from one domain encroaches into another one. These kinds of extensions have been pointed out above. Brackets indicate markers which, for the given domain, are emergent (e.g., Sln. *naj*) or marginal for some reason. Moreover, Table 3 does not include WH-words employed in embedded questions (on which see § 3.2).

Table 3: Complementation markers in South Slavic standard languages.

	Slovene	Serbian-Croatian	Macedonian	Bulgarian
specialized factive	—	*što (jer)*	*što*	*deto*
+ factual (strong epistemic support) = epistemically neutral → standard/default complementizer	*da*	*da (kako)*	*deka, oti*	*če*
– factual I (knowledge/belief-based)	*da (naj)*	*da*	*da*	*da*
– factual II (volition-based)	*da, naj,* INF	*da*	*da*	*da*

Table 3 (continued)

	Slovene	Serbian-Croatian	Macedonian	Bulgarian
perception (+ manner)	*kako*	*kako* (*gdje*)	*kako*	*kak*
similative ('as if')	*kot da* (+ indicative / conditional)	*kao* (+ *da, što*)	*kako da*	(*kato če (li), kato da*) (*sjakaš (da)*)
apprehension	—	—	(*da ne*)	(*da ne bi*)
embedded question ('if')	*ali, če*	*li*	*dali*	*dali*

2.3 Form of the predicate in the complement clause

For this parameter, the distinction between balanced and deranked clauses is crucial. I will therefore first comment on this notion (§ 2.3.1), before I will look at non-finite complements and possible contrasts with finite complements (§ 2.3.2).

As concerns argument marking in dependent clauses, in contemporary South Slavic, these are practically not marked differently than arguments in main clauses. Exceptions are object NPs of perception CTPs, which behave "janus-faced" (§ 2.2.5), and arguments of action nominals, which are anyway most debatable as clausal complements (§ 3.3).

2.3.1 On deranking

The 'balanced – deranked' distinction goes back to Stassen (1985: 76–83) and refers to the strategies by which two interrelated SoAs are connected (apart from occurring in succession). Either the predicates in both cores are coded in an identical way, so that they might each occur in independent clauses, or the predicate in one of the two clauses is coded in a way that is not employed in independent clauses (e.g., with participles, converbs or nominalizations). The former strategy is called balancing, the latter deranking. Stassen's definition was modified by Cristofaro (2003: 55–57), who qualifies a clause as deranked if its predicate occurs in a form that "cannot occur in independent <u>declarative</u> clauses taken in isolation [...] regardless of how this is indicated" (2003: 57, emphasis added). Taken literally, this rigid restriction would lead to an exclusion of imperatives, exclamatives and miratives, optatives and similar directive speech acts: such clauses code independent illocutions, although they are not declarative. The same would apply to any sort of 'subjunctive' and whatever is subsumed under the label of insubordination (cf. Wiemer 2017 for a comprehensive account concerning Slavic). We thus have to be aware that under Cristofaro's narrower definition of deranking it is illocutionary distinctions alone which may lead to the qualification of a clause type as deranked.

What such a treatment of the 'balanced – deranked' opposition can mean in practice becomes evident if we consider the assessment of the tense-aspect restriction which we encounter all over the place in South Slavic, namely: the restriction of the present tense of pfv. verbs to combinations with *da*; see § 2.2.3. In any South Slavic language, such clauses can be subordinated or function as independent sentences (with directive, mirative or exclamative illocutions). Following Cristofaro (2003), pfv. present tense would *per se* be indicative of deranking, but this would not tell us much (if anything) about the syntactic status of the respective clauses. If, conversely, deranking were defined in the sense that dependent clauses are characterized by paradigmatic forms of the predicate which do not occur in independent clauses, the tense-aspect restriction mentioned before would not be indicative of deranking.

2.3.2 Non-finite predicates and possible contrasts with finite predicates

There are only three types of non-finite forms to be considered for contemporary South Slavic. All of them are rare, probably except for Slovene and Croatian, spoken in the northwestern corner of the territory (see below). One instance is the so-called shortened infinitive in Bulgarian, which is used (if at all) only with CTPs occupying the highest positions in the SIH that do not belong to complementation proper, anyway (see § 2.1), such as complex predicates with modals. Compare (114):

Bulgarian
(114) *T-oj   ne   sme-a   se   obadi.*
       3-M.SG   NEG   dare-PRS.3SG   REFL   answer[PFV].TR_INF
       'He does not dare answer.'
       (from Joseph 2016: 267; cf. also Mladenov 1929: 299)

The other two types are complements of perception CTPs with infinitives and uninflected participial predicates; the latter can be considered converbs.

Participial complements of perception CTPs are sometimes encountered in literary registers of Serbian-Croatian, but even there they are extremely rare (cf. Mihaljević 2009: 336–340 for Croatian). In Old Serbian, inflected participles disappeared very early, AcP-constructions are practically absent even in the earliest records and are attested only in folk poetry; see (115). This corresponds to a general retreat of participles (and of converbs; see below) from complementation in Slavic (Wiemer 2014b: 1640–1641).

Serbian folk poetry
(115) kada   mi   **te**   začu-ju   moj-e im-e
      when   1SG.DAT   2SG.ACC   hear[PFV].PRS-3PL   (my name)-ACC
      kliku-jući
      shout[IPFV]-SIM_INDECL
      'when they hear **you shouting** my name' (B: 19.60)

Their survival in marginal use has probably been due to Latin, then German influence, an exception being the use of uninflected participles in NcP-constructions of the passive (Grković-Major 2018a: 344–346).

Converbs[52] as complements of perception CTPs have practically fallen out of use. In Macedonian, for instance, we find examples in archaic genres and the 19th century folklore, where they functioned as equivalents of finite clauses with a manner complementizer (see § 2.2.5). Their syntactic status was ambiguous in the same way, since they could also be interpreted as modifiers of object-NPs (see 116). This was clearly the case for anteriority participles (with n/t-suffix) as in (117). Their interpretation as complements is supported by information structure: without these "additions" the utterances would hardly have a communicative value:

Macedonian
(116) Vide-l-e   go   taka   čin-ejḱi   roditel-i.
      see-LPT-PL   3.M.ACC   such   do[IPFV]-SIM_INDECL   parent-PL
      'The parents saw him doing so.'

(117) Pojde   v šarena   odaa,   Bojana   najde
      go[PFV].AOR-(3SG) in colorful   room   PN[F]   find[PFV].AOR-(3SG)
      zaspa-n-a.   (= kako spie)
      fall_asleep[PFV]-PP-SG.F
      'He went into a colorful room, he found Bojana (having fallen) asleep'
      (= as she was sleeping)
      (from Georgievski 2009: 73)

---

52 All Slavic converbs are paradigmatically isolated (and sometimes truncated) forms of formerly inflected participles (Wiemer 2014b: 1634–1638). In Slavic linguistics they are usually dubbed 'adverbial participles', which corresponds to their practically exclusive use in adverbial subordination.

Infinitival complements introduced by a complementizer have become obsolete even in the western part of South Slavic, where infinitives are still in use. For ancient attestations see (130) in § 2.4 from Old Church Slavonic texts of Macedonian provenance (13th–16th century).

In other respects, Slovene has most consistently preserved infinitives as heads of complements.[53] Predictably, these occur after verbs which induce a high degree of semantic integration, such as perception and control verbs; compare (118–120):

Slovene
(118) *Sliša-l   sem   ga   žvižga-ti.*   immediate
      hear-PST-(SG.M) AUX.PRS.1SG   3M.ACC   whistle[IPFV]-INF   perception
      'I heard him whistle.'

(119) *Misli-m   jo   kupi-ti.*   subject control
      think[IPFV].PRS-1SG   3F.ACC   buy[PFV]-INF
      'I think (= intend) to buy it.'

(120) *Reke-l   mi   je   ses-ti.*   object control
      say[PFV]-PST-(3SG)   1SG.DAT   AUX.PRS.3SG sit_down[PFV]-INF
      'He told me to sit down.'
      (Uhlik and Žele 2018b: 229–230)

The domain of perception CTPs remains most outstanding (see 118). Yet, even here the infinitive has survived only in the western periphery of the Slavic-speaking territory; we find them in Croatian as well (Mihaljević 2009: 322–336 for a generative analysis). As with participles and converbs, their rise and survival has been ascribed mainly to contacts with Latin, then Italian and German (Grković-Major 2018a, 2018b).

However, infinitival complements are used much more rarely in combination with verbs denoting directive speech acts (see 120) than with finite, i.e. *da*-headed, complements (Uhlik and Žele 2018b: 230). In a sense, this converges with a remark by Topolińska (2003: 315) about purpose clauses: "*da* alone appears only where there is no coreference between the first (subject) arguments of the two clauses", whereas for "the *da bi* construction the referential status of the subject arguments is irrelevant". If this is correct, adverbial subordination

---

[53] The supine, which has been preserved in Slovene as well, is only used in purpose clauses and therefore lies outside our field of investigation.

and clausal complementation converge with a preference for *da*-clauses in case of different-subject combinations – while *da* disfavors subordinate clauses with either infinitival and conditional predicates. Concomitantly, we would have an explanation why *da*-clauses in the conditional have remained comparatively well-represented in Slovene (see § 2.2.3): they are simply not constrained by coreference relations between the conjoined clauses, so that they can replace both infinitive clauses and clauses headed by *da* (+ pfv. present), but not vice versa. However, these assumptions require a solid usage-based investigation.

This postulate is supported by the research situation concerning Serbian-Croatian, where the choice between complementation devices has also been claimed to be related to the same subject (= subject control, infinitive preferred) vs different subject (= object control, *da* + V_{fin} preferred) criterion. The findings are inconclusive and variation rather appears to be a matter of areality and/or of diastratic differences: infinitives are no longer available as an option in the East Serbian Torlak dialects (M. Mirić, p.c.), while in the standard languages (Croatian, Serbian), we encounter phenomena which are not easy to subsume under some common denominators. The Štokavian region (on which the Croatian and Serbian standards are based) clearly constitutes a transition zone with a high degree of diastratic variation. For instance, the commissive (i.e. subject control) verb *obećati* 'promise' needs a complement in the future (121a), an infinitival complement is felt unnatural (121b); notably, a *da*-clause is entirely ruled out (121c) (Vrdoljak 2019: 241–242):

Croatian
(121) a. *Ivan je obeća-o Marij-i da*
 PN AUX.PRS.3SG promise[PFV]-PTS-(SG.M) PN-DAT COMP
 će do-ći.
 FUT.3SG come[PFV]-INF
 b. ?*Ivan je obeća-o Marij-i do-ći.*
 PN AUX.PRS.3SG promise[PFV]-PTS-(SG.M) PN-DAT come[PFV]-INF
 c. **Ivan je obeća-o Marij-i da*
 PN AUX.PRS.3SG promise[PFV]-PTS-(SG.M) PN-DAT COMP
 dođe.
 come[PFV].PRS-(3SG)
 'Ivan promised Marija to come (that he would come).'

In turn, Belić (2005a; 2005b) finds that *da*-clauses are preferred if the matrix clause codes an oblique argument which is coreferent with the subject of the complement clause (122b). This occurs particularly with some predicatives (for which see § 2.4); compare (122)–(123):

Serbian
(122) a. Tešk-o   je   prizna-ti   / da   prizna-m
          hard-N   be.PRS.3SG   confess[PFV]-INF   COMP   confess[PFV]-PRS.1SG
          zločin.
          crime-(ACC)
          'It is hard to confess to a crime.'   infinitive preferred

(122) b. Tešk-o   mi   je   prizna-ti /   da
          hard-N   1SG.DAT   be.PRS.3SG   confess[PFV]-INF COMP
          prizna-m   zločin.
          confess[PFV]-PRS.1SG   crime-(ACC)
          'It is hard <u>for me</u> to confess to a crime.'   *da*-clause preferred

Vrdoljak (2019) takes facts such as these to indicate that epistemic control (which is considered to be stronger with a dative experiencer, as in 122b) favors *da*-complements over infinitives. Concomitantly, the infinitive might be preferred when generic readings are possible (see 122a).

2.4 PoS of the complement-taking predicate

Gast and Diessel (2012) present a symmetrical classification of subordinate clauses resulting from a cross-application of the part-of-speech (PoS) of the CTP (verbal vs nominal attachment site) with the adjunct – argument distinction; see Table 4 (from Gast and Diessel 2012: 6):

Table 4: Four major types of subordinate clauses.

	nominal projection	verbal projection
adjunction	RELATIVE CLAUSE the house [that you bought]	ADVERBIAL CLAUSE He's angry [because she left]
complementation	NOMINAL COMPLEMENT HOUSE the fact [that he was angry]	VERBAL COMPLEMENT HOUSE He said [that he was angry].

© Gast, Volker & Holger Diessel. 2012. The typology of clause linkage: status quo, challenges, prospects. In Volker Gast & Holger Diessel (eds.), *Clause Linkage in Cross-Linguistic Perspective: Data- Driven Approaches to Cross-Clausal Syntax*, 1–36. Berlin & Boston: De Gruyter Mouton (p. 6, Table 1).

Complementation with other than verbal attachment sites (see the lower left corner of Table 4) has been a stepchild of research. An exception is Dixon (2005: 281–283), who drew attention that verb classes such as 'like' and 'annoy' constitute notional parallels to adjectival bases whose semantics implies sentient beings experiencing some cognitive or emotional state or carrying out a judgment ('good – bad', 'nice – ugly', 'likely – unlikely', 'true – false').

Two remarks should be made. First, complements of nominal attachment sites can in some respect be regarded as intermediary between clausal complements with verbal attachment sites and relative clauses (see § 3.2). They differ from the latter in that the linking element in complement clauses is not a constituent of this clause, while relativizers are constituents of the dependent clause (Lehmann 1984: 153–155).

Second, the label 'nominal complement clause' (in Table 4) comprises not only complements of nouns, but also those of adjectives, and one wonders whether complements to less well-delimited classes such as predicatives (see 123 and 124) should be considered subtypes of nominal or of verbal complement clauses. Of course, this question is derivative of well-known discussions concerning PoS-divisions.[54]

Croatian
(123) **Šteta,** što Marij-a ni-je doš-l-a.
shame COMP PN-NOM NEG-AUX.PRS.3SG come[PFV]-PST-SG.F
'It's a **pity** that Marija hasn't come.' (Wiemer 2019a: 110)

Slovene
(124) **Vide-ti** je, (kot) da prihaja
see-INF AUX.PRS.3SG as COMP come[IPFV].PRS-(3SG)
/ (kot) da bi prihaja-l.
as COMP COND-(3SG) come[IPFV]-PST-(3SG)
'It can be seen that / as though he is coming.'
(from Uhlik and Žele 2018b: 221)

---

[54] For instance, from a typological point of view, adjectives can, on the basis of their behavior properties and structural coding in different pragmatic functions (reference, modification, predication), be considered intermediate between nouns and verbs (Croft 2000). Predicatives as a word class are debatable, at least since they are parasitic on stems of nominal categories (nouns, adjectives; see 123), on infinitives (see 124) and on PPs. Yet, it cannot be denied that this fuzzy class is united by their ability to form the nuclei of clauses with non-canonical marking of arguments (Wiemer 2019a: 128–134).

Related cases are clauses attached to adverbs, or rather: to predicates which superficially look like adverbs; compare (125):

Macedonian
(125)   **Sekako <u>deka</u>** *vakvoto vozobnovuvanje ne može da se razgleduva nadvor od vlijanieto na drugite južnoslovenski literaturni jazici.*
'**Certainly** such a restoration [of the use of the *bi*-conditional; BW] cannot be considered without (an account of) the influence of other South Slavic standard languages.' (lit. '<u>certainly / for sure</u> that such a restoration...')
(Labroska 2018: 76)

Predicatives with an adverbial origin are probably the most widespread ones. In (125) complementation is explicitly marked with a canonical complementizer; without a complementizer, the expressions written in bold in (123)–(125) would rather count as modifiers of the whole clause and the sentence be monoclausal (see § 3.6). It is questionable whether copula ellipsis can be assumed in such cases (compare with *sekako e (deka)* P 'it is certain (that) P'), but even if this might turn out a viable analysis, the syntactic relation between the epistemic expression (CTP with propositional complement or propositional modifier) would not become less ambiguous. The reasons were discussed in § 1 (see Figure 1); for a discussion of the "copula problem" cf. Wiemer (2019a: 146–150).

With predicatives, the criteria of subclassification are the same as for other types of CTPs, including meaning alternations reflected by variable choice of the complementation technique, i.e., between finite and infinitival complement (cf. Belić 2005a; 2005b for Serbian) or between complementation markers, for instance (126):

Macedonian
(126) a. *Dobr-o   e   da   molč-iš.*   non-factive
         good-N   be.PRS.3SG   CON   be_silent[IPFV]-PRS.2SG
         'It would be good **that** you be silent.'
      b. *Dobr-o   e   što   molče-še.*   factive
         good-N   be.PRS.3SG   COMP   be_silent[IPFV]-IMPF.2SG
         'It is good **that** you kept silent.'

The same applies for the choice of complementizers arguably occurring after prepositions (as claimed, e.g., by Rudin 1986: 58 for Bulgarian); for instance (127):

Bulgarian
(127) a. ***Osven če njama pari...***   factive
'**Besides** the fact that s/he has no money...'
b. ***Osven da njama pari...***   non-factual
'**Unless** s/he has no money...'

Here we observe the usual contrast between default complementizer and *da* (cf. Milenkovska and Pančevska 2014: 188 for Macedonian). Other scholars treat such collocations as complex conjunctions (e.g., Ivanova 2014a: 141).

Notably, not all nominalizations are equally well-suited attachment sites of clausal complements as are equivalent (or even cognate) verbs. The reasons behind this are yet poorly understood; cf. Letuchiy (this volume) for a corpus-based exploration of underlying conditions in Bulgarian. Notwithstanding the lack of research in this domain, we can say that, like verbal predicates, clausal complements of nominal attachment sites can code either propositions or SoAs, and this notional distinction manifests itself in differing morphosyntactic behavior, provided there is a choice. Thus, either there is a choice between complementation markers (see 126a vs 126b above), or (outside of contemporary Balkan Slavic) infinitival complements tend to occur after nouns which code situations (SoAs) not located in time (see 128), while propositional arguments of nominals tend to be morphologically finite (see 129). The complementizer for both types of complements may be identical;[55] see examples from Church Slavonic documents of Macedonian provenance from the 14th and the 16th century:

(128) *prorok že daniilъ imě-še* <u>*obyčai*</u>
prophet-(SG.NOM) PTC PN-(SG.NOM) have-IMPF.3SG habit-(ACC.SG)
jako trišti na d<ь>nъ **poklanja-ti** *se b<og>-u.*
COMP thrice on day(-ACC) bow[IPFV]-INF REFL God-DAT
'the prophet Daniil had the <u>habit</u> **to bow** to god thrice a day.'
(Krninski damaskin, 16th. c.)

(129) *i da-s<tъ> <u>znamenie</u> jako* **zaid-etъ**
and give[PFV].AOR-3SG sign-ACC COMP go_down[PFV].PRS-3SG
sl<ь>nc-e vъ silom-ě. (Stanislavov prolog, 1330)
sun-NOM in PN-LOC
'and he gives a <u>sign</u> that the sun **rises** in Silom.'
(cited from Ǵurkova 2008: 99)

---

[55] Georgievski (2009: 34–38, 58–59, 62–67) lists nouns with *da*-complements, but does not consider possible contrasts with *če*-complements.

Compare these to verbal attachment sites:

(130) g‹lago›la emu duxovnikъ.
 ta   g‹lago›l-et   jako   po dvoju m‹e›s‹e›cě   **umre-ti**.
 and say[IPFV].PRS-3SG COMP   in two months   die[PFV]-INF
 'the priest said to him and <u>tells</u> him that after two months he has **to die**.'
 (Krninski damaskin, 16th. c.; Ǵurkova 2008: 94)

(131) <u>pověda-šę</u>   že   mu   jako   i‹su›sъ   nazarěninъ
 say[IPFV]-AOR.3PL PTC 3M.DAT COMP   Jesus-(NOM)   from_Nazareth
 mymoxod-itъ.
 pass_by[IPFV].PRS-3SG
 '<u>they told</u> him that Jesus from Nazareth **is passing by**.'
 (Radomirovo evangelie, late 13th c.; Ǵurkova 2008: 94)

When predicatives denoting perception have clausal arguments, the latter are usually finite, but since these predicatives do not allow for canonical subjects, their coding pattern is identical with the pattern of Copulative verbs (see § 2.2.5). See (124), which also shows an overlap with similative meaning.

2.5 Correlative pronouns

In the maximum template (Figure 2), correlative pronouns are given in brackets not only because they are often optional, but mainly because it is questionable whether the subordinate clause (= Core 2) functions as a core argument in relation to the matrix clause (= Core 1). Instead, it rather can be argued to complement the pronoun. This is how such complex sentences are treated, for instance, in GSBKE (1983: 313) and by Penčev (1999: 577). If this reasoning is adequate, the correlative pronoun bears some resemblance to nominal attachments sites, namely to those with propositional complements. Despite some reservations, Hansen, Letuchiy, and Błaszczyk (2016: 175–177) provide insights about the role of correlative pronouns, primarily in Russian. Most noteworthy is their finding that, if there is a choice between using and not using a correlative pronoun, the realization with the pronoun induces high degree of certainty or factivity, and with factive CTPs (e.g., Russ. *radovat'* 'make glad') they can always be used. This is why correlative pronouns sound bad with non-factive verbs or predicates that lack strong epistemic support (e.g., Russ. *Ja dumaju (*to) / znaju (to), čto včera šel sneg* 'I think / I know that yesterday it snowed'). See the following contrast (cited from Baschewa 2004: 74):

Bulgarian

(132) *Săžaljava-m* **za tova,** *če zaminava-š.*
regret[IPFV]-PRS.1SG for DEM COMP leave[IPFV]-PRS.2SG
'I regret (lit. *for this*) that you are leaving.' factive

(133) *Prinudi-xa go (*na tova) da zamine.*
force[PFV]-AOR.3PL 3.M.ACC on DEM CON leave[PFV]-(PRS.3SG)
(lit.) 'They forced him (*to this) that he leaves'
('They forced him to leave.') non-factual (volition-oriented)

As far as I know, no systematic research has been carried out on this topic in South Slavic languages. Hansen, Letuchiy, and Błaszczyk (2016: 211–212) compared some Bulgarian and Russian CTPs (with different grammatical persons) in corpora and preliminarily concluded that in Bulgarian correlative pronouns are used less frequently than with equivalent verbs in Russian. Bulgarian regularly employs correlative pronouns only in contrastive contexts,[56] but even then the proportion of correlatives is much lower than in Russian. Another of their findings was that correlative pronouns often turn out to be obligatory when combining with verbs that require an argument headed by a preposition. Furthermore, the semantic role of the clausal argument has an impact: reason and stimulus clauses favor (or even require) the use of a correlative pronoun (on this issue see also Letuchiy, this volume).

For Macedonian, we find only casual remarks, as e.g., in Tomić (2006: 436), who gives the example in (134), with *toa* 'this' occurring in a PP (Bulgarian equivalents are *tova* 'this' and *tam* 'there'; 2006: 472).

Macedonian

(134) *Došo-l* **do toa,** *da go sožaluva-at*
come[PFV]-LPT-(SG.M) To DEM CON 3M.ACC pity[IPFV]-PRS.3PL
si-te.
everybody.PL-DEF.PL
'He is in such a deplorable situation that everybody feels sorry for him.'
(lit. 'He came **to it** that everybody feels sorry for him.')

It is this demonstrative which the *da*-clause complements, and to which it relates cataphorically. Alternatively, one might argue that *došol do toa* forms one seman-

---

56 Otherwise, they can be interpreted as purpose or consecutive clauses (see ex. 43 in § 2.2.3.3).

tic complex which, as the predicate, is targeted by the *da*-clause. In the latter case, PPs, as part of the matrix clause, would just signal the argument relation with the embedded clause.[57] After all, these are special constructions with PPs, but it would be unjustified to claim that Macedonian PPs are particularly prone to taking clausal complements. Additionally, Tomić's claim (2006: 436) as though in older Macedonian all prepositions could take clausal complements lacks any substantiation (she herself gives neither examples nor references).

3 Grey zones and delimitation problems

The discussion of the role of correlative pronouns in complementation sentences has already brought us into a grey zone. This section is devoted to a couple of recurrent issues that are problematic either because complementation cannot easily be disentangled from related phenomena, or because structures that look like complementation sentences allow for alternative analyses.

3.1 How to distinguish complementation from complementation strategies?

The distinction made by Dixon (2006: 33–40) between complementation and complementation strategies hinges on the issue whether a clause can be treated as a core argument of some predicate (see § 1), regardless of its PoS (§ 2.4). Let us illustrate this point for the distinction between purpose and complement clauses with nominal attachment sites. This distinction is always difficult if the subordinator conflates both functions and the noun denotes a volition-related concept (including covert directive speech acts). Balkan Slavic *da* is a case in point (see 135–136). Purpose clauses can be distinguished from complement clauses with nouns of other semantic classes, first of all those which describe habits or some kind of law (see 137–139):

---

[57] This resembles object doubling by clitics, a technique commonplace in Balkan Slavic (and other Balkan languages). However, since the cataphoric function of correlative pronouns is much more widespread elsewhere (e.g., in Germanic and North Slavic), clitic doubling (which is a clause level phenomenon) and correlative pronouns in complementation do not appear to be connected directly.

Macedonian

(135) *Nužn-a   mu   be-še   jak-a <u>volj-a</u>   **da**   ne*
necessary-SG.F 3.M.DAT be-IMPF.3SG (some will)-SG.F CON NEG
otstapi   ot   polugoliot prizrak.
refrain[PFV]-(PRS.3SG) from (half-nakd ghost)-SG
'He needed some <u>will</u> (in order) not to refrain from the half-naked ghost.'

(136) *Od   karaul-a-ta   na most-ot   dad-ov*
from   guard[F]-SG-DEF.SG.F   on bridge[M]-DEF.SG.M give[PFV]-AOR.1SG
<u>*upatstv-o*</u>   *si-te   semejstv-a   **da***
instruction[N]-SG   all-DEF.PL family[N]-PL CON
trgna-t   kon   Nivici.
move[PFV]-PRS.3PL   toward   PN
'He gave an <u>instruction</u> from the bridge guard **that** the whole family should move toward Nivici.'
→ complementation or purpose adjunct?

(137) *Naš-i-te   žen-i   ima-at   <u>običaj</u>   **da***
our-PL-DEF.PL woman-PL have[IPFV]-PRS.3PL habit-(SG) CON
gi   plaša-t   deca-ta   so mnogu
3PL.ACC frighten[IPFV]-PRS.3PL children-DEF.PL with many
zaplašuvačk-i.
frightening_thing-PL
'Our women have the <u>habit</u> **that** they frighten the children with many frightening things.'

(138) *Sabrija   može   da   si   zeme   za   <u>prav-o</u>*
PN   can.PRS.3SG CON REFL.DAT take[PFV]-(PRS.3SG) for right-SG
***da**   raskažuva   za   nekoj   den*
CON   tell[IPFV]-(PRS.3SG) for some-(SG.M) day[M]-(SG)
od   život-ot   na   Boris.
of   life[M]-DEF.SG.M on   PN
'Sabrija can take the <u>right</u> to tell a story from some day of Boris' life.'
(from Georgievski 2009: 64–67)
→ complementation

In addition, the *da*-clause in (136) might alternatively be analyzed as a relative clause. This is the more a plausible option as *da*-clauses can also modify nouns denoting first-order objects, e.g. Mac. *Imaat <u>kuče</u> **da** gi čuva* 'They have a <u>dog</u> to protect them' (Tomić 2006: 434–435, 469 for Bulgarian, see also f. 35). We are thus dealing with a clause type in which purpose meaning, NP-modification and complementation are hard to disentangle.

Gradience in the transition from adverbial subordination to clausal complementation surfaces when we compare syntactic tests of subordination (cf. Hansen, Letuchiy, and Błaszczyk 2016: 195–197; Letuchiy, this volume). Not all constructions and/or complementation markers pass all of them, so that establishing which tests are passed and which are not may be considered a procedure to roughly assess to which degree relevant markers have acquired the behavior of a canonical complementizer (presumably regardless of the semantic contrasts which they participate in). We have already seen that Sln. *naj*-clauses can in principle be inserted within "their" matrix clause, although no authentic examples are known; however, *naj*-clauses can hardly be preposed (see § 2.2.4.2). This might be indicative of an implication saying that if preposing "works", then insertion should do so as well, but not necessarily vice versa.

In fact, Hansen, Letuchiy, and Błaszczyk (2016: 191–193) show that only well-established complementizers, but also complementation strategies (e.g., an adverbial subordinator "doing the duties" of a complementizer) can be fronted together with their clause. Compare Bulg. *če* and *dali* in (139) and (140) vs *kogato* 'when' in (141a) and (141b):

Bulgarian
(139) [**Če** t-oj e xubav] ne me
COMP 3-SG.M be.PRS.3SG handsome-(SG.M) NEG 1SG.ACC
iznenada.
surprise[IPFV]-(PRS.3SG)
'[That he is handsome] did not surprise me.'

(140) [**Dali** t-oj e xubav] njama značenie.
whether 3-SG.M be.PRS.3SG handsome-(SG.M) BE.NEG meaning
'[Whether he is handsome] does not matter.'
(from Rudin 1986: 45)

(141) a. Ne običa-m [kogato mi govorj-at kato
NEG like[IPFV]-PRS.3SG when 1SG.DAT speak[IPFV]-PRS.3PL like
na bebe].
to baby
'I don't like it when people talk to me as a baby.'
b. *[**Kogato** mi govorj-at kato na bebe], ne običam.
*'When people talk to me as a baby, I don't like.'
(from Hansen, Letuchiy, and Błaszczyk 2016: 218)

However, the situation is more complicated. For instance, some emotive factive verbs allow their clausal complement to be preposed (see 139), while others, like Sln. *veseliti se* 'be glad', do not; in either case, the complementizer is well established:

Slovene
(142) a. *Veseli-m   se,   [da   mi   piše-š].*
         rejoice[IPFV]-PRS.1SG REFL   COMP   1SG.DAT   write[IPFV].PRS.2SG
         'I'm glad [that you write to me].'
     b. **[Da mi pišeš], se veselim.*
         *'[That you write to me] I'm glad.'
         (adapted from Uhlik and Žele 2018b: 221)

Whether cognitive factive verbs are in general more "tolerant" to the linear position of their clausal complements (compare *That such research is required everybody knows / realizes*), remains to be established.⁵⁸ Certainly, many different factors (among them, information structure) will have to be taken into account. For the time being I only want to point out that the "weakly subordinative" behavior of complements to (some) emotive factives can possibly be explained based on their close relation to clauses which provide a reason for the fact stated in the main clause (see § 2.2.2.3). Causes usually do not belong to core arguments, which conditions their rather weak syntactic integration. Simultaneously, reasons are rather supplied after the presentation of facts to which they relate; this disfavors their preposition to main clauses whose content they justify.

Furthermore, the aforementioned postposition constraint resembles the behavior of complements in the function of subjects to certain nominal predicates. This peculiar sentence type occurs in copular structures which define a situation type or some general notion named by an abstract noun: 'X is Y', or 'X DEM Y', but with an inverted order 'Y is/DEM X'. Compare (143) from Slovene, in which *da*-clause = X/subject and *svoboda* 'freedom' = Y/predicate, and the Bulgarian example (144), in which the similative combination *kato da* fulfils the same function.⁵⁹

---

58 The same question applies to fronted embedded questions (with WH-words), as in Bulg. *Kolko vreme stoja taka, tja ne pomneše* '**How much** time she stood that way she didn't remember' (cited from Baschewa 2004: 75).
59 Possibly, *kato da* is just a free combination of the similative marker *kato* 'like' with the irrealis connective *da*, comparable to Sln. *kot da* (see 86).

Slovene
(143) Svobod-a   je,   **da**   lahko   dela-š
      freedom[F]-NOM.SG be.PRS.3SG COMP POSSIB   do[IPFV]-PRS.2SG
      po svoji volji.
      'Freedom is **that/when** you can do as you want.' (lit. 'according to your will')
      (from Uhlik and Žele 2018b: 214)

Bulgarian
(144) Tvorčestv-o-to   e   **kato da**   xvărlja-š
      creativity[N]-SG-DEF.SG.N be.PRS.3SG as_if   throw[IPFV]-PRS.2SG
      pism-a   v butilka.
      letter[N]-PL in bottle
      'Creativity is **like** throwing letters in a bottle.'
      (A. Dimova. Internet; cited from Wiemer and Kampf 2011: 64)

The inverted predicate-subject order naturally follows from the specific purpose of defining a general notion. This certainly is a marginal type of complementation: the *da*-clause definitely fills out a basic syntactic slot (subject position); we can hardly say that it complements the copula, instead it is the noun resp. the NP itself (*svoboda* in 143, *tvorčestvoto* in 144) which is the predicate.

In returning to tests of subordination, there is a third environment that could be used as such a test: whether a complementation marker can attach to nominal heads. However, from all data known to me (many of them are mentioned in this article), even emergent or "young" complementizers can attach to nouns. A good case in point is, again, Sln. *naj* (see § 2.2.4.2). Thus, the availability of nominal attachment sites provides only a weak test. It is obviously weaker than the insertion test, since "candidates" of complementizers pass them in constructed examples, but real attestations are difficult to find, while their occurrence with nominal attachment sites is well-attested.

3.2 Relation of complementation to free relatives and indirect questions

Dixon (2006) relegated free (or headless) relatives to complementation strategies, because they covertly refer to places and times; see (145–146). This is basically an ontological criterion, and one could extend it to manner (see 147) or other notions able to be modified by WH-words used to emphasize clause-initial focus in embedding. The natural question to arise from this consideration is where the borderline between modification of abstract ontological entities and complementation runs.

Serbian
(145) *nije ni primetio [**kad** se stišala galama].*
'he didn't even notice [**when** the noise went off].'

(146) *Jako je teško posle toga ustanoviti [**kuda** je taj novac otišao].*
'Afterwards it is very difficult to determine [**where** that money went].'

(147) *Uvoznici tvrde da niko da ne može garantovati [**kako** će do kraja godine izgledati kursna lista].*
'Importers claim that no one can guarantee what (= **how**) the exchange rate list will look like by the end of the year.' (Politika)
(from Alanović 2018: 170, 173, 176)

In his comprehensive study, Schmidtke-Bode (2014: 34–35) excluded free relatives and embedded WH-questions from complementation proper, because both form independent nuclei, in the sense that they foreground a nominal entity (cf. Lehmann 1984), but they do not as such relate to SoAs or propositions connoted in the matrix clause. However, contrary to free relatives, embedded WH-questions occupy "slots" for argument positions of predicates that function as CTPs (cf. Rudin 1986: 52–53 on Bulgarian). They cannot appear in place of any other argument and are more selective as for their CTPs (i.e., heads) than free relatives. This is certainly the reason why embedded WH-questions are usually included in complementation, while free relatives are not, despite their conspicuous similarities. This somewhat intermediate status of embedded WH-questions suggests some gradience in the transition from complementation proper to relatives or, as Dixon would have it, between reference to SoAs or propositions and reference to lower order (though abstract) objects.

Simultaneously, headless relatives and indirect questions undoubtedly supply important diachronic roads into clausal complementation (Schmidtke-Bode 2014: 35), for the same reason they are a valuable source of variation among potential complementizers. Many cases of WH-words in embedded questions are known which developed into complementizers. This, first of all, concerns *kak(o)* 'how' in all Slouth Slavic languages (cf. Petrović 2003 for Serbian). Prominent cases in point are Bulg. *deto* and Mac. *deka*, whose first element derives from *gd(j)e* 'where' (cf. Grković-Major, this volume: § 3.5) and which are now +factual complementizers. Croat. *gdje* itself has complementizer uses with perception

CTPs, which are however regarded as archaic and bookish (Mihaljević 2009: 319); see § 2.2.5. Among factive complementizers Serb.-Cr./Mac. *što* is the best known case, it derives from the general interrogative (or *relativum generale*) 'what' (Grković-Major, this volume: § 3.2). Other good cases to illustrate the relation to free relatives are complements after perception CTPs (cf. Bužarovska 2013, Mitkovska and Bužarovska, this volume); compare (148b) with (148a). The distinction between a complement clause and an embedded question may remain ambiguous. Here, intonation disambiguates: if the WH-word takes stress we are dealing with an indirect question; compare (148c) with (148b), in which capital letters indicate stress:

Macedonian
(148) a. *GLEdam **deka** / oti uči.*
           'I see **that** s/he is studying.'
       b. *GLEdam **kako / kade** uči.*   complementizer
           'I see that (< **how / where**) s/he is studying.'
       c. *GLEdam **KAko / KAde** uči.*   WH-word
           'I am observing **HOW / WHERE** s/he is studying.'
           (from Tomić 2006: 430)

Sonnenhauser (2015: 49) shows how "switches" between complementizer and embedded question occurred with Balkan Slavic *kako* in the 19th century. In turn, Hansen, Letuchiy, and Błaszczyk (2016: 199–200, 216–218) argue that Bulgarian employs interrogative variants of pronouns, i.e., without *-to*, in complement clauses, whereas variants with *-to* are used in complementation strategies, e.g., with *kogato* (see 135a in § 3.1). This looks like morphological differentiation associating with syntactic disambiguation. One wonders whether this process occurred only recently and in which chronological relation it stands to the uses of *kak(o)*, which continues its "janus-faced" existence in complementation proper and embedded questions.

Furthermore, Balkan Slavic *da*-clauses can become ambiguous between headless relatives and relative clauses modifying some generalized first-order object which occurs as an argument of the matrix predicate. Among other things, this happens with existential predicates like Mac. *ima* 'there is' (< *imam* 'have') as in (149) (cited from Tomić 2006: 434–435):[60]

---

[60] See (Tomić 2006: 469) for Bulgarian. Mitkovska and Bužarovska (this volume: § 3.4), present similar examples from Macedonian. Cf. also Bužarovska (2002) and Bužarovska and Tomić (2009) for more comprehensive accounts of such ambiguous contexts.

Macedonian

(149) Ima   što   da   kupi-š   vo ovoj dukan.
       have[IPFV]-(PRS.3SG) what CON buy[PFV]-PRS.2SG
       'There are things you can buy in this shop.' (more literally: 'There is what to buy in this shop.')

This syntactic ambiguity is predictable, given the proclitic properties of *da*, the non-clitic character of *što* 'what, something' and the indeterminate meaning of the latter. These conditions create another favorable environment of clause-union phenomena.

3.3 Nominalizations as clausal arguments

Nominalizations (a.k.a. action nominals, nomina actionis) are another complementation strategy mentioned by Dixon (2006: 34–38). The basic problem with regarding nominalizations as clausal complements arises from the fact that, although they can function as complements of predicative nuclei ("predication manifested in argument slots", Horie and Comrie 2000: 1; see § 1), only subsets of them show coding properties typical of clausal units (for the given language), even if their actionality features and other lexical properties (e.g., argument structure, or theta-grid) appear to be identical to their verbal bases. As Lehmann (1988: § 3.1.4) puts it: "the mere insertion of a verbal noun as a constituent of a sentence does not yet make this sentence syntactically complex". Nominalizations represent an extreme case of desentencialization, in terms of external syntax they behave like NPs; therefore, the first thing to check should be whether, and to which extent, their internal syntactic characteristics retain properties of verb phrases (VPs), or even of independent clauses. Compare, for instance,

(150) a. *I see (that) Albert is kicking the dustbin.*
      b. *I see Albert kicking the dustbin.*
      c. *I see Albert's kicking of the dustbin.*
      d. *I see Albert's kick(s) of the dustbin.*

Sentences (150a) and (150b) roughly convey an equivalent meaning: Albert is treating the dustbin in an unpleasant way, and the speaker of the utterance is perceiving this. (150a) slightly differs in that its finite complement induces propositional status, while in (150b)–(150d) the event is just described as ongoing, it may therefore be argued that these complements code SoAs. Consequently, only (150a) may alternatively be employed to denote the speaker's inference about Albert's current activity without having immediate perceptual access to that activity. Regardless of this, the two-place argument structure **kick** (*Albert, dustbin*) is realized in the complements of all four sentences, and this structure *in toto* occupies a syntactic slot implied by the argument structure of *see*. This simple comparison demonstrates that semantic considerations are insufficient to claim that a complement has been embedded under a predicate as a clause. Likewise, saying that sentential nominals have the same content as sentences (Asher 1993: 149), only brings us back to the problems with notional definitions of clausal complementation pointed out in § 1.

In generative literature, nominalizations have been analyzed in accordance with the Mirror Principle (Baker 1985) assuming that "morphological derivations must directly reflect syntactic derivations (and vice versa)" (Markova 2010: 100). A similar approach is known after Borer as Parallel Morphology, which assumes V-raising from an NP-internal VP (cf. Rozwadowska 1997: 27–28; Siloni 1997: 4–5). Discussions have concerned the place at which verbal bases with nominal heads are merged at nodes above the VP, whether untensed verbal nodes dominated by determiner phrases (DPs) have to be assumed (Siloni 1997: 8), and at which step in the derivation (e.g., in relation to *v*P) verbal categories like aspect, or features like [± bounded], are specified.[61] However, apart from such "technical" details, in the generative literature on nominalizations, it is difficult to find a definition of 'clause'.

In fact, it seems that the issue of how embedded nominalized predicates relate to biclausality, and thus to clausal complementation (as defined in § 1), has hardly ever been addressed. In the literature on nominalizations one either does not find any definition of 'clause', or this notion is identified with "any syntagm containing one predication" (Lehmann 1988: § 1), "a sentence that contains one predicate" (Tallerman 2015: 77–78), or any constituent whose highest head is a verb (or a copula), whether finite or not (Testelec 2001: 256). See also the definitions given in § 1 (with 'proposition' often meaning simply 'predicate-argument structure'). In practice, discussing clauses becomes tantamount to talking about VPs, predicate-argument structures, or whatever their equivalents may be in a theory. Some scholars add that clauses 'house' or 'contain' such structures, so they are the syntactic correlates of predicate-argument structures, or of other abstract objects. However, usually, the formal properties of such "containers" for SoAs, propositions or facts remain unspecified.

---

[61] Compare, for instance, analyses proposed in Markova (2010: 99–106) for Bulgarian, in Bašić (2010) for Serbian, or the survey in Birtić (2008) for Croatian. Cf. also Tatevosov (2015: 244–325) for Russian and other languages.

Furthermore, a typology of nominalizations can be built on the ways we can refer to them in discourse. Asher (1993, 2000) and Peterson (1997: 129–172), among others, have extensively described the ways in which anaphoric expressions can refer to events, propositions and facts; these different abstract entities can be denoted by nominals. But these distinctions are, again, of a semantic (or ontological) nature, for which the notion of clause and the distinction between mono- and biclausality appear to be of no particular concern.

At least, across different theoretical convictions it appears to be acknowledged that (sets of) properties of clauses and of NPs, respectively, are gradable. Therefore, it makes sense to investigate action nominals from the point of view of which verbal properties are preserved and which nominal properties are acquired; these properties can be arranged on scales capturing properties of verbal heads.[62] The order of their acquisition or loss, respectively, correlates with layers (or categories). External layers like illocutionary force or tense are lost early, while, for instance, valency and aspect (or rather: actionality features) are lost later (cf. already Lehmann 1988: § 3.1). That is, in deverbal nominalization, layers related to discourse and syntax are affected earlier than layers which are more closely connected to lexical semantics (i.e. functions related to a root or stem). This yields two scales of nominalization which are associated with competing motivations: (i) adaptation of predicate-argument structures to the syntactic context vs (ii) reference to situations (actions, events or facts), i.e., pragmatic functions (Malchukov 2004, 2006). Correspondingly, nominalizations have been classified according to which arguments are coded, and how they are coded. These properties correlate with the degree to which action nominals acquire categories typical of NPs (e.g., articles, number, adjectival or genitive dependents); see the sentences in (150a)–(150d). This yields the following scale, reproduced from Koptjevskaja-Tamm (2015: 1199; cf. also Koptjevskaja-Tamm 1993):

| Sentential | > | Poss-Accusative | > | Ergative-Possessive | > | Nominal |

more sentence-like  more NP-like

Figure 5: Scale of sentence-like and NP-like dependent-marking in the major action noun patterns. © Koptjevskaja-Tamm, Maria. 2015. Action nouns. In Peter O. Müller, Ingeborg Ohnheiser, Susan Olsen & Franz Rainer (eds.), *Word-Formation: An International Handbook of the Languages of Europe*, vol. 2, 1195–1209. Berlin & Boston: De Gruyter Mouton (p. 1199, Fig. 67.1).

---

62 Such properties are discussed, for instance, in Abney (1987: 107–163), Grimshaw (1990: § 3), Rozwadowska (1997: 68–73).

Moreover, what seems to be commonly accepted, regardless of the adopted framework, is that there is some sort of harmony between the verbal noun in a syntactic core position and the predicate in terms of actionality features (or eventuality types). For instance, nouns derived from verbs denoting (atelic or telic) activities are good equivalents of HOW-complements (for which see § 2.2.5); compare (151a) with (151b). Concomitantly, these nouns are, as a rule, compatible with the same type of time adverbials as are the corresponding finite verb forms (see 152):

Slovene
(151) a. *Slišа-l* sem njegovo **pet-j-e**
hear-PST-(SG.M) AUX.PRS.1SG POSS.ACC.SG.M sing[IPFV]-NMLZ-ACC
(zapira-nj-e *vrat)*.
close[IPFV]-NMLZ-ACC door-(GEN.PL)
'I heard his **singing (closing of the door)**.'
b. *Slišа-l* sem da / kako poje
hear-PST-(SG.M) AUX.PRS.1SG COMP / how sing[IPFV].PRS-3SG
(zapira *vrat-a)*.
close[IPFV].PRS-(3SG) door-ACC.PL
'I heard that / how he was singing (closing the door).'
(adapted from Uhlik and Žele 2018: 229)

Serbian
(152) **Potpisiva-nj-e** dokumenat-a je dugo
sign[IPFV]-NMLZ-NOM.SG.N document-GEN.PL AUX.PRS.3SG long
traja-l-o.
last[IPFV]-PST-N
'The signing of the documents took a long time.'
compare: dugo potpisiva-o dokument-i
long sign[IPFV]-PST.SG.M document-ACC.PL
'he signed the documents for (?) a long time'
(from Bašić 2010: 42)

In turn, nouns denoting events are "harmonious" with verbs like 'happen' or 'occur'; see (153). However, events and processes can be telic or atelic, and all of them can be presented as facts (see 154 and 155c), as can states (see 139, also *John's* **honesty** *is well-known* or *They were happy about her* **pregnancy**). Thus, referring to facts hardly says anything about the actionality structure, either of nominalizations or of their verbal (or adjectival) equivalents that are able to form independent predicative nuclei. However, telicity is, in turn, compatible with (or indicated by) appropriate adverbials (*v 3 časa* 'in 3 hours' for telic events in 153, *po vreme na čestvaneto* 'during the celebration' for durativity in 154):

Bulgarian
(153) **Kraž-b-a-ta** stana v 3 čas-a.
 steal-NMLZ-SG.F-DEF.SG.F take_place.AOR-(3SG) in hour-COUNT
 'The **theft** took place at three o'clock.'
 (from Markova 2010: 101)

(154) **Kosit-b-a-ta** be-še včera
 mow-NMLZ-SG.F-DEF.SG.F be-IMPF.3SG yesterday
 (po vreme na čestvaneto na denja na blagodarnostta).
 'The **mowing** took place yesterday (during the thanksgiving celebration).'

Similarly, since Slavic action nouns do not bear tense features, their form alone does not allow to distinguish between propositions and SoAs (see some related discussion for Slovene in Uhlik and Žele 2018b: 229), let alone between propositions and facts. Neither of these distinctions manifests itself in any formal contrast, instead they hinge solely on the lexical semantics of the predicate of which the action noun codes an argument, and on how they can be referred to anaphorically.

Bulgarian
(155) a. *Vižda-m* **kăpa-n-e-to** *na deca-ta.*
  see.PRS-1SG bath[IPFV]-NMLZ-SG.N-DEF.SG.N on children-DEF.PL
  'I see the **bathing** of the children' (i.e. how the children are bathing). SoA
 b. **Razpada-n-e-to** *na sistem-a-ta*
  fall_apart[IPFV]-NMLZ-SG.N-DEF.SG.N on system-SG.F.DEF.SG.F
  e neizbežno / malko verojatno.
  'The **breakdown** of the system is inevitable / unlikely.' proposition
 c. **Zamărzva-n-e-to** *na rek-a-ta*
  freeze[IPFV]-NMLZ-SG.N-DEF.SG.N on river-SG.F-DEF.SG.F
  učudi *Stojan.*
  surprise[PFV]-(AOR.3SG) PN
  'The **freezing** of the river surprised Stojan.' fact
  (from Korytkowska and Małdżiewa 2002: 30, 11, and I. Krapova, p.c.)

Croatian
(156) a. *Jerk-o   čuj-e   Jurič-in-o*
PN-NOM hear[IPFV]-(PRS.3SG) PN-ADJV-ACC.SG.N
svira-nj-e   *klavir-a.*
play[IPFV]-NMLZ[N]-ACC.SG   piano-GEN
'Jerko hears Jurica's **playing** of the piano.'   SoA (time-located)

b. *Jurk-o   uči   Juric-u   **svira-nj-e***
PN-NOM teach[IPFV]-(PRS.3SG) PN-ACC play[IPFV]-NMLZ[N]-ACC.SG
klavir-a.
piano-GEN
'Jurko teaches Jurica the **playing** of the piano.'   SoA (not time-located)
(from Mihaljević 2009: 349–350)

c. *T-o   **hvata-nj-e**   je*
DEM-NOM.SG.N catch[IPFV]-NMLZ[N]-NOM.SG AUX.PRS.3SG
bi-l-o   nerazumn-o.
be-PST-SG.N   unreasonable-NOM.SG.N
'That **capture** was unreasonable.'   fact
(from Birtić 2008: 156)

Slovene
(157) *Sliša-l   sem   za   **izvolitev**   Trump-a.*
hear-PST-(SG.M) AUX.PRS.1SG about election[M]-(ACC.SG) PN-GEN
'I've heard about Trump's **election**.' (= 'about Trump being elected') fact
(M. Uhlik, p.c.)

Notice that all verbal nouns in (151–156) are derived from ipfv. stems, irrespective of the actionality of the eventuality and of its status as SoA, proposition or fact. The relation of aspect to verbal nouns leaves many open questions, but preliminarily we can say that it is not mainly aspect which drives the choice of stem in verbal nouns, but the inherent actionality features of the verb stem (Wiemer 2019b: 107–110 with further references).

After all, we are left with the issue whether South Slavic languages show any patterns in accordance with which the morphological make-up of action nominals correlates with their verbal behavior. We may furthermore ask whether such patterns become (and stay) productive, i.e., what are the restrictions under which they can be be applied to verbal stems (or roots).

Languages may tend to develop morphological distinctions between verbal nouns denoting processes and verbal nouns denoting events or propositions (including facts). Thus, in Bulgarian the former are marked with the suffix {ne}, they are derived productively from ipfv. stems,[63] whereas the latter are marked with {nie} and derive from the aorist or from the base of the passive participle (depending on the analysis) of either aspect (see 159a vs 159b); they often undergo metonymic shifts, usually toward the result (in accordance with their participial bases), which deprives them of verbal properties and brings them closer to nouns denoting first-order objects. Compare, for instance, Bulg. *săbira-ne*.IPFV 'collecting', *pada-ne*.IPFV *na kamăk* 'fall of a stone' vs *săbra-nie*.PFV 'meeting, assembly', *pade-nie*.PFV *na čovek* 'a man's (moral) decline' (Georgieva 1976; Popov 1985: 100, 103–106; Markova 2010: 95–96). These changes on an ontological level correlate with their more NP- vs more clause-like behavior in the syntax (see below).

These observations still leave us with our basic question: under which conditions can nominalizations be regarded as nuclei of separate clauses and, consequently, as clausal complements? As a possible symptom I would suggest the following: if a verbal noun realizes the verb's argument structure syntactically, but does not use the reflexive pronoun to mark coreference between argument NPs, or between an argument NP and a modifier within another argument NP, this indicates a clause boundary (otherwise: a c-domain) that cannot be "jumped over" by an anaphoric expression. For instance, (158a) contains a nominalized paraphrase of the complement clause in (158), but instead of the reflexive *si* it is the third-person pronoun *i* 'her' which marks coreference with the first argument (*Ala*) of the nominalization (*doverieto*); the reflexive would be ungrammatical (see 158b). This evidence might be regarded as indicative that in (158a) we are dealing with a biclausal structure, at least it behaves like such a structure.

Bulgarian
(158) *Zna-m,   če   Ala$_i$ se   doverjava*
      know-PRS.1SG   COMP   PN   REFL   trust[IPFV].PRS-(3SG)
      na koležka-ta$_k$ si$_i$.
      on colleague-DEF.SG.F   REFL.DAT
      'I know that Ala$_i$ trusts her$_i$ colleague$_k$.'

(158) a. *Zna-m   za   doverie-to   na Ala$_i$ kăm*
         know-PRS.1SG   about   trust[N]-DEF.SG.N   on PN   toward
         koležka-ta$_k$ i$_i$
         colleague-DEF.SG.F   3SG.F.DAT

---

[63] Stojanov (1976 [1966]) discusses the restricted range of pfv. bases of Bulgarian action nouns.

b. *Zna-m   za   doverie-to   na Ala$_i$ kăm
    know-PRS.1SG about   trust[N]-DEF.SG.N   on PN   toward
    koležka-ta   si$_j$.
    colleague-DEF.SG.F   REFL.DAT
    'I know about Ala$_i$'s trust in her$_j$ colleague$_k$.'
    (adapted from Korytkowska and Małdżiewa 2002: 30)

Another symptom of biclausality might be that true action nominals are barred from predicative use (cf. Bašić 2010: 43 on Serbian). In fact, it is hardly conceivable how a nominalized predicate-argument structure might predicate by itself. A more general answer to our question obviously depends on the place a nominalization occupies on the scale in Figure 5. Two points can be made, both of them comply with Dixon's (2006: 15) second requirement that complement clauses have the internal structure of a clause (see § 1); first of all, this means that a unit in question becomes the more a clause, the closer it approaches the argument coding pattern in declarative main clauses (see § 2.3.1 on deranking). The points will again be illustrated by drawing on Bulgarian.

First, the clausal properties of an action noun decrease with typical markers of NPs, such as articles (or other determiners). Thus, according to Markova (2010: 95), (159a) is more like a converb in that its internal argument is marked like an ordinary object after a verb.[64] This possibility is precluded if the verbal noun is combined with an article (159b), in which case the object of the verbal noun must be marked like an NP-internal modifier (with *na*), comparable to Engl. *of* or a genitival modifier in other Slavic languages:

Bulgarian
(159) a. [[[očak]-va]-n]-e   (*na) velik-a-ta   promjan-a
          wait-SFX-NMLZ-SG.N   of great-SG.F-DEF.SG.F   change[F]-SG
          'awaiting the great change'
      b. [[[očak]-va]-n]-e]-to   *(na) velik-a-ta   promjana
          wait-SFX-NMLZ-SG.N-DEF.SG.N of great-SG.F-DEF.SG.F change[F]-SG
          'the waiting for the great change'
          (glossing and brackets for scope adapted)

---

[64] Compare with (150b). Examples like (159a) are remarkable also because the most typical Slavic converbs ('adverbial participles') have practically been ousted from complementation (see § 2.3.2).

Second, there is a well-known distinction between eventive and non-eventive nouns (a.k.a. 'process vs result' or 'imperfect vs perfect nominals'); only the former allow, or even require, arguments to be coded syntactically, and they can be further divided into argument-structure and participant-structure nominals. This tripartite split is known from Grimshaw (1990) and shown in Table 5.[65] Its structure from top to bottom corresponds to Figure 5 read from left to right, i.e., the most clause-like nouns are argument-structure nominals (Markova 2010: 107–111). Only eventive nouns can be considered candidates of clausal complementation.

Table 5: Main classes of verbal nouns (Bulgarian examples).

		Grimshaw's (1990) term
argument-structure nominals (eventive)	internal arguments are coded obligatorily; external argument is coded optionally, but if coded, it denotes the agent/causer	Complex Event nominals
(160) [iz-p(e)]-java-n-e-to *(na pesen-ta) (ot Maria) [[PFX-sing]-SFX]-NMLZ-SG-DEF.SG.N of song[F]-DEF.SG.F from PN 'the singing *of* the *entire* song *on behalf of / by* Mary'		
participant-structure nominals (eventive)	internal arguments are coded optionally; if external argument is coded it can have different interpretations: agent/causer, source, possessor	Simple Event nominals
(161) [pro-d]-a-žb-a-ta (na stok-i) (ot Ivan) sell-ATHV-SFX-SG-DEF.SG.F of good-PL by / from PN 'the sale of goods *by / from* Ivan'		
(162) săbr-a-n-ie-to (na deputat-i-te) meet-ATHV-NMLZ-SG-DEF.SG.N of deputy-PL-DEF.PL 'the meeting *of* the deputies'		
result nominals (non-eventive)	no internal arguments	Result nominals
(163) [po-stroj]-k-a-ta (*na nov-a-ta sgrada) ot Ivan PFX-construct-NMLZ-SG.F-DEF.SG.F of new-SG.F-DEF.SG.F building[F]-SG by PN *'the construction *of* the new building *by* Ivan'		

---

[65] Just like the scale in Figure 5, this division should probably be treated as a gradient, at least Grimshaw's criteria do not always lead to clear-cut distinctions. Moreover, many simple-event nominals are not derived from verbal roots (or stems), e.g., *journey, joy, concert* (Koptjevskaja-Tamm 2015: 1197). Cf. Letuchiy (this volume) for more discussion.

Prefixation of verbal bases favors argument-structure nominals, and this correlates semantically with the fact that often prefixes introduce an additional causative argument (see 160). Remarkable is the fact that agent/causer (or causation) is more optional than internal arguments, or otherwise: there is an implicational hierarchy 'internal argument(s) > external argument', saying that the presence of an external argument implies the coding of internal arguments, but not vice versa (for some discussion concerning Croatian cf. Birtić 2008: 146).

3.4 Zero complementizers?

The notion of zero (or null) complementizer (or of zero-marked complementation) implies that something is omitted which normally is to be expected. Such an assumption may be premature. Optionality of complementation markers seems to be a more appropriate notion; it belongs to the same gradient as does obligatoriness, but is probably empirically more adequate and not theoretical, *a priori* commitment concerning an "omission" (or conversely an "insertion") of such a marker need be made (Kehayov and Boye 2016b: 850).

At a certain point, however, optionality causes that parenthetical use may become indiscriminable from CTPs with clausal complements. For instance, do the following utterances illustrate complementation with a zero complementizer, or is the first clause a parenthetical comment on the second, bracketed one?

Bulgarian
(164) *Včera si mislex [Ivan utre da me zavede na kino].*
       'I was thinking yesterday [Ivan could take me to the cinema tomorrow].'
       (from Krapova 2001: 115)

Slovene
(165) *Slišal je, [trgovci spretno nagovarjajo mimoidoče].*
       'He heard [dealers skillfully address passersby].'
       (from Uhlik and Žele 2018: 223)

The bracketed parts can be independent utterances, and from a communicative point of view, the first part can be backgrounded and then function as a parenthetical. Since this asymmetry works in both ways, i.e., either of the two clauses can be back- or foregrounded (see § 1), only an explicit complementizer can make clear whether there also holds a syntactic asymmetry, i.e., embedding. As the examples show, these considerations particularly apply to verbs for which clausal arguments appear to be strongly required.

There is a lack of research into the optionality of complementation markers in South Slavic, but we can confidently infer one observation. After all we said about different types of *da*-clauses in § 2.2.3 (and elsewhere), it is evident that, if *da* is considered a mood marker ('particle'), such clauses lack a complementizer. This applies to Balkan Slavic *da* in all its occurrences, and this is what researchers agree on. As for the western part of South Slavic the matter is more complicated: in all cases when *da* occurs as an alternative to the infinitive in complex predicates (i.e., after verbs occupying the highest ranks on the SIH) we may say that *da* is not a complementizer (in the sense defined in § 2.2); see ex. (26, 47) in § 2.2.3. It is however not a mood marker either, since the modality of the clause (if any) is induced by the other part of the predicate complex (auxiliar or phasal verb). Similarly, in biclausal sentences the TAM-restrictions for the *da*-clause follow from the semantics of the CTP (whether it induces low assertiveness or not), and *da* is simply a complementizer (see § 2.2.3.2).

As for combinations with *bi* (*da* + *bi*), it seems to be undisputed that *bi* marks the conditional (together with the *l*-form), so that *da* is a complementizer, again, which just combines with this mood marker and serves as its prosodical host, but has not fused with it to a new unit (see, for instance, ex. 168). This contrasts sharply with *da*'s closest equivalents in North Slavic; compare Russ. *čto|by*, Pol. *a|by*, Czech *že|by*, etc., all deriving from a clause-initial particle or pronoun and the first, enclitic part of a disjunctive subjunctive (or conditional) marker. Therefore, the distinction of complementizer vs mood marker does not entirely coincide with the distinction between da_1 and da_2 employed for Serbian-Croatian.

3.5 Double complementizers?

This issue is the converse of the issue just discussed.[66] Trivially, both perspectives depend on what we consider a complementizer. If we define complementizer combinations as the "co-occurrence in the complement structure of two or more elements, which can identify complements on their own" (Kehayov and Boye 2016b: 854), which includes complementation markers, then combinations such as (166)–(168) could be considered double complementizers:

---

66 The cases considered here differ from 'doubly filled Comp-positions', which have been discussed in recent versions of generativism. They can be illustrated with cases from Southern German dialects in which a dedicated complementizer is preceded by a WH-phrase (e.g., Alemannic *I woass it <u>wieviel</u> **dass** er für des Auto zahlt hät* lit. 'I don't know <u>how much</u> **that** he has paid for the car'); cf., for instance, Bayer (2015).

Bulgarian

(166) *Žen-a-ta sedna taka,*
(=43) woman[F]-SG-DEF.SG.F sit_down[PFV].AOR-(3SG) such-NOM.SG.F
če da me vižda.
COMP IRR 1SG.ACC see.PRS.3SG
'The woman sat in such a way **that** she could see me.'

Macedonian

(167) *Uča-m* **kako** *da pišuva-m so penkalo.*
(=46) learn[IPFV].PRS-1SG how CON write[IPFV].PRS-1SG with pen
'I'm learning **how** to write with a fountain pen.'

Slovene

(168) *Govori se,* **da naj** *bi se letos udeleži-l-i*
say[IPFV].PRS-(3SG) REFL COND REFL this_year attend[PFV]-PST-PL
conference.
conference
'Rumour has it **that** they're planning to attend to the conference.' (http://opus.nlpl.eu/)
(from Sonnenhauser, this volume: § 2.4)

Other cases in point might be a similative connective preceding a complementation marker, like Serb.-Cr. *kao da* vs *kao što* (see 92a and 92b in § 2.2.5), Sln. *kot da* or Bulg. *kato da* (see § 2.2.5, § 3.1).

If, however, we restrict ourselves only to elements which are considered core members of the complementizer category, cases such as these would not count as illustrations of double complementizers.

The problem, thus, boils down to the treatment of elements which occur after a dedicated (canonical) complementizer and which fulfil the following conditions:
(i) the unit can appear clause-initially,
(ii) it indicates some illocutionary function and/or weakens assertiveness, and
(iii) properties (i–ii) also apply in main clauses (independent utterances).

Balkan Slavic *da* fufils all these conditions, however it behaves as a clitic. A further condition may therefore be that the element in question must not be a clitic. But even then, such an element in combination with a canonical complementizer may be interpreted as a complementizer or as a 'particle' participating in the marking of 'analytic mood'. The probably most well-known example from South Slavic is Sln. *da naj* (Topolińska 2003, Sonnenhauser, this volume); see

(168). Usually, researchers treat these combinations as complementizer + 'modal/ illocutionary particle', but when *naj* (or *neka* in the other South Slavic languages) occurs clause-initially and by itself, analyses diverge. Uhlik (2018: 412) argues that *naj* can be considered a complementizer when it is not moved away from the clause-initial position. He admits that *da* is an exception, so that we get the combination *da naj*, "which is semantically identical with *naj* because *da* is semantically empty and can therefore be omitted"[67] (cf. also Uhlik & Žele 2018a: 106, f. 42). The opposite view is advocated by Topolińska (2003), who treats *naj* only as a particle, even if it is not preceded by *da*; in such cases it "accomodates" to the matrix clause predicate, which makes it a mood marker (2003: 314) and we eventually have to draw the same conclusion as for complementation without a complementizer as we did for Balkan Slavic *da* in § 3.4. Sonnenhauser (this volume), who gives a more comprehensive overview concerning the different treatments of *naj*, argues that *naj* can be both at once, clause-initial particle and complementizer: if it occurs in the scope of *da*, it just carries the illocutionary functions discussed in § 2.2.4.2; if it occurs alone it, as it were, "inherits" the complementizer function of *da*. This change in status obviously is achieved by frequent co-occurrence with *da*, but this is another issue requiring usage-based research.

This summary demonstrates how much assumptions about double complementizers depend on one's theoretical preconceptions, and that these assumptions mirror one's stance toward zero complementizers. A key for either perspective is the way in which one captures the relation between complementizers and (non-indicative) mood.

In particular cases, considerations about double complementizers may also hinge on scope relations with propositional markers that originate from adverbs or quantifiers. For instance, Hansen, Letuchiy, and Błaszczyk (2016: 198–199) draw attention to Bulg. *vse edno* 'all the same' (a "modal comparative marker"), which can be combined with the default complementizer *če*:

(169) Šte   mi   ob'jasnjava   **vse edno**   če
      FUT   1SG.DAT   explain[IPFV].PRS-3SG   all_the_same   COMP
      provincijata izxranvala Sofija.
      'He will explain me **that** [lit. *as if that*] the province is feeding Sofija.'

Here, the authors suggest, *vse edno* functions as a complementizer. However, in an alternative analysis this is simply a combination of the standard comple-

---

[67] "ki je pomensko enak z *naj*, ker je *da* pomensko izpraznjen in zato izpustljiv."

mentizer with a propositional modifier which scopes over the entire sentence. The fact that *vse edno* precedes *če* supports this analysis; if *vse edno* were an ordinary propositional modifier of a clause headed by *če*, we would expect it inside that clause, i.e., following on *če*. This brings us to the last point to be made.

3.6 Between complementation and propositional modification

In § 2.2.3.2 we came across combinations of *da* with a preceding morpheme marking some kind of irrealis in Macedonian. For convenience, I repeat one of the examples here:

Macedonian
(170)   *Mora **da** zarabotija mnogu pari.*
(=33)   'They must / probably have earned a lot of money.'

Here, the aorist is striking, as it is otherwise excluded after *da*. A plausible explanation for this is that we are no longer dealing with a *da*-clause, but *mora* and *da* tend to jointly constitute a propositional modifier (comparable to sentence adverbs or particles with epistemic and/or evidential functions). The analysis would thus look not like (171a), but like (171b); it implies that a biclausal sentence has become monoclausal:

(171)   a.   *Mora [**da** [zarabotija mnogu pari]].*   '[must be] [[that [P]]]'
        b.   >   *Mora **da** [zarabotija mnogu pari].*   'probably / evidently [P]'

It is doubtful that *mora + da* has really reached a stage of one complex unit (comparable to *kako da* or *da ne*, see §§ 2.2.5–6), but the modal *mora* 'must' can only combine with *da*, and if *da* stood alone 'confirmative tenses' would be inhibited. Thus, *mora* and *da* are mutually dependent, although they cannot really be considered to create a new lexical unit jointly modifying a proposition, yet (Wiemer 2014a: 150–161). Nonetheless, the process by which new propositional markers emerge appears to be more advanced in Macedonian than in Bulgarian, where, under identical conditions, aorist and imperfect are excluded even if evidential meanings (inferential or reportive) are intended, and only the present or the perfect are possible (I. Krapova, p.c.).

Importantly, the reanalysis of dependency relations, and the change from biclausal to monoclausal constituency, occurs only if the irrealis marker (in particular a modal auxiliary like *mora*) is used epistemically. It has scope over the entire proposition (and not over an SoA or, in syntactic terms, over a *v*P) only in these cases, so that we might think of it as a CTP (see 171a). Furthermore, the rise of propositional markers from predicate complexes with modal auxiliaries or other units with inflectional properties of verbs implies the loss of tense and agreement (i.e., person-number) marking.[68] Although the details of diachronic change remain to be discovered, the case of modal auxiliaries developing toward propositional markers (together with *da*) can be assumed to start from predicate complexes in the domain of non-epistemic modality, i.e. from monoclausal structures (not from clausal complementation), to epistemic uses of the modal. Consequently, the modal gains wide scope and can "detach" from the lexical verb in the complex, which results in a seemingly biclausal structure (if the epistemic modal can still be treated as a CTP), and ends up in a monoclausal structure with the lexical verb as the predicate and the former modal as a modifier of this structure (see [5]). *Da* remains as an irrealis-marker, but since functionally it is associated to the preceding modal more closely than to the following verb, the usual tense-aspect constraints do not apply any longer.

	Stage 1:		Stage 2:		Stage 3:
[5]	non-epistemic modal complex		epistemic modal		epistemic modifier
	modal scopes over SoA (*v*P)	⇒	modal scopes over proposition	⇒	scopes over proposition
	monoclausal		biclausal		monoclausal
	Examples: Macedonian				
	Deca-ta		*Mora da*		see (171)
	children-DEF		must CON		
	mora / mora-at		*došo-l.*		
	must / must-PRS.3PL		come[PFV]-LPT-(SG.M)		
	da dojd-at				
	CON come[PFV].PRS-3PL				
	tamu.				
	there				
	'The children must come there.'		'He must have come.'		

---

68 Cf. Hansen (2010, 2017) and Wiemer (2014a) on Balkan Slavic (and beyond). In the case of Serb. *mora (da)* and *biće (da)* (< *biti će* 'be.INF FUT.3SG') *da* seems to be optional (Kovačević 2008, 2009).

Mac. *kako da* as a complex 'as if'-connective (see § 2.2.5) must have evolved out of a similar competition, with loss of tense-aspect restrictions, but it developed out of a different source function, namely similarity and/or perception (Bužarovska 2006). Moreover, contrary to propositional modifiers originating from modals, *kako da* can be used as a complementizer and it thereby participates in biclausal structures. Plausibly, this development manifests a step that occurs after *kako da* has reached stage 3 in [5] (although on another path): at this stage *kako da* is just a propositional modifier ('particle'); if it occurs clause-initially and after a suitable predicate it can be interpreted as a complementizer of the latter's clausal argument. We thus have two paths of development after propositional scope has been acquired: one path leads into biclausality via syntactic tightening (e.g. *kako da*) as a clausal complement; the necessary condition is that the unit in question occurs right after a suitable predicate. The other path, on the contrary, pulls a unit (e.g. *mora (da)*) out of complementation and makes it a modifier of a single core; see [6].

[6] loss of syntactic tightness | syntactic tightening
> monoclausal propositional modification | > complement sentence

mora (da) | *kako da*
CTP | COMP
↓ | ↓
modifier [P]$_{Core}$ | Core1 − [COMP [P]]$_{Core2}$

Furthermore, as we saw in § 2.2.5, the Macedonian SEEM-verbs *izgleda* and *se čini* are suitable as CTPs for *kako da*. But they themselves can be used like particles which downtone epistemic support (see 172a). What is more, particles originating from either side of [6] may be combined. See (172c), where *se čini* does not show agreement with the (elliptic) subject of *poletaat*. Consequently, sentences like (172b) are syntactically ambiguous: either *izgleda* is an impersonal CTP and *kako da* a complementizer (or just a clause-initial particle, if zero complementizer is an issue; see § 3.4), or both are two particles combined with each other. Ambiguity does not arise with *izgleda deka*, since *deka* can only be interpreted as a complementizer (following after *izgleda*):

Macedonian
(172) a.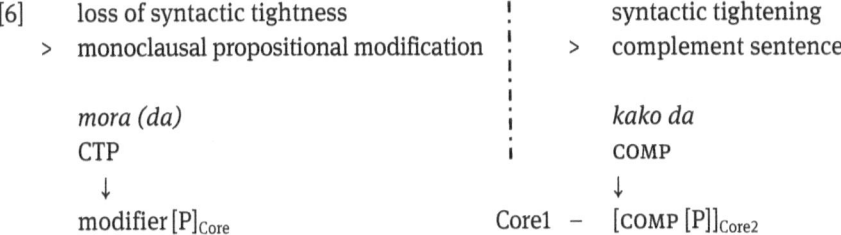
　　　　Izgleda
　　　　look.PRS.3SG(?)　　　ḱe　　poleta-at　　/ leta-at.
　　　　Kako da　　　　　　　FUT　fly[PFV].PRS-3PL　fly[IPFV].PRS-3PL
　　　　as if
　　　　'It seems they are about to fly / they are flying.'

b. *Izgleda   kako da / deka   ḱe   poleta-at.*
   look.PRS-(3SG)(?)   as if   COMP FUT   fly[PFV].PRS-3PL
   'It seems (as if ?) / that they are about to fly.'

c. *T-ie   se čini   kako da   ḱe   poleta-at.*
   3-PL   seem-(PRS.3SG)   as if   FUT   fly[PFV].PRS-3PL
   'They, it seems, fly. / Apparently, they are about to fly.'

That is, both units, left and right to the boundary between CTP and complement clause in [6] can behave like propositional modifiers. These observations also signify that (164c) does not represent subject-to-subject raising, but simply "fronting" of the clausal subject (L. Mitkovska, p.c.). Correspondingly, (172a) and (172c) can easily be treated as monoclausal, while the potential ambiguity of (172b) yields mono- vs biclausal readings.

In Bulgarian, with fronted topics, particles derived from petrified forms of SEEM-verbs can even move directly before a complementizer, as in (173):

Bulgarian
(173) *Ivan   i   Petăr   **izgležda**   **če**   sa*
       PN   and   PN   seem[IPFV].PRS-(3SG)(?)   COMP(?)   be.PRS.3PL
       pijan-i.
       drunk-PL
       'Ivan and Petăr seem to be drunk.', lit. 'Ivan and Petăr [it seems] that (they) are drunk.'

In this strange constellation, the coordinated subject agrees with the predicate in the complement (after *če*), but simultaneously *izgležda* 'seems' is the only possible CTP the complementizer *če* can attach to. If one does not want to claim that *izgležda* and *če* have merged into one complex unit (as Mac. *mora da* almost seems to have), the only reasonable assumption remains that *Ivan i Petăr* is a left-dislocated phrase at the "margin" of a sentence with an impersonal SEEM-verb and its clausal complement.

4 Conclusions and outlook

As emphasized in § 1, this survey of clausal complementation in South Slavic did not only pursue a descriptive purpose, but aimed at the creation of a grid of criteria suitable to the study of inner- and cross-linguistic variation in clausal complementation and its sources as well as the rise of clausal modifiers out of complementation markers of CTPs and, in this connection, the relation of clausal complementation to discourse prominence. The "ingredients" of clausal complementation had to be shown in a comprehensive, though not exhaustive, way. There are a wealth of phenomena which we only touched upon, as if encountering only the top of an iceberg: for instance, the emergence of complementizers and their syn- and paradigmatic distribution with older, inherited structures, first of all the *bi*-conditional. Variation would have increased considerably, if the survey had not been restricted to standard varieties and the contemporary situation (with only occasional comments on the rather recent diachronic background), and if it had accounted also for non-Slavic Balkan languages. However, this survey has fulfilled its function, if it supplies the basis for an application of the grid to diatopic, diastratic and diaphasic variation and to diachronic changes within South Slavic languages, against a general Slavic background, the areal background (as for the Balkans and the Mediterranean Sea) and a typological profile of the contemporary stage of South Slavic.

Let me thus conclude by first summarizing some of the benefits which the study of clausal complementation in South Slavic offers to a better understanding of issues relevant for general typology (§ 4.1), by subsuming the probably most salient features of South Slavic on a typological background (§ 4.2). Afterwards, I give a summary of the internal South Slavic differentiation of clausal complementation (§ 4.3). I will finish by pointing out some general desiderata (§ 4.4).

4.1 South Slavic as a polygon for general typological issues

On all of the levels mentioned before, the variation in South Slavic provides an especially rich test field for the study of emergent complementation structures. Since the role of morphologically non-finite structures has steadily decreased since the Middle Ages, and in Balkan Slavic almost no non-finite predicates are left, this richness, first and foremost, concerns complementation markers. Their separation from unbound markers of non-indicative mood ('analytical subjunctive' or else) proves to be particularly hard, because both categories inherently scope over clauses. The various systems of clitic rules and clusters, which we find, first of all, in Balkan Slavic, do not supply reliable indicators of semantic scope, and their significance as markers of dependent clauses comes close to zero. Van Lier (2009: 69, and passim) captured distributional properties of such markers in structural terms, according to which 'dependent clause markers' code "at the level of the D[ependent] C[lause] as a whole" or only "at the level of its nucleus". Complementizers belong to the former category, non-finite verb forms rather to the latter. Yet, what about clitics (Balkan Slavic *da*) or connectives that may, but need not, occur clause-initially (like Sln. *naj*)? The problem is aggravated by the fact that neither unbound or clitic mood markers nor units able to function as (clause-initial) complementizers are usually restricted to dependent clauses: syntactically independent *da*-clauses are commonplace, and many complementizers are heterosemic,[69] since they additionally occur as particles or other types of clause modifiers (usually related to the propositional content), e.g., Sln. *naj*, Mac. *da ne* and *kako da*. This situation raises the desire to provide better definitions of moods and complementizers. However well-defined these notions may be, we have to be aware that they take part in the same linguistic dimension: mood markers and complementizers form continua (or fuzzy categories) which, in structural terms, hit each other from opposite directions, provided the typical mood marker is regarded as a bound morpheme on the verb (of predicate complex), while complementizers typically are independent words occurring at the (left or right) boundary of clauses (see § 2.2). Notably, none of these properties is as such a reliable indicator of subordination, let alone of complementation (see § 2.2.3).

In this connection, another principled point is whether one allows for double complementizers. Any argumentation for (or against) such a notion is vulnerable, because any combination of clause-initial connectives can in principle be treated as (i) a combination of complementizer plus 'particle', (ii) a double complementizer, or simply (iii) a combination of two clause-initial connectives ('particles'). The case may be clear, in favor of (i) or (iii), for clause-initial *da* hosting the enclitic *bi* in western South Slavic, however much less so for Sln. *da naj* (see § 2.2.4.2 and Sonnenhauser, this volume). Sometimes two clause-initial morphemes start coalescing, but in South Slavic this has occurred only to a very limited extent (e.g., with Mac. *da ne*, Bulg. *da ne bi*; see § 2.2.6), contrary to what we observe in North Slavic (compare many complementizers with the fused irrealis-marker *-by* which cannot any longer be analyzed as a separate morpheme). Thus, distinguishing degrees of morphological fusion may be helpful in counting units as clause-initial connectives. However, a better indicator of the emergent rise of a new clausal connective out of two morphemes may be the loss of TAM-constraints which otherwise apply to clauses containing these morphemes. A good case to illustrate this is Mac. *kako da*: as a complementizer these two segments may be split, but nonetheless *da* no longer requires the verb to take forms of the present or the perfect (see § 2.2.5). If such phenomena were examined

---

[69] For this notion cf. Lichtenberk (1991). A related notion is 'transcategorization' (cf. Ježek and Ramat 2009).

more systematically on a crosslinguistic basis, the following tentative implicational relation could be tested:

[7] Hypothesis:
Changes in distributional (= behavioral) properties of complex clause-connectives precede their morphological fusion (= coding properties).

This relation is, of course, formulated in analogy to hierarchies of subject properties known since Keenan (1976). Similarly, the rise of propositional modifiers out of combinations with *da* (compare Mac. *mora da*) may be indicative of morphological coalescence as well, and in some cases – compare, again, Mac. *kako da* – the chronological relation between becoming a propositional modifier and being (re)interpreted as a complementizer is anything but clear (see § 3.6). On the other hand, TAM-constraints with clause-initial connectives may be loosened or lost altogether, as the use of *da* in western South Slavic shows, and this behavioral change has not brought about any morphological changes.

Another issue concerns the relation between the placement of complementation markers in linear sequences. As we saw in § 2.2, it can be problematic to define complementizers as elements that mark clause boundaries. Balkan Slavic seems to be a particularly favorable testing field to demonstrate how information structure may "overwrite" such boundaries, so that even canonical complementizers do not occur where they are otherwise "expected" (see § 2.2.3.3, § 3.6). We still need to know more about the mechanisms which trigger the pre- or postposition of topicalized, or focalized, NPs (or PPs) to a default complementizer, i.e., in cases there is a choice in linearization. Marked topics and foci favor preposition, and we may distinguish canonical complementizers like Bulg. *če* from "dubious" units like Balkan Slavic *da*, since the former (but not the latter) provide a choice of placement. But this choice causes variation which probably needs to be understood in interaction with preferences for the suprasegmental organization of the utterance.

4.2 Profile of South Slavic clausal complementation as a whole

First and foremost, the loss of non-finite complements belongs to this profile, practically entirely in the Balkans, but non-finite complements probably have been a minor option also in the western part since the Middle Ages (see § 2.3.2). In contrast to this, we observe a tendency toward developing a [± factual] distinction marked by complementizer choice, in particular with propositional complements, i.e., complements showing weak semantic integration (according to the SIH). This corresponds to similar tendencies in North Slavic and might be considered a more general feature of Europe's eastern half (Wiemer 2018). In South Slavic, inherited contrasts marked by an opposition, primarily, between infinitival and finite complements (introduced by *ěko, jako* 'that') have been replaced (or renewed) by contrasts between clause-initial connectives in Balkan Slavic (*da* vs Bulg. *če* / Mac. *deka*), whereas this contrast has partially remained in the distinctions between *da*-clauses with and without TAM-restrictions (hence Ivić's *nemobilan* vs *mobilan prezent*). Moreover, only Slovene shows a tendency toward contrasting *da* (as default complementizer) with *naj*, which is semantically much more specific than inherited *da* and betrays other properties characteristic of an only emergent complementizer.

This has already brought us to the internal differentiation of South Slavic.

4.3 Areality: main features of inner-South Slavic continua

The largest amount of internal differentiation is conditioned by changes in the relations between old and new complementation markers. These changes have led to splits between the (north)western and the (south)eastern (= Balkan Slavic) part, the most obvious and well-known case being the retention of irrealis-functions of *da*-clauses in Balkan Slavic, while in western South Slavic this unit has lost these functions. Simultaneously, *da* has been encroaching on the domain of specialized factive complementizers in Serbian-Croatian (*što, jer*), which developed from causal connectives, probably in separate waves (Grković-Major, this volume). The competition between factive and default (+factual) complementizers yields less clear-cut areal divisions (see § 2.2.2.1).

Consequently, in the western part of South Slavic, *da* has become the default device of attaching a finite clause to a verbal or nominal head (Topolińska 2003: an "all powerful connective", regarding Slovene). This is why Sonnenhauser (this volume: § 2.4) regards Sln. *da* as a marker of declarative force par excellence. However, this function is now largely restricted to complement clauses, both in Slovene and Serbian-Croatian. In main clauses (with independent illocutionary force) *da* has practically retained irrealis-functions: in Slovene *da*'s use in main clauses is anyway obsolete and rare, while in Serbian-Croatian it still appears to be more widely used with the same irrealis functions as it is in main clauses in Balkan Slavic (directive, optative, mirative, etc.). We may thus say that western South Slavic *da* acquired its status as standard complementizer concomitantly to the loss of irrealis functions and to the shrinking use as a syntactically independent particle.

Bulg. *če* has become the standard complementizer, but it still has usages as causal connective as well. Slovene apparently does not have this kind of specialized complementizers, and Serbian-Croatian shares an isogloss with Macedonian in using factive *što*, whereas Bulgarian employs the more recent unit *deto* (< **kъde-to* 'where + PTC'), which is also used as a relativizer. Instead, in Slovene a non-factual complementizer has been developing which is sensitive to the presence/absence of speaker and addressee in the current speech act: Sln. *naj* is excluded if both speech act participants are mentioned in the reporting complement sentence; with respect to this feature, *naj* creates a paradigmatic opposition with the standard complementizer *da* (see § 2.2.4.2). Geographically, we thus arrive at a polar distribution of [±factual] complementation: *da* (+factual) vs *naj* (−factual) in Slovene and *da* (−non-factual) vs Mac. *deka* / Bulg. *če* (+factual) in Balkan Slavic. Complementizer contrasts in the Štokavian area (Serbian-Croatian) are less clear-cut, and this area constitutes a transitional zone between Balkan Slavic and the northwestern edge with respect to the use of infinitival complements.

The split based on the status and use of *da* is clearly connected to the degree of its morphologization, which is advanced in Balkan Slavic. Here it follows from the tight integration into proclitic clusters oriented toward the verb (loss of promiscuous attachment); cf. Sims and Joseph (2019) for a systematic analysis. This way into more affix-like usage has to be distinguished from univerbation (leading to loss of morphological boundaries), which appears to be more prominent if *da* itself is the host of 2P-enclitics (compare, e.g., Mac. *da ne*, Bulg. *da ne bi* in § 2.2.3.4). However, this process also seems to be comparatively weakly represented all over South Slavic. Moreover, remarkably, the acquisition of verb-oriented properties as a proclitic is not related to clitic climbing at all, which is attested only in Serbian-Croatian and only in cases of high degree of semantic integration (§ 2.2.3.4).

Being innovative in terms of the loss of irrealis features of *da*, the western part is much more conservative in employing the inherited *bi*-conditional in clausal complementation (e.g., reported speech) and in adverbial subordination (e.g., conditionals, concessives). In Balkan Slavic *da*-clauses have largely taken over the domain of the *bi*-conditional. Within the western part Slovene differs from Serbian-Croatian in that is has not extended the *bi*-conditional to mark habitual action (see § 2.2.3). Nowhere have *da* and *bi* fused into an unsegmentable unit, maybe except some idioms (curses etc.) based on obsolete collocations.

In addition, the infinitive has remained an option only in the western part; but usage-based research is called for in order to establish its functional distribution in comparison with finite complements (headed by *da*). Among other things, the division between same-subject and different-subject complementation (including constructions with subject vs object control) requires thorough examination. The distribution between infinitival and *da*-headed complements is of interest only for complements with a high degree of semantic integration (see the left half of the SIH, Table 1).

Slovene can in many respects be considered structurally closest to North Slavic. This implies not only an assumed higher frequency of infinitival complements and of combinations of the neutral complementizer (*da*) with *bi* (+ *l*-form), but also the reduction of the past tense system (Topolińska 2003). To which extent impressions concerning a higher frequency load – and its implications for functional distribution – are justified should be investigated, again, in usage-based research. By a similar token, the relation between *da* + *bi* (+ *l*-form) and *da* + pfv. present in western South Slavic raises the question whether these two patterns of irrealis marking follow a unidirectional development toward ousting *da* + *bi*, or whether *da* + *bi* is undergoing a "renaissance". This question applies in particular to Slovene.

Finally, turning back to the southeastern part of South Slavic, Macedonian seems to be more advanced in the creation of new lexical units serving as propositional modifiers out of epistemic CTPs (compare *mora* + *da*) and in the creation of clause-initial connectives developing into complementizers (*kako da*, *da ne*). In this respect, Macedonian has a pattern that is more similar to Serbian (and Croatian) than to Bulgarian, but this picture may change if research starts digging deeper into uses encountered in spontaneous speech. The same applies to employing *kako* 'how' beyond the domain of direct perception and manner, namely as a +factual complementizer, first of all in Serbian and Macedonian (see § 2.2.5).

4.4 General desiderata

The maximum template provides an opportunity to pinpoint desiderata in ongoing discussions on clausal complementation and related matters. These desiderata persist mostly due to a lack of usage-based research, for which, in the first place, sufficiently annotated corpora are an indispensible tool. Although there are various questions that may be formulated in this respect, within the scope of this paper, only some can be briefly addressed here.

First, the distribution of complementation markers after particular CTPs, for instance, Bulg. *da* vs *če* (and similar cases) after 'hope' and 'promise'. Obviously, this question has to be investigated verb by verb and with multivariate techniques that help to relate token frequencies to functional diversification. Obviously, discussions about the morphosyntactic status of complementation markers (e.g., *da*) do not seem helpful. Analogous remarks apply to the choice of auxiliaries in the transition zone between mono- and biclausal structures, e.g., analytical causatives (see § 2.1), and to the relation between same-subject and different-subject constructions: how neatly does this opposition really match with preference for infinitival vs finite *da*-complements (in languages which still use the infinitive)? See § 2.3.2.

Second, as for Balkan Slavic *da* turning into a strictly verb-oriented proclitic, has this process been favored by a more frequent occurrence of elliptical subjects (within the *da*-clause) in comparison to nominal subjects (full NPs)? Or otherwise: how often could subjects be presumed from the context so that they were not expressed (i.e. elliptic)? In these cases *da* automatically occurs adjacent to the verb. This issue might be studied diachronically for Balkan Slavic varieties, but comparisons with modern Serbian-Croatian corpus data, first of all data consisting of non-standard speech, will certainly be helpful as well.

Third, what is the relation between *da* + pfv. present and the future (inflected *ću*... in Serbian-Croatian, *bom*... in Slovene) and between *da* + pfv. present and *bi*-conditional? All these elements occurring after *da* are strict 2P-enclitics, whereas in Balkan Slavic *da* and future markers (Bulg. *šte*, Mac. *ḱe*) exclude each other in paradigmatic verb forms and all of them are proclitic. What is the underlying mechanism leading to *da*'s proclitic behavior and its inclusion into clitic clusters in Balkan Slavic, but not in western South Slavic? Certainly, language contact (e.g., with Greek and Arumanian) is a factor, as concerns almost all phenomena encountered on the Balkans.

This brings us to the concluding general remark. To which extent does the internal South Slavic differentiation in clausal complementation pattern rather in accordance with larger areas of convergence, which sometimes seem to cut through the South Slavic territory, and to which extent can we still discern dialectal continua within South Slavic that had formed in times prior to standardization? In particular, for the splits discussed above, can we really say that there is no transition between varieties close to the Serbian standard and typical "Balkanized" varieties? It is hard to believe that transitions are absent. Evidently, East Serbian dialects (located in the Torlak, Timok region) can count as most valuable sources of information in this respect. This is only one of many questions which arise when we realize that variation of potentially any of the components of clausal complementation occurs on a dialectal (diatopic) level, on the tension between standardized and non-standard varieties (diastratic level), and that variation may also surface in registers of speech (diaphasic level). Last but not least, the areal and diastratic differentiation should be "mapped" onto diachronic development, since synchronic variation often mirrors different diachronic layers.

Abbreviations

CTP	complement-taking predicate
ipfv.	imperfective
pfv.	perfective
SIH	Semantic Integration Hierarchy
SoA	state of affairs

In glosses

1,2,3 – first, second, third person

ACC	accusative
ADJ	adjectival form
ADJV	adjectivizer
ADV	adverb form
AOR	aorist
ATHV	athematic vowel
AUX	auxiliary
BE.NEG	clausal negation (suppletive)
COMP	complementizer
CON	connective
COND	conditional (with *l*-form)
COUNT	count form (Bulgarian nouns)
DAT	dative
DEM	demonstrative
DEF	definite article
F	feminine
FUT	future
GEN	genitive
IMP	imperative
IMPF	imperfect
INF	infinitive
IPFV	imperfective
IRR	irrealis marker
LF	*l*-form (in conditional)
LPT	*l*-participle
LOC	locative
M	masculine
N	neuter
NEG	negation
NMLZ	nominalizer
NOM	nominative
PFV	perfective
PFX	prefix

PL	plural
PN	proper noun
POSS	possessive pronoun
POSSIB	possibility modal
PP	past participle
PP_INDECL	indeclinable past participle
PRS	present
PST	past
PTC	particle
REFL	reflexive marker
REFL_POSS	reflexive possessive pronoun
REL	relative pronoun
Q	question marker (= IF-complementizer)
SFX	suffix
SG	singular
SIM_INDECL	indeclinable present participle
TR_INF	truncated infinitive

References

Abney, Steven Paul. 1987. *The English noun phrase in its sentential aspects*. Cambridge, MA: PhD thesis.

Abusch, Dorit. 2010. Presupposition triggering from alternatives. *Journal of Semantics* 27. 37–80.

Aikhenvald, Alexandra Y. 2004. *Evidentiality*. Oxford etc.: Oxford U.P.

Aikhenvald, Alexandra Y. (ed.). 2018. *The Oxford Handbook of Evidentiality*. Oxford etc.: Oxford U.P.

Alanović, Milivoj. 2018. Rečenice sa dopunskom klauzom [Sentences with a complement clause]. In Predrag Piper (ed.), *Sintaksa složene rečenice u savremenom srpskom jeziku*, 91–197. Novi Sad: Matica Srpska; Belgrade: Institut za srpski jezik, SANU.

Anand, Pravan & Valentine Hacquard. 2013. Epistemics and attitudes. *Semantics and Pragmatics* 6. 1–59.

Asenova, Petja. 2002. *Balkansko ezikoznanie* [Balkan linguistics]. Veliko Tărnovo: Faber.

Asher, Nicholas. 1993. *Reference to abstract objects in discourse*. Dordrecht etc.: Kluwer Academic Publishers.

Asher, Nicholas. 2000. Events, facts, propositions, and evolutive anaphora. In James Higginbotham, Fabio Pianesi & Achille C. Varzi (eds.), *Speaking of Events*, 123–150. New York & Oxford: Oxford University Press.

Baker, Mark. 1985. The mirror principle and morphosyntactic explanation. *Linguistic Inquiry* 16–3. 373–415.

Bally, Charles. 1950. *Linguistique générale et linguistique française*. 3ème édition. Bern: Francke.

Baschewa, Emilia. 2004. *Objekte und Objektsätze im Deutschen und im Bulgarischen*. Frankfurt/M. etc.: Lang.

Bašić, Monika. 2010. On the morphological make-up of nominalizations in Serbian. In Artemis Alexiadou & Monika Rathert (eds.), *The syntax of nominalizations across languages and frameworks*, 39–66. Berlin & New York: De Gruyter Mouton.

Bayer, Josef. 2015. Doubly-filled Comp, *wh* head-movement, and derivational economy. In Marc van Oostendorp & Henk van Riemsdijk (eds.), *Representing structure in phonology and syntax*, 7–39. Berlin & Boston: De Gruyter Mouton.

Belić, Bojan. 2005a. *Complement verb variation in present-day Serbian*. Ohio: Ohio State University unpubl. PhD thesis.

Belić, Bojan. 2005b. Infinitive is difficult to lose: What governs variation of complements in unique control in Serbian. *Glossos* 6. 1–20.

Belyavski-Frank, Masha. 2003. *The Balkan conditional in South Slavic: A semantic and syntactic study*. Munich: Sagner.

Bezlaj, France. 1977. *Etimološki slovar slovenskega jezika* [Slovene etymological dictionary]. *I: A-J*. Ljubljana: SAZU.

Birtić, Matea. 2008. *Unutarnja struktura odglagolskih imenica u hrvatskome jeziku* [The internal structure of deverbal nouns in Croatian]. Zagreb: Institut za hrvatski jezik i jezikoslovlje.

Boye, Kasper. 2010. Evidence for what? Evidentiality and scope. In Björn Wiemer & Katerina Stathi (eds.), *Database on evidentiality markers in European languages*, 290–307. Berlin: Akademie Verlag. [*STUF – Language Typology and Universals* 63 (4)].

Boye, Kasper. 2012. *Epistemic meaning: A crosslinguistic and functional-cognitive study*. Berlin & Boston: De Gruyter Mouton.

Boye, Kasper & Peter Harder. 2007. Complement-taking predicates: Usage and linguistic structure. *Studies in Language* 31 (3). 569–606.

Boye, Kasper & Peter Harder. 2012. A usage-based theory of grammatical status and grammaticalization. *Language* 88 (1). 1–44.

Boye, Kasper & Petar Kehayov (eds.). 2016. *Complementizer semantics in European languages*. Berlin & Boston: De Gruyter Mouton.

Boye, Kasper, Eva van Lier & Eva Theilgaard Brink. 2015. Epistemic complementizers: a crosslinguistic survey. *Language Sciences* 51. 1–17.

Bresnan, Joan W. 1970. On complementizers: Toward a syntactic theory of complement types. *Foundations of Language* 6 (3). 297–321.

Browne, Wayles. 1986. *Relative clause in Serbo-Croatian in comparison with English*. Zagreb: Institute of Linguistics, University of Zagreb.

Bužarovska, Eleni. 2002. The purpose-modification continuum: purposive *da*-relative clauses in Macedonian. *Southwest Journal of Linguistics* 21 (1). 67–99.

Bužarovska, Eleni. 2006. Pathways of semantic change: from similarity to sensory evidential. *Slavia Meridionalis. Studia Linguistica et Balcanistica* 6. 185–211.

Bužarovska, Eleni. 2013. *Glagoli za auditivna percepcija: Semantika i sintaksa* [Verbs of auditive perception: Semantics and syntax]. Skopje: UKIM.

Bužarovska, Eleni & Olga Mišeska Tomić. 2009. Subjunctive relatives in Bulgarian and Macedonian. In Mila Dimitrova-Vulchanova & Olga Mišeska Tomić (eds.), *Investigations in the Bulgarian and Macedonian nominal expressions*, 204–229. Trondheim: Tapir Academic Press.

Bužarovska, Eleni & Liljana Mitkovska. 2014. Semantikata na glagolot *se nadeva*: izrazuvanje emocija ili stav? [The semantics of the verb *se nadeva* 'hope': expressing emotion or state?] *Makedonski jazik* LXV. 203–218.

Bužarovska, Eleni & Liljana Mitkovska. 2017. Aprexensivnite govorni činovi vo makedonskiot jazik [Apprehensional speech acts in Macedonian]. *Makedonski jazik* LXVIII, 121–130.

Bybee, Joan, Revere Perkins & William Pagliuca. 1994. *The evolution of grammar: Tense, aspect, and modality in the languages or the world.* Chicago & London: The University of Chicago Press.

Comrie, Bernard. 1993. Argument structure. In Joachim Jacobs, Arnim von Stechow, Wolfgang Sternefeld & Theo Vennemann (eds.), *Syntax: An International Handbook*, vol. 1, 905–914. Berlin & New York: Walter de Gruyter.

Cornillie, Bert & Paola Pietrandrea. 2012. Modality at work. Cognitive, interactional and textual functions of modal markers. *Journal of Pragmatics* 44. 2109–2115.

Cristofaro, Sonia. 2003. *Subordination.* Oxford etc.: Oxford U.P.

Croft, William. 2000. Parts of speech as language universals and as language-particular categories. In Petra M Vogel & Bernard Comrie (eds.), *Approaches to the typology of word classes*, 65–102. Berlin & New York: De Gruyter Mouton.

Čakărova, Krasimira. 2008. Funkcionalno-semantična xarakteristika na modalnite formi s *neka* v săvremennija bălgarski ezik [Functional-semantic properties of modal forms with *neka* in contemporary Bulgarian]. In Sigrun Comati (ed.), *Bulgaristica – Studia et Argumenta: Festschrift für Ruselina Nitsolova zum 65. Geburtstag*, 115–126. Munich: Sagner.

Deutscher, Guy. 2000. *Syntactic change in Akkadian: The evolution of sentential complementation.* Oxford: Oxford U.P.

Diewald, Gabriele. 1999. *Die Modalverben im Deutschen: Grammatikalisierung und Polyfunktionalität.* Tübingen: Niemeyer.

Dimitrova-Vulchanova, Mila. 1999. Clitics in the Slavic languages. In Henk van Riemsdijk (ed.), *Clitics in the languages of Europe*, 83–122. Berlin & New York: De Gruyter Mouton.

Dixon, R.M.W. 1995. Complement clauses and complementation strategies. In Frank R. Palmer (ed.), *Grammar and meaning: essays in honour of Sir John Lyons*, 75–220. Cambridge etc.: Cambridge U.P.

Dixon, R.M.W. 2005. *A semantic approach to English grammar.* 2nd edition. Oxford etc.: Oxford U.P.

Dixon, R.M.W. 2006. Complement clauses and complementation strategies in typological perspective. In R.M.W. Dixon & Alexandra Y. Aikhenvald (eds.), *Complementation: A cross-linguistic typology*, 1–48. Oxford etc.: Oxford U.P.

Dobrushina, Nina. 2012. Subjunctive complement clauses in Russian. *Russian Linguistics* 36. 121–156.

Egrè, Paul. 2008. Question-embedding and factivity. *Grazer Philosophische Studien* 77 (1). 85–125.

Evans, Nicholas. 2007. Insubordination and its uses. In Irina Nikolaeva (ed.), *Finiteness: Theoretical and empirical foundations*, 366–431. Oxford: Oxford University Press.

Feleško, Kazimjež [= Feleszko, Kazimierz]. 1974. Od problematikata na takanarečenata konstrukcija so *da* (Nekolku prašanja za diskusija) [On issues of the so-called *da*-construction (Some suggestions to be discussed)]. *Makedonski jazik* XXV. 137–144.

Feleszko, Kazimierz. 1979. Wokół południowosłowiańskiego coniunctivu [Around the South Slavic conjunctive]. *Studia z filologii polskiej i słowiańskiej* 18. 185–192.

Franks, Steven. 2008. Clitic placement, prosody, and the Bulgarian verbal complex. *Journal of Slavic Linguistics* 16 (1). 91–137.

Friedman, Victor. 1993. Macedonian. In Bernard Comrie & Greville Corbett (eds.), *The Slavonic languages*, 249–305. London: Routledge.

Friedman, Victor. 2000. Confirmative/nonconfirmative in Balkan Slavic, Balkan Romance, and Albanian, with additional observations on Turkish, Roamni, Georgian, and Lak. In Lars

Johanson & Bo Utas (eds.), *Evidentials in Turkic, Iranian and neighbouring languages*, 329–366. Berlin & New York: De Gruyter Mouton.

Friedman, Victor. 2004. The typology of Balkan evidentiality and areal linguistics. In Olga Mišeska Tomić (ed.), *Balkan syntax and semantics*, 101–134. Amsterdam & Philadelphia: Benjamins.

Friedman, Victor A. 2011. Tipologija na upotrebata na *da* vo balkanskite jazici [A typology of the use of *da* in Balkan languages]. *Makedonistički studii*. 43–52. Skopje: MANU.

Gast, Volker & Holger Diessel. 2012. The typology of clause linkage: status quo, challenges, prospects. In Volker Gast & Holger Diessel (eds.), *Clause linkage in cross-linguistic perspective: Data-driven approaches to cross-clausal syntax*, 1–36. Berlin & Boston: De Gruyter Mouton.

Gegovski, Dejan. 2014. Okolu subjektivnite komplementarni rečenici vo dijalektite na makedonskiot jazik [Around subject complement clauses in Macedonian dialects]. In Zuzana Topolinjska (ed.), *Subjunktiv so poseben osvrt na makedonskite* da-*konstrukcii* [The subjunctive with a special account of Macedonian *da*-constructions], 93–106. Skopje: MANU.

Georgieva, Elena. 1976. Kăm văprosa za semantičnata xarakteristika na otglagolnite săščestvitelni v bălgarskija knižoven ezik. (Opit za leksiko-gramatičeska prekategorizacija) [On the issue of the semantics properties of deverbal nouns in literary Bulgarian]. In Petar Pašov & Ruselina Nicolova (eds.), *Pomagalo po bălgarska morfologija. Glagol*, 440–462. Sofija: Nauka i izkustvo.

Georgievski, Georgi. 2009. Da-*rečenicata vo makedonskiot jazik* [*Da*-sentences in Macedonian]. Skopje: Institut za makedonski jazik "Krste Misirkov".

Giannakidou, Anastasia. 1998. *Polarity sensitivity as (non)veridical dependency*. Amsterdam & Philadelphia: Benjamins.

Giannakidou, Anastasia. 2009. On the temporal properties of mood: the subjunctive revisited. *Lingua* 1119. 1883–1908.

Givón, Talmy. 1980. The binding hierarchy and the typology of complements. *Studies in Language* 4. 333–377.

Gnjatović, Tena & Ranko Matasović. 2010. Evidencijalne strategije u hrvatskom jeziku [Evidential strategies in Croatian]. In Matea Birtić & Dunja Brozović Rončević (eds.), *Sintaksa padeža: Zbornik radova znanstvenoga skupa s međunarodnim sudjelovanjem* Drugi hrvatski sintaktički dani: *Osijek, 13.-15. studenoga 2008*, 89–99. Zagreb: Institut za hrvatski jezik i jezikoslovlje.

Gołąb, Zbigniew. 1954. Funkcja syntaktyczna partykuły *da* w językach południowo-słowiańskich (bulgarskim, macedońskim i serbo-chorwackim) [The syntactic function of the particle da in South Slavic languages (Bulgarian, Macedonian and Serbian-Croatian)]. *Biuletyn polskiego towarzystwa językoznawczego* XIII. 67–92.

Gołąb, Zbigniew. 1964a. The problem of verbal moods in Slavic languages. *International Journal of Slavic Linguistics and Poetics* VIII. 1–36.

Gołąb, Zbigniew. 1964b. *Conditionalis typu bałkańskiego w językach południowosłowiańskich: ze szczególnym uwzględnieniem macedońskiego* [The Balkan-type conditional in South Slavic languages: with a special account of Macedonian]. Wrocław etc.: Ossolineum.

Grickat, Irena. 1975. *Studije iz istorije srpskohrvatskog jezika* [Studies concerning the history of Serbian-Croatian]. Belgrade: Zavod za udzbenike.

Grimshaw, Jane. 1990. *Argument structure*. Cambridge, Massachusetts & London: The MIT Press.

Grković-Major, Jasmina. 2018a. The development of perception verb complements in the Serbian language. In Jasmina Grković-Major, Björn Hansen & Barbara Sonnenhauser (eds.), *Diachronic Slavonic syntax: The interplay between internal development, language contact and metalinguistic factors*, 339–360. Berlin & Boston: De Gruyter Mouton.

Grković-Major [Grković-Mejdžor], Jasmina. 2018b. Razvoj klauzalne dopune kognitivnih predikata u srpskom jeziku [Development of cognitive predicate clausal complements in Serbian]. In Rajna Dragićević & Veljko Brborić (eds.), *Srpska slavistika: Radovi srpske delegacije na XVI međunarodnom kongresu slavista. Tom 1, Jezik* [Serbian Slavic studies: Contributions of the Serbian delegation on the XVI International Congress of Slavists], 89–105. Belgrade: Savez slavističkih društava Srbije.

Grković-Major, Jasmina. 2020. *Da*-clauses (connectives). In Marc L. Greenberg (ed.), *Encyclopedia of Slavic Languages and Linguistics online*. Brill: Leiden. https://referenceworks.brillonline.com/browse/encyclopedia-of-slavic-languages-and-linguistics-online (accessed Sepember, 14, 2020).

Gurkova, Aleksandra. 2008. *Sintaksa na složenata rečenica vo makedonskite crkvnoslovenski rakopisi* [The syntax of the complex sentence in Macedonian Church Slavonic manuscripts]. Skopje: Institut za makedonski jazik "Krste Misirkov".

GSBKE (1983): Popov, Konstantin (ed.). 1983. *Gramatika na săvremennija bălgarski knižoven ezik, t. 3: Sintaksis* [A grammar of contemporary literary Bulgarian, vol. 3: Syntax]. Sofia: Izdat-vo na Bălgarskata Akademija na Naukite.

Halpern, Aaron. 1996. Introduction. In Aaron Halpern & Arnold Zwicky (eds.), *Approaching second: Second position clitics and related phenomena*, ix–xxiii. Stanford: CSLI Publications.

Hansen, Björn. 2010. Constructional aspects of the rise of epistemic sentence adverbs in Russian. In Björn Hansen & Jasmina Grković-Major (eds.), *Diachronic Slavonic syntax. Gradual changes in focus*, 75–86. Munich etc.: Sagner. [Special issue *Wiener Slawistischer Almanach*, 74].

Hansen, Björn. 2017. What happens after grammaticalization? Post-grammaticalization processes in the area of modality. In Daniël Van Olmen, Hubert Cuyckens & Lobke Ghesquière (eds.), *Aspects of grammaticalization: (Inter)Subjectification and directionality*, 257–280. Berlin & Boston: De Gruyter Mouton.

Hansen, Björn, Alexander Letuchiy & Izabela Błaszczyk. 2016. Complementizers in Slavonic (Russian, Polish, and Bulgarian). In Kasper Boye & Petar Kehayov (eds.), *Complementizer semantics in European languages*, 175–223. Berlin & Boston: De Gruyter Mouton.

Hauge, Kjetil Rå. 1999 [1976]. The word order of predicate clitics in Bulgarian. *Journal of Slavic Linguistics* 7 (1). 89–137.

Hausman, Klaus. 1956. *Der Potential im Mazedonischen*. Göttingen: unpubl. doctoral thesis.

Hengeveld, Kees & J. Lachlan Mackenzie. 2008. *Functional Discourse Grammar*. Oxford etc.: Oxford U.P.

Holvoet, Axel. 2008. Secondary predicates in Baltic. In Christoph Schroeder, Gerd Hentschel & Winfried Boeder (eds.), *Secondary predicates in Eastern European languages and beyond*, 125–140. Oldenburg: BIS.

Holvoet, Axel. 2016. Semantic functions of complementizers in Baltic. In Kasper Boye & Petar Kehayov (eds.), *Complementizer semantics in European languages*, 225–263. Berlin & Boston: De Gruyter Mouton.

Holvoet, Axel & Jelena Konickaja. 2011. Interpretive deontics. A definition and a semantic map based on Slavonic and Baltic data. *Acta Linguistica Hafniensia* 43 (1). 1–20.

Hooper, Joan & Sarah Thompson. 1973. On the applicability of root transformations. *Linguistic Inquiry* 4 (4). 465–497.

Horie, Kaoru. 2001. Complement clauses. In Martin Haspelmath, Ekkehard König, Wulf Oesterreicher & Wolfgang Raible (eds.), *Language Typology and Language Universals: An International Handbook*, vol. 2, 979–993. Berlin & New York: De Gruyter Mouton.

Horie, Kaoru & Bernard Comrie. 2000. Introduction. In Kaoru Horie (ed.), *Complementation: Cognitive and functional perspectives*, 1–10. Amsterdam & Philadelphia: Benjamins.

Ivanova, Elena Ju. 2014a. Russkie paralleli bolgarskoj *da*-konstrukcii [Russian parallels to the Bulgarian *da*-construction]. In Zuzana Topolinjska (ed.), *Subjunktiv so poseben osvrt na makedonskite* da-*konstrukcii* [The subjunctive with special concern for the Macedonian *da*-constructions], 106–161. Skopje: MANU.

Ivanova, Elena Ju. 2014b. Aprexensiv v russkom i bolgarskom jazykax [The apprehensive in Russian and Bulgarian]. *Studi Slavistici* XI. 143–168.

Ivanova, Elena Ju. 2018. Častica *by/bi*: značenie, upotreblenie, sintaksis (russko-bolgarskie paralleli) [The particle *by/bi*: meaning, use, syntax (Russian-Bulgarian parallels)]. In Zuzana Topolinjska (ed.), *Statusot na modalnata morfema* bi *vo makedonskiot jazik i nejzinite funkcionalni ekvivalenti vo drugite slovenski i neslovenski jazici* [The status of the modal morpheme bi in Macedonian and its functional equivalents in other Slavic and non-Slavic languages], 49–74. Skopje: MANU.

Ivanova, Elena Ju. & Alla A. Gradinarova. 2015. *Sintaksičeskaja sistema bolgarskogo jazyka na fone russkogo* [The syntactic system of Bulgarian in comparison to Russian]. Moscow: JaSK.

Ivić, Milka. 1970. O upotrebi glagolskih vremena u zavisnoj rečenici: prezent u rečenici s veznikom *da* [On the use of verbal tenses in the dependent clause: the present tense in clauses with the conjunction *da*]. *Zbornik za filologiju i lingvistiku* 13 (1). 43–54.

Jačeva-Ulčar, Elka. 2014. *Da*-konstrukciite vo crkvnoslovenskite rakopisi od makedonska redakcija [The *da*-constructions in the Church Slavonic manuscripts of Macedonian recension]. In Zuzana Topolinjska (ed.), *Subjunktiv so poseben osvrt na makedonskite* da-*konstrukcii* [The subjunctive with special concern for the Macedonian *da*-constructions], 162–169. Skopje: MANU.

Ježek, Elisabetta & Paolo Ramat. 2009. On parts-of-speech transcategorization. *Folia Linguistica* 43 (2). 391–416.

Joseph, Brian. 2016. The semantics and syntax of complementation markers as an areal phenomenon in the Balkans, with special attention to Albanian. In Kasper Boye & Petar Kehayov (eds.), *Complementizer semantics in European languages*, 265–292. Berlin & Boston: De Gruyter Mouton.

Jurkiewicz-Rohrbacher, Edyta, Björn Hansen & Zrinka Kolaković. 2017. Clitic climbing, finiteness and the raising-control distinction. A corpus-based study. *Jazykovedný časopis* 68 (2). 179–190.

Karttunen, Lauri. 1971. Some observations on factivity. *Papers in Linguistics* 4 (1). 55–69.

Karttunen, Lauri. 1973. Presuppositions and compound sentences. *Linguistic Inquiry* 4 (2), 169–193.

Keenan, Edward. 1976. Towards a universal definition of 'subject'. In Charles N. Li (ed.), *Subject and topic*, 303–333. New York etc.: Academic Press.

Kehayov, Petar & Kasper Boye. 2016a. Complementizer semantics – an introduction. In Kasper Boye & Petar Kehayov (eds.), *Complementizer semantics in European languages*, 1–11. Berlin & Boston: De Gruyter Mouton.

Kehayov, Petar & Kasper Boye. 2016b. Complementizer semantics in European languages: Overview and generalizations. In Kasper Boye & Petar Kehayov (eds.), *Complementizer semantics in European languages*, 809–878. Berlin & Boston: De Gruyter Mouton.

Kemmer, Suzanne & Arie Verhagen. 1994. The grammar of causatives and the conceptual structure of events. *Cognitive Linguistics* 5 (2). 115–156.

Kiparsky, Paul & Carol Kiparsky. 1970. Fact. In Manfred Bierwisch & Karl E. Heidolph (eds.), *Progress in linguistics*, 143–173. The Hague: De Gruyter Mouton.

Kolaković, Zrinka, Edyta Jurkiewicz-Rohrbacher & Björn Hansen. 2019. Clitic Climbing, the Raising- Control Dichotomy and Diaphasic Variation in Croatian. *Rasprave Instituta Za Hrvatski Jezik i Jezikoslovlje* 45 (2). 505–522.

Koptjevskaja-Tamm, Maria. 1993. *Nominalizations*. London & New York: Routledge.

Koptjevskaja-Tamm, Maria. 2015. Action nouns. In Peter O. Müller, Ingeborg Ohnheiser, Susan Olsen & Franz Rainer (eds.), *Word-Formation: An International Handbook of the Languages of Europe*, vol. 2, 1195–1209. Berlin & Boston: De Gruyter Mouton.

Korytkowska, Małgorzata & Wiara Małdżiewa. 2002. *Od zdania złożonego do zdania pojedynczego (nominalizacja argumentu propozycjonalnego w języku polskim i bułgarskim)* [From the complex sentence to the simple sentence (the nominalization of the propositional argument in Polish and Bulgarian]. Toruń: Wyd-wo UMK.

Kosta, Peter & Anton Zimmerling. 2014. Slavic clitic systems in a typological perspective. In Lilia Schürcks, Anastasia Giannakidou & Urtzi Etxeberria (eds.), *The nominal structure in Slavic and beyond*, 441–487. Berlin & Boston: De Gruyter Mouton.

Kovačević, Miloš. 2008. Je li glagolski oblik *mora* uvijek glagol? [Is the verb form *mora* always a verb?] *Radovi filozofskog fakulteta* 10 (1). 35–47.

Kovačević, Miloš. 2009. Glagolske alolekse kao modalne riječi [Verb allolexes as modal words]. *Naučni sastanak slavista u Vukove dane* 38 (1). 73–86.

Kramer, Christina Elizabeth. 1986. *Analytic modality in Macedonian*. Munich: Sagner.

Kramer, Christina Elizabeth. 1992. Analytic modality in South Slavic. In Henry R. Cooper, Jr. & John D. Treadway (eds.), *Bulgaria Past and Present*, 113–122. [*Indiana Slavic Studies* 6 / *Balkanistica* 8].

Krapova, Iliyana. 1998. Subjunctive complements, null subjects and case checking in Bulgarian. *University of Venice Working Papers in Linguistics* 8 (2). 73–93.

Krapova, Iliyana. 2001. Subjunctives in Bulgarian and Modern Greek. In María Luisa Rivero & Angela Ralli (eds.), *Comparative syntax of Balkan languages*, 105–126. Oxford etc.: Oxford U.P.

Krapova, Iliyana. 2010. Bulgarian relative and factive clauses with an invariant complementizer. *Lingua* 120. 1240–1272.

Krapova, Iliyana, Tomislav Sočanac & Björn Wiemer (forthcoming-a). Factivity. In Marc L. Greenberg & Lenore A. Grenoble (eds.), *Encyclopedia of Slavic Languages and Linguistics*. Leiden: Brill.

Krapova, Iliyana, Tomislav Sočanac & Björn Wiemer (forthcoming-b). Veridicality. In Marc L. Greenberg, & Lenore A. Grenoble (eds.), *Encyclopedia of Slavic Languages and Linguistics*. Leiden: Brill.

Kratzer, Angelika. 1981. The notional category of modality. In Hans-Jürgen Eikmeyer & Hannes Rieser (eds.), *words, worlds, and contexts: New approaches in word semantics*, 38–74. Berlin & New York: De Gruyter Mouton.

Kratzer, Angelika. 2012. *Modals and conditionals: New and revised perspectives*. Oxford etc.: Oxford U.P.

Kroeger, Paul R. 2005. *Analyzing grammar: An introduction*. Cambridge etc.: Cambridge U.P.
Labroska, Veselinka. 2018. Funkciite na partikulata BI vo zapadnoto makedonsko narečje [The functions of the particle BI in the western Macedonian dialect]. In Zuzana Topolinjska (ed.), *Statusot na modalnata morfema bi vo makedonskiot jazik i nejzinite funkcionalni ekvivalenti vo drugite slovenski i neslovenski jazici* [The status of the modal morpheme bi in Macedonian and its functional equivalents in other Slavic and non-Slavic languages], 75–88. Skopje: MANU.
Laskova, Laska. 2009. Imperfekt i pluskvamperfekt v podčineni *da*-izrečenija sled glagoli za văzprijatie [Imperfect and pluperfect in dependent *da*-clauses after verbs of perception]. *Bălgarski ezik (Priloženie)*.
Lehmann, Christian. 1984. *Der Relativsatz: Typologie seiner Strukturen; Theorie seiner Funktionen; Kompendium seiner Grammatik*. Tübingen: Narr.
Lehmann, Christian. 1988. Towards a typology of clause linkage. In John Haiman & Sandra A. Thompson (eds.), *Clause combining in grammar and discourse*, 181–225. Amsterdam & Philadelphia: Benjamins.
Levshina, Natalia. 2015. European analytic causatives as a comparative concept. Evidence from a parallel corpus of film subtitles. *Folia Linguistica* 49 (2). 487–520.
Lichtenberk, František. 1991. Semantic change and heterosemy in grammaticalization. *Language* 67. 475–509.
Lindstedt, Jouko. 2010. Mood in Bulgarian and Macedonian. In Björn Rothstein & Rolf Thieroff (eds.), *Mood in the languages of Europe*, 409–421. Amsterdam & Philadelphia: Benjamins.
Lyons, John. 1977. *Semantics*, vol. 2. Cambridge etc.: Cambridge U.P.
Malchukov, Andrej. 2004. *Nominalization / verbalization: constraining a typology of transcategorial operations*. Munich: Lincom.
Malchukov, Andrej. 2006. Constraining nominalization: Function/form competition. *Linguistics* 44/45. 973–1009.
Markova, Angelina. 2010. The syntax of deverbal nominals in Bulgarian. In Artemis Alexiadou & Monika Rathert (eds.), *The syntax of nominalizations across languages and frameworks*, 93–128. Berlin & New York: De Gruyter Mouton.
Marques, Rui. 2009. On the selection of mood in complement clauses. In Lotte Hogeweg, Helen de Hoop & Andrej Malchukov (eds.), *Cross-linguistic semantics of tense, aspect and modality*, 179–204. Amsterdam & Philadelphia: Benjamins.
Mauri, Caterina & Andrea Sansò. 2012. What do languages encode when they encode reality status? *Language Sciences* 34. 99–106.
Mauri, Caterina & Andrea Sansò. 2016. The linguistic marking of (ir)realis and subjunctive. In Jan Nuyts & Johan van der Auwera (eds.), *The Oxford Handbook of Mood and Modality*, 166–195. Oxford etc.: Oxford U.P.
Mihaljević, Milan. 2009. The structure of complements of verbs of perception in Croatian. In Steven Franks, Vrinda Chidambaram & Brian Joseph (eds.), *A linguist's linguist: Studies in South Slavic linguistics in honor of E. Wayles Browne*, 317–353. Bloomington, Indiana: Slavica.
Milenkovska, Sonja & Angelina Pančevska. 2014. *Da*-konstrukcii kako argumenti na predikati od vtor i tret red (makedonski ~ polski) [*Da*-constructions as arguments of second- and third-order predicates (Macedonian ~ Polish)]. In Zuzana Topolinjska (ed.), *Subjunktiv so poseben osvrt na makedonskite da-konstrukcii* [The subjunctive with a special account of the Macedonian *da*-constructions], 178–192. Skopje: MANU.

Mirić, Mirjana. 2018. Upotreba/izostavljane subjunktivnog markera *da* u konstrukcii futura prvog u timočkim govorima [The use/omission of the subjunctive marker da in the construction of Future I in the Timok dialects]. In Svetlana Ćirković (ed.), *Timok. Folkloristička i lingvistička terenska istraživanja 2015–2017* [Timok. Field work on the folklore and the language, 2016–2017], 201–218. Knjaževac: Narodna biblioteka "Njegoš".

Mitkovska, Liljana. 2018. Možniot način nadvor od uslovniot period vo sovremeniot makedonski jazik [The potential mood outside of the conditional sentence in contemporary Macedonian]. In Zuzana Topolinjska (ed.), *Statusot na modalnata morfema bi vo makedonskiot jazik i nejzinite funkcionalni ekvivalenti vo drugite slovenski i neslovenski jazici* [The status of the modal morpheme bi in Macedonian and its functional equivalents in other Slavic and non-Slavic languages], 97–118. Skopje: MANU.

Mitkovska, Liljana & Eleni Bužarovska. 2015. Variation in clausal complementation: Macedonian and Bulgarian predicates *hope* and *believe*. In Branimir Belaj (ed.), *Dimenzije značenja*, 189–242. Zagreb: Zagrebačka slavistička škola.

Mitkovska, Liljana, Eleni Bužarovska & Elena Julvanova. 2017. Apprehensive-epistemic *da*-constructions in Balkan Slavic. *Slověne* 2017 (2). 57–83.

Mladenov, Stefan. 1929. *Geschichte der bulgarischen Sprache*. Berlin & Leipzig: De Gruyter & Co.

Mønnesland, Sven. 1972. Semantic factors in the syntax of nominal subordinate clauses in Serbo-Croatian. *Scando-Slavica* 18. 145–157.

Moiseeva, Nadežda. 1998. Verbs of perception in Russian. In Markus Giger, Thomas Menzel & Björn Wiemer (eds.), *Lexikologie und Sprachveränderung in der Slavia*, 153–164. Oldenburg: BIS.

Narrog, Heiko. 2005. Modality, mood, and change of modal meanings: A new perspective. *Cognitive Linguistics* 16 (4). 677–731.

Narrog, Heiko. 2009. *Modality in Japanese: The layered structure of the clause and hierarchies of functional categories*. Amsterdam & Philadelphia: Benjamins.

Nikolaeva, Irina. 2013. Unpacking finiteness. In Dunstan Brown, Marina Chumakina & Greville G. Corbett (eds.), *Canonical morphology and syntax*. Oxford etc.: Oxford U.P., 99–122.

Nikolaeva, Irina. 2016. Analyses of the semantics of mood. In Jan Nuyts & Johan van der Auwera (eds.), *The Oxford Handbook of Mood and Modality*, 68–85. Oxford etc.: Oxford U.P.

Noonan, Michael. 2007. Complementation. In Timothy Shopen (ed.), *Language typology and syntactic description*: Volume 2, *Complex constructions*, 52–150. Cambridge etc.: Cambridge U.P.

Nuyts, Jan & Johan van der Auwera (eds.). 2016. *The Oxford Handbook of Mood and Modality*. Oxford etc.: Oxford U.P.

Padučeva, Elena V. 2005. Èffekty snjatoj utverditel'nosti: global'noe otricanie [Effects of suspended propositions: global negation]. *Russkij jazyk v naučnom osveščenii* 10. 17–42.

Penčev, Jordan. 1999. Sintaksis [Syntax]. In Todor Bojadžiev, Ivan Kucarov & Jordan Penčev (eds.), *Săvremenen bălgarski ezik. Fonetika. Leksikologija. Slovoobrazuvane. Morfologija. Sintaksis* [Contemporary Bulgarian. Phonetics. Lexicology. Word formation. Morphology. Syntax], 498–655. Sofia: Petăr Beron.

Peterson, Philip L. 1997. *Fact, proposition, event*. Dordrecht etc.: Kluwer Academic Publishers.

Petrović, Vladislava. 2003. Upotreba veznika *kako* i *da* u komplementnoj klauzi srpskog jezika [The use of the conjunctions *kako* and *da* in the Serbian complement clause]. *Slavia Meridionalis* 4. 35–44.

Petkova-Schick, Ivanka. 1973. Zur Problemstellung und Modellierung der bulgarischen "да"-Konstruktion. *Zeitschrift für Slawistik* 18 (2). 273–280.

Philippaki-Warburton, Irene. 1994. The subjunctive mood and the syntactic status of them particle *na* in Modern Greek. *Folia Linguistica* 28 (3–4). 297–326.

Piper, Predrag. 1998. O kondicionalnosti u prostoj rečenici [On conditionality in the simple sentence]. *Južnoslovenski filolog* LIV. 41–58.

Pitsch, Hagen. 2020. Bulgarian *da* as a Non-Indicative Placeholder. In Teodora Radeva-Bork & Peter Kosta (eds.), *Current developments in Slavic languages. Twenty years after (based on selected papers from FDSL 11)*, 229–241. Berlin etc.: Lang.

Popov, Konstantin. 1985. Za otglagolnite săščestvitelni na *-nie* [About deverbal nouns ending in *-nie*]. In Konstantin Popov (ed.), *Iz istorijata na bălgarskija knižoven ezik*, 99–117. Sofija: Izdatelstvo na BAN.

Popović, Ljudmila. 2018. Ob osobom slučae temporal'nogo upotreblenija potenciala v serbskom i drugix slavjanskix jazykax [On a particular kind of temporal use of the potential in Serbian and other Slavic languages]. In Zuzana Topolinjska (ed.), *Statusot na modalnata morfema bi vo makedonskiot jazik i nejzinite funkcionalni ekvivalenti vo drugite slovenski i neslovenski jazici* [The status of the modal morpheme bi in Macedonian and its functional equivalents in other Slavic and non-Slavic languages], 131–157. Skopje: MANU.

Ransom, Evelyn N. 1986. *Complementation: its meanings and forms*. Amsterdam & Philadelphia: Benjamins.

Rentzsch, Julian. 2015. *Modality in Turkic languages: Form and meaning from a historical and comparative perspective*. Berlin: Schwarz.

Rizzi, Luigi. 1997. The Fine Structure of the Left Periphery. In Liliane Haegeman (ed.), *Elements of grammar* 281–337. Dordrecht: Kluwer.

Roberts, Ian & Anna Roussou. 2003. *Syntactic change: A minimalist approach to grammaticalization*. Cambridge etc.: Cambridge U.P.

Rothstein, Björn & Rolf Thieroff (eds.). 2010. *Mood in the languages of Europe*. Amsterdam & Philadelphia: Benjamins.

Rozwadowska, Bożena. 1997. *Towards a unified theory of nominalizations: External and internal eventualities*. Wrocław: Wyd-wo Uniwersytetu Wrocławskiego.

Rozwadowska, Bożena. 2000. Event structure, argument structure and the 'by'-phrase in Polish nominalizations. In Peter Coopmans, Martin Everaert & Jane Grimshaw (eds.), *Lexical specification and insertion*, 329–347. Amsterdam, Philadelphia: Benjamins.

Rudin, Catherine. 1986. *Aspects of Bulgarian syntax: complementizers and WH constructions*. Columbus: Slavica.

Schmidtke-Bode, Karsten. 2014. *Complement clauses and complementation systems: A cross-linguistic study of grammatical organization*. Jena: unpubl. PhD thesis.

Siegel, Laura. 2009. Mood selection in Romance and Balkan. *Lingua* 119. 1859–1882.

Siloni, Tal. 1997. *Noun phrases and nominalizations: The syntax of DPs*. Dordrecht etc.: Kluwer Academic Publishers.

Simons, Mandy 2013. Presupposing. In Marina Sbisà & Ken Turner (eds.), *Pragmatics of speech actions*, 143–172. Berlin: De Gruyter Mouton.

Sims, Andrea D. & Brian D. Joseph. 2019. Morphology versus syntax in the Balkan verbal complex. In Iliyana Krapova & Brian D. Joseph (eds.), *Balkan syntax and (universal) principles of grammar*, 99–150. Berlin & Boston: De Gruyter Mouton.

Smirnova, Anastasia. 2012. The semantics of mood in Bulgarian. *Chicago Linguistics Society (Proceedings)* 48. 547–561.

Snoj, Marko. 2016. *Slovenski etimološki slovar* [Slovene etymological dictionary]. 3rd edition. Ljubljana: Založba ZRC. https://fran.si/193/marko-snoj-slovenski-etimoloski-slovar (accessed March, 16, 2020).

Sonnenhauser, Barbara. 2015. Functionalising syntactic variance: declarative complementation with *kako* and *če* in 17th to 19th century Balkan Slavic. *Wiener slavistisches Jahrbuch. Neue Folge* 3. 41–72.

Spencer, Andrew & Ana R. Luís. 2012. *Clitics. An introduction.* Cambridge etc.: Cambridge U.P.

Stassen, Leon. 1985. *Comparison and universal grammar.* Oxford: Basil Blackwell.

Stjepanović, Sandra 2004. Clitic climbing and restructuring with "finite clause" and infinitive complements. *Journal of Slavic Linguistics* 12 (1). 173–212.

Stojanov, Stojan. 1976. Otglagolni săščestvitelni s nastavka *-ne* ot svăršeni glagoli [Deverbal nouns with the ending *-ne* derived from perfective verbs]. In Petar Pašov & Ruselina Nicolova (eds.), *Pomagalo po bălgarska morfologija. Glagol,* 427–436. Sofija: Nauka i izkustvo. [First printed in *Ezik i literatura,* kn. 2 (1966), 39–48.]

Szucsich, Luka. 2010. Mood in Bosnian, Croatian and Serbian. In Björn Rothstein & Rolf Thieroff (eds.), *Mood in the languages of Europe,* 394–408. Amsterdam & Philadelphia: Benjamins.

Švedova, Nina Ju. (ed.). 1980. *Russkaja grammatika* [Russian grammar]. Moscow. Nauka.

Tallerman, Maggie. 2015. *Understanding syntax.* 4th edition. London & New York: Routledge.

Tatevosov, Sergej G. 2015. *Akcional'nost' v leksike i grammatike: Glagol i struktura sobytija* [Actionality in the lexicon and the grammar: The verb and event structure]. Moscow: JaSK.

Testelec, Jakov G. 2001. *Vvedenie v obščij sintaksis* [An introduction into general syntax]. Moscow: Izd-vo RGGU.

Thieroff, Rolf. 2010. Moods, moods, moods. In Björn Rothstein & Rolf Thieroff (eds.), *Mood in the languages of Europe,* 1–29. Amsterdam & Philadelphia: Benjamins.

Tiševa, Jovka. 2001a. Podčinitelno svărzvane v složnoto izrečenie. Komplementizatorite v bălgarskija ezik [Dependent binding in the complex sentence. Complementizers in Bulgarian]. In Svetla Koeva (ed.), *Săvremenni lingvistični teorii: Pomagalo po sintaksis* [Contemporary linguistic theories: A guide on syntax], 164–173. Plovdiv: Izd-vo na Universitetot văv Plovdiv.

Tiševa, Jovka. 2001b. Svoboden ili fiksiran e slovoredăt na klitikite? [Is the order of clitics free or fixed?] In Vasilka Radeva (ed.), *Bălgarskijat ezik prez XX vek* [The Bulgarian language through the 20th century], 64–70. Sofija: Akademično izd-vo "Prof. Marin Drinov".

Tiševa, Jovka. 2008. Za statuta na *li* v bălgarskoto izrečenie [On the status of *li* in the Bulgarian sentence]. In Sigrun Comati (ed.), *Bulgaristica – Studia et Argumenta: Festschrift für Ruselina Nitsolova zum 65. Geburtstag,* 298–311. Munich: Sagner.

Todorović, Nataša. 2015. *The indicative and subjunctive* DA-*complements in Serbian: A syntactic-semantic approach.* Frankfurt etc.: Lang.

Tomić, Olga Mišeska. 2006. *Balkan sprachbund morpho-syntactic features.* Dordrecht: Springer.

Tomić, Olga Mišeska. 2012. *A grammar of Macedonian.* Bloomington, Indiana: Slavica.

Topolinjska, Zuzana [Topolińska, Zuzanna]. 2014. Organizacija na ne-faktivnata zona na verbalniot sistem vo makedonskiot i vo polskiot jazik [The organisation of the non-factual zone in the Macedonian and the Polish verb system]. In Zuzana Topolinjska (ed.), *Subjunktiv so poseben osvrt na makedonskite* da-*konstrukcii* [The subjunctive with a special account of the Macedonian *da*-constructions], 218–229. Skopje: MANU.

Topolińska, Zuzanna. 2003. Means for grammatical accommodation of finite clauses: Slovenian between South and West Slavic. *Sprachtypologie und Universalienforschung* 56 (3). 306–322.

Topolińska, Zuzanna. 2006. /+ factive/, /+ modal/. In Ireneusz Bobrowski & Krystyna Kowalik (eds.), *Od fonemu do tekstu: Prace dedykowane Profesorowi Romanowi Laskowskiemu* [From the phoneme to the text: Contributions dedicated to prof. Roman Laskowski], 373–377. Cracow: Lexis.

Topolińska, Zuzanna. 2008a. Factivity as a grammatical category in Balkan Slavic and Balkan Romance. In Zuzanna Topolińska (ed.), *Z Polski do Macedonii. Studia językoznawcze, tom 1: Problemy predykacji*, 173–184. Cracow: Lexis.

Topolińska, Zuzanna. 2008b. 'Neka'-konstrukciite i nivniot status vo slovenskite glagolski sistemi ['Neka'-constructions and their status in the verb systems of Slavic languages]. In Zuzanna Topolińska (ed.), *Z Polski do Macedonii. Studia językoznawcze, tom 1: Problemy predykacji* [From Poland to Macedonia. Linguistics studies, vol. 1: Problems of predication], 217–223. Cracow: Lexis.

Uhlik, Mladen. 2018. O *naj* in *pust'* v slovensko-ruski sopostavitvi [On *naj* and *pust'* in a Slovene-Russian comparison]. *Slavistična revija* 66 (4). 403–419.

Uhlik, Mladen & Andrea Žele. 2017. Semantičeskie i sintaksičeskie osobennosti glagolov *bati se* 'bojat'sja' i *upati (se/si)* 'nadejat'sja; otvaživat'sja' v slovenskom predloženii [Semantic and syntactic peculiarities of the verbs *bati se* 'fear' and *upati (se/si)* 'hope; dare' in the Slovene sentence]. *Slovenski jezik – Slovene Linguistic Studies* 11. 87–109.

Uhlik, Mladen & Andreja Žele. 2018a. *Da*-predloženija pri glagolax želanija i pobuždenija v slovenskom jazyke [*Da*-sentences after verbs of wish and inducement in Slovene]. *Voprosy jazykoznanija* 2018 (5). 87–113.

Uhlik, Mladen & Andreja Žele. 2018b. Predmetni *da*-odvisniki v slovensko-ruski sopostavitvi [Object clauses introduced by *da* in a Slovene-Russian comparison]. *Slavistična revija* 66 (2). 213–233.

van Lier, Eva. 2009. *Parts of speech and dependent clauses: A typological study*. Utrecht: LOT.

Van Valin, Robert D., Jr. 2005. *Exploring the syntax-semantics interface*. Cambridge etc.: Cambridge U.P.

Viberg, Åke. 1983. The verbs of perception: A typological study. *Linguistics* 21 (1). 123–162.

Viktorova, Kalina. 2009. Funkcionalen razvoj na *da*-konstrukcijata v săvremennija bălgarski ezik [The functional evolution of the *da*-construction in contemporary Bulgarian]. In Valentin Stankov & Kalina Viktorova (eds.), *Problemi na gramatičnata sistema na bălgarskija ezik – glagol* [Problems of the Bulgarian grammatical saystem – the verb], 304–345. Sofija: Akademično izdatelstvo "Prof. Marin Drinov".

von Waldenfels, Ruprecht. 2015. Grammaticalization of 'give' in Slavic between drift and contact: Causative, modal, imperative, existential, optative and volative constructions. In Brian Nolan, Gudrun Rawoens & Elke Diedrichsen (eds.), *Causation, permission, and transfer: Argument realisation in GET, TAKE, PUT, GIVE and LET verbs*, 107–127. Amsterdam & Philadelphia: Benjamins.

Vrdoljak, Ivana. 2019. *Complementizers in interaction: Exploring the conceptual basis of the Serbian/Croatian complementation system from a typological perspective*. Mainz: JGU unpubl. PhD thesis.

Wiemer, Björn. 2014a. *Mora da* as a marker of modal meanings in Macedonian: on correlations between categorial restrictions and morphosyntactic behavior. In Elisabeth Leiss & Werner Abraham (eds.), Modes of modality. modality, typology, and universal grammar, 127–166. Amsterdam & Philadelphia: Benjamins.

Wiemer, Björn. 2014b. Umbau des Partizipialsystems. In Tilman Berger, Karl Gutschmidt, Sebastian Kempgen & Peter Kosta (eds.), *Die slavischen Sprachen: Ein internationales*

Handbuch zu ihrer Struktur, ihrer Geschichte und ihrer Erforschung, Band 2, 1625–1652. Berlin & Boston: De Gruyter Mouton.

Wiemer, Björn. 2017. Main clause infinitival predicates and their equivalents in Slavic: Why they are not instances of insubordination. In Łukasz Jędrzejowski & Ulrike Demske (eds.), *Infinitives at the syntax-semantics interface: A diachronic perspective*, 265–338. Berlin & Boston: De Gruyter Mouton.

Wiemer, Björn. 2018. On triangulation in the domain of clause linkage and propositional marking. In Björn Hansen, Jasmina Grković-Major & Barbara Sonnenhauser (eds.), *Diachronic Slavonic syntax: The interplay between internal development, language contact and metalinguistic factors*, 285–338. Berlin, Boston: De Gruyter Mouton.

Wiemer, Björn. 2019a. On illusory insubordination and semi-insubordination in Slavic: Independent infinitives, clause-initial particles and predicatives put to the test. In Karin Beijering, Gunther Kaltenböck & María Sol Sansiñena (eds.), *Insubordination: Theoretical and empirical issues*, 107–166. Amsterdam & Philadelphia: Benjamins.

Wiemer, Björn. 2019b. Tipologija akcional'nosti: svojstva finitnoj klauzy, klassifikacija glagolov i edinyj podxod k slovoizmenitel'nomu i derivacionnomu vidu [Typology of actionality: properties of the finite clause, verb classification, and a uniform approach to inflectional and derivational aspect]. *Voprosy jazykoznanija* 2019 (1). 93–129. Review of: Tatevosov, Sergej G. 2015. *Akcional'nost' v leksike i grammatike: Glagol i struktura sobytija*. Moscow: JaSK. And Tatevosov, Sergej G. 2016. *Glagol'nye klassy i tipologija akcional'nosti*. Moscow: JaSK.

Wiemer, Björn. (forthcoming). *Major apprehensional strategies in Slavic: a survey of their areal and grammatical distribution*. In: Faller, Martina, Eva Schultze-Berndt & Marine Vuillermet (eds.): *Apprehensional constructions (in a cross-linguistic perspective)*. Berlin: Language Science Press.

Wiemer, Björn & Veronika Kampf. 2011. Inventarisierung und Analyse lexikalischer Evidenzialitätsmarker des Bulgarischen: Adverbien, Partikeln und Prädikative (I). *Zeitschrift für Balkanologie* 47 (1). 46–76.

Alexander Letuchiy
Clausal complements of certain nominalizations in Bulgarian: Relevant parameters

Abstract: In this paper, the distribution of complement clauses with some nominalizations (deverbal and deadjectival nouns) in Bulgarian is considered. The central question is which factors influence the (in)ability of the derived noun to host a complement clause with which the base verb or adjective was compatible. Although the behavior of complement clauses is predicted by some semantic parameters, their distribution cannot be reduced to syntactic or actional classes, as in Grimshaw's (1990) account. In fact, the distribution of complement clauses with nouns in Bulgarian is regulated by several features: (i) real (non-prospective) vs. irreal (prospective) semantics of the embedded clause; (ii) the modifier / argument status of the 'complement' clause; (iii) semantic role characteristics; (iv) the opposition of generalized names of situations (generic situations) vs. names of single occurrences; (v) Grimshaw's nominalization types (actional classes). The main parameter seems to be the opposition of generic situation vs. occurrence, which takes into account both actional classes and semantic roles. I also consider two other parameters that may also be relevant for the (im)possibility of complement clauses but are not elaborated on in detail, since their relevance is questionable: namely, (vi) the syntactic position of the complement clause and (vii) the opposition of the complementizers *da* vs. *če*. An additional problem considered in the article is the distribution of the indefinite vs. definite forms of head nouns in constructions with complement clauses. The general conclusion is that the distribution of noun complement clauses is highly affected by semantic and lexical factors and that it cannot be accounted for by a single factor.

Acknowledgements: The reported study was funded by RFBR and National Science Foundation of Bulgaria (NSFB), project number 20-512-18005. I am grateful to the editors, Björn Wiemer and Barbara Sonnenhauser, for the invitation to participate in this volume, their useful remarks and discussion. I equally thank my colleagues Pavel Rudnev, Anna Volkova, Mikhail Knyazev, Fedor Golosov and participants of the conference "Typology of morphosyntactic parameters" (Moscow, 2018) for fruitful discussion of similar Russian data. Last but not least, I thank Ivan Derzhanski and Vesela Simeonova for their native speaker judgments.

Alexander Letuchiy, HSE University, Moscow, Staraya Basmannaya ul., 21/4,
e-mail: Alexander.letuchiy@gmail.com

https://doi.org/10.1515/9783110725858-003

Keywords: complementation, nominalization, reality, definiteness, Bulgarian, actional class, modifier, argument

1 Introduction

In this paper, I will examine the behavior of nominalizations with complement clauses in Bulgarian. The main problem related to them is that deverbal nouns are often incompatible with complement clauses, even if their base verbs are compatible with them. This fact contrasts complement clauses to nominal arguments, which are generally retained in nominalization.[1] Some nominalizations (1) are incompatible with complement clauses, while others (2) allow them (both base adjectives, namely, *stranno* 'strange' and *vъzmožno* 'possible', take complement clauses):

(1) **Strannost-ta da obsъd-im tova*
  peculiarity-DEF.F.SG COMP.IRR discuss.PFV-PRS.1PL this.N.SG
  Intended: 'The peculiarity to discuss it.'

(2) *vъzmožnost-ta da obsъd-im tova*
  possibility-DEF.F.SG COMP.IRR discuss.PFV-PRS.1PL this.N.SG
  'The possibility to discuss it.'

The main question I pose is which parameters are responsible for the (in)compatibility of the given nominalization with a complement clause. Theoretical approaches to complements of nouns significantly vary across theories. Below some of the existing accounts are considered in brief.

1.1 Grimshaw's account of the distribution

One of the main accounts of noun complement clauses is put forward by Grimshaw (1990): she states that the (in)ability of nominalizations (nominals) to host complement clauses can be explained by their classification into Complex Event, Simple Event and Result Nominals. The main opposition is between Complex

---

[1] Other differences between complement clauses and nominal arguments are analyzed, for instance, by Davies and Dubinsky (2009) and Letuchiy (2012).

Event and Result nominals.[2] Complex Event Nominals (CEN) are similar to the base verb in their actional properties and argument structure (3), while Result Nominals (RN) significantly differ from the base verb in various respects (4):

(3) *The destruction of the city by the enemy (in three hours).*

(4) *a complete destruction / an impressive building*

The Result nominal in (4) refers to the resulting state of the place. Neither aspectual / temporal characteristics of the dynamic event that preceded the state, nor its participants can be expressed. Simple Events occupy an intermediate position, representing a generalized situation, not having argument structure in the proper sense and temporal modififers (often they are generic) as in (5b):

(5) a. *The event / race / trip / exam took a long time / took place at 6.00 p.m.* (Grimshaw 1990: 59).
 b. *the meeting of the members (*in two hours)*

Under this type, the situation can be characterized with its general aspectual properties, but usually it does not refer to a single event and does not have participants expressed (in what follows, we only consider Complex Event and Result Nominal). According to Grimshaw's view, only Complex Event nominalizations really have argument structure, while other types of nominals host modifiers. For instance, *examination* can be either a Complex Event or a Result Nominal. When used as a Complex Event Nominal, it is compatible with an explicitly expressed agent and patient, as well as a designation of temporal properties of the situation (e.g., *The examination **of** the patient* (Patient) **by** *the doctor* (Agent) **took a long time** (temporal properties)). When used as a Result nominal, it is incompatible with an Agent and, usually, also a Patient expression (*The examination (*of the patient *by the doctor)* **was on the table**), but can only have modifiers. Grimshaw does not propose a single test to distinguish modifiers from arguments. However, she

---

[2] A small remark should be made about the terms 'nominal' and 'nominalization'. Nominalization is a process of deriving a nominal from a non-nominal word or the derived nominal itself. Grimshaw uses the term 'nominal' because she does not restrict her analysis to derived nominals. I mainly use 'nominalization' to emphasize that the nouns I consider are all derived – however, in general, I do not make any difference between 'nominals' and 'nominalizations'. At the same time, I understand that nouns like *strax* or *navyk* are not morphologically derived from verbs or verbs of any other part of speech, but rather semantically correlate with verbs *boja se* 'be afraid' and *navikna* 'be used to'.

points out that the semantic properties of Complex Event Nominals (compatibility with aspectual modifiers) match their syntactic properties: the tendency to occur with the expressed subject and object of the base verb (as is the case with the noun *examination* in the dynamic reading). Thus, result nominals normally do not tolerate argument expression. By contrast, if a noun incompatible with aspectual modifiers and with subject expression allows object expression, it is likely that this 'object' of the base verb is a modifier, not a complement of the nominalization. Grimshaw also states that RN take complement clauses more readily than CEN. According to her, the ability of Result nominals to take complement clauses proves that complement clauses are not real arguments – hence their possibility with the type of nominals that does not take nominal arguments.

1.2 Alternative syntactic accounts

The most radical point of view is presented by Stowell (1981), who argues that deverbal nouns cannot have real arguments (neither argument structure as a whole in the proper sense, nor sentential arguments in particular). Cinque and Krapova (2016) make the account proposed by Stowell (1981) more explicit. They suppose that clausal complements of nouns are relative clauses, though different types of complements have different syntactic organizations. A similar account is adopted by Simeonova (2019). She shows that complement clauses can be analyzed as relative clauses, though they are formally different from the main, core class of relative clauses. For instance, Bulgarian complement clauses are rarely marked with the subordinator *deto*, or relative pronouns with *-to*, typical for 'standard' relative clauses in Bulgarian.

Another line of research goes back to Lehmann's (1984: 46, 153–155) study of relative clauses and their relations with complement clauses. Lehmann proposes a test for distinguishing those two classes: he claims that (at least in German) relative clauses are compatible with indefinite NPs, while complement clauses are not:

Relative clause:
(6) a. *Ein Faktum, das nicht zutrifft, ist ein schwarzer Schimmel.*
         'A fact that is not true is a black mold.'
Complement clause:
     b. **Ein Faktum, dass es nicht zutrifft, beunruhigt uns alle.*
         Intended: 'A fact that it is not true worries all of us.'

However, this account is mainly valid for languages with indefinite articles. In Bulgarian, which has no indefinite articles, the opposition of definite vs. indefinite NPs behaves in another way with complement clauses (see Section 4). As I show in Section 4, the presence / absence of the definite article or an NP without an article does not seem to disambiguate between relative and complement clauses: both nouns with and without an article can host complement clauses, the distribution of definite and indefinite head nouns depends on other factors.

I am grateful to an anonymous reviewer for the idea that lexical elements marking indefiniteness (in particular, the pronoun *edin* 'one, some') may work in Bulgarian in the same way as an indefinite article. However, it seems that it is not confirmed by the language data: for instance, examples of the combination *edno čuvstvo če* 'a / some / one feeling that' are easily found by Google search:

(7) *Ostavja   edn-o   čuvstvo,   če   lipsv-at*
    leave.IPFV.PRS.3SG one-N.SG   feeling   COMP   miss.IPFV-PRS.3PL
    argument-i.
    argument-PL
    '(This) leaves a / some feeling that (he has) no arguments.'

1.3 Knyazev's pragmatic / referential account of the distribution

Knyazev (2014) shows that Grimshaw's classification is useful but insufficient to account for the properties of nominalizations. He proposes that complement clauses are favoured if the nominalization occupies the predicate position and lacks concrete reference. He claims, for instance, that for such Russian nominals as *dokazatel'stvo* 'proof', *ponimanie* 'understanding' and *strax* 'fear', the (in)ability to take CCs depends on their position and, correspondingly, on their referential properties. Among the parameters that are relevant, Knyazev mentions the predicate position, referential properties and the focus status (all of them favour complementation with nouns). For instance, *ponimanie* 'understanding' is best compatible with complement clauses when it is used in the argument position of the existential possessive construction with the verb *byt'* 'be', as in (8):

Russian:
(8) *U   Van-i   by-l-o   ponimani-e   čto*
    at   Vanja-SG.GEN be-PST-SG.N   understanding-SG.NOM   COMP
    nado   čto-to   menja-t'.
    necessary.PRAEDIC   something.ACC   change.IPFV-INF
    'Vanja understood (lit. 'At Vanja, there was an understanding') that one should change something.' [Knyazev 2014: 24]

The proposed account is relevant for some examples under analysis (in general, we did not check the head nouns and complements under analysis for Knyazev's parameters). The best example is the noun *dokazatelstvo* 'proof'. In most of the examples found in the Bulgarian National Corpus this noun occupies the focus position.

(9) *Tova   šte   e   nedvusmislen-o   dokazatelstvo   če*
    this.N FUT   be.PRS.3SG   unambiguous-N   proof   COMP
    v   Kalimport   tajno   se   e   namesti-l-ø
    in   Kalimport   secretly REFL   BE.PRS.3SG   move.PFV-PERF.PART-M.SG
    nov   igrač.
    new   player
    'This is an unambiguous proof that a new player has moved secretly to Kalimport.'[3]

However, the problem is that Knyazev (i) does not consider infinitive complements (infinitives can have distributions different from that of finite complements) and (ii) does not address the fact that some nominalizations are incompatible with complement clauses in any position.

The problem with most existing accounts is that they seek to regard complements of nominalizations uniformly. They do not give much attention to the fact that some nominalizations are compatible with complement clauses and others are not. Nor are they interested in the fact that even the class of complement-taking nouns is semantically and, perhaps, syntactically heterogeneous. I am trying to fill this lacuna. My article focuses on the lexical aspect of the problem in the sense that my main question is "Why do some nominals take complement clauses and others do not, even if both are derived from complement-taking predicates?"

In what follows, I will try to explain the (in)ability of Bulgarian nominalizations to host complement clauses and the choice between definite vs. indefinite forms of the head noun in the relevant constructions. I will show that, though both Grimshaw's and Knyazev's accounts are helpful, they are insufficient. Several parameters must be taken into account. The article is organized as follows. In Section 2, I sketch the Bulgarian system of complement clauses. Section 3 is central for the study: here we discuss the distribution of complement clauses with nominal heads. In Section 4, the definiteness of the head noun

---

[3] A similar factor may be occurrence of the head noun with a 'lexical function' in terms of Apresjan (1974), Mel'chuk et al. (1984). This term denotes a lexicalized context like Russian *ispytyvat' čuvstvo* 'have a feeling' (lit. 'experience a feeling') that is functionally close to systematic derivational mechanisms.

in noun complement constructions is discussed. In conclusion, some general claims, relevant for the data, are made (Section 5). Most of the data used in this study were taken from the Bulgarian National Corpus (BNC, http://search.dcl.bas.bg/). Statistical figures are also based on this corpus, unless marked otherwise. I used native speakers' judgments only sporadically and only in addition to corpus examples and figures. In those cases, the diagnostic contexts were evaluated by two native speakers: Ivan Deržanski and Vesela Simeonova.

2 Key properties of the Bulgarian complementation system

In this section, I briefly outline the properties of the Bulgarian complementation system: this system is rather poor compared, for instance, to the Russian one; the opposition between real vs. irreal situations is significant for the way of marking the embedded situation; finally, the opposition of adjunct vs. argument embedded clauses is not always clear.

2.1 Poor system of complementizers

Bulgarian can be called a language with a rather poor complementizer system (see (Hansen et al. 2016) for details). The majority of contexts is covered by two markers: *če* 'that' and *da* 'to, in order to, so that'. The use of *če* induces that the event has been realized or its probability is discussed, as in epistemic contexts (in most cases the event is given strong epistemic support). By contrast, *da* is mainly employed to designate that the event cannot be ascribed any truth-value (e.g., with embedded directive speech acts), or, as for epistemic contexts, its proposition gains low support from the speaker. For instance, its content refers to someone's wish or situations when the speaker does not fully support its propositional content. The inventory of verb classes, which allow the use of *da*, is basically the same as for *čtoby*-clauses in Russian, as described by Dobrušina (2016) and corresponds to the typological tendencies described by Noonan (2007). It includes modal verbs and auxiliaries, causative verbs, phasal verbs, and so on. To some extent, *da* fulfils the functions that infinitive has in some other languages, because Bulgarian lacks an infinitive. Some less canonical verbs taking *da*-clauses are logical proof verbs, such as *dokazvam* 'prove'. Example (10) shows a construction with *da* hosted by *dokazvam*. In general, argumentation and logic predicates tend to be compatible with *če*, but here *da* is more appropriate due to the negative context.

(10) *Săd-ăt   namira   če   po   delo-to   ne*
     court-DEF.M.NOM think.IPFV.PRS.3SG COMP about case-DEF.N NEG
     se   dokazva   da   e   nalice skljuèn
     REFL prove.IPFV.PRS.3SG   COMP.IRR BE.PRS.3SG present signed
     meždu stran-i-te   dogovor   za   zaem.
     between side-PL-DEF.PL   agreement of   loan
     'The court believes that it is not proven that a loan agreement is signed between the sides.'

Če is a complementizer *sensu stricto*. It is always situated in the clause-initial position, typical for complementizers. By contrast, *da*, as noted in many studies, has a double function in the grammatical system. It is a means of complementation and, at the same time, a marker of subjunctive mood (see Wiemer 2017: § 3.3; 2018: §§ 3.2–3.4). This is why *da* tends to be situated immediately before the lexical verb. In these cases, the subject of the embedded *da*-clause (*ljubovta mu* in (11)) is situated before *da*, thus, in terms of linear sequence it seems to belong to the main clause.[4]

(11) *Bog iska   ljubov-ta   mu   da   preliva*
     God want.IPFV.PRS.3SG love-DEF.F he.DAT COMP.IRR pass[ipfv].PRS.3SG
     črez   nas kăm drugi-te.
     through us   to   other-DEF.PL
     'God wants his love to pass through us to others.'

The precise feature responsible for the distribution of complementizers is not so obvious. It is apparently related to the contrast between 'real' and 'irreal' contexts relevant for many of the world's languages (see Noonan's (2007) and Plungjan's (ed., 2004) typological work).

The semantic contrast between 'real' and 'unreal' clauses calls for an explanation. Several semantic features have to do with the opposition of realis and irrealis:

---

4 It might be tempting to analyze these constructions as instances of raising in terms of Culicover (1997), Culicover and Jackendoff (1997, 2005), and Polinsky (2013). However, no behavioral tests seem to show that *ljubovta* is syntactically in the main clause in (11).

1) Factivity: factive vs. non-factive (whether or not the embedded predication is presupposed to be true).
2) Degree of reality: real vs. hypothetical vs. counterfactual (whether or not the embedded predication is realized, can be realized or known not to have occurred).
3) Types of modality: Epistemic vs. deontic

For a comprehensive discussion see Plungjan (2011), Mauri & Sansò (2012, 2016).The factive vs. non-factive distinction is not the factor which determines the distribution of *da* and *če*. For instance, *če* is compatible with both factive (*znam* 'know') and non-factive (*mislja* 'think') predicates. The degree of reality is relevant for the distribution, but is not considered here because it is mostly reflected in adjunct (mainly conditional) clauses. In argument clauses, the distribution is not explained by this feature: for instance, it is hardly possible that *običam da* 'love' denotes an event with a lower reality status than *mislja če* 'think'. It seems that the opposition between epistemic vs. deontic meaning (and between modal predicates vs. predicates of cognition and opinion) is the most significant for the Bulgarian data. According to Yanakiev and Kotova (2003) and Hansen, Letuchiy and Blaszczyk (2016), the default complementizer marking realized and epistemically neutral situations is *če* 'that'. It is opposed to *da* 'for, in order to' that is often used in modal and irreal contexts, for instance, with semantics of wish, necessity, and so on.

(12) *Iska-m   da   mi   se   obadi-š.*
     want.IPFV-PRS.1SG COM.IRR   I.DAT REFL call.PFV-PRS.2SG
     'I want you to call me.'

(13) *Zna-m   če   šte   mi   se   obadi-š.*
     Know.IPFV-PRS.1SG COMP FUT   I.DAT REFL call.PFV-PRS.2SG
     'I know that you will call me.'

A sort of tendency is valid here: while verbs with a volitional component (*iskam* 'want') are typically used with *da*, verbs with an epistemic component (e.g., 'think') are mainly used with *če*.[5] Moreover, the presence of an epistemic component can favour *če* even if the volitional component is also present: this is the case of 'hope' that can be used with *da*, but equally well with *če*. On

---

5 See Uhlik, Želje (2018) on the distribution of the similar irreal complementizer *da* in Slovene.

the other hand, the verb *nadjavam se* is opposed to *mislja* 'think', which only marks an opinion and is only used with *če:* it only codes the subject's opinion (the situation is epistemically marked as possible), but no positive / negative relation or wish to make the situation realize. Note that addition of negation to the matrix verb, as in Russian (see Dobrushina 2016), can change its combinational properties.

2.2 Opposition of adjunct vs. argument clauses

Another opposition comes to mind when people discuss complementation, namely, the opposition of adjunct vs. argument dependent clauses. It is especially relevant, because, as mentioned before, the argument status of noun complement clauses has been doubted by Stowell (1981) and others. Cross-linguistically, adjunct vs. complement clauses often differ not only in their marking (see Cinque and Krapova (2016), Simeonova (2019), but also in their syntactic behavior. The criteria were first introduced by Ross (1967) in his influential dissertation. Ross noted, for instance, that adjunct clauses tend to resist extraction of any material (e.g., for question formation); for clausal complements, the restriction is not so strict. I illustrate the point with Russian examples; Russian behaves quite predictably in this respect. In (14), an element of the adjunct purpose clause cannot be extracted; the same is possible in (15) with an element of a complement clause.

Russian:
(14) *Čto   ty   priše-l-Ø   čtoby   ja   tebe
     what   you.NOM   come.PFV-PST-SG.M   in.order.to   I.NOM   you.DAT
     skaza-l-Ø?
     say.PFV-PST-SG.M
     Intended: 'What did you come in order for me to tell you?'

(15) Čto   ty   xoče-š   čtoby   ja   tebe
     what   you.NOM   want.IPFV-PRS.2SG   IRR.COMP   I.NOM   you.DAT
     skaza-l-Ø?
     say.PFV-PST-SG.M
     'What do you want me to say you (lit. 'What do you want that I told you?)?'
     (Testelec 2001: 204)

In Bulgarian, the restriction on wh-extraction from adjunct clauses does not seem to be strict. One of our native speakers judged both variants of (16) (with wh-extraction from purpose clauses) as grammatically correct. The other claims that only the version with *da*, but not with *za da*, sounds normal.[6] These data contrast with examples like (14) in Russian, normally judged as ungrammatical.

(16) Kakvo   si   došъ-l-ø   da / ?za da
      what   be.2SG.PRS   come.PFV-PERF.PART-M.SG   to   in.order.to
      kupi-š
      buy.PFV-PRS.2SG
      'What did you come to buy / in order to buy.'

Note, however, that the purpose clause with *da*, according to Krapova (this volume), has special syntactic properties, while the island features of *za da*-clauses have to be additionally checked with other native speakers.

For nominalizations, the problem of delimiting adjunct and argument clauses is far more complicated than for verbs. The wh-extraction test is not applicable here because of the island restriction valid for nominalizations: according to Ross (1967), in most languages he dealt with nominalizations obey the Complex NP Constraint: this means that no element can be extracted from a clause hosted by a nominal head, irrespective of their adjunct or argument status. Thus, from the operational point of view, the question of whether complement clauses of nouns are really complements (= have argument properties) or whether they are closer to modifiers is complicated and has no easy solution.

3 Complement clauses of nominalizations

I turn now to the focus of the paper. As mentioned before, the key issue is nominalizations (deverbal nouns) and their compatibility with complement clauses. In many languages, nominalizations do not always retain clausal complements of the base verb (see sections 1.1–1.2). For instance, in Russian, the noun *bojazn'* 'fear', derived from the verb *bojat'sja* 'fear, be afraid', mostly hosts infinitives, though the base verb is compatible both with infinitive clauses and with finite clauses with *čto:*.

---

6 See Gusev (2004), Stojnova Ms., (2016) with arguments for the fact that in Russian, infinitive complements of motion verbs can also have some argument properties.

(17) *On   bo-it-sja   navredi-t'   /   čto   ego*
     he.NOM   be.afraid.IPFV-PRS.3SG-REFL   hurt.PFV-INF   COMP   he.ACC
     osudj-at.
     condemn.PFV-FUT.3PL
     'He is afraid of hurting someone / that he will be judged'

(18) *bojazn'-Ø   navredi-t'   /   ?čto   ego   osudjat.*
     fear-SG.NOM   hurt.PFV-INF   COMP   he.ACC   condemn.PFV-FUT.3PL
     'the fear of hurting someone / that he will be judged '

The entire range of complement-taking predicates is rather complicated to sketch here. I focus on the following classes of Bulgarian predicates and predicate nouns:
1) Emotional predicates: *straxuvam (se)* 'frighten / be afraid' (the deverbal noun *strax* 'fear'), *bezpokoja se* 'worry' (*bezpokojstvo* 'worry'), *običam* 'love' (*obič / ljubov* 'love'), *učudvam (se)* 'surprise / be surprised' (*učudvane* 'surprise').
2) Cognition predicates, both with a modal component ('hope') and without it ('think'), *mislja* 'think' (*misъl* 'thought'), *znam* 'know' (*znanie* 'knowledge'), *nadjavam se* 'hope' (*nadežda* 'hope').
3) Evaluative predicates, including modal ones: *važno (e)* '(it is) important' (*važnost* 'importance'), *vъzmožno (e)* '(it is) possible' (*vъzmožnost* 'possibility'), *stranno* '(it is) strange' (*strannost* 'strangeness, peculiarity').
4) Logic / argumentation predicates: *dokazvam* 'prove' (*dokazatelstvo* 'proof'), *otkrivam* 'find out, discover' (*otkritie* 'discovery').
5) Speech act predicates: *objasnjavam* 'explain' (*objasnenie* 'explanation').

As I will demonstrate below, several features will be shown to be relevant to a certain degree for the (in)compatibility of Bulgarian nominalizations with complement clauses. They can be formulated as oppositions (i) between the prospective (following the main event) vs. retrospective (preceding the main event or taking place simultaneously); (ii) between dependent clauses which are arguments in the proper sense vs. modifiers and, correlated to it, (iii) between complement clauses with the role of content vs. other semantic roles; (iv) between generic situations and names of single occurrences / individual realizations, and (v) between Grimshaw's Complex Event vs. Result Nominals (see section 1.1). Some other features and oppositions, e.g., the opposition between complement clauses in different syntactic positions, may also be relevant, but they will not be discussed here in much detail.

Deverbal nouns (e.g., *strax* 'fear' from *straxuvam se* 'be afraid') are analyzed here together with de-adjectival ones, such as *strannost* 'strangeness' from *stranno e* 'it is strange' or *stranen* 'strange'. Note that only complement clauses with the complementizers *če* and *da* are tested, and sometimes indirect questions are used in examples. Among patterns that were not included are constructions with a correlative pronoun *tova* (*strax ot tova če* 'the fear of the fact that') and combinations like *tozi fakt če* 'the fact that'. The reason why they were excluded was that these complex markers include a nominal component and whether they have nominal properties (properties of NP arguments) or verbal properties (properties of complement clauses) is not predictable.

All figures are based on data from the Bulgarian National Corpus (http://search.dcl.bas.bg/). Table 1 below shows the number of structures with complement clauses of verbs in the first and third persons as compared to structures with complement clauses of nominalizations (in definite and indefinite forms and with a possessive pronoun).

The columns include the following figures:
- column 2: the number of 1SG PRS or AOR forms immediately followed by the complementizer;
- column 3: the number of 3SG PRS forms immediately followed by the complementizer;
- column 4: the number of nominalizations immediately followed by the complementizer (without / with the article);
- column 5: the number of nominalizations with the definite article immediately followed by the possessive pronoun *mu* 'his' and then the complementizer. This figure was not counted for de-adjectival nominals.

For some verbs for which the actual present context is unnatural, the number of 1SG and 3SG forms are given also for the perfective verb in the aorist. For non-verbal predicates like *važno* and *vozmožno*, which do not have person forms, the relevant data is in column 3.

Table 1: Number of examples with a nominalization and a complement clause, compared to the frequency of the base verb / adjective.

Verb + complementizer	1SG PRS / AOR with the complementizer	3SG PRS / AOR with the complementizer	NMLZ + complementizer	NMLZ + DEF + mu + complementizer
bezpokoja se če 'worry that'	59	51	*bezpokojstvo če* 32 *bezpokojstvoto če* 9	*bezpokojstvoto mu če* 0
bezpokoja se da 'worry that'	8	9	*bezpokojstvo da* 10 *bezpokojstvoto da* 1	*bezpokojstvoto mu da* 0

Table 1 (continued)

Verb + complementizer	1SG PRS / AOR with the complementizer	3SG PRS / AOR with the complementizer	NMLZ + complementizer	NMLZ + DEF + mu + complementizer
čuvstvam če 'feel that'[7]	810	448	čuvstvo če 1668 čuvstvoto če 11679	čuvstvoto mu če 14
dokazvam če 'prove that'	69	1282	dokazatelstvo če 2230 (the real number of different examples is >357) dokazatelstvoto če 132 (the real number of different examples is 107)	Dokazatelstvoto mu če
nadjavam se če 'hope that'	9608	1498	nadežda če 2186 nadeždata če 3109	nadeždata mu če 16
nadjavam se da 'hope that'	4415	2696	nadežda da 2036 nadeždata da 2374	nadeždata mu da 14
objasnjavam če 'explain that'	285 (objasnjix če 590)	738 (objasni če 3777)	objasnenie če 193 objasnenieto če >600	Objasnenieto mu če 7
običam da 'love to'	3934	4726	ljubov da 0 ljubovta da 0 obič 0 običta 0	običta mu da 2 ljubovta mu da 0
otkrivam če 'discover that' (IPF)	249	477	otkritie če 104 otkritieto če 394	otkritieto mu če 1
otkrija če 'discover that' (PF)	1877	4021		
razbiram če 'understand that' (IPF)	3297	3029	razbirane če 93 razbiraneto če 204	razbiraneto mu če 2
razbra če 'understand that' (PF)	10096	18043		

---

7 If for a given verb no line for a particular pattern is listed (e.g., the pattern with *da* for *čuvstvam* 'feel', this means that the search has not been carried out due to alleged low frequency of this pattern.

Table 1 (continued)

Verb + complementizer	1SG PRS / AOR with the complementizer	3SG PRS / AOR with the complementizer	NMLZ + complementizer	NMLZ + DEF + mu + complementizer
rešix če[8] 'decide that'	5316	10807	rešenie če 192 rešenieto če 619	rešenieto mu če 0
rešix da 'decide to'	6939	21572	rešenie da 1798 rešenieto da 675	rešenieto mu da 131
straxuvam se če 'be afraid that / to'	3061 <	793 <	strax če 2005 straxъt / straxa če 701	straxъt mu če 5
straxuvam se da 'be afraid to'	1288 <	2034 <	strax da 3153 straxъt / straxa da 372	straxъt mu da 11
učudvam se če 'be surprised that'	345	45	učudvane če 33 učudvaneto če 1	učudvaneto mu če 1
važno e če 'it is important that'		582	važnost če 0 važnostta če 1	
važno e da 'it is important to'		2589	važnost da 0 važnostta da 10	
vъzmožno e če 'it is possible that'		2176	vъzmožnost če 25 vъzmožnostta če 45	
vъzmožno e da 'it is possible to'		9152	vъzmožnost da 18064 vъzmožnostta da 6209	
znam če 'know that'	22825 (16366 znam + 6459 znaja)[9]	12570	znanie če 24 znanieto če 106	znanieto mu če 0

Note that sometimes, the figures can be distorted by contexts like (19), where the dependent clause is not a complement of the noun it follows, but of the matrix verb:

(19) Iskam strax mu da namaljava.
want.IPFV-PRS.1SG fear his COMP.IRR decrease.IPFV.PRS.3SG
'I want his fear to decrease.'

---

8 The verb reša 'decide' is listed and counted in columns 2 and 3 in the forms of aorist, because it occurs rather rarely in present tense forms.
9 The verb znam / znaja 'know' has two alternative 1SG PRS forms znam vs. znaja. As they seem to be synonymous, here they are counted together.

These contexts were filtered out when the nominalization is not too frequent, but in the case of highly frequent nominalizations, this filtration would take too much time.

It should also be noted that the results of the search of the Bulgarian corpus are sometimes imperfect for other reasons. For instance, sometimes the same examples appear more than once. In such cases, the following strategy was used: in cases when the result, automatically shown by the corpus, was about 100 or less, the number of relevant, non-repeating results was counted manually. If the number was several hundred examples or more, the automatically generated number was inserted into the table. However, it seems intuitively correct to assume that the distortions are not highly significant for the purposes of my research. At least, the Google search shows that the classes of nominals taking complement clauses regularly, taking them rarely and those that take them never or almost never are reflected correctly by the corpus (note that not all head nouns were searched for in Google).

To interpret the data in Table 1, I divide the nominalizations into three statistical classes (taking complement clauses regularly vs. rarely vs. almost never, see Table 2 below). This statistical classification does not seem to be affected by the special features of the corpus. The three groups are represented in Table 2.

Table 2: Statistical grouping, based on the frequency of complement clauses with nominalizations.

Nominalizations	Number of constructions with clausal complements of nominalization	Number of constructions with clausal complements of the finite verb
Dokazatelstvo če 'proof that', *vъzmožnost da* 'possibility to', *nadežda da / nadežda če* 'hope to / that' (with each of the two complementizers), *čuvstvo če* 'feeling that', *strax da / strax če* 'fear that / to' (with each of the two complementizers), *otkritie če* 'discovery that' *rešenie da* 'decision to'	> 2000 (only for *otkritie* about 500)	The same or less than for nominalizations
vъzmožnost če 'possibility that', *važnost da* 'importance to', *razbirane če* 'understanding that', *znanie če* 'knowledge that', *rešenie če* 'decision that'	10–210	>2000
važnost če 'importance that', *ljubov da* 'love to', *obič da* 'love to', *interes* 'interest' with indirect questions	0–10	>2000

The first group includes *vъzmožnost* 'possibility' with the complementizer *da*, *nadežda* 'hope' (in both patterns), *čuvstvo* 'feeling', *strax* 'fear' (in both patterns), *otkritie če* 'discovery that', *dokazatelstvo* 'proof', *rešenie* with *da* 'decision'. Not only do these nouns take complement clauses, but also some constructions are either more frequent or have a similar frequency as the base constructions with *vъzmožno* '(it is) possible', *nadjavam se* 'hope', *straxuvam se* 'fear', and so on. Here also belong *učudvane* 'surprise' with *če* and *bezpokojstvo* 'worry, concern' with both markers, not mentioned in Table 2. The number of examples where the verbal head and the nominal head are used with complement clauses is roughly equal, yet both the verbal and the nominal head are rather rare.

In the second group, we include the nouns *vъzmožnost* 'possibility' (with the complementizer *če*), *važnost* 'importance' with *da*, *razbirane če* 'understanding', *znanie če* 'knowledge', *rešenie če* 'decision'. These nouns rarely occur with complement clauses (compared to complement clauses hosted by the base verb or adjective), but these constructions are nevertheless found and sometimes are either judged by native speakers as acceptable or as partly acceptable.

Finally, the third group consists of *važnost* with *če*, as well as *ljubov* and *obič*, both meaning 'love', and *interes* 'interest' (contrary to other nouns, the noun *interes* was analyzed in its combinations with indirect questions). These heads are almost never found with complement clauses in the BNC and were usually judged unacceptable by the two native speakers. Some examples occur in the Google search sample, not shown here (e.g., *interes koj e toj* 'the interest into / of who he is'), but they are found only sporadically, whereas their base verbs and adjectives are often found with complement clauses (more than 2000 occurrences for each head).

Table 3 is the most illustrative one. Here, two proportions are compared: the proportion of constructions with complementizers among all uses of a noun (e.g., *bezpokojstvo* 'worry') and the proportion of constructions with complementizers among all uses of the base verb (e.g., *bezpokoja se* 'worry (intr), be worried').

In column 2, the number of examples with the first and the third person + a complementizer from Table 1 is summed up. The figure in column 3 is the sum of all uses of the verb in the first and the third person. The proportion of uses of the base predicate with a complement clause is shown in column 4. In column 5, the constructions with a head and a complementizer are counted, including three types of constructions (with an article on the head noun; without an article on the head noun; with a possessive clitic). In column 6, all uses of the given noun with and without an article are counted. The proportion of uses with the complement clauses among all uses of the nominal is shown in column 7. Finally, column 8 represents the proportion of constructions with a complementizer headed by a nominal (column 7) divided into the proportion of complement clauses hosted by

Clausal complements of certain nominalizations in Bulgarian: Relevant parameters — **177**

Table 3: Frequency of constructions with complement clauses with nouns in relation to their frequency with base verbs / predicatives.

Verb + complementizer	Verb with a complement clause	Total	Frequency with the complement / total	Noun with a complement clause	Total	Frequency with the complement / total	Ratio of complements with nouns / ratio of complements with verbs
bezpokoja se če 'worry that'	110	821 + 1072 = 1893	0.058	41	5343 + 1732 = 7075	0.0058	0.1
bezpokoja se da 'worry that'	17	821 + 1072 = 1893	0.0089	11	5343 + 1732 = 7075	0.0017	0.19101124
čuvstvam če 'feel that'	1258	9008 + 23791 = 32799	0.038	13361	25042 + 19536	0.684	18
dokazvam če 'prove that'	1351	270 + 3252 = 3522	0.3836	2362	10140 + 1102 = 11242	0.210	0.54744526
nadjavam se če 'hope that'	11106	19865 + 3979 = 23844	0.4658	5311	19149 + 9322 = 28471	0.1865	0.40038643
nadjavam se da 'hope that'	7111	19865 + 3979 = 23844	0.298	4424	19149 + 9322 = 28471	0.1554	0.52147651
objasnjavam 'explain that'	1023	2182 + 7693 = 9875	0.1036	800	9097 + 2515 = 11612	0.069	0.66602317
običam da 'love to'	8660	20450 + 17905 = 38355	0.2258	2	6018 + 1684 = 7702 (*obič*) 27017 + 18559 = 45576 (*ljubov*)	0.000037	0.00016386
otkrivam če 'discover that' (IPF)	726	1157 + 4552 = 5709	0.127	499	3442 + 1958 = 5400	0.0924	0.727559055

(continued)

Table 3 (continued)

Verb + complementizer	Verb with a complement clause	Total	Frequency with the complement / total	Noun with a complement clause	Total	Frequency with the complement / total	Ratio of complements with nouns / ratio of complements with verbs
otkrija če 'discover that' (PF)	5898	7007 + 15967 = 22974	0.2567				0.359953253[10]
razbiram če 'understand that' (IPF)	6326	33508 + 106936 = 140444	0.045		299 5531 + 1628 = 7159	0.042	0.93333333
razbra če 'understand that' (PF)	28139	21658 + 38547 = 60205	0.467				0.08993576
rešix če[11] 'decide that'	16123	13824 + 42242 = 56066	0.2876		811 35940 + 17304 = 53244	0.0152	0.05285118

(continued)

---

10 Since the noun *otkritie* 'discovery' corresponds either to the perfective verb *otkrivam* or to the imperfective one *otkrija*, the proportion is counted separately: 0.727559055 is the result of dividing the proportion of noun complement clauses into their proportion with the imperfective verb; 0.359953253 is yielded by dividing the proportion of noun complement clauses into their proportion with the perfective. Both results are rather high compared to the rest of sample. In principle, the list of lexemes includes some other nouns that correspond to two possible verbs (e.g., *dokazatelstvo* may correspond to the imperfective *dokazvam* or perfective *dokaža* 'prove'), but due to the lack of space I do not take two verbal lexemes in all these cases.

11 The verb *reša* 'decide' is listed and counted in columns 2 and 3 in the forms of aorist, because it occurs rather rarely in present tense forms.

Table 3 (continued)

rešix da 'decide to'	28511	13824 + 42242 = 56066	0.5085	2604	35940 + 17304 = 53244	0.0489	0.09616519
straxuvam se če 'be afraid that'	3854	6510 + 4605 = 11115	0.3467	2711	41532 + 5846 + 6745 = 54123	0.05	0.1442169
straxuvam se da 'be afraid to'	3322	6510 + 4605 = 11115	0.2989	3536	41532 + 5846 + 6745 = 54123	0.0653	0.21846771
učudvam se če 'be surprised that'	390	874 + 440 = 1314	0.2968	35	5809 + 889 = 6698	0.005	0.01684636
važno e če 'it is important that'	582	8072	0.072	1	2372 + 1024 = 3396	0.00029	0.00402778
važno e da 'it is important to'	2589	8072	0.3207	10	2372 + 1024 = 3396	0.0029	0.00904272
vъzmožno e če 'it is possible that'	2176	32073	0.0678	70	42139 + 12904 = 55043	0.0013	0.01917404
vъzmožno e da 'it is possible to'	9152	32073	0.285	24273	42139 + 12904 = 55043	0.441	1.54736842
znam če 'know that'	35395	16366 + 37448 = 53814	0.6577	130	3266 + 2814 = 6080	0.0214	0.03253763

a verb (4). In other words, column 8 shows to which extent the derived nominal retains the frequency of the use with complement clauses, characteristic of the base verb.[12]

Table 4 further interprets the data and represents the subgrouping of nominalizations based on the values in column 8 of Table 3. The data from Table 4 mainly agrees with the subgrouping shown in Table 2. For instance, most nominals from the first class of Table 2 belong to the first or the second class of Table 3 (except for the nouns *strax* 'fear' and *rešenie* 'decision'[13]). Nouns from the third class of Table 2 are all in the last two classes of Table 4.

Table 4: The ratio of complement clause constructions with nouns compared to the same ratio with their base verbs.

Nominalizations	Number with nouns / number with verbs
vъzmožnost da 'possibility', *čuvstvo če* 'feeling that'	> 1
dokazatelstvo 'proof', *nadežda da* 'hope', *objasnenie* 'explanation', *otkritie* 'discovery' (in comparison to the imperfective aspect), *razbirane* 'understanding' (in comparison to the imperfective aspect)	Between 0.5 and 1
nadežda če 'hope', *otkritie* 'discovery' (in comparison to the perfective aspect) 'interest' with indirect questions, *strax da* 'fear'	Between 0.2 and 0.5
bezpokojstvo da 'worry', *strax če* 'fear'	Between 0.1 and 0.2
bezpokojstvo če 'worry', *rešenie* 'decision' with *če* and *da*, *razbirane* 'understanding' (in comparison to the perfective aspect), *učudvane* 'surprise', *znanie* 'knowledge'	Between 0.01 and 0.1
ljubov 'love', *obič* 'love', *važnost* 'importance'	Less than 0.01

Now I will examine the parameters relevant for complementation with nouns one by one. I will try to apply each parameter to the data of the tables above. I will begin with the opposition of prospective vs. non-prospective complements. Next, follow two related features: the syntactic opposition of modifiers vs. com-

---

[12] In what follows, we often refer to the main figure of Table 3 (the figure in column 8) simply by 'the proportion in Table 3' or 'the value in Table 3'.
[13] While the noun *strax* is rather high in Table 4 (and this is related to the value of Feature 1 it has, see Section 3.1), the noun *rešenie* behaves in a peculiar way: Table 4 shows that it rarely hosts complement clauses, though it has the values of all features that favor complementation. At the moment, I do not have an explanation of this fact: perhaps, it shows the idiosyncratic nature of noun complementation or points to the existence of parameters I did not take into account.

plements and the semantic opposition of the ontological type of content modifiers vs. other types of complements. Then, I will address the semantic opposition of the generic situation vs. single occurrence. Finally, at the end, I will check the data against Grimshaw's opposition of Complex Event vs. Result Nominal.

Note that not all factors are independent from each other. However, each of the factors is useful for accounting for the behavior of some subclass of head nouns.

3.1 Feature 1. Prospective (irreal) vs. non-prospective (real) complements

The first feature is the temporal localization of the embedded event with respect to the main one and the reality of the embedded event:

(Rule 1) In the emotional class, head nouns compatible with embedded events that have been realized (as a single event or as a repeated / habitual event) have less chance to host a complement clause than head nouns compatible with embedded events that have not yet been realized (either will be realized in the future or will not be realized at all).[14]

Some head nouns denote that an emotion, utterance or another sort of situation occupies a time interval prior to the interval of the embedded situation (e.g., *boja se* 'fear'). With others, the emotion is based on the event that is realized, which is the case with *učudvane* 'surprise'. We call the former type of nouns and contexts prospective or unreal and the latter non-prospective or real. The borderline between 'prospective' and 'unreal' is vague: very often, if the embedded situation is located in time after the main situation, it is possible that the former will not take place at all. The tendency, formulated above as Rule 1, explains why *ljubov* 'love' and *učudvane* 'surprise' are not freely compatible with complement clauses, contrary to *strax* 'fear' (for *učudvane*, the proportion of complement clauses of the noun in Table 3 is 0.01684636, which is much lower than for *strax* (0.1442169 and 0.21846771, depending on the complementizer); for *ljubov*, almost no complement clauses are found, the proportion being 0.00016386). The noun *strax* very often hosts a complement clause that refers to an unreal situation: in a context like 'the fear that someone will rob me', it is presupposed that the situation has not become real at the moment

---

14 Note that this factor is at least partially covered by two more general factors: namely, syntactic status (modifier vs. argument) and semantic role (content vs. another). However, I discuss it here, mainly because the temporal localization and / or reality of the stimulus is a semantic parameter particularly important for description of emotional lexemes (see Iordanskaja 1992, among others).

of speech. Retrospective contexts seem to be also possible for this head noun, but peripheral compared to prospective ones. The nouns *učudvane* and *ljubov* behave differently. *Učudvane* is derived from a factive verb: thus, *učudvane če P* 'surprise that P' presupposes that P has been realized. With *ljubov da P* 'love to P' the reality of P is not presupposed, since P is non-specific: for instance, in 'Peter likes walking' no specific walk is discussed. However, it is very probable that Peter has at least once walked and even that he walks rather often. Thus, the embedded situation **does not need** to be realized, but is **likely to be** realized. This is why both *učudvane* and *ljubov* host with complement clauses more rarely than *strax*.

Some verbs are used both in prospective and non-prospective contexts. Interestingly, nouns formed from them behave according to Rule 1: they are used mainly in prospective contexts. This is the case with the verb *bezpokoja (se)* 'worry' (prospective (20) and non-prospective (21)) vs. the noun *bezpokojstvo* 'worry', which is mainly prospective or unreal, as in (22).

(20) *Tajno se bezpoko-i če tova šte se*
     secretly REFL worry.IPFV-PRS.3SG COMP this.N FUT REFL
     sluč-i.
     happen.PFV-PRS.3SG
     'He secretly worried that this will / might happen.'

(21) *...me bezpoko-i če prez tezi posledn-i 2.5-3*
     I.ACC worry.IPFV-PRS.3SG COMP during this.PL last-PL 2.5-3
     mesec-a nie si igra-em na promen-i.
     month-NUM we.NOM REFL.DAT play.IPFV-PRS.1PL on change-PL
     'It worries me that during the last 2,5-3 months we are (only) pretending to change (something).'

(22) *Za prъv pъt uset-i bezpokojstvo če se e*
     for first time feel-AOR.3SG worry COMP REFL be.PRS.3SG
     otkъsna-l-Ø ot xora-ta.
     separate.PFV-PERF.PART-SG.M from people-DEF.PL
     'For the first time, he worried that he was separated from other people.'
     (it is unclear whether he is really separated from the other people).

Note that for *bezpokojstvo*, due to its prospective use, the proportion in Table 3 is rather high (0.1 and 0.19101124, depending on the complementizer), though for *strax*, which is only prospective, the proportion is greater.

At the same time, the use of some nouns contradict Rule 1 formulated above. For instance, *navik* 'habit', usually combines with complements that denote repeated actions, but is compatible with complement clauses, as in (23). The reason can be that it does not belong to the emotional class.

(23) Navik   da   se   vod-i   dnevnik
      habit   COMP.IRR   REFL   lead.IPFV-PRS.3SG   diary
      'The habit of writing a diary.'

3.2 Feature 2. 'Modifiers' vs. 'real arguments'

The second contrast opposes complement clauses that are real syntactic arguments of their head nouns with complement clauses that are modifiers. Although in all contexts under analysis, complement clauses introduce a semantic argument of the head noun (e.g., if a person worries, (s)he worries about something), syntactically only some complement clauses behave like arguments. Others are rather modifiers of the head noun. I propose two tests for the argument / modifier status and argue the contrast to be relevant for the possibility of complementation.

The opposition of arguments vs. modifiers is based on two criteria:
1) modifier-type complements can be referred to with pronouns that are adjective-like modifiers (e.g., *drug* 'another, other', *tozi* 'this', *takъv* 'such'). In other words, they are syntactically parallel to adjectival units that are typical modifiers (adjuncts in the generative parlance).

The possibility of this test is proven by the fact that nominal arguments typically cannot be referred to by adjectival pronouns. Consider, for instance, (24), where *kartinata* 'picture' is a nominal argument of the head noun *opisvane* 'description':

(24) opisvane   na   kartina-ta
      description   of   picture-DEF.F.SG
      'description of the picture'

Of course, (24′) is possible but only with *tazi* referring to 'the description that has been previously mentioned'. The use of the pronoun *tazi* referring to the object of description (the picture) is impossible, and it is highly probable that the object of description will occur in (24′), with the pronoun:

(24′) tazi   opisvane   (na   kartina-ta)
      this   description   of   picture-DEF.F.SG
      'this description (of the picture)'

2) modifier-type complements are typically not syntactically obligatory and can be omitted from the sentence. Note, however, that the contrast between obligatory and non-obligatory syntactic units in Slavic languages is often motivated pragmatically and is not a reliable syntactic criterion.

(Rule 2) Complement clauses of nouns tend to behave as modifiers, not as arguments. It is rare that a complement clause of a noun behaves as an argument in the proper sense.[15]

Rule 2 seems to be well compatible with the fact that nouns tend to take modifiers, rather than arguments, but is not fully predictable. Recall that some head nouns can take argument NPs and PPs, e.g., *ljubovta kъm rodinata* 'love to the motherland'. In these cases, argument NPs and PPs do not show any modifier properties. Grimshaw (1990) addresses the contrast between arguments and modifiers, but she does not regard it as a separate feature of the particular complement clause. She claims that modifiers (not real arguments) are associated with Result nominals.

The contrast between arguments and modifiers and its relevance for complementation can be best illustrated by stative nominals. *Strannost* 'peculiarity' and *važnost* 'importance' do not take complement clauses (the proportion in Table 3 is 0.00402778 or 0.00904272 for *važnost*, depending on the complementizer, which is among the lowest values in the whole sample), while *vъzmožnost* 'possibility' takes CCs very frequently (in Table 3, the proportion is 1.54736842 for the uses with *da*), and these CCs behave as modifiers. Complementation is illustrated by (25):

(25) *Samo   če   sъštestvuva   i   druga   vъzmožnost   če*
     only   that exist.IPFV.PRS.3SG and   another.F.SG possibility   COMP
     cjal-a-ta   taja   rabota e   rezultat na recesija.
     all-F.SG-DEF.F this.F.SG work   be.PRS.3SG result   of recession
     'However, there exists another possibility: that all this work itself is a result of the recession.'

The complement clause of the noun *vъzmožnost* is a modifier regarding the first criterion formulated above. It can be replaced with an adjectival pronominal element. In (26), *tazi* 'this (F)' refers to the complement clause (*this possibility* = 'the possibility to **take the award**'), thus, the clausal complement of *vъzmožnost* satisfies condition 1 above: it can be syntactically parallel to adjectival pronouns.

---

[15] Note that when we talk about ability or inability of a particular noun to take a modifier or an argument, this only refers to the fact that its complement clause has properties of a modifier or an argument. We do not make a stronger claim that **all** complement clauses or NPs that they host are only modifiers or only arguments.

(26) [Nikoj ne se iznenada, kogato Galaxad vze nagradata ot imeto na xorata na Lancelet].
Obiknoveno   dava-xa   tazi   vъzmožnost   na
usually   give.IPFV-IPF.3PL this.F   possibility   to
novoposveten-ija   ricar.
recently.knighted-M.SG.ACC   knight
'[Nobody was surprised when Galahad took the award on behalf of Lancelet's people]. Usually the knights who have recently been knighted received such an opportunity.'

When *važnost* and *strannost* take complement clauses (very rarely), they do not seem to behave like complementizers (no contexts with adjectival pronominal units, as in (26), are found). This is one of the reasons for the rarity of such contexts.

Similarly, the argument vs. modifier distinction is valid in the emotional domain. The fact that *ljubov* 'love' is incompatible with complement clauses can be related to this distinction. With *ljubov*, the complement would be an argument, and not a modifier. For instance, the adjective pronoun *tazi* 'this (f)' in the combination *tazi ljubov* 'this love' can only refer to 'love directed to somebody' or 'love that has already been mentioned', but not to 'love to do something that I mentioned'. *Tazi* here cannot refer to the content of love. In (27), anaphora sounds odd:

(27) Običa-še   da   pe-e.   Tazi   ljubov...
      like.IPFV-IPF.3SG   COMP.IRR   sing-PRS.3SG   this.F.SG   love
      'He loved to sing. This love...'

By contrast, with *čuvstvo* 'feeling', taking complement clauses, the content of the feeling can be referred to by *tozi čuvstvo* 'this feeling'. Not surprisingly, the proportion in Table 3 is very high for this head noun (18, the highest in the whole sample).

At the same time, Feature 2 does not account for some aspects of complement clause distribution. Some complement clauses of nouns fail the test for modifier status and are, therefore, arguments. For *dokazatelstvo* 'proof', the proportion of complement clauses is high, yielding 0.54744526 in Table 3. However, the complement clause of *dokazatelstvo* is not a modifier. The complement clause denotes the fact being proven, and it cannot be referred to by adjectival modifiers like *kakъv* 'which' or *tozi* 'this' that can only refer to the arguments by means of a proof or a way of proving something. Of course, the combinations *kakvo dokazatelstvo* 'which proof' or *tova dokazatelstvo* 'this proof' are possible, but no examples were found where they mean 'the proof of this / which fact'. They are only used in the meaning 'the proof / way of proving that has been mentioned'.

3.3 Feature 3. Ontological properties: Complements with the property of content vs. other roles

The difference in the modifier / argument properties of the complement clause often correlates with the difference in semantic roles of the complement clause. Complementation is mostly possible with nouns if the complement clause can be described as the content of the property or an abstract notion like emotion, cognitive act or utterance.

Definition. A constituent is a content expression only if it specifies the precise nature of the situation denoted by the head noun (for instance, clarifies material and / or cognitive objects that constitute the nature of the situation). A content constituent does not exist separately, without the main situation.

Thus, the head noun has a special ontological property: it denotes a complex abstract object that can be reformulated as a set of propositions (thoughts, words, and so on). For instance, 'discovery' is described as a set of propositions revealed by a scientist, while 'feeling' is reformulated as a more concrete emotion or a group of emotions. We describe someone's feelings by mentioning what emotions they include. By contrast, 'fear' can be described in two ways:

(28) (i) Fear includes the proposition 'wolves will come'. (CONTENT)
 (ii) There is a possibility that wolves will come. This possibility makes someone be afraid (STIMULUS).

The typical criterion of the content complement is the possibility of overt and / or covert copular constructions, as in (29) and (30):

(29) *The main conclusion was that rats are intelligent.*

(30) *The research team reached an interesting conclusion – that rats are intelligent.*[16]

In (29), the copula *was* is present and it states the equivalence relation between *the main conclusion* and the content of conclusion. In (30), no overt copula is expressed, but in fact the meaning of the sentence is 'The research

---

[16] Here I adopt an assumption that the copular construction can simply check the syntactic properties of nominalization but not change its semantics and / or syntactic properties. This 'zero hypothesis' can, of course, be refuted by detailed studies of copular constructions which are, however, outside the scope of this paper.

team reached an interesting conclusion, [and this conclusion is / was] that rats were intelligent'. Thus, the nature of the conclusion is clarified by the use of a complement clause. Another crucial property of content complements is that, typically, they do not exist autonomously from the situation denoted by the head noun. For instance, in (29) and (30), the claim 'that rats are intelligent' only exists as the content of the conclusion. We know nothing about the epistemic status of this claim, it is unclear if the rats are intelligent in the real world. By contrast, in contexts like *It frightened me that it was dark* the situation 'it was dark' occurred before the main situation 'I was frightened' and independently of it.

(Rule 3) The tendency is that **complement clauses clarifying the content of the head noun have a better chance to be compatible with the nominal head than complement clauses with another semantic role.**[17]

The content vs. non-content distinction is most productive for describing complements of stative nouns. It is easy to show that the syntactic difference between *vъzmožnost* and *strannost* is reflected in the difference in ontological types. With *vъzmožnost* 'possibility', the complement clause behaving as a modifier defines the content of possibility. It is possible to say something like (31), with a covert copular construction:

(31) [V   tezi   klas-ove   igrač-i ima-t   mnogo   vъzmožnosti]
     Naprimer   da   igra-ete   v   njakolko igr-i   ednovremenno.
     for.instance COMP.IRR   play.IPFV-PRS.2PL in   several   game-PL simultaneously
     '[In these classes players have many opportunities]. For instance, (one of these opportunities is) to play several games simultaneously.'

In (31), if the second sentence was not added after the head noun, the utterance would be unclear, though grammatically correct. This is because the complement clause clarifies what is the best possibility – thus, what its content is. With *strannost*, dependent NPs have the role of 'bearer of property', and not the role of content. This is why no construction like (31) with a complement clause is possible. Thus, for *strannost* both the syntactic and semantic parameters prevent the head noun from having a clausal complement. Similarly, *ljubov* is incompatible

---

[17] Grimshaw (1990: 70–106), Bejan (2005: 189–192) mention the relevance of the content property as typical for complement clauses / modifiers: she says that in examples like *Their announcement that the position has been filled was a surprise*, "the complement specifies the content" of the announcement (Bejan 2005: 190). However, they do not focus on the semantic role as a separate parameter. They rather think that having a content complement correlates with the result reading of the head noun, as opposed to the complex event reading.

with complement clauses, and this fact is also explicable from the value of Feature 3. The nominal argument of *ljubov* (the person, object or situation that is loved) does not have a content role: it is a stimulus. The hypothetical complement would also be a stimulus that exists independently from love itself, but not the content. Recall that the NP hosted by *ljubov* is an argument, and not a modifier (Feature 2).

In other words, the contrast in the ontological type exists in the emotion class. With nouns like *strax* with prospective semantics, the complement clause can have a semantic role of content of emotion (though it seems that there are equally contexts where the complement of *strax* has the role of stimulus). With *ljubov*, complements can only have the role of stimulus. Why must we say that with 'fear' the complement clause consists of content of emotion, while with 'love' it does not? It seems that complements of nouns denoting a prospectively-oriented emotion ('fear') can be assigned the role of content (see below): the emotion has no practical real ground, what causes it is the **probability** of a future situation, which is, thus, contained in the emotion itself, and does not occur before the emotion. Non-prospective emotions are linked to elements of reality ('love' presupposes that the object of love already exists). This is why the complement clause is a stimulus, a reason of love, rather than its content. The embedded situation exists in the real world by itself, and not just as a part of the emotional process.[18]

The fact that *strax* can have a content complement and *ljubov* cannot is verified by the copula criterion:

(32) Strax-ъt   mu   e   če   neminuemo šte   se
     fear-DEF.M.SG.NOM he.DAT   be.PRS.3SG   COMP   inevitably FUT   REFL
     zaraz-i.
     infect.PFV-PRS.3SG
     'His fear is that he will be infected inevitably.'

---

[18] Note that verbs like English *frighten* or its equivalents in some languages (Bulgarian *strax-uvam* 'frighten', Russian *pugat'* 'frighten') have both prospective and non-prospective readings (examples like *It frightened me that she didn't feel well* are perfectly acceptable and found on the Internet). However, it seems that the nominal *strax* 'fear' with complement clauses in Bulgarian is mainly used in prospective contexts, which is predictable given the tendency formulated in 3.1 (in the emotional class, complement clauses are mainly compatible with prospective / unreal nominals). In the prospective use, the stimulus of the fear does not exist before the emotion, which makes the situation with *strax* also predictable from Feature 3.

(33) *Ljubov-ta   mu   e   da   pluva
     fear-DEF.F.SG   he.DAT   be.PRS.3SG   COMP.IRR   swim.IPFV.PRS.3SG
     v   more-to.
     in   sea-DEF.N
     Intended: 'His love is to swim in the sea' (not found).

As mentioned above, the complement of *strax* can equally have the role of stimulus. Thus, the complement clause has mixed properties, which will be relevant for the distribution of definite vs. indefinite forms of the head noun (see below). At the same time, the crucial thing is that the complement of *strax* **can** have the role of content. In this case, the situation denoted by the complement does not exist autonomously from the main situation.

An interesting illustration for the content vs. non-content distinction comes from the fact that with some nouns that are able to take content and non-content arguments complement clauses can only denote the content of the head noun. For instance, the nominal *objasnenie* 'explanation' only occurs with a complement clause if the latter clarifies the content of the explanation ('the explanation containing the following arguments'). By contrast, when the noun *objasnenie* denotes an explanation in the sense 'discovering reason of some situation', 'explanation given for something', the complement clause is impossible. This intuition is confirmed by the fact that with a complement clause, *objasnenie* can occur in a copular construction:

(34) *Naj-udobno-to*   *objasnenie*   *be-še*   *če*
     SUP-convenient-DEF.N   explanation   be-IPF.3SG   COMP
     ima-l-o   *iztičane*   *na*   *atomn-i*
     have.IPFV-PERF.PART-SG.N   leak   of   nuclear-PL
     e
     be.PRS.3SG
     tajn-i.
     secret-PL
     The most convenient explanation was that some 'leak' of secrets related to the nuclear industry has taken place.'

At the same time, the content vs. non-content distinction does not account for the whole distribution of complement clauses. There are head nouns that take complement clauses, but these clauses are not modifiers and do not have the semantic role of content. An interesting case is the noun *nevъzmožnost* 'impossibility', which takes complement clauses, as in (35):

(35) Drazn-eše   go   nevъzmožnost-ta   da
    annoy.IPFV-IPF.3SG he.ACC   impossibility-DEF.F COMP.IRR
    otkri-e   ubediteln-a   pričina   za   ubijstvo-to.
    open.PFV-PRS.3SG   convincing-F.SG   reason   for murder-DEF.N
    'The impossibility of finding a plausible (lit. 'convincing') reason for the murder bothered him.'

Of course, the complement of this noun cannot clarify the content because impossibility, due to its negative semantics, is not conceptualized as a set of possible (or impossible) situations. It is incompatible with the copular construction:

(36) *Naj-glavna-ta   nevъzmožnost   e   da   mu
    SUP-main-DEF.F   impossibility   be.PRS.3SG   COMP.IRR   he.DAT
    govorja.
    speak.IPFV.PRS.1SG
    Intended: 'The main impossibility (for me) is to talk to him.'

Moreover, the clausal complement of *nevъzmožnost* is an argument rather than a modifier. It is impossible to refer to the complement clause using adjectival pronouns like *tazi* 'this (F)'.

However, the noun takes complement clauses, as in (35), which contradicts the general property of other property names like *strannost* 'strangeness', *važnost* 'importance', and so on. The same unusual property characterizes the cognate noun *nevozmožnost'* in Russian. Perhaps, the reason is that the property meaning itself is less focused in the use of *nevъzmožnost* than in the use of *važnost* or *strannost*. However, another possible explanation is that *nevъzmožnost* simply borrows a pattern from the noun *vъzmožnost* without negation.

The same is true for the 'data processing' nominal *dokazatelstvo* 'proof'. Its complement clause, as in (9), repeated here as (37), does not clarify the content of the proof, but denotes the fact being proven (the content clause is only manifested in the copula construction, as in (38)). Thus, the accessibility of complementation with *dokazatelstvo* is not explained by Factor 3. By contrast, *otkritie* 'discovery', as (39) shows, has a content complement clause.

(37) (=9) Tova   šte   e   nedvusmislen-o   dokazatelstvo če
        this.N   FUT   be.PRS.3SG   unambiguous-N   proof   COMP
    v   Kalimport   tajno   se   e   namesti-l-Ø
    in   Kalimport   secretly   REFL   be.PRS.3SG   move.PFV-PERF.PART-SG.M
    nov   igrač.
    new   player

(38) Dokazatelstvoto   mu   e   če   magnetism-a
     proof-DEF.N   he.DAT   be.PRS.3SG   COMP   magnetism-DEF.M.ACC
     mož-e   da   min-e   prez   edn-a   dъska.
     can.IPFV-PRS.3SG   COMP   pass.IPFV-PRS.3SG through one-F   board
     '[Leedskalnin thinks that there is what he calls 'magnetic substance' around each atom. This substance consists of particles smaller than a photon]. His proof of this fact is that magnetism can, for instance, go through a board, and photons are unable to do this.'

(39) Otkritie-to   mu   e,   če   vsjaka   vizitka
     discovery-DEF.N   he.DAT   be.PRS.3SG   COMP   each   visit.card
     kazva-Ø   dostatъčno mnogo   za   nejniy-a   pritežatel.
     say.IPFV-PRS.3SG   rather   much   about   her-DEF.M.ACC   possessor
     'His discovery is that any business card can tell you (rather) much about its possessor.'

The two parameters – the ontological property of having content (and content arguments) and the argument vs. modifier distinction – apparently correlate with each other. Content complements tend syntactically to be modifiers. This is not surprising at all. Content complements only clarify the nature of the head noun but do not introduce a new participant autonomous from the head noun. This is why, syntactically, they tend to be modifiers. The only problem with the two parameters under analysis is that they are not intuitive. It is unclear why, for instance, the complement of *strannost* cannot be interpreted as 'the precise content of the property 'strange'' ('the strange property that is X'), and *ljubov* as 'the content of love that is described as love to do something' ('his love can be precisely formulated as'). Or, for instance, why does *sigurnost* 'certainty' take a content complement, while for *interes* this is impossible?[19]

---

19 I am thankful to an anonymus reviewer for pointing out that the content vs. non-content participant distinction (perhaps, together with the real vs. unreal complement opposition) can be accounted for using the distinction of intensional vs. extensional contexts. I basically agree with this claim, but given that the notion of intensionality is related to reality and the semantic role in a complex way, its integration into the current version of the paper would be inconvenient. I leave the issue of applying this contrast to future studies.

3.4 Feature 4. Generic situations vs. single occurrences

The problem of parameters mentioned here is that each of them accounts only for a part of our sample: for instance, stative nouns like *strannost* are best described by Features 2 and 3, while *dokazatelstvo* is better covered by Grimshaw's aspectual opposition (see Feature 5 for detail). I propose a new parameter that seeks to account for the whole picture: namely, the opposition of the generic **situation** to single **occurrence.** By the **generic situation** I mean the reading in which the nominalization can denote a generalized situation with no reference to the number of occurrences and / or the specific participants. For instance, in (40), *ubijstvo* means 'killing animals, perhaps, for many times':

Russian:
(40) On   by-l-Ø   obvin-en   v   ubijstv-e
      he.NOM   be-PST-SG.M   accuse.PFV-PART.PASS.PST.SG.M   in   killing-SG.LOC
      zver-ej.
      animal-PL.GEN
      'He was accused of killing animals.'

What is relevant here is the very fact that someone killed animals, it does not matter how many and when: (40) can refer to multiple acts of killing animals that took place at different times. Of course, (40) can also be used to denote one act of murder, but this is irrelevant here. What is relevant, is that the generic meaning is also possible. By contrast, in (41), with no argument mentioned, the noun *ubijstvo* 'murder' can refer only to one murder:

Russian:
(41) On   by-l-Ø   obvine-n   v   ubijstv-e.
      he.NOM   be-PST-SG.M   accuse.PFV-PART.PASS.PST.SG.M   in   killing-SG.LOC
      'He was accused of a murder.'

(Rule 4) The data show that **complementation is mostly characteristic of head nouns that mark a single occurrence of the situation.**

Let us look at some arguments in favor of this parameter.
1. Some nouns of 'data processing' like 'proof' that can alternate between the generic situation and the single occurrence reading take CCs only in the latter reading. For instance, both *dokazatelstvo* 'proof' and *otkritie* 'discovery' can be used to express either single occurrences or a generic situation. However, they are compatible with CCs only in a single occurrence reading, as the oddness of (43) and (45) shows:

(42) otkritie-to   na   naj-glavni-te   zakon-i   na fizika]
     discovery-DEF.N   of   SUPERL-main-DEF.PL   law-PL   of physics
     'the discovery of the main physical laws [always takes lots of time]'

(43) #otkritie-(to)   kak   e   ustroen-a   priroda-ta
     discovery-(DEF.N)   how   be.PRS.3SG organized-F.SG   nature-DEF.F
     Intended: 'discovery of how nature is organized'

(44) Pri   dokazatelstvoto   na   teorem-i
     at   proving-DEF.N.SG   of   theorem-PL
     'in the course of proving theorems' (each theorem is proved separately)

(45) #Dokazatelstvo-(to)   če   vseki   ot   nix   e
     prove-DEF.N   COMP   everyone   from   they.OBL   be.PRS.3SG
     vinoven.
     guilty.M
     Intended: 'The proof that each of them is guilty'

Example (43) is either unacceptable or highly dubious in the relevant sense because the head noun *otkritie* is used here as a generic (or repeated) situation, and not a single occurrence ('discovery of multiple and very different aspects of the organization of nature'. Example (45) is acceptable, but only in the meaning where guilt is proven for all the people together, and cannot denote a situation where guilt is proven separately for each person. By contrast, with nominal arguments, the same nouns can serve as names of generic situations. In (42) and (44), *otkritie* and *dokazatelstvo*, respectively, refer to a generalized situation which has a different argument in each individual case. In (42), a different law is discovered in every case, while in (44), different theorems are proven, but the singular form is possible for the generic process.

Note that Grimshaw's account is hardly valid for this verbal noun. *Dokazatelstvo* does not always behave as a result noun – for instance, in (46), it probably points to the process of proving something (= Complex Event) but is compatible with a complement clause.

(46) Za   dokazatelstvo-to   če   izgarjanij-a-ta   ne   bja-xa
     for   proving-DEF.N   COMP   burn-PL-DEF.PL   NEG   be-AOR.3PL
     težk-i   zaspa-x.
     hard-PL   fall.asleep.PFV-AOR.1SG
     'Because I wanted to prove (lit. 'for proving') that the burns were not serious,
     I (deliberately) fell asleep . . .'

2. The same distinction is valid for cognitive nominals, such as the nominals *priznanie* 'declaration, confession, recognition' and *znanie* 'knowledge'. The noun *priznanie* is compatible with complement clauses in different readings (e.g., 'recognition (of some facts, e.g., by state authorities)' or 'declaration (that someone loves another person)'). However, in each of them, *priznanie* is a single occurrence. With a nominal argument, *priznanie* can also denote a generic situation. *Znanie* also behaves as a single occurrence with complement clauses (meaning that it refers to one item of knowledge by one set of people in one situation). By contrast, with NP arguments, *znanie* and *priznanie* can denote a generic situation (for instance, referring to several people and / or several objects of knowledge). Grimshaw's account can hardly account for this fact. Knowledge is stative (contrary to learning something), and it is difficult to classify *znanie* as a Complex Event or Result Nominal. Note, though, that *znanie* has a rather low value in Table 3 (0.03253763), perhaps, because its complement clause does not have the role of content.

I will now show that the single occurrence account covers both accounts that have been considered before. First, single occurrences tend to be denoted by **result nouns**. When the nominalization denotes one occurrence of an event, it is likely that this event has already taken place, and is separable from other possible occurrences. The result is more perceivable and more easily located in time and space. Second, when a nominalization denotes one occurrence of a situation, it is natural if it has **modifiers**. It is already known which occurrence we speak about. Thus, a complement clause can add some (perhaps, unnecessary) information to the description of the event, but does not add an obligatory participant.

The opposition of a single occurrence vs. generic situation seems to be correlated with the (in)ability of the head noun to be pluralized. For example, of the emotion nouns, only *strax* 'fear', is regularly pluralized (2217 occurrences of the plural form *straxove* are found in the BNC). As mentioned above, *strax* can have a complement with the role of stimulus. For the plural *bezpokojstva* 'worries', 312 uses are found (if the plural is chosen, it can, just as in the case of *strax*, reflect the fact that there are several occurrences of the situation 'be worried'). The situation with *ljubov* 'love' is different. Although it is found in plural in 109 cases, they mainly denote the situation of love to another person, and not to a situation. Finally, *učudvanija* 'surprises' is only found once, which corresponds to the fact that *učudvane* denotes a situation in the proper sense and occurs with complement clauses more rarely than 'fear' and 'worry'. However, outside the emotional class, plural forms can hardly serve as a reliable criterion of the single occurrence vs. generic situation distinction.[20]

An important remark should be made here. The generic situation vs. single occurrence opposition cannot be claimed to be the only possible factor to explain the distribution of complement clauses. The differences between complement-taking nominals and those that are incompatible with complements can be accounted for by combining the previous factors with Grimshaw's opposition. However, the opposition of generic situation vs. single occurrence is perhaps the factor that covers the widest set of cases (including 'minimal pairs' where the same noun takes NPs vs. CCs), and this is why it is useful in the analysis.

3.5 Feature 5. Grimshaw's opposition: Result vs. Complex Event reading of the head noun

The opposition of Complex Event Nominals and Result Nominals, introduced by Grimshaw (1990), is useful for the description of Bulgarian nominalizations, but only to some extent. Some cases confirm the relevance of Grimshaw's classes. In those cases, a noun cannot take complement clauses if it denotes a dynamic situation, a process of communication, and so on (in Grimshaw's terms, if it is a Complex Event Nominal). However, they are compatible with complement clauses when they have a stative reading (Grimshaw's Result Nominals), when the process phase, actional and temporal properties are irrelevant.

Among the nouns that mainly behave according to Grimshaw's classification we find *dokazatelstvo* 'proof', that shows the relevance of Grimshaw's actional classes. The vast majority of examples represent the proof as a result, and not as a process.

(47) *tova   šte   e   nedvusmislen-o   dokazatelstvo   če   v*
     this.N FUT be.PRS.3SG unambiguous-N   proof   COMP   in
     Kalimport tajno   se   e   namesti-l-Ø   nov igrač.
     Kalimport secretly REFL be.PRS.3SG move.PFV-PERF.PART-M.SG   new player
     'This will be an unambiguous proof that a new player secretly moved to Kalimport.'

---

[20] As pointed out by an anonymous reviewer, an additional test can be the (im)possibility of temporal and aspectual modifiers, such as *včerašen* 'yesterday's' or *postojanen* 'repeated, constant' with head nouns. I leave this test to future studies.

However, as mentioned in 3.4, even in this case, some non-result examples, such as (46), are found. In other words, the tendency that mainly result nominals take complement clauses is confirmed on Bulgarian data but is not a strict rule. The relevance of Feature 5 is proven by the fact that for some head nouns, the possibility of using a complement clause is not accounted for by Features 1 or 2. At the same time, the applicability of Grimshaw's (1990) classes is restricted. The main restriction is that many nominalizations are derived from stative predicates and are *a priori* stative. Here belong, for instance, nouns like *strannost* 'strangeness', *važnost* 'importance', *vъzmožnost* 'possibility'. Yet, they behave differently with respect to complementation. Thus, Grimshaw's distinction cannot be responsible for cases like this.

3.6 Other features

In this section, I will briefly mention the features that are not highly relevant for the (im)possibility of complementation (or the degree of their relevance remains unclear). Their list includes the syntactic position of the complement and the opposition of complementizers *če* vs. *da*.

3.6.1 Syntactic position of the complement in the base structure

The syntactic position can be responsible for the contrast between *sigurnost* 'sureness' taking complement clauses vs. *strannost* 'strangeness', *važnost* 'importance' that normally do not take them. All of them are derived from adjectives *siguren* 'sure', *stranen* 'strange' and *važen* 'important' by means of the same suffix *-ost*.

(48) Vie   zatvъrždava-te   sigurnost-ta   mu   če   se
     you.NOM   confirm.IPFV-PRS.2PL   sureness-DEF.F   he.DAT COMP   REFL
     e   doveri-l-Ø   imenno   na   vas.
     be.PRS.3SG   trust.IPFV-PERF.PART-M.SG   precisely on   you.ACC
     'You confirm his sureness that he trusted precisely you.'

(49) *strannost-ta   da   prav-ime   tova
     strangeness-DEF.F   COMP.IRR   do.IPFV-PRS.1PL   this
     Intended: 'The strangeness for us to do it.'

The syntactic difference may result from the fact that in the base structure with the adjective, the complement clause occupies different positions. With *strannost* and *važnost*, it is initially a subject of the construction ('the fact P is strange') and is syntactically obligatory.

With *sigurnost*, the complement clause is initially in the position of a peripheral argument (compare (50a) to (50b) where the same adjective expresses the same argument in a prepositional phrase:

(50) a. *Siguren   sъm   če   šte   pobedj-a.*
        sure   be.PRS.1SG   COMP   FUT   win.PFV-PRS.1SG
        'I am sure that I will win.'
     b. *Siguren   sъm   v   pobeda-ta.*
        sure   be.PRS.1SG   in   victory-F.SG
        'I am sure of victory.'

The subject position of (50) is occupied by the Experiencer ('I'), and there is no direct object position. It is well known that peripheral arguments lower than the DO in the syntactic hierarchy do not change their position under nominalization (see Ljutikova 2017). They are not obligatory either in the base structure or in the derived structure (with a nominalization). This is why the peripheral argument of *sigurnost* can be retained.

3.6.2 The choice of irreal complementizer *da* vs. real complementizer *če*

The syntactic strategy of complementation has never been systematically considered as a factor of (im)possibility of a complement clause with a nominal head. For Bulgarian, we could compare complement clauses with the "irreal" complementizer *da* and the "real" complementizer *če* in their ability to be hosted by nominalizations. However, the figures of Table 1 do not confirm the relevance of this feature. Among the nouns allowing for either *da* or *če* (*vъzmožno, nadjavam se, bezpokoja se*), only with the head noun *vъzmožnost* is the proportion of *da* with the noun more significant than with the predicative *vъzmožno*.

Da also outranks *če* with some head nouns that normally do not take complement clauses: for the noun *važnost*, for instance, only one example is found for the combination with *če* and 11 for the variant with *da* (here belong (51) and (52)). However, this distinction is not statistically significant due to the very low frequency of these examples.

(51) *Nikoj   ne   mož-e   da   mi*
     nobody.NOM NEG   can.IPFV-PRS.3SG   COMP.IRR   I.DAT
     otnem-e   važnost-ta   da   razkazva-m
     take.away[pfv]-PRS.3SG   importance-DEF.F   COMP.IRR   tell.IPFV-PRS.1SG
     če   mi   se   e   sluči-l-o.
     COMP   I.DAT   REFL   be.PRS.3SG   happen.PFV-PERF.PART-N.SG
     'Nobody can deny (lit. 'take it away from me') the importance of the fact that I am telling it, that it happened to me.'

(52) *Razočarovan   ot   neuspex-a   i   sъznavašt   mnogo   dobre*
     disappointed   by   fail-DEF.M.ACC   and   realizing   very   well
     važnost-ta   da   zaem-e   ukreplenie-to.
     importance-DEF.F   COMP.IRR   occupy.PFV-PRS.3SG   fortification-DEF.N
     '... disappointed by his failure and realizing very well that it is important (lit. 'the importance') to occupy the fortification.'

Speakers' judgments do not show a high degree of relevance of the complementizer choice either. Nominalizations like *važnost* 'importance' and *strannost* 'peculiarity, strangeness' are not accepted by native speakers, irrespective of the complementizer chosen. One of our native speakers regards all examples like (53)-(54) as strictly impossible. The other speaker supposes that (53) is slightly better than (54) but also not fully acceptable:

(53) *?Govor-eše   za   strannost-ta   da*
     speak.IPFV-IMPF.3SG   about   strangeness-DEF.F   COMP.IRR
     obsъžda-me   Petko   sega.
     discuss.IPFV-PRS.1PL   Petko   now
     'He said that it is strange (lit. 'about the strangeness') to discuss Petko now.'

(54) **Govor-eše   za   strannost-ta   če   Petko*
     speak.IPFV-IMPF.3SG   about   strangeness-DEF.F   COMP   Petko
     zakъsnjava.
     be.late.IPFV.PRS.3SG
     'He said that it is strange (lit. 'about the strangeness') that Petko is late.'

In general, we can see that the (im)possibility of the predicate noun to take complement clauses is not crucially related to the choice of complementizer.

3.7 Summary: Relevant features

I conclude that the distribution of behavior of nominalizations can only be predicted if we have several features: (a) prospective / non-prospective; (b) argument vs. modifier; (c) content vs. non-content semantic role of the complement clause; (d) occurrence vs. situation in the proper sense; and (e) Grimshaw's Complex Event vs. Result distinction. As Table 5 shows, the most relevant are features (b) and (c), strongly correlated to each other, as well as (d).

In the class of property nouns, which are similar to each other in respect to aspectual properties and lexical semantics, complementation is only possible for those nouns with which the complement clause has the role of content and is in fact a modifier, rather than a real argument. The noun 'impossibility' constitutes an exception. The situation in the other classes is more complicated. For instance, in the class of emotional nouns like *strax* 'fear', *bezpokojstvo* 'worry' and *ljubov* 'love', complementation is primarily possible for nouns that **can** have the role of content (prospective nouns) and impossible or dubious when a hypothetical complement clause would have the role of stimulus (retrospective nouns like *ljubov* 'love'). However, even with prospective nouns, the complement clause can equally have the role of stimulus (e.g., stimulus of the fear). Thus, the distinction between content vs. non-content complements is not clear-cut here.

The semantic feature 'content / non-content ontological status' is tightly linked to the syntactic distinction of argument vs. modifier. The status of content, for instance, favors modifier constructions. Content clauses do not introduce an argument as a referent, distinct from the head noun. In contexts like 'the hope that we will win', the clause 'that we will win' makes the the designation 'the hope' more precise. As mentioned above, the argument / modifier (or the content / non-content) parameter is distinct from the aspectual opposition proposed by Grimshaw (1990). We showed that property nouns like *strannost* 'strangeness' or *vъzmožnost* 'possibility' are very similar to each other aspectually, though their complement clauses have different positions and semantic status.

The best property to generalize the behavior of complement clauses in Bulgarian seems to be the situation proper vs. occurrence contrast introduced here. Head nouns better host complement clauses when they denote a single occurrence of the situation, not a generalized situation.

Table 5 below sums up the applicability of each parameter. All nouns under analysis are marked for five parameters: (i) content vs. non-content complement; (ii) complement which is a real argument vs a modifier; (iii) prospective vs. retrospective context; (iv) Result (static) vs. Complex Event (dynamic) read of the construction; and (v) situation proper vs. occurrence.[21]

Table 5: Features of nominalizations in Bulgarian.

	content / non-content	modifier / argument	Prospective / non-prospective	static (Result) / dynamic (Complex Event)	Single occurrence / generic situation
dokazatelstvo	N	A	N	+S / –D	O
*ljubov	N	A	N	S	S
učudvane če?	N	A	N	S	O
učudvane da?	N	A	N	S	O
*važnost če	N	A	P or N	S	S / O
??važnost da	N	A	P or N	S	S
bezpokojstvo	C	A or M	P / N	S	S / O
bezpokojstvo da	C	M	P	S	S / O
strax če	C or N	A or M	P	S	O
strax da	C or N	A or M	P	S	O / S
znanie če	C or N, rather C	A or M	P or N	S	O / ??S
*interes kakvo	C or N, rather C	A?		S	S
cuvstvo če	C	M	P	S	O
nadežda če	C	M	P	S	O
nadežda da	C	M	P	S	O
objasnenie	C	M	N	S / D*	O
otkritie	C	M	N	S	O
razbirane	C or N, rather C	M	P or N	S	O / S
rešenie če	C	M	P	S	O
rešenie da	C	M	P	S	O
vъzmožnost če	C	M	P	S	O
vъzmožnost da	C	M	P	S	O

The table shows a strong correlation between the first two parameters (content / non-content and modifier / argument), which was noted above. The correlation between these two parameters and the prospective / non-prospective feature is

---

[21] This last parameter is only applicable to some nominals under analysis. For instance, nouns like *ljubov* 'love' are derived from static verbs which do not have a dynamic reading.

weaker. The majority of nouns allowing complement clauses has the values (1) prospective, (2) modifier, (3) content, (4) occurrence, and (5) static (Result). At the same time, the fifth parameter (Result / Complex Event) is not always relevant for the (im)possibility of complement clauses in our sample, though it is relevant for other contexts, described by Grimshaw in detail.

4 Article on deverbal nouns

In this section, I will consider an additional feature relevant for noun complementation: namely, the category of definiteness of the head noun. The nominalization can have or lack a definite article. Table 1 shows that the distribution of definite vs. indefinite forms is different for different head nouns. In Bulgarian, definiteness is marked with the definite article that distinguishes gender in the singular (-ъt / -a in masculine, -ta in feminine, and -to in neuter gender) and has a common form -te / -ta for plural (the choice of the article form in plural depends on the form of the plural marker).

It should be noticed that the link between definiteness and the presence of complement clauses can be analyzed in two ways. First, it is possible that definiteness is a separate factor influencing the (im)possibility of complement clauses. Second, it can be claimed that, vice versa, the presence and properties of complement clauses result in definiteness of some deverbal nouns and indefiniteness of others. Below I choose the second line of analysis. Although the presence of the complement clause itself does not always make the use of an article obligatory, it divides the head nouns in two classes, for the first of which the use of an article is rare and for the second frequent and even default.

If we look thoroughly at the data in Table 1, we will see that the nominals under analysis fall into three classes (only some of the nouns are listed below): some of them are primarily used with complement clauses in their definite forms, others are mainly used in the indefinite form, finally, for the third class, the two forms are almost equally frequent.

1) Occurring primarily in the indefinite form: *vъzmožnost* 'possibility', *bezpokojstvo* 'worry', *strax* 'fear'
2) Occurring primarily in the definite form: *čuvstvo* 'feeling, sense', *otkritie* 'discovery', *rešenie* (with *če*) 'decision', *objasnenie* 'explanation'
3) Occurring in the definite and indefinite form with almost the same frequency: *nadežda* 'hope'

The first opposition is between **self-suficient** and **not self-sufficient** head nouns. The prevalence of indefinite forms is primarily found with the name of concrete emotions, such as *strax* 'fear', *bezpokojstvo* 'worry' and *učudvane* 'surprise'. The information that a person experiences fear, surprise or worry is in a sense self-sufficient: we see the type of emotion, though do not understand its content and reason. Thus, these head nouns only need an article if the speaker points to a concrete (e.g., mentioned above in his / her speech) type of surprise and worry. The complement clause does not **classify** the emotion, but makes clear its content and reason. By contrast, nouns favoring definite forms are not self-sufficient. They do not say much about the experiencer's emotional state on their own, as nouns like *strax* 'fear' do. Here belong *znanie* 'knowledge', *razbirane* 'understanding', *čuvstvo* 'feeling', *otkritie* 'discovery', *vъzmožnost* 'possibility', as well as *navik* 'habit', not considered here. It is not useful to say that a person knows something, feels something or that something is possible, while not saying what we are talking about. Thus, the prevalence of definite forms is characteristic for head nouns that have an obligatory semantic argument with the role of **content**, and the head should be not **self-sufficient**.

A related feature is that the definite use favors modifier clauses denoting content and disfavors arguments proper with non-content roles. The proportion of definite uses is greater for head nouns with modifier clauses, such as *nadežda* 'hope', than for ones with argument proper clauses, such as *strax*. We can formulate the difference between 'primarily definite' and 'primarily indefinite' head nouns in the following way:

(55) i. Nouns that have non-content complement clauses or can have either content or non-content clauses, such as *strax* and *bezpokojstvo*, mostly occur without an article. At the same time, it is unclear why *vъzmožnost* mostly occurs without an article.
 ii. Nouns that have a content clause with the status of the modifier and cannot be identified without the embedded situation (are not self-sufficient), such as *čuvstvo* and *otkritie*, mostly occur with an article (the number of definite forms outranks the number of indefinite forms) or are equally frequent with and without it.

Some minimal pairs show that nouns with content complements are really used with a definite article more frequently than those with other types of complements. Here belongs the pair *dokazatelstvo* 'proof' vs. *otkritie* 'discovery', mentioned in Section 3.6. As mentioned, *otkritie* has a content clause, while *dokazatelstvo* does not. *Otkritie* is a primarily definite noun, while *dokazatelstvo* is primarily indefinite.

At the same time, the proposed analsysis faces some problematic cases when the behavior of a noun conflicts with our expectations. For instance, it is surprising that *vъzmožnost* 'possibility' belongs to the primarily indefinite group (6209 definite and 18064 indefinite forms). Perhaps, this means that the complement of this head noun can have a non-content reading ('possibility of [the situation that] Peter will be late'). Interestingly, the noun *nevъzmožnost* appears much more frequently with the definite article: examples like (56) with an article are more frequent than those like (57) without an article (462 and 383 occurences in the corpus, respectively):

(56) *Izdava   nevъzmožnost-ta   da   bъde   pisatel.*
     show[ipfv].PRS.3SG impossibility-DEF.F COMP.IRR   be.FUT.3SG   writer
     'It shows the impossibility of being a writer.'

(57) *nevъzmožnost   da   se   izvъrš-at*
     impossibility   COMP.IRR REFL   carry.out.PFV-PRS.3PL
     izsledovatelski-te   procedur-y.
     research-DEF.PL   procedure-PL
     'Impossibility of carrying out research procedures' (lit. 'for the research procedures to be carried out').

Of course, according to the formulation in (55i-ii) above, *nevъzmožnost* had to disfavor the definite article. *Nevъzmožnost* is a property, and its complement does not have the role of content. The case of 'possibility' and 'impossibility' makes us consider the possibility that the surprising figures result from the non-uniformity of the use of the article. I propose that we have to distinguish between two types of article uses. They can be called 'classifying' and 'individuating'. For the description of Bulgarian complementation, mainly the classifying type is relevant.

The classifying type of definiteness: 'the abstract object denoted by the noun X with a complement clause P is definite because the stimulus, content or other element denoted by P is different from the stimuli or contents that other referents of X have. Under this reading, in the construction *vъzmožnost-ta da se porazxod-im* [possibility-DEF.SG.F COMP.IRR REFL walk-PRS.1PL] 'the possibility for us to walk', the word *vъzmožnost-ta* is definite because it denotes the possibility to walk as opposed to other possibilities (e.g., to smoke, to swim in the sea or to play chess). It, thus, does not require any contextual support to be definite.

The discourse type of definiteness: 'the abstract object denoted by the noun X with a complement clause P is definite because the same referent has already been mentioned or is referentially accessible to the speaker and the addressee.

Under this reading, in the construction *vъzmožnost-ta da se porazxod-im* [possibility-DEF.SG.F COMP.IRR REFL walk-PRS.1PL] 'the possibility for us to walk', the word *vъzmožnost-ta* is definite because this possibility to walk has already been mentioned.[22]

Some problematic cases, such as *nevъzmožnost* 'impossibility', which is primarily definite, can be explained by the discourse use of the article: in the examples where the definite form *nevъzmožnost-ta* 'the impossibility' is used, the article is used because the fact that P is impossible has already been mentioned. We expect that the two uses of the article also differ statistically. To show this, let us compare the use of several nominals with a prepositional phrase with *na* 'of' to their use with a complement clause. We expect that if the definite form of the nominal mainly has a classifying use with a complement clause, the percent of definite forms will be larger with complement clauses than with *na*-phrases: complement clauses are often content modifiers that clarify the nature of the head noun, while this function is not characteristic of *na*-phrases. By contrast, the discourse use of the article does not seem to be linked to the distinction between complement clauses vs. *na*-phrases: either a construction with a complement clause or a structure with a PP can have been previously mentioned in the discourse. This difference is confirmed by the data of Table 6. Head nouns that have an article with CCs more often than with PPs are marked with bold, and these results are more explainable than just the proportion of the definite form (Table 1). For instance, let's take the pair *vъzmožnost* vs. *nevъzmožnost*. *Vъzmožnost* is used with the definite article more frequently if there is a complement clause. By contrast, with *nevъzmožnost*, the presence of the article is even more frequent with nominal arguments, which presupposes the discourse use of the article. The same distinction is found in the cognitive group. The presence of the complement clause favors the definite article with the noun *otkritie*, but not with *dokazatelstvo* – the latter, by contrast, shows a greater frequency of definite forms when used with an NP argument. Thus, only with *otkritie* does the definite article have a classifying function and is it favored by the presence of the complement clause that explains the nature of the discovery. With *dokazatelstvo*, the large number of definite forms with NPs demonstrates the discourse function of the article: perhaps, *dokazatelstvo* is used in the definite form when the author speaks about an individual, concrete proof (e.g., the proof that has been proposed for an argument in the discussion or a mathematical theorem and is known from the pretext). Finally, in the emotional group, the head noun *čuvstvo*

---

[22] It seems that the demonstrative pronoun *tozi* 'this' also has these two types of uses, but this discussion is beyond the scope of this article.

'feeling, sense' demonstrates the prevalence of the definite form only when used with a complement clause, which also confirms the classifying function of the article. The same is true for the nominal *strax* 'fear', though the proportion of definite uses is rather low even with a complement clause.

Table 6: Proportion of definite vs. indefinite forms with complement clauses and with nominal arguments.

	- DEF	+ DEF	Proportion (+ DEF / − DEF)
nevъzmožnost da 'impossibility to'	383	462	1.21
nevъzmožnost na 'impossibility of'	43	68	1.58
vъzmožnost da 'possibility to'	18064	6209	0.34
vъzmožnost na 'possibilty of'	3698	839	0.23
čuvstvo če 'feeling that'	**1668**	**11679**	**7**
čuvstvo na 'feeling of'	5649	1937	0.34
otkritie če 'discovery that'	**104**	**394**	**3.79**
otkritie na 'discovery of'	**235**	**495**	**2.11**
dokazatelstvo če 'proof that'	2230	132	0.06
dokazatelstvo na 'proof of'	309	131	0.42
strax če 'fear that'	2005	701	0.35
strax ot 'fear of'	14551	2339	0.16

If we only consider the nouns marked with bold, we will see that these are mainly head nouns with a content modifier, with the exception of *strax*, which is compatible with content modifiers, as well as with stimulus complements.

5 Conclusions

In this paper, I analyzed the distribution of complement-taking nouns and nouns that are incompatible with complement clauses in Bulgarian. The results show that Bulgarian nominalizations significantly vary in their ability or inability to take complement clauses. It turns out that the following parameters define the (im)possibility of complement clauses: (i) real (non-prospective) vs. unreal (prospective) semantics of the embedded clause; (ii) the modifier / argument status of the 'complement' clause and (iii) the content / non-content semantic role; (iv) the opposition of generic situations vs. single occurrences of the situation and (v) Grimshaw's nominalization type (actional class).

The first three parameters are correlated to each other and to the semantic class of the head noun: for instance, 'retrospective' feelings and emotions, such as 'surprise' and 'love', are not well compatible with complement clauses, because their hypothetical complements would have the role of stimulus and the status of 'real' arguments. By contrast, the 'prospective' feeling 'fear' has a complement clause with the role of content. The reason is that in the prospective class, the emotion is not directed to any real situation. Thus, there is no independent (or partially independent) stimulus argument. What we consider to be the stimulus of someone's fear, is in fact a modifier which helps to define the nature and the content of the fear. The situation is more complicated with *bezpokojstvo* 'worry', which can be either prospective or retrospective. We propose that our distinctions cannot be reduced to one parameter, though the most relevant opposition in our sample is between complement clauses with different semantic roles (content / non-content complement clauses).

The opposition of 'generic situations' and 'single occurrences' (3.4), introduced here, is, perhaps, the most important parameter. On the one hand, it correlates with the actional class: for instance, result nouns tend to denote definite realizations and not just an indefinite number of realizations of the situation. Second, for the behavior of stative nominals like 'possibility', 'importance' or 'strangeness', that is not accounted for by Grimshaw's classes, the single occurrence vs. generic situation opposition is also relevant. Only stative nouns that behave as names of single occurrences can take complement clauses.

We have also determined that the differences between head nouns do not always follow from Grimshaw's classification. For instance, both *važnost* 'importance' and *vъzmožnost* 'possibility' denote the property of the situation which, in turn, is denoted in the complement clause. They can hardly be argued to belong to different Grimshaw classes. This leads us to the conclusion that the semantics of the head noun is also relevant: concrete properties, such as 'importance', 'strangeness' and others disallow complement clauses, while nouns like 'possibility' are compatible with them. This semantic parameter can be formulated in other terms: property nouns are mainly compatible with complement clauses that clarify the content of the head noun. They make the semantics of the head noun more explicit, e.g., make it clear which possibility we are speaking about. At the same time, the two types of property nouns also differ in the syntactic respect: with *važnost*, the complement clause would really be an argument, while with *vъzmožnost*, the complement clause occupies in reality a modifier position. Note though, that the precise syntactic status of complement clauses may require additional syntactic tests. The same opposition between content and non-content complements (and, correspondingly, between modifiers and 'real arguments') is relevant outside the property class, but not to the same degree. For instance, in the cognitive class, both *otkritie* 'discovery' and *dokazatelstvo* 'proof' are compatible with complement clauses, though the clause has the role of content in the former case and another role in the latter one. In this case, Grimshaw's classes can be relevant: both *otkritie* and *dokazatelstvo* are result nouns.

In other words, Grimshaw's (1990) opposition of Result Nominals vs. Complex Event Nominals does not seem to account for the whole set of Bulgarian data. Her other claim, that nominals are not case licensers and usually do not have real arguments, can be true for an even greater part of the data. We noted that 'real arguments' are less acceptable for nouns than modifiers. This claim is to be checked by syntactic tests, but it seems natural to suppose that the noun *vъzmožnost* has a complement clause that modifies the head noun (this is why it can be referred to an adjectival pronoun); the reason is that for *važnost*, the complement must be case-marked (just as genitive NPs), while for *vъzmožnost*, this is not the case. However, the complement of *dokazatelstvo* does not behave as a modifier. As mentioned before, the generic situation vs. single occurrence account can also be relevant here.

It appears that some head nouns choose the definite, and others the indefinite form. The presence / absence of the article is regulated by semantic and syntactic factors: the prevalence (or, at least, high frequency) of definite forms is characteristic of head nouns that have an obligatory complement clause with modifier properties and a content semantic role (cf. *otkritie* 'discovery'). The highest proportion of definite uses is characteristic of nouns with a very general meaning like *čuvstvo* 'feeling' that are not interpretable without their complement clauses. If the complement can have either content or non-content properties, and the complement situation exists autonomously from the head noun, indefinite forms tend to prevail. However, some particular cases remain unclear: for instance, it is unexplained why *otkritie* 'discovery' is primarily used in the definite form, and for *vъzmožnost* 'possibility', the indefinite form is more frequent. A more detailed semantic and syntactic analysis is necessary to account for this sort of individual difference.

I conclude that all features, mentioned above: the retrospective vs. prospective type, the content vs. non-content semantic role, the modifier vs. argument status, the Result vs. Complex Event reading, and generic situation vs. single occurrence, are only concurring factors that can be relevant for the (im)possibility of complementation. Neither of them can be regarded as the sole factor describing all the cases under analysis. In general, our data confirm Grimshaw's claim that complement clauses are mostly not canonical arguments of their head nouns. However, the fact that complement clauses of nouns are not canonical arguments is not reducible to one feature: complement clauses are different from canonical arguments in multiple respects. This, in turn, leads us to the conclusion that the set of possible complements of nouns is not automatically inherited from the base predicate, but rather licensed separately by the noun.

Abbreviations

1, 2, 3	1st, 2nd, 3rd person
AOR	aorist
COMP	'real' / default complementzer *če*
COMP.IRR	'unreal' complementizer *da*
DAT	dative
DEF	definite article
F	feminine gender
FUT	future tense
IPF	imperfect
M	masculine gender
N	neuter gender
NOM	nominative
PERF.PART	perfect participle (*l*-participle)
PL	plural
PRS	present tense
REFL	reflexive
SG	singular
SUP	superlative

References

Apresjan, Jurij D. 1974. *Leksičeskaja semantika* [Lexical semantics]. Moscow: Nauka.

Bejan, Camelia. 2005. Nominalizations in English and German. Bucharest: Bucharest University dissertation. Unpublished PhD thesis.

Cinque, Guglielmo & Iliyana Krapova. 2016. On noun clausal "complements" and their non-unitary nature. *Annali di Ca' Foscari. Serie occidentale* 50. 77–107.

Culicover, Peter & Ray Jackendoff. 2005. *Simpler syntax*. Oxford: Oxford University Press.

Culicover, Peter. 1997. *Principles and parameters: An introduction to syntactic theory*. Oxford: Oxford University Press.

Culicover, Peter & Ray Jackendoff. 1997. Semantic subordination despite syntactic coordination. *Linguistic Inquiry* 28. 195–217.

Davies, William, and Stanley Dubinsky. 2009. On the existence (and distribution) of sentential subjects. In Donna B. Gerdts, John C. Moore & Maria Polinsky (eds.), *Hypothesis A/hypothesis B: Linguistic explorations in honor of David M. Perlmutter*, 111–128. Cambridge, MA: MIT Press.

Dobrušina, Nina R. 2016. *Soslagatel'noe naklonenie v russkom jazyke: Opyt issledovanija grammatičeskoj semantiki* [Subjunctive mood in Russian: A study of grammatical semantics]. Prague: Animedia.

Grimshaw, Jane. 1990. *Argument structure*. Cambridge, MA: MIT Press.

Gusev, Valentin Ju. 2004. Celevyje konstrukcii pri glagolax dviženija: aktanty ili sirkonstanty? [Purpose constructions with motion verbs: arguments or adjuncts?] *International symposium on typology of the argument structure and grammatical relations in languages spoken in Europe and North and Central Asia*. Kazan: Kazan State University.

Hansen, Bjoern, Alexander Letuchiy & Isabella Blaszczyk. 2016. Complementizers in Slavonic. In Kasper Boye & Petar Kehayov (eds.), *Complementizer semantics in European languages*, 175–224. Berlin & Boston: De Gruyter Mouton.

Iordanskaja, Lidia N. 1992. Popytka leksikografičeskogo tolkovanija gruppy russkix slov so značeniem čuvstva [Towards a lexicographic description of a group of Russian words with semantics of feeling]. *Mašinnyj perevod i prikladnaja lingvistika* [Machine translation and applied linguistics] 13. 13–26.

Kayne, Richard. 2008. Antisymmetry and the lexicon. *Linguistic Variation Yearbook* 8. 1–31.

Knyazev, Misha. 2014. Structural licensing of sentential complements: evidence from Russian noun-complement constructions. In Larisa Avram (ed.), *Bucharest Working Papers in Linguistics* 2, 21–45. Bucharest: Bucharest University Press.

Lehmann, Christian. 1984. *Der Relativsatz (Typologie seiner Strukturen. Theorie seiner Funktionen. Kompendium seiner Grammatik)*. Tübingen: Narr.

Letučij, Aleksandr B. 2012. O nekotoryx svojstvax sentencial'nyx aktantov v russkom jazyke [On some properties of complement clauses in Russian]. *Voprosy jazykoznanija* 5. 57–87.

Ljutikova, Ekaterina A. 2017. *Struktura imennoj gruppy v bezartiklevom jazyke* [The structure of noun phrase in a language without an article]. Moscow: Jazyki slavjanskoj kul'tury.

Mauri, Caterina & Andrea Sansò. 2012. What do languages encode when they encode reality status? *Language Sciences* 34. 99–106.

Mauri, Caterina & Andrea Sansò. 2016. The linguistic marking of (ir)realis and subjunctive. In Jan Nuyts & Johan van der Auwera (eds.), *The Oxford Handbook of Mood and Modality*, 166–195. Oxford: Oxford University Press.

Mel'čuk, Igor' A., Aleksandr K. Žolkovskij et al. 1984. *Tolkovo-kombinatornyj slovar' russkogo jazyka. Opyt semantiko-sintaksičeskogo opisanija russkoj leksiki* [Explanatory and combinational dictionary of Russian. Semantic and syntactic descriptions of Russian lexics]. Vienna: Wiener Slawistischer Almanach.

Pazel'skaya, Anna. 2006. Argument structure in Russian deverbal nouns in *-nie*. Handout for a talk at the FDSL 2006 conference.

Plungjan, Vladimir A. & Anna Ju. Urmančieva (eds.). 2004. *Irrealis i irreal'nost'*. Moscow: Gnozis.

Polinsky, Maria. 2013. Raising and control. In Marcel den Dikken (ed.), *The Cambridge Handbook of Generative Syntax*, 577–606. Cambridge: Cambridge University Press.

Simeonova, Vesela. 2019. Flavors of predicate modification. In Eszter Ronai, Laura Stigliano, Yenan Sun (eds.), *Proceedings of CLS 54 Conference*, 477–492. Chicago: Chicago University Press.

Stowell, Tim. 1981. *Origins of phrase structure*. Cambridge: Massachusetts Institute of Technology dissertation.

Stojnova, Natal'ja M. Celevoj infinitiv [The infinitive of purpose]. Ms.

Stojnova, Natal'ja M. 2016. Kontrol' bessojuznogo celevogo infinitiva pri glagolax kauzacii dviženija v russkom jazyke: dannye NKRJa (Control of the infinitive in Purpose Constructions with Causation-of-motion Verbs in Russian: Evidence from the Russian National Corpus). In Vladimir P. Selegej (ed.), *Komp'juternaja lingvistika i intellektual'nye texnologii* 15 (22). *Trudy konferencii "Dialog-2016"*, 733–745. Moscow: RGGU.

Testelec, Jakov G. 2001. *Vvedenie v obščij sintaksis* [Introduction to general syntax]. Moscow: RGGU.

Uhlik, Mladen & Andreja Žele. 2018. *Da*-predloženija pri glagolax želanija i pobuždenija v slovenskom jazyke [*Da*-sentences with wish and causation verbs in Slovene]. *Voprosy jazykoznanija* 5. 87–113.

Ross, J.R. 1967. *Constraints on variables in syntax*. Cambridge: Massachusetts Institute of Technology dissertation.

Wiemer, Björn. 2017. Main clause infinitival predicates and their equivalents in Slavic: Why they are not instances of insubordination. In Łukasz Jędrzejowski & Ulrike Demske (eds.), *Infinitives at the Syntax-Semantics Interface: A Diachronic Perspective*, 265–338. Berlin & Boston: De Gruyter Mouton.

Wiemer, Björn. 2018. On triangulation in the domain of clause linkage and propositional marking. In Björn Hansen, Jasmina Grković-Major & Barbara Sonnenhauser (eds.), *Diachronic Slavonic Syntax*, 285–338. Berlin & Boston: De Gruyter Mouton.

Iliyana Krapova
Complementizers and particles inside and outside of the left periphery: The case of Bulgarian revisited

Abstract: The paper discusses the organization of the left periphery in Bulgarian and argues that it has a rich articulation guided by the general syntactic principles as established on a wide cross-linguistic basis. Bulgarian shows several points of dissociation with respect to the original theoretical template established by Rizzi's 1997 seminal work. The paper discusses these points and brings new empirical evidence about the hierarchical ordering of complementizers in Bulgarian. The evidence shows that the declarative complementizer is merged in a low position within the left periphery and may optionally raise to the position related to the illocutionary force of the embedded clause, while the interrogative complementizers dispose of different and higher dedicated positions, as inferred from their relative order with respect to different types of contrastively focussed phrase. The paper also discusses the controversial modal particle *da* and argues that it does not occupy a position within the left periphery but given the independently established left peripheral positions, a mechanism is proposed about how its modal and finiteness features are related to selection and to veridicality as the guiding principle behind the organization of the left periphery of Bulgarian.

Keywords: Bulgarian, left periphery, complementizer, complement clause, illocutionary force, declarative, interrogative, polarity, indirect questions, unselected questions, topic, Aboutness Topic, Given Topic, Contrastive Topic, focus, Contrastive Focus, question particle, (non-)veridicality, propositional predicate, mood, modal marker, realis-irrealis, factive, finiteness

1 Introduction

In this paper, I will discuss the syntax of Bulgarian complementizers from the point of view of Rizzi's (1997) theory that embedded clauses have a left periphery which is richer than usually thought. The term *left periphery* refers to that area of the syntactic representation of the clause where various contextually relevant

---
Iliyana Krapova, University Ca' Foscari of Venice, Dorsoduro 3199, Venice, Italy,
e-mail: krapova@unive.it

https://doi.org/10.1515/9783110725858-004

sentential elements are encoded in order for the sentence to connect to preceding discourse. In embedded clauses, this is also the area where complementizers are located whose main function is to serve as syntactic elements connecting the matrix with the embedded clause. Following the Split CP approach originally proposed by Rizzi (1997), I will show that the left periphery of the embedded clause of Bulgarian is a richly articulated area and contains various positions organized in a hierarchical way. To do so, I will look in more detail at the syntax of the complementizer system of Bulgarian in relation to those discourse properties that express the informational articulation of the structure. Most authors that have worked on Bulgarian complementizers so far (Rudin 1993, Rudin et al. 1999; Bošković 2001; Franks and Rudin 2005; Dukova-Zheleva 2010, a.o.) have posited a single C position hosting each particular complementizer and have proposed various adjunction positions to deal with discourse-related phrases. In this paper, I will argue that a Split CP approach offers more precise and more refined theoretical tools that can help us account for issues of both order and interpretation of the elements potentially (co-)occurring within the CP area of the Bulgarian clause. The syntactic analysis I will propose will therefore seek to account for some not quite well understood phenomena regarding the interaction between Topic/Focus phrases on the one hand and the complementizer area on the other.

Like other Balkan languages, Bulgarian is a language with quite a rich complementizer system whereby, as I will argue, each complementizer occupies a distinct syntactic left peripheral position consistent with its functional-semantic specification. In this paper, I will consider the declarative complementizer *če* 'that' and the interrogative complementizers *dali* and *li* 'if/whether'. For lack of space, other conjunctions and relative pronouns used as complementizers will remain outside the scope of the paper: the conditional complementizer *ako* 'if', the relative complementizer *kogato* 'when' used to introduce adverbial (temporal) clauses and the two factive *wh*-complementizers *deto* 'that' and *kak* 'how'. Concerning the complementizers under study, I will discuss the preliminary hierarchy shown in (1), harmonized with the template discussed in Wiemer (this volume) and will advance arguments as to their relative order with respect to other elements that occupy distinct positions within the left periphery:

(1) CORE 1 (matrix clause) COMP 1   COMP 2 (dependent clause)
　　　　　　　　　　　　dali/li   če

The paper is organized as follows. In section 1, I briefly introduce the basic conceptual tenets that underlie the view, elaborated originally in Rizzi (1997) and further elaborated in a series of works (see Rizzi 2001, 2013, 2014; Rizzi and Bocci 2017), namely that all languages avail themselves of a Split CP system in which categories like complementizers, question operators, modal particles and other "function words" that languages use to connect CORE 2 to CORE 1 target different functional projections in the space between them.

In section 2, I discuss general issues of distribution and selection involving the complementizers under study and their relative order with respect to the discourse projections that inhabit the COMP area. In section 3, I discuss the syntactic status of the much debated particle *da*, sometimes argued to be a complementizer of the irrealis type, and will show that it does not belong to the CP domain but is rather a modal particle within the functional domain of CORE2, in accord with my previous work on this topic (Krapova 2001).

2 The left periphery of CORE2 according to Rizzi (1997)

In the Government and Binding framework of Chomsky (1981), only one head position and only one maximal projection position, i.e. only one position where a phrase XP can appear, are available on the left of the subject (NP). This is illustrated in the following structural representation:

(2) [$_{CP}$ XP [C [$_{IP}$ NP [$_{Infl}$ Agr(eement) M(ood) T(ense) [$_{VP}$ V]]]
                    $\underbrace{\hspace{6cm}}_{\text{CORE2}}$

In (2), CORE 2 corresponds to what in standard generative grammar terms is known as IP involving the various CORE2-internal functional projections related to verbal tense, mood and agreement and located outside of the lexical projection of the V system (VP). Although C(OMP) too is a syntactic head, it is fundamentally different from the functional array of projections in CORE2 in that it can only host complementizers, connectors or particles serving to introduce the subordinate IP clause and to connect it to CORE1, as in *John thinks **that** Mary left*.

It is generally assumed that the category 'complementizer', introduced as early as Bresnan (1972) and further elaborated in Chomsky (1986), conflates two functions: syntactically, it indicates clause type, which, in its traditional understanding, captures basic structural properties of clauses that underlie their interpretation, i.e., whether the clause is a root or a subordinate one, or whether it is a declarative, an interrogative, an imperative or an optative.[1] Complementizers also signal the conversational uses conventionally associated with the various clause types: thus a declarative complementizer introduces a declarative clause corresponding to an assertion, an interrogative complementizer – a clause corresponding to a question, while a modal complementizer of sorts typically introduces a modalized clause expressing a requirement or a wish (Portner 2009: 258).

Rizzi (1997) proposes that these distinctions are structurally represented in a uniform way across languages. Apart from this conceptual claim he also advances the hypothesis that the CP does not correspond to a single maximal projection but should rather be conceived as an "area" or "zone" hosting various functional projections with a fixed semantic/functional specification and rigidly ordered among each other as in (3).

(3) V_{matrix}....[$_{ForceP}$ Force[Topic [Focus.... [$_{FinP}$ Finiteness   [$_{IP}$]]]]]]
     CORE 1   CP-area   CORE 2

The two projections – ForceP and FinP – delimit the boundaries of the CP area and are located at the interface with CORE1 and CORE2, respectively. The projection of ForceP encodes properties relating to clause type and illocutionary force. ForceP is the highest projection of the CP domain, one that establishes a local relation with CORE1 and is directly accessible to it for the purposes of selection (the main predicate or some other element within CORE 1, e.g. the head of a relative clause). The projection that closes off the CP domain from below is Fin(iteness)P expressing distinctions pertaining to the (non-)finiteness character of CORE 2, i.e., information that "faces the inside, the content of the IP embedded under it" (Rizzi 1997: 283). As the label indicates, the role of Fin is to structurally distinguish finite from non-finite embedded clauses, but it also encodes related properties pertaining to tense,

---

[1] Clause types (also labelled sentence moods) express concepts related to belief, knowledge, truth and the speaker's commitment to the truth of the proposition (Nordström 2010: 41), so they are also closely related to distinctions like *realis-irrealis* or *factual-non-factual* (see Wiemer this volume), which also determine the choice of verbal mood (indicative vs. subjunctive) within CORE2. Thus, while an assertion would typically be encoded in the indicative, a request or a wish would typically be encoded in the subjunctive. Even though there is a close correspondence between clause type and illocutionary force, Portner (2009) notes that the two should be kept apart because the correspondence is not absolute. For example, (i) has the clause type of an assertion but its illocutionary force is that of a request:

(i) *I wonder if you can tell me the time.*

In what follows, I will assume that as far as sentence structure is concerned, clause type matches illocutionary force at least in typical contexts, leaving aside the pragmatic aspects of the relation between clause type/sentence mood and illocutionary force/speech act mood. See also Cristofaro (2003) and Nordström (2010) for a discussion regarding embedded clauses.

agreement and modality. These properties are then "passed down" to CORE2 and in general serve as some sort of "instruction" about the exact morphological make-up of the embedded verb. As an abstract conceptual category, Fin correlates with those language specific morphological properties encoded in the Infl space of CORE2 (see (2) above) that are responsible for anchoring of the embedded tense to the speech context, as well as for the various mood distinctions expressed on the embedded verb or on other elements (such as negation, location markers, etc.). For example, a declarative embedded clause i.e., one whose Force is marked as declarative,[2] would typically have its Fin specified as [+finite] in virtue of having independent temporal reference and indicative modality. On the other hand, the Fin of a modalized clause, given the variety of modal meanings languages express, can be specified for one or more features from the domain of non-indicative modality, often correlating with non-finiteness or with temporally dependent event anchoring. This then will determine the choice of a subjunctive or an infinitive, or of some other type of non-affirmative mood marking on the verb according to the morphological inventory of the language.[3] In more recent accounts, Fin is also exploited as a host for other abstract features relating the embedded clause to the context of speech, like Speech Act distinctions, Speech event anchoring, Assertion Time, logophoricity, etc. (see discussion and references in Eide 2016).

Interspersed between Force and Fin are the discourse-related projections like the ones hosting topicalized and focalized phrases. There is ample evidence that in many languages such phrases occupy left-peripheral positions, so assuming these positions to be fixed within the CP domain they can serve as useful diagnostics for evaluating the positional evidence coming from the distribution of complementizers and their interpretive import with respect to both CORE1 and CORE2. For example, Rizzi argues that, in Italian, the complementizers *che* 'that' and *di* 'of' (the infinitival complementizer) have a different distribution with respect to topics or focussed phrases: such phrases follow the declarative complementizer *che* but precede the prepositional complementizer *di* so that they are ordered as in (4):

---

[2] Quite obviously, Force has access to the informational content encoded in Fin and *vice versa*, so that if for example the clause represents an assertion embedded under a declarative complementizer (e.g., after 'bridge' verbs like *say*, *believe*, etc.), the indicative would be chosen. If on the other hand the clause expresses a requirement, a wish or an order, embedded under a modal complementizer, the subjunctive will be chosen (if the language possesses such morphology) or a special type of tense marking.

[3] Rizzi's system thus aptly differentiates the broader category of *modality* that can be said to featurally reside in Fin from the more narrow category of mood, which is by necessity instantiated within the IP domain/CORE2. "[M]ood correlates with a verbal form and composes a paradigm within the verbal system of a certain language, whereas the instantiations of modality are not necessarily associated with the verb" (Sampanis 2012: 72). See also Quer (2006) and a discussion in Palmer (2001).

(4) Force   Top   Foc   Fin [+/-finite]
    che   topic focus di

Left peripheral topics and focus contribute to the informational organization of the embedded clause via two well-known articulations: Topic-Comment and Focus-Presupposition.[4]

The order in (4) is thus a direct reflex of the fact that topic and focus phrases have interpretive (semantic-pragmatic) properties which force them to move to a dedicated position (criterial head) within the left-periphery (Top, Foc) for purposes of discourse-scope (Rizzi 2014). Apart from positional evidence justifying the relative order between the two complementizers (an empirical generalization) there are also conceptual reasons behind this order (an explanatory generalization). Since the syntactic component of natural language is at the interface with the sound system on the one hand (given the specific intonational contours with which topics and focussed phrases are pronounced), and with the semantics and pragmatics system on the other (given the ways they connect to previous discourse in terms of notions such as *newness* and *givenness*) it is expected that at the "[a]t the interfaces, the criterial heads and features activate the relevant interpretive routines of semantic-pragmatic interpretation, and determine the appropriate prosodic contour assignment, respectively" (Rizzi and Bocci 2017: 12). Therefore, in Rizzi's understanding pragmatic properties are directly encoded in syntax and interfere with other elements located in the left periphery. See also Grimshaw's (1979: 317) conclusion: "treating complement selection syntactically is possible only if the relevant aspects of semantic interpretation are built into syntactic structure".

Parametric variation may regard cross-linguistic selectional differences (i.e., which elements of CORE1 select which kinds of lexically filled C positions) but also number and order of the available C positions. All of these depend on

---

[4] According to Rizzi (2014), the head Top takes the entire complement as its Comment, while the head Foc takes the entire complement as its Presupposition:

(i) [. . . . . . .] Top [. . . . .]
     'Topic'   'Comment'
(ii) [. . . . . . .] Foc$_x$ [. . . . .]
     Focus$_x$ 'Presupposition'

Foc$_x$ refers to the particular kind of focus import in the left periphery: contrastive, corrective, exhaustive or mirative (see discussion in Dal Farra 2016; Bianchi et al. 2015, 2016, and below). Presupposition refers to notions like *givenness*, as in the classical terminology going back to Jackendoff (1972) and Chomsky (1972). Rizzi also notes that as far as (i) is concerned, the interpretive conditions on comments are extremely weak: presumably the only requirement is that the comment should contain focal information, just to make the statement informative.

language-specific properties of grammar. Certain languages like the Balkan ones, given their more analytic character, exploit a greater number of lexical items in a finer-grained left periphery, which allows for a greater freedom of combinations among the complementizers themselves as well as with respect to discourse phrases (Roussou 2000, 2010; Hill 2002, 2004, a.o.). On the other hand, Slavic languages seem to use a more limited number of complementizers (basically three – a declarative, an interrogative, and a subjunctive one) and moreover, they appear to have fixed positions within the CP area. This however does not exclude the possibility that complementizers can be multifunctional in some cases and may target more than one position (cf. e.g., Kašpar 2015 on *že* 'that' in Czech).

Although Rizzi's (1997) argument is based mainly on Italian, it served as a benchmark for pursuing interesting comparative analyses.[5] It was soon extended to Romance and Germanic, where complementizers like *che* (*que* of Romance), as well as English *that*, German *dass*, etc. lexically realize the Force position in finite clauses and are to be distinguished from prepositional complementizers like e.g., English *for*, *di/de* of Romance, etc. which typically lexicalize the lower (non-finite) Fin position and are also relevant for the purposes of Case assignment to the embedded subject as in e.g., English *I want for* [*John*-Acc] *to leave* (exceptional case marking).

The goal of this section was to make it clear that although Rizzi's elaboration of the CP area (see in particular Rizzi 2013, 2014) incorporates a number of theory-internal premises, e.g., the role of the interface conditions, the necessity of a phrase to undergo movement to the left periphery for discourse-scope/interpretive reasons, etc., his conclusions have a much wider empirical validity than usually expected from a generative-type approach.

3 Exploring the Bulgarian left periphery

In this section, I will explore the left periphery of the Bulgarian embedded clause and will discuss some syntactic and semantic facts that have not been observed so far but in my view are highly relevant for understanding the precise distribution of the declarative and the interrogative complementizers.

---

5 Rizzi's theory is part of what is known as "the cartographic research project" within generative linguistics whose basic idea is that syntactic representations are complex objects consisting of sequences of hierarchically organized functional elements" (Rizzi and Bocci 2017: 1) and moreover, that there is a systematic matching between morphosyntactic and semantic features and functional projections, providing "as precise and detailed maps as possible of syntactic configurations" (Cinque and Rizzi 2010: 58).

3.1 Distribution of declarative and interrogative complementizers

The complementizer system of Bulgarian contains several functional items that can be said to occupy a left peripheral position given that they appear to the left of the embedded subject marking the edge of IP (for an early account see Krapova 2002): the declarative complementizer *če* 'that' and the interrogative markers *dali* 'if/whether' and *li* (the clitic variant of *dali*). The complementizer status of these lexical elements (particles in more traditional descriptions) is well-established since early work on Bulgarian generative syntax (Rudin 1986; Penčev 1998). More attention has been given to the particle *li*, which according to some early accounts (Izvorski 1995) does not belong to the complementizer system but is a marker of focalization. See Dukova-Zheleva (2010) for an extensive recent account and § 3.3.2 for more details. Also debatable from point of view of distribution, position and interpretation are the properties of the modal particle *da*. As is well-known, this particle is typically (though not exclusively) related to the expression of modality in constructions usually labelled 'Balkan-type subjunctives'[6] and evolved as a result of the characteristic loss (or drastic reduction) of the infinitive in the Balkan languages. The concept 'Balkan subjunctive' however has turned out to be rather misfortunate since there is no verbal subjunctive morphology in these languages, though the verb in the indicative may show signs of either finiteness or of non-finiteness according to the specific syntactic configuration in which the 'subjunctive' occurs (see Krapova and Cinque 2018 for more details). This ambiguity, arguably attributed to the modal particle itself, raises the question of its syntactic position within the Infl area of CORE2 or – alternatively – within the C-domain (see Rivero 1994; Rudin 1993; Krapova 1999, 2001, and especially Pitsch 2018 for a thorough discussion of many different types of *da*-clauses). (5) provides an initial illustration of the declarative and the interrogative complementizers, and of the modal particle, whose special status and syntactic properties will be discussed in § 4.

(5) a. *Ivan smjata, če Marija e štastliva*
   Ivan thinks   that Maria is happy
   'Ivan thinks that Maria is happy'
  b. *Ivan pita dali Marija e štastliva*
   Ivan asks if   Maria is happy.
   'Ivan asks if Maria is happy'

---

[6] In each Balkan language, the 'subjunctive' is rendered by a combination of a modal marker/particle and a temporally restricted finite verb form. See Mitkovska and Bužarovska (this volume).

c. *Ivan iska   Marija da e štastliva.*
   Ivan wants Maria DA is happy
   'Ivan wants Maria to be happy'

Recall that within a Split CP approach as the one I adopt here, the highest left peripheral position, Force, indicates the clause type properties of the embedded clause and its illocutionary force. Given that *če*-complements are declarative subordinate clauses whose illocutionary force is that of an assertion, while *dali*-complements are interrogatives whose illocutionary force is that of a yes-no question,[7] *če* and *dali* can be said to occupy the position of Force. At first sight, this seems reasonable in view of the complementary distribution seen in (6):

(6) a. *Petăr smjata, **če/*dali** manastirăt   e napusnat*
       Peter thinks   that/*if   monastery-DET is deserted
       'Peter thinks that/*if the monastery is deserted'
   b. *Petăr se   čudi   *če/ dali   manastirăt   e napusnat*
       Peter REFL wonders *that/if   monastery-DET is deserted
       'Peter wonders *that/if the monastery is deserted'

These selectional properties may be taken to show that Force itself bears the specification [+/-Q] which then gives the distinction between a clause with a declarative and with an interrogative illocutionary force. As both of these clause types are morphologically and syntactically finite, in the sense that they are not restricted temporally or aspectually, we can suppose that when illocutionary force is overtly signaled in Bulgarian, the lower projection in the C-domain, Fin, remains phonologically empty or null. However, Fin can be said to contain mood features since the indicative of *če*- and *dali*-complements stands in sharp contrast to the 'subjunctive' *da*-complements, which are always referentially dependent and temporally/aspectually restricted (admitting typically present tense and perfective aspect on the embedded verb). See (7) and examples in (8):

(7) CORE1   Force   Fin   CORE2
              +/−Q   [+indicative]
              Modal   [+subjunctive]

---

[7] For the time being I will concentrate on *dali* reserving § 2.5 for a discussion of the syntactic and semantic differences with *li*.

(8) a. *Petăr smjata, če Ivan šte kupi /   šte kupuva/   e kupil kăštata*
   Peter thinks that Ivan will buy-PF/will buy-IMPF/is bought house-DET
   'Peter thinks that Ivan will buy/will be buying / has bought the house'
   b. *Petăr pita dali   Ivan šte kupi/   šte kupuva/   e kupil kăštata*
   Peter asks whether Ivan will buy-PF/will buy-IMPF/is bought house-DET
   'Peter asks whether Ivan will buy/ will be buying / has bought the house'
   c. *Petăr se nadjava Ivan da kupi/ *kupuva/   *šte kupi /e kupil kăštata*
   Peter hopes   Ivan DA buy-PF/*buy-IMPF/*will buy/is bought house-DET
   'Peter hopes that Ivan will buy/has bought the house'

3.2 Semantic selection of declarative and interrogative complements and the issue of Illocutionary force

(9) and (10) summarize the classes of predicates that may select for a *če*-complement or for a *dali*-complement:

(9) *Če*-complements are selected by:
   a) propositional attitude/epistemic verbs (*mislja* 'think', *smjatam* 'consider', *vjarvam* 'believe', etc.),
   b) verbs of communication (*kazvam* 'say', *tvărdja* 'claim', etc.) and
   c) verbs of intellection/cognitive predicates (*znam* 'know', *razbiram* 'understand', etc.).
   d) emotive predicates (*săžaljavam* 'regret', *radvam se* 'be glad', *măčno mi e* 'be sad', etc.)

(10) *Dali*-complements are selected by interrogative predicates: e.g., *čudja se* 'wonder', *pitam* (se) 'ask (myself)', etc.

Without going into detail for lack of space, it seems plausible to assume that the distribution of the complementizer *če* is dependent on the veridicality status of the complement with which it combines. Giannakidou (1998, 2009) defines veridicality as a propositional function that entails the truth of its complement: "F is veridical iff Fp entails p – that is, if whenever Fp is true, p is true too. F is nonveridical if Fp does not entail p – that is, if when Fp is true, p may or may not be true" (Giannakidou 2016: 186). All of the verb classes in (9) involve truth entailment in the sense of introducing a proposition with an independent truth value, i.e., one that can evaluated for truth or falsity. An indicative *če*-complement, embedded in a positive and declarative main clause, denotes a proposition that is either objectively true/factive, (9c,d), or is evaluated as true (subjective veridicality) by the main clause subject or the speaker (9a,b). This implies that at least one epistemic agent is committed to the truth value of this proposition.[8]

Interrogative predicates on the other hand are non-veridical. Questions denote propositions that leave open the truth value of the proposition; yes-no questions in particular are also polar since they comprise a set of two mutually exclusive propositions {p, ¬p} corresponding to the yes- and the no-answer (Hamblin 1973). As indicated by the negative tag in (11), and argued by Dukova-Zheleva (2010), and Callegari (2018), *dali* is a polar complementizer.

(11) *Pitax te   dali   Ivan si   e vkâšti   sega (ili ne)*
     I.asked you-CL.ACC   whether   Ivan REFL   is at-home now   (or not)
     'I asked you if Ivan was at home now'

Dali-clauses are also used for what Adger and Quer (2001) label 'unselected embedded questions' which do not strictly correspond to a question but to a proposition whose truth value is left open (undetermined). Such contexts present another instance of non-veridical clauses alongside selected *dali*-questions. See examples in (12) below. Interestingly, non-selected 'questions' in Bulgarian are available only with the predicates of class (9c) above, namely with the class of objective veridicals/cognitive factives. Given that factive complements contain a presupposition, i.e., their truth is anchored or taken for granted in the speech context or in shared world knowledge, the function of *dali* in such contexts is precisely that of suspending the presuppositional meaning usually associated with such complements. This however is possible only if the factive predicates of (9c) are negated, questioned or used in a conditional form; otherwise *dali* cannot be felicitously used. Note furthermore that *dali* is incompatible with the emotive predicates of (9d) even if the latter are negated, questioned or used in a conditional form. Such predicates correspond exactly to the class of 'true factives' in the sense of Karttunen (1971), also known as 'strongly veridical' or 'hard'

---

[8] According to Baunaz (2016), *če* is non-veridical with verbs of saying. I adopt here the particular concept of veridicality proposed by Giannakidou (1998, 2009). Note that with verbs of saying, Bulgarian morphologically distinguishes between indicative and evidential moods on the embedded verb. In this paper, I leave evidentials aside, but if the embedded verb is marked with the indicative, the unmarked reading is that the subject believes or knows that the proposition corresponding to the embedded clause is true. This is what Giannakidou labels 'subjective veridicality': the epistemic state of the subject, rather than that of the speaker, is homogeneous, epistemically settled. On the contrary, the semantic import of the evidential is that of an epistemic weakener, i.e., the subject (and the speaker) does not have full knowledge or belief that p is true. This is due to the fact that the evidence for the embedded assertion is partial, i.e., second-hand, which in any case constitutes a less reliable source of knowledge (Giannakidou 2018).

presupposition triggers. As such, they stand apart from the rest of the (factive) complement-taking predicates in that the presuppositional reading they give rise to cannot be (easily) suspended (on some pragmatically determined cases of presupposition suspension with true factives, see Karttunen 1971).[9]

(12) a. *Petar ne znae   dali   Ivan si   e vkăšti   sega* (ili ne)
Peter not knows whether Ivan SELF is at-home now (or not)
'Peter does not know whether Ivan is at home now (or not)'
b. *Petar znae li, dali   Ivan si   e vkăšti sega?* (ili ne)
Peter knows Q whether Ivan SELF is at-home now (or not)
'Does Peter know whether Ivan is at home now (or not)?'
c. *Ako znaex   dali   Ivan si   e vkăšti   sega* (ili ne),
if I.knew whether Ivan SELF is at-home now (or not),
štjax   da   ti   kaža
I.would DA you.CL.DAT I.tell
'If I knew whether Ivan was at home now I would have told you'

Suspension of the presupposition does not lead to a change in the functional meaning of the interrogative complementizer: much like in selected questions, *dali* has polar semantics and as indicated by the negative tag in (12), introduces a set of propositions {p, ¬p} although since the set in this case is not a question set *per se*, a yes-no answer is not required in substitution of the two opposite values of *p*.[10] Thus, all *dali*-clauses have an identical semantics (as well as an identical syntax) and can be argued to differ only in terms of the higher selector: interrogative *dali* would be selected by interrogative predicates, while non-interrogative *dali* would be selected by a class of non-veridical expressions like matrix negation, question or conditional (unselected *dali*). As these elements are operators,

---

9 Cognitive factives are well-known to be special with respect to presupposition triggering. In particular, such predicates may lose their presuppositional readings in precisely the contexts illustrated in (12), where the predicate is in the scope of some non-veridical operator like negation, question or conditional. Karttunen's (1971) original distinction was between 'true/full factives' and 'semi-factives'. In later work on the topic, the more general distinction between 'hard' and 'soft' presupposition triggers has been adopted (see also Abbott 2006; Simons 2007).
10 Note that a sentence like (i) is not ungrammatical but *dali* here introduces what Egrè (2008) refers to as the true answer of a question, i.e., the *dali*-clause has an intentional rather than an extensional meaning:

(i) *Petăr znae dali   Ivan si   e vkăšti sega*
Peter knows whether/*if Ivan REFL is at-home now
'Peter knows whether Ivan is at home now'

the sensitivity of *dali* to their semantic properties argues in favor of treating this complementizer as a (non-veridical) operator itself.

A property of *if*-clauses in English, shared by selected *dali*-clauses, is that according to context, they may give rise to alternative answers rather than those drawn from the polar set ({p, ¬p}). For example, a question like (11) can also be answered with e.g., (*Ne*), *Ivan otide na kino* 'Ivan went to the movies'; (*Ne*), *Ivan zamina za čužbina* 'Ivan went abroad', etc., i.e., with a proposition that can be drawn from a contextually relevant set containing p and alternatives to ¬p. Unselected *dali*-'questions', on the other hand, seem to pattern more with English *whether*-clauses, which are strictly polar, at least according to the analysis of Bolinger (1978) cited in Godard (2002) (for a different view, see Adger and Quer 2001).[11]

As mentioned, the selection issues seen above for *dali* do not arise for the declarative complementizer *če* 'that': *če*-complements introducing a presupposition remain immune to matrix operators like negation, question or a modal operator. See examples in (13) where the symbol ≫ indicates the respective presupposition. Therefore, *če* has no operator semantics inherited from its diachronic predecessor – Slavic *čъto* 'what', related to Russian *čto*, cf. Hansen, Letuchiy, Błaszczyk 2016):

(13) a. *Petar ne znae, če Ivan si e vkăšti sega* ≫ Ivan is at home now
Peter not knows that Ivan REFL is at-home now
'Peter doesn't know that Ivan is at home now'
b. *Petar znae li, če Ivan si e vkăšti sega?* ≫ Ivan is at home now
Peter knows Q that Ivan REFL is at-home now
'Does Peter know that Ivan is at home now?'
c. *Može bi znaeš, če Ivan si e vkăšti sega* ≫ Ivan is at home now
maybe you.know that Ivan REFL is at-home now
'Perhaps you know that Ivan is at home now'

The selection issues discussed above raise a problem for the Split CP approach. Given that *če* is always selected (cf. the ungrammaticality of (14a)), while *dali*

---

11 *Whether*-complements present the speaker with a strict choice between alternatives. "[W]hether appears to imply something about laying hold of information. The speaker has already taken the alternative possibilities under consideration and wants to make up his mind about them." (Bolinger 1978: 96). Of course, there is no one-to-one correlation between *dali* and *if/whether* according to context. Some unselected questions in English do not allow *whether*, cf. *I don't know *whether/if John is at home now*. The reason that *dali* takes over both complementizers in English can plausibly be attributed to the fact that, unlike English *if* or Greek *an* 'if' (Roussou 2010, see also discussion in Adger and Quer 2001; Haegeman 2010), the Bulgarian interrogative complementizer cannot be used in conditionals.

(together with the modal marker *da*) are free to occur in both main and embedded ones, as shown in (15), we might want to say that the non-interrogative complementizer is in fact not a force marker but an obligatory clausal subordinator selected by verbal (14b) or nominal (14c) heads.[12] Pure subordinators have been argued to differ from true force markers in a number of languages, e.g., Korean (Bhatt and Yoon 1992), and Hungarian (Brody 1990). And Roussou (2000), too, proposes for Modern Greek that *oti* 'that' can optionally realize the Subordinator position suggested by Rizzi (1997: 328) as a potential site above Force precisely in order to account for such languages (16):[13]

(14) a. (*Če) *Ivan pristiga dnes.*
*that Ivan arrives-IMPF today
intended: 'Ivan is arriving today'
b. *Mislja, *(če) Ivan pristiga dnes*
I.think that Ivan arrives-IMPF today
'I think that Ivan is arriving today'
c. *Novinata/tova, če Ivan pristiga dnes*
news-DET/this-DET that Ivan arrives-IMPF today
'The news/the fact that Ivan is arriving today'

(15) a. *Dali Ivan pristiga dnes?*
whether Ivan arrives-IMPF today
'Is Ivan arriving today?
b. *Ivan da idva/dojde tuk vednaga!*
Ivan DA comes-IMPF/PF here immeidately
'Ivan should come here right away!'

---

[12] Rizzi's system allows for this. In previous work (Krapova and Karastaneva 2002), we suggested that *če* spells out a feature relevant to clausal subordination relying on a footnote in Rizzi's paper (1997: 328) in which he envisions the possibility that the CP field could be a tripartite system, consisting of a SubordinatorP, a ForceP and a FinitenessP.

[13] From this perspective, languages like English and Romance, which do not formally distinguish embedded illocutionary force and subordination, conflate the expression of these two distinct categories into a single complementizer with a composite semantic specification. Other authors have opted for different solutions regarding the highest C position. For example, according to Ambar (2010) the topmost projection should rather be specified as +/−AssertionP whose purpose is to connect the sentence to a certain type of speech act, while Speas (2004) has argued in favor of a SpeakerP hosting features relevant for epistemic and evidential modality and the speaker's evaluation of truth. In this paper, we will assume that the highest C position is Force. Other alternatives will be explored in future work, in particular Radford's (2018: 270–287) proposal for an additional projection FACTP below ForceP, reserved for factive complementizers like *deto* 'that-factive', *kak* 'how', and *kak taka* 'how come'.

(16) Subordinator > Force > Fin
    če   dali/da

The examples discussed in § 3.1 argue however against treating *če* as a pure subordinator: as seen in (6) above, it is incompatible with any type of [+Q] specification within the embedded clause, whether the [+Q] feature is carried by *dali* or by some wh-marked element (17). Also, *če* never introduces a modalized clause such as the embedded imperative in (17b) which instead must contain the subjunctive marker *da*.[14] The data in (17) thus show that selectional requirements are strictly observed in Bulgarian declarative complements (formulated as a requirement in (18)), and that *če* conflates the expression of illocutionary force and subordination without formally distinguishing between these two categories.

(17) a. *Marija me   popita   *če/ koj/dali   idva   utre*[15]
        Maria me-CL.ACC asked   that/who/if   comes   tomorrow
        'Maria asked me who is coming tomorrow/if she is coming tomorrow'
     b. *Kazax, (*če) Marija   da   dojde   vednaga*
        said-1SG that Maria   DA   comes   immediately
        'I said that Mary should come right away'

---

14 The complementizer *če* can combine with *da* in unselected purpose-(like) clauses like (i) introduced by *taka* 'so':

(i) *Skrij   ja   v drehite,   taka če da ne ja namerjat*
    hide-IMP it-CL.ACC in clothes-DET so that DA not it-CL.ACC they.find
    'Hide it in your clothes so that they can't find it'

Complex complementizers can also result from combinations of *če* and a preposition: *văpreki če* 'although', *makar če* 'although, even though' etc. and are used in various types of adverbial clauses. Plausibly, such complementizers are merged as a single element in view of the requirement that the two components that they are made of must be adjacent.

15 The wh-word and the interrogative complementizer are in complementary distribution. This shows that both have a +Q feature which suffices for the clause to be interpreted as interrogative. Bulgarian thus differs from languages which instantiate the so-called Doubly Comp filter in allowing both the specifier of Q (the wh-word) and the Q head to co-occur, see (i) from Dutch:

(i) Ik vraag me af wie of dat er   morgen kommt
    I   ask me AF who if that there tomorrow comes
    (Koopman 2000: 342)
(ii) Doubly Filled Comp Filter: When an overt wh-phrase occupies the Spec of some CP, the head of that CP must not dominate an over complementizer (Haegeman 1994: 423)

Koopman (2000) argues that three CP projections are involved in the analysis of Dutch complementation: *wie* sits in the specifier of a WH-projection, *of* in the head of a Q projection, and *dat* in a lower C position.

(18) *Če* 'that' must be selected by a verbal or nominal head.

The fact that *če* is underspecified for subordination, clause type and factivity, can be taken to imply that this complementizer can occupy more than one position in the left periphery. In the next section, we will see, on the basis of the distribution of topics, that *če* may in fact occupy a C-position lower than Force. The complementizer *dali*, which was shown to be indifferent to semantic selection, must be merged in a position compatible with its operator properties. Logically, this difference in complementizer behavior could be due to the fact that, unlike *če*, *dali* has a more specific compositional make-up, involving the modal particle *da* and the interrogative clitic/focus particle *li*. (See § 3.4. for details and Callegari 2019 for a proposal that *dali* is syntactically composed of these two elements). If both *če* and *dali* are merged in positions different from Force, then we must ensure that some mechanism of feature transmission connects any C position(s) below Force to Force itself, so that the respective selectional requirements be satisfied wherever that is required.

3.3 Left dislocated topics, contrastive focus and complementizer ordering

As mentioned above, one of the arguments that is often adduced in favor of a split CP approach to the clausal left periphery comes from the relative position of discourse elements with respect to the particles of the complementizer system. In the most detailed version of Rizzi's (1997) system shown in (19), Topics must follow Force and precede the lowest CP position Fin, while there is a unique position in which focalized phrases can surface.

(19) V_{matrix}. ...[$_{ForceP}$ Force [Topic [Focus [Top. ... [$_{FinP}$ Finiteness [$_{IP}$]]]]]]

In this section, we will see more arguments in favor of postulating (distinct) C positions for the complementizers *če* and *dali*. The arguments will come from the distribution and the interpretation of left dislocated topicalized expressions. Focalized phrases and their relative order with respect to the rest of the left periphery will be discussed in § 3.4.

3.3.1 Multiple Topics in the Bulgarian left periphery

One important property of Topics in Bulgarian is that they can either follow or precede complementizers. Consider (20) indicating in parentheses the available positions for the topicalized phrase:

(20) a. *Mislja (na Ivan) če (na Ivan$_i$) kolegite mu$_i$ podarixa samo cvetja*
 I.think (to John) that (to John) colleagues-DET his they.gave only flowers
 za roždenija den
 for birthday-DET
 'I think that to John his colleagues gave only flowers for his birthday.'
 b. *Čudja se (na Ivan) dali (na Ivan$_i$) kolegite mu$_i$ podarixa samo cvetja*
 I.wonder (to Ivan) if (to Ivan) colleagues-DET his they.gave only flowers
 za roždenija den
 for his birthday-DET
 'I wonder if to John his colleagues gave only flowers for his birthday'

The left dislocated constituents in both examples are in the left periphery preceding the embedded subject and are resumed by a clitic. Clitic left dislocation is a common topicalization device in Bulgarian used to refer to a previously introduced discourse antecedent (Arnaudova 2002). There is however a difference in interpretation between the two Topic positions in (20). In the pre-complementizer position, topicalization signals that the speaker wants to introduce the topic constituent (*Ivan*) as highlighted or salient for the purposes of the conversation or to reintroduce it into discourse as a new topic to be commented on in the future conversation. The post-complementizer occurrence of the clitic left dislocated constituent on the other hand is simply an instance of a familiar or given topic in the sense of Schwarzschild (1999) whereby the dative argument is not highlighted but simply refers to an antecedent known from previous discourse. In other words, the topic in this case resumes background information shared by the discourse participants. Following a proposal by Bianchi and Frascarelli (2010), I will consider these two instantiations of the left dislocated topic constituents as corresponding to two different types of Topic: A(boutness) Topic (used for topic shift) and G(iven) Topic (used for topic continuity). The topic found to the left of *če/dali* matches the description offered by Bianchi and Frascarelli, from both a pragmatic and a syntactic point of view: it is obligatorily clitic resumed and must be unique. If this is indeed correct, then Bulgarian surprisingly reveals a case of an embedded A-Topic. G-Topics on the other hand can but need not be clitic resumed, in accord with other (independent) principles guiding the probability of clitic resumption. For example, as Cinque and Krapova (2008) have shown, direct objects show a higher propensity for resumption in Bulgarian left dislocation structures, as compared to indirect objects introduced by the dative-like preposition *na* 'to'. Additionally, (21b) which illustrates that a Topic can indeed be recursive but in order for that to be the case, it must show up after *če* and *dali*, i.e., it must be a G-Topic as expected under Bianchi and Frascarelli's approach:

(21) a. *Mislja, če   [na decata]   [knigite]   (im)*
I.think that to children-DET books-DET (to-them-CL.DAT)
gi razdadoxa.   ošte   na părvija učeben   den
them-CL.ACC gave already on first-DET school-Adj day
'I think that they gave the books to the children already on the first day of school'
b. *Čudja se   dali   [na decata]   [knigite]*
wonder-1SG whether   to children-DET books-DET
sa   (im)   gi are-3PL razdali ošte   na   părvija
are-3PL (to them.CL.DAT) them.CL.ACC gave-3PL already on first-DET
učeben   den
school-Adj day
'I wonder if they gave the books to the children already on the first day of school'

Based on the above data, the following preliminary template can be envisaged: given that Force splits the topic area delimiting the space where an A-Topic can occur form that where a G-Topic can occur, then the A-topic can be said to occupy the specifier position of Force, thus appearing to the left of the complementizers, while one or more G-Topics (as indicated by the asterisk in (22)), may show up in to the right of Force:

(22)   CORE1 [A-Topic [Force G-Topic* [CORE 2]]]]
                       če/dali

But things are more complicated than (22) would seem to suggest, especially when we consider a third type of Topics, namely C(ontrastive) topics. C-Topics, like G-Topics, mark a constituent as given, but differently from the latter, involve contrast among alternatives: "the function of CT-marking is to signal that the topic denotation belongs to a contextually salient set" (Bianchi and Frascarelli 2010: 72). From a syntactic point of view, one characteristic property of C-Topics in Bulgarian is the obligatory absence of clitic resumption (Arnaudova 2002, 2010). Consider for example (23):

(23) *Pomnja, če* [c-Topic *na Ivan*]   *podarixme* [*parfjum*]_F, *a* [c-Topic *na Marija*] [*cvetja*]_F
    remember-1SG that to Ivan   gave-1PL   perfume   and   to Maria   flowers
    'I remember that to Ivan we gave as a present a perfume, and to Maria flowers'

In (23), the second conjunct introduces a contrast set with two alternative values (Marija, cvetja) for the phrases (Ivan, parfjum) in the first conjunct. Following Büring's (2003) analysis,[16] the second element in the contrastive set is focus marked, and the contrastive topic is given by the first element. This is because contrastive topics can be represented as answers to *wh*-questions, with the focus marked element substituting for the wh-word in a question like 'x was given what as a present?', and the contrastive topic substituting x in the same question. Since the value of x must be chosen from a contextually salient set of available alternatives ({Ivan, Marija} in (23)), the contrastive reading of both topic phrases obtains, each unique in its own clause.[17]

Consider now the linear order of a C-Topic with respect to the complementizers *če* and *dali*. As shown by (24), a contrastive topic can only follow *če* and *dali*, though the position to the left of *dali* is inaccessible to this kind of topics (Rudin 1991: 432):

---

[16] Büring (2003) has argued that this set can be identified as a set of alternative wh-questions (question set) and that the function of the contrastive topic is to replace the value of the respective wh-word from the relevant wh-question. Thus, for example, (i) can be thought as an answer to (ii):

  (i) [FRED]_CT ate [the BEANS]_F and [MARY]_CT ate [the FISH]_F.
  (ii) Who ate what? (the superquestion)
     → Who ate the beans?
     → Who ate the fish?

The first step is to replace the focussed term with a wh-word and front the latter, yielding the question:

  (iii) What did Fred eat?

The second step is to form from this a set of alternative questions by replacing the contrastive topic (Fred) with some alternative to it: this is a set of questions of the form:

  (iv) What did x eat?

The contrastive topic thus provides a value for x and can be answered by propositions: {Fred ate the beans; Mary ate the fish}.

[17] It remains to be seen whether C-Topics are indeed unique in Bulgarian, as Bianchi and Frascarelli (2010:63) suggest on the basis of Italian. Multiple C-Topics have been argued to exist in a multiple *wh*-language like English. In a footnote, Bianchi and Frascarelli (2010, fn. 24) cite the following example from Culicover (1996: 35):

  (i) *I insisted that* THAT *book, to* ME, MAXIM *gave, and* THIS *book, to* YOU, SASHA *gave.*

Bulgarian is a multiple *wh*-fronting language, so multiple contrastive topicalization should in principle be possible theoretically. I leave that issue for further research.

(24) a. *Pomnja* (_C-Topic_ na Ivan) *če* (_C-Topic_ na Ivan) *podarixme* [*parfjum*]_F_
I.remember (to Ivan) that (to Ivan) we.gave-as-a-present perfume
togava, a na Marija samo cvetja
then but to Maria only flowers
'I remember that to Ivan we gave a perfume as a present then, but to Maria [we gave as a present] only flowers'

b. *Pitax te* (*_C-Topic_ *na Ivan*) *dali* (_C-Topic_ *na Ivan*) *podarixme*
I.asked you-CL.ACC (to Ivan) if to Ivan we.gave-as-a-present
parfium togava, a na Marija samo cvetja.
perfume then, but to Maria only flowers
'I asked you if to Ivan we gave as a present a perfume then, and only flowers to Maria'

If C- Topics are ordered with respect to both an A-topic and an G-Topic, as argued by Bianchi and Frascarelli (2010)[18] and indicated in (25), we end up with the templates in (26), where all available positions of the complementizers are summarized with respect to the three types of peripheral Topics:

(25) Aboutness Topic > Given Topic* > Contrastive Topic

(26) a.   A-Topic   G-Topic*   C-Topic
              ↑   ↑   ↑
              če   če   če
     b.   A-Topic   G-Topic*   C-Topic
              ↑   ↑
              dali   dali

The fact that *če* though not *dali* can appear following a C-Topic makes it plausible to assume that this complementizer disposes of an additional lower position which is banned for *dali*. I suggest that the lowest position in (26a) can plausibly be identified as Fin – the projection that closes off the CP field and also signals the morpho-syntactic information relevant for distinguishing between indicative and non-indicative clauses. In Fin, *če* can be preceded by all types of Topics, while in any of the higher positions indicated in (26a) the declarative complementizer can be preceded by a G-Topic (G-Topic > *če*) or followed by a G-Topic

---

18 The order assumed in Bianchi and Frascarelli (2010) is different: A-Topic > C-Topic > G-Topic. The data from Bulgarian thus show that this order is subject to parametric variation.

(*če* > G-Topic). Apparently, the two higher positions in (26) coincide for the two complementizers. Plausibly, then, we can identify the highest position targeted by *če* and *dali* as being that of Force, given that it distinguishes between the unique A-Topic and the rest of the Topic field. In § 3.4, however, I will give evidence that Force is not always accessible to the interrogative complementizer. As for the intermediate position, the comparison between (26a) and (26b) might be taken to imply that the two complementizers can surface in the (head of the yet unidentified XP) position preceding the C-Topic.

(27) A-Topic G-Topic **XP** C-Topic

Rizzi (2001 seq) argues that the position hosting interrogative complementizers within the left periphery is Int(errogative)P (see (28)), a dedicated functional position different from and lower than Force. Int also hosts a dedicated operator (*Op*) in its specifier responsible for the interpretation of yes-no questions (see also Grimshaw 1994, Roberts 1993, Haegeman 2012):[19]

(28) [$_{ForceP}$ Force . . . [$_{IntP}$ Op Int] . . .Fin
   dali

It seems reasonable to suppose that given the operator properties of *dali*, this complementizer is also merged in Int (like its Italian counterpart *se*), and assuming that there is an empty *Op* in the specifier of IntP, *dali* could share with the latter a Q feature, in accord with standard principles of Spec, head agreement. A question arises at this point: if Int is the functional projection where *dali* is merged, is this position also accessible to the declarative complementizer, given

---

19 Rizzi treats Int as an operator position in both main and embedded clauses in Italian hosting the abstract yes-no operator, as well as certain *wh*-adverbials like the reason adverbial *why*, which occupies the specifier of Int. (i) illustrates that this might be a reasonable suggestion also for Bulgarian 'why'-phrases: such phrases, differently from the *wh*-argument *kakvo* 'what' in (ii), can either follow or precede a topicalized phrase and can thus be argued to surface in a higher position than the one reached by *wh*-arguments, at least in embedded questions:

(i) *Pitam se   na Ivan   zašto (na Ivan)   mu   podarixa samo cvetja*
    I.ask REFL to Ivan-Topic why (to Ivan-Topic) him-CL.DAT they.gave only flowers
    za roždenija den.
    for birthday-DET
    'I am wondering why to Ivan they gave only flowers for his birthday'
(ii) *Pitam se   na Ivan kakvo (*na Ivan) mu   podarixa   za roždenija den.*
     I.ask REFL to Ivan what   (*to Ivan) him-CL.DAT they.gave   for birthday-DET
     'I am wondering what they gave as a present to Ivan for his birthday?'

the complementary distribution between the two complementizers? As a consequence, what would be the correct featural specification of Force, given the template in (7) above?

To answer these questions, let us suppose that the intermediate position XP in (27) that *če* has access to does not coincide with the position of Int in (28). This is motivated by the fact that the declarative complementizer has no operator properties and has a non-interrogative specification. I will label this position Verid(icality)P, a label which seems suitable in view of the selectional properties of the verb classes in (9). Let us furthermore assume that VeridP is lower than IntP but contiguous to it so that each complementizer occupies the respective head position according to its featural specification (+Q or -Q). This is illustrated in (29) which also captures the relative order of the two complementizers with respect to both G-Topics and the C-Topic:

(29)   A-Topic > Force > G-Topic* > Int > VeridP C- Topic > Fin
                       dali če   *če*

Given that a C-Topic necessarily follows *če* (and by transitivity also *dali*), VeridP can be said to mark the distinction between *givenness/topicality* on the one hand, and *contrast* on the other. From a discourse point of view, VeridP identifies the Topic field to its left and marks the start of the Comment in the Topic-Comment articulation of the clause, with C-Topics belonging to the Comment and requiring a focused phrase as part of the contrast set, as we saw above. In view of the syntactic and semantic affinities between contrastive topics and contrastively focalized phrases, VeridP can be said to mark off the area of focalization, characterized by the feature [+contrast].

I suggest that the position VeridP is also related to other interpretational differences between *če*-clauses and *dali*-clauses. Recall that apart from predicates selecting for a +Q complement, *dali* can also introduce unselected embedded questions. See (12a) repeated here as (30a). Recall also that *če*-complements appearing under factive predicates are not sensitive to the presence of a matrix non-veridical operator and preserve the factive presupposition, see e.g., (13a) above repeated here as (30b):

(30) a. *Petar ne znae   dali   Ivan   si   e   vkăšti sega* (ili ne)
        Peter not knows whether Ivan   REFL   is at-home now   (or not)
        'Peter doesn't know whether Ivan is at home now (or not)'
     b. *Petar ne znae,   če   Ivan si   e vkăšti sega.* >> Ivan is at home now
        Peter not knows that Ivan REFL is at-home now
        'Peter doesn't know that Ivan is at home now'

Standing with our previous suggestion that the *dali* can be licensed through selection either by a matrix Q predicate or by a non-veridical operator, while *če* has no operator properties and must be selected by a higher verbal selector, Int and Verid should be two distinct positions each with a different effect on the truth of the embedded proposition. Factive verbs, in particular, contain a variable feature as part of their lexical representation (Roussou 2010). When this variable is licensed by a matrix propositional operator (e.g., negation in (30)), a dependency relation is created between the matrix factive verb and the embedded operator C position Int hosting *dali*. This mechanism ensures that the embedded clause has no truth value (see discussion in Roussou 2010 and Oehl 2007). When Int is not present, Verid hosting *če* discharges the variable thus creating an independent truth domain for the embedded clause.

One last point regards the multiplicity of C positions and the issue of complementizer spell-out. A plausible analysis of the multiple positions seen above is to assume that complementizers can move around the available Topic positions provided they target a compatible higher hierarchic position in the Split CP domain. Different works propose a relation between Fin and Force, and various authors view this relation in terms of movement from one position to the other (Ledgeway 2000, 2006; Roussou 2000; Rizzi 2013; Radford 2018, a.o.). For example, Ledgeway argues that in Southern Italian dialects (see also Roussou 2000 for a similar proposal regarding Modern Greek) the respective complementizer *ca* 'that' originates in Fin (in virtue of marking declarativity/finiteness) and from there moves to Force passing across the various discourse-related positions (Topics, Focus) in a successive cyclic fashion (as also indicated by the different morphological shapes *ca* can assume). A clear indication that complementizer movement is indeed available cross-linguistically comes from the possibility of simultaneously spelling out two complementizer copies in the two positions. Radford (2018) shows this to be the case in colloquial English where *that* can lexicalize five C positions within the Split CP field: Force, Rep(ort), Rel(ative), Sub(ordinator), Fin. Radford cites different contexts where more than one position hosting *that* can be spelled out as a (secondary) copy of *that* (recomplementation), see (31a,b). Additionally, various examples are adduced from different oral registers pointing that two (copies of) different complementizers can co-occur in complex clauses such as (32):

(31) a. *I put it to him* [Force **that**] *with such a huge event and with so many vessels on the water* [Fin **that**] *safety should be the number one priority* (Radford 2018: 122, ex. (33d))

b. *I wanted to know* **whether** *in such a situation,* **whether** *it could adversely affect my LLM application* (Radford 2018: 175, ex. (134b))

(32) *I just don't know* [Int Op **whether**] [Fin **that**] *they will have the same attitude.*
(Radford 2018: 154, ex. (95a))

Since multiple spell-out of complementizer copies is not available in Bulgarian, as far as I can tell, and neither are "double" complementizer clauses like (31), we have to assume that whenever *če* and *dali* occupy positions different from Force,[20] Force itself remains empty although it is accessible for complementizer movement, in case an A-Topic is projected, as sketched in (26) above. Accessibility is ensured by the matching featural specification of the split C positions (or by some agreement mechanism in the sense of Rizzi 2013), as indicated in (33). One consequence of (33) is that it ensures that the relevant functional information can be passed over from Fin, Verid and Int to Force making Force ultimately available for the purposes of selection from the predicate of CORE1; cf. Rizzi's (2013) Search relation, and Radford (2018) for an alternative mechanism of top-down feature percolation.

(33) CORE1 A -Topic Force G-Topic IntP Verid P C-Topic Fin   CORE2
                        -Q/+Q   Q   -Q   -Q [+indicative]

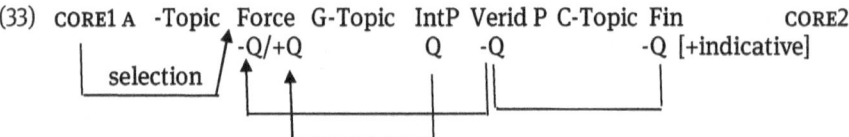

To summarize so far, the effect of multiple topicalization on the distribution of complementizers has brought us to revise the preliminary conclusion that the declarative and the interrogative complementizers necessarily occupy Force. Based on the premise that languages need not lexicalize illocutionary force in the highest C position Force, we argued that the interrogative complementizer in Bulgarian can be spelled out in its merge position, Int, but may subsequently raise/move to Force and be spelled-out in this position producing the alternative order in which G-Topics follow *dali*. The declarative complementizer on the other hand starts out from the position of Fin and can subsequently move to Verid (in case a C-Topic is present) or to a [-Q] Force in case of one or more G-Topics. Note that either complementizer can be spelled out in just one of the available positions, leaving the others phonologically empty or null. If on the other hand, no Topic is projected, these positions amalgamate and a single C is projected (Rizzi 1997: 314). To account for the complementary distribution between the declarative and the interrogative complementizer, we can thus assume that Fin and Verid project only if Int does not project, and *vice versa*, so the complementary distribution between the declarative

---

20 According to Rizzi (1997: 314), null or empty Comps are available only when Topic and Focus are projected.

and the interrogative complementizer seen in (6) above and repeated below as (34) can be derived from the structure of the split CP itself rather than from the conceptual necessity of occupying the same unique C position.

(34) a. *Petăr smjata,* ***če/*dali*** *manastirăt   e napusnat*
Peter thinks   that/*if   monastery-DET is deserted
'Peter thinks that/*if the monastery is deserted'
b. *Petăr se čudi   *če/ **dali**   manastirăt   e napusnat*
Peter wonders *that/if   monastery-DET is deserted
'Peter wonders *that/if the monastery is deserted'

One last note concerns the specification of clause type within the left periphery of CORE2. Two possibilities can be considered here, which I leave without further discussion. According to Rizzi and Shlonsky (2007: 35), apart from Force, Fin should also be involved in the specification of clause type:[21] in case Force is not filled by a complementizer, the embedded sentence can still get interpreted as declarative by default. In other words, Fin inherits the clause types specification of Force when the latter is phonologically empty. Under the alternative assumption that CP does not contain empty positions, then Fin should somehow be involved in the specification of clause type/declarative force, so that a (+finite) or (+indicative) Fin should always produce a declarative clause even in the absence of Force. Roberts (2004) argues that the very selection of Fin as [+finite] preempts declarativity (Stowell 1981), i.e., a clause with just a finite Fin is interpretatively equal to a clause with [+declarative] Force.

To summarize so far, the fine-grained order we arrived at so far is thus the one given in (35):

(35)   CORE1 [A-Topic [ForceP [G-Topic [IntP [VeridP [C-Topic [FinP]]]] CORE2

3.3.2 Focus in the left periphery

Focus phrases, in particular those related to the expression of contrast, are well-known to occupy left-peripheral positions and to exhibit operator properties cross-linguistically (Kiss 1998, Horvath 2010, Bianchi 2019). Focus is relevant for

---

[21] In later work, Rizzi seems to posit instead complementizer movement claiming that the normal derivation of a *that*-clause proceeds by first merging *that* in Fin where finiteness is expressed, and on a second step, by moving it to Force for checking of the Force feature (see Rizzi and Shlonsky 2007; Rizzi 2014).

the informational articulation of the embedded structure so it must correspond to a special "dedicated" position, where the focalized constituent gets interpreted in terms of discourse-scope much like the positions dedicated to the expression of topics (Rizzi 2014: 37).

Typically, contrastively focalized elements represent new information provided by the speaker for the purposes of contrast with what he/she considers to be knowledge on part of the interlocutor (as well as part of the shared common ground between the discourse participants).[22] To quote from Zubizarreta (1998): "Contrastive Focus makes a statement about the truth or correctness of (certain aspects of) the presupposition provided by its context statement." (p. 10). Thus, Contrastive Focus (hence forward CF) affects the truth conditions of the clause[23] and articulates the clause into a Focus -Presupposition information structure.

As in many other languages, the special function of contrastive focus in Bulgarian is signalled prosodically by the high pitch contour on the contrastively focussed phrase, conventionally indicated with capital letters in the examples.[24]

---

[22] Unlike Contrastive Focus, Information focus is the domain of new (non-presupposed) information and has been described as the new part, or what is being said about the topic or as the information of the sentence that makes contribution to the hearer's knowledge store (Vallduví 1992, and in particular Arnaudova 2001). The two types of focus are frequently associated with different representations. New information focus is typically realized in-situ, and its realization is guided by principles like the Nuclear Stress Rule, while contrastive focus often involves movement to a left peripheral position,

[23] Left peripheral focus is not constrained to contrastive interpretation; in Italian, for example, it seems to have a corrective or a mirative import rather than a contrastive one (Bocci, Rizzi, Saito, 2018: 12; Bianchi, Bocci and Cruschina 2015, 2016; see also Dal Farra 2018 for a discussion). Corrective focus is introduced for the purpose of correcting part of a previously made statement (assertion) or a commonly shared assumption not shared by the speaker, while mirative focus has a confirmative value: it requires confirmation of a piece of information which is considered unlikely compared to alternatives. All these types of focus share a prosodic contour such that the focalized phrase is pronounced with a high pitch contour and/or is more heavily accentuated. As far as Bulgarian is concerned, in the absence of more detailed studies, I will assume that left peripheral focus is of the contrastive type, although it can in some cases be used for corrective purposes, i.e., for denying or correcting a previous assertion or presupposition that the speaker does not share.

[24] Bulgarian can also express contrastive focus in situ. See (i) as compared to (ii) where the same constituent appears preverbally, and is plausibly moved to the left periphery:

(i) *Ivana iska* KOLA (*ne kăšta ili nova rabota*).
 Ivana wants CAR (not house or new job)
 'It is a car that Ivan wants' (not a house or a new job)
(ii) KOLA *iska Ivana __* (*ne kăšta ili nova rabota*)
 CAR wants Ivana (not house or new job)
 'It is a car that Ivana want' (not a house or a new job).

Contrastive interpretation arises from the contrast between the focussed phrase, e.g. *vino* in (36), and at least one other parallel element from a closed set of alternatives as indicated by the explicit or implicit tag. (36) shows that contrastive interpretation depends on the type of the embedded clause: in a declarative clause, (36a), focus negates the potential alternatives indicated by the negative tag, while in interrogative clauses containing a polarity complementizer *dali*, (36b), focus introduces one out a set of potential alternatives which bear the same value for the variable corresponding to the focussed constituent. As Bianchi and Cruschina (2016) argue, the set must contain more than one alternative so that the speaker chooses the single alternative which according to him/her satisfies the context description:

(36) a. *Kaza,* [*če* [Focus *VINO* [IP *šte nosjat za partito t*]]] (*ne rakija, limonada....*)
said that WINE will they.bring to party-DET (not rakia, lemonade)
'He/she said they would bring wine to the party (not rakia, lemondade, etc.)'
b. *Pitax te* [*dali* [Focus *VINO* [IP *šte nosite za partito t*]]
I.asked you-CL.ACC if WINE will you.bring-PL for party-DET
(*ili rakija, limonada...*)
(or rakia, lemonade...)
'I asked you if it is wine that you will bring to the party (or rakia, lemonade, etc.)'

Furthermore, contrastive focus appears to follow two of the three types of topicalized phrases we discussed in § 3.3.1. above: it follows both A-Topics and G--Topics, so with (35) in mind, and comparing (36) with (37), we can establish that the position of CF is below the position of Int, where *dali* is merged, and as a consequence, also below the highest position where *dali* reaches, i.e., Force, taking thus Focus (and the G-Topic) in its scope. In a moment, I will review evidence that Bulgarian disposes of a second left peripheral focus position and that consequently, this language does not conform to one basic tenet of Rizzi's CP approach: the left periphery may host a unique focalized constituent. (37c) further shows that CF can also occur above the complementizer *če*.

Prosodic marking of course is not enough to claim that there is a separate Foc projection in Bulgarian with quantificational properties in the left periphery. I will however show that in order for a preverbal constituent to receive a contrastive focus, certain syntactic conditions have to be met indicating that left peripheral focus obeys more stringent contextual conditions, yet to be determined precisely.

(37) a. *Pitax   te   (na Ivan) dali (na Ivan) VINO*
       I.asked- you-CL.ACC (to Ivan) if   (to Ivan) WINE
       šte (mu)   nosite   (ili rakija, limonada…)
       will (him-CL.DAT) you.bring   (or rakia, lemonade, etc.)
       lit. 'I was asking you if to Ivan it is wine that you will bring (him)'
   b. *Kaza,   (na Ivan) če (na Ivan) VINO šteli   da (mu)   nosjat.*
       He/she.said (to Ivan) that (to Ivan) WINE would.EVID DA (him-CL.DAT) they.bring
       lit. He/she said that to Ivan it is wine that they would bring (him)'
   c. *Kaza   VINO   če   na Ivan šteli   da (mu)   nosjat*
       he/she.said WINE that to Ivan would.EVID DA (him-CL.DAT) they.bring
       'He/she said that it is wine that they would bring to Ivan'

Note that a sequence of a contrastive topic and a contrastive focussed phrase is unavailable in Bulgarian. I take this to indicate that these two types of contrastive phrases are in complementary distribution and as a consequence that they occupy the same position. If this is correct, we can suppose that the left periphery of Bulgarian embedded clauses contains a position, labelled ContrastP in (38), which is accessible to both C-Topics and C-Focus phrases:

(38)   Force > G-Topic* > Int > VeridP > ContrastP > Fin

Contrast always involves quantification of alternatives, so whichever element surfaces in this position must have operator properties (operator topic and operator focus). In its left peripheral position, the XP expressing the contrast binds a gap (a variable, or a full unpronounced copy of XP,[25] Rizzi 2014: 37) in the original position from which the XP moves. This explains why CF phrases cannot be clitic resumed much like contrastive topics. The chain formed in this way ([XP$_i$ … t$_i$]) allows for the preservation of the original semantic interpretation of XP (e.g., as an argument of *bring* in (36)) and delimits the rest of the clause as presupposed (and therefore part of the Focus-Presupposition articulation of the embedded clause).

3.4 *Dali* interrogatives and contrastive focus

As mentioned above, *dali* shares the semantics of polar questions and has been labelled a polar operator (Dukova-Zheleva 2010; Callegari 2019) akin to the disjunction operator *ili* 'or', which is also a polarity item. Dukova-Zheleva (2010)

---

[25] This type of focus is not semantically restricted since any type of phrase can undergo focus movement.

has shown that when the embedded sentence does not contain a contrastively focussed constituent, *dali* takes the entire embedded proposition in its scope. The proposition is then interpreted with respect to the polar set which according to the classical Hamblin-type semantics of embedded interrogatives (Hamblin 1973), involves only two mutually exclusive alternatives: {p, ¬p}. In this set, p corresponds to the proposition denoting the positive answer, as in (39b), and ¬p to the one denoting the negative answer, as in (39c):

(39) a. *Pitax te   dali   šte xodiš   na kino   tazi večer.*
        I.asked you-CL.ACC if   will you.go to cinema this evening
        'I asked you if you will go to the cinema tonight'
    b. *Da, šte xodja na kino   tazi večer*
        Yes, will I.go to cinema this evening
        Yes, I will go to the cinema tonight'
    c. *Ne, njama da xodja na kino   tazi večer.*
        No, won't DA I.go to cinema this evening
        'No, I won't go to the cinema tonight'

(39a) can also receive (40) as an answer:

(40) *Ne, šte ritam futbol s prijatelite*
     No, will I.play football with friends-DET
     'No, I will play football with my friends'

In (40), the interpretation is computed not with respect to the negative alternative ¬p (39c) but with respect to a set containing *p* and other alternatives to *p* (Rooth 1992), so that a positive answer will involve *p* while a negative one will involve at least one other alternative which the speaker finds more likely. The availability of (40) shows that *dali* can generate a set of alternatives rather than just a polar set (Bianchi and Cruschina 2016). When asking the question, the speaker presupposes that one proposition in a set of salient propositions of the form "you will do x tonight" is true, and asks whether the proposition expressed by *p* "you will go to the cinema tonight" is in fact the one that is true (Bianchi 2019).

Note that such a wide scope interpretation of *dali* requires the entire embedded proposition to constitute new information. New information focus is well-known to allow for focus spreading so that every sentential constituent can be within the scope of *dali* (unless there is a Topic, in which case the scope of *dali* is not computed with the respect to the Topic, which in any case is taken for granted or given, but over the entire Comment (41b) or over a focus constituent, *vino* 'wine' in (41c), contained in the Comment).

(41) a. *Pitax   te   (na Ivan) dali (na Ivan) [šte mu   nosite*
      I.asked   you-CL.ACC (to Ivan) if   (to Ivan will him-CL.DAT you.bring
      vino]
      wine
      'I was asking you if you were going to bring wine to Ivan'
   b. *Ne, šte   mu   kupim   samo cvetja*
      No, will him-CL.DAT   we.buy   only flowers
      No, we will buy him flowers only'
   c. *Ne, šte   mu   nosim   edna rakija*
      No, will him-CL.DAT we.bring one rakia
      No, we will buy him a bottle of rakia'

Given these scope possibilities and the fact that as a polar operator *dali* always interferes with the focus structure of its complement, it is plausible to assume that *dali* itself bears a focus feature. As Callegari (2019) hypothesized, the focus feature on *dali* can plausibly be related to the morphological make-up of this complementizer, which incorporates the focus particle *li*, i.e., the clitic variant of *dali* (see next subsection for details). Moreover, *li* itself is akin to the disjunctive/polar operator *ili* 'or' pointing that focus and polarity are closely related and can have effects on the morphological level. In the next section, however, we will see that *li* and *dali* do not occupy the same position in the left periphery of the embedded clause.

Let's see now what the effect of CF is on the interpretation of embedded *dali*-questions. As observed by Dukova-Zheleva (2010), in such cases a *dali*-question is interpreted not with respect to the propositional alternatives that make part of the focus set but with respect to the focussed constituent itself, leaving the rest of the clause as part of the background information (presupposed). (42) illustrates this narrow focus:

(42) *Pitax   te   dali*[+foc] [CF *za*   SOFIA] *Ivan šte pătuva* (ili za Varna, Plovdiv ...)
     I.asked you if   to   SOFIA Ivan will he.travels (or to Varna, Plovdiv..)
     'I asked you if Ivan was going to travel to Sofia (or to Varna, Plovdiv, etc.)'

In discussing the interaction between the polarity operator and Focus in Bulgarian, Dukova-Zheleva (2010) argues that in cases like (42), the focussed phrase generates a set of focus alternatives (here, too, the focus set is by necessity a superset of the denotation of the focussed constituent), which provide possible answers to the question (Varna, Plovdiv, etc.). As this is reflected in the focus structure of the answer, (42) can be answered as (43a), or as (43b), while the rest of the sentence is presupposed, i.e., part of the shared knowledge:

(42) a. *Da, za Sofia* ~~Ivan šte pătuva~~
 Yes, to Sofia Ivan will he.travels
 b. *Ne, za Plovdiv* ~~Ivan šte pătuva~~   (Varna, . . .)
 No, to Plovdiv Ivan will he.travels   (Varna, . . .)

Dukova-Zheleva's account thus requires that the focus alternatives are introduced below the operator *dali*. This is crucial for the Rooth-type account to focus that Dukova-Zheleva adopts: *dali* must occupy a position immediately above the position of CF in order to allow for scope to be computed only with respect to this constituent rather than to the entire proposition, as in (39) above.

Somewhat surprisingly, however, in (43) we observe that a focussed constituent can also precede *dali*. We thus establish that *dali* can be surrounded by two Focus positions, though they can be realized only one at a time:

(43) *Čudja se/ Pitam te   (za SOFIA) dali   (za SOFIA) Ivan šte pătuva*
 I.wonder/I.ask you-CL.ACC (to SOFIA) if   (to SOFIA) Ivan will he.travels

As shown by the empirical evidence discussed below, there are important interpretational differences between these two focus positions. First, the higher focus position is incompatible with focalizing adverbs like *daže* 'even' but can only be accompanied by the focalizing adverb *samo* 'only':

(44) a. *Čudja se samo/*daže/*săšto i   za SOFIA dali Ivan šte pătuva*
 I.wonder only/*even/*also and to SOFIA if Ivan will he.travels
 (*ili i   za Varna, Plovidv* . . .)
 (or and to Varna Plovdiv, . . .)
 'I am wonderting if it is only to Sofia that Ivan will travel' (or also to Varna, Plovdiv, etc.)'
 b. *Čudja se dali samo/daže/săšto i   za SOFIA Ivan šte pătuva*
 I.wonder if only/even/also and to SOFIA Ivan will he.travels
 'I am wondering if Ivan will travel only/even/also to Sofia'

(44) shows that the higher Focus position may host a constituent with an exhaustive interpretation, while the lower Focus position may host a constituent with a pure contrastive focus interpretation. The behaviour of the higher focussed phrase is reminiscent of the English cleft constructions and of the Hungarian focus moved to the preverbal focus position (Exhaustive Focus) (Horvath 2010). In the account put forward by Kiss (1998) for Hungarian, exhaustive contrast is achieved via exclusion of alternatives. For example, in (44), the Focus phrase/cleft asserts the value for which the predicate (*travel*) holds by excluding all other

alternative values (Varna, Plovdiv..) for which the predicate could potentially hold and which are part of the natural expectations of the interlocutor. It is in this sense that clefting and Hungarian-style contrastive focus specify uniqueness provided by *only* as opposed to *even* and *also* which presuppose non-uniqueness (are non-exhaustive) and thus cannot be clefted/focussed. (45) shows that clefting must obey similar restrictions (Horn 1969, Sornicola 1988, Nelson 1997, Kim 2012):

(45) *It is only/*even John that Peter introduced to Mary.*

(45) contains the presupposition that Peter introduced x to Mary, and that out of a set of individuals present in the domain of discourse, John (the clefted constituent) was the only one that satisfies the description, i.e., x = John.

Similarly, (44)a from Bulgarian contains the presupposition that Ivan will travel to x, and that Sofia is the only relevant alternative, i.e., x = Sofia.

While in Hungarian contrast is always exhaustive (Horvath 2010) requiring movement to the left periphery as opposed to other type of focussed constituents, which do not, Bulgarian seems to feature a more fine grained focus articulation. This language has no special cleft construction but to render the difference between clefting and contrast resorts to a distinct focus position, which can be targeted by focus movement.

Another distinction between the two positions regards the possibility of focussing an existential quantifier. Compare:

(46) a. *Čudja se   (*njakoj) dali (njakoj)   vse pak njama da prieme*
         I.wonder (*someone) if (someone) after all   won't   DA he.accepts
         našata   pokana
         our-DET invitation
         'I wonder if someone will accept our invitation after all'
      b. *Čudja se (*vsičko)   dali vsičko   si   kazax.*
         I.wonder (*everything) if (everything) REFL   I.said
         'I am wondering if I said everything I had to say'

The existential quantifier is excluded also in English cleft constructions, confirming that the higher focus position in Bulgarian is indeed cleft-like:

(47) **It is someone/everything that he saw.*

We therefore need to recognize that there are two positions available for contrastive phrases at least as far as Bulgarian is concerned and that the position of *dali* distinguishes the two Focus positions due to its operator properties. Note however, that in (44b) the focalizing adverb *only* is compatible with the lower contrastively focussed phrase as well. Plausibly then, both focussed constituents share a [contrastive focus] feature but their compositional make-up in addition contains finer-grained focus features (Dal Farra 2018), like e.g. [+contrastive, ± exhaustive] or [+contrastive, +exhaustive].[26] Given that exhaustivity implies contrast, the lower C-Foc position can simply be labelled [contrastive], while the higher one must be specified as [+exhaustive], (48). As a consequence, other contrastive phrases, whether topicalized or focalized, are excluded.

(48)   Force   C-Foc[+exhaustive]   Int   C-Foc/Top[contrastive][27]

Putting together (48) with (38) above, repeated here as (49), we arrive at the template in (50) which is now enriched with the two CF positions: one above Int, reserved for exhaustivity, and one below Int, shared by topics and focussed phrase bearing the feature [contrastive]. Recall, that in order to make sense of the distribution of G-topics either following or preceding *dali*, we postulated in § 3.3.1 that the complementizer can optionally raise to the higher Force position, which however is not an operator position. When *dali* spelled-out in Force, the order *dali* > G-Topic(s) falls out but it becomes impossible to distinguish the two focus positions. This suggests that movement of the interrogative complementizer to Force is not optional and may take place only under certain circumstances, i.e., topicalization does not interfere with such a movement, while focalization does:

(49)   Force > G-TopicP* > Int > Verid > ContrastP > Fin

(50)   Force > G-TopicP* > CFoc[+exhaustive] Int Verid ContrastP > Fin

---

26 In fact, exhaustive focus has been shown to constitute one kind of contrastive focus, so what Kiss (1998) labelled 'contrastive focus' in order to explain Hungarian left peripheral focus was later revisited in terms of 'exhaustivity', which was found to correspond more closely to the syntactic and the semantic properties of Hungarian left peripheral focussed phrases (Horvath 2010).
27 Positing more than one focus position in the left periphery goes against Rizzi's observation (see also Frascarelli 2000 and Brunetti 2004) that there is a single dedicated position in the left periphery associated with focus. Other studies propose two fixed positions (Belletti 2001, 2004; Benincà and Poletto 2004). Given the distinct types of focus constructions mentioned in fn, 23, languages may plausibly dispose of different left peripheral positions where contrastively focussed phrases can move to for interpretative purposes. Whether these positions are activated or not depends on language-specific considerations.

3.5 The syntax of the particle *li*

Much work of the '90s has been dedicated to establish whether this particle is a complementizer or not. According to the more widespread view (Rudin 1997; Rudin et al 1999; Bošković 2001, and Franks 2005), *li* is a complementizer located outside IP, in C, and is endowed with a special focus feature triggering movement of XP (or a V) to its left. V-*li* movement produces a neutral yes-no question (51b), while XP-*li* movement (51a) produces a focus structure with XP pronounced in a marked way. Either one or the other option can be realized, though not both simultaneously, possibly as a consequence of the Doubly Filled Comp Filter stated in fn. 15. The complementizer analysis sketched in (52) is motivated by the complementary distribution of *li* with other complementizers, and also by its clause-typing properties as an interrogative marker like non-clitic *dali*.

(51) a. *Čudja se* [$_{XP+li}$ *na KINO li*]   *šte xodiš tazi večer*
    I.wonder   to CINEMA Q   will you.go this evening
    'I am wondering if you will go to the cinema tonight'
  b. *Čudja se* [$_{V+li}$ *šte xodiš li*]   *na kino tazi večer*
    I.wonder   will you.go Q   to cinema this evening
    'I am wondering if you will go to the cinema tonight'

(52) a. [$_{CP}$ XP [$_C$ li] [$_{IP}$ XP]]
  b. [$_{CP}$ [$_C$ V li [$_{IP}$ V

Another view holds that *li* is a focus particle and as such occupies a lower Foc position (Izvorski 1995; Dukova-Zheleva 2010). As both types of analysis work with a single C position, the choice is between this position and a lower Foc position, intermediate between C and IP.

(53) [$_{CP}$ Int/Q [$_{FocP}$ Foc   [$_{IP}$]]]
                li$_{+Q}$

Both analyses assume that *li* has a Q feature as well as a focus feature but differ with respect to how these two features are represented syntactically – under the regular position Q/Int supplied with a focus feature or under a different Focus position supplied with +Q feature. The question is thus about the syntactic nature of *li*: an interrogative particle or a focus marker?

Following the alternative semantics approach to focus proposed by Rooth (1992), Dukova-Zheleva (2010) argues that in (53), whereby *li* is in Foc (i.e., in the head of our ContrastP), it can either take the entire proposition in its scope (wide focus, all-focus, (54a)) or scopes over the only constituent which occupies its specifier (narrow focus, contrastive focus (54b)).

(54) a. OP Int/Q [$_{FocP/ContrastP}$ Foc V+li$_{+Q}$] [IP]]
b. OP Int/Q [$_{FocP/ContrastP}$ XP Foc li$_{+Q}$] [IP]]

Since *li* itself is within the scope of the polar operator, it is to be expected that the effects on interpretation of *li* in Foc should be comparable to those of *dali*-questions. In other words, whether it is the focus projection that is filled or the immediately higher Q/Int projection should be immaterial to interpretation given that they realize the same combination of Q and Foc features. This is confirmed, as (55) and (56) show: a *dali*-question can be paraphrased as a *li*-question regardless of scope:

(55) a. *Bašta ti   pita   dali šte xodiš   dovečera na*
      Father your he.asks if will   you.go tonight   to
      kino (ili šte praviš nešto drugo).
      cinema (or will you.do something else)
      'Your father is asking if you will be going to the cinema tonight (or you will be doing something else)'
   b. *Bašta ti   pita   šte xodiš   li dovečera na*
      Father your he.asks will you.go Q tonight   to
      kino (ili šte praviš nešto drugo).
      cinema (or will you.do something else)
      'Your father is asking if you will be going to the cinema tonight (or you will be doing something else)'

(56) a. *Bašta ti   pita   dali na KINO   šte xodiš dovečera*
      Father your he.asks if   to CINEMA will you.go tonight
      (ili šte praviš   nešto   drugo)
      (or will you.do   something else)
   b. *Bašta ti   pita na KINO   li šte xodiš ovečera (dili šte praviš nešto drugo).*
      Father your asks to CINEMA Q will you.go tonight (or will you.do something else)
      'Your father is asking if you will be going to the cinema tonight (or you will be doing something else)'

From the surface order of (56b) we cannot infer which position the contrastively focussed phrase *na kino* 'to the cinema' occupies. Recall that we postulated two focus positions around Int(*dali*) with slightly different semantic features (see

(50) above). Given that the lower focus position may contain various sorts of contrastively focussed phrases, while the higher one may contain exhaustive focus only, we can use this as a test to verify which exact position *li* occupies in narrow focus XP *li*-questions:

(57) *Bašta ti   pita   [G-Top decata]   samo/*daže/*săšto i   na* KINO   *li*
     father your asks   children-DET only/*even/*also and   to CINEMA Q
     šte (gi)   vodiš   dovečera?
     will (them-CL.ACC) you.take tonight
     lit. 'Your father is asking you if only to the cinema you will be taking the children tonight?'

(57) shows that focalizing adverbs like *even* and *also* are banned from combining with the focus particle *li*. Another piece of evidence comes from the ban on existential quantifiers to precede *li* (58).

(58) **Pitam te*   NJAKOGO/VSEKI   *li šte vodiš*   s   *teb na kino*
     I.ask you-CL.ACC SOMEONE/EVERYONE Q will you.take with you to cinema
     lit. 'I am asking you if you will be taking someone/everyone to with you the cinema'

Assuming that these distributional restrictions are syntactic and relate to the fact that the position of exhaustive focus is unavailable for non-unique adverbs, as well as for quantifiers with referentially dependent/non-specific readings (*someone, everyone*), it seems plausible to affirm that although *li* is merged as a focus particle in the position of Foc/Contrast in (54), this complementizer reaches the superordinate position of Int where it can take in its scope the contrastively focused XP. It also emerges from the data that XP cannot reach the higher Foc position given that it cannot receive an exhaustive interpretation as shown by (58) above. We can this assume that XP moves to the specifier of Int, (52a), so that a Spec,head relation can be established between Int hosting *li* and the specifier of the same projection. Head-movement of *li* to Int, though not further than Int, will also explain the fact that (G-)topics can linearly precede the XP-*li* complex, as we saw in (57) above.

(59)   Force > G-TopicP* > FocP[exhaustive] > Int > Verid > ContrastP > Fin
                                              li   *li*

If *li* surfaces in Int, the position where the complementizer *dali* is merged, as we argued in the preceding section, then one can imagine that the focus particle does indeed make part of the compositional make-up of the interrogative complementizer which would then be rightly considered as the non-clitic version of *li*. It is quite plausible that the use of *li* as an interrogative complementizer is contingent on its focus properties and that this focalizing Slavic particle dating back to earlier stages of the language has been reanalyzed as an interrogative complementizer precisely because of the superordinate Int projection which licenses C-Foc/Contrast in the left periphery (as we saw above, polarity properties and focus are closely related from a semantic point of view). Claiming however that all occurrences of *dali* are synchronically formed in syntax by combining the modal particle *da* and the focus particle *li* (Callegari 2019), as sketched in (60) below,²⁸ is more ambitious and more difficult to evaluate. It is not uncommon for languages to compose two elements with operator semantics in order to form more complex complementizers with operator properties, e.g., English *whether* composes a *wh-* feature and the existential *either*.

(60)   IntP   VeridP   Foc/ContrastP
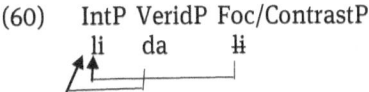

In some recent proposals, embedded yes-no *if*-questions in English pattern with *if*-conditional clauses in terms of complementizer choice and semantic make up. Both contain a *World* operator (Bhatt and Pancheva 2006; Haegeman 2010) or a projection WorldP that specifies the truth value of the clause via a feature *world* with a value [actual] or [possible] (Arsenijević 2009). WorldP could be taken to correspond to my VeridP with the modal particle *da* occupying this position in (59), in alternative to declarative *če*. And, as mentioned above, non-veridicality is relevant for the semantic interpretation of *dali*-clauses.

Even though such a line of thought appears quite attractive, there are at least two counterarguments that can be pointed out specifically for Bulgarian.²⁹ First, if *da* and *li* occupy different projections, it is not clear how they come to form a derived

---

28 Callegari does not make use of the Split CP framework: for her *li* occupies the Focus position. I adapt her proposal to my theoretical instruments,

29 Recall from § 3.4 above that *dali* is related (like *li*) to the disjunctive operator *ili* 'either/or' itself decomposable into 'and' + *li*. If *da* and *ako* 'if-conditional' share the *World* operator meaning, then *dali* differs from *ako* in that it has an additional component not present in *ako* 'if', namely a focus feature. In other words, both *(da)li* and *ako* 'if' would signal that the event is possible, not actual, i.e., not true in the actual world of the discourse (irrealis) but the additional focus meaning of *da+li* coming from the disjunction part of its morphological make-up '(either) or' partitions the possible worlds in which the event might take place into *p* worlds and non-*p* or alternative worlds. From this point of view English (and Italian, Greek), as well as all languages which employ a single complementizer for both interrogative and conditional clauses, capitalize

complementizer. One could imagine that *da* moves to the left of *li* if the latter has reached Int but this type of movement appears problematic under the present proposal: in such case, *li* would skip the intermediate Verid position occupied by *da* in (60), in violation of the Head movement constraint, which requires movement to be local (Travis 1984). Alternatively, it can be assumed that complex syntactic heads are derived by m(orphological)-merger (Matushansky 2006), but in order for m-merger to apply, *da* should be claimed to occupy the head of *li*'s specifier in Foc giving rise to an atomic though derived head. This however would predict that no further syntactic movement is available, given the post-syntactic nature of m-merger. In other words, it becomes less clear how to derive the interrogative syntax of *dali*, in case no movement to Int is posited. While this issue needs further investigation, the predominant view on the syntax of the subjunctive particle (first proposed by Rudin 1992) goes against treating it as a complementizer situated in a C-related position; in fact, it is dubious that *da* ever reaches the left periphery. See also §4.

A second counterargument against the claim that *dali* is formed in the syntax comes from the fact that this complementizer always selects an indicative IP, while *da* selects a Balkan-type subjunctive. If *dali* were the syntactic spell out of *da* + *li*, it would be expected to trigger a subjunctive, contrary to fact. However, the two *da*s can co-occur in those contexts in which *dali* and *da* can combine independently, it is the modal marker *da* that determines the 'subjunctive' morphology on the embedded verb, as well as its interpretation. See (61) as an example:

(61) *Ne znaeše   dali da govori   li   da mălči.*
    not he/she.knew if   DA he/she.talk or DA he/she.be-silent
    'He/she didn't know whether he/she should talk or be silent'

Even if one posits two copies of *da* – one merged in the head of VeridP, and another one merged in a lower position within the CP hierarchy, say Fin, we still need to know why the subjunctive effects get obviated only in case *da* combines with *li* though not in case *da* appears as an independent lexical item. I thus take (61) to show that *dali* is stored in the lexicon as an independent complementizer lexically composed of the modal marker and the focus/Q particle.

To summarize, in this section, we argued that *li* is akin to the disjunctive operator *ili* 'or' whose main function is to select among alternatives. These alternatives can be realized on the level of the proposition or on the level of the constituent which occupies the specifier of *li*. We also argued that even though *li* is merged

---

on the common meaning component, while Bulgarian capitalizes on their meaning difference. This point needs further elaboration which I leave for future research.

in the contrastive focus position (C-Foc/Contrast), and may take in its specifier a contrastively focalized phrase, it does not stay in this position but must move to the superordinate Int head in order to be interpreted as a question operator, sharing with the non-clitic *dali* the features focus and polarity.

3.6 Putting the orders together

Combining the various bits and pieces of the analysis discussed so far, we arrive at the following partial map of the Bulgarian left periphery. In (62), only positions at merge are indicated:

(62)   V A-Topic Force G-Topic* C-Focus   Int   Verid ContrastP   Fin
                                    +exhaustive   +contrastive
                                                        dali   *li*   *če*

Several important conclusions have been reached so far. First, (62) gives the structure where *če* and *dali* are merged in the left periphery: Fin and Int, respectively. Second, we discussed the availability of complementizer movement across the positions of topics and focus, proposing that such movements can indeed be postulated for Bulgarian as well: a) movement of the declarative complementizer to Verid thereby coming to linearly precede ContrastP hosting a contrastive topic or focus; b) movement of both the declarative and the interrogative complementizer *dali* to Force thereby coming to linearly precede one (or more) G-Topic; c) movement of the clitic complementizer *li* to Int, thereby forcing a focussed constituent to occupy its specifier.

The available positions of the three complementizers are summarized in (63):

(63) a. CORE1 V [A-Topic [ForceP *če* [G-Topic* [VeridP (*če*) [C-Topic/C-Focus [FinP (*če*) [CORE2]]]]]]]
 b. CORE1 V [A-Topic [ForceP *dali* [G-Topic* [C-Focus +exhaustive [IntP (*dali*) [C- Focus +contrastive [CORE2]]]]]
 c. CORE1 V [A-Topic [ForceP [G-Topic* [C-Focus +exhaustive [IntP *li* [C-Focus +contrastive]]]]]

Furthermore, there are restrictions on the availability of projected material. Thus, movement of *dali* from Int to Force cannot take place due the need of differentiating between the two types of C-Focus (exhaustive and contrastive) only one of which can project in the Bulgarian left periphery. Positing movement of the complementizer *dali* from Int to Force would predict the order *dali* > C-Focus when the latter is marked as [+exhaustive], which we saw is unavailable in Bulgarian.

The clitic variant of *dali, li*, is merged in the lower C-Focus/Contrast position, but the similar restrictions regarding the distribution and the interpretation of the two types of Focus force *li* to move to the position of *dali*, i.e., Int. In this position, (see (57) above), one or more G-Topics can precede the XP/V-li complex, as confirmed by the data.

As for A-Topics, they obviously do not count for selection, given that an A-Topic can precede *če* and *dali* in the highest available complementizer position Force. Given that a higher selector can "see through" a Topic, and thus select a +Q or -Q complement, then we have to assume that at least as far as Bulgarian is concerned, the configuration of the left periphery need not be local: the higher verb does not need to linearly precede the complementizer in order to able to select it (see the agreement mechanism in (33) above). This is an important difference of Bulgarian with respect to the rest of Slavic.

If locality is indeed a requirement, an alternative solution could be exploited, namely that the highest projection in the left periphery is not Force but some additional projection akin to SubordinatorP, as in Rizzi (2001). In §3, we concluded that *če* does not have the properties of a pure subordinator. A question arises at this point whether A-topics sit outside the left periphery. Krifka (2001: 25) argues that A-Topics constitute "a speech act by itself, an initiating speech act that requires a subsequent speech act like an assertion, a question, command or curse about the entity that was selected". In a similar vein, Bianchi (2014) regards topic shifting as indicating a separate speech act which is then conjoined to the speech act expressed by the following clause, as illustrated in (64):

(64) [$_{\&P}$ [$_{Top}$ Those petunias,] & [$_{ForceP}$ Force$_{[decl]}$ they are very nice]] (Bianchi 2014)

For comparable data from Modern Greek, where too topics can precede the declarative complementizer, Roussou (2000) has adopted the solution that *oti* 'that', which itself is marked as (+declarative), (subordinator), can optionally raise to the position of Subordinator, as opposed to the factive complementizer *pu*, which is merged directly in the higher Sub position. In Krapova (2010), I discussed the correlation between factivity and complementation, and I argued that indeed, topics, in particular an A-Topic, cannot surface in front of the complementizer *če* when selected by a factive verb like *regret*.

(65) *Săžaljavam, [knigite] če   [na Peter] Ivan ošte ne   mu   gi
      I.regret   books-DET that   to Peter Ivan yet not him-CL.DAT them-CL.ACC
      is vărnal
      is given-back
      lit. 'I regret that as for the books, Ivan hasn't returned them to Peter yet'

If these data are confirmed, and if the highest position of the Bulgarian left periphery turns out to be related to factivity, labelled C$_{Fact}$ in (66), then the declarative complementizer *če* can be found, according to the type of clause, in each of the complementizer positions theoretically available in the CP field (Fin, Verid, Force and C$_{Fact}$):

(66) C$_{Fact}$ A-Topic Force G-Topic C-Focus Int Verid C-Focus/Topic Fin
      ↑   ↑   ↑
      └─────────┴──────────────────────┴──────────────────────────────┘

The implication of (66) would be that *če* is maximally underspecified with respect to the features of these projections and can thus transit across the entire CP field. I leave for future work a more precise analysis of A-topics and their relative order with respect to the various types of complementizers in virtue of factivity.

4 *Da*: a modal particle or a complementizer in the left periphery?

In this section I briefly consider the Bulgarian modal particle *da* which introduces subjunctive clauses. In our discussion of the compositional make-up of the interrogative complementizer *dali* in §3.5, we hinted that *da* has no access to the C-domain even though it may seem that certain properties of *da* are shared with those of the declarative complementizer.

4.1 Veridicality issues

As in many other languages, the Bulgarian subjunctive does not seem to be associated with a specific kind of modality or mood. *Da*-clauses can be main, selected or unselected.

Since *da* occurs in a variety of clauses, it is difficult to associate this particle with a single description: in root contexts a *da*-clause can be an imperative, an optative, or a counterfactual (among others).

(67) a. *(Kazax) da   dojdeš   vednaga!*
        (I.said) DA   you.come   immediately
        'I told you to come here immediately'
    b. *Nadjavam se/dano   da   imaš   kăsmet!*
        I.hope   /let's hope DA   you.have luck
        'I hope/let's hope you will be lucky'

c. *Da beše   učil,   šteše   da   spolučiš.*
   DA you.were studied you.would DA you.succeed
   'If you had studied, you would have succeeded'

In embedded contexts a *da*-clause, depending on the class of verbs that selects it, can correspond to monoclausal 'restructuring' configuration or a bi-clausal control structure or a bi-clausal subjunctive configuration of the Romance type (see Krapova and Cinque 2018 and §4.5 below for further discussion).

In a series of papers, Giannakidou (1998; 2009:1887) proposes that the subjunctive is non-veridical, i.e., it creates a semantic space in which the sets of worlds compatible with what the individual knows are partitioned into *p* and non-*p* worlds. Additionally, Giannakidou argues that non-veridicality is what all subjunctives share cross-linguistically. A slightly different idea of the distinction between veridical and non-veridical contexts in the prism of the distinction between indicative and subjunctive modality is presented in Smirnova (2012: 24) for Bulgarian:

(68) Function of mood in Bulgarian
   a. The subjunctive presupposes that the domain with respect to which the embedded proposition p is evaluated, i.e. $\cap f(\alpha)(w)$ is non-homogeneous: some worlds in $\cap f(\alpha)(w)$ are p worlds and some worlds are not-p worlds.
   b. The indicative presupposes that $\cap f(\alpha)(w)$ is homogeneous: all worlds are p worlds or all worlds are not-p worlds.

Based on these definitions, Smirnova establishes that the criterion underlying mood choice is "epistemic commitment" to the truth of a proposition. Giannakidou (2016) further establishes a link between (non)veridicality and epistemic commitment: "a fully committed speaker is in a veridical epistemic state, which is a state with only worlds where the proposition is true" (p. 187). This by necessity requires the choice of an indicative *če*-complement. However, not all indicative-selecting verbs come with such a presupposition. For example, a sentence like (69a)

(69) a. *Ivan vjarva/smjata,   če opasnostta   e silno   preuveličena*
   Ivan believes/thinks that danger-DET is strongly overestimated
   'John believes/thinks that the danger is highly overestimated'

is obviously true for John (the believer) though not necessarily for the speaker who need not commit himself/herself in any possible way to the truth of the proposition, and can thus produce the following continuation:

(69) b. ….., *no az znam, če   opasnostta   e   seriozna.*
       but I I.know that   danger-DET   is   serious
       'but I know that there is a real danger'

To deal with the difference in commitment, Giannakidou proposes that veridicality (and epistemic commitment) is always relativized to an epistemic anchor. Anchors are the individuals asserting the sentence,[30] and both the speaker and the main clause subject can function as such, producing differences on the commitment scale in accord with the semantics of type of matrix verb. Since mood choice is a direct outcome of whether a truth inference of the complement clause is available to at least one epistemic agent, predicates can also be divided into veridical or not: veridical predicates allow for such relativized commitment to truth, while non-veridical predicates allow no such commitment.[31] I cannot go into a discussion of the various types of predicates in Bulgarian in relation to the concept of veridicality, but the important thing to note is that all verbs that may select for a subjunctive in Bulgarian, e.g., propositional attitude verbs like 'want', 'hope' and 'suggest' are non-veridical, i.e., they never introduce a proposition that is evaluated as true in all possible worlds. According to Giannakidou (2009, 2016), the main function of the subjunctive is to signal that a certain proposition p is left open (p is not entailed or presupposed):[32] in Smirnova's terms, the domain with respect to which p is evaluated are partitioned into p and non-p worlds, cf. (68a) above. Consequently, the subjunctive indicates that speaker (or the main clause subject) is in a weak(er) epistemic state.[33] Weaker epistemic states correlate with reduced confidence or with a low(er) degree of belief in the actual truth of the proposition. See also Siegel (2009: 1878): "in Balkan, indicative is correlated with a higher degree of certainty on the part of the subject than is subjunctive".

---

[30] That the sentence is asserted can be shown by the fact that an evidential cannot be used after *believe*-verbs in Bulgarian. Such predicates accept only an indicative or a subjunctive in certain cases. This shows that the evidential always involves the speaker and can be used as a test for distinguishing between the veridicality status of the proposition with respect to either the speaker or the subject.
[31] Giannakidou (2016) also proposes that veridicality is coded via a matching mechanism between the selecting verb and the mood of its complement.
[32] Other non-veridical contexts include questions, modal verbs and adverbs, imperatives, conditionals, the future, disjunctions, *before* clauses.
[33] Epistemic states are sets of worlds compatible with what the individual anchor knows or believes.

4.2 Non-veridicality properties of *da*

In view of the above discussion, and in confirmation to our previous analysis, veridical complement clauses in Bulgarian are expected to be indicative, and to also contain the declarative complementizer *če* (in opposition to *dali*-clauses which are indicative but create a non-veridical domain). Recall that we argued that this complementizer may occur in more C-positions among which particularly relevant for veridicality are Fin and Verid.

Now what about *da*? Are these positions also relevant for *da*? This might appear plausible if it can be shown that VeridP can be specified as [± veridical] with *če* alternating with the modal marker *da* in the head of VeridP. The specification of Fin will thus be free from modality features and will contain instead only features relevant to the realization of the clause as finite or non-finite. Below, we will see that in certain selected contexts *da* also expresses syntactic non-finiteness and would thus alternate with *če* along two dimensions – veridicality and finiteness. (7) above would thus be revised as (70):

(70) CORE1   Force   Verid   Fin   CORE2
             +/-Q   [+indicative]   finite
             Modal   [+subjunctive]   non-finite

4.3 *Da* in C?

Pitsch (2018) summarizes the two analyses that have been proposed: *da*-complements are full CPs and *da* is a complementizer in a C position; *da*-complements are regular IP clauses and *da* is a modal particle internal to CORE 2/IP and located in the head of a special projection dedicated to mood features and labelled MoodP, as originally suggested by Rivero (1994) on the basis of its complementary distribution with the future marker *šte* which, too, requires strict adjacency with the (present tense) finite verb. The ambivalence of *da* as a complementizer vs. mood marker is replicated in debates about the status of the virtually identical particles *na*, *să*, *të* in Modern Greek, Romanian, Albanian, respectively, so the controversy goes outside the limits of a language-specific analysis and assumes a wider significance (Rivero 1994; Roussou 2000, 2009; Dobrovie-Sorin 1994; Turano 1994, a.o.; see also discussion in Wiemer this volume).

There are arguments and counter-arguments for each position, as my own earlier work has also shown (Krapova 1999, 2001). On the one hand, both *če* and *da* are free functional morphemes and as such are excellent candidates for a left peripheral position. The various type of left dislocated phrases, as well as of focus phrases are all ordered above *da*, similarly to *če* when the latter can be shown to occupy the lowest C position Fin. For example, as (71) illustrates, a G-Topic, (71a), a C-Topic, (71c), and a contrastive Topic (71b) must precede the modal particle.

(71) a. *Predlagam* [G-Topic *na Ivan*] [C-Foc *TI*] *da mu kažeš*
I.suggest to Ivan YOU-NOM DA him-CL.DAT you.tell
kakvo e našeto rešenie.
what is our-DET decision
'I suggest that it should be YOU who will let Ivan know what our decision is'
b. ?*Nadjavam se* [C-Topic *edna kniga*] [*Ivan*]_F *da mi podari*
I.hope one book Ivan DA me-CL.DAT gives,
a [C-Topic *druga*] [*ti*]_F *da mi kupiš.*
and another YOU-NOM DA me-CL.DAT you.buy
'I hope that Ivan will give me for free one book, and that you will buy me a second one'
c. *Iskam* [G-Topic *tazi kniga*] [_IP *Ivan da mi ja podari*]
I.want this book Ivan DA me-CL.DAT it-CL.ACC gives
Lit. 'I want that this book, Ivan gives it to me as a present'

In each of these sentences, the particle *da* appears next to a subject. Note that while (71a) gives no indication as to whether the subject occupies the C-Foc/Contrast position of the left periphery or has been focussed in situ, (71b) makes it clear that the subject must be occupying the canonical position of Spec,IP/CORE2. Recall also our previous conclusion that there is only one C-Top/Foc position in the left periphery (see §3.3.1–§3.3.2 and the structural representation in (65) above), as well as the examples in (23)–(24) above attesting that second conjunct of a contrast set is focus marked in situ. I take these data to show that *da* is sensitive to subject properties and must be adjacent to an overt (or null) subject, marking the left boundary of the IP/CORE2 (71c). With the subject appearing on the opposite side of *če* and *da* (compare for example (71) with (63a) above), we have a clear indication that the lowest structural position of *če* 'that' is higher than (the highest position of) *da*. If the former is Fin (66), then the latter is not part of the left periphery.

4.4 Veridicality and double mood choice

As mentioned above, the complementary distribution between the indicative complementizer and the subjunctive particle arises not as a result of the syntactic position they occupy but as a result of the selectional properties of the main predicates *in lieu* of veridicality. A potential counterexample comes from a small group of selecting predicates which feature a double mood choice. Note, however, that the meaning of the verb changes according to whether the complement is introduced by *če* or by *da*. For example, in (72a) below the complement of *hope* introduces a homogeneous domain in the sense of (68b) above (all worlds are either *p* worlds, or ¬*p* worlds, where *p* = Peter has left, and ¬*p* = Peter hasn't left). This returns a meaning that we can label 'weakly assertive' which goes together with a high(er) certainty about the existence of a point in time in which the leaving event has taken place. In (72b), on the other hand, *hope* expresses a preference reading and denotes an attitude (Farkas 1992; Giannakidou 2016). In this case, the *da*-complement introduces a non-homogeneous domain in the sense of (68a) above, and the interpretation of *hope* is similar to that of a preferential predicate like *want* (the worlds in which Peter has left are preferred over worlds in which Peter has not left).[34] Note that a *when*-clause is available as an adverbial clause only under the scope of *da* (and the main verb *hope*) where it does not anchor the proposition to any particular time. This also explains why the *when*-clause is ruled out in (72a): it is simply incompatible with the resultative meaning of the present perfect which bans temporal anchoring:

(72) a. *Ivan se nadjava,   če Petăr e zaminal (*kogato ti   si   dojdeš).*
        Ivan REFL hopes   that Peter is left (*when   you-NOM REFL you.come
        'Ivan hopes that Peter will have left (*when/by the time you come back home'
     b. *Ivan se nadjava Petăr da e zaminal, kogato ti   si dojdeš*
        Ivan REFL hopes Peter   DA is left   when   you-NOM REFL you.come
        'Ivan hopes that Peter will have left when/by the time you come back home'

The relation between mood choice and veridicality and/or epistemic commitment is further strengthened by examples like those in (73a)-(74a), featuring respectively the so-called polarity subjunctives (Quer 2001, 2009) and subjunctives in questions producing an epistemic meaning (Giannakidou 2009, 2016: 183). These

---

34 Anand and Hacquard (2013) have argued for a multicomponent analysis of predicates such as *hope*, claiming that they contain a doxastic component, which triggers indicative selection, and a preference/bouletic component, which triggers subjunctive selection. The indicative example in (72a) is thus interpreted in a doxastic sense (i.e., in the epistemic model of the anchor *i* (= Ivan), there is a world compatible with Ivan's beliefs where he wins), whereas the subjunctive example in (72b) is interpreted in a more bouletic sense, referring to Ivan's preference (i.e., in the epistemic model of *i* = Ivan there is one world, call it the ideal world, where Ivan wins and which is more desirable to him than the worlds in which he does not win).

subjunctive types are available with propositional attitude predicates like e.g., *vjarvam* 'believe', *mislja* 'thinks' which exhibit a double mood choice: while they typically take an indicative *če*-complement, a switch to a *da*-clause gets licensed by several (non-veridical) operators (in the sense of Giannakidou 1995, 1998). In fact, these operators coincide with the ones that allow for an unselected *dali*-clause, as discussed in §3.2, namely matrix negation, the question operator, as well as modal expressions of possibility like *maybe, perhaps* (not illustrated here). The indicative on the other hand scopes over any of these matrix operators, cf. (73b)-(74b):[35]

(73) a. *(Ne) vjarvam   Marija da ima PhD .
        not I.believe   Maria DA has PhD
        'I don't believe Maria has a PhD'
     b. (Ne) vjarvam,   če Marija ima PhD.
        (not) I.believe   that Maria has PhD
        'I don't believe Maria to have a PhD'

(74) a. Vjarvaš   li Marija da ima PhD?
        you.believe Q Maria DA has PhD
        'Do you believe Maria has a PhD?'
     b. Vjarvaš   li, če Marija ima PhD?
        you.believe Q that Marija has PhD
        'Do you believe that Maria has a PhD?'

The function of matrix negation in (73) and of the Q operator in (74) is to remove the veridical reading inherent in the *če*-clause so that the embedded proposition is no longer evaluated as true in any individual's epistemic model. Giannakidou's approach would predict that such contexts would require a subjunctive complement, so the fact that a *če*-complement is still available in such non-veridical environments can perhaps be handled better under Smirnova's proposal, which, as mentioned above, relies on the notion of epistemic commitment. Whatever the correct explanation for the relation of mood choice to veridicality or epistemic commitment, the above examples seem to show that just like *če*, *da* must also be related to the C-position Verid, although the particle itself, for reasons we saw in the examples (71), cannot surface phonologically in this position. The rele-

---

[35] This is well documented in the literature (Farkas 1992, Manzini 1994, among others). Negation and the question operator license the subjunctive in complements of epistemic predicates also in Romance (Quer 2009). See also Siegel (2009) for Balkan languages.

vance of a special position within the left periphery related to veridicality or to the speaker's epistemic commitment as a function of his/her evaluation of the truth of the complement clause merits further research. Here, I propose that there is some feature transmission mechanism ensuring that the particle gets related somehow to the left periphery. One can imagine that *da* is merged in some Mood projection inside IP, as in the classical analysis of Rivero (1994), but that depending on context the feature(s) carried by *da* are copied onto the Verid head for reasons of interpretation under selection or under non-veridical operators of sorts. The modal force is then passed over to Force. I leave for future research the exact implementation of this proposal:

(75) Force   Topic field   Verid   Contrast   Fin   [$_{IP}$ Mood
      Modal   -veridical   +finite   *da*

4.5 *Da* as marker of ±finiteness

Apart from its veridicality-related property, the functional specification of *da* must also involve a finiteness-related feature. Note that all *da*-clauses involve a morphologically finite verb form but as I show in Krapova (2001), the syntactic expression of (non)finiteness in Bulgarian correlates with Tense and subject identity. Pitsch (2018) examines carefully various types of *da*-clauses and confirms the conclusion that wherever a complement has a [-T] specification, i.e., wherever embedded tense is interpreted as strictly simultaneous (realized morphologically as present tense) with the tense specification of the matrix clause, *da* can be argued to be syntactically non-finite and thus to correspond to an infinitive in a language with infinitives. On the other hand, wherever a complement is specified for Tense, i.e., has a [+T] specification, referentially independent in terms of tense, and denoting a proposition with a distinct time frame, then it can be said to correspond to a true subjunctive. As a consequence, the embedded subject can be identical or not with the main subject. Thus, subject (non-)identity follows from the competition of the two moods (subjunctive vs. infinitive) (Farkas 1992; Krapova 2001; Pitsch 2018; Wiemer this volume). A 'subjunctive'-like verb like *očakvam* 'expect' in (76a) allows for an overt embedded subject with disjoint reference, while an 'infinitive'-like verb like *znam* 'know (how)/be able' in (76b) does not in spite of the agreement inflection on both the main and the embedded verb:

(76) a. *Šefăt   očakva   (ti)   da si   podadeš ostavkata*
          boss-DET   expects   you-NOM   DA REFL   you.give resignation-DET
          'The boss expects you to resign'

b. *Ivan znae (*toj)   da pluva'*
   Ivan knows he-NOM   DA swims
   'John can swim'

Krapova and Cinque (2018) give the following list of predicates that select an infinitive-like *da*-complement, (75), arguing in favour of a monoclausal approach to their syntactic union on the basis of various transparency effects:

(77) a. modals: *moga* 'can', *trjabva* 'must', *može* 'it is possible'
   b. aspectuals and implicatives: *započvam* 'start', *spiram* 'stop', *svăršvam* 'finish', *opitvam se* 'try', *uspjavam* 'manage, succeed'
   c. motion verbs: *otivam da* 'go and do (something)'
   d. verbs of knowing[36]/ability: *znaja da* 'know how'/'can', *uča se da* 'learn how'

Modals, aspectuals and motion verbs combine with clausal projections smaller than a clause in many languages. They are thus comparable to the "restructuring" predicates well-known from Romance (Rizzi 1982, Cinque 2006). Several notes are in order regarding the classification in (77). First, the two predicates in (77d) *znaja da* 'know how' and *uča se da* 'learn', which is the inchoative version of *know how*, meaning 'come to know how', can be made to converge with the class of modals in virtue of their interpretation as predicates of mental (or internal) ability, synonymous with one of the meanings of English *can*, as in e.g., *Znam da pluvam* (lit. I.know DA I.swim 'I can swim'). Second, the class of aspectuals in (77b) has been extended to also comprise certain implicative verbs like *zabravjam* 'forget to', *uspjavam* 'succeed/manage to', which can be viewed as aspect-related in that they express notions akin to conative aspect (*try to*, *attempt to*), frustrative/success aspect (*fail to*, *forget to*, *(not) succeed/ manage to*). As demonstrated by Cinque (1999, 4.2.8.), non-Indo-European languages often express these aspects via grammatical suffixes, incorporated into the verb stem, much like what happens with prototypical aspectual notions such as inceptive (*begin to*), terminative (*stop* V–ing), completive (*finish* V–ing). Third, motion verbs in Bulgarian also require the subjunctive when expressing the distance covered to reach an endpoint at which the event takes place, as in e.g., *Otivam da kupja mljako* 'I.go DA I.buy milk 'I go and buy milk'. All the syntactic classes in (77) share the defining properties of Romance restructuring predicates: strict co-reference between the matrix subject and the understood subject of the embedded verb resulting

---

[36] I use the less formal term 'knowing' here in order to distinguish the ability sense of *znaja da* 'know how' from the epistemic sense of *znaja* 'know' which requires a *če* 'that'-clause.

in their obligatory semantic identity (as manifested by the obligatory agreement-feature matching between the two verbs); absence of deictic Tense properties of the embedded verb; impossibility of Nominative case assignment in the 'embedded' domain, cf. (76b).[37]

Cinque (1999) has shown that what are standardly considered IP-internal and unique categories of Mood, Tense and Aspect should be seen as a rich and fine-grained domain comprising various functional projections associated with different types of interpretations and observing a strict relative order. These functional projections can host verbs, adverbs and other elements dedicated to expressing modal/temporal/aspectual meanings. See (78) taken from Cinque (2006: 91, 93) and illustrating the relevant projections corresponding to the classes of (77):

(78) [$Mod_{epistemic}$ [$Mod_{possibility}$ [$Mod_{obligation}$ [$Asp_{terminative}$
    trjabva 'must'   *može* 'it's possible' *trjabva* 'have to'   *spiram* 'stop'
    [$Asp_{inceptive}$ [$Mod_{ability}$ [$Asp_{frustrative/success}$ [$Mod_{permission}$ ...
    započvam 'begin'   *moga* 'can^{1}'   *uspjavam* 'manage'   *moga* 'can^{2}'
    [$Asp_{completive}$ [V_{infin}]]]]]]]]]]
    svăršvam 'finish'   *da*+V

Since all of the functional verbs in (78) must combine with *da*, the hierarchy suggests that in similar 'restructuring' environments *da* is a sort of infinitive marker functionally equivalent, as indicated informally in (78), to the infinitive suffix in languages with infinitival morphology.

The hierarchical ordering of functional projections in (78) can also accounts for multiple sequences of *da*-complements. Such constructions, exemplified in (79) below, follow rigid ordering principles which would be hard to account if *da* were to occupy a single Mood projection. For example, the fact that the only interpretation available in (79) is the one in which the possibility modal takes the deontic ones (ability or permission) in its scope cannot be made to follow from any independent syntactic requirement on the order of clauses. On the contrary, in an approach that postulates a sequence of dedicated functional verbs associated with a specific interpretation, the correct interpretations simply follows

---

[37] Krapova and Cinque (2018) structurally distinguish between subjunctive-selecting predicates (e.g., *otkazvam* 'refuse') from infinitive-selecting ones (i.e., those in (77)) by arguing that in the former case strict coreference results from exhaustive control in a bi-clausal configuration, while in the latter case, the embedded verb's lexical subject raises to the subject position of the restructuring verb in a strictly monoclausal configuration (much like what happens with auxiliaries). The reader is referred to that work for details about other types of *da*-clauses in bi-clausal structures exhibiting obviation effects (as in (76a) above similar to Romance subjunctives.

from the order of the projections themselves without any further stipulation, thus predicting the two available interpretations in (i) (whereby the first appearance of *možem* 'we can' is interpreted in its 'possibility' reading, while the second occurrence of the same verb has the reading of 'ability' or 'permission'). The opposite combinations in (ii) are correctly excluded by the predictions of the hierarchy:

(79) [$_{CP}$ [$_{IP}$ pro *možem* [*da* [$_{FP}$ *možem* [*da* [$_{VP}$ *vlezem*]]]]]
we.can DA we.can DA we.enter
(Krapova 1998:118)
  (i) 'It is possible for us to be able to enter'; 'It is possible for us to be permitted to enter'
  (ii) '*We are able for it to be possible for us to enter'; *We are permitted for it to be possible for us to enter'.

Given that *da* can introduce different types of infinitival verbal complements to restructuring verbs, as well as different types of regular modalized clauses (e.g. after classes of verbs as those in (80), which unlike the verb classes in (77) take a regular CP complement rather than a reduced one, the possibility exists that the modal marker does not occupy a single position within the clause. In (78) we hinted at a possible interpretation of *da* as part of the embedded VP area of restructuring verbs, while with the predicates in (80) *da* seems related to modality rather than to the expression of functional non-finiteness:

(80) a. Preference predicates (volitionals and predicates of desire): *iskam* 'want', *želaja* 'desire'[38]
  b. Commissive predicates: *obeštavam* 'promise'

---

38 Krapova and Cinque (2018) argue that desideratives are ambiguous between an infinitive or a subjunctive-taking predicate so they may enter in either a monoclausal or in a biclausal structure, see (i). This structural ambiguity is shared by Romance, see (ii):

(i) a. *Iskam* [$_{VP}$ *da živeja*]   (monoclausal)
      I.want-   DA I.live
      'I want to live'
   b. *Iskam* [$_{CP}$ *ti*   *da živeeš*]   (biclausal)
      I.want you-NOM DA you.live
      'I want you to live'
(ii) a. *Voglio vivere*
      'I want to live (infinitive)'
    b. *Voglio che tu viva.*
      'I want that you live (subjunctive)'

c. Directives: *kazvam da* 'tell to', *săvetvam* 'advise', *porăčvam* 'order', *zapovjadvam* 'order'
d. Permissives: *pozvoljavam* 'allow', *zabranjavam* 'forbid'
e. Epistemics: *vjarvam* 'believe', *mislja* 'think' (see (73)a, (74a) above)

If these classes of verbs categorially select for a CP complement, then it appears plausible that *da* gets inserted in particular functional positions within the IP area (see the map in (78)), activating upon merge the functional content of these positions. An embedded imperative, for example, would activate in its derivation the projection Mod$_{obligation}$ (81a) where *da* spells out the content of a deontic modal (cf. English *should*). And this might be said to be the case with the other directive verbs in (80c). Permissives, on the other hand, can be said to involve the activation of Mod$_{permission}$, while epistemic predicates may involve the activation of different modal projections, for example Mod$_{possibility}$ in (81b) where *da*'s functional content is comparable to that of a possibility modal or of an adverb like *može bi* 'maybe'. This is confirmed by the paraphrase with a *če*-clause which unlike the *da*-clause can combine with modal adverbs like e.g., *može bi* 'maybe' producing the exact same interpretation:

(81) a. *Lekarjat   mi   kaza   da počivam poveče* (Mod$_{obligation}$)
        doctor-DET him-CL.DAT he.told DA I.rest   more
        'The doctor told me that I should rest more"
    b. *(ne) Vjarvam   (*može bi) da ima   (*može bi) lek za tazi bolest* (Mod$_{possibility}$)
        (not) I.believe (*maybe) DA there-is (*maybe) cure for this disease
        'I (don't) believe in the possibility of curing this disease'
    Cf. *(ne) Vjarvam, če može bi ima   (može bi) lek za tazi bolest*
        (not) I.believe that maybe there-is (maybe) cure for this disease
        'I (don't) believe that there can exist a cure for this disease'

This of course is a very tentative proposal. As is well-known, the list of verbs that select for a *da*-complement is quite long, and the range of constructions involving *da* is difficult to capture in a unified way (see also Wiemer this volume). A finer grained compositional analysis of the lexical features of selecting verbs is needed before we can gain a clue to what motivates selectional preferences and restrictions, i.e., why certain verbs combine with certain types of *da*-complements – a notoriously difficult question that remains unresolved until present day.

To summarize, in this section we have looked at structural and semantic properties of the Bulgarian modal marker *da*. But the important thing to note here is that *da*-complements can be of various sizes, as also argued for by Todorović (2012) on the basis of data from Serbo-Croatian but with a different theoretical apparatus. It is in any case not accidental that basically the same classes of verbs that select *da* in Bulgarian also select the respective modal particles present in the rest of the Balkan languages. I therefore converge with Siegel (2009) and Pitsch (2018) that *da* is a vacuous element although I do not agree with these authors that *da*-complements do not add anything to sentence semantics. In my view, *da* spells out functional features like tense/finiteness and mood in accord with the hierarchy in (78) according to whether the *da*-complement constitutes an independent syntactic domain or not. In the former case, i.e., when the *da*-complement is part of a full-fledged CP, I suggest that *da*'s features are copied onto the C positions of Fin and Verid, the former obligatory finite, i.e., endowed with the feature [+T], and the latter endowed with the feature [+subjunctive]. This accords well with Rizzi's proposal that Fin expresses distinctions pertaining to the (non-)finiteness character of CORE2, i.e., information that "faces the inside, the content of the IP embedded under it" (Rizzi 1997: 283). As for the role of Verid, we can suppose that its semantic function is to serve as an epistemic anchor for the embedded proposition (possibly via a *World* operator, as mentioned in 3.5 above).

(82)   CP ..... Verid + subjunctive] ... Fin[+T]   ...

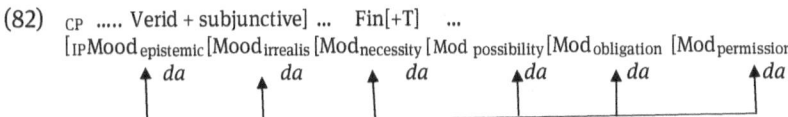

If on the other hand, the *da*-complement is selected by a modal, an aspectual, a motion verb or a verb of *knowing how*, the entire complex constitutes a monoclausal domain, in which case, *da*'s function equals that of an infinitive(-like) marker introducing a VP denoting an event rather than a proposition. This then is responsible for the host of effects that are related to monoclausal non-finite expressions, like the lack of an independent temporal specification, the obligatory lack of an overt nominative subject preceding *da* (which has raised to the subject position of the entire IP, as indicated by the trace in (83)), as well as other transparency effects (discussed in detail in Krapova and Cinque (2018):

(83)   [$_{CP}$ [$_{IP}$ Subject NP [Modal/Aspectual/Motion V^1 [t *da* + V^2]

5 Conclusion

In this paper, I proposed some modification of the original analysis of Rizzi (1997) and I hope to have shown, using data drawn from Bulgarian, that the CP area connecting CORE1 to CORE2 constitutes a rich functional domain comprising different types of complementizers as well as discourse phrases. Rizzi's work opened an important theoretical perspective on the syntactic and semantic dependencies between CORE1 and CORE2 and the ways they are encoded in the left periphery of CORE2 and determine some of the structural and semantic properties of CORE2 itself.

I argued that the projection labelled by Rizzi Fin(iteness), where presumably the declarative complementizer *če* in Bulgarian is merged, cannot handle the distribution of Topics emerging from the Bulgarian data, so I proposed an additional projection VeridP on top of FinP, hosting not only the raised complementizer *če* 'that' but also features copied from the various IP-internal modal projections hosting the modal marker *da*. I also reviewed the other C positions where the declarative complementizer *če* and the interrogative one *dali/li* 'if/whether' can surface arguing that the left periphery of the Bulgarian embedded clause is structured in a hierarchical way. In order to establish the precise dimensions of the CP hierarchy, I had to discuss some old-standing issues relevant to the positions and the variety of discourse phrases like topics and focus. I also argued that Force may not be necessarily filled by an overt complementizer but that it must be connected to the lower CP area via some feature transmission mechanism.

At the same time the above observations have shown that traditionally used concepts like *realis-irrealis* are insufficient to explain the wide variety of structural instantiations of the complementizers and the particles found in the Bulgarian functional domain, whether in the left periphery or within CORE2. To take one example, propositional attitude predicates are expected to select an *irrealis* complement but in Bulgarian and in Slavic more generally they take an indicative as in regular assertions. The modal particle *da*, too, cannot be viewed as a simple *irrealis* marker. Instead, as I tried to show, it functions as a default marker of non-veridicality, which is why it is compatible with a wide variety of modal meanings within the independently established functional hierarchy of Cinque (1999). I also showed that the complexity of this particle goes beyond the expression of modality in that with a particular class of predicates it is exploited as a marker of non-finiteness comparable to a morphological infinitive.

References

Abbott, Barbara. 2006. Where have some of the presuppositions gone. Drawing the boundaries of meaning: Neo-Gricean studies, In Betty J. Birner & Gregory Ward (eds.), *Pragmatics and Semantics in Honor of Laurence R. Horn*, 1–20. Amsterdam & Philadelphia: Benjamins.
Adger, David & Josep Quer. 2001. The syntax and semantics of unselected embedded interrogatives. *Language* 77. 107–133.

Ambar, Manuela. 2016. On finiteness and the Left Periphery: Focussing on Subjunctive. In Joanna Błaszczak, Anastasia Giannakidou, Dorota Klimek-Jankowska & Krzysztof Migdalski (eds.), *Mood, Aspect, Modality revisited. New Answers to Old Questions*, 125–176. Chicago: The University of Chicago Press.

Anand, Pranav & Valentine Hacquard. *2013*. Epistemics and attitudes. *Semantics and Pragmatics* 6. 1–59.

Arnaudova, Olga. 2001. Prosodic Movement and Information Focus in Bulgarian. In Steven Franks, Tracy Holloway King & Michael Yadroff (eds.), *Annual Workshop on Formal Approaches to Slavic Linguistics. The Bloomington Meeting 2000*, 19–36. Ann Arbor: Michigan Slavic Publications.

Arnaudova, Olga. 2002. Clitic Left Dislocation and Argument Structure in Bulgarian. In Jindřich Toman (ed.), *Proceedings of FASL* 10, 23–46. Michigan Slavic Publications.

Arnaudova, Olga. 2010. *Focus and Bulgarian Clause Structure. Word Order Variation and Prosody*. VDM Verlag.

Arsenijević, Boban. 2009. Correlatives as types of conditional. In Anikò Lipták (ed.), *Correlatives cross-linguistically*, 131–156. Amsterdam & Philadelphia: Benjamins.

Belletti, Adriana. 2004. Aspects of the low IP area. In Liugi Rizzi (ed.), *The Structure of CP and IP*, 16–51. New York: Oxford University Press.

Benincà, Paola & Cecilia Poletto. 2004. Topic, Focus and V2: Defining the CP Sublayers. In Liugi Rizzi (ed.), *The Structure of CP and IP*, 52–75. New York: Oxford University Press.

Bianchi, Valentina & Silvio Cruschina. 2016. The derivation and interpretation of polar questions with a fronted focus. *Lingua* 170. 47–68.

Bianchi, Valentina. 2019. Spelling Out Focus-Fronting Chains and Wh-Chains: The Case of Italian. *Syntax* 22 (2–3). 146–161.

Bianchi, Valentina & Mara Frascarelli. 2010. Is topic a root phenomenon? *Iberia* 2. 43–88.

Bianchi, Valentina, Giuliano Bocci & Silvio Cruschina. 2015. Focus Fronting and Its Implicatures. In Enoch Aboh, Jeannette Schaeffer & Petra Sleeman (eds.), *Romance Languages and Linguistic Theory* 2013, 1–20. Amsterdam & Philadelphia: Benjamins.

Bianchi, Valentina, Giuliano Bocci & Silvio Cruschina, 2016. Focus Fronting, Unexpectedness, and the Evaluative Dimension. *Semantics and Pragmatics* 9. 1–54.

Bhatt, Rajesh & James Yoon. 1992. On the composition of Comp and parameters of V-2. *Poceedings of the West Coast Conference on Formal Linguistics* 10. 41–53.

Bhatt, Rajesh & Roumyana Pancheva. 2006. Conditionals. In Martin Everaert & Henk van Riemskijk (eds.), *The Blackwell Companion to Syntax*, 638–687. Malden, MA: Blackwell. http://www.rcf.usc.edu/~pancheva/bhatt-pancheva_syncom.pdf (accessed 20 April 2020)

Bocci, Giuliano, Luigi Rizzi & Mamoru Saito. 2018. On the incompatibility of wh and focus. *Gengo Kenkyu* 154. 29–51

Bolinger, Dwight. 1978. Yes-no questions are not alternative questions. In Henry Hiz (ed.), *Questions*, 87–105. Holland: Reidel.

Bošković, Željko. 2001 *On the Nature of the Syntax-Phonology Interface: Cliticization and Related Phenomena*. Amsterdam: Elsevier Science.

Bresnan, Joan. 1972. *Theory of Complementation in English Syntax*. MIT dissertation.

Brunetti, Lisa. 2004. *A Unification of Focus*. Padova: Unipress.

Brody, Michael. 1990. Some remarks on the focus field in Hungarian, In John Harris (ed.), *University College London Working Papers* 2. 225–251.

Büring, Daniel. 2003. On D-Trees, Beans, and B-Accents. *Linguistics and Philosophy* 26 (5). 511–545.

Callegari, Elena. 2019. The relative order of foci and polarity complementizers: a Slavic perspective. University of Oslo (ms.)
Chomsky, Noam. 1972. *Language and Mind*. New York: Harcourt Brace Jovanovich Inc.
Chomsky, Noam. 1981. *Lectures on Government and Binding*. Dordrecht: Foris.
Chomsky, Noam. 1986. *Barriers*. Cambridge: MIT Press.
Cinque, Guglielmo. 1999. *Adverbs and Functional Heads*. New York: Oxford University Press.
Cinque, Guglielmo. 2006. *Restructuring and Functional Heads. The Cartography of Syntactic Structures*, vol. 4. New York: Oxford University Press.
Cinque Guglielmo & Luigi Rizzi. 2010. The cartography of syntactic structures. In Bernd Heine & Haiko Narrog (eds.), *The Oxford Handbook of Linguistic Analysis*, 51–65. New York: Oxford University Press.
Cristofaro, Sonia. 2003. *Subordination*. Oxford: Oxford University Press.
Culicover, Peter. 1996. On distinguishing A'-movements. *Linguistic Inquiry* 27 (3). 445–463.
Dal Farra, Chiara. 2018. Towards a Fine-Grained Theory of Focus. *Annali di Ca' Foscari. Serie Occidentale* 52. 39–63.
Hoop, Helen de. 1992. *Case Configuration and Noun Phrase Interpretation*. University of Groningen dissertation.
Dobrovie-Sorin, Carmen. 1994. *The Syntax of Romanian: Comparative Studies in Romance*. Berlin & New York: Mouton de Gruyter.
Dukova-Zheleva, Galina. 2010. *Questions and Focus in Bulgarian*. University of Ottawa dissertation.
Eide, Kristin Melun. 2016 Introduction. In Kristin Melun Eide (ed.), *Finiteness Matters. On finiteness-related phenomena in natural languages*, 1–44. Amsterdam & Philadelphia: Benjamins.
Enç, Murvet. 1991. The Semantics of Specificity. *Linguistic Inquiry* 22. 1–25.
Franks, Steven. 2005. Another look at *li* placement in Bulgarian. *The Linguistic Review* 23 (2). 161–211.
Franks, Steven & Catherine Rudin. 2005. Bulgarian clitics as K heads. In Steven Franks, Frank Y Gladney & Mila Tasseva-Kurktchieva (eds.), *Formal Approaches to Slavic Linguistics. The South Carolina Meeting*, 104–116. Ann Arbor, Michigan: Michigan Slavic Publications.
Frascarelli, Mara. 2007. Subjects, Topics and the Interpretation of Referential pro. An interface approach to the linking of (null) pronouns. *Natural Language and Linguistic Theory* 25. 691–734.
Frascarelli, Mara & Roland Hinterhölzl. 2007. Types of topics in German and Italian. In Kerstin Schwabe & Susanne Winkler (eds.), *On Information Structure, Meaning and Form*, 87–116. Amsterdam & Philadelphia: Benjamins.
Giannakidou, Anastasia. 1998. *Polarity Sensitivity as Nonveridical Dependency*. Amsterdam & Philadelphia: Benjamins.
Giannakidou, Anastastia. 2009. The dependency of the subjunctive revisited: Temporal semantics and polarity. *Lingua* 119. 1883–1908
Giannakidou, Anastasia. 2016. Evaluative Subjunctive and Nonveridicality. In Joanna Błaszczak, Anastasia Giannakidou, Dorota Klimek-Jankowska & Krzysztof Migdalski (eds.), *Mood, Aspect, Modality revisited. New Answers to Old Questions*, 177–217. Chicago: The University of Chicago Press.
Goddard, Cliff. 2002. Yes or no? The complex semantics of a simple question. In Peter Collings & Mengistu Amberber (eds.), *Proceedings of the 2002 Conference of the Australian Linguistic Society*, 1–7. http://www.als.asn.au (accessed 01/10/2020)

Grimshaw, Jane. 1979. Complement selection and the Lexicon. *Linguistic Inquiry* 10. 279–326.
Grimshaw, Jane. 1981. *Argument Structure*. Cambridge: MIT Press.
Grimshaw, Jane. 1994. Minimal s and clause structure. In Barbara Lust, Margarita Suñer & John Whitman (eds.), *Syntactic Theory and First Language Acquisition: Cross-linguistic perspectives*. Vol. 1 *Heads, projections and learnability*, 75–83. Hillsdale, NJ: Lawrence Erlbaum.
Haegeman, Liliane. 1994. *Introduction to Government and Binding Theory*, 2nd ed. Oxford: Blackwell.
Haegeman, Liliane. 2010. The movement derivation of conditional clauses. *Linguistic Inquiry* 41 (4). 595–621
Haegeman, Liliane. 2012. *Adverbial Clauses, Main Clause Phenomena, and the Composition of the Left Periphery*. Oxford: Oxford University Press.
Hamblin, Charles L. 1973. Questions in Montague English. *Foundations of Language* 10. 41–53.
Hansen, Björn, Alexander Letuchiy & Izabela Błaszczyk. 2016. Complementizers in Slavonic (Russian, Polish and Bulgarian). In Kasper Boye & Petar Kehayov (eds.), *Semantic functions of complementizers in European languages*, 175–223. Berlin & Boston: De Gruyter Mouton.
Hill, Virginia. 2002. Complementizer phrases in Romanian. *Rivista di Linguistica*, 14 (2). 223–248.
Hill, Virginia. 2004. On left periphery and focus. In Olga M. Tomić (ed.), *Balkan Syntax and Semantics*, 339–354. Amsterdam & Philadelphia: Benjamins.
Horn, Laurence R. 1969. A pressupositional analysis of *only* and *even*. *Papers from the 5 th Regional Meeting of the Chicago Linguistic Society* 5, 98–107
Horvath, Julia 2010. Discourse Features, Syntactic Displacement and the Status of Contrast. *Lingua* 120 (6). 1346–1369.
Izvorski, Roumyana. 1995. *On Wh-Movement and Focus Movement in Bulgarian*. Paper presented at CONSOLE 2 (1993). University of Tübingen.
Jackendoff, Ray S. 1972. *Semantic Interpretation in Generative Grammar*. Cambridge, MA: MIT Press.
Kašpar, Jiři 2015. Czech left periphery: a preliminary analysis. *Linguistica Brunensia* 64 (1). 71–88.
Kim, Jong-Bok. 2012. On the syntax of it-cleft constructions: A construction-based perspective. *Linguistic Research* 29 (1). 45–68.
Kiss, Katalin É. 1998. Identificational Focus versus Information Focus. *Language* 74. 245–273.
Koopman, Hilda. 2000. *The syntax of specifiers and heads*. London: Routledge.
Krapova, Iliyana. 1998. Modal verbs and modality of *da*. *Annals of the University of Plovdiv. Scientific works – Philology* 36 (1). 111–120.
Krapova, Iliyana. 1999. Subjunctive Complements, Null Subjects and Case Checking in Bulgarian. In Istvan Kenesei (ed.), *Crossing Boundaries*, 239–261. Amsterdam & Philadelphia: Benjamins.
Krapova, Iliyana. 2001. Subjunctive in Bulgarian and Modern Greek. In Maria-Luisa Rivero & Angela Ralli (eds.), *Comparative Syntax of Balkan Languages*. 105–126. New York: Oxford University Press.
Krapova, Iliana. 2002. On the left periphery of the Bulgarian sentence. *University of Venice Working Papers* 12. 107–128.
Krapova, Iliyana & Tsena Karastaneva. 2002. On the structure of the CP field in Bulgarian. In Mila Dimitrova-Vulchanova, Donald L. Dyer, Iliyana Krapova & Catherine Rudin (eds.), *Balkanistica*. 15. 293–321.
Krapova, Iliana & Guglielmo Cinque. 2008. Clitic Reduplication constructions in Bulgarian. In Dalina Kallulli & Liliane Tasmowski (eds.), *Clitic doubling in the Balkan Languages*, 257–288. Amsterdam & Philadelphia: Benjamins.

Krapova, Iliyana & Guglielmo Cinque. 2018. Universal Constraints on Balkanisms. A Case Study: The Absence of Clitic Climbing. In Iliyana Krapova & Brian Joseph (eds.), *Balkan Syntax and (Universal) Principles of Grammar*, 151–191. Berlin & Boston: De Gruyter Mouton.

Krifka, Manfred. 2001. For a structured account of questions and answers. In Caroline Féry & Wolfgang Sternefeld (eds.), *Audiatur vox sapientiae. A Festschrift for Achim von Stechow*, 287–319. Berlin: Akademie Verlag.

Landau, Idan 2004. The scale of finiteness and the calculus of control. *Natural Language and Linguistic Theory* 22. 811–877.

Ledgeway, Adam. 2000. *A comparative syntax of the dialects of southern Italy: a minimalist approach*. Oxford & Boston: Blackwell.

Ledgeway, Adam. 2006. The dual complementizer system in southern Italy: spirito Greco materia romanza? In Anna Laura Lepschy & A. Tosi (eds.), *Rethinking language in contact: the case of Italian*, 112–126. Oxford: Legenda.

Matushansky, Ora. 2006. Head movement in linguistic theory. *Linguistic Inquiry* 37. 69–109.

Nordström, Jackie. 2010. *Modality and Subordinators*. Amsterdam & Philadelphia.

Oehl, Peter. 2007. Unselected embedded interrogatives in German and English. S-selection as dependency formation. *Linguistische Berichte* 212. 403–437.

Palmer, Frans 2001. *Mood and Modality*. Cambridge: Cambridge University Press.

Penčev, Iordan. 1998. *Sintaksis na săvremennija bălgarski knižoven ezik*. Plovdiv: Plovdiv University Press.

Pitsch, Hagen. 2018. Bulgarian moods. *Journal of Slavic Linguistics* 26 (1). 55–100.

Portner, Paul. 2009. *Modality*. Oxford: Oxford University Press.

Quer, Josep. 2001. Interpreting mood. *Probus* 13. 81–111.

Quer, Josep. 2006. Subjunctives. In Martin Everaert and Henk van Riemsdijk (eds.), *The Wiley Blackwell Companion to Syntax*. 2nd ed., 660–684. Hoboken, NJ: John Wiley and Sons.

Radford, Andrew. 2018. *Colloquial English. Structure and Variation*. Cambridge: Cambridge University Press.

Rivero, Maria-Luisa. 1994. Clause Structure and V-Movement in the Languages of the Balkans. *Natural Language and Linguistic Theory* 12. 63–120.

Rizzi, Luigi. 1982. *Issues in Italian Syntax*. Foris: Dordrecht.

Rizzi, Luigi. 1997. The Fine Structure of the Left Periphery. In Liliane Haegeman, (ed.), *Elements of grammar*, 281–337. Dordrecht: Kluwer

Rizzi, Luigi. 2001. On the position of "Int(errogative)" in the left periphery of the clause. In Guglielmo Cinque & Giampaolo Salvi (eds.), *Current Studies in Italian Syntax. Essays offered to Lorenzo Renzi*, 287–296. Amsterdam: Elsevier.

Rizzi, Luigi. 2013. A Note on Locality and Selection. In Yoichi Miyamoto, Daiko Takahashi & Hideki Maki (eds.), *Deep Insights, Broad Perspectives: Essays in Honor of Mamoru Saito*, 325–341. Tokyo: Kaitakusha.

Rizzi, Luigi. 2013. Notes on cartography and further explanation. *Probus* 25 (1). 197–226.

Rizzi, Luigi. 2014. The cartography of syntactic structures: locality and freezing effects on movement. In Anna Cardinaletti, Guglielmo Cinque & Yoshio Endo (eds.), *On Peripheries. Exploring Clause Initial and Clausa Final Positions*, 29–59. Tokyo: Hituzi Syobo Publishing.

Rizzi, Luigi & Giuliano Bocci. 2017. Left periphery of the clause: primarily illustrated for Italian In Martin Everaert and Henk van Riemsdijk (eds.), *The Wiley Blackwell Companion to Syntax*. 2nd ed., 2171–2200. Hoboken, NJ: John Wiley and Sons.

Rizzi, Luigi & Ur Shlonsky. 2007. Strategies of subject extraction. https://www.researchgate.net/publication/235909691_Strategies_of_subject_extraction (accessed 22 March 2020)

Roberts, Ian. 1993. *Verbs in diachronic syntax*. Dordrecht: Kluwer.
Roberts, Ian. 2004. The C-system in Brythonic. Celtic languages and the EPP. In Luigi Rizzi (ed.), *The structure of IP and CP. The cartography of syntactic structures*, vol. 2, 297–328. Oxford: Oxford University Press.
Rooth, Mats. 1992. A theory of focus interpretation. *Natural Language Semantics* 1. 75–116.
Roussou, Anna. 2000. On the left periphery: modal particles and complementisers. *Journal of Greek Linguistics* 1. 65–94.
Roussou, Anna 2009. In the mood for control. *Lingua* 119. 1811–1836.
Roussou, Anna 2010. Selecting complementizers. *Lingua* 120 (3). 582–603.
Rudin, Catherine. 1986. *Aspects of Bulgarian Syntax: Complementizers and wh constructions*. Columbus: Slavica Publishers.
Rudin, Catherine. 1991. Topic and Focus in Bulgarian. *Acta Linguistica Academiae Scientiarum Hungaricae* 40 (3/4). 429–447.
Rudin, Catherine. 1992. The complementizer system of Modern Standard Bulgarian. *Indiana Slavic Studies* 6 / *Balkanistica* 8. 123–130.
Rudin, Catherine. 1993. On Focus Position and Focus Marking in Bulgarian Questions. In *Proceedings of FLSM* 4, 252–265. Department of Linguistics, University of Iowa.
Rudin, Catherine. 1997. Kakvo li e li: Interrogation and focusing in Bulgarian. *Balkanistica* 10. 335–346.
Rudin, Catherine, Christina Kramer, Loren Billings & Mathew Baerman. 1999. Macedonian and Bulgarian *li* Questions: Beyond Syntax. *Natural Language and Linguistic Theory* 17. 541–586.
Sampanis Konstantinos 2012. The Modern Greek subjunctive mood and its semantic features. In Georgia Fragaki, Thanasis Georgakopoulos & Charalambos Themistocleous (eds.), *Current Trends in Greek Linguistics*, 66–93. Cambridge: Cambridge Scholars Publishing.
Schwarzschild, Roger. 1999. Givenness, AvoidF and other constraints on the placement of accent. *Natural Language Semantics* 7. 141–177.
Siegel, Laura. 2009. Mood selection in Romance and Balkans. *Lingua* 119 (12). 1859–1882.
Simons, Mandy. 2007. Observations on embedding verbs, evidentiality, and presupposition. *Lingua* 117(6). 1034–1056.
Smirnova, Anastasia. 2012. The semantics of mood in Bulgarian. *Proceedings from the Annual meeting of the Chicago Linguistic Society* 48(1). 547–561.
Sornicola, Rosanna. 1988. "It-clefts and wh-clefts: Two awkward sentence types." *Journal of Linguistics* 24. 343–379.
Speas, Margaret. 2004. Evidentiality, logophoricity snd the syntactic representation of syntactic features. *Lingua* 114. 255–277.
Stowell, Tim. 1982. The tense of infinitives. *Linguistic Inquiry* 13. 561–570.
Todorović, Nataša. 2012. *The Indicative and Subjunctive* da-*complements in Serbian. A Syntactic-Semantic Approach*. University of Illinois at Chicago dissertation.
Travis, Lisa. 1984. *Parameters and Effects of Word Order Variation*. MIT dissertation.
Turano, Giuseppina. 1994. *Le dipendenze sintattiche dell'albanese*. University of Calabria dissertation.
Vallduví, Enric. 1992. *The Informational Component*, New York, Garland.
Zubizarreta, Maria-Luisa. 1998. *Prosody, Focus and Word Order*. Cambridge, Mass.: MIT Press.

Liljana Mitkovska and Eleni Bužarovska
Clausal complementation of visual perception verbs in Balkan Slavic

Abstract: The paper discusses the complementation patterns of visual perception verbs in standard Macedonian (M) and Bulgarian (B). The focus of the investigation is placed on the three clausal complement patterns of the central visual perception verbs: *gleda/vidi* in Macedonian and *gledam, viždam/vidja* in Bulgarian. To establish the current functional distribution of the complement patterns of the above verbs the authors conduct an in-depth analysis of a large number of examples from standard Macedonian and Bulgarian. The quantification of the data serves to discover structural and semantic factors that influence the choice of a given complement pattern. It depends on two important semantic oppositions cutting across the closed system of perception verbs: the aspectual distinction between states and activities, and the distinction between immediate and mental perception. The obtained results show that the two indicative patterns *kako/kak* and *deka/če* specialize for different types of perception in both languages, while the differences in distribution of subjunctive *da*-complements indicate a slightly different status of *da* in these languages. The analysis of the current complement distribution in both languages sheds light on the principles behind the semantic motivation of complementation patterning and helps account for the universal principles responsible for this syntactic regularity.

Keywords: immediate perception, mental perception, subjunctive, negation, semantics

1 Introduction

The paper examines the role of verbal semantics in the choice of complement patterns of visual perception verbs in two Balkan Slavic languages, Bulgarian (B) and Macedonian (M).[1] These verbs encode a perceptual relation between the viewer and

---

[1] Examples marked with 'M' are from Macedonian and with 'B' from Bulgarian.

Liljana Mitkovska, AUE-FON University, Skopje, North Macedonia, e-mail: liljana55@yahoo.com
Eleni Bužarovska, Ss. Cyril and Methodius University, Skopje, North Macedonia,
e-mail: elenibuzarovska@t-home.mk

https://doi.org/10.1515/9783110725858-005

the object of perception, which may be an entity or an event/situation. Possible clausal complementation patterns with verbs of visual perception in Balkan Slavic involve dependent clauses introduced by the complementizers *kako/kak, deka/če*,[2] the preverbal modal particle *da*, interrogative proforms, such as *koga/kogato* 'when', *kolku/kolko* 'how many', *kako* 'as', *što/kakvo* 'what' etc., and question particles such as *dali*. The focus of our study is on the Complement Clause (CC) patterns with *kako/kak, deka/če,* and *da*. We investigate three clausal complement patterns with the basic verbs of visual perception *gleda/vidi* in standard Macedonian and *gledam, viždam/vidja* in standard Bulgarian[3] and establish their distribution in each language. The first pattern is represented by a *kako/kak*-clause (1), the second employs a *deka/če* clause (2) and the third is realized by a *da*-clause (3).[4]

(1) *Vidov* **kako** *lugeto begaat od teatarot.*
    see-AOR.1SG COMP man-DEF.PL run-PRS.3PL from theater-DEF
    'I saw people running from the theater.' (M/mkd-news.com)

(2) *Vidov* **deka** *taa gi ima site moi omileni knigi.*
    see-AOR.1SG COMP she 3PL.ACC.CL have-PRS.3SG all my favorite books
    'I saw that she has all my favorite books.' (M/bride.mk)

(3) *Nikogaš ne sum ja videl* **da** *prosi.*
    Never NEG be-PRS.1SG 3SG.F.ACC.CL see-PRF.1SG SBJ beg-PRS.3SG
    'I have never seen her beg.' (M/hajdpark.mk)

Our main hypothesis is that the distribution of these complements tends to be semantically motivated depending on whether the visual verb expresses an immediate sensory experience (1), i.e. perception of the actual occurrence of some situation, or a mental state of knowledge resulting from the cognitive representation of this perceptual experience (2) and (3). The perceiver obtains knowledge of the perceived situation on the basis of the highest type of direct evidence, which is visual rather than auditory (Willett 1988: 59), thus signalling that s/he considers the observed situation as a fact.[5]

---

[2] These isofunctional complementizers are given in the following order: Macedonian/Bulgarian.
[3] Following tradition, Macedonian verbs are given in the 3sg.prs. indicative, but Bulgarian verbs are given in the 1sg.prs. indicative.
[4] The subjunctive particle *da* is glossed SBJ.
[5] Verbs of visual perception may have metaphorical or metonymical extensions into domains other than knowledge, illustrated in *Go gledam kako tatko* 'I see (i.e. consider) him as a father', *Gledaj da ne zadocniš*. 'Be careful not to be late.' etc. These extensions are not discussed here.

The main goal of the paper is to determine and compare the functional zones of each complement type in both languages, which should help discover the reasons for their distribution. By providing an explanation for the distributional differences between the complement types in the two closely related languages we aim to shed light on the nature of clausal complementation with visual perception verbs. For that purpose we conducted an analysis on a large number of attested examples from two genres: contemporary literature and web based texts (journals, blogs, chats, forums). The analysis addresses the following research questions grouped according to the investigated domains:

a. Is there a form–meaning correlation in the distribution of the three complement clause (CC) types in relation to the semantics of the perception verb predicates?
b. What are the semantic distinctions between the CC types? How do the CC types relate to mood distinctions and degrees of finiteness?[6]
c. What is the role of tense, grammatical aspect and participant foregrounding in the choice of the complement pattern? How does negation affect the choice of CC types?
d. What are the distributional differences between the examined CC patterns in the two languages?

The organization of the paper is as follows. Section 2 contains an overview of the semantics and syntax of visual perception verbs discussed in general linguistic literature and in Bulgarian and Macedonian scholarship. Section 3 presents the results of the analysis of the collected examples with basic perception CC patterns in the two languages. Section 4 discusses and compares the discourse-syntactic strategies characteristic of these patterns, while section 5 accounts for the differences between the examined CC patterns in these languages. The paper ends with a brief conclusion about the theoretical implications of the analysis for a deeper understanding of clausal complementation in Balkan Slavic.

---

6 We view the category of finiteness as a scalar phenomenon dependent on a number of parameters, such as subject realization, agreement, tense, syntactic opacity and independent clausehood. It reflects the level of integration of the subordinate event in the main event (Nikolaeva 2007: 8–10).

2 Theoretical background

In this section we present some basic views on CC employed in the ensuing analysis, as well as brief explanation of the CC markers in Balkan Slavic.

2.1 The semantics of clausal complementation of visual perception verbs

Clausal complementation is broadly defined as the process of integration of clauses in argument positions, so complement clauses function as arguments of the matrix clause predicate. Such clauses are integrated in the syntactic structure of the main clause to various degrees, reflecting the level of semantic integration of the two events. One accepted view in analyzing the semantics of the various relation types is that the semantics of the complement taking predicate (CTP) indicates the relation between the integrated events (e.g. Noonan 1985/2007). For instance, Cristofaro (2003: 122) suggests drawing a distinction between CTPs that entail no semantic integration (Knowledge, Propositional attitude, Utterance) and those that allow different levels of semantic integration (Phasal > Modals > Manipulatives (MAKE) > Manipulatives (ORDER), Desideratives, Perception), which has been cross-linguistically validated.[7] On the other hand, Nicolova (2008b: 263) claims that apart from the semantics of the main predicate, the relation between the two events also depends on other factors: negation, person in the main clause, as well as tense and illocutionary force of the main clause.

Furthermore, the level of integration can vary depending on the ontological status of the subordinate event. Distinctions have been made between: second-order entity and third-order entity (Lyons 1977), event vs. fact (Vendler 1967, Dixon 2006), predication level as state of affairs vs. propositional level as propositions (Dik and Hengeveld 1991), among others. According to Boye (2010: 4), these divisions "virtually all amount to the same ontological distinction between, respectively, entities which can be located in time, said to occur, etc., and entities which have a truth value". Such differentiation is related to the status of the subordinate event as asserted or not, known as 'the level of grounding' in Cognitive Grammar (Langacker 2008: 438). The exponents that indicate the status of the CC are either segments traditionally called complementizers or the non-indicative mood of the subordinate

---

[7] There are, however, typologically sensitive points of form-function mapping in the hierarchy which diverge from the usual patterns (Wiemer 2014), such as CCs conveying factual, but backgrounded information, complements of CTPs coding negative propositional attitudes, complements of commissive and apprehensional CTPs.

predication, or both. In line with Noonan's (2007: 55) definition of complementizers as "a word, particle, clitic or affix, one of whose functions it is to identify the entity as a complement", the two are often collapsed (Nordström 2010).

Time reference in the complement clause is another indicator of dependency status. While the time in independent clauses is related to the time of the speech act, in the dependent clause it varies along the CC cline. Noonan (1985/2007) distinguishes predicates with independent time reference (ITR) and with dependent time reference (DTR). The latter either do not have explicit tense marking (verbal adjectives or action nominals) or employ reduced tense markers (as in *da*-constructions).

The semantic status of the dependent predicate is also a contentious issue in the literature. The two oppositions: factuality/non-factuality and factivity/non-factivity are often blurred in Bulgarian and Macedonian literature. Following Wiemer (2017; this volume), we understand factuality as a dimension that refers to the epistemic judgment of the thruth of the proposition contained in the complement; hence these complements can be modified by adverbs denoting neutral or strong epistemic support (*likely, possibly, certainly, undoubtedly* etc.).[8]

2.2 Situations expressed by visual perception verbs

The syntactic behaviour of perception verbs depends on two important semantic oppositions cutting across the closed system of perception verbs: (a) the aspectual distinction between states and activities, and (b) the distinction between immediate and mental perception.

The first distinction is based on the inherent aspectual properties of the verb. In visual perception, as in the rest of the sensory modalities, the perceiver may be engaged in a controlled activity of perceiving something (*look, watch*) or experience a perceptual state caused by a stimulus (*see*). We refer to states as non-agentive and to activities as agentive verbs. This distinction is often lexicalized cross-linguistically especially in the highest two modalities on the so-called sensory hierarchy, visual and auditory (Viberg 1983),[9] present in the examined

---

[8] Wiemer (2017: 274) points to the frequent confusion of the terms 'factual' and 'factive'. The latter in its traditional sense (Kiparsky/Kiparsky 1970) applies to verbs which presuppose the truth of their propositional complements even under negation. Factivity is not a gradable value compared to factuality: factual clauses can be downtoned since epistemic support can be modified.
[9] One of the earliest typological taxonomies of perception verbs is presented in Scovel (1971) based on data from several languages. He divides the verbs of each modality into stative (e.g.,

languages as well: *gleda₁* vs. *gleda₂/vidi* (Macedonian) and *gledam* vs. *viždam/ vidja* (Bulgarian). In Macedonian, the non-agentive *vidi* has lost its imperfective counterpart compensating for this lexical gap with *gleda₂* in mental perception uses. Bulgarian *vidja*, as other Slavic languages, has an imperfective counterpart: *viždam*. Thus in Macedonian *gleda* can be both agentive and non-agentive, but not in Bulgarian. The agentive verbs *gleda* in both languages have prefixed perfective counterparts (*pogledne/pogledna*) which do not take propositional complements and so they are not included in this analysis.

The second opposition involves the distinction between immediate and mental perception (Dik and Hengeveld 1991), also known as direct and indirect. It is reflected in the form of the complement and the choice of a subordinating morpheme. Verbs of vision obtain direct perception reading when the perceived situation coded in the complement temporally coincides with the act of perception. Once the perceiver sees some event (intentionally or not), its mental representation becomes integrated in his/her knowledge system. This entails that vision verbs acquire evidential function when they denote coming to understanding and knowledge. In evidential uses, these verbs usually assert the truth of their complements, since they provide direct evidence for it.

In view of the fact that evidentiality covers "the kinds of evidence a person has for making factual claims" (Anderson 1986: 276), verbs of vision, as mentioned above, obtain evidential meaning when they report knowledge of some situation. However, their employment in evidential strategies or uses does not entail that perception verbs are true evidentials.[10]

Given the relation between the visual and the cognitive domain, the visual perception of a situation (the percept) triggers its mental representation in our knowledge system (the concept). Therefore, it is sometimes difficult to separate the mental state of knowledge from the physical experience that gives rise to it. Moreover, knowledge about a certain event may result from an inference: a viewer may arrive at a conclusion about the factualness of an event relying on situational clues. To account for this overlap between direct and mental perception, Dik and Hengeveld (1991: 240) suggest an additional division distinguishing primary mental perception, i.e. knowledge acquired through direct, visual perception of the event, from secondary mental perception referring to knowledge obtained by inference from direct physical evidence (cf. Johanson 2003: 282). We apply this additional distinction in the analysis of the collected examples because we

---

hear), active (*listen*) and resultative (*sound*). In Rogers (1974), they are named cognitive (*see*), active (*look at*) and flip visual verbs (*look*).
10 Aikhenvald (2004: 121) refers to this choice of complements as "evidential-like distinctions", as opposed to Whitt (2010), who considers perception verbs as lexical markers of evidentiality.

believe that a finer classification of the data will help account for the distributional differences of complementation patterns in Balkan Slavic. Thus, three categories are distinguished: (a) immediate perception (IP), taken to be expressed by the *kako/kak* pattern with agentive and non-agentive verbs, (b) primary mental perception based on visual experience (MP1), (c) and inference-based secondary mental perception (MP2); both MP1 and MP2 are evidential strategies: for conveying mental perception they typically employ non-agentive verbs in the *deka/ če* pattern. Thus agentivity as a semantic feature[11] participates in the choice of a clausal complement. Agentive visual verbs encode immediate perception excluding mental perception uses, which entails that they do not license the declarative complement pattern (*deka/če*).

(4) Jas vnimatelno gledam kako/*deka toj doaǵa.
 I carefully watch-PRS.1SG COMP he come-PRS.3SG
 'I carefully watch him coming/*that he is coming.' (M)

In MP1 function, the speaker reports about the event immediately after its observation or in the last stage thereof, becoming aware of its factuality. In MP2 function, the speaker claims that some event occurred for a fact upon perceiving the effects of this event in the form of visual clues. Thus, in uttering *Vidov deka doaǵa* 'I saw that he was coming' the speaker states that someone arrived because s/he witnessed the event unfolding, while in *Vidov deka došol* 'I saw that he had arrived' the speaker concludes about someone's arrival on the basis of perceived clues.

Furthermore, temporal relations between the act of perception and the observed event play a crucial role in indicating the distinctions: immediate perception involves only a simultaneity relation (*I saw him enter the room*) as opposed to a more flexible time reference in mental perception. Apart from simultaneity (*I saw that he didn't know about the accident*), mental perception involves precedence (*I see that the he has arrived, his car is here*) or subsequence relations (*I see that he is leaving, he is getting dressed*).

In evidential use a visual perception verb denotes a change of mental state in the perceiver who, via direct observation (MP1) or inference (MP2), learns that the perceived situation or event is part of reality.

---

[11] The agentivity of perception verbs can be established by several semantic tests (Fillmore 1968, Gruber 1976, Cruse 1973), one being the addition of adverbs like *carefully*.

2.3 Clausal complementation of visual perception verbs in Balkan Slavic

In Slavic (and other) languages, the distinction between immediate and mental perception correlates with particular complementation patterns.[12] This distinction is observed in South Slavic: in Bulgarian, *kak* with perception verbs "emphasizes the process itself" rather than the fact of occurrence of that process, the latter rendered by the semantically empty general complementizer *če* (Hansen, Letuchiy, and Błaszczyk 2016: 215). Equally, there is common consensus that *deka* in Macedonian and *če* in Bulgarian are typical indicative complementizers which introduce a CC of mental predicates.[13] They indicate the speaker's epistemic commitment to the truth of the propositional content expressed in the embedded clause, irrespective of the world they belong in, real or imagined. They specialize for the less integrated situations, considered as factual, i.e. assertive. These complementizers of Slavic origin came into use relatively late (around 14th century).[14]

In both Macedonian and Bulgarian, clauses introduced with *kako/kak* code directly perceived events. In both languages the status and distribution of *kako/kak* has not been fully determined and it is not clearly distinguished from its use as a pure interrogative pronoun marking dependent clauses, in parallel to *koga* 'when', *kade/kăde* 'where' etc. This could be attributed to the adverbial manner nuances in its meaning, which can sometimes be detected even in straightforward complementizer positions.[15]

It is generally accepted that the finite but temporally unanchored *da*-construction (*da*+present tense form) replaced the Slavic infinitive in Balkan Slavic and is regarded as one of the core Balkanisms (Joseph 1983, Topolińska 2008b, 2010, Lindstedt 2000, Assenova 2002, Friedman 2011 among others). This construction has taken on multiple functions in both languages. For instance, Kramer (1986) claims that in Macedonian the particle *da* has four main functions: directive, conditional, subordinate-modal and subordinate-aspectual, some occurring in both independent and dependent uses. Bulgarian exhibits a similar

---

12 In Russian, the difference is conveyed by the choice of a complementizer; thus Aikhenvald (2004: 121) notes: "The conjunction *kak* implies direct perception..., while the conjunction *čto*, a general complementizer, implies that what the speaker actually perceives is a clue, or basis of an inference which may give an idea about the situation."
13 Minova-Ǵurkova (1994), Ammann and van der Auwera (2004).
14 See Grković-Mejdžor (2010).
15 The different nature of Bulgarian *kak* with perception verbs has been noticed in Laskova (2013: 6), who considers it to be a "desemanticized interrogative pronominal adverb".

functional distribution, while in the other South Slavic languages *da* is active in the indicative domain.[16]

Although the modal nature of the *da*-construction in Balkan Slavic CC is generally acknowledged, its morpho-syntactic status is still a debated issue in linguistics. In Bulgarian it is traditionally called a conjunction (Dejanova 1985, GSBKE 1983, Assenova 2002) or a complementizer (Nicolova 2008a, Krapova 2001, Aleksova and Tiševa 2000), though there are also suggestions that "in some positions *da* is a proclitic modal particle, but in others a subordinating conjunction" (Assenova 2002: 151). The term "modal complementizer" is also used by Ammann and van der Auwera (2004) for *da* and the corresponding particles in other Balkan languages. Gołąb (1964: 18) points out that "the particle *da* in Bulgarian and Macedonian represents a "preverbal" morpheme whose position is always proclitic regarding the finite verb it specifies modally"; in fact, this modal morpheme is syntactically bound with the verb it precedes.[17] Following Topolinjska (2008a: 56), we consider the term (modal) particle or morpheme most appropriate.

When we talk about the *da*-construction we have in mind the *da*-clause[18] which is subject to tense restrictions and is employed in functions similar to those of morphologically marked subjunctives. As a mood marker, *da* has unique aspectual and temporal properties. Namely, in complement clauses the particle *da* is followed by a verb inflected for present tense or less frequently *esse*-perfect (to highlight anterior time relation to the main clause event),[19] so definite past tenses (imperfect and aorist) as well as future tense are disallowed.

It is generally considered that *da* marks the modal status of the complement clause it is heading. Gołąb (1964: 17) suggests that in Bulgarian and Macedonian *da* marks a special mood, "optative-subjunctive". Topolinjska (2000, 2008a) advocates the idea that the *da*-construction is comparable to the subjunctive mood in the Romance languages, despite the fact that it is not a bound morphological marker. She founds her claims on typological studies, where "subjunctive is the term given to special verb forms or markers that obligatorily occur in certain subordinate clauses" (Bybee, Perkins, and Pagliuca 1994: 121). Topolinjska (2000) argues that the definition of the subjunctive should not be confined to morphologically bound morphemes, but should be based on functional criteria. The *da*-construction is a

---

[16] The change lasted from the 13th to 15th century; it is supposed to have begun in the west and north spreading to the east and south (Grković-Mejdžor 2004; this volume).
[17] Rudin (1986) analyzed *da* in Bulgarian as a modal (subjunctive) particle.
[18] The terms *da*-clause/construction refer to clauses both in dependent and independent use.
[19] Cf. Gołąb (1964), GSBKE (1983), Dejanova (1985), Kramer (1986), Nicolova (2005), Topolinjska (2008), to mention just a few. Landau (2004: 820) maintains that "tense restrictions are a hallmark of subjunctive complements".

typical subjunctive mood marker because it occurs in dependent clauses expressing non-actualized, non-factual, omnitemporal, future, habitual events. It is "a dependent proposition whose modal-temporal characteristic depends on the super-ordinate predicate" (Bybee, Perkins, and Pagliuca 1994: 132).

This view is not adopted in traditional Bulgarian grammars mostly because *da*-forms may occur in assertive contexts such as perception verb complements (cf. Genadieva-Mustafčieva 1970). However, Smirnova (2011) argues that "embedded *da* forms in Bulgarian should be analyzed as subjunctive based on morphological properties, temporal properties, and the distributional pattern" (Smirnova 2011: 183–187). Similarly, Aleksova and Tiševa (2000: 94) suggest that "[d]ue to the temporal, modal and aspectual restrictions of the embedded *da*-clause, the status of *da*-constructions should be revisited" (Aleksova and Tiševa 2000: 115).

When comparing the CC with *da* and those with *deka/če* the accepted view is that the difference between them rests on the truth value properties assigned to the embedded event: *deka/če* generally presents events as facts, while *da* presents the event as something possible, wished or expected (Assenova 2002: 153, Ǵurkova 2015a: 8–9, GSBKE 1983: 332, Minova-Ǵurkova 1994: 247 among others). Indeed, Ammann and van der Auwera (2004: 349–350) have pointed out that there is a striking parallelism in the way realis vs. irrealis[20] content in complement clauses is formally marked in all Balkan languages via the opposition between a declarative complementizer and a modal morpheme linked to the verb. Therefore they claim that this complementizer split should be considered as yet another Balkanism, on a par with the other firmly established shared features, such as clitic doubling.

On the scale of event integration presented above, the *da*-clause tends to mark complement clauses of predicates that are characterized by stronger integration. It is the only option with Phasals, Modals, Manipulatives and Desideratives, while Utterance and Cognition predicates, lacking integration "capacity", usually take an indicative marker. Perception predicates allow different levels of semantic integration (Cristofaro 2003), which is reflected in the choice of either *da* or *deka/če*, depending on various factors. Negation has been noticed to play an important role, but questions also suspend factuality.

(5) *Ne pomnja da săm go viždal*
    NEG remember-PRS.1SG SBJ be-PRS.1SG 3SG.M.ACC.CL see-PRF.SG
    u tjah.
    at their's
    'I don't remember seeing him at their place.' (B)

---

20 As understood in Ammann and van der Auwera (2004).

(6) *Znaeš   li   njakoj   da   piše/   e pisal*
    knowPRS.2SG PRT someone SBJ write-PRS.3SG write-PRF.3SG
    po tozi văpros?
    on this question
    'Do you know if someone has written about this issue?' (B)

Though integrated in some syntax studies (Topolińska 2008b, Minova-Ǵurkova 1994, Bužarovska 2013), the topic of variability in perception verb complements has been rather understudied in Macedonian grammars. On the other hand, the variability between *da* and *če* has been extensively discussed in the Bulgarian literature (Laskova 2009, Ivanova and Gradinarova 2015, Nicolova 2008b, Aleksova and Tiševa 2000, Assenova 2002, Penčev 1993), albeit with less devotion to *kak* (with the exception of Laskova 2009, Ivanova and Gradinarova 2015: 264). In general, these authors often have different views on the motivation for the use of the *da*-pattern: for instance, Aleksova and Tiševa (2000) advocate free variation between *da* and *če*, while Nicolova (2008b) points out the affinity between negated matrix predicates and *da*-complements.

2.4 Hypotheses

In view of the existing variation of the clausal complements with visual perception verbs, the main purpose of our investigation is to examine the frequency of each syntactic pattern and the possible criteria that govern its choice. Drawing on the previous discussion, we posit several hypotheses about the semantic motivation of the clausal complements of visual verbs.

1. Given the cognitive base of the distribution of visual perception CC patterns, we assume that the same semantic opposition governs the choice of complement patterns in the two Balkan Slavic languages: the *kako/kak* pattern is used for immediate and *deka/če* for mental perception.
2. The second hypothesis pertains to the role of subjunctive *da*-constructions as perception complements. Considering the non-factual nature of such clauses in Balkan Slavic, we presume that in both languages they occur in contexts of low assertiveness (in particular under negation or in pragmatically marked situations).
3. The third hypothesis concerns the difference in the distribution of *da*-complements in the two examined languages. The form-function symmetry is assumed to be obscured in Bulgarian by the use of the *da*-pattern in the domain of immediate perception. This leads to the conclusion that the distribution of perception complements in Macedonian is semantically more regular than in Bulgarian.

3 Data analysis

The data for the analysis consist of a large body of attested examples (920 in Macedonian and 1024 in Bulgarian) which reflect the standard and colloquial use of CC patterns with verbs of vision. Sentences with these verbs were randomly excerpted from contemporary Macedonian and Bulgarian literature[21] and from internet sources (mainly press and blogs) and then classified according to the matrix verb and the CC pattern. Tables 1 and 2 present the distribution of the attested examples with each CC pattern in the two genres. There is a slight difference in the number of examples in the patterns, which may indicate functional differences: the *kako* pattern seems to be more often encountered in Macedonian than *kak* in Bulgarian, where *če* prevails. The reasons for such distribution will be examined in the analysis below. A more striking difference was noticed in the occurrence of *da*-clauses: in Bulgarian approximately the same percentage was detected in literature and internet texts, while in Macedonian such clauses were not encountered in the literature texts. This could be due to the pressure of the standard norm, which sanctions the use of *da* in indicative sentences.

Table 1: Distribution of the three CC patterns in Macedonian.

Mac	kako			deka			da		
	Fiction	Internet	Total	Fiction	Internet	Total	Fiction	Internet	Total
gleda	93	55	148	50	76	126	1	9	10
vidi	88	175	263	112	98	210	9	154	163
Total	181	230	411	162	174	336	10	163	173
				920					

The tables show that the distribution of the patterns *kako/kak* and *deka/če* differs considerably in the two languages: the *kako*-pattern in Macedonian makes up 46.67 % (411 tokens) in the examined sample, while its Bulgarian counterpart has a narrower distribution with 30.46 % (312 tokens). The opposite tendency is noted in the distribution of *deka* and *če*-pattern: *deka* is present with 36.52 %

---

[21] From Macedonian novels by Božin Pavlovski, Kočo Urdin, Jovan Boškovski, Petre M. Andreeevski and stories by Branko Varošlija, Blaže Minevski, Živko Čingo, Vase Mančev, Ace Gogov, Krste Čačanski, Kalina Maleska, Rumena Bužarovska. Novels by the following Bulgarian authors were analysed Anton Dončev, Bogomil Rajnov, Dimităr Talev, Georgi Ganev, Jordan Hadžiev, Miroljuba Benatova, Petăr Dimkov, Petăr Ruščukliev, Petja Bočilova, Svoboda Băčvarova, Tihomir Dimitrov, Todor Dimitrov, Vera Mutafčieva, Vesel Cankov, Viktor Paskov.

Table 2: Distribution of the three CC patterns in Bulgarian.

Bul	kak			če			da		
	Fiction	Internet	Total	Fiction	Internet	Total	Fiction	Internet	Total
gledam	50	86	136	1	37	38	1	6	7
viždam	26	33	59	82	56	138	16	23	39
vidja	62	55	117	168	158	326	70	94	164
Total	138	174	312	251	251	502	87	123	210
						1024			

(336 tokens) compared to a more frequent *če* represented by 49 % (502 tokens). The use of the *da*-pattern in both languages does not exhibit radical differences, though it is more common in Bulgarian (20.5 %) than in Macedonian (18.8 %).

In what follows, we analyze each pattern in the two languages separately and draw conclusions about their similarities and differences. We examine the type of perception expressed by each pattern (IP, MP1 or MP2) and how this is related to the type of events perceived and the time relations between the perceiving and the perceived event. The two events may be simultaneous (overlapping) or the perceived event may be anterior or posterior to the perceiving event. In case of simultaneous events, the tense in the dependent clause may be independent, reflecting the real time, or dependent when the time reference of the perceived event is interpreted in relation to the time of the perceiving event.

3.1 *kako/kak* complement clauses

In Macedonian, the *gleda kako* pattern expresses immediate perception (IP) of an event (7); but the MP1 interpretation, found in a few examples, is also available (8). The tense of the subordinate verb is overwhelmingly interpreted via the tense in the superordinate clause. The subordinate verb is in the perfect if it encodes a dynamic process (8) but if it refers to a series of events the present (i.e. dependent) tense is used (7).

(7) *Na televizija   gledav   kako   bankite se zatvaraat*
    on television   see-IMPF.1SG   COMP   banks   REFL close-PRS.3PL
    edna po druga.
    one after another
    'I saw on TV that banks closed one after another.' (M/srekja.mk)

(8) *Gledam   kako   vo gornata vilica   i   se potkršila*
    see-PRS.1SG COMP   in upper-DEF jaw   3SG.F.DAT.CL REFL break-PRF.3SG
    trojkata
    third-DEF
    'I can see that the third tooth in her upper jaw has been chipped.' (M/RB)

In Bulgarian, the embedded clauses after *gledam kak* have similar semantic and structural properties: they mainly express immediate perception (IP) of an event overlapping with the perception act. The tense of the subordinate verb can be independent (9) or dependent (10).

(9) *Gledah   gi   kak   se păhnaha*
    watch-IMPF.1SG   3PL.ACC.CL COMP   REFL get-IMPF.3PL
    pod   bjufeta   da   tărsjat   kraka na balerinata.
    under   cupboard-DEF   SBJ   look for-PRS.3PL leg of ballerina-DEF
    'I watched them get under the cupboard to look for the ballerina's leg.' (B/GG)

(10) *Možeh   da ja   gledam s časove   kak   govori.*
     can-IMPF.1SG SBJ 3SG.F.ACC.CL   watch-PRS.1SG with hours COMP   talk-PRS.3SG
     'I could watch her speak for hours.' (B/TD)

In Bulgarian, MP1 interpretation arises under the same conditions as in Macedonian, mostly with abstract embedded events (11).

(11) *No kato   gledam   kak   hamburgerăt   izmestva   svetini*
     but when   see-PRS.1SG COMP   hamburger-DEF   replace-PRS.3SG jewels
     v bălgarskoto hranenie,   započvam da go vzemam po-naseriozno tova dviženie.
     in Bulgarian cuisine   I start to take this trend more seriously
     'But when I see the hamburger replace all the jewels of Bulgarian cuisine, I start to take this trend even more seriously.' (B/VC)

Anterior events are rarely encoded in the dependent clause implying an inferential MP1 interpretation (12).

(12) *Ruskijat president   može da bădespokoen,   kato gleda*
     Russian-DEF president   can SBJ be unfazed   when see-PRS.3SG
     kak   bežanskata kriza   razdeli   Evropa.
     COMP   migrant-DEF crisis   divide-PRF.3SG   Europe
     'The Russian president can be unfazed as he sees the migrant crisis divide Europe.'(B/e-vestnik.bg)

The verb *viždam* (B) lacks a non-agentive lexical counterpart in Macedonian. The non-agentivity of *viždam* seems to affect the semantics of the embedded event in the pattern *viždam kak*, a property reflected in the preference for abstract (13) rather than physical activity verbs (14) in the attested examples. The former verbs lean towards MP1 interpretation, while the latter encode IP.

(13) ... toj viždaše   kak   vsički sa   nedovolni...
         he see-IMPF.3SG COMP   all   be-PRS.3PL dissatisfied
      '... he could see that everyone was dissatisfied ...' (B/DT)

(14) *Viždam   go   kak   se približava ...*
      see-PRS.1SG 3SG.M.ACC.CL COMP   REFL approach-PRS.3SG
      podava mi štafetata.
      hand me baton-DEF
      'I see him approach and... hand me the baton.' (B/GG)

Temporal relations of anteriority, with both imperfect and aorist (15) also impose the MP1 interpretation of activities.

(15) *Az se văzmuštavam,   kato viždam   kak   Turcija*
      I REFL irritate-PRS.1SG when see-PRS.1SG COMP   Turkey
      se vărna nazad   po otnošenie na pravata na ženite.
      REFL go-PST.3SG back   concerning rights of women-DEF
      'I get irritated seeing Turkey go back on women's rights.' (B/e-vestnik.bg)

The pattern *vidi kako* (M) is mainly used for immediate perception (16), but MP1 interpretation is found in one third of the examples (17 and 18).

(16) *Vide   kako   Blagoj mu   mavnuva   so*
      see-AOR.3SG COMP   Blagoj 3SG.M.ACC.CL wave-PRS.3SG with
      rakata   i   isčeznuva   od   sobata.
      hand-DEF   and   disappear-PRS.3SG from   room-DEF
      'He saw Blagoj wave his hand at him and disappear from the room.' (M/KU)

In some constructions with a verb in the aorist (17) and in abstract situations (18) the borderline between immediate and primary mental perception may be blurred, decreasing the difference between *kako* and *deka*.

(17) Vidov   kako   ḱesata so kutijata   padna   vrz
      see-AOR.1SG   COMP   bag-DEF with box-DEF fell-AOR.3SG upon
      glavata na Lile.
      head-DEF of Lile
      'I saw the bag with the box fall on Lile's head/I saw that the bag with the box fell . . .' (M/RB)

(18) Vo nekolku navrati, na forumov   vidovme   kako
      in several times   on forum-DEF   see-AOR.1PL   COMP
      Osmanliite   imale   vo mnogu aspekti uspešna država.
      Ottoman-DEF.PL   have-PRF.PL   in many aspects   successful state
      'Several times on this online forum we have seen that the Ottomans in many aspects had an effective government.' (M/isl.zaednica.com)

The pattern *vidja kak* (B) is used predominantly for immediate perception, while the MP1 interpretation is rare in the attested examples. Independent tense uses are more frequently encountered in *kak*-clauses with the verb *vidja* (19) than with *viždam* and *gledam*, though dependent tenses are also encountered (20).

(19) . . .vidjaha   kak   ostanalite deca   se pokačiha   na
      see-IMPF.3PL   COMP   remaining-DEF children   REFL climb-IMPF.3PL on
      lipata . . .
      linden tree-DEF
      'They saw the remaining children climb the linden tree . . .' (B/SB)

(20) Lazar go   vidja   kak   mu
      Lazar 3SG.M.ACC.CL   see-AOR.3SG   COMP   3SG.M.DAT.CL
      pravi   znaci s glava.
      make-PRS.3SG   signs with head
      'Lazar saw him giving him signs with his head.' (B/DT)

The MP1 interpretation is obtained with states and abstract events (21), and in rare cases with states resulting from anterior events (22).

(21) Toj se prosna   po grăb   i   az   otnova   vidjah
      he   REFL lie-AOR.3SG on back   and   I   again   see-AOR.1SG
      kak   ot   očite   mu   izvira   samota.
      COMP   from   eyes-DEF   3SG.M.DAT.CL   spring-PRS.3SG loneliness
      He lay on his back and I again saw that loneliness wells in his eyes.' (B/GG)

(22) Šte   go   vidiš   balona   kak   se   e
     FUT   3SG.M.ACC.CL   see-PRS.2SG balloon-DEF   COMP   REFL be-PRS.3SG
     puknal.
     burst-PRF.SG
     'You will see that the balloon has burst.' (B/e-vestnik.bg)

3.2 *deka* and *če* complement clauses

The *gleda deka* (M) pattern expresses both types of mental perception though MP2 examples are more numerous than MP1.[22] In MP2 interpretation the speaker's conviction of the truth of the assertion derives from directly observed clues, but the grounds for making an evidential statement is often not clear (23–25). All tenses can be used in the subordinate clause.

(23) *So svoi oči   gledame   deka   inteligencijata   uporno*
     with own eyes   see-PRS.1PL   COMP   intelligentsia   stubbornly
     se marginalizira.
     REFL marginalize-PRS.3SG
     'We see with our own eyes that the intellectuals...have been persistently marginalized.' (M/facebook.com)

(24) *Gledaš   deka   te   omaskariv?*
     see-PRS.2SG   COMP   2SG.ACC.CL   trick-PST.1SG
     'Don't you see that I tricked you?' (M/MM)

(25) *Ne gledaš   deka   site   bogovi   ḱe završat   vo*
     NEG see-PRS.2SG   COMP   all   gods   FUT end-PRS.3PL   in
     pesja čelust?
     dog's jaws
     'Can't you see that all gods are going to end up in dog's jaws?' (M/VA)

Fewer examples have MP1 interpretation. In such cases *gleda* presupposes that a situation coded by the dependent clause is true because its factuality can be deduced from some visible evidence at the moment of speaking, either with

---

[22] Stylistically marked *oti* is used in the literature register as a synonym of *deka*. In our sample it was used only by one author.

dynamic events (26) or states (27). The subordinate verbs are predominantly in present tense.

(26) Gi   potkreva   klepkite   i   gleda
     3PL.ACC.CL raise-PRS.3SG   lids-DEF   and   see-PRS.3SG
     deka   tie   ušte   go   tepaat.
     COMP   they   still 3SG.M.ACC.CL   beat-PRS.3PL
     'He raises his eyelids and sees that they are still beating him.' (M/PA)

(27) Ušte   gledame   deka   ima   turisti vo Dojran.
     still   see-PRS.1PL   COMP   have-PRS.3SG   tourists in Dojran
     'We see that there are still tourists in Dojran.'(M/mkd-news.com)

States in CCs of perception verbs are more likely to be used with MP1 interpretation, while activities that overlap with the act of perception, as in (27), are primarily conceived as immediate perception. However, since perception and knowledge are intertwined, a complementizer can be employed to foreground one of the interpretations.

In both functions *gleda* allows the use of the asyndetic pattern via the omission of *deka*. The matrix clause can be used parenthetically (28).

(28) Ama,   gledam,   nikoj   ništo   ne kupuva.
     but   see-PRS.1SG   none   nothing   NEG buy-PRS.3SG
     'But, I see, no one buys anything.' (M/PA)

Negation of the perceiving event produces some extra effects. The negated *gleda* acquires the meaning close to 'know' in MP1 (29) and 'think' in MP2 interpretation (30).

(29) Ne   gledate   li   deka   štrajkuvame?
     NEG   see-PRS.2PL   PRT   COMP   strike-PRS.1PL
     'Don't you see that we are on strike?' (M/KU)

(30) Ne   gledam   deka   Z   go   napravil   krivičnoto
     NEG   see-PRS.1SG   COMP   Z   3SG.M.ACC.CL   do-PRF.3SG   criminal-DEF
     delo   za   koe   se tereti.
     act   for   which   REFL accuse-prs.3sg
     'I don't see that Z has committed the crime he is accused of.' (M/grid.mk)

The pattern *gledam če* (B) is used to encode both types of mental perception. Since *gledam* is agentive we do not expect it to occur with *če*, as previously indicated. However, there are many such examples in the internet press and blogs, but not in the literature. It may indicate a tendency for neutralization of the opposition between *gledam* and *viždam* (B) in the spoken language. We encounter *gledam če* with similar semantic interpretations as in the Macedonian pattern: MP1 interpretations prevail in colloquial examples (31). Anteriority of embedded event is signaled by the *esse*-perfect, which suggests the existence of observable or inferential clues for making the claim (32).

(31) *Gleda,   če   kelnera   nosi   činija   i*
     see-PRS.3SG COMP   waiter-DEF   bring-PRS.3SG plate   and
     dărži   s   prăst   păržolata.
     hold- PRS.3SG   with   finger   porkchop- DEF
     'He sees that the waiter is bringing a plate holding the porkchop with his finger.' (B/bodliv.com)

(32) *Gledam,   če   dneska văv fejsbuk   vsički   sa*
     see-PRS.1SG   COMP   today on facebook   all   be-PRS.3PL
     stanali   hristijani.
     become-PRF.PL   Christians
     'I see that nowadays everybody has become a Christian on Facebook.' (B/facebook.com/ivo.siromahov)

With *viždam če* (B), as expected, MP2 interpretations prevail in both registers examined. In most of the examples the embedded event is abstract (33).

(33) *Eto,   viždaš,   če   edinijat   boksjor   e...   po-dobăr*
     here   see-PRS.2SG   COMP   one-DEF   boxer   be-PRS.3SG   better
     ot   našija.
     than   ours-DEF
     'Here, you see that one of the boxers is . . . better than ours.' (B/e-vestnik.bg)

(34) *...i   sam   viždaše,   če   taka   se   podgotvjaše*
     and   himself   see-IMPF.3SG   COMP   thus   REFL   prepare-3SG.IMPF
     ženitbata   mu   s   Božana.
     wedding-DEF   3sg.m.dat.cl   with   Božana
     '. . . and he saw himself that all this was leading to his wedding with Božana.' (B/DT)

Conclusions based on direct perceptual observation enforcing MP1 readings are rather rare (35). In such cases, as in the Macedonian sentence (26) above, the complementizer coerces a knowledge interpretation.

(35) *Viždam ja, če se zadava po ulicata,*
see-PRS.1SG 3SG.F.ACC.CL COMP REFL stroll-PRS.3SG along street-DEF
'I see that she is strolling down the street,
usmihnata i začervena ot studa.
with a smiling face ruddy with frost.' (orangecenter.bg/blog) *(B)*

The pattern *vidi deka* (M) is used for evidential functions (MP1 and MP2) with approximately the same distribution as *gleda deka*. The subordinate verb is found more often in independent (37), than in dependent tense (36). As stated in section 2.2, in MP1 uses, the perceiver sees the event unfolding (36) or in its final stage (37), which leads to his/her awareness of its factuality.

(36) *Se svrte i vide deka onie nabližuvaat.*
REFL turn-AOR.1SG and see-AOR.3SG COMP they approach-PRS.3PL
'He turned around and saw that they were getting closer.' (M/KU)

(37) *Vidovme deka voziloto ja skrši ... zaštitnata*
see-AOR.1PL COMP car-DEF 3SG.F.ACC.CL break-AOR.3SG security-DEF
ograda ...
fence
'We saw the car break the security fence ...' (M/dnevnik.mk)

MP2 interpretation is rendered when the subject comes to a conclusion that some event is true, upon perceiving its effects at the time of perception, which makes these verbs semantically close to knowledge acquisition verbs (realize, understand). They represent marginal cases in the perception domain, as in the examples below.

(38) *Na fejsbuk vidov deka soprugot me*
on facebook see-AOR.1SG COMP husband-DEF 1SG.ACC.CL
izneveruva.
cheat-PRS.3SG
'I saw on FB that my husband was cheating on me.' (M/vesti.mk)

(39) *Popot   vide   deka   Pejo ne   e*
    priest-DEF   see-AOR.3SG   COMP   Pejo NEG   be-PRS.3SG
    mnogu kriv za slučkata.
    very guilty for incident-DEF
    'The priest saw that Pejo was not very guilty of what had happened.'
    (M/itarpejo.org)

The Bulgarian equivalent pattern *vidja če* is also employed for expressing mental perception. MP1 situations comprise both events evolving at the time of perception (40) or immediately perceived states (41) which serve as a base for the mental representation of the event.

(40) *Kogato   izljazohme,   vidjah,   če   Elica   plače.*
    when   exit-IMPF.1PL   see-AOR.1SG   COMP   Elica   cry-PRS.3SG
    'When we went out I saw that Elica was crying.' (B/AD)

(41) *Vidjah,   če   Ašraf   beše   sam.*
    see-AOR.1SG   COMP   Ašraf   be-IMPF.3SG   alone
    'I saw that Ašraf was alone.' (B/MB)

MP2 meanings are found both with simultaneous and anterior (42) events. A perception verb in reflexive passive is usually interpreted as 'it is obvious' because everyone can see the existing situation (43). Such predicates can be considered marginal cases of perception, just like the Macedonian examples (38) and (39) above.

(42) *...vidjah,   če   njakoj   e   kopal   i*
    see-AOR.1SG   COMP   somebody   be-PRS.3SG   dig-PRF.SG   and
    pokril   kopanoto...
    cover-PRF.SG   hole-DEF
    'I saw that someone had been digging here and had carefully covered the place.' (B/AD)

(43) *Vidja se,   če   semejstvoto   ne   e   v   razvod.*
    see-PRS.3SG REFL   COMP   family-DEF   not   be-PRS.3SG   in   divorce
    'It can be seen that the family is not divorced.' (B/e-vestnik.bg)

3.3 Summary of the *kako/kak* and *deka/če* CCs

The analysis makes it clear that the two patterns specialize for different types of perception, which is summed up in Table 3. Basically, *kako/kak* patterns specialize for IP, but MP1 is also possible in certain contexts, while *deka/če* express only mental percepcion, inclined towards MP2 interpretations. In Macedonian this division is clear-cut, while in Bulgarian it gets fuzzy at two points: *viždam kak* is mainly used with abstract events which get MP1 interpretation, and *gledam če* favoures MP1, because of the agentive bias of the verb.

Table 3: Interpretation of the type of perception with CC patterns of perception verbs in Macedonian and in Bulgarian.

Macedonian patterns	IP	MP1	MP2	Bulgarian patterns	IP	MP1	MP2
gleda kako	✓✓	✓		gledam kak	✓✓	✓	
				viždam kak		✓	✓
vidi kako	✓✓	✓		vidja kak	✓✓	✓	
gleda deka		✓	✓✓	gledam če		✓	✓
				viždam če		✓	✓✓
vidi deka		✓	✓	vidja če		✓	✓✓

Meaning distribution could be related to some structural parameters. It is obvious that aspect and tense of the subordinate verb does not crucially affect the interpretation, while the type of event and time relations do so to some degree. MP1 interpretation in the *kako/kak* clause does not fit the basic semantics of this pattern, but it arises under specific conditions, in particular
a. with abstract events (e.g. 11 and 18), and
b. anterior events (e.g. 8 and 12), especially with bounded events in the aorist (e.g. 12 and 15).

In both contexts, the overlap between the perceiving and the perceived event is weakened.

A distinctive feature of the *deka/če* pattern is its specialization for coding mental perception. Both MP1 and MP2 were attested, though MP2 is the typical interpretation. MP1 arises in contexts that lean towards immediately perceived events, such as:

a. events evolving at the time of perception (e.g. 26 and 31),
b. immediately perceived states with no presupposed triggering event (e.g. 28 and 43),
c. concrete events, rather than abstract (e.g. 31 and 36).

The MP2 interpretation occurs in a different type of contexts:
a. Most often only the effects of some event are perceived (e.g. 23 and 32);
b. This correlates with the fact that in MP2 dynamic events are not simultaneous: the perceived event is usually anterior to the perceiving one (e.g. 24), rarely posterior (e.g. 25);
c. If the verb expresses a simultaneous activity, it is of a vague, imprecise nature, such as 'prepare' in (34), which presupposes some more concrete activities, which are not overtly stated.

In both languages, the two patterns overlap in MP1 interpretation, and even though each pattern combines with different properties to give rise to such interpretation, the patterns are interchangable. In such situations, visual and mental experiences are inseparable; it seems that the choice of a complementizer imposes the desired interpretation of the observed event. In MP1 situations *deka/če* implies a change in focus: the perceiver becomes aware of the observed event. However, the use of *kako/kak* in the same situation foregrounds the perceptual experience related to an IP interpretation. Correspondingly, in (44) the replacement of *deka* with *kako* is grammatical but results in a subtle meaning change: with *kako* the speaker merely reports what s/he sees, but *deka* creates an inference that the speaker has realized the possible effects of the observed event (see also examples 26 and 35 above).

(44) *Vidov   deka   so   ogromna brzina mi*
     see-AOR.1SG   COMP   with   enormous speed   1SG.DAT.CL
     se približuva   avtomobil.
     REFL approach-PRS.3SG   car
     'I saw that a car was coming towards me at the speed of light.'
     (M/ubavinaizdravje.mk)

In MP1 *kako/kak* clauses (as well as in some IP ones), the complementizer can be replaced by *deka/če*, which promotes the mental perception reading. Compare examples (7a) and (13a) with the corresponding examples (7) and (13) above, which employ *kako/kak*.

(7a) Na televizija gledav   deka   bankite   se zatvaraat
      on TV   watch-IMPF.1SG   COMP   banks-DEF   REFL close-PRS.3PL
      edna po druga.
      one after other
      'I saw on TV that banks closed one after another.' (M)

(13a) ... toj viždaše   če   vsički   sa   nedovolni ...
           he see-IMPF.3SG   COMP   all   be-PRS.3PL   dissatisfied
      '... he could see that everyone was dissatisfied ...' (B)

MP2 situations differ considerably from both IP and MP1 in that they are situated purely in the mental domain. Replacing *deka/če* by *kako/kak* in MP2 clauses results in manner interpretation of the latter complementizer, not in MP1 (23a).

(23a) So svoi oči   gledame   kako   inteligencijata ...   se
      with own eyes   see-PRS.1PL   COMP   intelligentsia-DEF   REFL
      marginalizira.
      marginalize-PRS.3SG
      'We see with our own eyes how the intellectuals ... have been marginalized.' (M)

3.4 *da* complement clauses

Macedonian *da*-complements of visual verbs occur predominantly in modalized contexts: negative and interrogative matrix clause, or expressive (unexpected, rare) and temporally unanchored (omnitemporal, repetitive) situations. In all these situations a special emphasis is put on the CTP.[23] Under negation, the perception verb negates only the visual act, so the *da*-clause does not indicate that the speaker asserts or denies the truth of the perceived situation, but expresses non-commitment to its truth. Therefore, such negated constructions serve as a pragmatic strategy for epistemic distancing. By emphasizing that a certain situation has never (or nowhere) been witnessed by the perceiver (or anyone else) the speaker undermines the truth of the *da*-complement.

In Macedonian, the *gleda da* pattern appears only under negation and has a substandard flavor responsible for its rare use; the standard opts for the *deka* pattern.

---

23 We are grateful to the anonymous reviewer for this observation.

(45) *Ne gledam   da   se trudi   i   da   pokažuva*
NEG see-PRS.1SG SBJ REFL try-PRS.3SG and SBJ show-PRS.3SG
deka me saka.
COMP me loves
'I don't see him trying or showing that he loves me.' (M/femina.mk)

In Bulgarian, *gledam da* is also infrequent, but the few examples (mostly from the internet) are affirmative. They reveal that the pattern allows two interpretations: IP and MP1. The former usually pairs up with dynamic habitual events (46) and the latter with states (47) coded in the complement clause.

(46) *Gledam   go   da   tancuva   ot godini...*
see-PRS.1SG 3SG.M.ACC.CL SBJ dance-PRS.3SG from years
'I have seen him dance for years...' (B/sanovnik.bg)

(47) *...gledam   go   da   njama*
see-PRS.1SG 3SG.M.ACC.CL SBJ not-have-PRS.3SG
psihični otklonenija.
psychological deviations
'... I can see that he has no psychological deviations.' (B/novetrading.bg)

The pattern *vidi da* in Macedonian is represented by 163 examples (154 from the internet and only 9 examples from literature). Since the bulk of such *da*-constructions originate from blogs and interactive forums, such discrepancy reflects the colloquial use of *da*-complements with perception verbs. Another salient feature of this pattern is a pronounced affinity with negation. The number of examples with negated perception verbs is five times higher than with affirmative and interrogative ones. The subordinate verb is not aspectually restricted, though the imperfective form is more common (51–53).

The analysis of Macedonian examples shows that this pattern tends to be used in referentially unanchored contexts, often compounded by marked information structure to express denial of existence, surprise, indignation, and other kinds of subjective stance. More than half of the examples contain direct objects foregrounding the CC subject with low referentiality status, such as indefinite pronouns (*nikoj* 'noone', *nešto* 'something' etc.) illustrated in (48) and (49) or temporal indefinite adverbs (*nikogaš* 'never', *nikade* 'nowhere', *dosega* 'until' etc), illustrated in (50).

(48) Nikogo   ne vidov   da   se šeta   niz pazarot
     noone   NEG see-AOR.1SG SBJ REFL walk-PRS.3SG in market-DEF
     so eden domat vo kesa.
     with one tomato in bag-DEF
     'I haven't seen anyone walking through the market with one tomato in the bag.' (M/kajgana.com)

(49) Vakvo nešto   dosega ne   sum   videl   da   se pravi
     such thing   before NEG be-PRS.1SG   see-PRF.SG   SBJ REFL do-PRS.3SG
     javno.
     publicly
     'Such a thing I haven't seen before to be done in public.' (M/vecer.mk)

(50) Nikade   ne vidov   da   štrajkuvaat   producenti.
     nowhere   not see-AOR.1SG SBJ strike-PRS.3PL   producers
     'Nowhere have I seen producers strike.' (M/slobodenprostor.com)

In affirmative clauses, *da*-complements also favor expressive contexts. Adverbs and adverbials such as *samo* 'only', *edinstveno* 'only', *konečno* 'at last', *retko* 'seldom', *prvpat* 'first time' occupy the focus position. The speaker testifies that it is highly unusual (or provides some other subjective evaluation) for the subject to be involved in the event coded in the *da*-complement (51).

(51) Prv pat   za vreme na negoviot mandat   go   vidovme
     first time   for time of his term   3SG.M.ACC.CL   see-AOR.1PL
     da   dojde   kaj   nas.
     SBJ   come-AOR.3SG   at   1PL.ACC
     'It was the first time during his term that we saw him visit us.' (M/vest.com.mk)

The *da*-pattern may also occur in omnitemporal and repetitive contexts, mostly with the perfect form of *vidi* (10 of 14) suggesting acquired knowledge (MP1).

(52) Sum   videl   da   se slučuvaat   i počudni raboti.
     be-PRS.1SG   see-PRF.SG.M   SBJ   REFL happen-PRS.3PL and stranger things
     'I've seen stranger things happen.' (M/lakers.mk)

In Bulgarian, *gledam da*, *viždam da* and *vidja da* patterns are considerably more frequent compared to Macedonian. Examples with *vidja da* are by far the most frequent. In the examples from the literature and internet texts the embedded clauses predominantly contain dynamic predicates (53–54), while states are rare (55). Apart from the prevalent present imperfective form, the embedded verb can be perfective (bounded), as in (53) or in the perfect (54), the latter encoding an anterior event.

(53) *Ne vidja   nikoj   da   si   složi   nadpis*
     see-AOR.1SG nobody   SBJ   REFL.DAT.CL   put- PRS.3SG slogan
     "Az săm Izraelec".
     I am an Izrealite
     'I haven't seen anyone use a slogan "I am an Izraelite".' (B/e-vestnik.bg)

(54) *Da kaže   kakvo   napravi   s cenite na lekarstvata,*
     SBJ tell-PRS.3SG what   do-AOR.3SG   with prices of medications
     če   nešto   ne viždam   da   sa   padnali.
     COMP   somehow   NEG see-PRS.1SG SBJ   be-PRS.3PL   drop-PRF.PL
     'He should say what he did about the prices of medications, I don't see them fall.' (B/e-vestnik.bg)

(55) *Kăde   vidja   Avstrija   da   ima   atomna centrala ... ?*
     where   see-AOR.2SG   Austria   SBJ   have-PRS.3SG   nuclear plant
     'Where did you see that Austria has a nuclear power plant ... ?'
     (B/e-vestnik.bg)

Although *da*-clauses occur with negated perception verbs (53–54), they do not dominate in the attested examples (only 30 of 210), as it is the case with Macedonian where the absence of visual perception entails speaker's non-commitment to the truth of the *da*-complement. In (56) the speaker claims that the kitten drinks water because she was seen it doing so (*če*-complement), but it cannot be asserted whether she eats or not (*da*-complement).

(56) *Vidjah   ja   če   pie   voda,   no   ne*
     see-AOR.1SG   3SG.F.ACC.CL   COMP   drink-PRS.3SG   water   but   NEG
     săm   ja   viždala   da   jade.
     be-PRS.1SG   3SG.F.ACC.CL   see-PRF.SG   SBJ   eat-PRS.3SG
     'I saw that it drank water, but I haven't seen it eat.' (B/kotkite.com)

Similarly to Macedonian, we find non-negated *da*-clauses in emphatic utterances, such as questions (57), exclamations (58) and in expressive contexts (59).

(57) Možeš   li   da   si   predstaviš   kogo
     can-PRS.2SG PART   SBJ   REFL.DAT.CL imagine-PRS.2SG   whom
     vidjah   da   tancuva   na   ploštadkata?
     see-AOR.1SG   SBJ   dance-PRS.3SG   on   dance-floor-DEF
     'Can you imagine who I saw dancing on the dance floor?' (B/PR)

(58) De se čulo i vidjalo   găska   da   plaši   bivol?!
     where was heard and seen   goose   SBJ   frighten-PRS.3SG   ox
     'Where have you seen a goose frighten an ox?' (B/e-vestnik.bg)

(59) Samo   tam   mozeš   da   vidiš   pop matarist ...
     Only   there   can-PRS.2SG   SBJ   see-PRS.2SG   priest motorbiker
     'Only there you can see a priest on a motorbike ...' (B/e-vestnik.bg)

What distinguishes Bulgarian *da*-clauses used as CCs of perception verbs is the frequent occurrence of such clauses in affirmative contexts without any particular pragmatic marking (here referred to as 'neutral' contexts). Our examples show that *da* is always used to express events simultaneous with the act of perception, yielding immediate perception reading (60). However, *da* may be used to imply indeterminacy as to the intended interpretation. In (61) the speaker's satisfaction may be understood to arise from seeing someone read his/her book or from the realization of the fact that people know his/her books.

(60) ... v tozi moment   vidja   da   sliza   ot kolata   Virdžinija.
         in that moment   see-AOR.3SG   SBJ   exit-PRS.3SG   from car-DEF   Virginia
     '... at that moment he saw that Virginia was getting off the car/ Virginia getting off the car.' (B/JH)

(61) Veče imam 9 publikuvani knigi i strašno se radvam
     'I have already published nine books and it pleases me immensely
     kogato   vidja   njakoj   v metro   da   čete
     when   see-PRS.1SG   someone   in subway   SBJ   read-PRS.3SG
     njakoja od tjah.
     some of them
     when I see someone reading /that someone is reading one of them on the subway.' (B/e-vestnik.bg)

Our data confirm the claims of some authors that in Bulgarian *da* can also be used in affirmative clauses. Most of them (for instance GSBKE 1983, Grickat 1975, Ivanova and Gradinarova 2014) claim that *da* does not decrease factualness and is in free variation with *če* and *kak*. While GSBKE (1983: 334–335) advocates their interchangebility in the indicative mood, Grickat (1975: 170) notes the tendency of the Bulgarian *da* to penetrate into the sphere of *če* (as in *Viždam **da** vărvjat voinici* 'I see soldiers passing').[24] Assenova (2002: 264–265), on the other hand, invokes suspension of the subjunctive vs. indicative opposition in perception verb complements to account for the interchangability between *kak/če* and *da*.[25]

4 Discourse-syntactic strategies in Bulgarian and Macedonian

An important syntactic property of perception verb complements, triggered by pragmatic considerations, is the occurrence of an NP functioning as a direct object (DO) to the matrix verb, together with a clausal complement. Typically, this direct object is coreferential with the subject of the embedded clause. In English and some other Germanic languages, where the verb of the embedded clause is expressed with some non-finite verb form these structures are explained as resulting from a syntactic movement called subject to object raising. Sonnenhauser (2015) uses this term when describing complement clauses in 18th and 19th century Bulgarian. Cinque (1995) refers to such clauses in Italian as "pseudo-relative". He rejects the three previously proposed ways of analyzing such clauses, putting forward the small clause analysis instead. This issue has been discussed in Bulgarian syntax, and although there is consensus regarding the discourse distinction between complement clauses with an additional NP object and those without it, the syntactic status of such objects and the embedded clause remains a debatable issue (Rudin 1986, Aleksova and Tiševa 2000, Laskova 2013, Sonnenhauser 2015, Ivanova and Gradinarova 2015, Ivanova 2016). For Macedonian, Bužarovska (2013), analyzing verbs of auditory perception, uses the term "complement-relative" clauses, and con-

---

[24] The occurrence of *da* in affirmative contexts is common in verbs of cognition as well, but in such cases the *da*-construction, while keeping its modal meaning, foregrounds the hypotheticality of the main predicate, as in *Vjarvam toj veče da e pristignal tam* 'I believe that he has already arrived there.' (Ivanova and Gradinarova 2014: 264–265). Similar conclusions regarding the Macedonian and Bulgarian verbs *se nadeva/nadjavam se* 'hope' and *veruva/vjarvam* 'believe' were reached in Mitkovska and Bužarovska (2015).
[25] The author shows that such complement variation exists in other Balkan languages providing Albanian, Romanian and Greek translation of the Bulgarian sentence *Čuva se samo cafarata mu tažno da/če sviri*. 'Only his flute is heard to play sadly' (Assenova 2002: 165).

siders them an intermediate class sharing properties of both complement and relative clauses.

In their basic constructions, verbs of perception code the perceiver as the subject and the stimulus as a direct object NP (DO) or as a clausal complement (CC) encoding a perceived situation. There are various strategies to focus the viewers' attention on the main participant of the embedded situation. In sentences with a direct object and a clausal complement, the DO of the matrix clause is typically coreferential with the elliptical subject in the embedded clause (62). It may be optionally realized in the complement clause to achieve emphasis (63).

(62) a. *Otnovo **ja** viždah kak rešitelno trgava* ...
again 3SG.F.ACC.CL see-IMPF.1SG COMP resolutely set off-PRS.3SG
'Again I watched her set off resolutely...' (B/JH)
b. ***Gi** vide kako nabližuvaat.*
3PL.ACC.CL see-AOR.3SG COMP approach-PRS.3PL
'He saw them approaching.' (M/KU)

(63) a. *Vidjah **go** če **toj** vleze prez*
see-AOR.1SG 3SG.M.ACC.CL COMP he enter-AOR.3SG through
službenija vhod...
official-DEF entrance
'I saw him, that he got in through the official entrance...' (B/dariknews.bg)
b. *...mi se ispolni srceto koga **ja***
1SG.DAT.CL REFL fill-AOR.3SG heart-DEF when 3SG.F.ACC.CL
*vidov **taa** kako se smee...*
see-AOR.1SG she COMP REFL laugh-PRS.3SG
'... my heart filled with joy when I saw her smile ...' (M/femina.mk)

It has been suggested that the DO of the matrix clause and the complement clause function as a single complement to the matrix predicate, known as 'small clause' (e.g. Cinque 1995). Aleksova and Tiševa (2000) adopt such an analysis for Bulgarian *da-* and *če-*clauses with verbs of perception, considering that in (64) *Ivan* forms a constituent together with the *da/če-*clause.

(64) *Az vidjah Ivan da/če tiča.*
I see-AOR.1SG Ivan SBJ/COMP run-PRS.3SG
'I saw Ivan run/that he was running.' (B)

A similar position is taken by Ivanova and Gradinarova (2015) and Ivanova (2016), who discuss the complement clauses of perception verbs as a kind of depictive constructions, using the Russian term 'predikativnoe opredelenie' (predicative attribute/modifier).[26] A similar view is expressed by Sonnenhauser (2015), who considers the matrix DO coreferential with the embedded subject as a result of subject-to-object raising, leading to greater syntactic integration of the matrix and embedded clause. However, there is a different view regarding this question, according to which perception verbs in Bulgarian can have two arguments: an NP object as well as a clausal complement (Rudin 1986: 70, Laskova 2013: 6).[27] According to this view, the subject of the lower clause does not occur on the surface for discourse-pragmatic reasons; hence there is no "raising", but ellipsis. Regardless of the formal description, it is obvious that these different syntactic constructions do not have identical communicative goals: the CC, as the only argument of the matrix clause, foregrounds the perceived event, whereas the presence of the main participant of the viewed event in the matrix clause foregrounds the participant. We will refer to such CC types as "participant foregrounding".

The attested examples show that both Macedonian and Bulgarian employ participant foregrounding strategy by positioning the embedded clause subject as a DO of the perception predicate, but diverge in their distribution along the CC patterns examined here. It should be pointed out that both languages have flexible word order permitting positioning of the embedded clause subject before the complementizer, which is considered marked word order (Rudin 1986: 24), as illustrated in (65). In CCs with perception verbs such constructions could be structurally ambiguous in written language, especially in Bulgarian. In Macedonian, ambiguity arises with indefinite NPs, but definite DOs always require a clitic before the verb, thus if *Ivan* is considered a DO of the matrix clause it would be signaled with the clitic *go* (66). Bulgarian does not exhibit such regular clitic doubling, which makes it difficult, if not impossible, to determine the syntactic affiliation of a fronted NP subject.[28]

---

[26] Ivanova (2016: 46) cites Koeva (2006), who holds the view that the small clause functions as a complement clause, and poses the question of the number of arguments in the structure of the perception verbs which have both a DO and a clause. She claims that the clause should be considered an argument of the matrix verb, while the DO is a realization of the argument of the embedded clause.

[27] From the typological point of view, Dixon (2006: 7) suggests that there is a possibility of a subclass of verbs which require a DO and an 'extension to core' filled by a complement clause.

[28] This has been pointed out in Bulgarian linguistics (Ivanova 2016: 45) by Penčev and other authors, some of them pointing out the role of prosody in disambiguation. See also Aleksova and Tiševa (2000).

(65) a. *Vidov   Ivan   kako/deka   ja   premina*
       Vidjah   Ivan   kak/če   preseče
       see-AOR.1SG Ivan   COMP/SBJ   3SG.F.ACC.CL cross-AOR.3SG
       ulicata. (M)
       ulicata. (B)
       street-DEF
       'I saw Ivan cross the street/I saw that Ivan crossed the street.'
   b. *Ne vidov   Ivan   da   ja   premina   ulicata.* (M)
       Ne vidjah   Ivan   da   preseče   ulicata. (B)
       NEG see-AOR.1SG Ivan   SBJ   3SG.F.ACC.CL cross-AOR.3SG street-DEF
       'I didn't see Ivan cross the street.'

(66) a. *Go   vidov   Ivan   kako   ja*
       3SG.M.ACC.CL   see-AOR.1SG Ivan   COMP   3SG.F.ACC.CL
       premina   ulicata.
       cross-AOR.3SG   street-DEF
       'I saw Ivan cross the street.' (M)
   b. *Ne go   vidov   Ivan   da   ja*
       NEG 3SG.M.ACC.CL see-AOR.1SG Ivan   SBJ   3SG.F.ACC.CL
       premina   ulicata.
       cross-AOR.3SG   street-DEF
       'I didn't see Ivan cross the street.' (M)

Such ambiguity also occurs with the indefinite pronouns which often appear before the complementizer or the *da*-particle in the nominative instead of prescribed accusative: *nekoj/nikoj* vs. *nekogo/nikogo* 'someone' (M) and *njakoj/nikoj* vs. *njakogo/nikogo* 'someone' (B). Since in both languages there is a tendency for leveling the difference between the subject and object forms in colloquial speech, the syntactic position of the pronoun cannot be determined (67).

(67) a. *Ne vidjah   **nikoj**   da   protestira.*
       NEG see-AOR.1SG   noone   SBJ   protest-PRS.3SG
       'I didn't see anyone to protest.' (B)
   b. *Toj videl   **nekoj**   kako   vleguva   vo kuḱata.*
       he see-PRF.3SG   someone   COMP   enter-PRS.3SG in house-DEF
       'He saw someone entering the house.' (M)

Tables 4 and 5 present the numbers and rates of occurrence of participant foregrounding constructions[29] (i.e. "outside" the complement clause) attested in the Macedonian and Bulgarian examples, respectively. For Macedonian, the total number of such examples is presented, compared to the number of all examples attested in that class. Because of the great number of indeterminate cases in Bulgarian examples, we counted separately the number of short pronominal objects[30] (where there is no ambiguity), and nominal objects, as the latter may embody different constructions.

Table 4: The distribution of participant foregrounding constructions in the Macedonian examples.

Mac	kako				deka				da			
	gleda		vidi		gleda		vidi		gleda		vidi	
	FG	total	FG	total	FG	total	FG	total	FG	total	FG	total
Fict.	33	93	38	88	1	50	0	112	0	1	7	9
Inter.	22	55	33	175	0	76	1	98	0	9	58	154
total	55	148	71	263	1	126	1	210	0	10	65	163
TOTAL	126 FG /411 all (30.66%)				2 FG /336 all (0.6%)				65 FG /173 all (37.57%)			

Table 5: The distribution of participant foregrounding constructions in the Bulgarian examples.

Bul	kak						če						da					
	gledam		viždam		vidja		gledam		viždam		vidja		gledam		viždam		vidja	
	CL	NP	CL	NP	CL	NP	CL	NP	CL	NP	CL	NP	CL	NP	CL	NP	CL	NP
Fict.	10	1	3	0	10	0	0	0	0	2	1	0	0	6	5	23	17	
Inter.	9	10	0	0	7	1	17	4	14	1	34	1	4	1	7	6	11	64
total	19	11	3	0	17	1	17	4	14	1	36	2	4	1	13	11	34	81
clause	39 (12.5%)						67 (13.35%)						51 (24.28%)					
NP	12 (3.85%)						7 (1.39%)						93 (44.29%)					
TOTAL	51 FG /312 all (16.35%)						74 FG /502 all (14.74%)						144 FG /210 all (68.57%)					

With *kako/kak* patterns the DO in the matrix clause occurs more often in Macedonian (68) than in Bulgarian (69). The overall representation is twice as frequent, with 30.66% vs. 16.35%. In both languages the foregrounded participant

---

29 Abbreaviated as FG (foregronding) in Tables 4 and 5.
30 Abbreaviated as CL (clitic) in Table 5.

is mainly realized by an accusative clitic pronoun. Nominal objects are rare (68b and 69b) displaying occasional ambiguity in Bulgarian (70). In Macedonian these objects refer to unspecified entities and may be considered topicalized rather than foregrounded subordinate subjects (71).

(68) a. *Ukočen od šok* ***ja*** *gledav kako po*
stiff from shock 3SG.F.ACC.CL see-IMPF.1SG COMP up
skalite se kačuva.
stairs-DEF REFL climb-PRS.3SG
'Petrified from a/the shock, I watch **her** climbing the stairs.' (M/mk/vesti/scena)

b. *Za prvpat* ***ja*** *vidov* ***mojata koleška*** *da*
for fist time 3SG.F.ACC.CL see-AOR.1SG my colleague-F SBJ
zapira so rabotata.
stop-PRS.3SG with work-DEF
'It was the first time I saw **my colleague** stop working.' (M/KM)

(69) a. *Možeh da* ***ja*** *gledam s časove*
can-IMPF.1SG SBJ 3SG.F.ACC.CL watch-PRS.1SG with hours
kak govori.
COMP talk-PRS.3SG
'I could watch **her** speak for hours.' (B/TD)

b. *... gledam* ***gi*** ***lekarite*** *kak se săbirat ...*
see-PRS.1SG 3PL.ACC.CL doctors-DEF comp REFL gather-PRS.3PL
'... I can see **the doctors** gathering ...' (B/e-vestnik.bg)

(70) *Vidjah* ***cara na frankite*** *kak jade i pie.*
see-AOR.1SG king of French COMP eat-PRS.3SG and drink-PRS.3SG
'I saw the **French king** eating and drinking.' (B/AD)

(71) *Vide* ***i drugi drugari*** *kako čekaa pred*
see-AOR.3SG and other friends comp wait-IMPF.3PL before
železnata vrata.
iron-DEF door
'He saw **some other friends** waiting in front of the iron door.' (M/KU)

It seems that participant foregrounding indicates immediate perception, where the attention of the viewer can zoom in on the participant, backgrounding the event. Mental perception disprefers foregrounding, as in such cases the observation of the event leads to a relevant conclusion.[31] Participant foregrounding is rarely encountered with *viždam kak* (B), which may be related to the predominantly abstract nature of the embedded event with those verbs (compare examples 11 and 12 above).

The divergence between the participant foregrounding constructions in the two languages is even greater in the basic indicative patterns *deka* and *če*. While the use of the matrix DO is extremely rare and unusual for Macedonian (72), it is generally accepted and quite common in Bulgarian (73), as pointed out by Aleksova and Tiševa (2000) and Ivanova (2016). The fact that the bulk of these examples were found in Internet texts (as in 72–73) suggests that they reflect a colloquial style.[32]

(72) Ušte   koga   **go**   vidov   deka   vleguva
      already   when   3SG.M.ACC.CL   see-AOR.1SG   COMP   enter-PRS.3SG
      vo   salata   si   pomisliv   deka   e
      in   hall-DEF   REFL.DAT.CL   think-AOR.1SG   COMP   be-PRS.3SG
      dojden   kako provokator.
      come-PART.M.SG   as provocator
      'The moment I saw **him** enter the courtroom, I realized that he came to provoke.' (M/star.dnevnik.com.mk)

(73) Vidjah   **ja**,   če   nakucvaše,   kato
      see-AOR.1SG   3SG.F.ACC.CL   COMP   limp-IMPF.3SG   as
      se približavaše.
      REFL approach-IMPF.3SG
      'I saw that **she** was limping as she was coming closer.' (B/wqpwqp.blog.bg)

In most situations, MP1 interpretation is more likely, but in Bulgarian there are examples where the *če*-clause expresses inferential knowledge (74).

(74) Viždam   **gi**,   če   sa   seriozni momčeta,
      see-PRS.1SG   3PL.ACC.CL   COMP   be-PRS.3PL   serious lads
      no   ograničeni.
      but   limited
      'I see that these lads are serious, but narrow-minded.' (B/forum.e-therapy.bg)

---

[31] This is evident in the following example: *Koga vide kako ispienite obrazi na tie sto gi sproveduvaat se stegaat, sfati oti se ludo gladni.* (KU) 'When he saw the prisoners' cheeks twitching he realized that they were starving.' (M)

[32] For some native speakers they are not stylistically marked.

It seems that in *deka* and *če*-clauses situations with foregrounded participants are closer to immediate perception reading. The mention of the main participant of the perceived event in the matrix clause yields immediate perception interpretation, on which mental perception is based. However, contrary to the claim of closer integration of the two events by participant foregrounding, this indicative pattern displays a split between the perceptual act of an entity and its mental representation.

The data presented in Tables 4 and 5 show that participant foregrounding is most typical for the *da*-pattern in both languages, with some relevant differences. In Macedonian, *kako-* and *da*-patterns behave similarly in respect to foregounding of the participant in the perceived event; this participant is usually topical, hence requiring the use of the DO clitic (68a and 69a). Only in rare cases of special emphasis is the object NP also realized (68b and 69b).

In Bulgarian, clear cases of participant foregrounding, with a DO clitic, are less represented in our sample (75), while examples with the subject NP preceding *da* are considerably more frequent (76). As pointed out, in writing, it is impossible to determine if the NP belongs to the matrix clause, but it is predominantly placed between *da* and the perception verb.

(75) *Vidjah* **ja** *da izkačva pătekata kăm*
see-AOR.1SG 3SG.F.ACC.CL SBJ climb-PRS.3SG path-DEF to
Prevala, ...
Prevala
'I saw **her** climb up the path towards Prevala, ...' (B/AD)

(76) *...eto vidjah* **Goran** *da lovi păstărva v edin vir.*
there see-AOR.1SG Goran SBJ catch-PRS.3SG trout in one pond
'...there – I saw **Goran** fishing trout in a pond.' (B/AD)

Another strategy for topicalizing the subject of the perceived situation is to place it at the very beginning of the matrix clause (77). It can be unclear where it belongs syntactically, but in example (78) it is undoubtedly the extracted embedded subject (the pronoun has a subject form). Such topicalization of the main participant in the perceived event is especially characteristic for Macedonian where it seems to play a special pragmatic role in triggering the use of *da* even in affirmative contexts. Positioning the subject of the embedded event at the beginning of the sentence, with or without change in the syntactic status is closely related to the nature of the *da*-clause.

(77) *Dvesta i osemnadeset čerkvi vidjah da săbarjat*
Two hundred and eighteen churches see-AOR.1SG SBJ shatter-PRS.3PL
novite mjusjulmani.
new-DEF Muslims
'Two hundred and eighteen churches I saw the new Muslims to ruin ...'
(B/AD)

(78) *I toa sum videl da se sluči*
and this be-PRS.1SG see-PRF.SG SBJ REFL happen-AOR.3SG
veli eden postar čovek.
says one older man
'**That** I have seen happen, too, says an older man.' (M/star.vest.com.mk)

Indefinite pronouns are often encountered in the focus; if they are not marked for case their status is ambiguous (79), but a pronoun marking the DO clearly belongs with the perception verb (80).

(79) *Nikoj ne sum videl da spori*
noone NEG be-PRS.1SG see-PRF.SG SBJ argue-PRS.3SG
so Komisijata ...
with commission-DEF
'I haven't seen anybody argue with the Commission ...' (M/press24.mk)

(80) *Nikogaš nikogo ne sum videl da*
never nonone.ACC NEG be-PRS.1SG see-PRF.SG SBJ
gleda emisija ... na MTV.
watch-PRS.3SG show on MTV
'I have never seen anybody watching shows ... on MTV.' (M/forum.it.com.mk)

5 Distribution of the analyzed CC patterns: comparison

In what follows, we summarize the findings regarding the similarities and differences of the examined CC patterns in Bulgarian and in Macedonian. The main features of the *kako/kak* pattern are the following: it is mainly used for immediate perception and less so for primary mental perception. MP1 interpretation obtains mostly with perceived states and abstract events. Participant foregrounding is common, though found more frequently in Macedonian. In our collection of examples it features twice as frequently in Macedonian: in 30.66% of the examples with *kako*, compared to 16.35% in Bulgarian. Foregrounded constructions do not render mental perception meanings, especially in Macedonian. Anterior observed events also contribute to the MP1 interpretation. The tense in the CC tends to be interpreted in relation to the tense of the CTP, but independent tense uses are also common with no tense and aspect restrictions. Generally, the patterns with *gleda* in both languages favor relative use of tense in the complement clause.

The main properties of *deka/če* complements include the following: in both languages these patterns are dedicated for primary (MP1) and secondary mental perception (MP2). There is a slight tendency for clauses with non-agentive verbs to express MP2 functions, which is not maintained in Bulgarian *gleda*. This might be due to the confusion of *gledam* and *viždam* in the colloquial register. The tense of the subordinate verb occurs in both independent and dependent uses in the patterns with the non-agentive verbs *vidi* and *viždam/vidja*, but the *gleda* pattern employs only dependent tenses. MP2 interpretation tends to be rendered by independent tenses, whereas MP1 readings prefer the dependent present. Bulgarian negated matrix verbs do not co-occur with the perfect,[33] unlike Macedonian (see example 31). Participant foregrounding, though atypical for these patterns, is found in Bulgarian examples of both styles, but especially among those from the Internet. The few attested Macedonian examples are highly colloquial.

The analysis of Macedonian and Bulgarian examples shows that *da*-complements do not have equal distribution in the two languages, which indicates a different status of *da* in perception complements. Table 6 summarizes the differences between *da*-complements in the two languages.

Table 6: Differences between Macedonian and Bulgarian examples in the use of *da*-clauses.

BULGARIAN	MACEDONIAN
– Only 17% occur with negated perception verbs	– Occur mostly with negated perception verbs (around 80% of the examples)
– More examples in neutral[34] context	– Few examples in neutral context[35]
– More imperfective verbs	– More perfective verbs
– More concrete perceived events	– More abstract perceived events
– Occur in literature and have no pronounced stylistic marking	– Almost absent in the literature, found in blogs and the press, colloquially marked

---

33 Aleksova and Tiševa (2000) claim that the following sentence is ungrammatical: **Ne viždam, če Ivan e došăl/e idval/e pristignal.* 'I don't see that Ivan has come/ arrived'.
34 This term is used for a number of affirmative, non-emphatic contexts.
35 The examples sound unusual due to several reasons: religious contexts, Serbian influence or literal translations from English.

It is obvious that *da*-complements differ in Macedonian and Bulgarian at syntactic, semantic and stylistic levels. Most significantly, in Bulgarian we find them in neutral contexts, while in Macedonian *da*-complements occur almost exclusively in non-assertive contexts (negative, interrogative, expressive and temporally unanchored situations). This difference was confirmed in a brief questionnaire conducted among native speakers of Macedonian (50 respondents) and Bulgarian (34 respondents). They were asked to mark the acceptability of 10 sentences with *da*-clauses as complements of visual perception verbs on a Likert scale from 1 to 5 (1 indicating unacceptable and 5 fully acceptable). Summarized results are presented in Table 7.

Table 7: Questionnaire results.

	Neutral context	Negated context	Interrogative context	Emphatic context
Bulgarian mean	4.12	3.65	4.36	4.41
Macedonian mean	1.77	3.10	4.05	4.35

As expected, Bulgarian speakers accepted the sentences with *da*-clauses in neutral contexts much better than Macedonian speakers. The results of the three examples expressing immediate perception were similar to those in (81). This sentence was fully accepted in Bulgarian (81b) with a mean of 4.56 in contrast to Macedonian (81a), where the acceptance mean was 1.86.

(81) a. *Po eksplozijata   vidovme   vo dvorot   da   vleguvaat*
     b. *Sled vzriva   vidjahme   v dvora   da   nahluvat*
        after blast-DEF   see-AOR.1PL   in yard-DEF SBJ   enter- PRS.3PL
        voeni avtomobili. (M)
        voenni avtomobili. (B)
        military cars
        'Right after the explosion, we saw military cars driving into the yard.'

The sentence in which the complement clause conveys mental perception was equally unacceptable with a mean of 1.64 for Macedonian speakers (82a) and 1.17 for Bulgarian ones.

(82) a. *Vidov   da   toa   rešenie   e   pravilno.*
        see-AOR.1SG   SBJ   this   decision   be-PRS.1SG   correct
        'I saw that this decision is correct.' (M)

b. *Vidjah,   da   rešenieto   za reforma   e   pravilno.*
   see-AOR.1SG SBJ   decision- DEF for reform   be-PRS.3SG correct
   'I saw that this decision for reform is correct.' (B)

It appears that Bulgarian speakers accept the *da*-pattern coding a perceived event that overlaps with the act of perception (81b), but they reject *da*-complements when they expresse inference-based perception as in (82b). This supports the findings of the present investigation and the claims in Bulgarian linguistic literature on complement clauses (GSBKE 1983, Grickat 1975, Ivanova and Gradinarova 2014, Assenova 2002 among others).[36] In non-assertive contexts, there is no significant difference between the reactions of Macedonian and Bulgarian speakers. Curiously, the acceptance of these sentences in interrogative and expressive contexts is higher than the acceptance of the negated perception clauses in both languages. This could be explained by the fact that negation allows for subjective interpretation as to the speaker's commitment to the truth of the dependent predication, while the other two marked contexts require the use of the *da*-construction more regularly.

To conclude, the distribution of the *da*-pattern with verbs of vision is constrained in Macedonian by modal factors related to the epistemic status of the complement clause. It could be argued that these constraints are looser in Bulgarian, which has resulted in a wider distribution of this pattern. Given that *da*-complements cover part of the immediate perception domain, they compete with the *kak*-pattern, which explains the lower frequency of the Bulgarian *kak*-pattern compared to its Macedonian counrepart (see Table 1 and 2).

6 Conclusion

The data-driven analysis of the three CC patterns of verbs of vision in Macedonian and Bulgarian has confirmed our first hypothesis about the semantic motivation of perception verb complements. In both languages the iconicity principle has led to a semantically motivated regularization of complementation patterns: *kako/kak*

---

[36] The occurrence of *da* in affirmative contexts is common in verbs of cognition as well, but in such cases the *da*-construction, while keeping its modal meaning, foregrounds the hypotheticality of the main predicate, as in *Vjarvam toj veče da e pristignal tam* 'I believe that he has already arrived there.' (Ivanova and Gradinarova 2014: 264–265). Similar conclusions regarding the Macedonian and Bulgarian verbs *se nadeva/nadjavam se* 'hope' and *veruva/vjarvam* 'believe' were reached in Mitkovska and Bužarovska (2015).

specialize for immediate perception and *deka/če* for mental perception. However, primary mental perception (MP1) may employ both patterns, which indicates its intermediate semantics between direct and indirect perception. This atypical interpretation of the *kako/kak*-clauses is triggered by stative and resultative matrix predicates, leading to the extension of these complementizers into the mental perception domain, especially in Macedonian.

The conducted analysis supports the second hypothesis involving the occurrence of subjunctive *da*-complements in specific semantic-pragmatic environments. It was shown that apart from negative contexts, subjunctive complements commonly occur in expressive contexts, as well. This agrees with the observation that the subjunctive may be triggered by certain semantic properties of the embedding context (Giannakidou 2009: 1888). Interestingly, Bulgarian *da*-complements have no pronounced stylistic function, compared to their colloquial role in Macedonian.

Despite the similarities, it was shown that the distribution of the *da*-clauses with perception verbs differs in the two languages, as stated in the third hypothesis. Predicates with asserted complements in Macedonian choose the indicative (*deka*- and *kako*-clause), whereas under matrix negation mental perception verbs may select between the indicative and the subjunctive CC pattern. Assertiveness is related to the truth-value assessment and factuality of the perceived event. Because *da*-complements cannot be assessed in terms of true or false they display variability in modally-marked contexts. Namely, negated factual immediate perception verbs pair up with the *kako*-pattern, while semi-factual mental verbs of vision choose the *deka*-pattern or the *da*-pattern (*Ne vidov deka/da dojde Vera*. 'I didn't see Vera arrive'). In Bulgarian, the adherence to the semantic opposition immediate vs. mental perception is blurred due to the expansion of the *da*-clauses into the functional domain of the two indicative complement clause types. Under matrix negation it occurs with both types of perception, especially when IP and MP1 partly overlap. Moreover, it is found in affirmative contexts expressing immediate perception readings, which is confirmed by a lower number of *kak*-complements compared to *kako*-complements in the analyzed data. We assume that the wider scope of the the *da*-pattern in Bulgarian may be due to the underspecified semantics of *da*, which, unlike in Macedonian, bears the inherited traces of the adjunctive *da*. It competes with *kak* in the domain of immediate perception, but the role of the factors that determine the distribution of the two structures needs to be further investigated.

Given the more restricted use of subjunctive complements in Macedonian, it can be concluded that their distribution is constrained by modal factors related to the epistemic status of the embedded proposition. In Bulgarian, these constraints are looser, resulting in a wider distribution of the *da*-pattern. This leads to the assumption that the semantic delineation between assertive and non-assertive complements is stricter in Macedonian than in Bulgarian, which, in turn, testifies to a typological tendency in the center of the Balkan Sprachbund.

References

Ammann, Andreas & Johan van der Auwera. 2004. Complementizer-headed main clauses for volitional mood in the languages of South-Eastern Europe – a Balkanism? In Olga Mišeska Tomić (ed.), *Balkan syntax and semantics*, 293–314. Amsterdam: Benjamins.
Aikhenvald, Alexandra Y. 2004. *Evidentiality*. Oxford: Oxford University Press.
Aleksova, Krasimira & Yovka Tiševa. 2000. Bulgarian *da*- and *che*-clauses after verbs of perception. *Papers from 3th conference on FASSBL. University of Trondheim. Working Papers in Linguistics* 34. 97–108.
Anderson, Lloyd B. 1986. Evidentials, paths of change, and mental maps: Typologically regular asymmetries. In Wallace Chafe & Johanna Nichols (eds.), *Evidentiality: The linguistic encoding of epistemology*, 273–312. Norwood: Ablex.
Assenova, Petya. 2002. *Balkansko ezikoznanie: Osnovni problem na balkanskija ezikov săjuz* [Balkan linguistics: Fundamental problems of the Balkan Linguistic Union]. V. Tărnovo: Faber.
Boye, Kasper. 2010. Reference and clausal perception-verb complements, *Linguistics* 48 (2). 391–430.
Bužarovska, Eleni. 2002. Svrznicite na zavisni rečenici so nadgraden predikat na vizuelna percepcija (vo tekstovite na Joakim Krčovski i Krninskiot Damaskin) [Clausal connectors with verbs of visual perception (in texts by Joakim Krčovski and Krnin damascinus)]. *Slavistički studii* 10. 76–94.
Bužarovska, Eleni. 2013. *Glagoli za auditivna percepcija* [Verbs of auditory perception]. Skopje: UKIM.
Bybee, Joan, Revere Perkins, & William Pagliuca. 1994. *The evolution of grammar: Tense, aspect, and modality in the languages of the world*. Chicago: University of Chicago Press.
Cinque, Guglielmo. 1995. The pseudo-relative and ACC-ing constructions after verbs of perception. In Guglielmo Cinque (ed.), *Italian syntax and universal grammar*, 244–275. Cambridge: Cambridge University Press.
Cristofaro, Sonia. 2003. *Subordination*. Oxford: Oxford University Press.
Cruse, Alan D. 1973. Some thoughts on agentivity. *Journal of Linguistics* 9. 11–23.
Cuyckens, Herbert & Frauke D'hoedt. 2015. Variability in clausal verb complementation: The case of admit. In Paul Rickman, Juhani Rudanko & Jukka Havu (eds.), *Perspectives on complementation: Structure, variation and boundaries*, 77–100. London: Palgrave Macmillan.
Dejanova, Marija. 1985. *Podčineni izrečenija săs* da *v săvremenija slovenski knižoven ezik, v sravnenie s bălgarski* [Dependent clauses with *da* in contemporary literary Slovene in comparison with Bulgarian]. Sofija: BANU.
Dik, Simon & Kees Hengeveld. 1991. The hierarchical structure of the clause and the typology of perception verb complements. *Linguistics* 29. 231–259.
Dixon, Robert M. W. 2006. Complement clauses and complementation strategies in typological perspective. In Robert M. W. Dixon & Alexandra Y. Aikhenvald (eds.), *Complementation: A cross-linguistic typology*, 1–48. New York: Oxford University Press.

Fillmore, Charles. 1968. In Emmon Bach & Robert T. Harms (eds.), *The Case for Case*, 1–88. New York: Holt, Rinehart and Winston.
Friedman, Victor A. 2011. Tipologija na upotrebata na *da* vo balkanskite jazici. In Zuzana Topolinjska & Marjan Marković (eds.), *Makedonistički studii* [The typology of the use of *da* in Balkan languages], 43–52. Skopje: MANU.
Genadieva-Mutafčieva, Zara. 1970. *Podčinitelnijat săjuz da v săvremennija bălgarski ezik* [The subordinate conjunction *da* in the contemporary Bulgarian language]. Sofija: BANU.
Giannakidou, Anastasia. 2009. The dependency of the subjunctive revisited: Temporal semantics and polarity. *Lingua* 119. 1883–1908.
Givón, Talmy. 2001. *Syntax. A functional-typological introduction*. Vol. I. Amsterdam: Benjamins.
Ǵurkova, Aleksandra. 2008. *Sintaksa na složenata rečenica vo makedonskite crkovnoslovenski rakopisi* [The syntax of simple sentences in Macedonian Church Slavonic manuscripts]. Skopje: IMJ.
Ǵurkova, Aleksandra. 2015a. Specifičnosti na kompletivnite svrznici vo makedonskiot i vo drugite južnoslovenski jazici [Specific features of the complementizers in Macedonian and other South Slavic languages]. *XXXI naučna konferencija na XLVII megunaroden seminar za makedonski jazik, literatura i kultura, Ohrid 14–15 juni 2014*. 7–18.
Ǵurkova, Aleksandra. 2015b. Svrznikot *da* vo makedonskite crkvenoslovenski tekstovi vo sporedba so drugite južnoslovenski redakcii na crkvenoslovenskiot [The conjunction *da* in Macedonian Church Slavonic texts in comparison with other South Slavonic reductions of the Church Slavonic language]. *Slovo* 65. 1–20.
Gołąb, Zbigniew. 1964. The problem of verbal mood in Slavic languages. *International Journal of Slavic Linguistics and Poetics* 8. 1–36.
Grickat, Irena. 1975. *Studije iz istorije srpskohrvatskog jezika* [Studies from the history of Serbocroat]. Beograd: Narodna biblioteka Srbije.
Grković-Major, Jasmina. (this volume) Development of emotion predicates in Serbian.
Grković-Mejdžor, Jasminka. 2004. Razvoj hipotaktičkog *da* u starosrpskom jeziku [The development of the hypotatctic *da* in Old Serbian]. *Zbornik Matice srpske za filologiju i lingvistiku* 471 (2). 185–203.
Grković-Mejdžor, Jasminka. 2010. O konstrukcii akuzativa s participom (tipološki i kognitivni aspekti) [On accusative with participle constructions (typological and cognitive aspects)]. *Južnoslovenski filolog* 66. 187–204.
Gruber, Jerome. 1967. Look and see. *Language* 43. 937–948.
GSBKE 1983: *Gramatika na săvremenniă bălgarski knižoven ezik, T. III, Sintaksis* [Grammar of the contemporary Bulgarian literary language]. Sofia: BAN, Institut za bălgarski ezik.
Hansen, Björn, Alexander Letuchiy & Izabela Błaszczyk. 2016. Complementizers in Slavonic. In Kasper Boye & Petar Kehayov (eds.), *Semantic functions of complementizers in European languages*, 175–223. Berlin & Boston: De Gruyter Mouton.
Ivanova, Elena Ju. & Alla A. Gradinarova 2015. *Sintaksičeskaja sistema bolgarskogo jazyka na fone russkogo* [The syntactic system of Bulgarian compared to Russian]. Moskva: JaSK.
Ivanova, Elena Ju. 2016. *Da*-konstrukcija v pozicii predikativnogo opredelenija v bolgarskom jazyke [*Da*-construction as predicative modifier in Bulgarian]. In O. V. Vasiljev & Z. K. Šanov (eds.), *XXI Deržavinskie čtenija: Sovremennye i istoričeskie problemy bolgaristiki i slavistiki*, 41–50. Sankt Petersburg: Filologičeskij fakultet.
Johanson, Lars. 2003. Evidentiality in Turkic. In Alexandra Y. Aikhenvald & Robert M. W. Dixon (eds.), *Studies in Evidentiality*, 273–290. Amsterdam: Benjamins.

Joseph, Brian. 1983. *The synchrony and diachrony of the Balkan infinitive: A study in areal, general and historic linguistics*. Cambridge: Cambridge University Press.
Kirsner, Robert S. & Sandra A. Thompson. 1976. The role of pragmatic inference in semantics: A study of sensory verb complements in English. *Glossa* 10. 200–240.
Koneski, Blaže. 1986. *Istorija na makedonskiot literaturen jazik* [The history of the Macedonian literary language]. Skopje: Kultura.
Kramer, Christina E. 1986. *Analytic modality in macedonian*. Munich: Sagner.
Krapova, Iliyana. 2001. Subjunctives in Bulgarian and modern Greek. In Maria Luisa Rivero & Angela Ralli (eds.), *Comparative syntax of Balkan languages*, 105–126. Oxford: Oxford University Press.
Landau, Idan. 2004. The scale of finiteness and the calculus of control. *Natural Language and Linguistic Theory* 22. 811–877.
Langacker, Ronald W. 2008. *Cognitive grammar: A basic introduction*. Oxford: Oxford University Press.
Laskova, Laska. 2013. Parametri na situacii, izrazeni v izkazvane s glagol za percepcija: lice, čislo, status i vreme [Parameters of situations expressed by perception verbs: person, status and tense]. *Littera et Lingua Series Dissertationes* 5. 1–19.
Minova-Ǵurkova, Liljana. 1994. *Sintaksa na makedonskiot standarden jazik* [Syntax of the Macedonian standard language]. Skopje: Rading.
Mitkovska, Liljana & Eleni Bužarovska. 2015. Variation in clausal complementation: Macedonian and Bulgarian predicates Hope and Believe. In Branimir Belaj (ed.), *Dimenzije značenja*, 189–242. Zagreb: Zagrebačka slavistička škola.
Nicolova, Ruselina. 2005. Glednata točka i upotrebata na vremenata v složnite săstavni izrečenija s mentalni predikati v bălgarskija ezik [Point of view and the use of tenses in complex sentences with mental predicates in Bulgarian]. *Jubileen slavističen sbornik s dokladi ot Meždunarodnata slavistična konferencija Slavjanska filologija v Jugozapadnija universitet „Neofit Rilski"*, 312–324. Blagoevgrad: Jugozapaden universitet "Neofit Rilski".
Nicolova, Ruselina. 2008a. *Bălgarska gramatika, Morfologija* [Bulgarian grammar: morphology]. Sofija: Universitet Sv. Kliment Ohridski.
Nicolova, Ruselina. 2008b. Problematika na složenite izrečenija s komplementi v bălgarskija ezik. [On complex sentences with complements in Bulgarian]. *Južnoslovenski filolog* 64. 261–272.
Nikolaeva, Irina. 2007. Introduction. In Irina Nikolaeva (ed.). *Finiteness. Theoretical and empirical foundations*, 1–19. Oxford: Oxford University Press.
Noonan, Michael. 1985/2007. Complementation. In Timothy Shopen (ed.), *Language typology and syntactic description*, vol. 2: *Complex constructions*, 52–150. Cambridge: Cambridge University Press.
Nordström, Jackie. 2010. *Modality and subordinators*. Amsterdam: Benjamins.
Nuyts, Jan. 2001. *Epistemic modality, language and conceptualization*. Amsterdam: Benjamins.
Palmer, Frank R. 2001. *Mood and modality*. Cambridge: Cambridge University Press.
Penčev, Jordan. 1993. *Bălgarski sintaksis: upravlenie i svărzvane* [Bulgarian syntax: government and binding]. Plovdiv: Plovdivsko universitetsko izdatelstvo.
Rogers, Andrew. 1974. *Physical perception verbs in English*. Los Angeles: University of California dissertation.
Rudin, Catherine. 1985. *Aspects of Bulgarian syntax*. Columbus: Slavica Publishers.
Scovel, Tom. 1971. A look-see at some verbs of perception. *Language Learning* 21 (1). 75–84.

Smirnova, Anastasia. 2011. *Evidentiality and mood: Grammatical expressions of epistemic modality in Bulgarian*. Columbus: Ohio State University dissertation.

Sonnenhauser, Barbara. 2015. Functionalising syntactic variance: Declarative complementation with *kako* and *če* in 17th to 19th century Balkan Slavic. *Wiener Slavistisches Jahrbuch* 3. 41–72.

Topolinjska, Zuzana. 2000. *Polski-makedonski: gramatička konfrontacija. Studii od morfosintaksata* [Polish-Macedonian: grammatical confrontation. Studies in morphosyntax]. Skopje: MANU.

Topolinjska, Zuzana. 2008a. *Polski-makedonski: gramatička konfrontacija. Razvitok na gramatičkite kategorii* [Polish-Macedonian: grammatical confrontation. The development of grammatical categories]. Skopje: MANU.

Topolińska, Zuzanna. 2008b. Factivity as a grammatical category in Balkan Slavic and Balkan Romance. In Zuzanna Topolińska: *Z Polski do Macedonii: Studia językoznawcze, problemy predikacji* 1, 173–184. Kraków: Lexis. [Reprint from: *Slavia Meridionalis* 1 (1994). 105–121.]

Topolińska, Zuzanna. 2010. The Balkan sprachbund from a Slavic perspective. *Zbornik Matice srpske za filologiju i lingvistiku* 53 (1). 81–115.

Večerka, Radoslav. 1996. *Altkirchenslavische (Altbulgarische) Syntax, vol. 2: Die innere Satzstruktur Die innere Satzstruktur*. Freiburg: Weiher.

Vendler, Zeno. 1967. *Linguistics in philosophy*. Ithaca, NY: Cornell University Press.

Viberg, Ake. 1983. The verbs of perception. A typological study. *Linguistics* 21. 123–162.

Wiemer, Björn. 2014. On the markedness of (non)factive clausal complements and its relation to hierarchies of semantic groups of CTPs. Presented at the *36 Jahrestagung der DGfS*, 5–7 March 2014, Marburg, workshop on *Clausal complementation and (non)factivity*.

Wiemer, Björn. 2017. Main clause infinitival predicates and their equivalents in Slavic: Why they are not instances of insubordination. In Łukasz Jędrzejowski & Ulrike Demske (eds.), *Infinitives at the syntax-semantics interface: A diachronic perspective*, 265–338. Berlin & Boston: De Gruyter Mouton.

Wiemer, Björn. (this volume) A general template of clausal complementation and its application to South Slavic: Theoretical premises, typological background, empirical issues.

Willett, Thomas. 1988. A cross-linguistic survey of the grammaticization of evidentiality. *Studies in Language* 12. 51–97.

Whitt, Richard J. 2010. *Evidentiality and perception verbs in English and German*. Bern: Lang.

Cited sources for examples from the literature (novels and collections of short stories)

Macedonian: (BP) Božin Pavlovski, (KM) Kalina Maleska, (MM) Mitko Madžunkov, (KU) Kočo Urdin, (PA) Petre M. Andreeevski, (RB) Rumena Bužarovska.

Bulgarian: (AD) Anton Dončev, (DT) Dimităr Talev, (GG) Georgi Ganev, (JH) Jordan Hadžiev, (MB) Miroljuba Benatova, (PR) Petăr Rusčukliev, (SB) Svoboda Băčvarova, (TD) Tihomir Dimitrov, (VC) Vesel Cankov.

Chapter III: **Complementation in space**

Marc L. Greenberg
Antemurale innovationis: Clausal complementation in the Slovene Mura River (Prekmurje) dialect and its Balkan parallels

Abstract: The paper discusses the opposition between two complementizers/subordinators, *da* vs. *ka*, in Prekmurje Slovene. The forms were used up through the first half of the 20th century to distinguish between irrealis (*da*) and realis (*ka*) propositions. In the discussion the available evidence is examined in order to establish more precisely the conditions for the distribution of the two forms. In addition, the diachrony and diatopy of the forms are considered in both South Slavic and broader Slavic contexts.

Keywords: complementizers, conjunctions, peripheral conservatism, Freising Folia, infinitive loss, irrealis/realis, epistemic modality, reanalysis, subordinators, supine

1 Preliminaries

As has been pointed out in the organizing materials for the workshop that led to the present volume, the South Slavic languages provide exemplary material for understanding the diversity in structures of clause combining, not only because of the striking internal dialect differentiation and standardization of several related varieties of Slavic, but also because of the range of language-contact situations encountered in this region. To this one might add also the fact that South Slavic represents speech varieties that descend from Common Slavic due to migration, dating from the sixth century CE, a time when the relatively uniform language began to differentiate into significantly divergent forms, including syntactic reorganization. In this respect, our understanding of the pathways to development are much clearer in phonology and morphology than in syntax (see Greenberg 2017: 521). Notably, the system of clause combining through participial constructions, including the dative absolute, as well as constructions with infinitives and supines, yielded to analytical means of clause combining and subordination in which daughter dialects selected inherited morphological material (verbal

---

Marc L. Greenberg, University of Kansas, Dept. of Slavic & Eurasian Languages & Literatures, 1445 Jayhawk Blvd., Rm. 2080, Lawrence, KS 66045-7594, USA, e-mail: mlg@ku.edu

https://doi.org/10.1515/9783110725858-006

morphology, pronominal forms, particles, etc.) and repurposed it, while the older system of participial subordination was retained in circumscribed systems in the grammars of individual languages and dialects (see Andersen 1970; Ambrazas 1990; Friedman and Joseph 2019).

1.1 Broader implications

The title of the present paper begins with a reference to issues that were raised in earlier papers by this author leading to this one (Greenberg 2011, 2019). Those papers discussed a distinction in subordinators in the Prekmurje dialect of Slovene distinguishing between what were referred to as "realis" *ka* and "irrealis" *da*, where the latter is the cognate form to the generalized subordinator *da* found in both standard Slovene and the Bosnian/Croatian/Montenegrin/Serbian (BCMS) standards. The Prekmurje distinction had hitherto gone unnoticed in the scholarly literature on the dialect. The earlier papers noted the surprising parallel between this distinction in Prekmurje and in core Balkan *Sprachbund* languages (Modern Greek, Albanian, Macedonian, Bulgarian, Balkan Romani, Romanian) vs. its absence in BCMS and the remainder of Slovene and asked whether the contrast may have been a common Prekmurje-Balkan innovation, despite the geographical discontinuity between Prekmurje Slovene, which lies at the northern periphery of the South Slavic area, and the Balkans in south-eastern Europe (Greenberg 2011, 2018; see also Amman and van der Auwera: 300–301 and Mitkovska and Bužarovska, this volume). There are at least some reasons to think this might be the case, as the Prekmurje dialect (including its literary and standard varieties) is in many respects an anomalous dialect of Slovene (Greenberg 2013). It is distinct from the neighboring Kajkavian Croatian dialect, and it has been noted to have similar innovations as those in geographically non-contiguous speech varieties further to the east (Ivić 1958: 30 with respect to BCMS; Schallert and Greenberg 2007 with respect to Bulgarian). In terms of location, we might have expected Prekmurje to pattern with the erstwhile "Pannonian" Slavic space, where we find, for example, common dialect innovations (dating to the 11th c and earlier) crossing from the northern tier of South Slavic (Slovene, Kajkavian Croatian) into West Slavic, notably Slovak (see Krajčovič 1974: 142–149, 314–318; Greenberg 2000: 40–41). Were it to be the case that the Prekmurje dialect agreed in significant ways with the Balkan developments and failed to fit into the geographical contiguity with the generally conservative neighboring Slovene and Croatian Kajkavian dialects, this would overturn the traditional conceptualization of the way that South Slavic dialects pattern. The earlier papers concluded that the Prekmurje contrast is an internal innovation, though they did not elaborate the processes as fully as will be undertaken in the present paper.

1.2 The special position of Prekmurje

The other reference (*antemurale*) acknowledges the fact that Prekmurje was incorporated into the Hungarian feudal structures following the Hungarian "land-taking" (*honfoglalás*) in the tenth century, and consequently the communication paths between groups of Slavic speakers in this region with and in the German March who were to become the future Slovenes gradually broke down. With the rise of Turkish incursions in the 16–17th cc. the Prekmurje region itself became *cordon sanitaire* toward the south, with relics of fortifications still extant, hence the region's Hungarian name *Őrség* 'defense territory' (Županič 2009: 17). This historical circumstance gives us a general external framework to hypothesize why the Prekmurje dialect diverges from its neighbors.

1.3 Organization of the paper

As in the other papers in this volume, the present paper employs as a heuristic tool the template framework outlined in Wiemer (this volume) and the acronyms adopted therein.[1] In the following exposition I shall address the topic and its subthemes as follows: Section 2 will deal with the theoretical, diachronic, and diatopic considerations of the problem, that is, placing the rough semantic distinction *da* (irrealis) vs. *ka* (realis) in a framework in order to tease out the conditions that determined the choice of each of the complementizers/subordinators (2.1). Sections 2.2–2.7 place the problem in a historical-comparative and diatopic perspective, taking into consideration the origins of the forms (going back to Proto-Indo-European), their semantic development, and the distribution of their configurations in South Slavic languages and dialects. Section 3 focuses on the distribution and attestation of the phenomenon in Prekmurje Slovene. This section is divided into two parts: 3.1 covers the attested period from the 18th century to the first half of the 20th century, when the distinction was still in effect; section 3.2 covers the second half of the 20th century, where the distinction has collapsed in favor of a general complementizer/subordinator *ka*, though some relic uses persist. In section 4 the analysis is synthesized and discussed.

---

[1] I am grateful for advice and grammaticality judgments regarding BCMS from colleagues Siniša Habijanec, Mate Kapović, Anita Peti-Stantić, Nikola Predolac, and Julijana Vučo. I have also received helpful advice from Victor Friedman and Marko Snoj as well as the editors of the volume, Barbara Sonnenhauser and Björn Wiemer. The usual disclaimers apply.

2 Theoretical, diachronic, and diatopic considerations

2.1 Earlier observations on the *ka: da* contrast

The contrast under focus in this paper is the Prekmurje Slovene opposition described in Avgust Pavel's (ostensibly normative, albeit de facto quite descriptive) Prekmurje Slovene Grammar (Pavel 1942; see also Greenberg 2013), where he notes that the conjunction *ka* is favored in dependent clauses where the proposition is asserted as factual (his terms: Hung *valódi*, PrSl *resznicsen* 'true') and *da* is favored in clauses that present potential actions or events (Hung. *teljesülhető, mogôcsen* 'possible') (§ 446). The contrast had been observed earlier, e.g., by Kühar, who glosses *ka* as Germ 'daß', Sl 'ker' and *da* as Germ 'wenn' (Kühar 1911: 48). Accordingly, in (1) the preference for *ka* is conditioned by the verb 'said, asserted' in the CTP, while in (2) *da* is preferred because of the future-oriented perfective aspect, marking a potential state, of the verb in the dependent clause (DC). (The orthography follows Hungarian pronunciation rules.)

(1) *Pravo   mi   je   **ka (da)** mi   zavszema zavüpa.*
    He.said   to.me   AUX-PR.3SG COMP   to.me   fully   trusts
    'He told me that he completely trusts me.' (Pavel 1942 § 436)

(2) *Zavêszt,   **da (ka)** szkoro ozdraví   ga   je   neszkoncsno*
    awareness COMP   soon   recovers.PFV.3SG   him   AUX   endlessly
    razveszelíla.
    pleased
    'The notion that he would soon recover pleased him to no end.' (Pavel 1942 § 437)

2.2 Further examination of the *ka: da* contrast

The formal opposition at stake here between two complementizers would tempt the structuralist to assume a binary opposition – whether equipollent or privative – between two corresponding semantic primes, which could be roughly categorized as "realis" (*ka*) and "irrealis" (*da*), though we hasten to acknowledge the pitfall of recognizing (ir)reality *a priori* as a category, as pointed out in Bybee's oftcited article (Bybee 1998). The dynamic nature of the opposition, whether viewed synchronically (e.g., in Pavel 1942, 2013, as illustrated in the examples [1, 2], above) or diachronically (historical examples in the exposition below), suggests that the underlying cognitive notions may yield to finer internal distinctions, e.g., speaker's commitment to a potential state of affairs (SoA) as real vs. irreal, or even the emotional state of the speaker. As we shall see, the Prekmurje situation takes the inherited subordinating conjunction *da* ("irrealis") and opposes it to the conjunction *ka* ("realis"), where the latter is extended into the domain of the former, eventually eliminating the distinction by the end of the 20th century. In the exposition we will attempt to sketch the indicators that point to the shape of the cognitive map by referring to the co-occurrence of tense-aspect-mood (TAM) in the complement-taking predicate (CTP) and dependent-clause predicate DC with the variability in complementizers, using, as appropriate, both traditional grammatical terms (indicative, etc.) and abstract notions. As a basic descriptive framework for analyzing the finer-grained analysis of the conditions for *da* vs. *ka*, we use as a point of departure the discussion of epistemic modality in Chung and Timberlake 1985: 242–244. In this work, though the focus is on epistemic modality as signaled in the morphology of verbs in various languages, the notional framework used applies in our case both to the indexicality of the complementizer/subordinator as well as the categories expressed in the verb in the CTP and the DC. Epistemic mode refers to the "actuality of an event in terms of alternative possible situations, or worlds" while restricting "the notion of alternative worlds to those that the speaker considers to be in some sense reasonably close to the actual world" (1985: 242).

2.3 South Slavic context

In contrast to the Balkan Slavic languages, the Prekmurje dialect (just as Slovene and neighboring Kajkavian Croatian) lacks special verbal forms for evidentiality (the opposition between witnessed and non-witnessed situations, a separate morphosemantic problem from the epistemic mode, discussed just above, which is of concern here), as well as (along with northern Slavic languages) absolute vs. coordinated past tense. Following the division of the South Slavic languages into western (Slovene, BCMS) and eastern (Bulgarian, Macedonian) subzones, the generalization of the *da*-complementizer as a subordinating conjunction and complementizer is thought to have been widespread in Western South Slavic, if only one possibility for marking subordination, by the end of the tenth century in the (Latin-rite) Freising Folia for both realis and irrealis propositions, as is the case for standard Slovene and BCMS. In the eastern subzone, canonical OCS largely reserved *da* for non-factual propositions both in independent and dependent clauses (Lunt 2001: 161; Večerka 2006: 227), though in some instances the DC could also have been factual (Vaillant 1977: 226).

2.3.1 Balkan Slavic parallels

The distinction in epistemic modality between complementizers *ka: da* in Prekmurje Slovene is reminiscent of a similar phenomenon in Balkan Slavic (and non-Slavic) languages, e.g., the Bulgarian contrast betwen *če* and *da* in such examples as in (3) and (4) (examples from Leafgren n.d.: 43).

(3) *Na sedem godini za părvi păt otkrix,* **če**
On seven years for first time discover.AOR.1SG COMP.FACT
'At seven years old I discovered for the first time
Djado Mraz e izmislen ot vъzrastnite.
Santa Claus COP.3SG made.up.PAST.PASS.MASC.SG by adults.DEF.PL
that Santa Claus is made up by adults.'

(4) *Mnogo iskam* **da** *ti kaža nešto.*
Much want.PRS.1SG COMP.NON-FACT you.DAT tell.PRES.1SG sth
'I really want to tell you something.'

The evidence suggests that the epistemic mode of potential, unrealized events or actions in the DC, marked by *da*, are the common point of departure for both the Prekmurje and Balkan Slavic contrasts, whether or not the oppositions of the type *ka : da :: če : da* were common to all of South Slavic at some earlier time. Otherwise, Slovene stands in contrast to the Balkan Slavic languages and central Slovene dialects share at least the first, albeit minimal, stage of infinitive loss (i.e., development of a short infinitive in -*ree*t, in contrast to the full infinitive in -*ti* found in Prekmurje Slovene, detected already in central and southern Slovene dialects by the 16th c., Ramovš 1952: 149–150), which is otherwise most fully developed in the core Balkan Slavic languages, Macedonian and Bulgarian, a precursor to the spread of *da*-clauses (moreover, such a contrast is found in disparate languages of the world, on which see Nordström 2010: 166ff). With regard to features other than *ka : da*, the Prekmurje dialect is more conservative than both Balkan Slavic and central Slovene in that it has fully preserved the segmental and accentual properties that distinguish the infinitive and the supine. Both standard and Prekmurje Slovene (as well as, for that matter, Kajkavian Croatian) use the infinitive and supine in circumstances where Balkan Slavic languages would (today) allow the substitution of *da* + finite-verb constructions. Overall, Prekmurje Slovene has more possibilities for clause combining, including the use of present and past active participles that had been lost in central Slovene by the nineteenth century. It is therefore at least plausible that the *ka : da* contrast is an archaism in Prekmurje Slovene, just as other features that set this area off from the rest of Slovene and varieties of BCMS.

The Prekmurje dialect shares with Slovene and other South Slavic languages the inherited modality signaled by *da* at the beginning of a clause. What has innovated in Prekmurje Slovene is the development of a new, default complementizer/subordinator *ka*, absent in other varieties of Slovene (nor is it found in Kajkavian Croatian), which has developed in opposition to inherited modal *da*. This opposition arose some time before the early 18th century and most likely several centuries before it, as we find variation signaling the weakening of the modal opposition already in the earlier texts and, by the time the twentieth century arrives, the opposition is already in decline, captured in the normative grammar of Prekmurje Slovene written in 1942, but is no longer extant in the speech of native speakers raised after the Second World War.

2.4 Diachronic development of *da* complementizer

The (provisional) contrast between *realis* and *irrealis* elaborated for Prekmurje Slovene, where modal *da* is the marked member of the opposition is not unexpected in its Slavic context. In OCS the particle *da* in earlier attested Slavic introduces clauses indicating intention, potential, hypothetical and possible propositions, as in example (5):

(5) bъdite   i   molite   sę   **da**   ne   vъnidete   vъ   napastъ
    you.watch and   you.pray   REFL   COMP   NEG   you.enter   into   temptation
    'Watch and pray lest you enter into temptation.'
    (Matt. 26:41, various OCS mss.)

Diachronically, the modal *da* comes from a lative particle originating in a demonstrative pronoun (< PIE *doh_2) (Kopečný, Polák, and 1980:148–49, Snoj 2009/2015: s.v.), though other explanations as to its origin have been proposed (see also Grković-Major, this volume). It is generally assumed that in BCMS and Slovene *da* spread from potential to indicative propositions as its modal semantics weakened (Grickat 1975:73–78). It is thought that the spread progressed from west to east, a process that Grickat terms a "Balkanism in regression" (Grickat 1975:74), presumably on the basis of the attestations of this usage in the early 11th-century Freising Folia, as in example (6).

(6) Tose   uueruiu   u Bog   i   i
                        uzemogoki   u iega Zin   u Zuueti Duh,
    also   believe.1SG in God   and   and
                        almighty   in his   in Holy Spirit
                                        son
    da   ta   tri   imena   <sunt>   edin   Bog
    COMP   these   three   names   <are>   one   God
    'I also believe in God almighty and his Son and in the Holy Ghost **that** these three names are one God . . .'
    (FF III)

2.5 Diachronic development of *ka* complementizer

The conjunction/complementizer *ka* originates in a lative or instrumental pronominal form IE *k^weh_2, cognate with Latin *quā* 'in what manner?, by what means?, whereby?, how?' (Sihler 1995: 268, Snoj 1996: 190–91; Perseus 4.0). These senses are still reflected in the the semantic range of Prekmurje pronominal *ka*, which can express causality, as in (7 a, b).

(7) a. *Nej   je   mogo   priti,   ka   je*
       NEG   AUX.3SG   can.PST.PTCP   come.INF   COMP   AUX.3SG
       üšo.
       fell PST.PTCP
       'He could not come, because it was raining.'
    b. *Zato   je   prišo,   ka   bi   dug*
       Therefor AUX.3SG   come.PST.PC   COMP   COND   debt
       vöplačo
       pay.PST.PTCP
       'He came in order that he could pay (his) debt.'
       Mukič 2005, s.v. *kå*

The form is attested with various semantic developments, as in Polish dialectal (8a) and Bulgarian (8b) examples, as reported in (Kopečný 1980: 325). These illustrate the archaic lative meaning and the change from the spatial metaphor to a mental-map metaphor, respectively.

(8) a. *Ka   ta   idziesz.*
       whither thither go.pres.2sg
       'Where are you going?'
   b. *Ka   smo   to   čuli,   taka   go   kazvame.*
       What AUX.3SG that.   heard.PL so   it.ACC.SG tell.PRS.3SG
       'What we have heard, thus we tell it.'

The element *ka-* is also presumed to be the basis for the formation of the Slovene and Kajkavian pronoun *kaj* 'what' < **ka-jь* (Snoj 1996). The relic form *ko*, glossed as 'what,' is also found in Carinthian Slovene phrases adduced in Zdovc 1972 (109), reproduced in (9a–c).

(9) a. *Ko   pa   je?*
       What FOC be.PRS.3sg
       'What is it?' / 'What's the matter?'
   b. *Ko   pa   bo?*
       What FOC be.FUT.3sg
       'What's will it be?' / 'What's gonna happen?'
   c. *Ko   pa   sə   rekli?*
       What FOC AUX.3PL say.PST.PTCP.PL
       'What did they say'

These correlate to to Prekmurje Slovene, as illustrated in example (10), which appears in Mukič 2005: 143.

(10) *Kå   gé?*
      What be.PRS.3SG
      'What is it?' / 'What's the matter?'

In contrast to the Carinthian dialect of Slovene (which has the compounded form characteristic of most of Slovene and Croatian Kajkavian **ka-jь* > *k,ói* ~ *qói* – Zdovc 1972:55, 134), in Prekmurje Slovene (stressed) *kà* is the normal form for the pronoun 'what.' There is good reason to think that the non-compounded from is the identical form in both Carinthian and Prekmurje Slovene. As I have pointed out in Greenberg (2000:65), rounded **a* was preserved longer in Carinthian and Pannonian dialects of Slovene, at least until the post *jer*-fall, as these two areas failed to merge strong *jers* with the reflex of **a*. Finally, returning to the aforementioned temptation to connect the Prekmurje dialect development to Balkan Slavic developments, it is enticing to see a connection between Prekmurje and Macedonian with the *deka : da* (roughly realis : irrealis), given the superficial resemblance of the forms and their function. As it turns out, however, *deka* is built from **(kъ)dě* 'where' + a particle *-ka* that is widespread as a suffixal extension in standard and dialectal Macedonian appearing with pronouns and adverbs of time, as well as the interrogative *deka* 'where' as in the example in (11), provided by Victor Friedman (p.c., see also Friedman 2015).

(11)   *Deka*   *ti*   *e*   *kukjata?*
        Where   you.DAT   be.PRS.3SG   house.DEF
        'Where is your house?'

Regarding the subordinator *da*, however, the Macedonian situation is indeed parallel to the development in Prekmurje in that it preserves the inherited Slavic irrealis semantics from Proto-Slavic.

2.6 Slovene context

In at least two respects, the Prekmurje dialect's strategies for clause-combining differ from standard Slovene. Crucially, the Prekmurje dialect is more conservative with regard to the means of subordinate clause formation than Standard Slovene; with regard to the South Slavic dialect continuum, it is more conservative with regard to the preservation of the infinitive (vs. its loss) (see also Friedman and Joseph 2019). First, the use of participles, especially the present active (*-oč-/-eč-*) and past active (*-[v]š-*) participles have remained longer in robust use in Prekmurje and eastern Slovene dialects, which lent this material to the standardization process of modern standard Slovene in the nineteenth century, in contrast to the central dialects around the capital, Ljubljana, where participial constructions as clause-forming elements had already gone out of use (Jesenšek 1998) (see also discussion in 2.3). Second, the Prekmurje dialect retains the contrast in form between the infinitive and supine in contradistinction to the colloquial language as spoken in the central areas of Slovenia (notably, the urban spoken language of Ljubljana). Thus, Prekmurje has *pìti* 'drink-INF', *pît* 'drink-SUP' while colloquial central (Upper Carniolan) Slovene has *pı̏t* (or with local variations in vowel reduction, e.g., *pə̏t, pĕ̏t*) 'drink-INF', *pît* 'drink-SUP', corresponding to orthographic *piti, pit*. The innovative central Slovene infinitive presents a puzzle, since both the reduction of short-stressed *-i-* to *ə* and loss of the final *-i* are attributable to the "modern vowel reduction," a process that began in the 16th century. However, the acute-stressed short vowel in the infinitive should have been preserved as short only if it were in the final syllable by the 15th century, implying that the loss of final *-i* preceded the lengthening of non-final acute-stressed syllables (see

Greenberg 2000: 128, 147). This suggests that the central Slovene "short infinitive" arose (for morphological, rather than phonological, reasons) prior to the fifteenth century, which is to say that, pitch-accent contrasts between the infinitive and supine aside, the terminal shape of the two forms had become conflated to -*t*. This fact is interesting for at least two reasons: one, the loss of final -*i* in the infinitive has been noted as the first stage of the loss of the infinitive in the Balkan Slavic languages (see Joseph 1983: 139 for details), placing the nascent process in central Slovene together with those of Balkan Slavic in such a way that it is evidently not a function of geographical diffusion, as well as placing Prekmurje outside of the innovative zone (note also that acute lengthening never took place there); and, two, the ongoing loss of the infinitive (and supine) is a precursor to the expansion of *da*-clauses in Balkan Slavic languages. These facts suggest that the processes of change in the infinitive and supine forms may be structure-driven in South Slavic, e.g., the loss of final -*i* in the infinitive does not result in conflation with the supine, where it survives, since the two are distinguished by word-prosody in Western Balkan Slavic, and at least not entirely a function of contact change. Further, they suggest by extension that the parallel development in subordinate-clause marking between Prekmurje and Balkan languages is not a common innovation but a parallel development, each motivated by local conditions.

2.7 Slovene and BCMS context

Though standard Slovene employs *da* as the default subordinating conjunction, *da* also has clause-marking functions that are relics of its earlier, richer semantics. At the beginning of a main clause, *da* marks optative constructions, often with an emotional color, such as urgency or threat, as illustrated in example (12).

(12) Da   te   nikoli več   ne   vidim   tukaj!
     OPT   you.ACC.SG   never   again NEG   see.PRS.1SG   here
     'May I never see you here again!'

As in Slovene, main-clause-initial *da* in BCMS (Štokavian) can also be used to signal emotionally charged direct commands, as in example 13.

(13) Da   te   ne   vidim   više   ovd(j)e/ovđe!
     OPT   you.ACC.SG   NEG   see.PRS.1SG   further   here
     'May I never see you here again!'

Optative usages in Štokavian are fossilized in lexicalized wishes and curses, derived from phrases, such as *dabogda* 'I hope, let's hope' (< *da bog da* 'May God give'), or *dabo(g)me* 'of course' (< *da bog me* [verb.TR] 'may God [verb.TR] me').

2.8 Peculiarities of *da* in BCMS

As mentioned above, the Kajkavian dialect today has *da*-complementation as in the rest of BCMS and there has been no mention in the literature of *ka*-complementation. This is worth noting to avoid the tacit assumption that Štokavian-based BCMS standards stand in for the non-Štokavian varieties of Croatian. In this sense, the Prekmurje contrast can be viewed as a local development on the notion that what does not go for central Slovene can sometimes be found in Kajkavian. Though Kajkavian *da*-complementation by and large agrees with Štokavian, in one subtle way it differs from it in that *da* is also used to mark reported speech, as illustrated in example (14) (Lončarić 1996: 131).

(14) Pita   ribiča,   da   kaj   mu   da   za
     ask.PRS.3SG fisher.ACC.SG   COMP   what   him.DAT   give.3sg   for
     toga   dečka.
     this   child.acc.sg
     'He asks the fisherman: "What will you give [me] for that child?"' (Kajkavian)

Colloquial Štokavian permits this usage, as well, though *da* is inserted (where Ø would be neutral) to *emphasize* reported speech (Mate Kapović, p.c.), as in example (15).

(15) Kad   mu   priđe   milicajac   i   pita   ga
     When   him.DAT   come.3SG   cop   and   ask.3SG   him.ACC.SG
     da   što   to   čita   . . .
     COMP   what   this   read.3SG
     'When the cop comes and asks him "What are you reading. . ."' (Štokavian)
     (internet forum http://hpgf.org/viewtopic.php?style=10&f=8&t=1738 accessed 26 October 2019).

In this respect, both in Kajkavian and Štokavian *da* functions as a marker of reported speech, apparently obligatorily in the former and optionally in the latter. The matter deserves further investigation, given that these comments are based on limited data, especially regarding Kajkavian.

2.9 Idiosyncrasy of the Prekmurje evidence

Another discrepancy in this regard between the Prekmurje dialect and the Balkan Slavic languages is in the material available for examining the phenomenon in question. The time horizon for attestation of the Prekmurje dialect begins in the first quarter of the eighteenth century with translations of the New Testament, devotional texts, a relatively small number of ephemeral texts for local consumption (calendars, newspapers) (see Jesenšek 2005), a Hungarian-language grammar of a proposal for standard Prekmurje Slovene (Pavel 1942, 2013), dialect texts (Pavel 1917, 1918), and the occasional attempt to revive the Prekmurje literary language (e.g., Ftičar 2004, 2006). The corpus of canonical Prekmurje texts, from which the dictionary of Old Literary Prekmurian (Novak 2006) is sourced, dates from 1715 to 1886 (Novak 2006: viii–ix). Furthermore, the *da* : *ka* contrast in the generation born after the Second World War has apparently been lost in favor of the complete generalization of *ka* as a general marker of complementation/subordination. This means that understanding the contrast requires triangulation from the heterogeneous attestations rather than working with the testimony and internal knowledge of native speakers.

3 The distribution of *da*, *ka* in the Prekmurje dialect

3.1 The Prekmurje situation up to 1942

In this section the distribution of the subordinating markers are described from extant materials up to the composition of Pavel's 1942 grammar, after which the project to standardize the Prekmurje dialect was abandoned.

In transcripts of oral narrative (Pavel 1917, 1918),[2] we can observe when these two principles are set in tension with each other. Thus, in example (16), where the narrative frame is about wish-making, the same verb of speaking is used, but the DC contains a wish that is intended to be fulfilled.

---

[2] Examples from Pavel 1917 and 1918, once so designated as from this source, are noted by page numbers alone, which do not overlap, i.e., 1917 = pp. 161–187, 1918 = 263–282. Some of the phonetic details of the transcription are simplified in the paper, as they are irrelevant to the topic.

(16) D'äs san právla, **da** bi d'äs nàjràj ńuvoga
    I   AUX said   COMP COND I most.of.all their
    inaša   mèila.
    servant have
    'I said that I would like most of all to have your-[extra-deferential] servant.'
    (Pavel 1918: 265)

Though the same verb *praviti* 'say' is used in the CTP of both examples (1) and (16), the illocutionary force differs in that in (1) the speaker expresses commitment to the proposition in the DC, while in (16) the DC contains a proposition that may or may not be realized and is independent of the volition of the speaker. In example (17) the speaker is the impersonal 'they' and the verb in the CTP asserts that what follows in the DC is a truth valid for all time, again favoring *ka*.

(17) Právijo,   **ka**   so   brăzglafci   dűšä   têstä
     they.say   COMP   are   headless.ghosts souls those
     präminôčă   dicé,   štăra brăzi   kr̀sta märjéjo.
     passing.away   children which without   baptism they.die
     'They say that the headless ghosts are the souls of passed-away children who die without baptism.'
     (Kühar 1911: 57)

3.2 Analysis of distribution of *ka* : *da*

Verbs of perception in CTP consistently trigger *ka*-complementation in the DC, as in examples (18–20). This comports with the notion that perception is an affirmation of something observed and, accordingly, knowledge acquired in the real world, rather than a potential action or event.

(18) Eden pa   'znyih   vidoucsi, **ka** je   ozdravo; povrno
     One   and from.them   seeing   COMP   AUX   healed   turned
     ſze   je   zvelikim   glászom   dicsécsi   Bogà.
     REF   AUX with.great   voice   glorifying   God
     'One of them, seeing that he was healed, came back, praising God in a loud voice'
     (Küzmič 1771: 229, Luke 17:15)

(19) *Vido   je,   **ka**   je   žalosten.*
     He.saw AUX   COMP is   sad
     'He saw **that** he is sad.'
     (Novak 2006: Jožef Bagary 1886, s.v. *viditi*)

(20) *Zaglȁdno   jä,   **ka**   nikša   škatla   dòj   po   vòudi   plàva.*
     He.noticed AUX   COMP some   box   below on   water   floats
     'He saw **that** some box was floating on the water.'
     (Pavel 1918: 269)

Pavel states in his prescriptive grammar that *da* is preferred after verbs expressing emotions, as illustrated in (21, 22), though other clause linkers may also occur in the DC responding to the question *zakaj* 'why': *ár* 'because', *jer* 'because' e.g., *Szilje je lepô, ár szmo dobro letino meli* 'The grain is good, because we had a good harvest' (§ 444).

(21) *Trno   me   veszelí,   **da (ka)**   szi   zse   pá   zdrav.*
     very   me   pleases   COMP   AUX-2SG already   again   healthy
     'I am very pleased **that** you are healthy once again'
     (Pavel 1942 § 444)

Thus the expression of an emotional state such as *biti žalosten* 'be sad' in the CTP tends to trigger the appearance of *da*, as noted descriptively in a transcribed folktale (22)

(22) *Kà   bi   näbi   bűu   žàlostän   – právi   srmák –*
     How   COND   NEG-COND   was   sad   says   wretch
     ***da**   san   tòi   dèitäcä   òudo!*
     COMP AUX-1SG this   baby   sold
     '"How would I not be sad," said the wretch, "**that** I have sold this baby!"'
     (Pavel 1917: 175)

3.2.1 Combination with conditional *bi* and purpose clauses

Pavel asserts that *da* also marks potential, unrealized states or events, noting in Pavel 1942 that DCs of purpose require *da bi* (i.e., with the addition of the conditional-optative marker) and cannot be marked with *ka* or *ka bi*, implying that speakers are likely to produce the latter. The prohibition on *ka bi* is perhaps Pavel's normativist intervention, as such constructions abound in the historical texts, e.g.,

(23) ki   je   na   pouli;
    whichever be.3SG   on   field.LOC.SG
    naj   ſze   ne   povrnè   k onim;
    OPT.COMP   REFL   NEG   return.3SG to them.DAT
    ſtera   je   za   ſzebom   niháo,
    which.N.ACC.PL be.3SG after self.INS   leave.PST.PTCP.M.SG
    ka   bi   vzeo   gvant   ſzvoj
    COMP   COND   take.PST.PTCP.M.SG   cloak.M.ACC.SG   one's.OWN.M.ACC.sg.
    'whoever is in the field, may he not return to those things that he has left behind, **so that** he may take his cloak'
    (Küzmič 1771: 144, translating Mark 13:16)

Küzmič 1771 has 270 instances of *da bi* against 156 instances of *ka bi*, indicating that *ka* had become a possibility alongside *da* in purpose clauses (alongside *naj*, as evidenced in the example 23) even in the eighteenth century. By inference we may surmise that the addition of *bi* sufficiently weakens the epistemic force of *ka : da* so that either form is acceptable in this combination. Pavel also points out that purpose clauses may be substituted with the supine, as in 24.

(24) *Bozsi*   *szin* *je*   *priso*   *szvêt* **odrêsit**
    God's.NOM.Sg.m   son   AUX.3SG   come.PST.PTCP.M.SG   world   save.SUP
    'God's son came to **save** the world'
    (Pavel § 445)

As in standard Slovene, the supine occurs only in a clause following a verb of motion.

3.2.2 Future readings in the CTP

Similarly, future tense propositions are read as potential, favoring *da*. In example (25) the text is immediately preceded by a statement proposing a soon-to-be, but as yet unrealized, world in which the Prekmurje written language will be fully developed and put into use for the production of literature (*Pride csasz, i ne je dalecs, gda bomo vu nasen maternom jeziki csteli dobra, csedna, postena, düsi i teli hasznovita dela* 'There will come a time, and not long from now, when we will be able to read good, beautiful, honest, works, useful for soul and body alike, in our mother tongue'.)

(25) *Niscse   nemre   prebraniti **da**   vszaki   bode*
     nobody   cannot   prohibit   COMP   each   FUT-3SG
     csteo   kaj   dobroga   vu   szvojem   jeziki...
     read   something good   in   own   language
     'Nobody can prevent **that** each will be able to read something good in one's own language...'
     (*Kalendar* 1915, cited in Jesenšek 2005: 90)

Scanning the whole of the 1771 Gospel, no examples of DC with *ka* + future were found, though examples, as in (26) of *da* + future are attested.

(26) *hodta   za   menom   i   vcsinim   váj;*
     you.two.walk   after   me   and   I.shall.make-PFV you.two
     da   *bodeta lüdi   ribicsa*
     that   you.shall.be of.people two.fishermen
     'follow me and I shall make you fishers among men.'
     (Küzmič 1771: 104; Mark 1:17)

3.3 The Prekmurje situation from the second half of the 20th century

3.3.1 Reduction and elimination of *da*

As mentioned earlier, the contrast between *da* and *ka* has apparently been lost in the generations that came of age after the Second World War, an observation from my own fieldnotes as well as the confirmation of a native-speaker researcher at ZRC SAZU, Mojca Horvat (p.c.).[3] This would seem additionally confirmed by the absence of any examples of *da*-complements in the recent Porabje dialect dictionary by Mukič (2005), which reflects the variety of the Prekmurje dialect spoken on the Hungarian side of the border and, as such, the variety that would have had the fewest opportunities for influence from standard Slovene. Examples (27–29) are provided with the equivalent standard Slovene and standard Hungarian translations, in this order, as they are presented in the dictionary. Example (27) represents the control case, since its obvious reading is factual, where the

---

[3] My fieldwork, conducted in the late 1980s, focused on phonology and accentual paradigms in inflected words, so any notes that included information about clause combining would have been collected unsystematically.

CTP presents a circumstance that is asserted to be observable in the real world. Accordingly, *ka* would be the expected conjunction and so it is.

(27) PSn Kå   tåu   za   déla,   **ka**   tåk   prklínjaš?
         what   this   for   matters COMP   so   you.cuss
     StSn Kaj   se   to   pravi   **da**   tako kolneš
         what   REFL   this   says   COMP   to   you.cuss
     'What's up with that, that you are cussing so much?' (Hung. *Micsoda dolog, így káromkodni?*)
     (Mukič 2005, s.v. *délo*)

Example (28 a, b) presents a purpose clause in the DC, which would have historically favored *da bi* in Prekmurje Slovene, but here *ka bi* is instead attested.

(28) a. PSn Záto   je   príšo,   **ka bi**   dúg   võpláčo.
             for.that AUX-3SG   came   COMP COND   debt   paid
     b. StSn Zato   je   prišel, **da bi**   poravnal svoj   dolg.
             for.that AUX-3SG   came   COMP COND   paid   own   debt
     'He came in order to pay his debt' (Hung. *Azért jött,* **hogy** *rendezze az adósságát*)
     (Mukič 2005, s.v. *ka¹*)

Example (29 a, b) presents both a future and (as yet) unrealized circumstance in the DC, though the CTP frames the assertion as an epistemic commitment to a future world. As such, the choice of the conjunction could have gone either way, but, again, only *ka* is attested. A factual and causal DC also takes *ka*, as in (30 a, b).

(29) a. PSn Nakåno   je   **ka**   nede   več   píu.
             decided   AUX-3SG   COMP   NEG-FUT-3SG more   drink
     b. StSn Odločil   se   je,   **da**   ne bo
             decided   REFL   AUX-3SG   COMP   NEG FUT 3SG
             več   pil.
             more   drink
     'He decided **that** he would no longer drink.' (Hung. *Megfogadta,* **hogy** *nem iszik*)
     (Mukič 2005, s.v. *nakåniti*)

(30) a. PSn *Nèj   je   mógo   príti, **ka**   je   dèž*
             not   AUX-3SG could   come   COMP   AUX-3SG rain
     b. StSn *Ni   mogel   priti, **ker**   je   dež*
             neg-aux-3sg   could   come   because AUX-3SG rain
             ùšo   šel
             went   went

'He couldn't come **because** it was raining' (Hung. *Nem tudott eljönni, **mert** esett*)
(Mukič 2005, s.v. *ka²*)

Perhaps the most compelling example is (31 a, b), in which the main clause frames the event as future and the subordinate clause presents a potential, but ultimately unrealizable action, both of which would have historically favored *da*. Here, again, *ka* is attested.

(31) a. PSn *Tåk   te   v rít   brsnen,*
             so   you   in butt   I.shall.kick
             ka   *boš*   *lèto*   *k trístau vragón!*
             COMP   you.shall fly   to 300 devils
     b. StSn *Tako   te   bom   sunil   v rit,*
             so   you   I.shall   kick   in butt
             da   *boš*   *videl*   *tristo hudičev*
             COMP   you.shall see   300 devils

'I'm gonna kick you so hard in the butt that you are going to fly to the moon!' (Hung. *Úgy fenékben billentelek, hogy attól koldulsz*)
(Mukič 2005, s.v. *rít*)

Finally, there is evidence from an epistolary memoir by the Prekmurje native journalist Jože Ftičar (1930–2017), who was a sophisticated writer of standard Slovene in his career, was trained as a dialectologist, but in the memoir wrote in a consistent rendering of the dialect that in general terms conforms to the norm outlined by Pavel (1942, 2013), though using the *gajica* orthography as in standard Slovene (Ftičar 2004, 2006). Ftičar's native village was Gomilica in southeastern Prekmurje, which in terms of the internal divisions of the dialect is furthest from that spoken in Porabje (north) though closer to Pavel's native village of Cankova (west) (see Greenberg 1993 for details). Nevertheless, after scanning some 20 pages of text, I found that the distribution of *ka: da* is clear-cut, where *ka* is the default and *da* may occur only in combination with the conditional marker *bi*.

In example (32) the factual-signaling *ka* is expected and attested, as the CTP contains a verb of perception and the DC contains an observed event in the real world.

(32) Vídin,   **ka**   vaj   víno   podéžgalo...
    see.1sg   COMP   you.DU   wine   fired.up.PST.PTCP.N.SG
    'I see that the wine has fired the two of you up...'
    (Ftičar 2006:16)

Examples (33) and (34), in which the DC is a purpose clause, would have earlier favored *da*, but instead we find *ka*. Example (34) would be the stronger case for *da*, given that the DC is hypothetical, while example (33) represents a potential action that is also understood to have been realized. Only in example (35) is *da* triggered in a DC with a hypothetical circumstance that is entirely in an imaginary world, suggesting that the use of *da* has now, at least in Ftičar's idiolect, restricted to non-real-world hypothetical actions or circumstances.

(33) ...je   stópo   žnjin   na škêgen,   **ka bi**   bole   čüu...
    AUX-3SG   stepped   with.him   onto barn   COMP COND   better   heard
    '...he stepped with him into the barn **in order to** better hear...'
    (Ftičar 2006: 17)

(34) ...stávek   je   dünola   tak   glasno,   kak   **da**   **bi**
    sentence   AUX-3SG   she.blurted   so   loudly   as   COMP   COND
    ga   strèskali   ...   plivánuš   Sàkovič   s prèdgance
    it   they.thundered   Father   Sàkovič   from pulpit
    '...she blurted out the sentence so loudly **that** it was **as if** Father Sakovič had thundered it from the pulpit...'
    (Ftičar 2006: 22)

Note also in (35) that *ka* (*da*) *bi* have not fused, as they still admit intervening clitics.

(35) ...se bránijo   dicé,   **ka** se ne **bi**   zêmla   prêveč
    REFL they.defend   children   COMP REFL NEG COND   land   too.much
    razfrčkala...
    divided...
    '...they oppose the children, so that the land wouldn't be divided up too much...'
    (Ftičar 2006: 20)

4 Discussion and conclusion

Above we have described the rise and fall of an opposition between two complementizers/subordinators *da* : *ka* in Prekmurje Slovene, which bears a resemblance to a parallel phenomenon in Balkan Slavic and other Balkan *Sprachbund* languages. The Prekmurje development is, however, independent of the Balkan one, as the generalization of *da* as a general marker of subordination had reached the northern limit of the South Slavic territory by the 11th century, as evidenced by the Freising Folia (ex. 4). The general meaning of *ka* as marker of 'real, factual' propositions and *da* as 'possible, potential' ones was recognized by native grammarians in the early part of the 20th century (Kühar, Pavel, see section 2.0). Pavel noted that the distribution of the markers was of a probabilistic nature, where the expected marker occurs more frequently in the contexts noted in examples (1, 2).

With regard to the internal, notional reticulation of reality status in Prekmurje Slovene as signaled by *ka* : *da*, we may draw some inferences from the data examined. Assertion of fact and commitment to the truth value of the proposition in the subordinate clause seems to be the fundamental notion anchoring the use of the *ka*-subordinator, as indicated by the consistent use of *ka* with CTPs containing verbs of perception and DCs containing a proposition presented as witnessed and having taken place in the world, as in examples 18–20. In a parallel fashion *verba dicendi* are treated the same (example 17). Standing outside of the epistemic modality noted by Chung and Timberlake (section 1.1), CTPs expressing a state of emotion trigger *da* in the DC (examples 21, 22) and override the factual-signaling function of *ka*. What is at stake in Prekmurje Slovene is that there are at least two distinctions operating with the *ka* : *da* contrast, one opposing real vs. irreal and another opposing description vs. emotion/evaluation. .

CTP future propositions require *da* and, at least through the 18th century, *ka* appears to have been excluded from future-oriented DCs (examples 25, 26). DCs with the combination of *da + bi* (conditional marker), with a statistical prevalence of *da bi* over *ka bi*, are noted in 18th-century texts (section 3.13). Furthermore, in the end period when the subordinator opposition has nearly collapsed in favor of the generalization of *ka*, *da bi* persists sporadically in 20th c. attestations, as in example (34), as contrasted with *ka bi* uses (33, 35) from the same author. To summarize, up through the first half of the 20th century, *da* clauses in Prekmurje Slovene were favored in the context of epistemic modality where either futurity or conditionality are expressed; an emotional state of the speaker overrides the notion of epistemic modality. Those that hew to or are asserted to be identical to or close to the actual world condition *ka*-clauses. In the second half of the 20th century the opposition collapses in favor of *ka*, removing the marked member of the opposition.

It is tempting to speculate about additional, non-structural causation for the collapse of the opposition in favor of *ka* as the general subordinator. In part it is clear, both from the attestations and from the optionality indicated by Pavel's *Sprachgefühl*, as articulated in his grammar, that the notional motivations underlying the forms had been labile as early as the earliest texts in the first part of the 18th c. and that *da* was the marked, *ka* the unmarked form. In this sense the erosion of the system in favor of the unmarked form is unsurprising. However, when regarded in a sociolinguistic perspective, taking into consideration the connections between Prekmurje Slovene both with central Slovene and the Kajkavian dialect, which both pattern with (Štokavian-based) BCMS in generalizing *da*, it raises the question of why Prekmurje remained resistant to the overall western South Slavic tendency. Here there may be an additional motivation that speaks to a preference for linguistic style, that is, linguistic identity, which has served to sharpen the contrast between the dialect and its neighbors cf. the sentiment expressed in the example in example 25. As this issue had not been addressed in the literature and we now lack the generation of speakers who could verify this potential motivation, the matter must remain speculative.

To summarize the developments described in this paper we can sketch the following processes as presented in Table 1.

Table 1: Proposed chronology of developments.

Balto-Slavic to Slavic (up to ca. 1000 AD)	Participial subordinating construction yield to COMP-headed subordinated clauses.
by 1000 AD	modal COMP *da* prevails in South Slavic
12th c. AD on	Infinitive loss in eastern South Slavic, spreading gradually westward.
by 1500	Short infinitive in central and southern Slovene dialect reflects nascent infinitive loss, which north-eastern Slovene (Prekmurje) remains conservative.
by 18th c.	Prekmurje develops factual *ka* COMP, competing with *da* COMP.
2nd half of 20th c.	All but relic usage of *da* bith COND *bi* is replaced by *ka* comp in Prekmurje.

Abbreviations

BCMS   Bosnian, Croatian, Montenegrin, Serbian
CTP   complement-taking predicate
DC   dependent clause
FF   Freising Folia (Bernik, Faganel, et al. 1992)
Germ   German
Hung   Hungarian
PSn   Prekmurje Slovene
StSn   Standard Slovene

References

Ammann, Andreas and Johan van der Auwera. 2004. Complementizer-Headed Main Clauses for Volitional Moods in the Languages of South-Eastern Europe. In Olga Mišeska Tomić (ed.), *Balkan Syntax and Semantics*, 293–314. Amsterdam: Benjamins.

Ambrazas, Vytautas. 1990. *Sravnitel'nyj sintaksis pričastij baltijskix jazykov* [Comparative syntax of participles in the Baltic languages]. Vilnius: Mokslas.

Andersen, Henning. 1970. The Dative of Subordination in Baltic and Slavic. In Thomas F. Magner & William R. Schmalstieg (eds.), *Baltic Linguistics*, 1–9. University Park & London: The Pennsylvania State University Press.

Bernik, France & Jože Faganel et al. 1992. *Brižinski spomeniki* [The Freising Folia]. Ljubljana: Slovenska knjiga.

Bulgarian National Corpus http://dcl.bas.bg/bulnc/

Bybee, Joan. 1998. 'Irrealis' as a Grammatical Category. *Anthropological Linguistics* 40 (2). 257–271.

Chung, Sandra and Alan Timberlake. 1985. Tense, Aspect, and Mood. In Timothy Shopen (ed.), *Language Typology and Syntactic Description, vol. 3: Grammatical Categories and the Lexicon*, 202–258. Cambridge: Cambridge University Press.

Friedman, Victor A. 2015. Sometimes a Cigar is Just a Cigar: Bulgarian and Macedonian QUIPs and Their Relatives. In Ljudmila Popović, Dojčil Vojvodić & Motoki Nomachi (eds.), *U prostoru lingvističke slavistike / Inside the Space of Slavic Linguistics*, 768–776. Belgrade: University of Belgrade.

Friedman, Victor A. & Brian D. Joseph. 2019. The Importance of Slovene for Understanding Balkanisms. In Stephen M. Dickey & Mark Richard Lauersdorf (eds.), *V zeleni držéli zeleni breg. Studies in Honor of Marc L. Greenberg*, 79–89. Bloomington: Slavica Publishers.

Ftičar, Jože. 2004, 2006. *Za nápršnjek vedríne* [For a bit of optimism] I., II. Murska sobota: Stopinje

Greenberg, Marc L. 1993. Glasoslovni opis treh prekmurskih govorov in komentar k zgodovinskemu glasoslovju in oblikoglasju prekmurskega narečja [Phonological description of three Prekmurje village dialect systems and commentary on the historical phonology and morphology of the Prekmurje dialect]. *Slavistična revija* [The journal of Slavistics] 41 (4). 465–487.

Greenberg, Marc L. 1999. Multiple Causation in the Spread and Reversal of a Sound Change: Rhotacism in South Slavic. *Slovenski jezik / Slovene Linguistic Studies* 2. 63–76.

Greenberg, Marc L. 2000. *A Historical Phonology of the Slovene Languages*. Heidelberg: Winter.

Greenberg, Marc L. 2011. A Balkanism in Central Europe? Realis vs. Irrealis in Subordinate Clauses in Prekmurje Slovene. In Zbyněk Holub & Roman Sukač (eds.), *Dialektologie a geolingvistika v současné střední Evropě*, 8–18. Opava: Slezská univerzita v Opavě.

Greenberg, Marc L. 2013. Prekmurščina med slovanskimi jeziki [The language of Prekmurje among the Slavic languages]. In Avgust Pavel: *Prekmurska slovenska slovnica. Vend nyelvtan* [Prekmurje Slovene Grammar]. Zbirka Zora, v. 100. Marija Bajzek Lukač (trans.), Marko Jesenšek (ed.), 401–412. Bielsko-Biała, Budapest, Kansas, Maribor & Prague: Zora.

Greenberg, Marc L. 2019. Subordinating Conjunctions in the Slovene Trans-Mura River (Prekmurje) dialect and their Balkan parallels. In Donald L. Dyer, Brian D. Joseph, & Mary Allen Johnson (eds.), *The Current State of Balkan Linguistics: Celebrating Twenty Years of the Kenneth Naylor Lectures* [Special issue]. *Balkanistica* 32 (1). 209–222.

Grickat, Irena. 1975. *Studije iz istorije srpskohrvatskog jezika* [Studies in the history of Serbo-Croatian]. Belgrade: Narodna biblioteka SR Srbije.

Ivić, Pavle. 1958. *Die serbokroatischen Dialekte. Ihre Struktur und Entwicklung*. 1. Band: *Allgemeines und die štokavische Dialektgruppe*. The Hague: Mouton & Co.

Jesenšek, Marko. 1998. *Deležniki in deležja na -č in -ši* (= *Zbirka Zora* 5) [Participles and gerunds in -č and -ši = (Zora series)]. Maribor: Slavistično društvo Maribor.

Jesenšek, Marko. 2005. *The Slovene Language in the Alpine and Pannonian Language Area*. Cracow: Universitas.

Joseph, Brian. 1983. *The Synchrony and Diachrony of the Balkan Infinitive. A Study in Area, General and Historical Linguistics*. Cambridge: Cambridge University Press.

Kopečný, František, Václav Polák & Vladimír Šaur. 1980. *Etymologický slovník slovanských jazyků: Slova gramatická a zájmena* [Etymological dictionary of the Slavic languages: grammatical words and pronouns], vol. 2. Prague: Academia.

Krajčovič, Rudolf. 1974. *Slovenčina a slovanské jazyky* I. *Praslovanská genéza slovenčiny* [Slovak and Slavic languages I. The Proto-Slavic genesis of Slovak]. Bratislava: SPN.

Kühar, Števan. 1911. Národno blágo vogŕskij *Slovȁncof* [The cultural goods of the Hungarian Slovenes]. *Časopis za zgodovino in narodopisje* [Journal of history and ethnography] 8. 47–76.

Küzmič, Štefan (trans.). 1771. *Nouvi zákon ali Testamentom goszpodna nasega Jezusa Krisztusa* [The New Testament of our Lord Jesus Christ]. Halle.

Leafgren, John. No date. *A Concise Bulgarian Grammar*. SEELRC Grammars. http://www.seelrc.org:8080/grammar/mainframe.jsp?nLanguageID=9

Lončarić, Mijo. 1996. *Kajkavsko narječje* [The Kajkavian dialect]. Zagreb: Školska knjiga.

Lunt, Horace G. 2001. *Old Church Slavonic Grammar*. 7th edition. Berlin &New York: Mouton de Gruyter.

Mukič, Francek. 2005. *Porabsko-knjižnoslovensko-madžarski slovar* [Porabje-standard Slovene-Hungarian dictionary]. Szombathély: Zveza Slovencev na Madžarskem.

Novak, Vilko. 2006. *Slovar stare knjižne prekmurščine* [Dictionary of the old Prekmurje literary language]. Ljubljana: ZRC SAZU, Institut za slovenski jezik Frana Ramovša.

Noonan, Michael. 1985. Complementation. In Timothy Shopen (ed.), *Language Typology and Syntactic Description, vol. 2: Complex Constructions*, 42–140. Cambridge: Cambridge University Press.
Nordström, Jackie. 2010. *Modality and Subordinators*. Amsterdam: Benjamins.
Pavel, Avgust (Pável Ágost). 1917. Vend szöveggyüjtemény s az eddigi gyüjtések története [A collection of dialect texts in the Prekmurje language with the history of their collection to date]. *Nyelvtudomány* [Philology] 6 (3). 161–187.
Pavel, Avgust (Pável Ágost). 1918. Vend szöveggyüjtemény s az eddigi gyüjtések története (folytatás és vége) [A collection of dialect texts in the Prekmurje language with the history of their collection to date (continuation and conclusion)]. *Nyelvtudomány* [Philology] 6 (4). 263–282.
Pavel 1942 = Greenberg, Marc L. (editor and translator). 2020. *Prekmurje Slovene Grammar. Avgust Pavel's* Vend nyelvtan *(1942)*. Leiden: Brill.
Pavel, Avgust. 2013. *Prekmurska slovenska slovnica. Vend nyelvtan* [Prekmurje Slovene grammar. Wendish/Prekmurje Slovene grammar]. *Zora*, v. 100. Bielsko-Biała, Budapest, Kansas, Maribor & Prague: Zora
Perseus 4.0 = Gregory R. Crane (editor). *Perseus Digital Library* 4.0. http://www.perseus.tufts.edu/hopper
Ramovš, Fran. 1952. *Morfologija slovenskega jezika* [Morphology of the Slovene language]. Ljubljana: DZS.
Schallert, Joseph and Marc L. Greenberg. 2007. The Prehistory and Areal Distribution of Slavic *gъlčěti* 'Speak'. *Slovenski jezik / Slovene Linguistic Studies* 6. 9–76. http://dx.doi.org/10.17161/SLS.1808.4398
Sihler, Andrew L. 1995. *New Comparative Grammar of Greek and Latin*. New York: Oxford University Press.
Snoj, Marko. 1997. Kaj je kaj? [What is *kaj* 'what'?] In Jože Toporišič (ed.), *Škrabčeva misel* [Škrabec's thought] II: 187–192. Nova Gorica: Frančiškanski samostan Kostanjevica.
Snoj, Marko. 2009. *Slovenski etimološki slovar* [Slovene etymological dictionary]. 3rd edition. Ljubljana: ZRC SAZU. Online edition (2015): http://www.fran.si/193/marko-snoj-slovenski-etimoloski-slovar
Vaillant, André. 1977. *Grammaire comparée des langues slaves, tome V: la syntaxe*. Paris: Klincksieck.
Večerka, Radoslav. 2006. *Staroslověnština v kontekstu slovanských jazyků* [Old Church Slavic in the context of the Slavic languages]. Olomouc & Prague: Euroslavica.
Zdovc, Pavel. 1972. *Die Mundart des südöstlichen Jauntales in Kärnten: Lautlehre und Akzent der Mundart der "Poljanci"*. Wien: Böhlau.

Walter Breu
Complementisers in language contact. The influence of Italian *che* on South Slavic and Albanian in Molise and beyond

Abstract: This paper deals with complementisers introducing object clauses, mainly restricted to the complements of *verba dicendi*. Other clause types and their connectors are added in so far as they are formally connected with the complementisers by means of polysemy or pleonasm in at least one of the languages in contact. As this research is about minority varieties in Italy, or "micro-languages" as we call them, Standard Italian and local Romance dialects serve as dominant or model languages in the contact-induced changes observed in the replica languages. The introduction presents an overview of the actual and historical situation of Italo-Albanian and of the corresponding information on the Slavic micro-languages in Italy.

As for the role of complementisers in language contact, section 2 is dedicated to the interplay of the Albanian conjunctions *se* and *që*, both in the Balkan-Albanian Standard and in Italo-Albanian, including their opposition to complementation by means of the subjunctive. Section 3 deals with complementation in two Slavic micro-languages, Molise Slavic in southern and Resian in north-eastern Italy. In doing so, Standard Croatian (or rather the whole range of the Serbo-Croatian continuum) and Standard Slovene serve as points of comparison for a development without direct influence of Italian. Complementation in the Italian model language is discussed as a source for pattern and matter borrowing in both Italo-Albanian and Slavic. In Section 4 the Romance influence in all described alloglottic varieties is compared. The results of our study are presented in chapter 5, including an outlook for further research in other micro-languages in Italy that could confirm or relativize them in terms of grammatical developments in situations of total language contact with the same donor language.

Acknowledgements: My thanks go to the German Research Foundation DFG for their financial support of the field research in Molise and Val Resia (Italy), especially with regard to the current research project "Slavic verbal aspect in South and West Slavic linguistic enclaves" (University of Konstanz, since 2015). I would also like to express my gratitude to Giovanni Piccoli (Acquaviva, Molise), Maria Luisa Pignoli (Portocannone, Molise), Malinka Pila (Konstanz, on Resian), as well as Luigi Solano and his family (Frascineto, Calabria) for their assistance in collecting the data.

Walter Breu, University of Konstanz, Department of Linguistics, D- 78457 Konstanz, e-mail: walter.breu@uni-konstanz.de

https://doi.org/10.1515/9783110725858-007

Keywords: borrowing, complementisers, Italo-Albanian, language contact, Molise Slavic, Resian, verba dicendi

1 Introduction

Italy on the whole is very rich in non-Romance varieties of different language families. There are several Germanic micro-languages in the north, Slavic varieties in northern and central Italy, as well as Greek and Albanian varieties in the south. In the following, we will focus on Slavic and Albanian micro-languages, in particular, Resian in the north-eastern Region of Friuli-Venezia Giulia, Molise Slavic in the central Region of Molise (*centro-sud*), and Italo-Albanian. As for the latter, only the Albanian varieties of Molise and Calabria will be considered. See Figure 1 for the overall distribution of Slavic and Albanian in Italy.

Figure 1: The geographic distribution of Slavic and Albanian varieties in Italy.

The direct contrast between Albanian and Slavic in Molise with the same Italian dialect as the dominant contact variety is especially interesting, while Calabro-Albanian and Resian will serve as "triangulation" points of comparison. The minority languages of Italy addressed in the following have been in contact situations for centuries and have now entered a stage of "total" (or "absolute") language contact. This means that all the speakers of these varieties are fully bilingual with

Italian as their only "foreign" *Dachsprache*[1] (umbrella language). As a result of the historical and present influence of the dominant languages and varieties, many contact-induced changes have manifested themselves in these micro-languages on all linguistic levels and may be considered the main reason for their development into *Abstand* languages within their respective language families.

It is in such situations that the concept of a common diasystem or diagrammar of the two (or more) languages in question becomes evident. The concept of "diagrammar" is a theoretical model based on the hypothesis that multilingual speakers do not strictly separate the grammars of their two or more languages but combine them in the most economical way possible; see Breu (2011: 440) and Breu (2019b, 2020). It could be argued that the grammars of the individual languages in contact are synchronically derived from their diagrammar, i.e. a kind of common deep structure, by means of language-specific rules. The fewer the rules are, the more economical the management of the languages. Therefore, the reduction of such rules by means of a more and more comprehensive diagrammar is the overall "purpose" or direction of language change in total contact situations.

The reduction of rules is mainly the result of pattern borrowing,[2] in the sense of copying the internal structure by means of syntactic and semantic calques based on the model of the dominant language. It is mainly grammar that is deeply affected by means of calquing. But it is well known that pattern borrowing plays its part in the lexicon, too, in addition to matter borrowing being the main method of adaptation to the dominant language in this field.

1.1 Actual and historical situation of Italo-Albanian

Italo-Albanian, or *Arbëresh, Arb(ë)risht*, shares similar contact conditions with Molise Slavic, as both of them are spoken by minorities in southern Italy. Nevertheless, there are considerable differences with respect to the numbers of speakers and to the territories inhabited. While Molise Slavs live in a small compact area, see below 1.2, there are almost fifty Italo-Albanian villages, spread out across several regions from Molise via Campania, Basilicata, Apulia, and Calabria

---

[1] For the terminology on the sociolinguistic characteristics of micro-varieties used in this chapter, see Kloss (1978 [1952¹]; 1967) and especially the discussion of the terms "Dachsprache" and "*fremdes Dach*" in Muljačić (1989).

[2] Pattern (PAT) borrowing as the mechanism of copying only the structures of a model language (traditionally: *Strukturentlehnung*) is understood as the opposite of matter (MAT) borrowing (*Materialentlehnung*), referring to the integration of forms or morphemes of the donor language in question. For these terms and their usage in contact linguistics see, for example, Sakel (2007).

down to Sicily, with a higher concentration, however, in the North Calabrian province of Cosenza (Breu 1991). In Molise alone, there are four Arbëresh villages, Montecilfone, Campomarino, Portocannone and Ururi, of which Montecilfone is the most isolated one. Language fidelity of the younger generations has strongly declined in the last decades, especially in Campomarino, having given up its original Arbrisht variety almost completely.

Albanian immigration to Italy was a process manifesting itself in several waves from the 15th up to the 18th century and including also additional migration inside Italy. Linguistic evidence like the shift of intervocalic *n* to *r* (the Tosk "rhotacism") and the lack of an infinitive point to southern Albania and Greece with their Tosk dialect as the original homelands of the Italo-Albanians.[3]

The absence of an infinitive in Tosk and other characteristics like the formation of the future with *do* 'to want' are typical for the Balkan languages. While Italo-Albanian generally agrees with Tosk dialects in these differentiating criteria, there are also contentious points like the formation of the future with *kam* 'to have', resembling in this respect the Geg future, where *kam* however combines with the infinitive, whereas in Italo-Albanian it combines with the subjunctive like *do* in Tosk: *kam me bâ* (Geg), *do të bëj* (Tosk), *ka(m) t bëj* (Italo-Albanian) 'I will make'. For this reason, some linguists claim the Italo-Albanian future to be a mixture of both dialects. On the other hand the Italo-Albanian future could also be claimed a result of Romance influence; for discussions see Altimari (2005) and Breu (2011: 156–158).

Like in the case of the other minorities in Italy, their actual number of speakers can only be estimated, with figures running from some tens of thousands up to one hundred thousand. Due to the extension of the Italo-Albanian territories, many Italian dialects have played a role in the contact-induced development of the Italo-Albanian varieties, but just as in the case of the varieties of the Slavic minorities, Standard Italian is nowadays the main source of foreign influences.

---

3 The two Albanian main dialects (or dialect groups) are Geg in the north and Tosk in the south with the river Shkumbin in central Albania separating them. Today's Albanian standard language shows mainly Tosk characteristics. Geg, traditionally spoken also outside Albania proper in Kosova and western Macedonia, is more conservative, for example in keeping the original intervocalic *-n-*, becoming *-r-* in Tosk, and the original nasal vowels, denasalized in Tosk, e.g. *bâna* vs. *bëra* 'I made' AOR.1SG . The Geg infinitive is formed by adding the particle *me* to a special form of the past participle, for example *me bâ* 'to make'.

1.2 Actual and historical situation of the Slavic micro-languages in Italy

Molise Slavic is still spoken in the coastal hinterland of the Province of Campobasso, about 35 kilometres away from the Adriatic Sea, in the southern Italian Region of Molise. Nowadays, this Slavic-speaking area, having been larger in the past, is restricted to the territory of three bordering municipalities with the villages of Acquaviva Collecroce, San Felice del Molise, and Montemitro in their centres. There are only about one thousand persons left who actively use Molise Slavic or are at least able to understand it, out of an overall number of less than two thousand inhabitants of these villages.[4]

Language knowledge and behaviour differs from one village to another, with the smallest village, Montemitro, being most conservative with respect to both the influence of language contact and language usage. In San Felice only very few older people still use their Slavic variety, while Acquaviva, historically considered the cultural centre of the Molise Slavs, is situated in the middle between these two extremes. In this paper, all examples are taken from the Acquaviva dialect.[5]

From a genealogical point of view, Molise Slavic belongs to the Štokavian-Ikavian dialect group of Bosnian-Croatian-Serbian (Serbo-Croatian) with examples like *mblika* 'milk', different from the Croatian Jekavian standard *mlijeko* and the Serbian Ekavian standard *mleko*, and likewise *lit* 'summer', contrary to Croatian *ljeto* and Serbian *leto*. This and other linguistic characteristics, as for example the absence of the ending -$\bar{a}$ in the genitive plural of nouns, show that, in addition to determining the moment in time in which the separation of the main body of Štokavian speakers occurred, the ancestors of the Molise Slavs probably emigrated to Italy from the Herzegovinian Neretva valley in the 16th century (Rešetar 1911: 78–89).

After the immigration, their South Slavic variety first came under the influence of the Romance dialect of Molise (Molisan). After Italy's unification in 1861, Standard Italian acquired its role as an additional donor language. As for grammar, most contact-induced changes in Molise Slavic seem to go back to the first centuries after the Slavic settlement in Molise, as they can best be explained from dialectal models. Italian (together with its local southern varieties) has

---

[4] For a comparison of the demographic development of Molise Slavic and Molise Albanian in the last two centuries, see Breu (2018).

[5] For an overview of the differences between the individual Molise Slavic dialects on all linguistic levels see Breu (2017: 16–72). In the present paper only a phonological differentiation has to be mentioned, namely "akanye", the pronunciation of unstressed short *e* and *o* as *a*, which has an effect on the form of the borrowed complementiser; see below. Akanye is found in Acquaviva and San Felice, while it is absent in Montemitro.

always been the only umbrella language for Molise Slavic, while Slavic standard varieties, for example Standard Croatian, have never played any substantial role in everyday life in the Molise Slavic villages.

Resian is still spoken in a few little villages with four main dialects. In contrast to Molise Slavic, it belongs to the Slovene *phylum* with Standard Slovene as its nearest relative among the Slavic standard languages.[6] But just like Molise Slavic, Resian is a micro-language with a "foreign roof", as Standard Italian and to a far lesser extent Friulian are its only umbrella languages (*Dachsprachen*). Standard Slovene has never played a substantial role in its history. In spite of its geographical position close to Slovenia, due to which it cannot figure among the linguistic enclaves in the proper sense, high mountains have practically prevented direct contact between Resia and the Slovene dialects beyond the border since the very immigration of the ancestors of modern Resians, which took place about a thousand years ago. Besides the Romance varieties, (Austrian) German seems to have had some contact influence on Resian, too.

2 Albanian complementisers in language contact

In Albanian both complementisers and the subjunctive have a role in complementation, though with clearly different functions.[7] This is true for Standard Albanian as well as for Italo-Albanian. Furthermore we will be claiming in the following that there is a functional difference between the single complementisers, too.

2.1 Complementisers and subjunctive in Standard Albanian

Standard Albanian has two concurring complementisers introducing object (and subject) complements, *se* and *që* 'that'. Though grammars do not hint at any substantial difference in usage,[8] it seems that *se* shows factuality (1) including strong

---

6 The classical description of the Resian dialect goes back to Baudouin de Courtenay (1895). For a modern description of the Resian dialect of San Giorgio see Steenwijk (1992). As for language contact, works like Pila (2017) on contact-induced change in the verb system could be mentioned. On the whole, very little has been said about Resian syntax. For a comparison of Resian and Molise Slavic in some parts of their grammars see, for example, Benacchio (2009) and Breu and Pila (2020).
7 For Albanian complementation in the context of the Balkan *Sprachbund* see Joseph (2016).
8 Actually, authors seem rather unsure in this respect. For example, Prifti (1971: 260) states that "Lidhëzat „se" dhe „që" duket se në disa raste mund të përdoren njëra në vend të tjetrës pa

epistemic support, while *që* expresses a dubitative or distancing connotation (2) based on weak or even negative epistemic support.[9] Both complementisers are followed by finite verbs in the indicative. On the other hand, intentionality and other non-realized situations, briefly termed 'non-factual' in the following, are the domain of the subjunctive clauses,[10] introduced by the pure (analytic) subjunctive without an additional conjunction (Buchholz and Fiedler 1987: 514); but see pleonastic *që* below. Note that the Albanian subjunctive is formed in a complex analytic way, by means of the subjunctive particle *të*. This particle then combines with subjunctive verb forms, different from the indicative ones in the second and third singular of the present tense and in all present tense forms of the auxiliaries *kam* 'have' and *jam* 'be' with the exception of the 1st and 2nd person plural. Examples are (3a) with the present subjunctive *vijë* 'come', different from the corresponding indicative *vjen*, and (3b), containing a verb form without a difference between indicative and subjunctive, the imperfect *sillte* 'bring'. This means that in the latter case the subjunctive particle *të* alone expresses the subjunctive, here reduced to *t'*, due to the following word-initial vowel. As Standard Albanian has no infinitive, infinitive objects of the type *he told her to come* in English, are, of course, excluded in this language, or rather, they are rendered by means of the subjunctive construction.

---

dallim kuptimi ... " [It seems that the conjunctions *se* and *që* may be used one instead of the other without a difference in meaning ...]. But then the examples he gives, in which *që* (with the indicative) according to him is not interchangeable with *se*, are by no means categorized. They only have in common that *që* is in front position of subject clauses, but this does not seem to be a decisive criterion. Buchholz and Fiedler (1987: 509–512), in their description of subject clauses, only indirectly hint at a possible lack of interchangeability of *që* (with the indicative) in not nominating *se* as equally possible with certain verbs meaning 'to happen, to occur' like *rastis, qëllon*. Further investigation is needed in this field outside of our research of the complementisers in object complements. What is really clear is that *që* is not interchangeable with *se* when combined with the subjunctive; see below.

9 This results from a detailed analysis of complement clauses in Ismail Kadare's novel *Koncert në fund të dimrit* [The concert at the end of the winter] and a number of other examples from the literature and from oral speech. But, for example, the comprehensive grammar of Buchholz and Fiedler (1987: 513–514) does not claim such a contrast. Its authors just state that with *verba dicendi* in statements about real facts *se* is used more frequently than *që*. Çabej (2002: 264) writes rather vaguely that *që* in object sentences in certain cases alternates with *se*. Joseph (2016: 269) simply states: "the indicative complementizers *që* and *se* are used, essentially interchangeably, with both factive and nonfactive complements".

10 Clauses coding non-realized situations either do not contain any proposition (e.g., those depending on desiderative or directive predicates), or the proposition(s) may be suspended, for example in conditional clauses, whose truth-values cannot be tested.

(1) Disa   banorë   thanë   **se**   kanë   frikë
    some   inhabitant:NOM.PL   say:AOR.3SG   COMP   have:PRS.3PL   fear:ACC.SG
    se   mund   të   dënohen.
    COMP   can   PTL   punish:PRS.SUBJ.PASS.3PL
    'Some inhabitants said **that** they are afraid **that** they could be punished.'

(2) Mos   më   thuaj   **që**   ke   frikë!
    NEG   1SG.DAT   say:IMP.SG   COMP   have:PRS.2SG   fear:ACC.SG
    'Don't tell me **that** you (allegedly) are afraid.'

(3a) I   thashë   **të**   vijë   me   mua.
     3SG.DAT   say:AOR.1SG   PTL   come:PRS.SUBJ.3SG   with   1SG.ACC
     'I told her **that** she **should** come with me.'

(3b) I   tha   stjuardesës   **t'**   i
     3SG.DAT   say:AOR.3SG   stewardess:DEF.DAT.SG.F PTL   3SG.DAT
     sillte   një   kafe.
     bring:IPRF.3SG   INDF   coffee:ACC.SG
     'He told the stewardess **that** she **should** bring him a coffee.'

In negative complement clauses *nuk* 'not' follows the complementiser combining to *që nuk* (4a) and *se nuk* (4b) respectively. When, however, the subjunctive is negated, instead of *nuk* the negative particle *mos* has to be inserted between the subjunctive particle and the finite verb as in example (4c).

(4a) Kuptohej   menjëherë   **që**   **nuk**
     understand:IPRF.PASS.3SG immediately   COMP   NEG
     kërkonte   asnjë   material.
     seek:IPRF.3SG   no   matter
     'One understood immediately **that** he (as it seems) did **not** look for any matter.'

(4b) Një   oficer   tankist   thoshte   **se**   **nuk**
     INDF   officer   tank.driver   sa:.IPRF.3SG   COMP   NEG
     zbatonte   urdhrin.
     execute:IPRF.3SG   order:DEF.ACC.SG.M
     'A tank officer said **that** he did **not** execute the order.'

(4c) *Ai   thotë   **të   mos** bëhet   panik*
    3SG.M.NOM say:PRS.3SG   PTL   NEG   make:PRS.PASS.3SG   panic
    rreth   furnizimit   me   energji.
    about   supply:DEF.ABL.SG.M   with   energy
    'He says that **no** panic should be made about energy supply.'

Both complementisers may be used pleonastically, for example *që* in combination with the subjunctive particle *të* in clauses coding non-realized situations, as in (5a), being absolutely equivalent to example (3a) above. The complementiser *se* is fairly frequent as a pleonastic element in embedded WH-questions, for example, by initiating a local object clause together with the interrogative pronoun *ku* 'where', see (5b). In example (5c) it combines with the conjunction *si* 'how' in an object clause as part of an interrogative sentence, initiated by the question particle *a*, (5d) is an example for a pleonastic combination of *se* with the conjunction *kur* 'when', in (5e) *se* combines with *ç'* 'what', and in (5f) with *kush* 'who'.[11]

(5a) *I   thashë   **që   të**   vijë   me   mua.*
     3SG.DAT   say:AOR.1SG   COMP   PTL   come:PRS.SUBJ.3SG   with   1SG.ACC
     'I told her [that] to come with me.'

(5b) *Ai   pyeti   stjuardesën   **se   ku**
     3SG.M.NOM   ask:AOR.3SG   stewardess:DEF.ACC.SG.F   COMP   where
     ndodheshin.*
     happen:IPRF.PASS.3SG
     'He asked the stewardess [that] **where** they were.'

(5c) *A   e   di   **se   si**   ka   qenë
     PTL   3SG.ACC   know:PRS.2SG   COMP   how   have:PRS.3SG   be:PTCP
     e   vërteta... ?*
     PTL   truth:DEF.NOM.SG
     'Do you know [that] **how** the truth was... ?'

(5d) *Kishte   pyetur   veten   **se   kur**   vallë   i
     have:IPRF.3SG   ask:PTCP   himself:ACC   COMP   when   well   3SG.DAT
     kishte   lindur   për   herë   të   parë*
     have:IPRF.3SG   born:PTCP   for   time.ACC.SG   CON.ACC first

---

[11] The *wh*-elements *ku, si, kur, ç', kush* connecting the indirect interrogative clause with the main clause, accompanied in the indirect object clauses (5b–f) by *se*, are homonymous with the corresponding interrogative pronouns, meaning 'where', 'how', 'when', 'what', and 'who'.

	kjo	dashuri				
	this.NOM.SG.F	love:NOM.SG.F				

'He had asked himself [that] **when** this love was possibly born in himself.'

(5e) *Ai donte të merrte vesh **se** ç'*
3SG.M.NOM want:IPRF.3SG PTL take:IPRF.3SG ear COMP what
murmuritej nën tokë.
murmur.IPRF.PASS.3SG under earth

'He wanted to understand [that] **what** was being murmured in the underground.'

(5f) *Silva deshi t-a pyeste*
S. want:AOR.3SG PTL-3SG.ACC ask:IPRF.3SG
***se kush** ishte ai.*
COMP who be:IPRF.3SG 3SG.M.NOM

'Silva wanted to ask [that] **who** he was.'

Embedded clauses containing yes-no questions are introduced by the complementiser *nëse* 'if, whether' in (6a); they are never doubled by *se*.[12] Alternatively, the interrogative particle *a* is used as a complementiser in such clauses, too. Contrary to *nëse* it appears also as a neutral question particle in interrogative (main) clauses, see (5c). In indirect interrogative clauses it allows for a pleonastic *se*, as in (6b). In negative indirect interrogative clauses the complementiser changes to *mos* (6c).

(6a) *Kramsi e pyeti **nëse** kishte dëgjuar*
K. 3SG.ACC ask:AOR.3SG COMP have:IPRF.3SG hear:PTCP
gjë për vizitën.
thing for visit:DEF.ACC.SG.F

'Kramsi asked him **if** he had heard something about the visit.'

---

[12] This is probably due to the fact that *nëse* itself is already a combination of the conditional conjunction *në* 'if' with the complementiser *se*, though in a word order different from *se* in its above-mentioned pleonastic usage. But note that a formal opposition similar to that between *në* and *nëse* also exists between the interrogative pronoun *pse* 'why' and the causal conjunction *sepse* 'because', here with *se*, indeed, preceding *pse*. There are some further peculiarities as *pse* is also a variant of *sepse* as a causal conjunction, whereas *nëse* is a frequent variant of *në* in conditional clauses.

(6b) *Mendoja* **se** *a mund të ketë lidhje*
 think:IPRF.1SG COMP if can PTL have:PRS.SBJV.3SG link
 kjo me Kinën.
 this.F with China:DEF.ACC.SG.F
 'I wondered, **if** this could have a link (= be connected) with China.'

(6c) *Do të pyes* **mos** *ka gjë.*
 AUX PTL ask:PRS.1SG NEG.COMP have:PRS.3SG thing
 'I will ask **if** there is **not** anything.'

With certain verbs the difference between an object clause, introduced by the complementiser *se*, and an object formed by means of the subjunctive may result in different lexical meanings of the verb. An example is the verb *mendoj*, showing its basic meaning 'think' in case of strong epistemic support, as in example (7a), but expressing 'intend', thus a non-realized (non-factual) situation, as in the object clause in (7b):[13]

(7a) *Ai* **mendonte** *se ishte vërtet*
 3SG.NOM.M think:IPRF.3SG COMP be:IPRF.3SG really
 një figurë tragjike.
 INDF figure:NOM.SG.F tragic:F
 'He **thought that** he really was a tragic figure.'

(7b) *Silva po* **mendonte** *të thoshte diçka gazmore.*
 Silva PTL think:IPRF.3SG PTL say:IPRF.3SG something joyful:F
 'Silva **was intending** to say something joyful.'

2.2 Complementisers and subjunctive in Italo-Albanian

Italo-Albanian does not show any differentiation corresponding to the Standard-Albanian division of the complementisers *se* and *që*.[14] On the other hand, Italo-

---

[13] See, for example Buchholz and Fiedler (1987: 514). By means of the particle *po*, added to finite forms of the imperfect as in (7b) or the present, Standard Albanian forms the progressive aspect periphrasis, here *po mendonte* 'was intending'.

[14] Italo-Albanian examples here and in the following have been collected in fieldwork on the spot, all of them checked again in recent times. No relevant differences with respect to age, gender and other sociolinguistic criteria have been noticed. The same is true for the Molise-Slavic examples below.

Albanian differs dialectally with respect to the only remaining declarative complementiser. So, in the Calabro-Albanian variety of Frascineto Albanian *se* has been preserved (8a), whereas in the Molise Albanian variety of Montecilfone it has been replaced by the loanword *ke* (8b), which corresponds to Standard Italian *che* (and its local variants).

(8a) Nusja   thot   **se**   ka   shor,
     bride:DEF.NOM.SG.F say:PRS.3SG COMP   have:PRS.3SG see:PRS.SUBJ.3SG
     ka   t   burthonj   gjithsej.
     have:PRS.3SG   PTL   show:PRS.SUBJ.3SG   all
     'The bride says **that** she has to see, has to show it all.' (Calabria)

(8b) Thonjën   gjith   **ke**   Munxhufuni   ka
     say:PRS.3PL   all   COMP   Montecilfone:DEF.NOM   have:PRS.3SG
     bukre   gra
     beautiful.F   woman.ACC.PL.F
     'All say **that** Montecilfone has beautiful women.' (Molise)

The possibility of expressing non-factuality or intentionality by means of the subjunctive continues to exist also in Italo-Albanian, see example (9) from Frascineto, with the reduced subjunctive particle *t*.[15]

(9) I   thash   **t**   **vinj**   me   mua.
    DAT.SG   say.AOR.3SG   PTL   come:PRS.SUBJ.3SG   with   1SG.ACC
    'I told him that he should come with me.' (Calabria)

In negative sentences the situation in both Italo-Albanian dialects in question resembles Standard Albanian in that the indicative negation particles *nëng* (Frascineto) and *ngë* (Montecilfone) are inserted into the complementation clause, introduced by the complementisers *se* (Frascineto) and *ke* (Montecilfone), resulting in (8a') *Nusja thot se **nëng** ka shor ...* and (8b') *Thonjën gjith ke Munxhufuni **ngë** ka bukre gra*. In an object clause expressing non-factuality (intentionality) both

---

15 In Italo-Albanian the common Albanian subjunctive particle *të* is sometimes omitted, see *ka (të) shor* in example (8a), or loses its final vowel even before consonants, as in *thash t vinj* in example (9). Often *ka të* 'has to', expressing deontic modality and also the de-obligative future, merges to a particle *kat*, being used in combination with the subjunctive either restricted to the singular alone or even in all forms of the present tense. In the imperfect the particle *kisht* < *kish + të* is used in such cases, for example, to express the future in the past; see Breu (1994: 366–369) for more details on verbal periphrases in Calabro-Albanian.

dialects insert the negation particle *mos* between the subjunctive particle and the finite verb, giving, for example, in Frascineto (9′) *I thash **t mos** vinj me mua*.

Special cases are verbs or constructions expressing fear. While in affirmative complements the normal complementiser is used, cp. *se* in the Calabro-Albanian example (10a), it may be omitted before the optional negative particle *mos*, see (10b), which means that *mos* itself may serve as a negative complementiser.

(10a) *Trëmbša* ***se*** *m prit me*
fear:IPRF.PASS.1SG COMP 1SG.DAT cut:PRS.3SG with
gërshëren
scissors:DEF.ACC.SG.F
'I feared **that** he would cut me with the scissors.'

(10b) *Kimi trëmbësir puru **mos** bënjën ndonjë*
have:PRS.1PL fear also COMP.NEG make:PRS.3PL some
dëm.
damage
'We are also afraid **that** they [**don't**] cause some damage.'

In Calabria, just like in Standard Albanian, the complementiser *se* is added pleonastically to the introducing *wh*-element of embedded interrogative clauses as in (11a–b).

(11a) *Do t shofsh **se** si*
want:PRS.2SG PTL see:PRS.SBJV.2SG COMP how
tundenj u këmben?
move:PRS.1SG 1SG.NOM leg:DET.ACC.SG.F
'Do you want to see [that] **how** I move my leg?'

(11b) *Shomi **se** ç bëri!*
see:PRS.1PL COMP what make:AOR.3SG
'Let us see [that] **what** he has done!'

In Molise Albanian this pleonastic method has been lost, as a consequence of the replacement of the complementiser *se* by the loanword *ke*, following its Italian source *che* in not being used in such cases. On the other hand, *ke*, in following Italian models, is used as part of compound conjunctions or adverbials, for example in the borrowings *vistu-ke* 'considering that' ← It. *visto che*, *datu-ke* 'as' ← It. *dato che*, *par-ke* 'seemingly' ← It. *pare che*, *dhopu-ke* 'after, when' ← It. *dopo che* and in calqued hybrids like the synonyms *vetëm-ke* and *mëse-ke*[16] 'only that', corresponding to Italian *solo che*. Such cases find their parallels in Molise Slavic; see 3.2 below.

2.3 Italian *che* as a source for pattern and matter borrowing

Italian *che* and its equivalents in the local dialects (Rohlfs 1969: 188–189) are highly polysemic in having quite a lot of different functions, from that of an interrogative pronoun 'what', over the aforementioned function as a complementiser, down to its functions as a relativiser and as a conjunction introducing causal and other subordinate clauses. Figure 2 is meant to illustrate some parts of this polysemy.

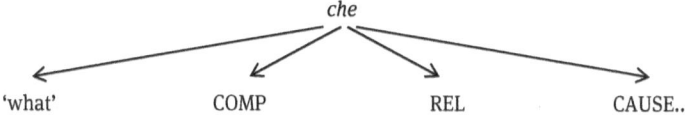

| | 'what' | COMP | REL | CAUSE… |

Figure 2: The polysemy of Italian *che*.

Italian or Molisan *che (chə)* serves both as the source form for matter borrowing and as a model for the adaptation to its polysemic semantic structure. For an overview of forms and functions with respect to the complementisers in the Albanian varieties, compared with the polyfunctional Italian *che*, see the upper part of Table 1. Among other things, Standard Albanian in the left column could reflect the original complexity of what was later to become Italo-Albanian at the time of the immigration of Albanians to Italy.

Table 1: The Albanian varieties between internal development and Romance influence.

	Albanian	ARB Calabria	ARB Molise	Italian
COMP (factual)	se	se	ke	che
COMP (+ connotation)	që			
REL	që	ç	ç	che
pronoun 'what'	ç			

---

[16] Note, by the way, that Molise-Albanian *mëse* 'only' could have preserved the original complementiser *se* as a constituent of its compound form. A similar case of this type is Albanian and Italo-Albanian *pse* 'because' < **për se* 'for that'.

If *që* really existed in the immigration dialects (of which we, unfortunately, do not have any written records),[17] the aforementioned absence of Albanian *që* as a complementiser in the Italo-Albanian varieties might be interpreted as a result of language contact. By replacing *që* with the unmarked *se* in Frascineto (Calabria), *se* has become as polyfunctional as its Italian equivalent *che* in the sphere of complementisers. This would be a case of pattern borrowing by semantic calquing. As becomes obvious from the information in the two rightmost columns, the same goal is reached in Montecilfone (Molise), by borrowing the Italian polyfunctional complementiser *che* itself (matter borrowing).

On the other hand, the lower part of Table 1 shows that the relativiser and the interrogative pronoun behave differently in the two Arbrisht dialects. It is worth noting that also in this case we have a merger based on the Italian polysemy of *che* as its model, but here Italo-Albanian takes *ç(ë)* 'what'[18] as the base form for calquing this polysemy.[19] As a consequence, the large-scale polysemy of the dominant model *che* corresponds to two different polysemic entities in the replica systems, or in other words, language contact led to a bifurcation of the overall polysemy of Italian *che* with the complementiser and other conjunctions, on the one hand, and the relativiser and the interrogative pronoun, on the other.

As for the role of Italian *che* and Italo-Albanian *se* and *ke* as causal conjunctions, see section 4 below. Furthermore, they serve as conjunctions in consecutive, final and comparative clauses and as free connectors with an only vague logical connection between individual clauses as in the Calabro-Albanian example (12a).

---

17 The oldest Italo-Albanian text is *Mbsuame e Krështerë* by Lekë Matrënga from 1592. It indeed already has *çë* 'what' as a relative marker, and *se* 'that' as a complementiser, while *që* is missing. But it is from Sicily. So it cannot necessarily be claimed the predecessor of the Calabrian and Molisan varieties in the present paper. In addition, it already shows other Italian influences, such that the adaptations in the field of complementisers and relativisers, described above, could have happened prior to the publication of this catechism. Anyway, in Gjon Buzuku's *Meshari*, the oldest Albanian book from 1555, *që* (though in its Geg form *qi*) is well documented in both functions it has preserved in modern Standard Albanian. The formal connection between *që*, *ç(ë)*, with an intermediate form *qish*, and *se* is a very complicated etymological problem. They all seem to have been derived from the same root *k^wi- 'what', though partially from different case forms and with a lot of analogy involved; see, for example, Çabej (2002: 264–265) and Matzinger (2006: 112, 143, 158).

18 In today's Standard Albanian, *ç'* is often expanded to *çka*, by adding the existential *ka* 'there is' to it.

19 See Breu (2019a) for *që* as a relative marker in Italo-Albanian. While the general statement by Turano (2011: 104) concerning the absence of *që* in the different Calabro-Albanian dialect of San Nicola dell'Alto in the Crotone district is confirmed by the data of the two dialects dealt with in this paper, we cannot agree on her assumption of its phonological development to *ç*. At least in our dialects, a direct phonetic development of the relative pronoun *që* > *ç* is excluded, and *ç* also in this case clearly corresponds to *ç* 'what'.

See also (12b) for a sentence, in which Calabro-Albanian *se* appears in a construction that from its very formation is a comparative clause, but which could also be interpreted as a temporal clause with *më par se*, literally 'more first than', as a compound conjunction meaning 'before'.

(12a) Vete   fjë   **se**   nani më   shkon.
      go:PRS.1SG sleep:PRS.1SG COMP   now   1SG.DAT   pass:PRS.3SG
      'I am going to sleep **as/because/and** then (the pain) will pass.'

(12b) Rijem   më   par   **se**   të   vet   fjëjem.
      stay:IPRF.1PL PTL.CMP   first COMP   PTL   go:PTL   sleep:IPRF.1PL
      'We stayed there before [than] going to sleep.'

3 Slavic complementisers in language contact

According to what was said in the introduction, we will concentrate on the situation in Molise Slavic with Resian as a triangulation point for a comparison with Italo-Albanian. Though these two Slavic micro-languages have different standard languages as their narrowest correlates in synchronic and diachronic respect, it is nevertheless useful for the theory of language contact to show parallelisms and contrasting developments in the field of their complementisers. In both cases we will take the respective standard language as a starting point, not pretending, however, that they necessarily preserved the historical situations preceding language contact in the minority languages.

3.1 Complementisers in Bosnian-Croatian-Serbian (BCS)

Traditionally, two more or less synonymous factual complementisers, not distinguishing between strong epistemic support and factive (i.e. presupposed) propositions, existed in the Serbo-Croatian dialect continuum, *da* and *što*, but with a strong predominance of *da* especially in the western parts. In modern Standard Croatian *da* is the only all-embracing complementiser; see example (13a). But even in the eastern parts of the continuum with *verba dicendi* almost exclusively *da* is used.[20] On the other hand, *što* is frequently used even in Croatian as

---

[20] This does, however, not exclude *što* as the general factual complementiser in eastern peripheral dialects or linguistic enclaves. One of them is Gallipoli Serbian, in which *š(t)o* frequently

a variant of *da* in constructions, expressing the emotional attitude of the speaker towards the given event, as in example (13b).²¹

(13a) *Rekao   sam   **da**   znam   ovu*
       say:PFV.PTCP.SG.M AUX.PRS.1SG COMP know:PRS.1SG this:ACC.SG.F
       ženu.
       woman:ACC.SG.F
       'I said **that** I knew this woman.'

(13b) *Radujemo   se,   **da ~ što** si   došao.*
       be.glad:PRS.1PL REFL   COMP   AUX.2SG come:PFV.PTCP.SG.M
       'We are happy **that** you have come.'

Complementisers concurrent with *da* in Croatian (and elsewhere) are *kako* 'how' and, more rarely in the standard, *gdje* 'where'; see examples (14a–b) from Raguž (1997: 421).²²

(14a) *Rekao   je   **da/kako** to   njemu*
       say:PFV.PTCP.SG.M AUX.3SG   COMP   this:N   3SG.M.DAT
       ne   bi   odgovaralo.
       NEG   COND.PTL   correspond:IPFV.PTCP.SG.N
       'He said **that** this would not have pleased him.'

---

replaces *da* in this function (Ivić 1994: 393). For a distribution of *da* in Serbo-Croatian dialects, including older times, see Zima (1887: 132–134). Grković-Major (this volume) deals with the complex development of complementisers in Serbian and the gradual penetration of *da* into the sphere of *što*, especially in the western territories. Standard Serbian is classified in this respect as being normalised on the basis of a conservative dialect. The rise of *da* as a complementiser in the western part of the Balkans is assumed to be due to Romance influence, which, however, is in sharp contrast to its contact-induced decline in Molise Slavic, see below.

21 See Raguž (1997: 414). The same variation is true for the Bosnian Standard (Jahić, Halilović, and Palić et al. 2000: 424). In this case *da ~ što* are not pure declarative complementisers, but possibly have a causal function or connotation; see Rječnik (1959–1962: 826–827). Such clauses, often governed by verbal complexes of the type *drago mi je, da ~ što ...* 'I like it that ... ', *žao mi je, da ~ što ...* 'I am sorry that ... ' are not object complements anyway, which does, of course, not exclude *da* and *što* from functioning as complementisers. In Serbian *što* seems even obligatory in these contexts, judging from Stevanović (1979: 891–892), who cites such examples only in his causal section, though with some reserve about this classification, and without any reference to a variation with *da*.

22 Raguž (1997: 421) states that with some verbs like *slušati* 'listen' (but not *ćuti* 'hear') or *gledati* 'observe' (but not *vidjeti* 'see') *da* is even excluded. But they obviously do not require a factive complement, as they refer to ongoing processes.

(14b) Vidio   je   **da/kako/(gdje)**   dolaze   pred
      see:PTCP.SG.M   AUX.3SG   COMP   come:PFV.PRS.3SG   before
      banku.
      bank:ACC.SG.F
      'He saw **that** he was arriving in front of the bank.'

In non-factual sentences the standard complementiser is again *da*, requiring the verb in the indicative and – as far as telic verbs are concerned – in the perfective aspect (15a). This means that – contrary to Albanian – complements are not differentiated according to their degree of epistemic support nor with respect to the distinction between factual and non-factual.[23] If the main verb is in the imperative, the particle *neka* may serve as a variant of the complementiser *da* in its non-factual reading (15b); see Raguž (1997: 315).

(15a) Rekao   mu   je   **da**   odmah
      say:PFV.PTCP.SG.M 3SG.M.DAT   AUX.PRS.3SG COMP   at.once
      dođe.
      come:PFV.PRS.3SG
      'He told him **that** he should come immediately.'

(15b) Reci   mu   **da ~ neka**   dođe!
      say:PFV.IMP.SG   3SG.M.DAT   COMP   come:PFV.PRS.3SG
      'Tell him to come!'

In addition to its function as a complementiser, *da* serves as a conjunction initiating several types of subordinate clauses, too, for example final, optative, conditional and consecutive clauses, partially combined with the *bi*-conditional of the verb. We cannot go into any detail here; see for example Raguž (1997: 300–301, 427–438) and the comprehensive description of the functions of *da* in Rječnik (1884–1886: 163–214).

In Standard Croatian free relative clauses are initiated by the relativiser *što*, formally identical with the interrogative pronoun *što* 'what', used in interrogative and embedded WH-questions (Raguž 1997: 397–401). Embedded yes-no questions, however, are linked to the main clause by the complex complementiser *da li* 'if' as in (16).[24]

---

23 In contrast to Albanian, negation does not have any influence on the choice of the complementiser either. In both cases *ne* 'not' is inserted before the verb in the subordinate clause.
24 The form *da* is also part of other complex connectors like *premda* 'though' (< *prem da*).

(16) Ne   znam   **da li** je   došao.
     NEG   know:PRS.1SG if   AUX.3SG   come:PFV.PTCP.SG.M
     'I don't know **if** he has come.'

3.2 Complementisers in Molise Slavic

The traditional complementiser *da* has completely lost this function in Molise Slavic, and so has *što*. Here the all-embracing complementiser is *ke ~ ka*,[25] borrowed from Italian.[26] It is insensitive to the degree of epistemic support. There is, however, a difference in the verb form combined with it in the complement clause.[27] On the one hand, factivity and strong epistemic support require an indicative form corresponding to the verb in the main clause in terms of the Romance *consecutio temporum* as in (17). But on the other hand, in adapting to the differentiation between factual and intentional (non-factual), expressed in Italian by *che* + indicative vs. subjunctive, a special intentional construction has developed. It is rendered by *ke ~ ka* and a deontic modal construction, also functioning as a de-obligative future (future of necessity, NEC), with the clitic marker *jimat* 'have, must' + infinitive, see example (18). It corresponds exactly to the southern-Italian colloquial future construction formed by *che* and the modal complex with inflected *dovere* 'must' + infinitive.[28]

---

25 This is also true for complement clauses with a causal connotation, governed by expressions or verbs conveying the emotional attitude of the speaker towards the given event, for which in Croatian both *da* and *što*, are possible.
26 Both variants *ke* and *ka* go back to Italian *che* and/or dialectal *chə/che* (Giammarco 1968: 514–515) as the basic integration form in Molise Slavic, which directly corresponds to *ke* as the only form used in the conservative dialect of Montemitro. Due to the phonological process of akanye, however, frequently changing unstressed short *e, o* to *a*, in the dialects of Acquaviva and San Felice, the normal form is *ka*. But some conservative speakers still use *ke* as a variant even in these two villages. In view of this distribution, Rešetar's (1911: 347) hypothesis of *ka* as the basic form with *ke* as an unstressed variety is problematic and even contradicts his own description of the relation between stressed and unstressed vowels (Rešetar 1911: 347).
27 Just like in Croatian and in contrast to Albanian, negation does not influence the choice of the complementiser. The negative particle normally is *ne* in both cases. With some verbs a special negative form exists, again identical in both cases, cp. *nenadaša* 'he did not know' in (17) with its positive equivalent *znadaša* 'he knew'. In (18) the negative equivalent to *maš* 'you must' would be *nimaš* 'you must not', like in the recorded sentence: *Ja sa ti rekla **ke** nimaša po utra tijalu!* 'I told you **that you should not go** into the pot!'.
28 The same is true for the local Molisan dialect, also replacing the subjunctive by a modal construction with *avé* 'to have, must'; see Piccoli (2005: 172–173). In principle, a similar construction is possible in Italo-Albanian, too, here in form of the aforementioned future with *kam* 'to have,

(17) Je   reka   ka   on   nenadaša
     AUX.3SG   say:PFV.PTCP.SG.M   COMP 3SG.M.NOM   NEG.know:IPRF.3SG
     nišča.
     nothing
     'He said **that** he did not know anything.'

(18) Sa   ti   rekla   ka   maš   hi
     AUX.1SG   2SG.DAT   say:PFV.PTCP.SG.F   COMP   must:PRS.2SG 3PL.ACC
     štrajit.
     remove:PFV.INF
     'I told you to **that** you **should** remove them.'

Just like in Italian, and without an equivalent in Standard Croatian, the intentional function is synonymously expressed also by an infinitival clause, introduced by the conjunction *za* 'for' as in (19). Its Italian equivalent is the infinitival complement preceded by the preposition *di* 'of', for example in the Italian translation of (19): *Ha detto loro di scendere*. In Molise Albanian such a construction is obviously impossible, due to the absence of an infinitive in its verbal system.

(19) Je   njimi   reka   **za**   **sa**   **skinit**   dol.
     AUX.3SG   3PL.DAT   say:PFV.PTCP.SG.M   for   REFL   descend:PFV.INF   down
     'He told them to descend [down].'

The infinitival construction in Molise Slavic is a syntactic calque from Italian, with the preposition *di* being replaced by Slavic *za*. The formation of such constructions introduced by the preposition *za* is a typical result of Romance influence,[29] found also in Resian; see below. It also occurs in other contexts, for example in final sentences of the type *za partit* '(in order) to leave' as in *Zec je sija* **za parti** *veča bolje* 'The hare crouched down to get a better start.'

Just like in Italian, the possibility of forming an infinitive construction like (19) depends on the referents of the two clauses. In the non-factual (intentional) sentence (19), it is possible, because the addressee of the main clause would also be the subject of the verb in the complement. The version with the overt subject

---

must' + subjunctive. But it is used only for strong obligation, not for a simple reference to a desired action in the future, which is always expressed there by the simple subjunctive without a complementiser.

29 Ivić (1958: 126) generally claims constructions of *za* + infinitive as "dem slavischen Sprachsystem vollkommen fremd" [completely alien to the Slavic language system].

in a subordinate clause as in (18) would also be possible, here: (19′) *Je njimi reka ka maju sa skinit dol* 'He told them that they should descend'.

This double solution corresponds to a similar variation in Standard Italian between the infinitive and the subjunctive solution, whereas in the local Molisan dialect the infinitive seems obligatory (Piccoli 2005: 172). On the other hand, in a factual example like (17) the infinitive construction is excluded in Molise Slavic, in spite of the referential identity of the subjects of the main and the subordinate clause, permitting it in Italian and obligatorily requiring it in the local Molisan dialect; cp. the Italian equivalents of (17): *Ha detto che non sapeva niente.* ~ *Ha detto di non sapere.*INF *niente.* This means that Molise Slavic, when compared to the Romance varieties, shows a third possibility in allowing for variation in the case of non-factual, just like Italian and in contrast to Molisan, and in requiring obligatorily the explicit complement clause in the case of factuality, contrary to Italian and even more to Molisan, where only the infinitive construction is possible.

As for the (marginal) complementisers *kako* and *gdje* in Standard Croatian, they do not have an equivalent in Molise Slavic as the corresponding interrogative pronouns, *kaka* 'how' and *di* 'where', basically do not show this function. If this is due to a contact-induced loss or to a later development of the complementising function of *kako* and *gdje* in Serbo-Croatian remains an open question.

In contrast to Molise Albanian *ke,* likewise borrowed from Italian *che,* but restricted to the realm of complementisers, Molise Slavic *ke* ~ *ka* have adopted the relativizing function of *che,* too. But they did not replace the interrogative pronoun *što* 'what', neither in questions nor in free relative / embedded interrogative clauses; see (Breu 2019a).

As mentioned above, the Italo-Albanian complementisers corresponding to Italian *che* have additional functions in other types of subordinate clauses. In the case of Molise Slavic we could mention, among other things, their usage as conjunctions in consecutive and final clauses as in (20a) and (20b) respectively (Piccoli 2005: 173–174). Example (20b) is ambiguous, as the subordinate clause might also be interpreted as a causal clause in the sense of 'because the wheat has to grow'. Apart from this, *ka* ~ *ke* also link main and subordinate clauses without any specific logical connection as in (20c), and they also serve as a conjunction in comparative clauses (20d).[30] For *che* introducing causal clauses see section 4 below.

---

30 All these cases are parallel to the usage of *chə/che* in dialectal Molisan. See for example the following comparative construction from the neighbouring dialect of Palata (thanks to Domenica Catino): [ˈmɛʎə ˈtardə kə ˈmajə] 'better late than never'.

(20a) *Je norko daždila* **ka**
AUX.3SG so.much rain:PTCP.SG.N COMP
su sa polagal sekolike njive.
AUX.3PL REFL flood:PFV.PTCP.PL all:NOM.PL field.NOM.PL
'It has rained so much **that** all fields have been flooded.'

(20b) *Neka daždi,* **ka** *ma rest žita.*
PTL rain:INF COMP must:PRS.3SG grow:INF wheat
'May it rain, so **that** the wheat will grow.'

(20c) *Štrega, kaka je pola* **ka** *maša*
witch how AUX.3SG go:PFV.PTCP.SG.F COMP must:IPRF.3SG
si ga po, je rivala
REFL.DAT 3SG.N.GEN go:PFV.INF AUX.3SG arrive:PFV.PTCP.SG.F
di vrata.
where door:NOM.PL
'The witch, when she went **as/when/because** she had to leave, arrived at the door.' (= The which, when she set out to leave, arrived at the door.)

(20d) *Jim veča ja* **ka** *on,*
have:PRS.1SG more 1SG.NOM COMP 3SG.M.NOM
na gošta veče.
one:ACC.SG.M year:ACC.SG.M more
'I have more **than** he, one year more.'

Italian *che*, apart from being a complementiser on its own, is also part of many compound conjunctions or adverbs like *finché, fintantoché* 'until', *dopo che* 'after, when', *senza che* 'without', *purché* 'if only' or *prima che* 'before', *cosicché* '(so) that'. They have either been borrowed in Molise Slavic, e.g. *fin-ka, fina-tand-ka, dòp-ka, sendza-ka, pur-ka,*[31] or they form calqued hybrid forms with the borrowed *ka* as a component like *prije-ka* 'before', *naka-ka* '(so) that'.[32] This is also true in those cases, in which *che* in Italian is optional (pleonastic) or rare, like *mentre ~ mentre che* 'during, when', appearing as *mendr ~ mendr-ka*. Sometimes the source is clearly dialectal, e.g. in *tramjend ~ tramjend-ka* 'during, when' and *kvaš-ka* 'as if' from local Romance. In contrast to Italian, in Molise Slavic *ke ~ ka*

---

[31] See section 2.2 above for similar cases in Molise Albanian.
[32] A special form of this kind, dealt with below in section 4, is *aje-ka* 'because', corresponding to Italian *perché*.

is clearly preferred in such cases, and it even shows up, where *che* is unusual in Italian as in *sikom-ka* 'as', corresponding to Italian *siccome*, and *pen-ka* 'hardly', corresponding to *appena*. But there is no pleonastic *ka* with the conjunctions in embedded interrogative clauses, neither in total ones, formed with the borrowed conjunction *si* 'if, whether', as for example in (21) below, nor in partial ones, with conjunctions like *di* 'where', *kaka* 'how' or *što* 'what'. So, there are no equivalents to Albanian pleonastic *se* 'that' in the above examples in (5) and their Calabro-Albanian equivalents like *se ku* 'where', *se si* 'how' and *se ç* 'what' in (11). In lacking such pleonasms, Molise Slavic has its parallel in Molise Albanian, likewise having borrowed Italian *che*; see 2.2 above.

Even verbs may combine with their complementiser in forming a kind of compound adverb, e.g. *par-ka* 'seemingly' ← It. *pare che* 'it seems that'. Furthermore, we find cases of meaning extension of newly formed compounds, especially with respect to *naka-ka* '(so) that', which has acquired the additional concessive meaning 'though', instead of borrowing or calquing Italian *benché* and in spite of the existence of the semantically near compound conjunction *pur-si* 'even if, though', calqued from Italian *anche se* or rather borrowed from its local equivalent *purə sə*.

On the other hand, in both Molise varieties combinations of the borrowed complementiser with interrogative pronouns in indirect interrogative clauses are absent. For example, Molise Slavic **di-ka* and Molise Albanian **ku-ke* are excluded, just like combinations of the type **dove-che* instead of *dove* 'where' in Italian and contrary to the inherited pleonastic formations of this type in Calabro-Albanian, here *se ku ~ ku* 'where'; see 2.2 above.

In embedded yes-no questions, Molise Slavic is again quite different from Croatian in not using *da li*, completely unknown in the micro-language, as a complementiser, but rather the loanword *si* 'if' as in (21).[33]

(21) *Sa   ja   nenadam   si   pa   mahu*
     now   1SG.NOM   NEG.know:PRS.1SG   if   then   must:IPRF.3PL
     platit   parekju.
     pay:PFV.INF   plane:ACC.SG.F
     'Now, I don't know **if** they had to pay the plane afterwards.'

The conjunction *da*, in Molise Slavic most probably functioning traditionally as a complementiser just like in Croatian, has been reduced to its optative function;

---

[33] The complementiser *si* is borrowed from local *sə/si*, but corresponds functionally also to Standard-Italian *se*, in both its functions, as a complementiser 'if, whether' and as the conjunction 'if', introducing conditional clauses.

see examples (22a–b). It is often combined with the *bi*-conditional, but in subordinate clauses like (22c) the present is also possible (Piccoli 2005: 173–174). In this case its function approaches that of the complementiser *ka* in non-factual (intentional) complements, though the optative meaning of the subordinate clause is expressed more directly.

(22a) «***Da bi*** ti **kalala** sajata teb s
 that PTL 2SG.DAT fall:PFV.PTCP.SG.F lightning:NOM.SG.F 2SG.DAT with
 njom!» sa ju rekla ja.
 3SG.F.INS AUX.1SG 3SG.F.DAT say:PFV.PTCP.SG.F 1SG.NOM
 '«The lightning may fall on you together with her!» I said to her.'

(22b) Bog **da bi** ma **pomoga** nonda di grem!
 God that PTL 1SG.ACC help:PFV.PTCP.SG.M there where go:PRS.1SG
 'God may help me there, where I go!'

(22c) Moli boga, **da bi** ga **pomoga**.
 pray:PRS.3SG god:ACC.SG.M that PTL 3SG.M.ACC help:PFV.PTCP.SG.M
 (~... **da** ga **pomogne**)
 that 3SG.M.ACC help:PFV.PRS.3SG
 'He prays to God **that** he should help him.'

Interestingly, even in Italian optative constructions *che* is used, for example in the Italian equivalent of (22a), *"Che ti cali la saetta a te insieme a lei", le dissi*, while *ke ~ ka* are excluded in Molise Slavic. Like in the aforementioned preservation of the interrogative pronoun, this is another case of the Slavic minority language not respecting the polysemy of the Italian model *che*. Here an explanation for this differentiating development may be found in the optative construction itself (*da* + conditional), of which *da* is an integral part that cannot be replaced so easily by a loanword as is the case with isolated conjunctions. Cases like the clearly less frequent variant of (22c) with the indicative after *da* could then have been kept due to their parallel usage with the conditional type.

There is also a reason for *što* 'what' being preserved as an interrogative pronoun in Molise Slavic, in contrast to the polysemic structure of Italian *che*. Actually, in colloquial Italian *che* as an interrogative pronoun has been almost completely replaced by *cosa*, originally meaning 'matter', e.g. Ital. *cosa vuoi?* 'what do you want?', corresponding to Molise Slavic *što hoš*. So, at least in colloquial Italian, there was no obligatory polysemic model including 'what' that should have been calqued or borrowed in Molise Slavic.[34]

Summing up what has been said about the three minority varieties in southern Italy, the polysemy of Italian *che* doubtlessly had a role in rearranging the system of complementisers and pronouns. But the borderlines between the different developments based on this polysemy are not congruent. The most important difference seems to be the merger of the interrogative pronoun with the relativiser in both Italo-Albanian varieties, while in Molise Slavic they remained separated, as the traditional interrogative pronoun *što* 'what' did not expand its functions to becoming a relativiser, or may have even lost it since immigration times. Furthermore, Albanian traditional *që*, functioning as a complementiser and as a relativiser, different from *ç* 'what', was replaced in both functions by the latter, which in this way became highly polysemic and resembles in this sense very much Italian *che*. On the whole, both micro-languages in contact follow different strategies of pattern borrowing, based both on the semantic structure of Italian *che*, but differing in the specific part of its polysemy they take as a model. So its full-range polysemy is copied, but either with the exception of the interrogative pronoun (Molise Slavic)[35] or including the interrogative pronoun, but with the exception of the complementiser (Italo-Albanian).

As for matter borrowing in the sphere of the complementiser, the isogloss runs across the Italo-Albanian varieties with Calabro-Albanian being conservative, whereas in Molise both the Slavic and the Albanian micro-language borrowed Italian *che*, though to a different extent with respect to its grammatical functions. It is the relative marker that makes the difference, as Molise Slavic *ke* (~ *ka)* also functions as a relativiser, whereas Molise Albanian *ke* does not. Why, contrary to Molise Slavic, the relativiser shares the same form with the interrogative pronoun in Italo-Albanian as a whole, seems to be an open question, if we do not claim this to continue a situation from historical stages of Albanian. In other words, a highly polysemic structure as in Italian *che* may be divided into

---

34 See Breu (2019a) for a similar argumentation in connection with not borrowing *che* as a relative pronoun in free relative clauses. As shown in this paper, there are, however, certain case forms of *što*, with the instrumental *kime* in the first place, playing a role in the realm of relativisers, at least for some speakers. But in the subject and the direct-object position of attributive relative clauses *što* is completely excluded as a relative marker. It could be added that at least some Molisan dialects have kept a special interrogative pronoun *ched*, also different from the complementiser and the relativiser (Giammarco 1968: 517).

35 Actually, Molise Slavic is a special case here, as not only part of the semantic structure of *che* is borrowed, but also the form *che* itself.

different partial models for the adaptation of the replica languages, dependent on language-specific characteristics.

3.3 Complementisers in Standard Slovene

The overall declarative complementiser in Slovene is *da* (23a–b), just like in Croatian, but in non-factual complements we normally find the particle *naj* as a complementiser (23c), optionally preceded by *da*.[36] We will not go into further details here.

(23a) Rekla   je,   **da**   pride.
      say:PFV.PTCP.SG.F AUX.3SG COMP come:PFV.PRS.3SG
      'She said **that** she will come.'

(23b) Rekel   je,   **da**   je   imela
      say:PFV.PTC.SG.M AUX.3SG COMP AUX.3SG have:PTCP.SG.F
      velike   probleme.
      big:ACC.PL   problem:ACC.PL
      'He said **that** she had had big problems.'

(23c) Učitelj   mu   je   rekel,   **(da) naj**
      teacher 3SG.M.DAT   AUX.3SG say:PFV.PTCP.SG.M   COMP
      odide.
      leave:PFV.PRS.3SG
      'His teacher told him **that** he **should** leave.'

3.4 Complementisers in Resian

Starting out from the rather similar situation in their respective standard language as a point of comparison, Resian seems to be less influenced by Italian *che* and its local variants than Molise Slavic. As a matter of fact, the examples in (24) and (25) show that Resian has preserved its traditional complementiser *da*.[37]

---

[36] See Sonnenhauser (this volume) for the role and historical development of the element *naj* and Toporišič (1984: 372–374, 530) for the range of functions of *da* in Slovene.
[37] Examples (24a–b) and (25) are taken from the texts of Baudouin de Courtenay (1895: 175, 12, 5), cited with his own orthography, whereas examples (26a–b) are from recent field research. I am grateful to Malinka Pila for letting me have them.

Example (24a) contains a factual complement clause, and so does (24b), showing furthermore that *da* is often used to introduce direct speech.

(24a) Swá   ràklá,   **dá**   mi   hréwa   po
      AUX.1DU say:PFV.PTCP.DU.M   COMP   1PL.NOM go:PRS.1DU on
      pôtь   zá   jĭtèt   jískat   judícьh.
      way:SG.DAT for   go:INF   seek:INF reason:SG.ACC
      'We [two] said **that** we were going our way [to go] to look for the common sense.'

(24b) E   rékal   úk,   **da**   «kán³⁸   vi   gréta?»
      AUX.3SG say:PFV.PTCP.SG.M   wolf   COMP   whither   2PL.NOM go:PRS.2DU
      'The wolf said [that]: «Where are you [two] going to?»'

The complement clause in example (25) is non-factual. Here *da*, abbreviated to *d* due to the initial *a-* of the next word, is combined with the imperative. Ježovnik (2015) claims this construction to be a syntactic loan from the Romance subjunctive.

As the Romance subjunctive and the *da* + imperative construction, having as their common basis a volitional or optative meaning, might be claimed non-transparent enough from a structural point of view for calquing, inherited patterns should, however, also be considered. See for example Dvořák (2005) on the syntax of Slovene imperatives, including those with the complementiser *da* preceding them. But in any case, the functional correspondence between the Italian and the Resian construction in the sense of Ježovnik's (2015) interpretation cannot be denied and certainly figures as a parallelism in the common diagrammar of bilingual Resians, even if the construction of *da* + imperative as such exists also in Standard Slovene (and beyond).

(25) Aŋ   je   prusìl,   **d**   aŋ   ga
     3SG.M.NOM   AUX.3SG   ask:PTCP.SG.M   COMP   3SG.M.NOM   3SG.M.ACC
     dej   spát   to   núħ.
     give:IMP.SG   sleep:INF   DEM.DIST.ACC.SG.F night:SG.ACC
     'He asked **that** he should let him sleep that night.'

---

38 In Baudouin de Courtenay's (1895: 12) original text, *kan vi* is amalgamated to *kami*, which he separated then in footnote *).

As the variation between the two examples in (26) shows, Resian, just like Molise Slavic, disposes also of a prepositional construction for expressing non-factivity, formed by *za* + infinitive and corresponding to Italian *di* + infinitive; cp. (26a) with the synonymous combination of *da* + imperative in (26b).

(26a) Si ti rakla **za prït.**
AUX.1SG 2SG.DAT say:PFV.PTCP.SG.F for come:PFV.INF
'I told you to come.'

(26b) Si ti rakla **da** ti prïdi.
AUX.1SG 2SG.DAT PTCP.SG.F COMP 2SG.NOM come:PFV.IMP.SG
'I told you **that** you should come.'

Apart from its function as a complementiser in declarative subordinate clauses, *da* has a lot of other functions, including its usage as a conjunction in consecutive and final clauses (Steenwijk 1992: 176), which seem to be traditional, too. Nevertheless they are supported by the polyfunctionality of Italian *che*.

Resian also has complex conjunctions reminding the Molise Slavic pleonastic formations with the complementiser *ke ~ ka* as the second element. But the hybrid formations in question, like (in Baudouin de Courtenay's notation) *apena k* 'hardly', *siccome ko* 'as', *dópo ka* 'after, when' or (Steenwijk 1992: 178–179) *fïn ki* 'until', *sebén ki* 'though', do not have a borrowed equivalent of the Italian complementiser *che* as their second component, but rather genuine Slavic elements from the sphere of the interrogative pronouns *ko(j)*, *ka(j)* 'what' and the relativiser *ki*; see below. Another hybrid type is formed with the help of the traditional complementiser *da*, for example *čɔ̈nča da* 'without', with the first element borrowed from Italian *senza* 'without'.

Let us now proceed immediately to a general comparative overview of the extent of Romance influence on the Albanian and Slavic varieties dealt with in this paper. Note, however, that the upper half of Table 2 in the following section 4 may serve as a summary of what has been said above about complementisers, relativisers, and the interrogative pronoun 'what' in the Slavic micro-languages, thus allowing for a direct comparison with the situation in the Albanian varieties in Table 1.

4 A comparison of the Romance influence in the sphere of complementisers

What we call the "sphere of complementisers" is defined by the whole range of phenomena connected by means of the functions of the polysemic element *che* in Italian in Figure 2 above, i.e. complementation, relative markers, the interrogative pronoun 'what' and causal conjunctions. The summarising Table 2, showing the overall Romance influence on Resian and Molise Slavic in these fields, is divided into three parts. Solid arrows symbolise matter borrowing, with borrowed elements in bold type, while interrupted arrows refer to pattern borrowing (calquing).

Table 2: Molise Slavic and Resian between internal development and Romance influence.

	Resian	Italian	Molise Slavic
COMP (factual)	da	che ⟶	**ka**
COMP (non-factual)	da	che ⟶	**ka**
infinitival construction (non-factual)	za	⟵---- di ----⟶	za
REL	ka, ki, **ke**	⟵ che ⟶	**ka**
pronoun 'what'	ko(j), (kaj)	che	što
CAUSE	ke	⟵-- che ⟶	ka
	ki, ka(j)		aje-ka
	par-da	⟵---- perché ----⟶	zašto-ka
	pokaj-ka		
	perké		**pr-ke**

As shown in the uppermost part of this overview, in Resian the traditional complementiser *da*, existing also in Standard Slovene, has preserved its functions as the basic complementiser in declarative sentences, whereas Molise Slavic, in contrast to Standard Croatian, has replaced it by (*ke* ~) *ka* borrowed from Italian *che*.[39] But both micro-languages show Italian influence in developing an infinitival construction with the preposition *za* in non-factual sentences, calquing Italian *di* + infinitive.

Including the information about Italo-Albanian and the contact-induced constructions for expressing non-factuality in the Slavic micro-languages, Table 3 sums up the complementisers in the four minority varieties dealt with in this paper. For

---

39 For the sake of better legibility only the forms of the akanye-dialect of Acquaviva have been listed here. In Montemitro we would, of course, have *ke* instead of *ka*.

the sake of simplicity Italian *che* was omitted here, with both matter and pattern borrowings set off in bold.

Table 3: A comparison of the complementisers in the Albanian and Slavic varieties in Italy.

	ARB Calabria	ARB Molise	Molise Slavic	Resian
COMP (factual)	*se*	**ke**	**ka**	*da*
COMP (non-factual)	subjunctive	subjunctive	*ka* + NEC	*da* + IMP
INF (non-factual)	–	–	+	+

The opposition between factual and non-factual (intentional) complements, kept in Italo-Albanian by means of the use of the subjunctive in the latter function, but originally missing in the Slavic varieties, was introduced into Molise Slavic by means of the adaptation to the local dialectal model of using the de-obligative future (NEC). In Resian the Romance subjunctive has been calqued by an imperative construction (IMP). Due to the lack of an infinitive in their systems, the Italo-Albanian varieties could not develop an infinitival construction similar to Slavic *za* + infinitive, calqued from the Italian *di*-complement.

The second part of Table 2 above refers to the relativisers and the interrogative pronouns, both homonymously expressed by *che* in Standard Italian. Molise Slavic borrowed *che* here only in its function as a relativiser, while it kept its traditional interrogative pronoun *što* 'what'. In Resian, in spite of their formal similarity to Italian *che*,[40] the relativisers *ka*, *ki* seem to be of Slavic origin, with *ki* serving as a relative marker in Standard Slovene, too.

The relativiser *ka* most probably goes back to a meaning extension of its traditional interrogative pronoun, whose full form is *kaj*, corresponding to *kaj* 'what' in Standard Slovene, but (now) rare in Resian. Here the variant *koj*, with its short form *ko*, is preferred. Originally 'what' was expressed in Slovene by *ka*, but has been preserved as such only in Venetian Slovene and in Resian. Today's standard form *kaj*, evidenced already in the 16th century, goes back to *ka* + asseverative particle *j* (Bezlaj 1982: 9 s.v. *káj*). In the 16th century *kaj* – but not *ka* – was also used

---

[40] Note that in Resian, contrary to *ka* in Molise Slavic, going back to *ke* (akanye), the very form *ka* could hardly be explained phonetically from an Italian source *che*. Note that *ka* is not used as a complementiser in Resian, in contrast to the Slovene *Prekmurje* dialect, where an existing opposition between *ka* and *da* even collapsed in favour of *ka*; see Greenberg (this volume). This reminds to some extent the Molise Slavic situation, at least, with respect to the withdrawal of *da*, whereas here *ke ~ ka* has been borrowed and contrasts with the interrogative pronoun *što* 'what', in its turn corresponding to *ka* 'what' in *Prekmurje* Slovene.

as a relative marker besides *kar < ka-re < *ka-že*. In modern Resian *kaj* is mostly restricted to the meaning of 'something'.⁴¹

There are also cases of a relative marker *ke*, fewer in number and probably borrowed from Italian *che*; see the abbreviated example (27) with *ke* besides the genuine (originally relative) Slavic *ki*, both functioning here as causal conjunctions.⁴²

(27) | Já | bon | mážal | tèt... | **ki** | já |
|---|---|---|---|---|---|
| 1SG.NOM | AUX.1SG | must:PTCP.SG.M | go:INF | because | 1SG.NOM |
| man | tèt | kár | je | dín, | **ké** | to |
| must:PRS.1SG | go:INF | when:REL | be:PRS.3SG | day | because | 3SG.N |
| jœ | na | hŭda | pôt... | | | |
| be:PRS.3SG | INDF.F | bad:F | way | | | |

'I will have to go... because I must go as long as it is day, because this is a bad way...'

The bipartition of the complementising functions of *da* and the block of relativisers and interrogative pronouns resembles the Molise-Albanian structure, where,

---

41 As this paper is not specifically addressed to etymological questions of Resian, we will not elaborate here on the difficult question if *ka(j)* and *ko(j)* go back to different sources, with the latter being connected to Slovene *ko* 'if, because, when' etc., or, less probably, if *ko(j)* is only a phonetic variant of *ka(j)*. In any case, Baudouin de Courtenay (1895: 399) explicitly explains *koj* in a footnote as "kaj". For our comparison it is important that the loanword *ke* is not used as an interrogative pronoun and that there are also genuine-Slavic forms, by means of which relativisers and interrogative pronouns may be kept apart, e.g. *ki: koj*, besides the polysemic form *ka*. The problem becomes still more intricate as a consequence of the fact that the individual Resian dialects are not homogeneous in this field, as for example *ka* as an interrogative pronoun seems to be restricted to the dialect of Stolvizza (besides *koj*), while the others only have *koj ~ ko*. Furthermore, *ka* as a relative pronoun is restricted to the dialects of Gniva and Oseacco, while in the San Giorgio and Stolvizza dialects in this function *ki* is used; see http://abaoaqu.maldura.unipd.it:8081/resianica/dictionaryForm.do (Resian online dictionary, accessed 18 July 2021). This means, above all, that a syncretism of the interrogative 'what' and the relativiser exists only from a cross-dialectal point of view, whereas they are kept apart in the single dialects by having their individual contrasting couples out of the overall set of *k*-forms, which all go back to different derivations (gender, cases) of the same Proto-Slavic root **k-*; see Bezlaj (1982: 30) for *ki*, (1982, 49–50) for *ko*, (1982: 7) for *ka*, and (1982: 9) for *kaj*. Resolving the puzzle of the formally and functionally overcrossing *k*-forms in Resian would require a special research on this topic.

42 They are mostly marked by means of italics in Baudouin de Courtenay (1895), his way of referring explicitly to borrowings. But there are also cases of *ke* without italics. It remains unclear, if the author considered them as variants of the basic forms *ki, ka*, just like the more reduced forms *k, kъ*, or if they simply escaped him.

however, it most probably is a result of language contact. The polysemy of Resian *ka* as a relativiser and as an interrogative pronoun could well be due to a partial adaptation to the semantic structure of Italian *che*, too, as at least Standard Slovene does not use *ka(j)* as a relativiser.

As mentioned above, the full form *kaj* was historically used as a relative pronoun in written Slovene, but we do not know if this was also possible in Resian, before Romance varieties started to influence it. In any case, claiming a Romance model for the extension of its meaning (functions) remains just a hypothesis. If it is confirmed, Resian could be a parallel case to the Italo-Albanian meaning expansion of *ç* 'what' to a relative marker. In any case, these two micro-languages differ from Molise Slavic, where the loanword *ke ~ ka* is used as a complementiser as well as a relative marker, whereas *što* functions only as the interrogative pronoun meaning 'what'. Compared with Standard Croatian, Molise Slavic *što* has even lost its once existing polysemy, comprising the function of a relativiser.[43]

Overall, it is worth noting that all variants of the micro-languages dealt with in this paper are strictly conservative with respect to the form of the interrogative pronoun in not borrowing it from the dominant varieties. On the other hand, only Molise Slavic (and partially Resian) has borrowed *che* as a relativiser. This situation is contrary to that of *che* as a complementiser, borrowed in the whole Molise area (but not in Resian and Calabro-Albanian), irrespective of the language family the micro-language in question belongs to. In other words, what we have is an implicational hierarchy for MAT borrowing in the given field: complementiser (particle) < relativiser (particle) < (interrogative) pronoun, with "<" symbolising 'before'.

The third part of Table 2 refers to causal conjunctions, one of which is again *che* in (mostly dialectal or colloquial) Italian, besides the more specific conjunction *perché* 'because' (Standard Slovene *ker*, Standard Croatian *jer*). The situation is still more varied here than in the other fields. To begin with, both Slavic micro-languages borrowed Italian *che*; for Resian see example (28a) from Baudouin de Courtenay (1895: 6). Furthermore, in Resian the use of the relativisers *ki* and *ka(j)* with the function of causal conjunctions could again be cases of

---

[43] This must not be mixed up with the interrogative pronoun *što*, introducing in Molise Slavic, among other things, free relative clauses, see above, an additional function of Resian *koj* 'what', too. In such cases, Resian *koj* may be preceded by the pleonastic complementiser *da* as in *An he vœdœt ... **da kój** prodáɜ twůj ońá* 'He wants to know, what your father sells.' (Baudouin de Courtenay 1895: 87). The same optional usage of the complementiser *da* occurs with other interrogative pronouns in indirect interrogative clauses like *da káku* 'how', *da zakój* 'why' (Steenwijk 1992: 176). This usage, unknown to Molise Slavic, corresponds to the pleonastic complementiser *se* in Albanian of the type *se ç* 'what', *se si* 'how' like in the Calabro-Albanian examples in (11).

pattern borrowing on the model of Italian *che;* see example (28b) with causal *kaj* from Baudouin de Courtenay (1895: 7).

(28a) *To   ħe   bìt   téško   za   jitìt   nútar...,*
      it   will:3SG   be   hard   to   go   inside
      ke   *tana   wráteh   sta   dwá   leóna.*
      COMP   at   door:LOC.PL   be:PRS.2DU   two   lion:DU.NOM
      'It will be hard to go in..., **because** at the door there are two lions.'

(28b) *An   ni   mǽšœ   béčou̯   nikár,*
      3SG.M   NEG   have:IPRF.3SG   money:GEN.PL   nothing
      káj   *am   bíl   búžac.*
      what   3SG.M   be:PTCP.SG.M   poor
      'He had no money at all, **because** he was poor.'

Molise Slavic, however, contrary also to Standard Croatian, does not use *što* 'what' as a causal conjunction, not even in constructions expressing the emotional attitude of the speaker towards the given event, in which Croatian *što* varies with the complementiser *da*, see section 3.1. The only traditional causal conjunction is *aje*, nowadays almost always combined with *che*, thus forming the hybrid compound conjunction *aje-ka* 'because' as in (29a), replaceable by the borrowed causal conjunction *pëke* ← Ital. *perché*.[44] The simple form *aje* is restricted to its function as an interrogative pronoun meaning 'why', i.e. as a synonym of the traditional pronoun *zašto*.

Note that *zašto* 'why' is the only traditional form of the interrogative pronoun in Molise Slavic, still used in both dialects considered as a variant of the forms *aje, jer*, which in their turn had been the traditional causal conjunctions; cf. Croatian *jer* 'because'. So, language contact has induced several subsequent restructurings in this field, based on the form and the polysemy of Italian *perché* 'why, because'. Starting from the original opposition between *zašto* 'why' and *jer* 'because', in a first step *jer* (and its local phonetic variants) also acquired the interrogative function of *zašto*, thus becoming its variant in the meaning 'why', while *zašto* in its turn, by the opposite development, based again on the polysemic model of *perché*, expanded to the meaning 'because'. In a further step, calquing of the internal structure of *perché* with the complementiser *che* as its component led to the compositional hybrid forms *aje-ka* and *zašto-ka*. Finally, the polysemic form *perché* → *pëke* itself was borrowed.

---

[44] The Molise-Slavic forms in Table 2 are again those of the Acquaviva dialect. In Montemitro, with its basic form *ke*, the hybrid forms are *jer-ke, er-ke, ajer-ke* 'because'.

In addition, a parallel hybrid form *zašto-ka* has been formed, consisting of the interrogative pronoun and the complementiser *ka*, a (possible but rather rare) variant of *aje-ka* in (29a). Another variant is the loanword *ka* itself in its causal meaning (29b).

(29a) Nisma   mogl   spat, **aje-ka**   bihu   fandazma.
      NEG.AUX.1PL can:PTCP.PL   sleep because   be:IPRF.3PL ghost:NOM.PL
      'We could not sleep, **because** there were ghosts.'

(29b) Biša   rajana   pur   s   menom   **ka**   ja
      be:IPRF.3SG furious:SG.F   also with 1SG.INS COMP   1SG.NOM
      sa   smijahu.
      REFL   laugh:IPRF.1SG
      'She was annoyed at me, too, **because** I was laughing.'

Based on the hybrid conjunctions, Molise Slavic has developed a system different from Italian with its ambiguity of *perché* as an interrogative pronoun and as a causal conjunction, by using hybrid (pleonastic) forms with the added complementiser *che* in the latter case, thus giving rise to the oppositions *aje: aje-ka* and *zašto: zašto-ka* = 'why': 'because'; see the direct opposition in the little dialogue (29c). When in such cases the direct borrowings *pëke* and *ka* are used, the ambiguity between 'why' and 'because' remains the same as in Italian.

(29c) «Ja   ne   moram   jiskodit!»   – «**Aje**?»
      1SG.NOM   NEG   can:PRS.1SG   get.out:PFV.INF why
      – «**Aje-ka**   su   škare   odekaj!»
      because   be:PRS.3PL   scissors   here
      "I can't get out!" – "**Why**?" – "**Because** there are scissors here!"

As for Resian, it also forms a hybrid conjunction, but in a clearly different way. The basis is again Italian *perché*, which, however, is decomposed into its components *per* 'for' + *che* 'what', with the polyfunctional *che* interpreted in terms of its function as a complementiser. The result is the hybrid calque *par-da* as in (30), composed of the borrowed element *par* ← *per* and the traditional complementiser *da*, replacing Italian *che*. In the examples we have come across up to now, like (30) from Baudouin de Courtenay (1895: 115), *par-da* is used only as a final conjunction, one of the functions of Italian *perché* besides its causal one; see also Steenwijk (1992: 177).

(30)   ... **par da**   ni   ba   ni   výdœly,   d   áŋ
       so that   3PL.NOM   PTL   NEG   see:PTCP.PL.M   COMP   3SG.NOM
       ha   pijé   pròč.
       3SG.ACC   lead:PRS.3SG   away
       '... **so that** they may not see that he is leading him away.'

In Resian there are also pleonastic forms with the meaning 'because'. In Baudouin de Courtenay's (1895) texts we find, for example, *pokaj-ka*, based on the traditional form *pokaj* 'why', combined with the pleonastic *ka* (interrogative and/or relativising). On the other hand, there is also *pokaj-da* 'why', with the complementiser *da* added to the basic form *pokaj*.[45] Finally, there is also the conjunction *perké* 'because' (Steenwijk 1982: 181), borrowed directly from Italian *perché*.

Calabro-Albanian *se*, apart from still being used as a complementiser, also functions as a variant of the causal conjunction *pse*; see the subordinate causal clause in (31a).[46] As this double usage of *se* is known also from Standard Albanian, this parallel to Italian *che* seems to be original, without any need to explain it by means of language contact. But, of course, language contact may have contributed to keeping this polysemy after the emigration to Italy. As for Molise Albanian, it goes parallel with Molise Slavic in using the borrowed complementiser *ke* additionally as a causal conjunction (31b).[47]

(31a) E   vën   gjith   esposto,   **se**
       and   put:PRS.3PL   all   exposed   COMP
       kan   e   shohen   gjindjat.   (Calabria)
       have:PRS.3PL   and see:PRS.3PL   people:DEF.NOM.PL
       'And they expose it all, **because** the people have to see it.'

---

[45] See, for example, the question with *pocai da* and the corresponding answer, introduced by *pocai ca* in the dialogue in paragraph 1424 of the Resian Catechism (Baudouin de Courtenay 1895: 459).

[46] Interestingly enough, Albanian in Greece (Arvanitika) went the opposite way, by using now *pse* 'because' (< *për se* 'for that') as a variant of the traditional complementiser *se*. On the other hand, there is also a pleonastic formation *se oti*, at least among male speakers, combining *se* with the Greek complementiser ότι (Sasse 1991: 394–395).

[47] In Italo-Albanian, not considered in Table 2, we have not found up to now a parallel hybrid form of *pse* 'because' combined with *ke* of the type *pse-ke*, which could only have developed in Molise, as only here the complementiser *ke* itself has been borrowed. This is contrary to the aforementioned parallelisms in the domain of compound and pleonastic conjunctions with the element *ke* both in Molise Slavic and Molise Albanian.

(31b) Ka   vemi   Këmvash **ke**   ka   fërmomi.   (Molise)
      have:PTL go:PRS.1PL   C.   COMP   have:PTL   sign:PRS.1PL
      'We have to go to Campobasso, **because** we have to sign (the contract).'

Calabro-Albanian has also borrowed Italian *perché* 'because', which serves as a variant of genuine Albanian *pse*, see example (32). In Molise Albanian normally only *pse* is used, while *perché* is restricted to sequences of code-switching from Italian. In this respect, it resembles the conservative Montemitro variant of Molise Slavic.

(32) Nëng   m   e   nxuar   jatroj,
     not   1SG.DAT   3SG.ACC   remove:AOR.3SG   doctor:DEF.NOM.SG.M
     perke   u   hrisja.   (Calabria)
     because   1SG.NOM   cry:IPRF.1SG
     'The doctor did not remove it (= the plaster) from me, **because** I was crying.'

There are quite a lot of further influences based on Italian *che* as a model for the structural reorganisation of the minority languages, which cannot be dealt with in this paper. But one of them should be mentioned, as it could lead to the grammaticalisation of a newly developed form in terms of a 'reportive evidential'. It is based on the local Italian impersonal form *dice* (*che*) 'it is said (that)', 'allegedly', literally 'says (that)', and appears in both alloglottic micro-languages of Molise; see examples (33a–b). Note that this happened by means of matter borrowing in Molise Slavic, while Molise Albanian shows pattern borrowing, resulting in a hybrid form, as the borrowed complementiser *ke* is added to the traditional Albanian verb *thom* 'say' in its 3rd person singular present.

(33a) **Dič-ka**   sa   čujaša   gruba.   (Molise Slavic)
      REP   REFL   feel:IPRF.3SG   bad
      'He **allegedly** felt bad.'

(33b) **Thote-ke**   errurën   solde.   (Molise Albanian)
      REP   arrive:AOR.3PL   money:PL
      '**It is said that** money has arrived.'

5 Summary and conclusion

In concluding, we will emphasise some central results of the contact-induced developments of the complementisers in Italo-Albanian and Italo-Slavic minority languages, due to the influence of the highly polysemic Italian *che* and its equivalents in the local Romance varieties. The polysemy of *che* was the reason for including other parts of syntax in this paper, especially relative and causal clauses with their respective introducing elements.

In all contact areas we find matter and pattern borrowings, though in a different distribution. In Molise, the central region of our investigation, *che* was borrowed directly in the Slavic and the Albanian varieties, but only in Molise Slavic do the borrowed variants *ke ~ ka* serve as both a complementiser and a relativiser, while in Molise Albanian borrowed *ke* is restricted to the complementising function. The Slovene-based Resian micro-language in north-eastern Italy and also Calabro-Albanian preserved their original complementisers *da* and *se* respectively, not borrowing *che* at all in this function. In contrast, they adapted to the polysemy of Italian *che* as a model for semantic calquing. So, in Calabro-Albanian *se* replaced also the original alternative complementiser *që*, and in Resian the traditional interrogative pronoun *ka* expanded its functions to that of a relativiser. The latter development is found also in both Albanian varieties (with respect to *ç* 'what'), but not in Molise Slavic, which preserved the interrogative pronoun *što* different from the borrowed relativisers *ke ~ ka*. As a consequence, Molise Slavic and Molise Albanian, though equally borrowing *che* as a complementiser, remain different with respect to its homonymy with the relativiser, present only in Slavic.

Again based on the characteristics of Italian *che*, causal conjunctions changed in different ways in the single contact areas: in this case both Slavic micro-languages borrowed *che*, while both Italo-Albanian varieties kept their original conjunction *pse*. The Italian alternative causal conjunction *perché*, having *che* as one of its constituents, led to several hybrid formations in Molise Slavic, which added *ke ~ ka* to the original conjunction *jer* (> *aje*) 'because' and to the original interrogative pronoun *zašto* 'why', thus restoring the original opposition between the conjunction (now with *che*) and the pronoun (without *che*), alien to Italian, on the basis of a preceding merger of both, due to the polysemy of Italian *perché* 'why, because'.

Besides fully borrowing Italian *perché*, Resian replaced *che* as a component of *perché* by its traditional complementiser *da*, which led to the hybrid form *par-da*. Italo-Albanian as a whole did not form hybrid causal conjunctions, and only Calabro-Albanian borrowed *perché* as a variant of the traditional causal conjunction *pse*, while Molise Albanian did not. But even Molise Slavic does not behave homogeneously in this respect, as only the dialect of Acquaviva borrowed *perché* (> *pëke*) as a free variant of *ka, aje-ka, zašto-ka,* while it is rather rare in the more conservative variety of Montemitro.

Apart from the restored opposition between the interrogative pronouns meaning 'why' and the causal conjunctions extended with the complementiser, another opposition has developed in Molise Slavic, differentiating factual and non-factual (intentional) statements. This was achieved by means of introducing a new type of complement clauses on the model of local Romance varieties, more precisely by combining its de-obligative future with the complementiser to express non-factuality (intentionality). While the differentiation between 'why' and 'because' is contrary to the Italian polysemy of *perché* 'why, because', the non-factual solution clearly copies the Romance differentiation.

Resian developed a contact-induced construction for non-factual (intentional) sentences, too, by combining the complementiser with the imperative, thus calquing the Romance combination of the complementiser with the subjunctive. What is more, both Slavic micro-languages have adopted the Italian (standard and dialectal) possibility of using an infinitival construction in case of referential identity between the main and the subordinated clause in non-factual sentences. This was achieved by means of the preposition *za* preceding the infinitive, i.e. by a construction clearly alien to the traditional Slavic grammatical structures.

On the whole, the model of the dominant varieties often overrides inherited structures in the alloglottic minority languages by copying the polysemy of *che* or even by borrowing it as a lexical element. But every single contact situation shows individual results based on the overall possibilities given by the Romance models. Sometimes the "genealogic" factor plays a role, especially the impossibility of adopting infinitive constructions in Italo-Albanian due to the lack of an infinitive. So, the inherited Albanian hypotactic construction with the pure subjunctive in non-factual (intentional) sentences remained absolutely untouched.

There are also some implications and restrictions with respect to the borrowed grammatical elements in the investigated varieties. So, if the relativiser is borrowed, then the complementiser is borrowed, too, but not the other way round. The interrogative pronoun is still more stable than the relativiser, as it is never borrowed. The complementiser can only become homonymous with the interrogative pronoun, if the functions of the latter are extended, not the other way round. In Slavic the interrogative pronoun and the complementiser remain different, but they merge in Albanian (though possibly already prior to the immigration). When the borrowed complementiser is used pleonastically in the source language, it is used in the same way in the replica languages and with the same restrictions, for example, by excluding the combination of *che* with interrogative pronouns in indirect interrogative sentences, contrary to the combination with adverbs serving as conjunctions. If the complementiser was not borrowed, however, there are no such restrictions, as show Resian *da koj* and Albanian *se ç* with their traditional complementisers pleonastically preceding the interrogative pronoun 'what'.

Comparing our results with contact-induced change in other minority languages in Italy could confirm or relativize them in terms of grammatical developments in situations of total language contact with the same donor language (and its local varieties). For example, the German-based Cimbrian variety of Luserna in Northern Italy, and the Greek-based varieties in Southern Italy corroborate our findings about the borrowability of Italian *che*, as Salentinian Griko (Rohlfs 1977: 98, 204) borrowed *ka*[48] from its local Romance neighbours both as a complementiser and a relativiser, while Cimbrian (Tyroller 2003: 234–236) borrowed *ke* only as a complementiser. This reflects the situation in Molise Slavic and in Molise Albanian respectively as well as the implicative order claimed above. On the other hand, the Calabro-Greek variety seems to be as conservative in this respect as Calabro-Albanian in not borrowing *che* at all (Rohlfs 1977: 97–98, 204). In future research, similar comparisons could be made with respect to the other contact-induced developments in this paper, and the role of the "genealogic" background of the individual micro-languages in the sense of their traditional structure could be analysed in more detail.

The alloglottic varieties in Italy are only one facet of an overall spectrum of linguistic enclaves, but fine-grained knowledge about the behaviour of their complementisers and the like could, hopefully, be an important contribution to a general theory of contact-induced grammatical change in situations of total language contact.

Abbreviations and glosses

1,2,3	1st, 2nd, 3rd person
ABL	ablative
ACC	accusative
AOR	aorist

---

48 In spite of its formal similarity to *che*, deriving from Latin *quid* and *quod* 'what', the form *ca* [ka], serving as a complementiser and a relativiser in the local Romance dialects, goes back to Latin *quia* 'because' (Rohlfs 1968: 195–196; 1969: 188–189). Actually, *ca* is also found in Molisan dialects (Giammarco 1968: 354), but the borrowed form *ke* in Molise Slavic and Molise Albanian clearly refers to the alternate complementiser *chə/che* as their source. In any case, these local differences are irrelevant for the process of borrowing in the minority languages itself.

AUX	auxiliary
CMP	comparative
COMP	complementiser
COND	conditional
CON	connector
DAT	dative
DEF	definite
DU	dual
F	feminine
GEN	genitive
IMP	imperative
INDF	indefinite
INF	infinitive
INS	instrumental
IPFV	imperfective
IPRF	imperfect
LOC	locative
M	masculine
N	neuter
NEG	negation
NOM	nominative
PASS	passive
PFV	perfective
PL	plural
PRS	present
PTCP	participle
PTL	particle
REFL	reflexive
REP	reportive
REL	relative
SG	singular
SUBJ	subjunctive

References

Altimari, Francesco. 2005. Il "futuro necessitativo" dell'albanese d'Italia: Influenza italo-romanza o arcaismo balcanico? In Walter Breu (ed.), *L'influsso dell'italiano sulla grammatica delle lingue minoritarie*, 1–12. Rende: Centro Editoriale e Librario.

Baudouin de Courtenay, Jan. 1895. *Materialien zur südslavischen Dialektologie und Ethnographie, I, Resianische Texte (gesammelt in den Jj. 1872, 1873 und 1877, geordnet und übersetzt von Baudouin de Courtenay)*. St. Petersburg.

Benacchio, Rosanna. 2009. Il contatto slavo-romanzo nel croato del Molise e nei dialetti sloveni del Friuli. In Lenka Scholze & Björn Wiemer (eds.), *Von Zuständen, Dynamik und Veränderung bei Pygmäen und Giganten*, 177–191. Bochum: Brockmeyer.

Bezlaj, France. 1982. *Etimološki slovar slovenskega jezika. Druga knjiga. K–O* [Etymological dictionary of the Slovene language. Second book. K–O]. Ljubljana: Mladinska Knjiga.

Breu, Walter. 1991. Zur aktuellen Situation in den nördlicheren italoalbanischen Kolonien. In Walter Breu, Hans Jürgen Sasse & Rolf Ködderitzsch (eds.), *Aspekte der Albanologie*, 1–16. Wiesbaden: Harrassowitz.

Breu, Walter. 1994. Forme verbali perifrastiche arbërisht. In Francesco Altimari & Leonardo M. Savoia (eds.), *I dialetti italo-albanesi*, 365–385. Roma: Bulzoni.

Breu, Walter. 2011. Il verbo slavomolisano in confronto con altre lingue minoritarie: mutamento contatto-dipendente, resistenza e sviluppo autonomo. In Walter Breu (ed.), *L'influsso dell'italiano sul sistema del verbo delle lingue minoritarie*, 149–184. Bochum: Brockmeyer.

Breu, Walter. 2017. *Slavische Mikrosprachen im absoluten Sprachkontakt. Glossierte und interpretierte Sprachaufnahmen aus Italien, Deutschland, Österreich und Griechenland. Band I. Moliseslavische Texte aus Acquaviva Collecroce, Montemitro und San Felice del Molise.* Wiesbaden: Harrassowitz.

Breu, Walter. 2018. La situazione linguistica nei paesi arbëreshë del Molise. In Lucija Šimičić, Ivana Škevin & Nikola Vuletić (eds.), *Le isole linguistiche dell'Adriatico*, 169–197. Canterano: Aracne.

Breu, Walter. 2019a. Partikeln und Pronomina im slavisch-romanischen Sprachkontakt. Zur Relativsatzeinleitung des Moliseslavischen in Süditalien. In Imke Mendoza & Barbara Sonnenhauser (eds.), *Relativisation strategies in a Central European perspective: Slavic and beyond* [Special issue]. *Zeitschrift für Slavische Philologie* 75 (1), 183–208.

Breu, Walter. 2019b. Morphosyntactic change in Slavic micro-languages: The case of Molise Slavic. In Andrii Danylenko & Motoki Nomachi (eds.), *Slavic in the Language Map of Europe*, 385–432. Berlin & Boston: De Gruyter Mouton.

Breu, Walter. 2020. Partitivity in Slavic-Romance language contact. The case of Molise Slavic in Italy. In Tabea Ihsane & Elisabeth Stark (eds.), *Shades of Partitivity: Formal and areal properties* [Special issue]. *Linguistics* 58 (3), 837–868.

Breu, Walter & Malinka Pila. 2020. Buduščee vremja i glagol'nyj vid pod vlijaniem jazykovogo kontakta v slavjanskix mikrojazykax Italii [Future tense and verbal aspect under the influence of language contact in the Slavic micro-languages of Italy]. *Revue des études slaves* 91 (4), 455–470.

Buchholz, Oda & Wilfried Fiedler. 1987. *Albanische Grammatik*. Leipzig: Verlag Enzyklopädie.

Çabej, Eqrem. 2002. *Studime etimologjike në fushë të shqipes* [Etymological studies in the field of Albanian]. *VI. NN-RR.* Tiranë: Akademia e Shkencavet e Republikës së Shqipërisë.

Dvořák, Boštjan. 2005. Slowenische Imperative und ihre Einbettung. *Philologie im Netz* 33, 36–73.

Giammarco, Ernesto. 1968. *Dizionario Abruzzese e Molisano. Volume Primo. A – E.* Roma: Edizioni dell'Ateneo.

Greenberg, Marc L. (this volume). Antemurale innovationis: Clausal complementation in the Slovene Mura River (Prekmurje) dialect and its Balkan parallels.

Grković-Major, Jasmina (this volume). The development of emotion predicate complements in Serbian.

Ivić, Pavle. 1958. *Die serbokroatischen Dialekte. Ihre Struktur und Entwicklung. Erster Band. Allgemeines und die štokavische Dialektgruppe.* 's-Gravenhage: Mouton & Co.

Ivić, Pavle. 1994. *O govoru Galipoljskih Srba* [On the dialect of the Gallipoli Serbs]. Novi Sad: Izdavačka knjižarnica Zorana Stojanovića.

Jahić, Dževad, Senahid Halilović & Ismail Palić. 2000. *Gramatika bosanskoga jezika* [Grammar of the Bosnian language]. Zenica: Dom Štampe.

Ježovnik, Janoš. 2015. Vezni naklon v rezijanščini [The subjunctive mood in Resian]. In Danila Zuljan Kumar & Helena Dobrovoljc (eds.), *Škrabčevi dnevi 8. Zbornik prispevkov s simpozija 2013*, 63–83. Nova Gorica: Založba Univerze.

Joseph, Brian D. 2016. The semantics and syntax of complementation markers as an areal phenomenon in the Balkans, with special attention to Albanian. In Kasper Boye & Petar Kehayov (eds.), *Complementizer semantics in European languages*, 265–292. Berlin & Boston: De Gruyter Mouton.

Kloss, Heinz. 1978 [1952[1]]. *Die Entwicklung neuer germanischer Kultursprachen 1800–1950*. Düsseldorf: Pädagogischer Verlag Schwann.

Kloss, Heinz. 1967. Abstand languages and Ausbau languages. *Anthropological Linguistics* 9 (7), 29–41.

Matzinger, Joachim. 2006. *Der Altalbanische Text* Mbsuame e Krështerë *(Dottrina cristiana) des Lekë Matrënga von 1592*. Dettelbach: Röll.

Muljačić, Žarko. 1989. Über den Begriff der *Dachsprache*. In Ulrich Ammon (ed.), *Status and function of languages and language varieties*, 256–277. Berlin & New York: De Gruyter.

Piccoli, Giovanni. 2005. L'influsso dell'italiano nella sintassi del periodo del croato (slavo) molisano. In Walter Breu (ed.), *L'influsso dell'italiano sulla grammatica delle lingue minoritarie*, 167–175. Rende: Centro Editoriale e Librario.

Pila, Malinka. 2017. L'uso dell'aspetto perfettivo al tempo presente nei dialetti sloveni della Val Resia e delle valli del Torre e del Natisone, 267–281. In Marina di Filippo & François Esvan (eds.), *Studi di linguistica slava*. Napoli: Il Torcoliere.

Prifti, Stefan. 1971. *Sintaksa e gjuhës shqipe* [Syntax of the Albanian Language]. Prishtinë: Universiteti i Prishtinës. [Tirana [1]1962]

Raguž, Dragutin. 1997. *Praktična hrvatska grammatika* [Practical Croatian grammar]. Zagreb: Medicinska Zaklada.

Rešetar, Milan. 1911. *Die serbokroatischen Kolonien Süditaliens*. Wien: Kaiserliche Akademie der Wissenschaften.

Rječnik 1884–1886 = *Rječnik hrvatskoga ili srpskoga jezika. Dio II. Četa – Đavli* [Dictionary of the Croatian or Serbian Language. Part II]. Zagreb: Jugoslavenska akademija znanosti i umjetnosti.

Rječnik 1959–1962. = *Rječnik hrvatskoga ili srpskoga jezika. Dio XVII. Sunce – Taj* [Dictionary of the Croatian or Serbian Language. Part XVII]. Zagreb: Jugoslavenska akademija znanosti i umjetnosti.

Rohlfs, Gerhard. 1968. *Grammatica storica della lingua italiana e dei suoi dialetti. Morfologia*. Torino: Einaudi.

Rohlfs, Gerhard. 1969. *Grammatica storica della lingua italiana e dei suoi dialetti. Sintassi*. Torino: Einaudi.

Rohlfs, Gerhard. 1977. *Grammatica storica dei dialetti italogreci (Calabria, Salento)*. München: Beck.

Sakel, Janette. 2007. Types of loan: Matter and pattern. In Yaron Matras & Jeanette Sakel (eds.), *Grammatical borrowing in cross-linguistic perspective*, 15–30. Berlin & New York: Mouton de Gruyter.

Sasse, Hans-Jürgen. 1991. *Arvanitika. Die albanischen Sprachreste in Griechenland. Teil I*. Wiesbaden: Harrassowitz.

Sonnenhauser, Barbara (this volume). Slovene *naj*: An (emerging) clausal complementiser?

Steenwijk, Han. 1992. *The Slovene dialect of Resia. San Giorgio*. Amsterdam: Rodopi.

Stevanović, M. 1979. *Savremeni srpskohrvatski jezik II* [The modern Serbo-Croatian language]. Belgrade: Naučna Knjiga.
Toporišič, Jože. 1984. *Slovenska slovnica. Pregledana in razširjena izdaja* [Slovene grammar. Checked and expanded edition]. Maribor: Založba Obzorja.
Turano, Giuseppina. 2011. Rapporto lessico-sintassi e contaminazione di forme linguistiche. Il caso dell'*arbëresh*. *Hylli i Dritës* 31 (2), 103–117.
Tyroller, Hans. 2003. *Grammatische Beschreibung des Zimbrischen von Lusern*. Stuttgart: Steiner.
Zima, Luka. 1887. *Sintaktične razlike između čakavštine, kajkavštine i štokavštine* [Syntactic differences between Čakavian, Kajkavian and Štokavian]. Zagreb: Jugoslavenska Akademija znanosti i umjetnosti.

Chapter IV: **Complementation in time**

Hanne Martine Eckhoff
The history of Slavonic clausal complementation: A corpus view

Abstract: Syntactic annotation of historical text, with no access to native-speaker intuitions, poses a number of problems to the annotator who is faced with the task of giving a single analysis of each sentence. This article reports on the experiences from annotating complementation structures in Old Church Slavonic and Old East Slavonic in the PROIEL and TOROT treebanks. Two case studies are examined: complement clauses in Old Church Slavonic and the history of Russian *čьto* 'what, which, that'. In the first case the annotation scheme is shown to work well in terms of interannotator agreement and retrievability. However, the price is that a large number of examples with *jako* 'that' are analysed as complement clauses with a subjunction, even though many of these examples are in fact ambiguous and *jako* can equally well be interpreted as a quotative particle followed by direct speech. The second case study looks at a development from situation where *čьto* could be taken to be an interrogative pronoun in all subordinated clauses, to a situation where a subjunction and a relative pronoun analysis are also available. This leads to a large number of ambiguous occurrences. The solution in TOROT is to analyse unambiguous interrogative pronoun and subjunction examples at face value, while all of the remaining occurrences are analysed as relative clauses. This makes the annotator's job manageable, but causes retrievability problems, since individual researchers will have to sift through the relative clause examples themselves.

Keywords: Ancient Greek, corpus linguistics, dependency grammar, Middle Russian, Old Church Slavonic, Old East Slavonic, treebanks, quotatives, reported speech

1 Introduction

This chapter describes and analyses Old Church Slavonic, Old East Slavonic and Middle Russian complementation structure on the basis of experiences with syntactic annotation of such structures in the PROIEL and TOROT treebanks. The chapter focuses on problems encountered when analysing ambiguous structures and struc-

Hanne Martine Eckhoff, University of Oxford, Lady Margaret Hall, Norham Gardens, Oxford OX2 6QA (United Kingdom), e-mail: hanne.eckhoff@mod-langs.ox.ac.uk

https://doi.org/10.1515/9783110725858-008

tures that are undergoing diachronic change, i.e. structures where it is not clear how the relationship between the complement-taking predicate, the complementiser (if any) and the dependent-clause verb should be analysed (cf. the template outlined in Wiemer, this volume). These structures often contain words, such as Old Church Slavonic *jako*, that signal subordination, but are not unambiguously complementisers, and such ambiguities are the main topic of my discussion. Old Church Slavonic is the earliest attestation of South Slavonic, and its inventory and distribution of complementation strategies can largely be seen as the diachronic source of the strategies found in modern South Slavonic languages, for example the role of *da*-clauses. The data from Old East Slavonic and Middle Russian illustrate a development that happened to various extents in all Slavonic languages, namely the reanalysis of interrogative and indefinite *čьto* 'what, something' as a complementiser and/or relativiser.

The PROIEL and TOROT treebanks use an enriched dependency grammar scheme which is combined with a rich inventory of part-of-speech labels in order to yield detailed analyses. The choice of part-of-speech label will usually determine the syntactic analysis: if the word signalling subordination is deemed to be a subjunction, it will be the head of the complement clause and a direct dependent of the complement-taking predicate. If it is deemed to be a "particle", or an interrogative pronoun or adverb, it will instead have its place inside the complement clause, yielding a very different analysis (for examples, see section 3). The system only allows a single analysis for each sentence, so even in clearly ambiguous cases, a choice must be made. This is a design choice that makes it necessary to accept that the chosen analysis may not always be ideal from a linguistic point of view. Instead the corpus builder's focus must be on retrieval: the ambiguous examples must be lemmatised and parsed in such a way that they can easily be retrieved. The retrieval of these examples may be further simplified by adding additional tagging in PROIEL/TOROT's customisable tagging layers, e.g. for person-reference conversion in complement clauses.

Two case studies demonstrate the advantages and problems of this annotation style, and become the backdrop for a discussion of the need to distinguish between various subordination types. The first case study is the situation in canonical Old Church Slavonic, where the system can be made to work well in terms of interannotator agreement and retrievability. In the second case study, an examination of the history of Russian *čьto* 'what, which, that', I look at a number of problems that arise when an element is often ambiguous between several part-of-speech labels (interrogative pronoun, relative pronoun, indefinite pronoun, subjunction), and what is more, clearly undergoing diachronic change. The result is a large number of ambiguous cases, which must be analysed so that they are easily retrievable as a group.

Section 2 presents the TOROT/PROIEL dependency annotation scheme. Section 3 discusses the application of the scheme to complement clauses and related structures.

Section 4 discusses how well the scheme works for canonical Old Church Slavonic data. Section 5 examines some problems raised by applying the annotation scheme to a diachronic Russian corpus. Section 6 is the conclusion.

2 Treebanks and annotation scheme

This chapter is based on experiences and data from two closely related dependency treebanks: The PROIEL treebank of early attestations of Indo-European languages, and the Tromsø Old Russian and OCS Treebank (TOROT). The PROIEL treebank,[1] at its core, is a parallel treebank of early Indo-European languages, containing the New Testament in Greek, Latin, Gothic, Classical Armenian, as well as in OCS. It contains a fully lemmatised and morphosyntactically annotated version of the Codex Marianus, which is also aligned at word token level with the Greek text. The TOROT treebank[2] is an expansion of the Slavonic part of the PROIEL corpus. For OCS, it contains the Codex Zographensis (with lemmatisation and morphological and partial syntactic annotation, also aligned with the Greek) and the Codex Suprasliensis with full lemmatisation and morphosyntactic annotation, as well as a number of other texts. In addition, it contains approximately 250,000 word tokens of fully annotated Old East Slavonic and Middle Russian from a variety of genres and times.

The PROIEL/TOROT annotation scheme is an enriched variety of dependency grammar. It deviates, for instance, from the analytical layer of Prague Dependency Grammar by using null verbs and conjunctions,[3] secondary dependencies and a richer set of relation label tags. This makes the formalism more expressive, but also more complicated to parse and query. The scheme also employs a relatively large set of part-of-speech tags, as well as detailed morphological tags, and analyses generally exploit the interplay between part of speech, morphology and syntax (for further details, see Haug and Jøhndal 2008, Eckhoff and Berdičevskis 2015, Eckhoff et al. 2018). This interplay is exemplified throughout this chapter. It should be noted that the current incarnation of the system requires that a single analysis be given for each sentence. That is, even in passages that are clearly syntactically ambiguous, we can currently present only one interpretation. This is a conscious design choice, since allowing for multiple analyses of individual sentences would complicate retrieval and might not be very good for annotation consistency. However, it is certainly not

---

[1] proiel.github.io, foni.uio.no:3000
[2] torottreebank.github.io, nestor.uit.no
[3] In this chapter the term "conjunction" is used to mean 'coordinating conjunction' – for subordinators the term "subjunction" is used.

unproblematic, as the history of Slavonic complementation demonstrates, since the design choice here results in large groups of systematically ambiguous examples. In the PROIEL/TOROT system, these examples can be dealt with in two ways: a) by making pragmatic and well-documented decisions about how to group ambiguous examples with unambiguous ones, and b) by adding customised tagging to minimise the efforts of individual researchers (see further section 4.1.1). Both solutions merely improve retrievability and reduce the manual effort of the corpus user. They do not necessarily contribute to the solution of the linguistic problem, which is arguably not the corpus builder's task.

3 Analysing complement clauses

The analysis of complement clauses relies on the interplay between dependency relations, relation labels and part-of-speech tag. Dependency grammar does not take word order into consideration, and constituent structure may only be indirectly derived from combining information from the word-order layer with the previously mentioned information. Thus, while a standard phrase-structure analysis would give both a subjunction such as *jako* and an interrogative such as *kъto* a place in the CP (head and specifier respectively), dependency grammar has no way of indicating this commonality and does not posit movement. However, the fact that both *jako* and *kъto* would be the leftmost element in the complement clause subtree is retrievable from the word-order layer. There is a relation label COMP which subsumes most complement clauses, but which is also used more generally for clausal arguments, such as infinitive "subjects" (1). Note that the label is not used in correlative structures, for which we use an apposition analysis, nor is it used for participle and infinitive structures deemed to have an external subject, for which there is a dedicated label XOBJ (2).

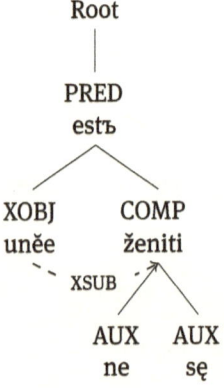

(1) unĕe estъ   ne   ženiti sę
    better be.PRS3SG not marry   REFL
    'it is better not to marry'
    (Mar. Mt. 19.10)[4]

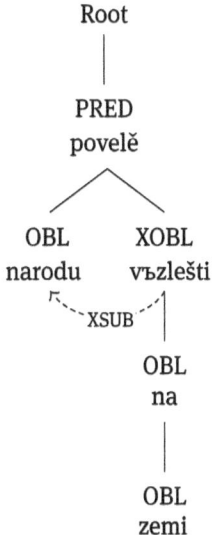

(2) povelĕ   narodu   vъzlešti   na   zemi
    order.AOR3SG people.DAT.SG lie-down   on   ground.LOC.SG
    'he ordered the crowd to recline on the ground'
    (Mar. Mk. 8.6)

As we see in (3) and (4), the head of a complement clause is labeled COMP. In (3), that head, *jako* 'that', is analysed as a subjunction.[5]

---

4 Note that the relation label AUX is used for all particle-like functors, from negation markers, reflexive markers and auxiliary verbs to discourse markers with full sentence scope. The scope is indicated by the attachment site, but since dependency grammar does not operate with VP (SUB and OBJ are both daughters of PRED), VP scope and full sentence scope cannot be differentiated. There is no part-of-speech label "particle", particle-like functors are normally classified as adverbs.

5 Part-of-speech labels are stored in the lemma layer of the annotation.

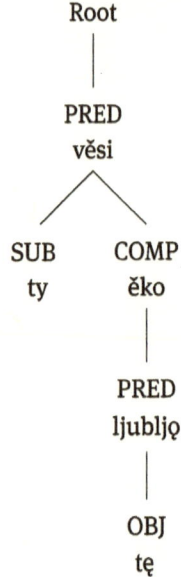

(3) ty   vesi   ěko   ljubljǫ   tę
    you.NOM.SG know.PRS2SG   that love.PRS1SG you.ACC.SG
    'you know that I love you'
    (Mar. John 21.15)

However, in (4), we see that the head of the complement clause is not a subjunction, but a verb. This is the PROIEL-style analysis of indirect questions.

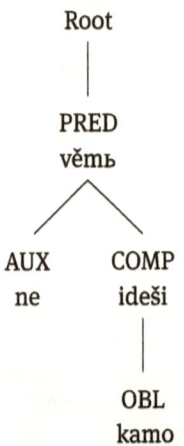

(4) ne   věmь   kamo   ideši
    not   know.PRS1SG whither   go.PRS2SG
    'I do not know where you are going'
    (Mar. Jh. 14.5)

In figure (4) we might like to think of *kamo* 'whither' as the complementiser, as we think of *jako* as the complementiser in (3). However, unlike *jako*, *kamo* is considered to have a syntactic role inside the complement clause – it is the goal argument of *ideši* 'go'.[6] Therefore it is analysed as such: it is taken to be the OBL argument of *ideši*, and as it would be in direct speech, its part of speech is deemed to be interrogative adverb. The role of head of the complement clause is therefore handed over to the main verb of the complement clause, again *ideši*. The analysis follows from the basic principle of dependency grammar, namely that every word has one and only one head. Since *kamo* is clearly the daughter of *ideši*, since it is its goal argument, it cannot also be the daughter of *věmь*. Thus, *věmь* is the only possible choice of head for *ideši*, and the relationship is still one of complementation. Therefore *ideši* itself must bear the COMP label holding for the whole subtree, even though *ideši* is clearly also the PRED of the subordinate clause.

Thus, we see that what part-of-speech label we assign to the complementiser has serious consequences for the rest of the analysis, since it decides what the head of the construction must be. If the complementiser is deemed to be a subjunction, such as *jako*, that subjunction is the head of the complement clause. However, if the complementiser is deemed to be an interrogative pronoun or adverb (such as *kamo*), or a "particle" of some other sort (typically interrogative *li*),[7] then the verb is deemed to be the head of the construction.[8] In the case of complex

---

[6] This is of course the case in any standard phrase-structure analysis as well, but the dual role of the interrogative pronoun would be dealt with by movement from inside the VP to SpecCP.

[7] As pointed out in footnote 4, there is no part-of-speech label "particle", particle-like functors are classified as adverbs.

[8] In practice, then, the vast majority of indirect questions can be retrieved by looking for finite verbs bearing the relation label COMP, conflating the ones with interrogative pronouns or adverbs with the ones with interrogative particles such as *li*. The exception would be indirect questions with non-finite verbs (for example modal infinitives). A query for finite verbs bearing the relation COMP would also capture constructions of the type *i bystъ vъ osmy denь pridǫ obrězatъ otročęte* 'and it happened on the eighth day (that) they came to circumcise the child' (Mar. Lk. 1.59), where *pridǫ* '(they) came' is analysed as a COMP dependent on *bystъ* '(it) happened'. The latter type of construction can be excluded from the query by requiring that the COMP must not be headed by *byti* 'be'.

complementisers such as *jako da*, we also have the problem of deciding which element should have subjunction status and which should be a mere particle.[9]

In the analysis of correlative structures (5), we do not use the COMP relation label at all. Instead, the correlative word, in this case *si* 'this', is taken to be the direct object of the complement-taking predicate *zapovědajǫ* 'command'. The complement clause is then taken to be an apposition (APOS) on the object.

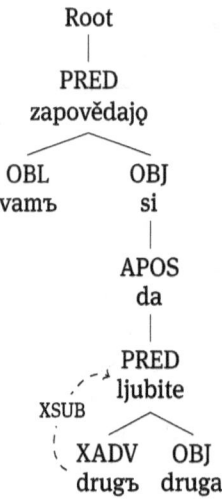

(5)   *si*   *zapovědajǫ*   *vamъ*   *da*   *ljubite*
these.ACC.PL   command.PRS1SG   you.DAT.PL   that   love.PRS2PL
drugъ   *druga*
other.NOM.SG   other.GEN-ACC.SG
'These things I command you, that you love each other'
(Mar. Jh. 15.17)

An obvious limitation of this analysis is that it conflates correlative structures with other appositional structures. This means that some manual sorting may be necessary to isolate only the correlative structures.

When a complement infinitive or participle is deemed to take one of the complement-taking predicate's arguments as its external subject, we use the XOBJ tag, which is generally used for arguments with external subjects (see also ex. 1–2).

---

9 An option would of course be to lump them together as a single multi-word complementiser. However, we have generally been very sparing with this type of solution in the PROIEL/TOROT analyses, preferring to attempt head-dependent analyses of as many phenomena as possible.

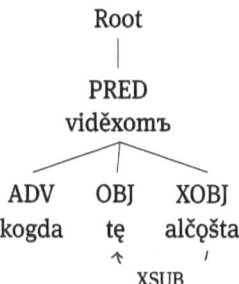

(6) kogda tę viděxomъ alčǫšta
    when you.ACC.SG see.AOR1PL hunger.PRSP.M.GEN-ACC.SG
    'when did we see you hungry (and feed you)?'
    (Mar. Mt. 25.37)

This type of structure is illustrated in (6). We see that *tę* 'you(SG)' is clearly the direct object of *viděxomъ* '(we) saw', but it is also the external subject of the participle *alčǫšta* 'hungering'. The participle is taken to be an argument of *viděxomъ*.

From a retrievability perspective, the analysis conflates complement-like infinitives with a number of other infinitives with external subjects that are not normally deemed to be complements, such as infinitives with phase verbs. To retrieve the complement-like ones, it is necessary to sort infinitive and participle XOBJs by their head verbs: only the ones that are headed by known complement-taking predicates (speech verbs, thought verbs, perception verbs) need to be selected.

4 OCS complementation: A well-behaved system?

How well do the outlined analyses describe the system attested in canonical Old Church Slavonic? To answer this question, I extracted data from the annotated and reviewed part of the PROIEL/TOROT treebanks. The data set comprises the Codex Marianus in its entirety, approximately two thirds of the Codex Suprasliensis, and a small selection of the Codex Zographensis (including all passages that cover lacunae in the Codex Marianus).[10] The dataset contains detailed information on each complement-taking predicate, the complementiser (if any) and the main verb of the dependent clause (including information on the Greek parallel for the Marianus and Zographensis data), as found in the following structures:

---

10 The full dataset and an R analysis script can be accessed at https://doi.org/10.18710/FY7R8N.

- All items with the relation label COMP that were dependent on a noun[11] or verb complement-taking predicate (null verbs and *byti* 'be' were excluded). Total: 1231 occurrences.
- All items with the relation label APOS (apposition) dependent on an item labeled OBJ, if the item labeled APOS was either a subjunction or a verb that was neither a participle nor the head of a relative clause. Total: 34 occurrences, but this also includes several other apposition types.

I will not consider complement infinitives and participles with external subjects (XOBJs) in this chapter.

4.1 Complement clauses with subjunctions

Table 1 gives an overview of the four most common subjunctions[12] found in the dataset, and how they combine with various TAM forms of the dependent-clause verb.[13] In this chapter I will only deal with *jako* 'that' and *da* '(so) that'.

Table 1: Most frequent subjunctions in the OCS dataset by tense/finiteness of the dependent-clause verb.

subjunction	null	present/future	infinitive	*l*-form	other finite
da	1	122	0	16	1
jako	130	344	4	18	135
jakože	1	10	2	0	4
ašte	0	23	0	0	5

4.1.1 *Jako*

Jako '(so) that' is certainly the most frequent subjunction, and the one that is used most freely with a relatively wide range of complement-taking predicates and dependent-clause verb TAM forms (Table 1). However, it is important to be aware

---

[11] This included only 12 occurrences of complement-taking predicate nouns, such as *zapovědь* 'commandment', *pritъča* 'simile', *glagolъ* 'word'.
[12] We also find analyses of *aky, eda* and *ježe* as subjunctions in complement clauses, but they only encompass 15 occurrences altogether, and I will not discuss them further in this chapter.
[13] When the TAM form is listed as "null", it means either that the dependent-clause verb is elliptic (a null copula or other verb ellipsis), or that there is no dependent clause under *jako*. The latter group is further discussed towards the end of section 4.1.1.

that the form *jako* is notoriously multifunctional in OCS: in PROIEL/TOROT there are as many as four lemmas on that form, all linked to a separate syntactic analysis.

There is, naturally, the subjunction 'that, so that, because'. The subjunction occurs both in complement clauses such as (3), and in adverbial clauses such as (7).

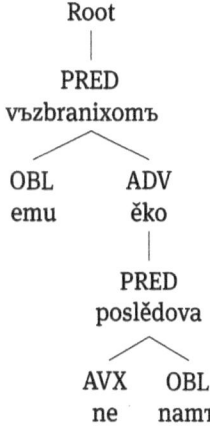

(7) vъzbranixomъ   emu.   ěko   ne   poslědova   namъ
    prevent.AOR1PL he.DAT.SG because   not   follow.AOR3SG we.DAT
    'we tried to prevent him because he was not following us'
    (Mar. Mk. 9.38)

However, there is also a relative adverb (8) and two separate "adverb" lemmas: one for the comparison word usages of *jako* (9), and one for the introductory discourse particle usage 'for', as illustrated in (10).

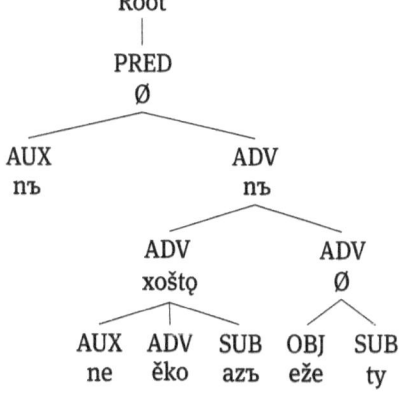

(8) nъ   ne   ěko   azъ   xoštǫ.   nъ   eže   ty.
    but   not   as   I   want.PRS1SG   but   which.N.ACC.SG   you.NOM
    'Yet not what I will, but what you will.'
    (Zogr. Mk. 14.36)

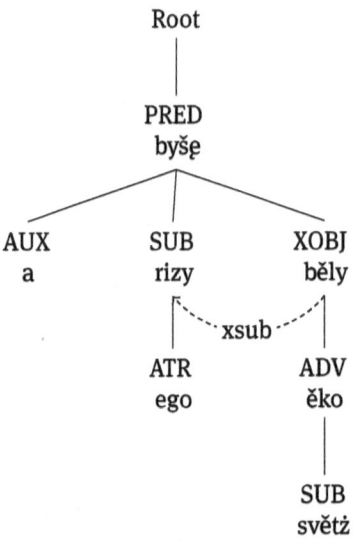

(9) a   rizy   ego   byšę   běly   ěko
    and   robes.NOM.PL   he.GEN.SG   be.AOR3PL   white.F.NOM.PL as
    světъ.
    light.NOM.SG
    'and his clothes became white as light'
    (Mar. Mt. 17.2)

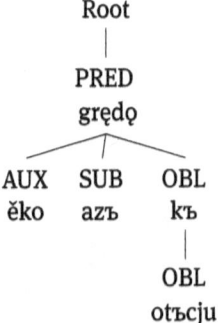

(10) ěko   azъ   kъ   otъcju   grędǫ.
     for   I.NOM to   father.DAT.SG go.PRS1SG
     '(He will do even greater things than these,) because I am going to the Father.'
     (Mar. Jh. 14.12)

When we look at the syntactic analyses, we see that in (3), *jako* is the head of a complement clause, in (7) it is the head of an adverbial clause, in (8) it is an adverbial inside a relative clause, in (9) it is analysed as the head of an abbreviated comparison construction, and in (10) it is taken to be a discourse particle with scope over the whole sentence, which is indicated by making it an auxiliary dependent on the main clause verb.[14] As different as these syntactic trees may look, it is not difficult to see *semantic* similarities between the four ostensibly separate lemmas. The difference in the trees is, however, the consequence of a highly syntactic approach to part-of-speech assignment.

The comparison word adverb lemma in (9) is doing much the same job as the relative adverb lemma in (8). Both are examples of comparison constructions. In (8), the comparison is not limited to a single item: Both the persons wanting something (Jesus, God) and what they want are compared. It is therefore reasonable to analyse the construction as a relative clause with an elided main verb, and *jako* is thus taken to be a relative adverb. In (9), on the other hand, the comparison is limited to a single item: *rizy* 'clothes' are compared to *světъ* 'light'. It is common to analyse such constructions, too, as elliptic, positing an underlying 'His clothes were white as light (is white)', since the compared element is interpreted and receives case according to its syntactic role in that elliptic sentence. However, this is not the only option. In PROIEL and TOROT we have opted for an abbreviated, non-elliptic analysis where the comparison element is a direct dependent of the comparison word *jako*, which may be more realistic. The price to pay for this analysis is, however, that we must posit both a relative adverb *jako* for structures such as (8), and a comparison adverb *jako* for structures such as (9). It is, perhaps, unlikely that the original language users perceived these as two separate items. However, it is not unlikely that there is a real difference between structure (8) and structure (9) in the language user's mind – abbreviated comparison constructions of this type are common cross-linguistically, and it is not clear that they are elliptic (see e.g. Lechner 2004 for extensive discussion). The part-of-speech distinction is thus primarily a device to allow the economic (and

---

14 See also footnote 4 on this type of analysis. As pointed out there, dependency grammar cannot distinguish between VP scope and full sentence scope, since it has no direct representation of phrases.

possibly realistic) analysis in (9) and thus ultimately improve retrievability in the treebank.

It also seems unlikely that the discourse particle ("adverb") *jako* in (10) is really separate from the subjunction *jako*, especially in the meaning 'since, because', as in (7). Rather, the difference appears to be that the discourse particle occurrences just do not have a likely candidate for a main verb in their vicinity.

Nonetheless, it is worth mentioning that this does not affect the *jako* complement clauses. None of the other *jako* lemmas occur with complement-taking predicates. Thus, the analysis makes the *jako* complement clauses very easily retrievable.

Thus, despite the multifunctionality of *jako*, there are many examples where it looks like a straightforward complementiser, apparently heading complement clauses that serve as core arguments of a typical complement-taking predicate, such as *viděti* 'see', *slyšati* 'hear', *věděti* 'know', *věrovati* 'believe' and *glagolati, rešti* 'say, tell' (cf. Dixon 2006). In 511 occurrences out of 631 in the dataset, the dependent clause may be interpreted as indirect speech or thought. These dependent clauses are not marked by changes in word order and mostly not in tense, as they are in English, but when necessary, pronouns and person reference are converted to fit the person reference of the complement-taking predicate's subject (typically from first person to third person, as in (12)). These conversions serve as evidence that OCS had an indirect-speech construction, which is not the case in all languages (cf. Dixon 2006:10, 28).

However, there is a complication in the form of "mixed speech" constructions (cf. the literature on *jako recitativum*, e.g. Collins 1996). Sometimes an apparently complement-taking verb has a dependent *jako*, which is then followed by something that must be considered *direct* speech, since pronouns and person agreement of the ostensible dependent-clause verb are retained in the form they would have in direct speech. In (11ab), for instance, *vasъ* 'you(PL)' has not been converted into *ixъ* 'them'. In PROIEL/TOROT we analyse these structures as two independent sentences, as demonstrated in (11a)[15] and (11b). We maintain the analysis of *jako* as a subjunction and a COMP dependent on the presumed complement-taking predicate, but treat the potential dependent verb and its dependents as a separate main clause. This is also the way we treat regular direct speech.

---

15 Note that introductory *i* 'and' is also treated as an auxiliary, on a par with discourse particles with scope over the full sentence. It is nonetheless assigned the conjunction part-of-speech label.

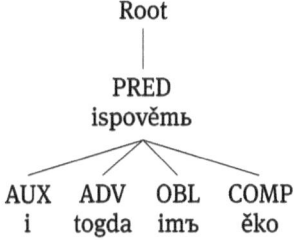

(11a) i   togda ispověmь   imъ.   ěko
       and   then   declare.PRS1SG they.DAT that

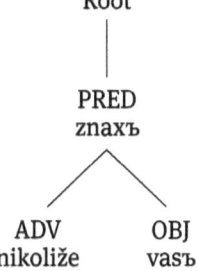

(11b) nikoliže znaxъ   vasъ
       never   know.AOR1SG   you.GEN.PL
       kai tote homologēsō autois hoti oudepote egnōn humas
       'And then will I declare to them, "I never knew you"'
       (Mar. Mt. 7.23)

These structures are frequent, both in the OCS dataset and in the parallel Greek.

Table 2: Presence and absence of mixed speech in OCS and Greek jako correspondences.

	Mixed speech in Greek	No mixed speech in Greek
Mixed speech in OCS	54	29
No mixed speech in OCS	7	387

There are 122 OCS mixed-speech occurrences in the dataset. 83 of these occurrences are in the Codex Marianus, which allows us to look at the Greek parallel

(Table 2).¹⁶ 74 of them have a Greek item corresponding directly to the OCS subjunction (in all cases this is the subjunction *hoti* 'that'), and out of these, 54 are examples of mixed speech in the Greek source text as well. However, 29 instances of mixed speech in the OCS text have no mixed-speech correspondence in the Greek. 20 of them are analysed as having plain complement clauses, and in the remaining 9 cases, the Greek text has direct speech instead of a complement clause or mixed speech.¹⁷ Among the OCS subjunction occurrences there are also seven mismatches of the opposite kind, i.e. Greek has a mixed-speech analysis, whereas OCS does not. It therefore seems likely that the mixed speech structures may have been a feature of both OCS and Greek. If we are to see the structure as an argument against a subjunction analysis of OCS *jako*, then it is also an argument against a subjunction analysis of Greek *hoti* 'that'.

As I have presented the data so far, the mixed-speech occurrences still appear to be in a clear minority (122 out of 631 *jako* subjunction occurrences). However, this is not as clear-cut as it may seem. An examination of all the *jako* complement clauses with dependent verbs in the third person (which are thus likely to have been converted) shows that only 7% of the examples (26 out of 370) have explicit agreement and/or pronoun conversions.¹⁸ An example is seen in (12), where the third-person *emu* 'him' reflects what must have been a first-person pronoun in direct speech. The rest of the examples – the vast majority – have no observable contrast: direct and indirect speech would have the same form, as in (13). This state of affairs has led several scholars to claim that OCS did not have an indirect speech construction at all (e.g. Xaburgaev 1974: 426).

(12) otъ tolě načętъ sъkazati učenikomъ svoimъ
from then begin.AOR.3SG show disciple.DAT.PL his.M.DAT.PL
ěko podobaatъ emu iti vъ ierusalimъ
that be-suitable.PRS.3SG he.DAT go to Jerusalem.ACC
'From that time Jesus began to show his disciples that he must go to Jerusalem'
(Mar. Mt. 16.21)

---

16 The remaining 39 occurrences are from the Codex Suprasliensis, which does not have an aligned Greek text in TOROT. There is a parallel Greek text in Zaimov and Capaldo 1982–83, but this is an adapted composite of multiple Greek texts which cannot reliably be used for syntactic studies.
17 The Greek text used in PROIEL is Tischendorf (1869–1872). It should be noted that in five of these cases, several other Greek New Testament manuscript variants, including the Byzantine Majority Text, also had mixed speech, while in four of the cases no major Greek text variant had mixed speech.
18 The tagged data subset can be found at https://doi.org/10.18710/FY7R8N.

(13) *sluxъ*   *bystъ*   *ěko* *vъ* *domu*   *estъ*
     rumour.NOM.SG be.AOR.3SG   that   in   house.LOC.SG be.PRS3SG
     'there was a rumour that he was in the house'
     (Mar. Mk. 2.1)

We thus have an interesting situation where neither a subjunction/complementiser analysis nor a quotative particle analysis of OCS *jako* is entirely satisfactory. There are groups of examples clearly in favour of each of the analyses. The examples with pronoun and person agreement conversion are evidence that there is an indirect speech construction that appears to be headed by *jako*, which would then be a subjunction. The "mixed speech" examples, on the other hand, is evidence that *jako* can be used to introduce *direct* speech and should perhaps be taken to be a quotative particle rather than a subjunction.[19] It is not obvious what to do with the large number of ambiguous examples, where either interpretation is possible.

In the PROIEL/TOROT analysis we have chosen to collapse them with unambiguous complement clause examples. We have also chosen to do without a quotative particle lemma, analysing even the mixed-speech occurrences of *jako* as subjunctions and COMP dependents of the complement-taking predicate. Given the standard analyses of other early attestations of Indo-European languages, this is not a controversial choice: these languages generally have complementising subjunctions and indirect-speech constructions. We believe that this is also an economic solution that makes retrieval of relevant examples as easy as possible. In the large group of ambiguous examples, we are able to signal that the putative *jako* complement clause is potentially a core argument of the complement-taking predicate. By taking *jako* in mixed-speech constructions as a COMP subjunction, we signal the close syntactic relationship between the three groups of examples. The best way of improving retrievability would be to add tags indicating person-reference conversion in COMP clauses in PROIEL/TOROT's customisable layer for such tags. In this way, all three types of examples could be distinguished perfectly without extra work for the analyst.

4.1.2 Da

The second most frequent subjunction in the dataset is *da* 'so that'. The subjunction has a clear purpose meaning, and the dependent-clause verb is restricted to the

---

[19] It is also possible to argue that the lack of conversion is not really an argument against subjunction status for *jako*, as many languages seem to have subjunctions that freely allow non-converted direct speech as well as converted indirect speech after subjunctions, for discussion see Aikhenvald (2004). However, such an approach could easily lead to circularity and will not be pursued here.

present indicative (14) and the conditional (i.e. *l*-form with *byti* auxiliary in the subjunctive), as seen in (15).[20] The present indicative is much more common – the conditional is only found in 16 out of 142 occurrences.

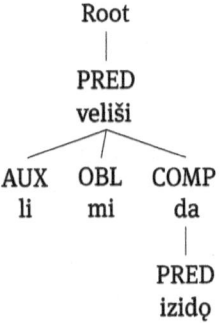

(14) veliši   li   mi   da   izidǫ
     order.PRS2SG PTC   I.DAT   that   out-go.PRS1SG
     'are you ordering me to go out?'
     (Supr. 48)

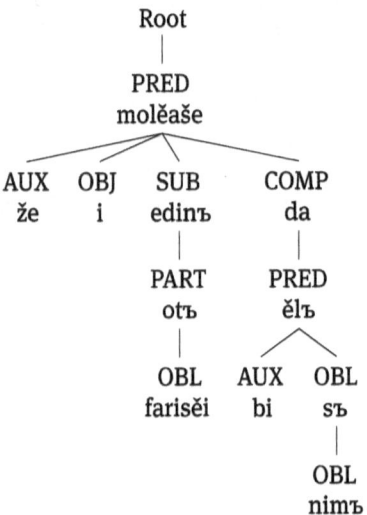

---

[20] Note that a few of them have an auxiliary that is technically in the aorist (*by* rather than *bi*), but the function is solidly conditional.

(15) *molěaše   že   i   edinъ   otъ*
    beg.IMPERF3SG PTC he.ACC one.NOM.SG of
    fariseǐ   da   bi   ělъ   sъ   nimъ
    Pharisee.GEN.PL that be.SBJV2SG eat.L-FORM.M.SG with he.INST
    'one of the Pharisees begged him to eat with him'
    (Mar. Lk. 7.36)

The complement-taking predicates involved overwhelmingly entail wishes and commands, the most common are *moliti* 'pray, beg' (47 out of 142 occurrences), *xotěti* 'want' (28 occurrences), *zaprětiti* 'berate, forbid' (8 occurrences) and *rešti* 'say' (8 occurrences). The latter always means 'tell someone to do something' in these constructions.

Like *jako*, *da* is also a multifunctional item that may occur with a very similar meaning even when there is no complement-taking predicate around: it regularly serves as a marker of a third-person 'imperative' (16).

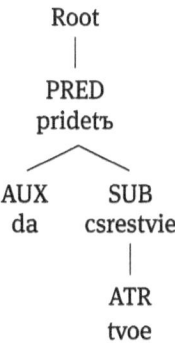

(16) *da   pridetъ   csrestvie   tvoe*
    that come.PRS1SG   kingdom.NOM.SG   your.M.NOM.SG
    'Your kingdom come'
    (Mar. Mt. 6.10)

In PROIEL/TOROT *da* in such constructions is classified as an adverb, which is the part-of-speech assignment we currently use for all types of indeclinable particle-like words, as well as for more conventional adverbs.[21] This part-of-speech assignment is combined with the regular syntactic analysis for all "particles" – it is taken to be an auxiliary dependent on the main verb. This analysis has the advan-

---

21 See also footnote 4.

tage of having a main verb – if we had analysed it as a subjunction, we would have had to posit an elliptic construction with an empty head verb node. The obvious disadvantage, however, is that an item that has largely the same function in (15) and (16) is analysed as two separate lemmas with separate parts of speech.

A similar challenge to the PROIEL/TOROT analysis practice is the fact that *jako* and *da* sometimes cooccur, as in (17).

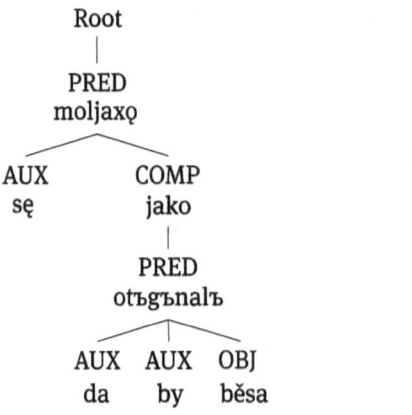

(17)   moljaxǫ   sę   jako   da   by   šelъ
       beg.IMPERF3PL   REFL   that   that   be.SBJV3SG   come.L-FORM.M.SG
       i   otъgnalъ [. . .]   běsa
       and   drive-out.L-PART   demon.GEN-ACC.SG
       'they begged that he should come and drive away (that devious) demon'
       (Supr 3)

In our analysis, *jako* is taken to be the subjunction and *da* a particle, but this decision is largely arbitrary. We see that the dependent-clause verb behaves as it frequently would with the *da* subjunction: it is in the conditional. We also see that the complement-taking verb is *moliti* 'pray, beg', which is by far the most common one with the *da* occurrences deemed to be subjunctions. Conversely, this is the only example in the data set where *moliti* takes a *jako* clause. Thus, there are arguments in favour of classifying the example as a *da* subjunction example instead. The question, then, would be what to do with *jako*. Looking back at section 4.1.1, one option would clearly be to take the *jako da* constructions as evidence in favour of analysing *jako* as a quotative particle.

4.2 Complement clauses without subjunctions

When there is no apparent subjunction, the complement clause is deemed to be headed by the dependent-clause verb. This is the case in various types of infinitive constructions and in indirect questions. In this chapter I will deal only with indirect questions.

A problem with later stages of Slavonic is that wh-words such as *kъto* 'who', *čьto* 'what' and *kako* 'how' take on new syntactic behaviour – they are reanalysed as relative pronouns, relative adverbs and subjunctions. In the current OCS dataset there is no evidence that they can ever be subjunctions – they always have a role in the subordinate clause. In (18), for example, *čьto* 'what' is the direct object of *gl(agole)ši*.

(18) ne   věmь   čьto   glši
     not   know.PRS1SG what.ACC.SG say.PRS2SG
     'I do not know what you are saying'
     (Mar. Mt. 26.70)

There is only marginal evidence suggesting that they can be relative pronouns or relative adverbs. It is clear, however, that they can be indefinite pronouns. This is demonstrated in (19), where *kъto* is an indefinite pronoun subject within a complement clause headed by *da*, and does not signal subordination.

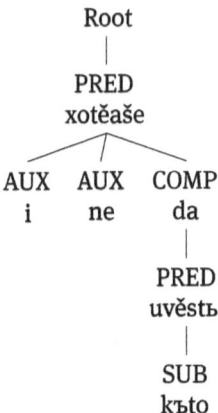

(19) i   ne   xotěaše   da   kъto   uvěstь
    and not   want.IMPERF3SG that anyone.NOM.SG   know.PRS3SG
    'and he did not want anyone to know'
    (Mar. Mk. 9.30)

Such indefinite pronouns are typically found in *ašte* 'if' and *da* 'so that' clauses. This means that dependent clauses with a wh-word as subordination marker are safely analysed as indirect questions (with very few exceptions). In the further history of Slavonic, however, this situation changes, and the complications that arise are discussed in section 5, with diachronic examples from East Slavonic.

4.3 Analysis, fit and facts

From an annotation perspective, the OCS complementation data fit neatly into the annotation scheme. It is easy for the annotators to make the decisions – the construction types are rarely confused. It is also easy to retrieve the various clause types in sensible groupings. However, as we have seen, this does not mean that the analyses are linguistically ideal. Are *jako* and *da* really subjunctions in complement clauses? Are some of the indirect questions really better understood as something else?

Another question that should be raised is whether (some of) the neatness comes from Greek. As Tables 3 and 4 show, OCS faithfully follows Greek in the choice of head part of speech in complement clauses. If Greek has a subjunction, so does OCS, if Greek has a verbal head, so does OCS. Table 4 also shows us that the OCS and Greek have standard subjunction correspondences: In the aligned

Table 3: Greek vs. OCS head part of speech in complement clauses (where the OCS subjunction has token alignment).

	Greek adverb	Greek interrogative adverb	Greek subjunction	Greek verb
OCS subjunction	1	2	465	0
OCS verb	0	0	0	148

Table 4: Most common Greek-OCS subjunction correspondences (where the OCS subjunction has a subjunction token alignment).

	ašte	da	jako
ei	15	0	0
hina	0	63	0
hopōs	0	6	0
hoti	0	0	382

part of the dataset, *jako* always translates *hoti*, *ašte* always translates *ei*, and *da* almost always translates *hina*. There is thus a chance that the underlying language system was more complex than the extant translated data suggest – both the translations in themselves and the annotated PROIEL/TOROT data.

5 Old Russian complementation: A system in flux

While OCS complement clauses could be annotated in a (perhaps deceptively) clean-cut and easily retrievable way, Old East Slavonic and Middle Russian challenge the annotation scheme in a much more serious way. I will exemplify these problems by looking briefly at the history of *čьto* 'what' in Russian, which is a good example of the types of reanalyses of wh-words that have occurred across Slavonic after the Common Slavonic era. The OCS dataset presented us with a situation where *čьto* could be analysed as *either* an interrogative pronoun *or* an indefinite pronoun. Of these two lemmas, only the former can signal subordination, and only in indirect questions, such as in (20). The latter can occur in subordinate clauses too, but it does not signal subordination. It typically occurs in conditional clauses such as (21), where the subordination is signalled by the subjunction *ašte*.

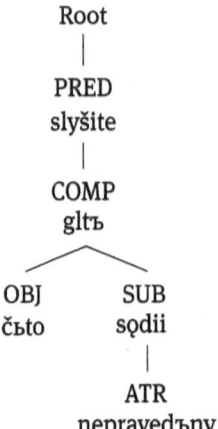

(20) slyšite čьto sǫdii nepravedъny gltъ
hear.IMP2PL what judge.NOM.SG unjust.M.NOM.SG say.PRES3SG
'Hear what the unjust judge says'
(Mar. Lk 18.6)

(21) i ašte esmъ kogo čimь
and if be.PRES1SG someone.GEN-ACC.SG something.INST.SG
obidělъ vъzvraštǫ četvricejǫ
offend.L-FORM.M.SG return.PRS1SG fourfold
'and if I have cheated someone of something, I will return it fourfold'
(Mar. Lk 19.8)

In Old East Slavonic and especially Middle Russian, however, it is no longer possible to analyse all subordinate clauses containing *čьto* as indirect questions. Even in the very earliest texts, there are examples where *čьto* must be considered a relative pronoun, or even a subjunction in a complement clause. In (22), from *Russkaja pravda*, one of the earliest Old East Slavonic sources, it is clear that *čьto* is a relative pronoun in a relative clause with an explicit nominal head (*těm*).

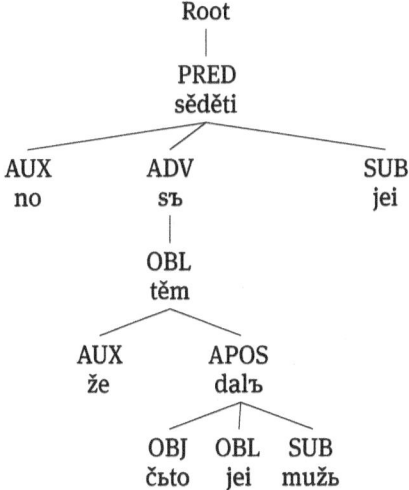

(22) no   čьto   jei   dalъ   mužь.
     but   what.ACC.SG she.DAT   give.l-form.M.SG   husband.NOM.SG
     s   těm   že   jei   sěděti
     with   that.INST.SG PTC   she.DAT   sit.INF
     'but what her husband gave her, that she can keep'
     (Russkaja pravda 102)

In (23), from late Middle Russian, we must consider *čьto* to be a subjunction, since it clearly has no syntactic role in the complement clause.

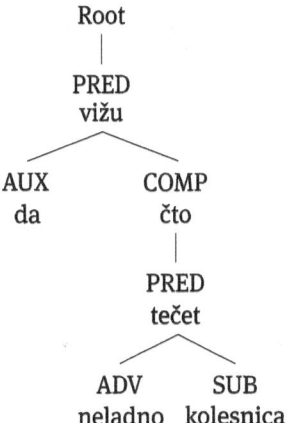

(23) *da   vižu   čto   neladno   kolesnica   tečetъ*
      and see.PRS1SG   that not-right wagon.NOM.SG   run.PRS3SG
      'and I see that the wagon is not running correctly'
      (Avvakum 26)

As soon as the data force us to allow these two types of analyses, however, many examples become ambiguous. It is not always clear whether something is a headless relative clause argument or an indirect question complement clause, nor is it always clear whether *čьto* has a syntactic role in the subordinate clause.[22] Since the PROIEL/TOROT annotation scheme requires the annotator to choose a single analysis in such situations, we made the decision to analyse all unclear examples as relative clauses. In such a scenario, all dependent clauses containing *čьto* are still taken as complement clauses if they are dependent on speech, thought or emotion verbs (or nouns). Within this group, if *čьto* clearly has no syntactic role in the subordinate clause, it is analysed as a subjunction, otherwise the clause is analysed as an indirect question. Outside this group, dependent clauses containing *čьto* are taken to be relative clauses if there is no other signal of subordination. In these cases, *čьto* is lemmatised as a relative pronoun, and the dependent clause is given the relevant syntactic relation label.

Thus, we are left with two groups of clear examples and one group of both clear and ambiguous examples that must be sifted through manually by interested researchers. There is also the possibility to ease the access to the group of potentially ambiguous examples by tagging the (un)ambiguous relative clauses as such in the customisable annotation layer.

6 Conclusions

This chapter highlights some of the advantages and problems with applying the PROIEL/TOROT annotation scheme to complementation structures in various stages of Slavonic. The annotation brings obvious advantages, in that the tagged data makes it easy to retrieve all potential complement clauses in OCS, Old East Slavonic and Middle Russian, and thus relieves the interested scholar of a lot of manual work. The analyses are in keeping with standard analyses of other early attestations of Indo-European languages, and have, at least for OCS, been easy to

---

22 An additional confounding factor is that conditional clauses, a common environment for the *indefinite* pronoun *čьto*, often lack subordinators in Middle Russian texts, which can cause even more ambiguities.

apply to the material. However, the scholar may not use the data without considering the inherent problems. Some problems are synchronic – an analysis choice may make the data look somewhat neater than they really are. The diachronic problems are more serious: Especially in cases of reanalysis, where large groups of examples may have ambiguous part-of-speech assignment and/or dependency attachment site, a scheme such as the PROIEL/TOROT one, where only one analysis can be assigned to each sentence, forces the analyst to assign non-optimal analyses to groups of ambiguous examples, leaving it up to interested scholars to sift through them. If possible, a conservative analysis should be used across a diachronic treebank, in the way the indirect question analysis has been in the PROIEL/TOROT treebanks. If that is not possible, it is necessary to make principled decisions about how to categorise ambiguous cases, and one may consider to add custom tags to sift ambiguous from unambiguous examples within a uniform group of analyses.

The reader should keep in mind that corpus annotation is very much a practical and descriptive endeavour. Retrievability should always be the first priority. Corpus analysis does not so much need to be "true" as consistent, well-documented and retrievable. It is, however, very important that it is detailed, especially in historical linguistics, where the data is sparse and therefore precious. One way of adding extra detail is to enrich the data with extra annotation layers: for instance with tags for semantics, and even for ambiguity.

References

Aikhenvald, Alexandra Y. 2008. Semi-direct speech. Manambu and beyond. *Language Sciences* 30. 383–422.
Collins, Daniel. 1996. The pragmatics of indirect speech in Old Church Slavonic and other early Slavic writings. In Adriaan A. Barentsen, B. M. Groen, Jos Schaeken & R. Sprenger (eds.), *Studies in South Slavic and Balkan Linguistics*, 21–86. Amsterdam: Rodopi.
Dixon, R. M. W. 2006. Complement clauses and complementation strategies in typological perspective. In R. M. W. Dixon & Alexandra Y. Aikhenvald (eds.), *Complementation. A Cross-Linguistic Typology*, 1–48. Oxford: Oxford University Press.
Eckhoff, Hanne Martine, Kristin Bech, Gerlof Bouma, Kristine Eide, Dag Haug, Odd Einar Haugen & Marius Jøhndal. 2018. The PROIEL treebank family: a standard for early attestations of Indo-European languages. *Linguistic Resources and Evaluation* 52 (1). 29–65.
Eckhoff, Hanne & Aleksandrs Berdičevskis. 2015. Linguistics vs. digital editions: The Tromsø Old Russian and OCS Treebank. *Scripta & e-Scripta* 14–15. 9–25.
Haug, Dag T. T. & Marius L. Jøhndal. 2008. Creating a Parallel Treebank of the Old Indo-European Bible Translations. In Caroline Sporleder and Kiril Ribarov (eds.). *Proceedings of the Second Workshop on Language Technology for Cultural Heritage Data* (LaTeCH 2008), 27–34.

Lechner, Winfried. 2004. *Ellipsis in Comparatives*. Berlin & New York: De Gruyter Mouton.
von Tischendorf, Constantin. 1869–1872. *Novum Testamentum Graece*. Leipzig: Hinrich.
Zaimov, Jordan and Mario Capaldo. 1982–1983. *Suprasŭlski ili Retkov sbornik*. [Codex Suprasliensis or the Codex of Retko.] Sofia: Bulgarian Academy of Sciences Press.
Xaburgaev, Georgij A. 1974. *Staroslavjanskij jazyk*. [Old Church Slavonic.] Moscow: Prosveščenie.

Jasmina Grković-Major
The development of emotion predicate complements in Serbian

Abstract: The evolution of complement clauses with emotion predicates (EPs) in the history of Serbian was shaped by both language-internal and contact-induced factors. In the process of creating hypotactic structures, motivated by the rise of transitivity and the ascent of configurationality as its manifestation, Serbian went through a phase of syntactic instability, being a fruitful ground for areal influences. Complementation strategies were initially governed by the semantics of EPs. Complements of non-factive EPs had an irrealis modality: (a) infinitive (coreferential agents) and (b) *da*-clauses (non-coreferential agents), which evolved from juxtaposed optative *da*-sentences. After *da*-complements were established in (b), they spread to the structures with coreferential agents (a). Factive EPs had several complementation strategies in Old Serbian: *jer(e)*-, *zato što*-> *zašto*-> *što*- and *gd(j)e*-clauses. Being in the state of flux, the system was exposed to two waves of innovation. Southern and southeastern dialects became part of the *Balkan Sprachbund* convergence area, retaining a split clausal complementation system (factive: non-factive) and promoting *gde* as the factive complementizer. The majority of dialects were subjected to the innovation wave coming from the west and southwest, as the result of Slavic-Romance language contacts. First *što*-clauses got narrowed to EPs, becoming a conjunction-factive complementizer, in opposition to the non-factive *da*-complementizer. Afterwards, factive *da*-complements, already established with other semantic classes of CTPs, entered non-factive EP constructions, advancing gradually at the expense of the *što*-clauses. This on-going change is a further step in generalizing factive *da*-complements.

Keywords: historical linguistics, complementation, emotion predicates, Serbian, što-clauses, da-clauses

---

Acknowledgements: This research was conducted within the project The History of the Serbian Language (N° 178001) financed by the Ministry of Education, Science and Technological Development of the Republic of Serbia.

Jasmina Grković-Major, Department of Serbian Language and Linguistics, Faculty of Philosophy, University of Novi Sad, Dr Zorana Đinđića 2, 21000 Novi Sad, Serbia, e-mail: jgrkovicns@gmail.com

1 Introduction

Contemporary complementation systems in the Indo-European languages are the result of a long-lasting development. Proto-Indo-European was a non-nominative language type, characterized by semantic alignment.[1] Apposition and agreement were the basic principles of sentence structuring, sentence elements being highly autonomous: a word was self-sufficient to indicate its role and there was no government of one word by another (Meillet 1908: 320–342). Since they had no transitivity feature, verbs had "absolute" meanings (Desnickaja 1984: 148) and only semantic valence.[2] Syntax was paratactic and semantic subordination was expressed by various nominal(-verbal) forms (double case constructions, compounds, verbal nouns, participles, absolute constructions, etc.) or by juxtaposition of simple sentences in which semantic subordination was contextually induced (cf. Lehmann 1980: 117–124).[3]

The gradual rise of transitivity in the proto-language and the daughter languages, among them Slavic, led to the creation of the nominative, syntactically aligned, configurational systems, where "semantic constituency turned into syntactic constituency" (Luraghi 2010: 226). This typological change comprised the dissolution of the old system of paratactic semantic subordination and the creation of complex sentences (Bednarczuk 1971: 160).

Development of syntactic alignment included the evolution of grammatical subject and object. As shown in Grković-Major (2010: 65–68), the pace of grammaticalization of the accusative object in Slavic has been proportional to the level of the predicate's semantic transitivity. The process first encompassed constructions with prototypical transitive, agentive verbs, such as causatives, but was much slower with experiencer predicates, especially emotion predicates (EPs). Some of them became reflexives already in Proto-Slavic (e.g.*bojati sę 'be afraid, fear'), keeping the genitive object,[4] and could have only causal NP adjuncts. This

---

[1] On semantic alignment generally see Donohue (2008: 24).
[2] *Semantic valence* refers to the number of participants in the event expressed by a verb, while *syntactic* (grammatical) *valence* refers to a number of arguments in a clause (Payne 2007: 169–170).
[3] In Hittite, for example, the oldest attested Indo-European language, "verbs which typically take Complement clauses in other languages are systematically found in paratactic constructions" (Luraghi 1990: 76).
[4] While the genitive object with this verb is still the only possibility in some Slavic languages, like Serbian, in some languages we see the recent rise of the accusative object as well. As Kuznetsova and Nesset (2015: 279–280) argue "in contemporary standard Russian the accusative is also used", although still rare, with 1% of such examples in their main corpus and 7% in the newspaper corpus (p. 266).

led us to the question whether the same force governed the establishment of complement clauses – objects within complex sentences. Therefore, we have been studying the rise of clausal complementation with different predicate classes (Grković-Major 2018a, 2018b). The aim of this paper is to analyze the rise of EP complements. EPs are of special interest in this respect since, as experiencer verbs, they have low transivity parameters (cf. Hopper and Thompson 1980: 252) and their "objects" have a specific semantic status.

Emotions are experiences or states evoked by different stimuli: by the perception of significant events or situations in the real world, present and past, or by those in our imagination (Milivojević 2014: 17–57).[5] They "usually have a clear relation to whatever elicited them" (MIT: 273), and are either "backward-looking" or "forward-looking", the first being "directed toward things, persons, or state of affairs that exist presently or have existed in the past", the latter are "directed toward future possibilities" (Gordon 1987: 25). Linguistically, this can be formalized in factive vs. non-factive complementation strategies with EPs in syntactically aligned languages. Factive complements with EPs represent an intersection of theme and cause. In *I am sorry that he did not come*, the complement denotes at the same time what my sorrow is about and what caused it. This is substantiated by the possibility to use different syntactic patterns, a complement or an adverbial clause: *I am sorry that he did not come* vs. *I am sorry because he did not come*. Non-factive EP complements are, on the other hand, future-oriented and represent an intersection of theme and goal: in *I hope that she will come* the complement expresses what my hope is about and to what possibility it is directed. This "double character" of EP complements gives them a special place in comparison to the constructions with other experiencer CTPs (perception and cognition).

The factivity status of EPs and their complements are interdependent. For example, Serbian *kajati se* 'feel sorry for something bad one did in the past (regret)' can only have a factive complement, while non-factive *želeti* 'wish' only a non-factive one. There is also a class of so-called ambiguous EPs (cf. Kiparsky and Kiparsky 1971: 360–361), which take both kinds of complements, e.g. Serbian *stideti se*: a) 'be ashamed (because of something)', factive and b) 'hesitate to do something because of the feeling of insecurity', non-factive. In such cases the complement type resolves EP polysemy.

Our corpus consists of texts written in vernaculars, not influenced by the Church Slavonic tradition, and it encompasses documents of different genres, from 12th century up to nowadays: charters, letters, legal codes, chronicles, novels etc. In order to capture the contemporary diatopic variation, we used data from

---

[5] On different theories about emotions see SEPh.

various dialectological and dialectographical studies (see Sources). No statistics of the phenomena investigated will be presented since the number of examples is not statistically significant. Namely, EPs are rare in the historical corpus, due to both linguistic and extralinguistic factors: a) EPs usually have NP complements, and b) the corpus of medieval documents consists predominantly of business and legal documents, a genre which does not favor emotional expressions.

Having in mind the gradual rise of hypotactic from paratactic structures we will use the terms C1 (Core1) and C2 (Core2), in accordance with the explanation given in Wiemer (this volume). This is additionally important when studying EPs, because of the semantic status of their objects and the possible developmental cline adjunct > argument, in order to not imply any syntactic relationship.

2 Non-factive complements

In case of non-factive EPs in C1, Old Serbian had two strategies, depending on whether the agents in C1 and C2 were coreferential or not, in accordance with the iconic principle that the stronger semantic integration of two clauses implies their stronger syntactic integration (Haiman 1983: 799).

2.1 Infinitival clauses

In cases of coreferential agents, EPs take the infinitive complement from the earliest documents:

(1) ako   hokete   vi   mьně   moje   ludi
     if   want[IPFV].PRS.2PL   you   I.DAT   my   people.ACC
     vratiti
     give.back[PFV].INF
     'if you want to give me back my people'
     (1252–54, PP 25[6])

Being the dative of a verbal noun in *-ti* by origin, the infinitive was marked as non-factive by its allative meaning. Since allative denotes a notion toward which an action or state is directed, when metaphorically transfered into the tempo-

---

[6] The number of the charter in the edition. All the examples are transliterated following the scientific ISO 9 transliteration norm.

ral domain it expresses posteriority in relation to the moment of speech, which explains its *irrealis* semantics.[7] Thanks to this, the Slavic infinitive cannot be used as a complement of perception verbs.[8]

In consonance with their semantic valence, non-factive, future-oriented EPs were constructed with semantically compatible datives in Proto-Slavic, including the verbal noun which later gave the infinitive. This is corroborated by the archaic structures with nominal dative complements of desiderative verbs, still found in Old Serbian:

(2) *jerъ   mi   **zlěmъ   dinaremъ**[9]   ne   htě*
    because I.DAT   bad.DAT.PL   dinar.DAT.PL   NEG   want[IPFV].PRS.3PL
    grъci
    grъci
    'Because the Greeks do not want bad dinars from me.'
    (1320, PP 43)

After the verbal noun in *-ti* was petrified and grammaticalized into the infinitive in Proto-Slavic, becoming a part of the verbal system, it was generalized as a non-factive complement, as witnessed by the following Old Serbian example with the polysemous verb *stideti se* a.'be ashamed (because of something)', b. 'be ashamed (to do something)', where it induces the non-factive reading of the predicate:

(3) *stydekje se*   *kъ   velikosti   vi*
    be.ashamed[IPFV].PRS.PTCP + REFL   to   Greateness.DAT.SG   you.DAT
    ***poslati**   je*
    send[PFV].INF   they.ACC.PL
    'being ashamed to send them to your Grateness'
    (1422, PP 525)

Exceptionally, and only in formulaic expressions (uttered by a ruler, in the sanction of charters), we find constructions with a non-agreeing participle complement. In such cases, the active present participle is with perfective stems:

---

[7] On universal connection between posteriority/futurity and modality see Lyons (1968: 310).
[8] Only rare cases are documented, as a result of language-contact situation (Grković-Major 2018a: 353).
[9] In the syntactically aligned contemporary Serbian, we have the grammaticalized accusative object instead: *Jer Grci neće **loš novac** od mene*.

(4) ě   sьmь   radъ   pravdu   **učine**
    I   AUX.1SG   willing justice.ACC execute[PFV].PRS.ACT.PTCP
    'I am willing to execute justice.'
    (1234, PP 10)

This is an inherited Proto-Indo-European complementation device (Ambrazas 1990: 132), testified by the early Slavic languages in a narrowed scope of usage, only with reflexive and passivized verbs (Večerka 1961: 65–67; Potebnja 1958: 156–160). In Old Serbian it became non-productive before the first written records and was preserved in formulaic sequences since ritual formulae were strictly ordered, sometimes keeping the intact structure for millenia. This shows that in analyzing data one must take into account the register/part of a document to which they belong.

In Proto-Slavic, EPs originally had a nominal complement dative + infinitive in constructions with non-coreferential agents (cf. Grković-Major 2011). This was an inherited Proto-Indo-European appositive double case construction, where the first dative denoted the agent while the action/state ascribed to him was expressed by the dative of the verbal noun, later infinitive. Such semantically aligned constructions are still seen in Old Church Slavonic, corresponding to the Greek accusative + infinitive (5).

(5) čajǫšte   *jemu*   *živu*   **byti**
    expect/hope[IPFV].PRS.PTCP   he.DAT   alive.DAT   be[IPFV].INF
    (Supr. 41v)
    Gr. προσδοκῶντες   ζῆν   αὐτόν
    expect/hope.PRS.PTCP   live.INF   he.ACC
    'expecting/hoping that he is alive'
    (NT)

2.2 *Da*-clauses

The system in which double cases expressed subordination was lost by the time of the first Old Serbian records. Instead of the dative + infinitive complement we find another strategy with non-coreferential agents: juxtaposition of independent sentences, the second of which was *da* + present tense. Its *irrealis* semantics is based on the optative meaning of the particle *da* (cf. Grković-Major 2004: 185–186). The fact that we are dealing with a juxtaposed sentence in (6) is shown by the presence of the pronoun *tvoja* 'your', while in a complex sentence it would have to be *moja* 'my':

(6) vi   ste   se   obekali   i   rekъli
     you   AUX.2PL REFL   promise[PFV].PST.PTCP   and say[PFV].PST.PTCP
     da   si   sěde   tvoě sela   svobodъno
     PRT.OPT.   REFL   exist [IPFV].PRS.3PL   your villages freely
     'You promised and said: Let your villages be free.'
     (1240, PP 16)

Such asyndetic constructions were the basis for the creation of *da*-complement clauses in general which started already in the 13th century, and by the end of the 14th century they were established (Grković-Major 2004). However, since juxtaposition was employed even after the stabilization of *da*-complements, it is sometimes hard to discern whether we are dealing with the asyndetic or the subordinate pattern with EPs:

(7) mi   voleli   bismo   **da**   je   veće
     we   like[IPFV].PST.PTCP   AUX.1PL   PRT.OPT/COMP?   COP.3SG   more
     °gdnu   Kostadinu
     lord.DAT   Kostadin
     a. 'We would like: May lord Kostadin have more.'
     b. 'We would like lord Kostadin to have more.'
     (1395, PP 247)

In resolving this problem several factors have to be accounted for: the semantics of the EP in C1, the TAM of both predicates in C1 and C2, and sometimes even a wider context. For example, since a syntactically independent optative *da*-sentence cannot have future tense,[10] its use in C2 is a sign of complementation (cf. Pavlović 2009: 35):

(8) upvamo   da   ćete   i   vi   dobrě   **učinit(i)**
     hope[IPFV].PRS.1PL   COMP   AUX.2PL   and   you   well   do[PFV].INF
     'We hope that you will do well too.'
     (1397, PP 270)

After *da*-complements developed in constructions with non-coreferential agents in C1 and C2, they started expanding to the constructions with coreferential agents at the expense of the infinitive:

---

10 At this period future tense was already grammaticalized in Old Serbian (Grković-Major 2012).

(9) hoće **da** imъ uzъme °crinu
    want[IPFV].PRS.3SG COMP they.DAT take[PFV].PRS.3SG money.ACC
    'He wants to take their money.'
    (1399, PP 274)

It is generally accepted that the non-factive *da*-complement is a *Balkan Sprachbund* innovation which spread from the southeast (Grickat 1975: 74). However, the first examples in our corpus are from the western dialects and, according to Pavlović (2009: 90), in Old Serbian documents written in the west they are even slightly more frequent than in those from the east. This indicates that another innovation wave must have come from the west, presumably under the influence of Romance varieties in the western part of the Balkans.[11] Already in Latin, EPs could take both the infinitive and *quod*-clauses, with a tendency to generalize the *quod* complement clause, preferred in the spoken language (Ernout and Thomas 1953: 297–298, 321), and the number of *quod*-clauses grew after the 2nd century (Drašković 1959–1960: 173).

It is not possible to give a precise account of the degree to which the complement clause has replaced the infinitive in present-day dialects since dialectal studies rarely investigate this matter. Judging from the available data we can only conclude that the infinitive is preserved in the majority of the western Serbian vernaculars, in varying degree (e.g. Vujović 1969: 348–349; Stanić 1977: 93–94; Kašić 1995: 346), while completely being lost in the southern and southeastern dialects, which belong to the *Balkan Sprachbund* (A. Belić 1905: 378). These two types of complements also exist in standard Serbian, and the scope of their usage depends on regional or individual preferences (Ivić 2005: 328). Apart from the regional differences in standard Serbian, the infinitive being more frequent in the west and southwest, the choice between the infinitive and *da*-complement is determined by certain syntactic factors (see e.g. Kravar 1953, Brozović 1953, Ivić 1972, Ivić 2005: 328–32).

3 Factive complements

3.1 *Jer(e)*-clause

The first emerging factive complementation type is with *jer(e)*, originating from PS **ježe* 'this'(< anaphoric neuter **je* + particle **že*, with rhotacism). This petrified

---

[11] We will further refer to these just as 'Romance', as opposed to Balkan Romance, which applies to the varieties which are a part of the *Balkan Sprachbund* and, as opposed to the majority of Romance languages, have two clause complementation systems.

deictic (in different forms) had a wide scope of usage in the early Slavic vernaculars. According to Kopečný and Plevačová (1980: 291), in the history of Slavic languages it had delimitative and interjective functions, it was used as a deictic, a *relativum generale*, and a "universal subordinator" (cf. Gast and Diessel 2012: 17), introducing different types of adverbial clauses as well as complement clauses. Its oldest records with EPs in C1 are found in Old Church Slavonic (10).[12] Interpreted as a pronominal accusative belonging to C1 (cf. Kopečný and Plevačová 1980: 292), it could be seen as an archaic "protoaccusative" meaning 'in reference to', which, depending on the context, renders all kinds of adverbial relations, among them causal.[13] They also exemplify the primary "absolute" meaning of EPs, which expressed the emotional state of the experiencer, while its cause was denoted by the adverbial accusative:

(10) *čjuždaahǫ sę*   **ježe** || *kъšněaše*
     marvel[IPFV].IMPF.3PL + REFL   this.ACC   tarry[IPFV].IMPF.3SG
     tъ   vъ   crъkъve
     he   in   temple.LOC
     'They marveled *in reference to* this: he tarried so long in the Temple.'
     (Mar. Lk 1:21)
     Gr. ἐθαύμαζον   ἐν   τῷ   χρονίζειν   ἐν   τῷ
     marvel.IMPF.3PL   at   ART.DAT tarry.INF   in   ART.DAT
     ναῷ   αὐτόν[14]
     temple.DAT   he.ACC
     'They marvelled that he tarried so long in the temple.'
     (NT)

On the other hand, *ježe* could also be seen as an emphatic, exclamative particle between the two sentences: 'And they marveled. Look! He tarried so long in the Temple' (cf. Trávníček 1956: 56). But in both possible explanations *ježe* was not part of C2.

---

12 In such cases *ježe* is interpreted as a complementizer or a causal conjunction (SS: 802, StbR II: 1265), but we believe that this is a projection of contemporary syntactic relations into the distant past, when sentence organization was quite different (cf. Kurc 1963: 10).
13 We use the term "protoaccusative" in order to differentiate it from the accusative case in the contemporary syntactically aligned systems. "Protoaccusative" was diachronically the first morphological case in Proto-Indo-European, and its remnants (the so-called *accusativus relationis*) are found in various Indo-European languages, among them Slavic, e.g. Serb. epic poetry: *Jovan majku*[ACC] *u pećinu kaže* 'Jovan told **about his mother** in the cave' (Grković-Major 2010: 67). Cf. Krys'ko (1997: 19–46).
14 The Greek text has an articular infinitive (ἐν τῷ χρονίζειν), which shows that the construction with *ježe* is Slavic.

Old Serbian developed *jer(e)*-clauses which, depending on the lexical semantics of the predicate in C1, had two main semantic interpretations: 'complement' and 'cause' (Pavlović 2009: 74–80, 242–243). Thus, as seen from (11), their interpretation with EPs is ambiguous: they could be seen as causal adjuncts or as transitional causal-complement clauses. However, such interpretations are made from the point of view of configurational syntax, where semantic structure is projected into syntactic structure. In Old Serbian at that time, "polyfunctional" particles and deictic expressions were in many cases still just a sign of subordination while the kind of subordinative relation was contextually induced, depending on the semantic content of C1 and C2 predications. The creation of the complex sentence will be a process by which such particles and deictics will turn into conjunctions and complementizers, formalizing semantic relations in it.

The boundary shift, by which *jer(e)* came to the initial position in C2, is proven by the placement of the enclitic *mu* after it (post-frontal, Wackernagel's position):

(11) jerъ   se   gospodarъ srъdi | **jerъ**
     because   REFL   master   be.angry[IPFV].PRS.3SG   because/COMP
     mu   něsmo   odpisali
     he.DAT   NEG.AUX.1PL write back[PFV].PST.PTCP
     'The master is angry because/that we did not write back to him.'
     (1400, PP 496)

After factive *da*-clauses were established at the end of the 14th century, *(j)er(e)* was being restricted to causal clauses in the majority of dialects, and this is the situation in the standard language today. However, it is, together with its shorter version *e*, still found in some dialects[15] as a complementizer and a causal conjunction with different verb classes, including EPs (e.g. Pešikan 1965; 211; Ćupić 1977: 178; Stanić 1977: 35; Pižurica 1981: 217; Jovanović 2005: 133):

---

15 We include dialectal data recorded in the 20th century only in reference to the conjunctions and complementizers investigated in this paper, whose development can be tracked in the historical documents. Besides, there are phenomena restricted to certain vernaculars or groups of vernaculars, e.g. the causal conjunctions/complementizers *te*, *a* etc. (cf. Barjaktarević 1966: 142–143). Dialects, as spoken varieties, do not have well developed hypotaxis. Their sentence structure is even today often closer to what we find in historical documents than to the hypotactic structures found in the present-day written standard language.

(12) čudin se   ere   ne   nauči
    be.amazed[IPFV].PRS.1SG + REFL because/COMP NEG learn[PFV].AOR.2SG
    što   bolje
    something   better
    'I am amazed because/that you did not learn something better.'
    (Miletić 1940: 573)

3.2 Correlative structures

The other strategy inherited from Proto-Slavic and witnessed by other early Slavic vernaculars (Bauer 1960: 289–291; Borkovskij and Kuznecov 2006: 482) was a correlative structure with a demonstrative in C1 (in different cases, depending on the semantics of the predicate) and *ježe* in C2. Its first records are from Old Church Slavonic, with *o* + Locative in C1, interpreted by Toporov (1961: 195–197) as a transitional case between a causal adjunct and an argument:

(13) plakaasta sę   i   tọžaasta   o   tomь |
    cry[IPFV].AOR.3DU + REFL and   grieve[IPFV].AOR.3DU   about that.LOC
    ježe   sьtvorista   zьlo   mnogo
    REL/DEM   create[PFV].AOR.3DU   evil   great
    'They (two) cried and grieved about the fact that they created great evil.'
    (Supr. 106r, Gr.–)

After the disappearance of the opposition between *j- and *k- pronoun types in Old Serbian, interrogatives spread into the syntactic positions formerly occupied by anaphorics. As a consequence, *što* (< PS *čьto), as *relativum generale*, replaced *ježe* in the structures with resumptive pronouns:

(14) namь   je   za   tozi   nedrago | **što**   bezь
    we.DAT   COP.3SG   for that   not pleasing   REL/DEM   without
    naše   vesti   čine
    our   knowledge   do[IPFV].PRS.3PL
    'We are displeased with what they are doing without our knowledge.'
    (1400, PP 459)

As opposed to *o* + locative in (13), C1 has *za* + pronominal accusative in (14), the most frequent causal NP in Old Serbian from the 12th–15th centuries (Pavlović 2006: 271). The prevalence of this structure in Old Serbian can be attributed to Romance influence, since Vulgar Latin expanded the usage of *pro eo quod*, literally 'for that which' in the causal meaning 'because' from the 5th century onward (Herman 2000: 92). The correlative pattern was preserved for centuries. Still in the works of Vuk Karadžić in the first half of the 19th century *za to* and *što* are not in a contact position in most cases (Kovačević 1998: 131). Later, with the merging of the preposition and the demonstrative, followed by a change in intonation (*za tô što*> *zàto što*), it became one of the compound causal conjunctions in standard Serbian.

3.3 *Zašto*-clause

Correlative *za to što* followed yet another developmental path: the loss of the demonstrative element in C1, found in many languages (Cristofaro 2003: 97): *za to što > zašto*, which gave a new conjunction covering different types of causal relations (cf. Pavlović 2009: 270–272). Since South Slavic differs from the situation in East Slavic (compare Russian *potomu čto*) and West Slavic (compare Czech *protože*), where the pronominal element was preserved, Grickat (1975: 133) considers this to be a language-contact phenomenon, noticing a similarity between Romance and Serbo-Croatian in the formation of causal clauses. Compound conjunctions such as the causal *post quod* became productive in Vulgar Latin (Herman 2000: 92).

The first examples with EPs are from the 15th century. This was concomitant with the boundary shift, with the newly created conjunction now in the initial position in C2, as seen by the position of the enclitic cluster (*ni*, *vi*, *ne*) after it:

(15) mnogo   ti   ni   je   usilno   i   žal | **zašto**
      very   you.DAT   we.DAT   COP.3SG   sorrowful   and   grief   because
      ni   **vi**   **ne**   upisaste
      we.DAT   you (PL)   NEG   write[PFV].AOR.2PL
      'We are very sorry and sad because you did not write to us.'
      (1404, PP 276)

For the next several centuries EPs were constructed with this kind of causal clauses:

(16) tuj   se   veseli   **zašto**   su   nokti   u   njega
      here   REFL   rejoyce[IPFV].PRS.3SG   because   COP.3PL   nails   at   him
      velici   i   jaci
      big   and   strong
      'He is rejoycing because his nails are big and strong.'
      (1715–1725, Ž: 19b)

Zašto was productive, competing with *jer* (see 3.1) and *što* (see 3.4), as shown by the texts written in different dialectal areas. It is still present in the vernaculars, especially in the southern and southeastern area, which belong to the *Balkan Sprachbund* (A. Belić 1905: 651; Mladenović 2001: 471; 2013: 391).

On the other hand, *zašto* was eliminated from the standard language. Vuk Karadžić, who standardized it in the first half of the 19th century, used *zašto* in his earlier works, but replaced it with *jer* in the later ones, e.g. in the second edition of the *Srpski rječnik* from 1852 (Kašić 1987: 1548) and in the second edition of *Serbian folk tales*:

(17) ti   više   da   ne   ideš   za   mnom, đe   se
     ti   više   da   ne   ideš   za   mnom, đe   se
     you more   IMP.PRT   NEG   go[IPFV].PRS.2SG after me   where   REFL
     ja   oglasim **zašto** neće   biti   dobro (SNP1: 7)
     ja   oglasim **jer**   neće   biti   dobro (SNP2: 184)
     I   appear because   NEG.AUX.3SG   be[IPFV].INF   good
     'Do not follow me any more where I appear, because it will not be good.'

As the result of his intervention *jer* prevailed over *zašto* in the standard language and became a causal conjunction covering a wide range of causal relations.

3.4 *Što*-clause

From the beginning of the 15th century we find *što* with the same syntactic functions as *zašto*. *Što* could be explained as the shortened version of *zašto*,[16] or as *relativum generale* (cf. [14]), which had an array of functions in early Slavic languages, among them to introduce causal clauses (Kopečný and Plevačová 1980: 133). The first example in our corpus is with a communicative verb expressing emotion *zahvaliti* 'express gratitude'. The fact that the conjunction *što* is in the initial position in C2 is shown by the placement of the enclitic cluster *ga ste* after it:

(18) zahvalismo | **što**   ga   ste   doslej   u
     thank[PFV].AOR.1PL   because   it.ACC   AUX.2PL   until now   at
     sebe   počteno   prědrъžali
     yourself.GEN   honestly   keep[IPFV].PST.PTCP
     'We thanked because you kept it with you honestly until now.'
     (1404, PP 440)

---

16 In the same way as, according to some authors, Russian *potomu čto* gave *čto* (Troicki 1959: 168).

This innovation wave came from the west, encompassing slowly the predominant part of the Serbian dialects. Still in the 19th century *što* was used both with EPs (19) and with other semantic classes of predicates (20) in C1:

(19) zdravo   joj   žao   bude   **što**   oca
     very   she.DAT   sorry   become[PFV].PRS.3SG   because   father.ACC
     nije   našla   kod   kuće
     NEG.AUX.3SG   find[PFV].PST.PTCP   at   home.GEN
     'She was very sorry because she did not find her father at home.'
     (SNP2: 171)

(20) ja   ću   tebe   učiniti   čestita,   **što**
     I   will   you.ACC   make[PFV].INF   honorable.M.ACC.SG   because
     si   me   od   nje   izbavio
     AUX.2SG   I.ACC   from   her   save[PFV].PST.PTCP
     'I will make you honorable because you saved me from her.'
     (SNP2: 183)

The 20th century brought changes, when *što* left the sphere of pure causality and got restricted to EPs, thus turning into a kind of conjunction-complementizer. Stevanović (1969: 856) points out that *što* appears in the standard language only if the main clause predicate denotes some "state or mood", and all the examples he lists are with EPs. The status of *što*-clauses with EPs is fuzzy. They are considered to be causal (Stevanović 1969: 856), "causal-explicative" (Grickat 1952; Ružić 2006: 136), or "causal-declarative" (Kovačević 1998: 127). In any case, they have a fuzzy, transitional status between an adverbial and a complement clause.

The same is true for the contemporary dialects where the subordinative *što* exists:

(21) ljutijo se   **što**   ga   nijesmo
     be.angry[IPFV].PST.PTCP + REFL   because/COMP   h.CC   NEG.AUX.1PL
     iščekali
     wait.for[PFV].PST.PTCP
     'He was angry because/that we did not wait for him.'
     (Stanić 1977: 36)

The rise of the *što*-clause embodies the principle of "the iconic expression of conceptual distance" (Haiman 1983: 783), showing that the process of clause-union is "an iconic reflection of the cognitive-semantic process of event integration" (Givón 2001: 89). While in present-day Serbian *zato što* (among other conjunctions) introduces causal clauses, the cause of an emotion, being its object at the same time, is expressed by the shorter form *što*.

3.5 *Gd(j)e*-clause

Another complementation strategy was with *gd(j)e* (< PS **kъde/ kъdě*), the spatial interrogative adverb 'where', ESJS 7: 391). This was an emerging late Proto-Slavic strategy, and in the history of North and South Slavic languages such clauses were contextually interpreted as adverbial (temporal, conditional, concessive, causal) or complement clauses (Kopečný and Plevačová 1980: 378–384). In Old Serbian from the 12th–15th centuries the *gd(j)e*-clause was fuzzy, its semantic interpretation being context-dependent, most frequently spatial (Pavlović 2009: 142–146). From the 15th century on it introduced diverse types of adverbial clauses (RJA, III: 122–124). However, its meaning is fuzzy, as in (22), where it could be interpreted both as causal and temporal conjunction:

(22) vi   ste   pečalni   bili   za   .i.   godištь, **gde**
     you   AUX.2PL   sad   be.PST.PTCP   for   ten   years   because/when
     ste   ne   svlačili   oružija   s   sebe
     AUX.2PL   NEG   take.off[IPFV].PST.PTCP   weapons   from   you
     a. 'You were sad for ten years because you did not take your weapons off.'
     b. 'You were sad for ten years, when you did not take your weapons off.'
     (RT: 256v)

Gd(j)e (also in the phonetic realization *đe*) exists today in many Serbian dialects as a causal conjunction with different verb classes (23), including EPs, where it could be also interpreted as a complementizer (24):

(23) neće   da   kaže   **đe**   ne   zna
     not.will.3SG   COMP   say[PFV].PRS.3SG   because   NEG   know[IPFV].PRS.3SG
     'He does not want to say because he does not know.'
     (Tešić 1977: 245)

(24) ljuti se   **đe**   mu   nijesmo
     be.angry[IPFV].PRS.3SG + REFL   because/COMP   he.DAT   NEG.AUX.1PL
     pomogli   juče
     help[PFV].PST.PTCP   yesterday
     'He is angry because/that we did not help him yesterday.'
     (Vuković 1938–39: 103)

It is particularly widespread in the Serbian dialects belonging to the *Balkan Sprachbund* (*gde*, *de*, *dek(a)*, *ge*), where it functions both as factive complementizer and a causal conjunction (e.g. A. Belić 1905: 649–651; Bogdanović 1987: 230; Ćirić 1999: 194), thus its status with EPs is fuzzy (conjunction-complementizer):

(25) potres⁰l se   **gde**   mu   umrela
     distress[PFV].PST.PTCP + REFL   because   he.DAT   die[PFV].PST.PTCP
     mati
     mother
     'He was distressed because/that his mother died.'
     (Bogdanović 1979: 131)

These dialects share this trait with Bulgarian and Macedonian vernaculars. In Bulgarian dialects we find *deto* (< *gde-to*, BER I: 328) in the same functions (Gerovă 1: 393), in Macedonian – *deka* (< *gde-ka*) (RMNP: 254). Grickat (1975: 182) points to the parallelism with Gr. *opoŭ* > *poŭ*, etymologically 'where', also a complementizer, causal conjunction and a relative. The complementizer based of the 'where' adverb is a *Balkan Sprachbund* feature (Sandfeld 1930: 107). However, as shown by the aforementioned North Slavic parallels, this was an original Slavic construction, whose expansion was just supported by language contacts in the Balkans.

The standard language exhibits rules which are the result of its codification. The subordinator *gd(j)e* existed in the native dialect of Vuk Karadžić, both with EPs (26) and other classes of predicates (27):

(26) pa   se   začudi   **gde**   sve   selo
     so   REFL surprise[PFV].AOR.3SG   because/that   whole   village
     peva
     sing [IPFV].PRS.3SG
     'So he got surprised because the whole village was singing.'
     (SNP2: 112)

(27) ne   htednu   mu   je   odmah   dati,
     NEG   want[PFV].PRS.3PL he.DAT   she.ACC   right away   give[PFV].INF
     gde   je   star   i   siromah
     because   COP.3SG   old   and   poor
     'They did not want to give her to him because he was old and poor.'
     (SNP2: 109)

Thus, its absence in Karadžić's original works is to be seen as the consequence of his normative work, by which it was eliminated. In the standard language we find it only in literary works, as a stylistic (dialectal) feature of certain authors (Kovačević 1998: 128).

3.6 *Da*-clause

The factive *da*-clauses, as a west South Slavic innovation, appeared in the 14th century in the western Serbian dialects and reached the eastern ones by the 15th–16th century. As already pointed out by Sedláček (1970) and Grickat (1975: 172), this was the result of the Romance influence. The classical Latin opposition between factive *quod* and non-factive *ut* was eradicated in favor of *quod* in Romance (Drašković 1959–1960: 176). This is corroborated by the fact that already in the 13th century factive *da*-clauses are found in Old Croatian (Čakavian) (Grickat 1975: 160), which was in close contact with Romance.

This innovation entered the structures with EPs only a few centuries later, first in Old Croatian, where the oldest attestation, according to RJA (2: 190), is from 1507, then western and southwestern Old Serbian dialects in the 17th century. The first example in our corpus is a correlative structure, where *da* simply replaced *što*: *za to što* (cf. [14]) > *za to da*:

(28) **za to** se veoma čudim **da** mi ne
for that REFL very surprise[IPFV].PRS.1SG COMP I.DAT NEG
o(d)g(o)varate
reply[IPFV].PRS.2PL
'This is why I am very surprised that you are not replying to me.'
(16th–17th c., Per.:13)

In the 17th century we see complement *da*-clauses replacing *što*-clauses in the southwest (29), and a century later in the northeast (30):

(29) kaje se **da** vam ga je
regret[IPFV].PRS.3SG + REFL COMP you.DAT it.ACC AUX.3SG
dao
give[PFV].PST.PTCP
'He regrets that he gave it to you.'
(1676, Dubr.: 605)

(30) *radue se* **da** *se e odъ ně čovekъ*
 rejoyce[IPFV].PRS.3SG + REFL COMP REFL AUX.3SG from her man
 na svetъ rodio
 into world.ACC bear[PFV].PST.PTCP
 'She rejoices that a man was born to this world from her.'
 (1793, DO: 1)

Since at that time in Vuk Karadžić's native dialect this feature did not exist, the norm of the standard language preserved the opposition between the two syntactic strategies with EPs: non-factive *da*-complements and factive *što*-clauses. However, factive *da*-complements with EPs began entering the standard language already in the 19th century:

(31) *ja se veseljah, odgovori Mijat* **da**
 I REFL rejoice[IPFV].IMPF.1SG reply[PFV].AOR.3SG Mijat COMP
 me je Bog doveo gdje se pravo
 I.ACC AUX.3SG God bring[PFV].PST.PTCP where REFL rightly
 sudi
 judge[IPFV].PRS.3SG
 'I was rejoicing, said Mijat, that God brought me to the place where they judge rightly.'
 (1875, SM: 222)

They became more frequent in the 20th century (Grickat 1952: 205–206; Kovačević 1998: 126–127). In present-day Serbian this is a widespread phenomenon, especially in colloquial speech. Grickat (1952: 206) states that this is the wrong usage of *da*, a "barbarism" under Italian or German influence. It is indeed a "wrong usage" from the standpoint of normative grammar, but this is undoubtedly an ongoing change taking place. Nonstandard features in the colloquial language reveal linguistic innovations (cf. Grković-Major 2015).

This gradual process is conditioned by different factors and here we will point out some of them.[17] The use of *da* instead of *što* does not change the factive status of the complement clause if something else in the complex sentence indicates it, as already noticed by Riđanović (1981: 11–12). For instance, *da* replaces *što* if: a) the CTP is factive (29), b) the DCP is in the perfect (30), c) some element

---

[17] The spread of *da*-complements at the expense of *što*-clauses has to be the subject of a separate and thorough investigation. Our aim is just to show that this is an ongoing, internally conditioned change.

in the wider context implicates the factive status of the complement, as in (32), where *podneti ostavku* 'resign' implies that the subject actually was a member of the government:

(32) *U decembru 1992. je   uz reči: stidim se*
 In December 1992 AUX.3SG with words be.ashamed[IPFV].PRS.1SG + REFL
 da   pripadam   ovoj   vladi,
 COMP belong[IPFV].PRS.1SG this.DAT government.DAT
 podneo   ostavku
 submitt[PFV].PST.PTCP resignation
 'In December 1992, after saying "I am ashamed that I belong to this government", he resigned.'
 (SrWaC)

Exceptions are the so-called polysemous predicates, such as "predicates of fearing", e.g. *bojati se*, whose meaning is specified by *što*-causal conjunction and non-factive *da*-complement.[18] When used in their primary sense, 'fear', they take *što*-clauses, indicating the cause of fear in the real world (33), while their *da*-complements denote an imagined object of anxiety, worry, suspicion, concern (34) or hesitation (35):

(33) *bojim se   što   je   ovo i   predizborna*
 be.afraid[IPFV].PRS.1SG + REFL because COP.3SG this also pre-election
 nedelja
 week
 'I am afraid because this is also the pre-election week.'
 (SrWaC)

(34) *bojim se   da   to   smišljeno*
 suspect.with anxiety[IPFV].PRS.1SG + REFL COMP that on purpose
 rade
 do[IPFV].PRS.3PL
 'I suspect (with anxiety) that they are doing that on purpose.'
 (SrWaC)

---

18 On such predicates in the standard Serbian see Moskovljević (2004: 58–59).

(35) *bojim se*   ***da***   *to*   *izgovorim*
      hesitate.with anxiety[IPFV].PRS.1SG + REFL   COMP   that   say[PFV].PRS.1SG
      'I hesitate (with anxiety) to say that.'
      (SrWaC)

4 Summary and conclusions

The development of complement clauses with EPs in the history of Serbian has been a long-lasting process, shaped by both language-internal and contact-induced factors. The internal language tendency toward hypotaxis was motivated by the typological change of Indo-European languages from the parent system with semantic alignment, lacking transitivity and configurationality to transitive, configurational systems with syntactic alignment. In the gradual process of creating hypotactic structures, Serbian went through a phase of instability with competing strategies and polyfunctional particles or deictic expressions evolving into markers of subordination. This instability was a fruitful ground for areal influences in the Balkans.

The evolution of factive / non-factive complementation has been governed by the semantics of the predicate in C1. Complements of non-factive EPs originate from linguistic forms with irrealis modality. In cases with coreferential agents in C1 and C2, Old Serbian used the infinitive, the complementation strategy inherited from Proto-Slavic. If the agents C1 and C2 were not coreferential, EPs had dative + infinitive construction in Proto-Slavic. By the time of the first Old Serbian documents the latter strategy was lost and instead we find juxtaposition of independent sentences, the second of which was an optative *da* + present tense sentence, semantically compatible with non-factive EPs. Such asyndetic constructions were the basis for the creation of non-factive *da*-complement clauses. In the course of time the infinitive has been withdrawing from structures with coreferential agents in favor of *da*-complements, with diatopic variation, including the dialects belonging to the *Balkan Sprachbund*, where it does not exist any more. Formulaic expressions, as petrified sequences retaining archaic syntactic structures, disclose another possibility: the non-agreeing participle, lost in prehistoric times.

A question that needs to be addressed is whether, and how, the former initial particle *da* in C2 "can be acknowledged as a complementizer" (Wiemer, this volume). In studying spoken languages, a reliable clue is the intonation contour, since the complex sentence, as well as the simple one, "must fall under a single intonation contour" (Givón 2009: 82). Left without such a diagnostic tool in diachronic studies we must look for other signs of C1 and C2 union. In the case of *da*-clauses, where the formation of the complement clause did not include a boundary shift, the indication of subordination (found in the corpus) is the future tense in C2 (since optative sentences could not have it).

Factive EPs had several emerging syntactic strategies. Since they imply that the cause of an emotion precedes it, they were initially constructed with causal NP adjuncts: a) demonstrative protoaccusative *jer(e)*, followed by a juxtaposed sentence expressing the cause of the emotion or b) demonstrative *za to*, followed by the correlative *što* introducing a clause expressing the cause of the emotion. The bond between C1 and C2 was further strengthened by the elimination of the demonstrative and the merge of *za što* > *zašto*. Another possibility was a *što*-clause, where *što* might be the result of the shortening of *zašto* > *što* or a *relativum generale*. The fourth road into factive clause was *gd(j)e*-clauses. All these conjunctions were fuzzy, and the interpretation of the relation between C1 and C2 still heavily depended on their semantic content. In time *što* left the sphere of pure causality, and got narrowed to EPs, becoming a kind of conjunction-factive complementizer, in opposition to the non-factive *da*-complementizer.

The rise of *jer(e)*, *zašto* and *što*-clauses included a boundary shift, bringing the conjunctions in the initial position of C2. A reliable diagnostic tool for the syntactic union of C1 and C2 in these cases are the enclitics. Since they are not permitted in clause initial position, their appearance after *jer(e)*, *zašto* and *što* indicates the (newly formed) subordinator movement to C2.

In the 16th–17th centuries factive *da*-complements, a west South Slavic syntactic innovation, which started spreading with other semantic classes of CTPs already in the late 14th century, entered factive EP constructions, first in the southwestern and western dialects. From then on, factive *da*-complements have been advancing at the expense of fuzzy causal-complement *što*-clauses and today they are a widespread phenomenon in colloquial Serbian. It is an ongoing syntactic change in the majority of Serbian dialects and the spoken varieties of the standard language. We argue that it is the final step in generalizing *da*-complements, as objects within complex sentence. However, the polysemous "predicates of fearing" (e.g. *bojati* se 'fear', factive; 'be anxious, hesitate', non-factive) still have factive *što*-clauses, because *da*-complements automatically induce their non-factive reading.

The pace of factive *da*-complement generalization was directly dependent on the lexical semantics of CTPs, i.e. their semantic transitivity. The reason this change started several centuries later with factive EPs than with other CTP classes lies in their low transitivity parameters and specific semantic content, because, as opposed to other verb classes, e.g. perception and cognition verbs, they imply cause, the content of an emotion being at the same time the cause of an emotion.

This is parallel with the grammaticalization of the accusative object in the Slavic simple sentence, which corroborates the language-internal role of transitivity in the development of complement clauses.

Serbian has been exposed to another wave of innovation. Its southern and southeastern dialects got typologically bound to the east South Slavic area. They retain the opposition factivity: non-factivity, formalized as *gde* / *dek(a)*-clauses: *da*-clauses. The factive 'where'-complement is also a lexical isogloss shared with the neighboring Macedonian and Bulgarian dialects. The emerging Old Serbian factivity *gd(j)e*-pattern, still found in many dialects as one of the possibilities, was given prominence by language contacts in the *Balkan Sprachbund* convergence zone.

As opposed to diatopic language variation, standard Serbian presents a uniform picture with non-factive *da*- vs. factive *što*-clauses with EPs. This is because: a) being based on one dialect, it still reflects the situation in that variety from the beginning of the 19th century; b) it was further subjected to standardization processes, and c) its norm, being conservative as the norm of any standard language, does not reflect the ongoing changes in the colloquial speech, which exhibit the generalization of factive *da*-complements. This brings us to an important methodological issue: language history and the history of the standard language are two different subjects, although their study is inseparable. Having in mind the diatopic syntactic complexity in South Slavic, with language continuums, transitional dialects and multiple innovation waves, not coinciding with "language boundaries", we should carefully approach the question of the systemic differences between languages and focus on the study of isoglosses.

Sources

Barjaktarević, Danilo. 1966. Novopazarsko-sjenički govori [The speeches of Novi Pazar and Sjenica]. *Srpski dijalektološki zbornik* XVI. 1–177.

Belić, Aleksandar. 1905. Dijalekti istočne i južne Srbije [Dialects of east and south Serbia]. *Srpski dijalektološki zbornik* I. 1–715.

Bogdanović, Nedeljko. 1979. Govori Bučuma i Belog Potoka [The speeches of Bučum and Beli Potok]. *Srpski dijalektološki zbornik* XXV. 1–178.

Bogdanović, Nedeljko. 1987. Govor Aleksinačkog Pomoravlja [The speech of the Aleksinac Morava region]. *Srpski dijalektološki zbornik* XXXIII. 7–302.

Ćirić, Ljubisav. 1999. Govori Ponišavlja [The speeches of Ponišavlje]. *Srpski dijalektološki zbornik* XLVI. 7–262.

Ćupić, Drago. 1977. Govor Bjelopavlića [The speech of Bjelopavlići]. *Srpski dijalektološki zbornik* XXIII. 1–226.

DO: *Sobranie raznyhъ nravoučitelnyhъ veščej vъ polzu i uveselenie* [A collection of useful and entertaining moralizing stories]. 1793. Dositeemъ Obradovičemъ. Vъ Viennĕ: Pri G. Stef. Novakovičĕ.
Dubr.: Komar, Goran Ž. 2012. *Ćirilična dokumenta Dubrovačkog arhiva* [Cyrillic documents of the Dubrovnik archive]. Herceg Novi: Društvo za arhive i povjesnicu hercegnovsku.
Jovanović, Miodrag. 2005. *Govor Paštrovića* [The speech of Paštrovići]. Podgorica: Univerzitet Crne Gore.
Mar.: Vatroslav Jagić (ed.). 1960 [1883]. *Quattuor Evangeliorum versionis palaeoslovenicae Codex Marianus glagoliticus*. Graz: Akademische Druck- U. Verlagsanstalt.
Miletić, Branko. 1940. Crmnički govor [The speech of Crmnica]. *Srpski dijalektološki zbornik* IX. 1–663.
Mladenović, Radivoje. 2001. Govor šarplaninske župe Gora [The speech of the župa Gora in Šar-planina]. *Srpski dijalektološki zbornik* XLVIII. 1–606.
Mladenović, Radivoje. 2013. *Govor južnokosovskog sela Gatnje* [The speech of the south Kosovo village Gatnja]. Beograd: Institut za srpski jezik SANU.
NT: *Novum Testamentum Graece*. http://www.academic-bible.com/en/online-bibles/about-the-online-bibles/ (accessed January 2017).
Per.: Goran Ž. Komar. 2013. *Ćirilična dokumenta Peraškog arhiva (1633–1851)* [Cyrillic documents of the Perast archive]. Herceg Novi: Društvo za arhive i povjesnicu hercegnovsku.
Pešikan, Mitar. 1965. Starocrnogorski srednjokatunski i lješanski govori [The oldmontenegrin speeches of the Srednji katun and the Lješan nahija]. *Srpski dijalektološki zbornik* XV. 1–284.
Pižurica, Mato. 1981. *Govor okoline Kolašina* [The speech of the Kolašin surroundings]. Titograd: CANU.
PP: Ljubomir Stojanović. 1929, 1934. *Stare srpske povelje i pisma I/1–2* [Old Serbian charters and letters]. Beograd: Srpska akademija nauka i umetnosti.
RT: Allan Ringheim. 1951. *Eine altserbische Trojasage*. Prague & Upsal: Imprimerie de l'état à Prague.
SM: Šćepan Mitrov Ljubiša. 1889. *Pripovijesti crnogorske i primorske* [Montenegrin and coastal stories]. U Dubrovniku: Nakladom knjižare Dragutina Pretnera.
SNP1: Vuk Stefanović Karadžić. 1821. *Srpske narodne pripovijetke* [Serbian folk tales]. U Beču.
SNP2: Vuk Stefanović Karadžić. 1853. *Srpske narodne pripovijetke* [Serbian folk tales]. U Beču: U štampariji Jermenskog manastira.
SrWaC: *Serbian web corpus*: http://nlp.ffzg.hr/resources/corpora/srwac/ (accessed February 2016).
Stanić, Milija. 1977. Uskočki govor II [The speech of Uskoci]. *Srpski dijalektološki zbornik* XXII. 1–157.
Supr.: *Codex Suprasliensis*: http://suprasliensis.obdurodon.org/ (accessed March 2016).
Tešić, Milosav. 1977. Govor Lještanskog [The speech of Lještansko]. *Srpski dijalektološki zbornik* XXII. 159–328.
Vujović, Luka. 1969. Mrkovićki dijalekat [The Mrkovići dialect]. *Srpski dijalektološki zbornik* XVIII. 73–399.
Vuković, Jovan. 1938–39. Govor Pive i Drobnjaka [The speech of Piva and Drobnjak]. *Južnoslovenski filolog* XVII. 1–114.
Ž: *Žitije kneza Lazara* [The vita of Prince Lazar]. Manuscript. University Library "Svetozar Marković", Belgrade, sign. Rs-42.

References

Ambrazas, Vytautas. 1990. *Sravnitel'nyj sintaksis pričastij baltijskix jazykov* [Comparative syntax of Baltic participles]. Vilnius: Mokslas.
Bauer, Jaroslav. 1960. *Vývoj českého souvětí* [Development of the Czech complex sentence]. Prague: Nakladatelství Československé akademie věd.
Bednarczuk, Leszek. 1971. *Indo-European parataxis*. Cracow: Wydawnictwo naukowe Wyższej szkoły pedagogicznej.
BER: *Bălgarski etimologičen rečnik*, 1– [Bulgarian etymological dictionary]. 1971–. Sofija: Izdatelstvo na Bălgarskata akademija na naukite.
Borkovskij, Viktor I. & Petr S. Kuznecov. 2006. *Istoričeskaja grammatika russkogo jazyka* [Historical grammar of the Russian language]. Moscow: Akademija nauk SSSR.
Brozović, Dalibor. 1953. O vrijednosti infinitiva i prezenta s veznikom da [On the value of the infinitive and of the present tense with the conjunction "da"]. *Jezik: časopis za kulturu hrvatskoga književnog jezika* 2 (1). 13–18.
Cristofaro, Sonia. 2003. *Subordination*. Oxford: Oxford University Press.
Desnickaja, A. V. 1984. *Sravnitel'noe jazykoznanie i istorija jazykov* [Comparative linguistics and the history of languages]. St. Petersburg: Nauka.
Donohue, Mark. 2008. Semantic alignment systems: What's what, and what's not. In Mark Donohue & Søren Wichmann (eds.), *The typology of semantic alignment*, 24–75. Oxford: Oxford University Press.
Drašković, Vlado. 1959–1960. Infinitiv iza predloga *à* i *de* kao dopuna finitnom glagolu u francuskom jeziku [The infinitive after the prepositions *à* and *de* as the complement of finite verbs in French]. *Južnoslovenski filolog* XXIV. 85–200.
Ernout, Alfred & François Thomas. 1953. *Syntaxe latine*. Paris: Libraire C. Klincksieck.
ESJS: Eva Havlová (ed.). 1989–. *Etymologický slovník jazyka staroslověnského*,1–. [Etymological dictionary of Old Church Slavonic]. Prague: Academia.
Gast, Volker & Holger Diessel. 2012. The typology of clause linkage: status quo, challenges, prospects. In Volker Gast & Holger Diessel (eds.), *Clause linkage in cross-linguistic perspective. Data-driven approaches to cross-clausal syntax*, 1–36. Berlin & Boston: De Gruyter Mouton.
Gerovă, Najden. 1895–1904. *Rěčnikă na blăgarskyj jazykă*, 1–5 [Dictionary of the Bulgarian language]. Plovdivă: Družestvena Pečjatnica "Săglasie".
Givón, Talmy. 2001. *Syntax: An introduction*, Vol. 2. Amsterdam & Philadelphia: Benjamins.
Givón, Talmy. 2009. Multiple routes to clause union: The diachrony of complex verb phrases. In Talmy Givón & Masayoshi Shibatani (eds.), *Syntactic complexity: Diachrony, acquisition, neuro-cognition, evolution*, 81–118. Amsterdam & Philadelphia: Benjamins.
Gordon, Robert M. 1987. *The structure of emotions: Investigations in cognitive philosophy*. Cambridge: Cambridge University Press.
Grickat, Irena. 1952. O jednom slučaju mešanja sveza *da* i *što* [On a case of mixing the conjunctions *da* and *što*]. *Naš jezik* III n.s. (5–6). 196–207.
Grickat, Irena. 1975. *Studije iz istorije srpskohrvatskog jezika* [Studies from the history of the Serbo-Croatian language]. Belgrade: Narodna biblioteka Srbije.
Grković-Major [Grković-Mejdžor], Jasmina. 2004. Razvoj hipotaktičkog *da* u starosrpskom jeziku [Development of the hypotactic *da* in Old Serbian]. *Zbornik Matice srpske za filologiju i lingvistiku* 47 (1–2). 185–203.

Grković-Major, Jasmina. 2010. The role of syntactic transitivity in the develoment of Slavonic syntactic structures. In Björn Hansen & Jasmina Grković-Major (eds.), *Diachronic Slavonic syntax. Gradual changes in focus* [Special issue]. *Wiener Slawistischer Almanach, Sonderband 74*, 63–74. Munich, Berlin & Wien: Sagner.
Grković-Major [Grković-Mejdžor], Jasmina. 2011. Praindoevropski dativ + infinitiv: poreklo i slovenski razvoj [Dative + infinitive: Its Proto-Indo-European source and Slavic development]. *Zbornik Matice srpske za filologiju i lingvistiku* LIV (1). 27–44.
Grković-Major [Grković-Mejdžor], Jasmina. 2012. Razvoj futura u starosrpskom jeziku [The development of the future tense in Old Serbian]. *Zbornik Matice srpske za filologiju i lingvistiku* LV (1). 83–104.
Grković-Major [Grković-Mejdžor], Jasmina. 2015. Supstandardne crte kao pokazatelj jezičke promene u toku [Substandard features revealing lingustic innovations]. In Ljudmila Popović, Dojčil Vojvodić & Motoki Nomaći (eds.), *U prostoru lingvističke slavistike. Zbornik naučnih radova povodom 65 godina života akademika Predraga Pipera*, 293–303. Belgrade: Filološki fakultet.
Grković-Major, Jasmina. 2018a. The development of perception verb complements in the Serbian language. In Jasmina Grković-Major, Björn Hansen & Barbara Sonnenhauser (eds.), *Diachronic Slavonic syntax: The interplay between internal development, language contact and metalinguistic factors*, 339–360. Berlin & Boston: De Gruyter Mouton.
Grković-Major [Grković-Mejdžor], Jasmina. 2018b. Razvoj klauzalne dopune kognitivnih predikata u srpskom jeziku [Development of cognitive predicate clausal complements in Serbian]. In Rajna Dragićević & Veljko Brborić (ed.), *Srpska slavistika. Radovi srpske delegacije na XVI međunarodnom kongresu slavista. Tom 1, Jezik*, 89–105. Belgrade: Savez slavističkih društava Srbije.
Haiman, John. 1983. Iconic and economic motivation. *Language* 59. 781–819.
Herman, József. 2000. *Vulgar Latin*. Translated by Roger Wright. The Pennsylvania University Press.
Hopper, Paul J. & Sandra A. Thompson. 1980. Transitivity in grammar and discourse. *Language* 56 (2). 251–299.
Ivić, Milka. 1972. Problematika srpskohrvatskog infinitiva [Problems related to the Serbo-Croatian infinitive]. *Zbornik za filologiju i lingvistiku* XV (2). 115–138.
Ivić, Milka (ed.). 2005. Predrag Piper, Ivana Antonić, Vladislava Ružić, Sreto Tanasić, Ljudmila Popović & Branko Tošović. *Sintaksa savremnoga srpskog jezika. Prosta rečenica* [Syntax of the contemporary Serbian language. The simple sentence]. Belgrade: Institut za srpski jezik, Beogradska knjiga & Matica srpska.
Kašić, Jovan. 1987. O *Srpskom rječniku* iz 1852. godine [On the *Serbian Dictionary* from 1852]. In *Srpski rječnik (1852)*, II, 1483–1744. Belgrade: Prosveta.
Kašić, Zorka. 1995. Govor Konavala [The speech of Konavli]. *Srpski dijalektološki zbornik* XLI. 241–386.
Kiparsky, Paul & Carol Kiparsky. 1971. Fact. In Danny D. Steinberg & Leon A. Jakobovits (eds.), *Semantics: An interdisciplinary reader in philosophy, linguistics and psychology*, 345–369. Cambridge: Cambridge University Press.
Kovačević, Miloš. 1998. *Sintaksa složene rečenice u srpskom jeziku* [The syntax of the complex sentence in the Serbian language]. Belgrade: Raška škola.
Kopečný, František & Hermina Plevačová (red.). 1980. *Etymologický slovník slovanských jazyků, sv. 2: Spojky, částice, zájmena a zájmenná adverbia* [Etymological dictionary of the Slavic

languages, 2: Conjunctions, particles, pronominals and pronominal adverbs]. Prague Academia.

Kravar, Miroslav. 1953. O «razlici» između infinitiva i veze da + prezent [About the "difference" between the infinitive and the connection da + present tense]. *Jezik: časopis za kulturu hrvatskoga književnog jezika* 2 (2). 43–47.

Krys'ko, V. B. 1997. *Istoričeskij sintaksis russkogo jazyka: Ob"ekt i perexodnost'* [Historical syntax of the Russian language: Object and transitivity]. Moscow: Indrik.

Kurc, Josef. 1963. Problematika issledovanija sintaksisa staroslavjanskogo jazyka [Problems in the study of Old Church Slavonic syntax]. In *Issledovanija po sintaksisu staroslavjanskogo jazyka*, 5–14. Prague: Izdatel'stvo Čexoslovackoj akademii nauk.

Kuznetsova, Julia & Tore Nesset. 2015. In which case are Russians afraid? *Bojat'sja* with genitive and accusative objects. *Journal of Slavic linguistics* 23 (2). 255–283.

Lehmann, Winfred P. 1980. The reconstruction of non-simple sentences in Proto-Indo-European. In Paolo Ramat (ed.), *Linguistic reconstruction and Indo-European syntax*. 113–144. Amsterdam & Philadelphia: Benjamins.

Luraghi, Silvia. 1990. *Old Hittite sentence structure*. London & New York: Routledge.

Luraghi, Silvia. 2010. The rise (and possible downfall) of configurationality. In Silvia Luraghi & Vit Bubenik (eds.), *Continuum companion to historical linguistics*, 212–229. London & New York: Continuum International Publishing Group.

Lyons, John. 1968. *Introduction to theoretical linguistics*. Cambridge: University Press.

Meillet, Antoine. 1908. *Introduction à l'étude comparative des langues indoeuropéennes. Deuxième édition corrigée et augmentée*. Paris: Hachette.

Milivojević, Zoran. 2014. *Emocije. Psihoterapija i razumevanje emocija* [Emotions. Psychotherapy and the understanding of emotions]. Novi Sad: Psihopolis institut.

MIT: *The MIT encyclopedia of the cognitive sciences*. 1999. Cambridge & London: The MIT Press.

Moskovljević, Jasmina. 2004. O distribuciji komplementizatora u savremenom srpskom jeziku [On distribution of complementizers in contemporary Serbian]. *Južnoslovenski filolog* LX. 57–65.

Pavlović, Slobodan. 2006. *Determinativni padeži u starosrpskoj poslovnopravnoj pismenosti* [Determinative cases in Old Serbian legal and business documents]. Novi Sad: Matica srpska.

Pavlović, Slobodan. 2009. *Starosrpska zavisna rečenica od XII do XV veka* [The Old Serbian dependent clause from the 12th to the 15th century]. Sremski Karlovci & Novi Sad: Izdavačka knjižarnica Zorana Stojanovića.

Payne, Thomas E. 2007[9]. *Describing morphosyntax. A guide for field linguists*. Cambridge: Cambridge University Press.

Potebnja, Aleksandr A. 1958. *Iz zapisok po russkoj grammatike. Tom I–II* [From the notes on Russian grammar]. Moscow: Akademija nauk SSSR.

Riđanović, Midhat. 1981. Upotreba zavisnih veznika *što* i *da* osvijetljena pojmom presupozicije [The notion of presupposition and the use of subordinate conjunctions *što* and *da* in Serbo-Croatian (s-c)]. *Književni jezik* 10 (4). 7–13.

RJA: *Rječnik hrvatskoga ili srpskoga jezika*. I–XXIV [Dictionary of the Croatian or Serbian language]. 1880–1976. Zagreb: Jugoslavenska akademija znanosti i umjetnosti.

RMNP: Todor Dimitrovski (red.). 1987. *Rečnik na makedonskata narodna poezija, tom II (D–S)* [Dictionary of Macedonian folk poetry]. Skopje: Institut za makedonski jazik "Krste Misirkov".

Ružić, Vladislava. 2006. *Dopunske rečenice u savremenom srpskom jeziku* [Complement clauses in the contemporary Serbian language]. Novi Sad: Matica srpska.

Sandfeld, Kristian. 1930. *Linguistique balkanique. Problèmes et résultats*. Paris: Librarie C. Klincksieck.
SEPh: *Stanford encyclopedia of philosophy*: Emotion. https://plato.stanford.edu/entries/emotion/ (accessed January 2016).
Sedláček, Jan. 1970. Srpskohrvatske potvrde o razvitku rečenica sa *da* u južnim slovenskim jezicima [Serbo-Croatian evidence of the development of *da*-clauses in South Slavic languages]. *Zbornik za filologiju i lingvistiku* XIII (2). 59–69.
SS: Ral'a M. Cejtlin, Radoslav Večerka & Emilie Blagova (eds.). 1994. *Staroslavjanskij slovar' (po rukopisjam X–XI vekov)* [Old Church Slavonic dictionary (based on the manuscripts from the 10th to the 11th centuries)]. Moscow: Russkij jazyk.
StbR: *Starobălgarski rečnik*, I–II [Old Bulgarian dictionary]. 1999–2009. Sofija: Izdatelstvo "Valentin Trajanov".
Stevanović, Mihailo. 1969. *Savremeni srpskohrvatski jezik II: Sintaksa* [Contemporary Serbo-Croatian language II: Syntax]. Belgrade: Naučna knjiga.
Toporov, Vladimir Nikolaevič. 1961. *Lokativ v slavjanskix jazykax* [Locative in Slavic languages]. Moscow: Akademija nauk SSSR.
Trávníček, František. 1956. *Historická mluvnice česká III. Skladba* [Historical grammar of Czech III. Syntax]. Prague: Státní pedagogické nakladatelství.
Troicki, V. I. 1959. K istorii sojuza *čto* v russkom jazyke [On the history of subordinator *čto* in the Russian language]. *Slavjanskoe jazykoznanie. Sbornik statej*, 160–169. Moscow: Akademija nauk SSSR.
Večerka, Radoslav. 1961. *Syntax aktivních participií v staroslověnštine* [Syntax of active participles in Old Church Slavonic]. Prague: Státní pedagogické nakladatelství.

Barbara Sonnenhauser
Slovene *naj*: An (emerging) clausal complementiser?

Abstract: Slovene *naj* (coarsely: 'let; should') is a highly multifaceted modal element. In the contemporary standard language, it occurs as a modal marker and figures in the formation of periphrastic predicates and complex clauses. With regard to the latter, *naj* has also been analysed as a clausal complementiser. In order to get a clearer understanding of its potential to contribute to complex clause formation, the present paper traces the development of *naj* from the earliest sources of the 16th century onwards. Carving out the semantic and syntactic changes underlying the emergence of its remarkable polyfunctionality, the features of 'non-assertion' and 'speaker-attitude' turn out as central semantic components. Both relate to the original imperative function of *naj*, which got lost in the course of its development. This semantic bleaching was accompanied by a functional expansion and an accumulation of structural options for *naj*. Whether these options include the function as a clausal complementiser emerges as an empirical question that needs to be discussed against the more general background of linguistic categorisation.

Keywords: assertion, cyclic development, deonticity, force, mood, quotative, speaker attitude, volition

---

Acknowledgements: The research for this paper has been carried out within the project *Language description as filter and prism: the 'individuality' of Slovene*, funded by the Swiss National Science Foundation SNSF (grant number 10001B_162970/1). This support is gratefully acknowledged. I am also very much indebted to Marjana Tišler for her native speaker judgements. Furthermore, I would like to thank Mladen Uhlik and Björn Wiemer for their valuable comments on earlier versions of this paper, and an anonymous reviewer for many helpful remarks.

Barbara Sonnenhauser, University of Zurich, Slavisches Seminar, Plattenstrasse 43, CH-8032 Zürich, e-mail: barbara.sonnenhauser@uzh.ch

https://doi.org/10.1515/9783110725858-010

1 Introducing *naj*

Slovene *naj* (coarsely: 'let; should') is a highly multifaceted modal element. In contemporary Slovene, it takes finite complements and figures in the formation of periphrastic predicates, see (1), and complex clauses, as in (2).[1]

(1) a. vsak naj ostane kar je in naj pokuša
 each naj remain.PFV.PRS.3SG what is and naj try.PRS.3SG
 naj bolje uspeti.
 the most succeed.PFV.INF
 'Let each remain what s/he is and (leat each) try her/his best to succeed.'
 (Topolińska 2003: 319)
 b. *naj vaša soseda jutri pride*
 naj your neighbour tomorrow come. PFV.PRS.3SG
 'Your neighbor shall / let your neighbor come tomorrow!'
 (Uhlik & Žele 2017: 95)

(2) a. *Rekel je, naj mu oprosti ...*
 he said naj him forgive. PFV.PRS.3SG
 'He said that he ought to be forgiven...' (Topolińska 2003: 313)
 b. *Končno sem mu ukazala, naj gre v posteljo*
 finally I told him naj go.(I)PFV.PRS.3SG to bed
 'Finally, I ordered him to to to bed [lit: that he should got to bed]'
 (Gigafida; DZS 2000)

The fact that in the complex structure in (2), the syntactic argument status and the modal characteristics of the embedded clause are signalled exclusively by *naj* is taken to indicate that it has acquired complementiser functions (Topolińska 2003: 313) and has been grammaticalised as a clausal complementiser (Uhlik 2018: 403). Thereby, *naj* emerges as a 'remarkable feature of Slovene' (Topolińska 2003), since this option is not available for cognate and semantically comparable

---

[1] In the literature, *naj* is referred to in different ways, e.g. as optative/hortative marker or as periphrastic imperative (summarised, e.g., in Roeder & Hansen 2006), as subjunctive (Stegovec 2019), as conjunction (e.g. Uhlik 2017) to mention just a few. Each of these denominations is based on a specific focus of analysis and specific theoretical assumptions which makes them hardly comparable or generalisable. In order to avoid invoking particular morphological, syntactic and/or functional associations and remain as agnostic as possible concerning the concomitant categorisations, the present paper will simply speak of '*naj*-structure', referring to *naj* and the element it attaches to.

elements in other Slavonic languages, such as BCS *neka*, Czech *at'* or Russian *pust'* (for a comparison of *naj* and *pust'* see Uhlik 2018).

The semantic contribution displayed by *naj* in these different uses has been described in terms of deonticity and as an interpretative device based on deontic use (Holvoet & Konickaja 2011), weak necessity (Roeder & Hansen 2006) or non-factivity (Topolińska 2003; note that Topolińska understands non-factivity in a broader sense, i.e. as encompassing non-factuality in the sense as defined by Wiemer, this volume), the syntactic manifestations in terms of 'independent' vs. 'dependent' uses (Topolińska 2003; Uhlik 2018; Uhlik & Žele 2017). This places *naj* within the domain of modality on the one hand, and within the system of clausal connection on the other. A possible link between these two functions consists in the assumption that modally marked structures tend to exhibit restricted assertiveness and hence a lesser degree of semantic independence, which in turn may provide a starting point for reanalysis in terms of a syntactic integration of two structures. The latter involves a scope extension of the element in question from event description to the description of a situation and its being semantically and/or syntactically headed by a structurally higher predicate.

Drawing on these intuitions, the present paper aims at elaborating the semantic and syntactic polyfunctionality of *naj* and sketching its development from a verb oriented modal element to an element serving as clausal connector, i.e. from a predicate related marker within one clausal structure to a marker connecting two predicates across clauses. In a further perspective, this will contribute to uncovering in more detail the variety of strategies of clausal complementation encountered in the South Slavic languages and the diversity in the underlying diachronic processes.

The paper is structured as follows: Section 2 reviews the main types of *naj* established in the previous literature. On this basis, the features of non-assertion and speaker-attitude will be suggested as the two central semantic contributions introduced by *naj* (Section 3). Section 4 provides a diachronic sketch illustrating the functional extension of *naj* that might have led to its contemporary polyfunctionalty. The question as to whether *naj* qualifies as a clausal complementiser will be addressed in the concluding Section 5, putting this question into the broader perspective of linguistic categorisation.

2 Polyfunctional *naj*

Due to its polyfunctionality in contemporary Slovene, a semantic characterization of *naj* is hard to obtain. Roeder & Hansen (2006: 165) regard it as "a word with diffuse semantics", Topolińska (2003) characterises it as expressing 'non-factivity'. Roughly speaking, four main types of *naj* have been distinguished in previous work (see, in particular, Roeder & Hansen 2006, Holvoet & Konickaja 2011, Messner 1980, Gradišnik 1981, Topolińska 2003, Uhlik 2018, Uhlik & Žele 2017):[2] mood marker, modal particle, adverbial conjunction and clausal complementiser. The former two are also summarised as independent, the latter as dependent uses (Topolińska 2003, Uhlik & Žele 2017). While these types are, of course, not clear-cut categories, elaborating their functional characteristics will serve as a first step towards determining the functional range of *naj*.

2.1 Mood marker

As a mood marker, *naj* is regarded to be part of a periphrastic permissive verbal paradigm, a function which is described already in the early grammars of Slovene (e.g. Kopitar 1808). Complementing the morphological imperative in the first and third persons, see (3) and (4), it is ascribed hortative and optative meanings, i.e. as expressing a speaker's wish with an appeal to carry out this wish addressed to the 1st and 3rd person and a speaker's wish addressed to all persons (on these conceptions of hortative and optative meanings see, e.g., Ammann & van der Auwera 2004: 343–344).

(3) *Ampak nihče mi ni rekel, naj neham delati*
but nobody me NEG tell.PST.3SG naj stop.PRS.1SG work.INF
'But nobody has told me, that I should stop working' (Gigafida; Delo Revije 2008)

(4) a. *Tisti [...] pa naj ne hodijo na Grmado ampak*
those but naj NEG go.PRS.3PL on Grmada but
naj ostanejo v planinski koči.
naj stay.PFV.PRS.3PL in mountain shelter
'Those should not climb the Grmada, but should stay in the mountain shelter.' (Gigafida; Novi tednik NT&RC 1998)

---

[2] Roeder & Hansen (2006) regard *naj* as an exponent of weak obligation, comparing it to Polish *mieć*; Holvoet & Konickaja (2011) propose an analysis in terms of 'interpretive deontics', comparable to Latvian *lai*. Messner (1980) and Gradišnik (1981) focus on *naj* as marker of hearsay or conjecture, discussing in particular the question whether these functions have arisen due to language contact with German. Topolińska (2003) is concerned with *naj* as a non-finite mood marker and as a means to accommodate finite clauses. Uhlik & Žele (2017) investigate its uses with the introduction of complements to desiderative and manipulative verbs, comparing it to the complementiser *da*; Uhlik (2018) compares *naj* to Russian *pust'*. Regarding *naj*-structures as an instance of embedded directives, Stegovec (2019) proposes an analysis in terms of 'perspectival control'.

b. *Zavarovalna vsota   naj ponuja   finančno brezskrbnost* [...]
   insurance sum   naj offer.IPFV.PRS.3SG financial carefereness
   'The insurance sum shall offer financial carefreeness.' (Gigafida; Delo FT 2007)

However, *naj* and the morphological imperative are not as neatly distributed as these descriptions suggest. On the one hand, the morphological imperative appears with inclusive first person dual and plural as well (as pointed out also by Stegovec 2019), see (5).

(5) *delajva   dalje*
    work.IPFV.IMP.DU   further
    'let us two work on' (Gigafida; Dnevnik 1997)

On the other hand, *naj* may appear – albeit rarely, and, according to a native speaker's judgement, somewhat markedly – in combination with morphological imperatives, (6).[3] Instances of *naj*+imperative can also be found in 16th century texts, see Trubar's translation of Mt 27,49 in (7).[4]

(6) *Vendar naj povej   da*
    but   naj tell.PFV.IMP.2SG   that
    'But you should say that' (Gigafida; Dolenjski list, 1997)

(7) *Pufti,   nai gledaimo,   aku Elias pride*   (TRB)
    let.IPFV.IMP.2SG   naj see.IPFV.IMP.2PL whether Elijah come.PRS.3SG
    'Wait, let us see whether Elijah will come to save him.' (Mt 27,49)[5]

In addition, *naj* is also attested with 2nd person indicative (noted also in Roeder & Hansen 2006), see (8). As with *naj*+imperative, this combination is judged odd by a native speaker informant. It is only rarely attested – but still, it is can be found.[6]

---

[3] A corpus search in Gigafida (carried out 9 Sept 2017) yielded 660 hits for '*naj*+verb.IMP', distance 2.
[4] The contemporary version has the 1st plural imperative *poglejmo*.
[5] All Slovene bible passages are taken from www.biblija.net, the English translations correspond to the English Standard Version as retrieved from https://biblia.com (note that not in all cases do they reflect the structure and semantics of the Slovene constructions).
[6] A search for *naj+greš* in Gigafida on April 05, 2019 yielded 16 hints.

(8) da raje   naj greš   čistit
     that better naj go.(I)PFV.PRS.2SG clean.SUP
     'that you better go cleaning' (Gigafida; 24ur.com 2010)

In its function as a mood marker, *naj* also appears in questions, be they rhetorical or direct (Topolińska 2003: 319), see (9a) and (9b). This is another distinguishing feature of *naj*, since this usage is not possible for functionally comparable markers in other Slavic languages, such as Russian *pust'* (Uhlik 2018: 409).

(9) a. *Kaj   naj napišem   v zapisnik?*
        what   naj write.PFV.PRS.1SG in record
        'What ought I to write in the record?' (Topolińska 2003: 319)
    b. *Naj pokličem   zravnika?*
        naj call.PFV.PRS.1SG doctor
        'Shall I call the doctor?' (Topolińska 2003: 319)

Obviously, thus *naj* differs from the imperative, but does not simply complement the morphological imperative paradigm. This suggests that its function needs to be elaborated in more detail.

As a mood marker, *naj* takes scope over the finite verb and is thus event related. While this also holds for the questions illustrated in (9), in questions of the type illustrated in (10a) it behaves differently. Here, *naj* appears after the finite verb and at least in this specific case seems to be correlated with different scope: It does not relate to the verb and the event it describes, as in (10b), but has larger scope over the proposition. These uses of *naj* come close to the functional type to be discussed in Section 2.2.

(10) a. *Obvladam   naj se?*
         control.IPFV.PRS.1SG naj REFL
         'Control myself?' (http://opus.nlpl.eu)[7]
         [I should control myself?]
     b. *Kako naj se obvladam?*
         how   naj REFL control.IPFV.PRS.1SG
         'How should I control myself?' (http://opus.nlpl.eu)

---

[7] Unless indicated otherwise, translations to examples from opus.nlpl.eu correspond to the parallel English texts in that corpus. In case they are too loose to substantiate the point to be made, they will be supplemented by more literal translations in square brackets.

2.2 Modal particle

As a modal particle, *naj* is ascribed meanings of doubt, (11), conjecture (12), and hearsay (13).

(11) *To   naj   bi mi zadostovalo   za ves mesec!*
      this naj   SUBJ me suffice.IPFV.SUBJ   for whole month
      'This is meant to suffice for me for the whole month!' ['this shall suffice for me']
      (Gradišnik 1981: 24)

(12) *In zdaj   naj   bi bil   Jeremy na zabavi?*
      and now   naj   SUBJ be.SUBJ   Jeremy at parti
      'And now Jeremy's supposedly at the party?' (http://opus.nlpl.eu)

(13) *Ruth,   po podatkih   naj   bi se pregon začel   v okolici La Brea*
      Ruth   according data   naj   SUBJ REFL pursuit begin.SUBJ   in vicinity La Brea
      ['According to the data the pursuit began']
      'Ruth, we're hearing reports that the pursuit began near the La Brea area'
      (http://opus.nlpl.eu)

This usage is discussed as being borrowed from German (see Messner 1980, Gradišnik 1981). With its uses as a iussive marker and an epistemic/evidential modal, German *sollen* 'shall, should' serves functions similar to *naj*. And similar to *sollen*, *naj* obviously extended its applicability from root-modal to epistemic/evidential contexts (see Zeman 2013 for a diachronic description of the emergence of reportive and quotative functions for German *sollen*), as in (14).[8] Following Boye, van Lier & Theilgaard Brink (2015: 3), these latter interpretations can be subsumed under the concept of 'justificatory support'.

(14)   *Naj   bi bila   očarljivo   [dekle; BS]*
       naj   SUBJ be.SUBJ   charming   [girl]
(14') *Es   soll   sehr hübsch   sein.*
       it   supposed.to   very beautiful be.INF
       'It [the girl, BS] is supposed to be charming.' (http://opus.nlpl.eu)

---

8 Whether or not the marking of hearsay or doubt is borrowed from German (the path from deonticity to meanings expressing justificatory support is quite frequently attested, see, e.g., Holvoet 2012 for Polish *mieć*), the main difference to the German constructions consists in the morphological makeup: While German has a finite modal verb plus infinitive, Slovene has a non-inflected marker plus finite verb. This is similar in structure to the possibility modal marker *lahko*, which likewise appears with a nominative subject and a finite verbal complement.

At the same time, *naj* covers uses of German *lassen* 'let'. In this function, *naj* is frequently preceded by an imperative form of *pustiti* 'let', (15), and appears also in older data, (15b), where the hearsay-function does not seem to be attested (see Section 4).

(15) a. *Pusti   ga,   naj gre*
       let.PFV.IMP.2SG him   naj go.(I)PFV.PRS.3SG
       'Just let him go.' (http://opus.nlpl.eu/)
       [lit: 'Let him, he shall go.']
   b. *Puſti   naj nyh Misa   bo   k'enimu ſhtriku*   (DAL)
       let.PFV.IMP.2SG naj their table be.FUT.3SG to them snare
   b'. *Njihova miza naj postane   zanka.*   (SSP3)
       their table   naj become.PFV.PRS.3SG snare
       'Let their table become a snare' (Rom 11,9)

Differently from the uses as mood marker discussed in Section 2.1, *naj* as a modal particle has scope over the proposition and assesses it with respect to its justificatory support. Importantly, the particular meanings ascribed to this usage of *naj* are not contributed by *naj* alone but are rather contingent on the subjunctive '*bi*+*l*-participle' (see also Hansen & Roeder 2006: 167; Uhlik 2018: 410–411). Again, thus, a closer look on the contribution of *naj* seems necessary.

2.3 Adverbial conjunction

In its 'dependent' uses, *naj* is restricted to clause-initial position (Uhlik 2018: 412). Semantically and/or syntactically it relates to the preceding predicate, which thereby functions as its head. Topolińska (2003) distinguishes two dependent functions for *naj*: adverbial conjunction and complementiser.

For *naj* as an adverbial conjunction, the semantic link to a preceding predicate is established by a feature of goal, concession or condition encoded in this predicate (Topolińska 2003: 314; see also Roeder & Hansen 2006). Examples of *naj* introducing concessive and conditional clauses are given in (16) and (17).

(16) *Naj jo tudi imajo,   ampak ne   na mojem dvorišču.*
     naj her also have.IPFV.PRS.3PL but not   in my backyard
     'Let them have her as well, but not in my backyard.' (Gigafida: rtvslo.si 2010)

(17) *Naj te kdo sliši,   pa bo zamera*
     naj you somebody hear.(I)PFV PRS.3SG EMPH be.FUT.3SG bad_mood
     'Should somebody hear you, bad mood will arise.' (SSKJ)

In these cases, however, the overall construction seems to add a decisive contribution to the interpretation,[9] while *naj* itself functions as a verbal modifier. It is thus questionable, whether these should be regarded as instances of 'dependent' *naj*, the more so as in both cases the *naj* clause could stand on its own, but with a jussive interpretation.

This is different in (18), where *daj* 'give' implies 'goal' (supported by the imperative form) and *naj* can be interpreted as spelling out to this feature.

(18)   *Daj mu denar,   naj   vozi   celo noč.*
       give him money   naj   drive.IPFV.PRS.3SG   whole night
       'Give him money, he shall drive / such that he drives the whole night through.'[10]
       (http://opus.nlpl.eu)

The structure in (18) consists of two clauses that are loosely connected; instead of being connected by a final relation (interpretation: 'such that he drives'), both may equally well stand on their own (interpretation: 'he shall drive'), in which case *naj* functions as independent marker (noted also by Topolińska 2003: 315). That is, the relation between the triggering predicate and *naj* arises from a discourse inference and is not syntactically determined; the presumed status of *naj* as adverbial conjunction is based on a discourse relation, less on syntactic grounds.[11]

The availability of these two options – discourse mediated biclausal structure and two separate clauses – also becomes apparent in (19), where there does not seem to be a goal-triggering predicate in the main clause. Here, *naj* may be interpreted (i) as final conjunction triggered by the directive component implied in the goal-oriented *na sodisce* 'to court', or (ii) as an independent mood marker relating to the verb *se izkaže* 'turn out'.

---

9 The conditional connection resembles the Russian 'conditional imperative construction', which is not restricted to 2nd person imperatives, but may as well contain wishes directed to 1st and 3rd persons (Fortuin & Boogart 2009: 647–648).

10 Translation BS; no English translation available in opus.nlpl.eu (German: 'Da, der Fahrer soll die Nacht durchfahren').

11 Note that here, the clause introduced by *naj* has to follow *dati*. This adds to the assumption of a less subordinate and more independent status of the *naj* structure (e.g. Weiss 1989 on the possibility of switching clauses as one indicator of the paratactic/hypotactic status of a complex clausal structure) and the involvement of a discourse relation.

(19) *Tako je prav, Janšo na sodišče, naj se izkaže*
that is right Janša to court naj REFL turn_out.PFV.PRS.3SG
ali je kriv ali ne.
wether is guilty or not
'That's the right way, [bring] Janša to court, (i) *such that* it will *turn out* /
(ii) It shall turn out whether he is guilty or not.' (Gigafida; 24ur.com 2010)

In sum, the difference between *naj* as an adverbial conjunction and as an independent mood marker is not clear cut. In the type of dependent usage discussed in this section, *naj* applies to a finite predicate and the event described by it. At the same time the inference of a semantic link to a predicate in a previous clause may arise, which then may be interpreted to function as a semantic, possibly also syntactic, head. Again, thus, the interpretations ascribed to *naj* do not seem to be triggered by this marker alone.

2.4 Complementiser

The second type of dependent usage mentioned by Topolińska (2003) is that of a 'non-factive' – that is, non-factual (see section 1) – complementiser. She takes the main difference to the adverbial conjunction function as consisting in 1) the syntactically relevant status of the structure introduced by *naj*, which fills in a valency slot opened by a head predicate, and 2) the triggering of a directive interpretation for the head predicate by *naj*. Both is the case in (20) and (21).

(20) *Rekel si naj bo luč in bila je.*
you said naj be.FUT.3SG light and it was
'You ordered there to be light and there was light.' (Gigafida; Dnevnik 2000)

(21) *Daniel Starman je predlagal naj*
Daniel Starman suggested naj
Spomenka raje sama odstopi
Spomenka better resign.PFV.PRS.3SG by herself
'Daniel Starman suggested Spomenka to better resign by herself.'
(Gigafida; Mladina 1992)

According to Topolińska (2003: 313), *naj* here functions as a signal "that there is a volitive component in the lexical meaning of the dominating predicate". This is comparable to the Balkan Slavic complementiser *da* (2003: 313), as illustrated in (22) for Macedonian (see Uhlik 2018 for *da* vs. *naj* as introducing complements to desiderative and manipulative verbs; Tomić 2012: 342–343 on the differences between statement and desire/intention induced by *deka*- vs. *da*-headed complements to *verba dicendi* in Macedonian):[12]

(22) a. *toj reče   deka*
       he   say.AOR.3SG that
       'he said that'
    b. *toj reče   da*
       he   say.AOR.3SG that
       'he ordered that / to'

If *naj* serves both functions – the filling in a valency slot and the triggering of a non-factual ('non-factive' in Topolińska's terms) interpretation for the head predicate – on its own, i.e. without the general complementiser *da*, Topolińska (2003: 314) regards it as a complementiser.

What needs to be accounted for then are combinations of *da* and *naj*, as in (23). Here, *naj* functions as a mood marker relating to the predicate, whereas *da* as a complementiser has scope over the structure headed by *naj*.

(23) a. *Rekel mi je,   da naj   vas pričakam*
       he told me   that naj you pick_up.PFV.PRS.1SG
       'He told me to pick you up.' (http://opus.nlpl.eu)
    b. *preden jim je reko da naj   hitro pridejo*
       bevor I told them   that naj quickly come.PFV.PRS.3PL
       'before I told them *that they should come* quickly' (GOS)

---

12 Elements such as Balkan Slavic *da* or Albanian *të*, too, may appear as part of a modally marked verbal form (the subjunctive), function in independent clauses and serve the formation of complex phrasal structures (see Widmer & Sonnenhauser 2020 for a comparison of Macedonian *da* and Albanian *të*). Differently from Balkan Slavic and Albanian, *naj* is less strictly tied to the verb and is used for complex predicate formation only in the cases discussed in this paper. Concerning the diachrony of Balkan Slavic *da*, one possible scenario starts from a verbal form, i.e. the imperative of *dati* 'give' (see Wiemer 2017: 325–326 for a brief overview of hypotheses), see (i)–(iv). Upon this scenario, the development of *da* and *naj* seems largely comparable.

(i)   Imperative of *dati* 'give'
(ii) Particle with volitional semantics
(iii) Usage after volitional and directive verbs > complementiser
(iv) Introduction of final and consecutive sentences > conjunction

The same holds for combinations of *da* and *naj*+subjunctive, see (24). Here, *naj*+subjunctive is in the scope of *da*, such that specific interpretation triggered by this combination, here: hearsay, is part of the clausal complement introduced by *da*. The overall structure is thus close to (13), with the source of information provided by a syntactically external predicate (*govori se* 'it is said').

(24) *Govori se,   da   naj bi   se letos*
      say.PRS.3SG REFL that   naj SUBJ   REFL this_year
      udeležili conference.
      attend.PFV.SUBJ conference
      'Word is they're planning to attend the conference.' (http://opus.nlpl.eu/)

Examples such as (25) provide additional support for the assumption that with the combination of *da* and *naj*, the attachment to the head predicate is achieved by *da*. A non-negated factive predicate like *vedeti* 'know'[13] should not allow for a clausal complement that is reduced in assertiveness. Hence, it is *da* that adds declarative force, while *naj* is in its scope and functions as modal particle applying to the subjunctive *bi poznali*.[14]

(25) *Vem,   da   naj bi poznali   pot do Zemlje.*
      know.PRS.1SG   that naj SUBJ know.IPFV.SUBJ way to Earth
      'I know they're supposed to know the way to Earth.' (http://opus.nlpl.eu)

Uhlik & Žele (2017: 106) list examples of *da naj* in which *da* seems to be optional, (26), and interpret *da naj* as a complex conjunction ("sočetanie v sojuznoj funkcii"). In these cases, they regard the 'cluster' *da naj* as semantically equivalent to *naj* (Uhlik & Žele 2017: 106, fn 42).

(26) *Zahtevam,   (da) naj   bo soba pospravljena.*
      demand.IPFV.PRS.1SG   (that) naj be.FUT.3SG room tidied_up
      'I demand the room to be tidied up' ['that the room be tidied up']
      (Uhlik & Žele 2017: 106)[15]

---

[13] Factive or propositional knowledge in Slovene is expressed by *vedeti*, while ability-related knowledge is expressed by *znati* (see Sonnenhauser 2017).
[14] That is, we are dealing here with two propositional scopes being inserted into each other, which makes this example even more interesting. I thank Björn Wiemer for pointing this out to me.
[15] In Russian, *čtoby*+subjunctive would be used: *Ja trebuju, čtoby komnata byla ubrana* (Uhlik & Žele 2017: 106).

The optionality of *da* under certain circumstances suggests that *naj* may indeed serve the complementising function on its own. As (27) shows, in the absence of *da* serving as complementiser, *naj* may assume a double function. Similar to (25), (27) has *naj* and a subjunctive predicate. Differently from (25), however, *naj* not only adds an attitude holder to the subjunctive *bi sukala* 'moves around', but also attaches this predicate and the overall clausal structure into the complement slot of *izvedeli* 'find out'. The attitude holder is provided by the matrix clause subject.

(27) *Neuradno smo izvedeli, naj bi se vsota sukala*
unofficially we found out naj be.SUBJ REFL sum move.SUBJ
okrog 100.000 nemških mark.
around 100.000 German mark
'We found out from unofficial sources that the sum (allegedly) moves around 100.000 D-Marks.' (Gigafida; Dnevnik 1997)

The data presented here show that *naj* ranges between independent and dependent uses. Both types may be activated in particular usage contexts. This oscillation provides first hints concerning the potential starting point for the diachronic functional extension of *naj*.

2.5 Summing up

In contemporary Slovene, *naj* requires a finite complement. The only restriction applying is 'non past', which fits the directive force of *naj*. In specific cases, *naj* contributes to complex structure building across predicates beyond the clausal level. This complex structure may be based on and inferred by a discourse relation (in particular in case of a preceding predicate carrying 'goal' as semantic feature) or syntactically required (if the preceding predicate opens up a valency slot).

The data presented in this section illustrate the difficulty involved in distinguishing *naj* as establishing an intra-predicate or an inter-predicate relation, i.e. *naj* as predicate-oriented marker vs. clausal marker, and – within the latter – conjunction and complementiser. This second question pertains to the nature of the relation between a head predicate and a predicative complement and the linguistic analysis of this relation. Since this, in turn, invites conceptual problems on a more theory-dependent level exceeding the issue of the status of *naj*, it is more constructive to focus on *naj* and its potential to contribute to complex clause formation. Even though this might not provide an answer to the question of how to distinguish complement clauses form adverbial clauses (and other types of complex clauses), it contributes to carving out those features of *naj* that permit it to serve a clause connecting function. These features will be illustrated in the following section.

3 Semantics

Both the syntactic versatility and the semantic polyfunctionality of *naj* require a closer look on its specific semantic contribution in the various syntactic contexts it appears in. This is also necessary to position *naj* within the modal system of Slovene and its system of clausal connectors. Two features turn out relevant in this respect: the specification of an attitude holder and the indication of a non-assertive context.

3.1 Attitude holder

One of the distinctive features of *naj* consists in the introduction of an attitude holder. This attitude holder may be introduced within the structure containing the *naj*-construction ('dependent' uses of *naj*) or provided by a predicate external to it ('independent' uses of *naj*).

3.1.1 Independent uses

As a mood marker, *naj* is functionally close to the imperative. Differently from the imperative, however, volition and permission expressed by *naj* may be imposed to and from attitude holders dissociated from the actual communicative situation and its speech act participants. In (28), with the imperative, addresser and addressees are part of the communicative situation, while in (29), with a *naj* structure, the source of volition is outside the situation.[16] The volitive attitude is directed towards the event denoted by the finite verb.

---

[16] Comparing (in)dependent *naj* with (in)dependent *da* to express imperative meanings, Uhlik & Žele (2017: 95, 111) regard the manifestation of the addressee as main difference between the two: it is 'indirect' with *naj* but 'direct' with *da*, i.e. outside the communicative situation or part of it, respectively. They do not consider the addresser, i.e. the source of volition. According to the analysis proposed here, the addresser/source of volition plays a crucial role for the semantic contribution of *naj* as well. In a recent paper, Stegovac (2019) takes the "ban on coreference between the attitude holder and the subject" (2019: 48) as characteristic features of dependent *naj*-structures and proposes an analysis in terms of 'perspectival control' for their specific relation to the matrix clause.

(28) *Delajmo   skupaj,   delajmo   razumno.*
    act.IPFV.IMP.1PL jointly act.IPFV.IMP.1PL   reasonably
    'Let's act jointly, let's work intelligently.' (Gigafida; 24ur.com 2010)

(29) *Mi, kmetje   pa naj bomo   lepo tiho in   naj delamo*
    we, farmers EXPR naj be.FUT.1PL nicely calm and   naj work.IPFV.PRS.1PL
    'We, farmers, *should be quiet* and *should work*.' (Gigafida; Kmečki glas 2009)

The interpretations of hearsay, conjecture, doubt (i.e. justificatory support, see Section 2.2) are tied to the combination of *naj* with a subjunctive predicate. These interpretations are not typical of either element on their own.[17] Examples such as (30) and (31) suggest that here, too, *naj* introduces an attitude holder which is not necessarily identical with the actual narrator and may also be implicit, see (32).

(30) *Po njihovih ocenah   naj   bi se trg   že letos*
    according their assessments   naj   SUBJ REFL market   already this year
    nekoliko umiril,
    somewhat calm_down.PFV.SUBJ
    'According to their assessment, the market is *supposed* to [lit. *should*] *calm down* somewhat already this year.' (Gigafida)

(31) *Po tvojem   naj   bi bil   edini*
    according you naj   SUBJ be.SUBJ   only.one
    'You made it seem like I was the only one.' (http://opus.nlpl.eu)

(32) *Ubil   naj   bi   tisto žensko   iz poročil,*
    kill.PFV.SUBJ   naj   SUBJ that woman   from news
    'They're saying he killed that woman on the news' (http://opus.nlpl.eu)

Serving as anchor of the non-actuality contributed by the subjunctive predicate, the attitude holder emerges as the source of justificatory support. Here, the attitude has situational scope, i.e. it relates to the proposition expressed by the clause headed by *naj*.

---

[17] This seems comparable to *lahko*, the other modal particle of Slovene combining with finite verbs. Its application to the subjunctive yields an epistemic interpretation, specifically, that of epistemic possibility (*naj*+subjunctive: epistemic necessity). The obvious assumption that *lahko*+SUBJ and *naj*+SUBJ complement each other as epistemic possibility / epistemic necessity constructions is still in need of empirical verification.

3.1.2 Dependent uses

In the dependent uses of *naj*, the attitude holder is introduced by a predicate outside the immediate clause structure containing the *naj*-construction, i.e. a predicate that serves as semantic and/or syntactic head. In (33), the matrix verb *povedati* 'tell' heads the structures introduced by *da* and, as can be seen from the coordination *in* 'and', *da*+*naj* in a parallel way. This suggests that here, *naj* still relates to the verb and that this complex appears in the scope of *da*. That is, *da* introduces a clause containing a complex predicate headed by *naj*, while *naj* introduces an attitude expressed by one of the speech act participants of the matrix clause. This attitude modifies the event description and thereby contributes to marking the illocutionary force of the complement to *povedati*.

(33) *Povedal nam je, da   Morrok ne obstaja   in   da naj*
     he told us   that Morrok not exist.IPFV.PRS.3SG and that naj
     se ne bojimo.
     not be_afraid.IPFV.PRS.1PL
     'He told us there was no morrok and that we shouldn't be afraid.'
     (http://opus.nlpl.eu)

In (34), *naj* allows for various interpretations: in parallel with *da* as introducing a syntactic complement to *reče*, i.e. as having scope over the proposition relating to an attitude holder specified by an external predicate, or as being within the scope of *da*, i.e. as event-related mood marker.

(34) *Pa mi reče,   da   sem res neumen   in   naj*
     and s/he told me that I am indeed stupid   and   naj
     si izberem   pomočnikov
     me select.PFV.PRS.1SG   assistants
     'And s/he told me, that I am really stuped and (that) I should select me assistants.' (Gigafida; Delo 2008)

In the absence of *da* in (35), the complement to *reči* seems to be attached by *naj* alone, i.e. it introduces indirect speech.

(35) *Mama me pošilja. Je rekla   naj pogledam,   če*
    Mum me sending   she told   naj look.PFV.PRS.1SG   whether
    imate   morda   svinjsko glavo
    have.IPFV.PRS.2PL   maybe   pig head
    'Mum is sending me. She asked me to look whether you maybe have a pig's head.' (Gigafida; Celjan 2002)

What is decisive again is the ability of *naj* to introduce an attitude holder potentially expressing an attitude different from or in addition to that of the narrator. That is, not only the addressee or target of volition / permission is 'indirect' (see Uhlik & Žele 2017), but also the addresser or source, i.e. the attitude holder. This attitude holder is provided by a predicate outside the clause containing the *naj*-structure, the attitude relates to the event described by the finite verb (conjunction) or the state of affairs (complementiser) in the scope of *naj*. By relating to an attitude holder in another clause, *naj* establishes an anchoring beyond the level of the clause it appears in and hence a relation to the discourse. Establishing a relation to the discourse is typical of elements at the left periphery of clauses, i.e. elements that qualify as conjunctions and complementisers.

Summing up so far, the interpretations available for *naj* mainly depend on and differ in the target of attitude – event or state of affairs – and the way in which an attitude holder is manifested (contributed by clause external predicate or not). The next question is, what kind of attitude this might be and in how far it contributes to the modal meanings indicated by *naj*.

3.2 Non-assertion

By the introduction of an attitude holder providing the source of volition/permission or the source of justificatory support, the event or situation in the scope of *naj* is assessed with respect to the 'actual world', which makes *naj* a modal element. Thereby, *naj*-structures are regarded as being close to the imperative (as a permissive marker; e.g. Toporišič 2004) and the subjunctive (by the feature of 'non-factivity'; e.g. Topolińska 2003), see above. However, as has been shown, *naj* does not simply supplement the imperative paradigm, since for most persons, both options are attested, including *naj*+morphological imperative, and it is not just another exponent of non-factivity alongside the subjunctive, since both may co-occur and only in combination yield the characteristic interpretations of hearsay, doubt.

What *naj*, the imperative and the subjunctive indeed do share is the feature of 'non-assertion' (in the sense of Palmer 2001). Manifested as counterfactual/hypothetical non-assertion, this feature covers the functions of the subjunctive, manifested as deontic non-assertion the functions of permission (*naj*) and volition (morphological imperative; *naj*). For deontic modality, an independently given source figures as modal background; in the case of *naj*, this source is provided by the attitude holder.

Differently from the imperative and subjunctive, *naj* does not code a particular manifestation of non-assertion as a stable meaning component, but simply contributes to its specification. Thereby, *naj* comes close to what Portner (1997) describes as 'mood-indicating modals', such as *may* in (36).

(36) a. *May you have a pleasant journey!*
     b. *Jack wishes that you may be happy.*

In (36), *may* is not necessary from a syntactic or semantic point of view, since the modal information – volition, judgement – is provided by other lexical and/or structural means, i.e. the optative construction *have pleasant journey* in (36a) and the verb form *wishes* in (36b). Nonetheless, its usage is not redundant (that is, 36a does not mean that the speaker wishes the wish to have a pleasant journey, and 36b does not mean that Jack wishes the wish for the addressee to be happy). Portner (1997: 190) takes this to suggest that in these cases, *may* "does not carry modal force of its own", i.e. does not double information, "but simply indicates that its clause has a particular conversational use or is in a certain kind of semantic context". As instances of 'notional mood' such mood-indicating elements concern "aspects of meaning [...] which contribute to the conversational force of a clause or which constrain the attitude someone has toward what it expresses" (Portner 1997: 182).

Naj behaves very much alike: It indicates that its context is non-assertive and marks its complement as being modified by an attitude holder. Its mood-indicating potential allows for the activation of various kinds of non-assertion, depending on the scope of *naj* (event, state of affairs), the morphological characteristics of its complement (indicative, subjunctive) and the presence of a semantic or syntactic head.

Putting the pieces together, the various functions of *naj* are based on the introduction of an attitude holder (from its original lexical meaning 'let'), the indication of non-assertion (from its original morphological imperative form) and the potential of introducing different scope relations (relating to the loss of its original part-of-speech, i.e. verbal, characteristics). The next question to be addressed is, whether the functional versatility can be related to a diachronic functional extension.

4 Diachronic sketch

As the discussion in Sections 2 and 3 has shown, the structural and semantic types extracted for the uses of *naj* cannot be understood as clear-cut categories. They rather form a continuum with oscillation between interpretations, in particular for *naj* as a verbal marker vs. *naj* as clausal connector. This might reflect a diachronic development in terms of functional expansion in parallel with changes in positions it may occupy in the syntactic structure. In the absence of quantitatively and qualitatively sufficient data, the following remarks only provide an approximation. This approximation is based on Pleteršnik's Slovene-German dictionary from the end of the 19th c. and on a comparison of various translations of the New Testament: Trubar's and Dalmatin's translations (TRB 1555-1577 and DAL 1584) as the oldest written sources of Slovene, Jernej Japel's (JAP 1784-1802) translation as reflecting an immediate pre-standard state,[18] and the contemporary version from 2003 (Osnovna izdaja; SSP3).

4.1 Origin

The entries in the dictionary of contemporary Slovene (SSKJ 2006) and Pleteršnik's Slovene-German dictionary from the late 19th c. (Pleteršnik 1894) provide a first indication of the diachronic development of *naj*. In both, *naj* appears as an element compatible with various syntactic contexts. Remarkably, only Pleteršnik but not SSKJ lists *naj* as an inflected verbal form, i.e. an imperative. As inflected verb, it attaches to various types of structures and may cover two different meanings: 'let', (37), and 'stop', (38). In the former meaning, *naj* may take infinitives as well as finite complements with and without *da* as a linking element,[19] in the latter, only infinitival complements are possible.

(37) *naj, najta, najmo, najte*, lass, lasst, lassen wir 'let, let us'
 – (z "da" 'with *da*'): *naj* da tvoja vest tebi govori, lass dein Gewissen zu dir sprechen [...] 'let your conscience speak to you'; *najte* da izvemo, lasst uns in Erfahrung bringen [...] 'let us find out'; *Najmo* da voda stoji, lassen wir das Wasser stehen [...] 'let us allow the water to stand' [...];

---

[18] In his grammar, Jernej Kopitar (Kopitar 1808) cites examples taken from Japelj.
[19] The fact that *da* and its omission are explicitly mentioned by Pleteršnik, might probably be interpreted to indicate a structure with *naj* belonging to the matrix clause with *da* introducing the complement clause.

- ("da" je izpuščen 'da is omitted'): *najte* se učimo, lasst uns lernen 'let us learn' [. . .]; *najte* vas vprašam, lasst mich euch fragen 'let me ask you' [. . .];
- (z infinitivom 'with infinitive'): *najmo* zvon hladiti, lasst uns die Glocke abkühlen 'let us leave the bell to cool down' [. . .]

(38) *naj, najta, najmo, najte*, z infinitivom, = nikar 'with infinitive, = 'in no case' *naj* me žaliti, beleidige mich nicht [. . .] 'do not insult me'; *naj* se groziti, drohe nicht [. . .] 'do not threaten' [. . .]; *najte* soditi, richtet nicht [. . .] 'do not judge'

Even though the meanings given for inflected *naj* are quite different – permission/volition on the one hand, (37), prohibition/warning in on the other, (38) – Pleteršnik gives the same origin for both: "skrčeno iz 'nehaj'" 'abbreviated from *nehaj*', i.e. deriving from *nehati*, which again originates from *ne hajati* 'not bother, not care'.[20] This seems contradictory, but only at first sight. Both interpretations constitute two manifestations of deonticity, with the differences relating to two different scopes of negation: narrow scope including only the auxiliary (do not bother, do = you should do, let do, i.e. permission/volition), wide scope including also the verbal complement (do not bother doing = stop doing, i.e. prohibition/ warning). In contemporary Slovene, the former is associated with the lexical verb *nehati* 'to stop', which functions as a phasal verb taking infinitival complements, the latter with the modal particle *naj* taking finite complements.

The phasal verb *nehati* and the particle *naj* may be combined, which shows that they indeed have different scope and are hence independent of each other, see (39a)–(39c); in (39c) *nehati* is used as a main verb without complement.

(39) a. *Naj   neha   noreti!*
       naj   stop.PRS.3SG freak.out. IPFV.INF
       'Listen!' (http://opus.nlpl.eu/)
       [lit.: 'He shall stop freaking out!']

---

20 See Pleteršnik's entry to *nehati*, which lists 'stop' and 'let' as two meanings : *neháti, -ȃm*, nav.: *nȇhati, -am*, vb. pf. 1) aufhören 'to stop'; *n. delati; nehaj me zmerjati* 'stop scolding me'; *dež, zima neha* 'the rain stops, the winter ends' [. . .]; – ablassen 'desist': *n. od dela* 'desist from work'; – 2) = pustiti, lassen 'let': *n. kaj* 'let s.th.' [. . .]; *ne neham vas sirote* 'I will not leave you as orphans' [. . .]; *nehaj me! = pusti me!* 'leave me alone!' [. . .] – = *odpustiti* 'forgive': *ves strašni dolg mu je nehal* 'he has forgiven him all debt' [. . .].

b. *Ampak nihče mi ni rekel,   naj   neham delati,*
   but nobody has told me   naj   stop.PRS.1SG work..IPFV.INF
   ko začnem   dobivati pokojnino.
   when begin.PRS.1SG receive.INF pension
   'But nobody has told me, that I should stop working, when I start to receive my pension.' (Gigafida: Delo Revije 2008)
c. *Poskušal sem   jo prepričati   naj   neha.*
   I tried   her convince.PFV.INF   naj   stop.PRS.3SG
   'I tried to get her to stop.' (http://opus.nlpl.eu)

The entries given in (37) and (38) not only show a semantic differentiation from the same etymological source into a phasal verb and a modal marker, they also show the emergence of *naj* as modal marker from a former imperative form. In the available corpora, only rare attestations of inflected *naj* in the permissive/volitional function can be found; they date to the 19th c., see (40a)–(40b).

(40) a. *najta   mene vama   za očeta   biti*
        let.IPFV.IMP.2DU   me you   as father be.INF
        'let me be a father for the two of you' (IMP; nl.ijs.si/imp; 1847)
    b. *najte   de   le v' nebefa   gledam*
        let.IPFV.IMP.2PL that just in heaven   look.IPFV.PRS.1SG
        '[you] let me just look into heaven [lit: let that I look]' (IMP; nl.ijs.si/imp; 1837)
    c. *Naj   se imata   rada!*
        naj   REFL have.IPFV.PRS.2DU   like
        'May they like each other!' (IMP; Žrtve, 1901)

The data presented here allow to derive a first insight into the historical development of *naj*: The (narrow scope) negated imperative form (*ne haj* > *naj*, *najte*, *najmo*, *najta*) of a lexical verb (*ne hajati* 'not bother') developed into an uninflected functional element (*naj*) by expanding its semantic and syntactic scope while at the same time restricting its complement to finite verbs. That is, the original imperative form has lost its inflectional morphology. Morphological information is provided on the verbal complement (inflection is in a way 'externalised') and is restricted by the non-assertive potential of the original imperative. From this, *naj* inherited its non-assertive potential, while the introduction of an attitude holder is a remnant of its former lexical semantics.

4.2 Independent uses: Verbal modifier

The non-inflecting particle *naj* is attested in its independent use already in the early Bible translations by Dalmatin (DAL) and Trubar (TRB) of the 16th c., see (41) and (42).[21]

(41) a. *Ony imajo Mosefsa inu Preroke,* naj *ony teiſte* poſluſhajo. (DAL)
 b. *Oni imaio Moiſeſa inu te Preroke,* nai *te iſte* poslushaio. (TRB)
 c. *Imajo Mojzesa in preroke, te* naj *poslušajo!* (SSP3)
 'They have Moses and the Prophets; let them hear them.' (Lk 16,29)

(42) a. *On je doſti ſtar, vpraſhajte njega,* naj *ſam sa ſe govory.* (DAL)
 b. *On ie ſtar ſadoſti, vprashaite nega,* nai *on ſam ſaſe gouori.* (TRB)
 c. *Dovolj je star. Sam* naj *govori o sebi.* (SSP3)
 'He is of age. He will speak for himself.' (Jn 9,21)

In general, most contexts which exhibit *naj* in the SSP3 display different constructions in JAP, DAL and TRB, whereby *naj* seems to appear more frequently in JAP than DAL and TRB. In addition, several more specific patterns seem to obtain.

For the two variations of deonticity expressed by *naj* in contemporary Slovene, i.e. permission and volition, preferences for different constructions can be found in DAL, TRB and JAP: for the permissive, the imperative of *pustiti* 'let' + infinitive tends to be used in DAL and TRB, whereas JAP has *naj* (43)–(44).

(43) a. *Takó* naj *vaša luč sveti pred ljudmi* (SSP3)
 b. *Taku* naj *fvęti vaſha luzh pred ludmy* (JAP)
 c. *Taku* puſtite *vaſho Luſh* ſvejtiti *pred Ludmy* (DAL)
 d. *Taku* puſtite *vasho luzh* ſueititi *pred ludmi* (TRB)
 'Let your light shine before others' (Mt 5,16)

(44) a. *Oni pa so še bolj kričali: »Križan* naj *bo!«* (SSP3)
 b. *Ali ony ſe ſhe bòl vpyli, rekózh:* Naj *bó krishan.* (JAP)
 c. *Ony ſo pak ſhe vezh vpyli, iuu ſo djali:* Puſti *ga* krishati. (DAL)
 d. *Oni ſo pag teim vezh vpyli inu giali.* Puſtiga Cryshati. (TRB)
 'But they shouted all the more, "Let him be crucified!"' (Mt 27,23)

---

[21] In these examples, *naj* is immediately pre-verbal in SSP3, while in DAL and TRB material may intervene between *naj* and verb. Whether this attests to a diachronic trend remains to be investigated.

For the volitional interpretation, *imeti* 'have', (45), *morati* 'must', the future tense (46) and the morphological imperative (47) prevail in JAP, DAL and TRB.

(45) a. *Rečeno je bilo: Kdor se loči od svoje žene,* naj ji dá *ločitveni list.* (SSP3)
 b. *Rezhenu je pak: de vſaki, katęri ſe bó od ſvoje shene lózhil,* imá *njęj en lozhitni lyſt* dati. (JAP)
 c. *Onu je tudi rezhenu: Gdur ſe od ſvoje Shene lozhi, ta* ima *njej en lozhitni lyſt* dati. (DAL)
 d. *Onu ie tudi rezhenu, kateri ſe lozhi od ſuie shene, ta* ima *neei* dati *en lozhitui lift.* (TRB)
 'It was also said, "Whoever divorces his wife, let him give her a certificate of divorce."' (Mt 5,31)

(46) a. *Gospod, kolikokrat* naj odpustim *svojemu bratu, če greši zoper mene??* (SSP3)
 b. *Goſpód, koliku krat bó grèſhil supèr mene mój brat, inu* bóm *njemu odpuſtil?* (JAP)
 c. *GOSPVD, kuliku krat* moram *tedaj mojmu Bratu odpuſtiti, kateri meni pregriſhi?* (DAL)
 d. *Goſpud kuliku krat ieſt* moram *muimu bratu, kir na meni pregrishi, odpuſtiti?* (TRB)
 'Lord, how often will my brother sin against me, and I forgive him?' (Mt 18,21)

(47) a. *Kdor ima ušesa,* naj posluša. (SSP3)
 b. *Katęri imá vuſhęſsa sa poſluſhat, tá* poſluſhaj. (JAP)
 c. *Kateri ima uſheſsa h'poſluſhanju, ta* poſluſhaj. (DAL)
 d. *Dur ima vshefa hposlushanu, ta* poslushai. (TRB)
 'He who has ears to hear, let him hear.' (Mt 11,15)

For the volitional optative, *da*+indicative is found alongside *naj* in the older texts, see TRB with *da* in (48) vs. *naj* in (49):

(48) a. Naj prideta *oblastnika sama semkaj* (SSP3)
 b. *Takú ne bó: Ampak* naj *ſamy pridejo,* (JAP)
 c. *Nikar taku, temuzh* naj *ony ſamy prideo* (DAL)
 d. *Nekar taku, temuzh de ſami prideio* (TRB)
 'Let them come themselves' (Apd 16,37)

(49) a. *Ali pa naj tile tukaj sami* povedo, (SSP3)
b. *Ali pak naj lety tukaj* povèdó, (JAP)
c. *Ali naj lety ſamy* povédo, (DAL)
d. *Oli nai lety oni ſami* poueido, (TRB)
'Or else let these men themselves say' (Apd 24,20)

There are also instances, in which DAL and TRB have *naj*, but not JAP and SSP3. In these cases, *naj* tends to appear as a complement to *pustite*, the imperative of *pustiti* 'let'. JAP and SSP3 prefer the imperative, see (50).

(50) a. Pustite, poglejmo, *ali bo prišel Elija in ga snel.* (SSP3)
b. Puſtite, poglęjmo, *aku Elias pride, inu njega doli ſname.* (JAP)
c. Puſtite, naj vidimo, *aku Elias pride, inu ga doli vsame.* (DAL)
d. Puſtite, nai gledamo, *aku Elias pride, nega doli ſnemat.* (TRB)
'Wait, let us see whether Elijah will come to take him down.' (Mr 15,36)

The above-cited bible passages allow to infer a gradual expansion of *naj* into non-assertive, directive contexts formerly occupied by other deontic expressions, and its becoming established as a selfcontained verb-related modal marker.

No instances of *naj* taking situational scope, i.e. in the hearsay function, could be found. This could be both an effect of the data basis, the New Testament, or an indication of a later development of these functions. The latter might be expected from what is known of the expansion of modal meanings, in this case possibly fostered also by German influence.

4.3 Dependente uses: Clausal connector

The prevailing strategy for introducing clausal arguments with final interpretation to *verba dicendi* in JAP, DAL and TRB is *da*+subjunctive instead of *naj* as in SSP3, see (51).[22]

(51) a. *In ko so ga zagledali, so ga prosili,* naj odide *iz njihovih krajev.* (SSP3)
b. *inu kadar ſo ga vględali, ſo ga proſsili,* de bi *prozh* ſhàl *od njih krajov.* (JAP)
c. *Inu kadar ſo ga vgledali, ſo ga proſsili,* de bi *prozh* ſhal *od nyh ſtrane.* (DAL)

---

[22] Differently from Russian (*čtoby*), the combination of complementiser and subjunctive particle never developed into a single marker. It could be speculated whether this has been blocked by the availability of *naj*.

d. *Inu kadar nega vgledaio, ga proffio,* de bi *on prozh* shal *od nih kraieu.* (TRB)
'And when they saw him, they begged him to leave their region.' (Mt 8,34)

As Topolińska (2003: 312–313) notes, *da*+subjunctive constitutes another strategy beyond *naj* in contemporary Slovene for the attachment of non-factual clauses. That is, the data in (51) might simply be an indication of the translators opting for this particular strategy and thus not tell so much about the functions of *naj*.[23]

In (52), JAP, DAL and TRB have *da*+indicative present. Since the interpretation is goal-oriented, this indicates the ability of *da* to induce non-assertive force, which is otherwise typical of Balkan Slavic, but neither of Slovene nor BCMS *da* (see also Greenberg, this volume). With the context being constant in (52), the difference between the *da*- and *naj*-structures is not related to a different kind of interpretation triggered by the choice of marker. This suggests that both have undergone a semantic development, with *naj* being preferred for final clauses in contemporary Slovene.[24] As has been mentioned above, if in contemporary Slovene predicates allow for a *da*- and a *naj*-complement alike, the difference consists in the addressee: it is direct for the former, indirect for the latter.

(52) a. *reci,* naj *ti kamni* postanejo *kruh* (SSP3)
b. *rezi,* de *letó kamenje kruh* poſtane (JAP)
c. *rezi,* de *letu Kamenje Kruh* poſtane (DAL)
d. *reci* de *letu kamine* bode *kruh* (TRB)
'command these stones to become loaves of bread' (Mt 4,3)

Another option found in older texts is an infinitival construction in contexts where contemporary Slovene has *naj*, (53).[25]

---

[23] In general, a closer look on the options available or preferred in the various dialects is necessary in order to see whether a particular development is indeed a language related development or related to the expansion of literacy based on a specific dialect serving as basis for an emerging norm. The latter seems to be the case for the relative pronoun *kdor*, which is gaining ground during the 18th c. not so much as a result of a language-internal development, but rather as an effect of the respective dialects constituting the basis for the emerging literary language and its spread in literary sources (Sonnenhauser 2019).

[24] As one reviewer pointed out, this might have let to a stable differentiation of meanings for *reči* in contemporary Slovene: informative *reči da* vs. manipulative *reči naj*.

[25] See Uhlik & Žele (2017) on the choice of infinitival complements after manipulative and desiderative verbs in contemporary Slovene. Even though in the examples discussed here, the usage of the infinitive might be due to the source texts, it still appears as an available option.

(53) a. *In velel je ljudem,* naj *sedejo po travi,* (SSP3)
 b. *Inu on je vkasal mnóshizam doli ſęſti na travo* (JAP)
 c. *Inu on je rekàl timu Folku doli ſeſti na travo,* (DAL)
 d. *Inu on ſapouei tim ludem doli ſeſti na to trauo.* (TRB)
 'Then he ordered the crowds to sit down on the grass' (Mt 14,19)

Evidence for an emerging potential of *naj* to function as clausal connector can be found in examples as (54). DAL and TRB both have two syntactically and semantically independent clauses; there is no overt element that would trigger the inference of semantic dependency. JAP has *naj* as initial element in an independent clause, for which a volitional interpretation is possible. This in turn may be related to some goal-oriented feature specified by *zaupati* 'trust' in the previous clause (see also Section 2.3). In SSP3, the *naj*-headed clause is orthographically presented as being more integrated and semantically connected to *zaupati* 'trust'. This allows for evidence for a reanalysis going on at clause boundaries.

(54) a. *Zaupal je v Boga,* naj *ga zdaj reši* (SSP3)
 b. *On je v' Bogá savupal:* Naj *ga sdaj ręſhi,* (JAP)
 c. *On je v'Buga vupal, ta njega sdaj odreſhi* (DAL)
 d. *On ie Vbuga vupal, ta nega sdai odreshi* (TRB)
 'He trusts in God; let God deliver him now,' (Mt 27,43)

Summing up, where contemporary Slovene has *naj*, the older translations in the majority of cases opt for another construction, in particular with respect to the 'dependent' uses of *naj*. A comparison of the parallel passages indicates the intrusion of *naj* into non-assertive contexts and allows to infer its basic clause combining potential.

4.4 Along the complementiser cycle?

The data presented in section 4.1–4.3 allow to sketch the potential diachronic development of *naj* from an inflected verbal form (imperative) towards an element that may assume clause connecting and complementiser-like functions. A brief summary of its formal development is provided in (55).

(55) a. *nehati* (< *ne hajati*) + verb.INF full-fledged verbal form
      'to let' ('NEG to bother')
   b. *naj* (< *nehaj*) + verb.INF imperative form
      'let' ('do not bother')
   c. *naj* + verb.FIN no morphological distinctions, modal particle
   d. *naj* + clause clausal connector

The semantic contribution of *naj* is based on a combination of 'non-assertion', inherited from the original imperative form, and the introduction of an attitude holder, inherited from the original lexical meaning 'not bother, let'. The morphosyntactic restriction towards an uninflected particle and the meaning generalisation towards indicating deontic non-assertion is related to an extension in syntactic functions from an independent marker taking a finite verbal complement to a clause initial element establishing an inter-clausal relation to a head predicate in the previous clause. One of the main triggers of syntactic change is reanalaysis, which in turn is made possible by surface structures open to various interpretations. For 'naïve' native speakers (differently from certain linguists), these various interpretations most probably do not constitute a matter of 'either – or', but a specific space of functional possibilities available within one and the same context.

In (56), orthography suggests that the author (or the person responsible for typesetting) might indeed have intended an interpretation of *naj* as a clausal connector. However, since both clauses are quite loosely integrated and could both stand on their own, *naj* seems to function both as a verb-related independent marker and a dependent use conditioned by a final feature implied by the action of adding (*primešamo* 'we add') described in the matrix clause. That is, *naj* oscillates between a VP modifying position and a structural position in the left periphery of a clause.

(56) *starega vina primešamo,*   [...]   *naj*
     we add old wine   naj
     bodo možilnost dobile
     be.FUT.3PL pubescence get.PFV.FUT.PL
     'We add old wine, such that they will obtain / let them get pubescence.'
     (IMP: Čebelarstvo, 1831)

The potential of being located in the left periphery and in a syntactic position typically assumed by clausal conntectors can be seen from minimally opposed cases as (57) and (58). In the (a)-examples, *naj* follows the general complementiser *da*. It is still event-related, i.e. *naj mu povesta* and *naj stražijo* are in the scope of the assertive force of *da* ('asked them that they should', 'ordered that they should').

That is, the syntactic subordination is contributed by *da*, while *naj* contributes non-assertion. In the (b)-examples, both features are combined in *naj* ('asked his brother to' / 'ordered them to').

(57) a. *jih je profil,   de   naj mu povefta,*
       he asked them that naj him tell.PFV.PRS.3DU
       'he asked them that they should tell him' (IMP: Zlata jabolka, 1844)
    b. *in brata prosil,   naj se nikar*
       and he asked his brother naj REFL on_no_account
       ne prenagli,
       NEG rush.PFV.PRS.3SG
       'and he asked his brother not to rush on no account'
       (IMP: Hirlanda, bretanska vojvodinja, 1851)

(58) a. *oskrbnik je zapovedal, da   naj stražijo   v veži*
       careteaker ordered   that naj stand_guard.IPFV.PRS.3PL in corridor
       'The caretaker ordered that they should stand guard in the corridor.'
       (IMP: *Rokovnjači*, 1881)
    b. *Vojakom je ukazal,   naj stražijo   v veži.*
       he ordered the soldiers   naj stand_guard.IPFV.PRS.3PL in corridor
       'He ordered the soldiers to stand guard in the corridor.'
       (IMP: Rokovnjači, 1881)

The syntactic parallel between *da* and *naj*, while at the same time differing in terms of force indication, can be seen in (59). Both elements fill in a valency slot opened up by *pisati* and *se veseliti*, respectively; *naj* indicates non-assertive (directive) force, triggered by its potentially goal-directed head predicate *pisati*, while *da* as a complement to the factive predicate *veselijo se* carries assertive force.

(59) *ino je fvoji ljubi materi pifal,   naj fe s' njim vefelijo,*
     and he.has to.his beloved mother written naj REFL with him be_happy.PRS.3PL
     de   je she tako bliso   fvetiga raja
     that be.PRS.3SG already so close earthly paradise
     'and he wrote to his beloved mother, that they[26] should be happy for him, that he is already so close to paradise on earth' (IMP: Življenja srečen pot, 1837)

---

[26] As a native speaker reviewer pointed out, the pronoun could also refer to 'mother', since third person pronouns were used in the sense of V-addressing. The exact referential specification does not have a bearing on the analysis.

The potential of *naj* to be interpreted as being located towards the left of the clause, i.e. in the position of a clausal connector, is supported by combinations of *naj*+morphological imperative, as in (60) and (61)

(60) [...], *ki nas spodbujajo, da naj uživajmo življenje*
   who motivated us that naj enjoy.IPFV.IMP.1PL life
   'who motivated us that we enjoy live' (Gigafida; Naša lekarna 2007)

(61) [...], *ki veli, naj ne govorimo po krivem,*
   who orders naj NEG say.IPFV.PRS.1SG wrongfully
   naj ne izdajajmo in naj ne delajmo
   naj NEG betray.IPFV.IMP.1PL and naj NEG do.IPFV.IMP.1PL
   drugim tega, kar ne želimo,
   to.others that which NEG wish.IPFV.PRS.1PL
   da bi drugi delali nam.
   that SUBJ others do.IPFV.SUBJ to.us
   who orders we should not wrongfully convict, should not betray and should not do to others, what we don't want others to do to us.' (Gigafida; Internet 2011)

Based on the fact that morphological imperatives are possible in subordinate clauses in Slovene (as described, e.g., in Dvorak 2005), see (62a) for contemporary and (62b) for 19th c. data, examples as (60) and (61) can be regarded as indicating that *naj* has uses in which it loosened its connection to the verb and moved to the left into a position occupied by elements such as the general complementizer *da*.

(62) a. *Sem rekla, de pridi!*
      I said that come.PFV.IMP.2SG
      I said that come! (Dvorjak 2005: 38)
   b. *Ateij! mati so rekli, da pojdite domu*
      Father! mother said that come.PFV.IMP.2PL home
      'Father! Mother said that you should come home.'
      (IMP; Bohinjec, Peter. Žganjar. 1890)

The possible steps involved in the reanalysis underlying the functional extension of *naj* from an independent modal marker towards an element with clause combining potential is illustrated in (63). That *naj* in (63c) indeed introduces an indirect speech construction is suggested by the coreference to the addressee signalled by the 3rd person.

(63) a. *Rekli so: naj   gospodje učitelj*
they said naj   gentlemen teachers
se marljivo trudijo
REFL diligently endeavour.IPFV.PRS.3PL
'The said: may / let the gentlemen teachers diligently make efforts.'
(IMP; Novice kmetijskih, rokodelskih in narodnih stvari, 1853)
b. *ji je rekel,   da   naj   plete nogavice*
he told her that naj knit.IPFV.PRS.3SG socks
'he told her that she should knit stocking' (IMP; Milan in Milena, 1913)
c. *Ciliki* [je] *rekel, naj stopi k njemu.*
he told Cilika   naj come.PFV.PRS.3SG to him
'he *told* Cilika *to* come to his side [lit.: she *should come*]' (IMP; Mohoričev Tone, 1886)

In addition, the set of potential matrix predicates seems to have widened from *verba dicendi* towards verbs potentially denoting a future-directed action, as *poslati* 'send' in (64).[27]

(64) *Res je,   da tudi sam   pošljem otroke,   naj*
it is true that also myself send.PFV.PRS.1SG children naj
si sperejo   usta z vodo
REFL wash_out.PRS.3PL   mouth with water
'It is true that I myself send the children to rinse [lit.: that they rinse] their mouth with water' (Gigafida; Dnevnik 2001)

Furthermore, the future-directedness may also be induced by *naj*, as in (65) for a verbal and in (66) for a nominal head. Differently from (63), the matrix predicates are not primary speech act verbs. And differently from (64), the *naj*-structure fills a valency slot and the future-directed, goal-oriented interpretation of the *naj*-structure is not induced by a meaning component of that head predicate. In all cases, the PFV present in the *naj* clause supports the future-directed interpretation.

(65) *To pomeni,   naj   stigmatizirani   sprejemajo*
this means   naj   stigmatized   receive.IPFV.PRS.3PL
prevladujoča merila normalnosti
prevailing standards of normality
'This means that the stigmatized should receive the standards of normality' (Gigafida; Dialogi 2008)

---

27 If *poslati* takes a verbal complement, it requires a supine. This indicates that goal-directedness is indeed a meaning component that may be activated with this verb.

(66) mnenja smo   naj   odstopi
      we are of the opinion naj resign.PFV.PRS.3SG
      'we are convinced that s/he should resign' (SSKJ)

These observations strongly suggest that *naj* has acquired the potential of serving as an indicator of directive force, syntactically located in the left periphery, i.e. the CP layer.

Thereby, the development of *naj* follows a frequently encountered path, which van Gelderen (2009, 2015) describes as 'complementiser cycle':

> "[...] the left periphery, or CP layer, is renewed. Phrases that are base generated in the VP (or vP) get to be fronted and then serve two functions. They are later reanalysed as CP layer elements, both of the main clause and of the embedded one. This can be seen as a cycle, namely a CP cycle." (van Gelderen 2009: 189)

Typically, this kind of cyclic development starts from an element having two functions (van Gelderen 2015: 172), i.e. as contributing to the event structure and to the sentence mood. As has been shown, *naj* behaves in a similar manner: Its functions range between the poles of intra-predicate marker modifying its complement predicate by introducing an attitude towards the event or situation description, and inter-predicate marker modifying the proposition state of affairs described by the *naj* structure by introducing an attitude it anchored in a previous clause on the other. This provides a starting point for a reanalysis of *naj* as potentially occupying different syntactic positions, which in turn underlies the extension of syntactic positions from a VP-internal, adverbal marker to an element located in the specifier of CP (illocutionary force marker) or the position of a C head.

5 To conclude: *naj* as clausal complementiser?

Having sketched a possible scenario for the morphosyntactic and semantic development of *naj* based on which its contemporary functional versatility can be accounted for, it is now possible to address the status of *naj* as a clausal complementiser. The question is not so much, whether *naj* 'is' or 'is not' a complementiser, but rather whether and to which degree it displays functions typical of complementisers. This leads to the problem of how to identify such functions. Here, one has to be careful to not apply ready-made categorical notions and distinctions that are in themselves problematic, such as that between arguments and adjuncts. In addition, one should avoid engaging in purely terminological discussions that do not help in describing and systematising the data, in particular when it comes to dealing with older varieties and cross-linguistic comparison.

One possibility to circumvent such pitfalls consists in starting from the most general function complementiser-like elements assume and decomposing it into smaller-scale features. The relevant function can be described as marking a particular element or structure to be part of a larger syntactic unit. From this description, which does not presuppose a specific syntactic or semantic approach, the three features given in (67) emerge as first candidates to characterise elements with respect to their function as clausal complementisers.

(67) A: embedding: the element serves the building-up of complex hierarchical predicational structures
→ vs. coordination on clausal level, adnominal modification on phrasal level

B: relation: the element serves to fill in a valency slot of a verbal or nominal structure
→ vs. adverbial conjunction on clausal level, prepositional dependencies on phrasal level

C: opacity: the element is not the target of agreement, i.e. it does not express a grammatical relation within the structure it embeds and it is not assigned features by the embedding head
→ vs. relativisation on clausal level, linking articles of the Albanian type on phrasal level

As to *naj*, it displays uses in contemporary Slovene, in which all three features are positively specified, such as (65) and (66) above. In other uses, feature (B) is not fulfilled, as in (19). In this case, feature (A) constitutes a possible interpretation via the inference of a discourse relation. Feature (B) is not fulfilled in all 'independent' uses of *naj*, i.e. restricted assertiveness does not necessarily correlate with syntactic dependency. Finally, feature (C) is given in all uses of *naj*.

Facing the manifold conceptions of what a complementiser 'is' or 'is not (yet)' and which syntactic and semantic aspects exactly an element should display in order to qualify as a complementiser, the above considerations might seem quite uninformed or ignorant. On the other hand, exactly this kind of categorically ignorant view seems necessary in order to prevent empirical analyses from ending up in discussions of categories as such. The features gained by decomposition allow to discriminate complementiser uses within the set of elements employed for complex VP and complex NP formation. Elements may correspond to these features to a smaller or larger degree, which is quite natural given that languages are in constant flux. To the degree an element displays these features it can be said to display (synchronic perspective) or be developing (diachronic perspective) clausal complementiser functions. That is, features like those suggested in (67) allow for an empirically founded diachronic and diatopic comparison and hence to capture and pin down variation.

References

Ammann, Andreas & Johan van der Auwera. 2004. Complementizer-headed main clauses for volitional moods in the languages of south-eastern Europe. In Olga Mišeska Tomić (ed.). *Balkan Syntax and Semantics*, 293–314. Amsterdam, Philadelphia: Benjamins.

Boye, Kasper, Eva van Lier & Eva Theilgaard Brink. 2015. Epistemic complementizers: a crosslinguistic survey. *Language Sciences* 51. 1–17.

Dvořák, Boštjan. 2005. Slowenische Imperative und ihre Einbettung. *Philologie im Netz* 33. 36–73.

Fortuin, Egbert & Ronny Boogaart. 2009. Imperative as conditional: From constructional to compositional semantics. *Cognitive Linguistics* 20 (4). 641–673.

Gelderen, Elly van. 2009. Renewal in the left periphery: economy and the complementizer layer. *Transactions of the Philological Society* 107 (2). 131–195.

Gelderen, Elly van. 2015. The particle how. In Josef Bayer, Roland Hinterhölzl & Andreas Trotzke (eds.), *Discourse-oriented syntax*, 159–174. Amsterdam, Philadelphia: Benjamins.

Gradišnik, Janez. 1981. Domneve z 'naj' [Presumptions with 'naj']. *Jezik in Slovstvo* 2 (1). 23–24.

Holvoet, Axel. 2012. Polish mieć and the semantic map of interpretive deontics. *Zeitschrift für Slawistik* 57 (2). 129–146.

Holvoet, Axel & Jelena Konickaja. 2011. Interpretive deontics: a definition and a semantic map based mainly on Slavonic and Baltic data. *Acta Linguistica Hafniensia* 43 (1). 1–20.

Kehayov, Petar & Kasper Boye. 2016. Complementizer semantics in European languages: Overview and generalizations. In Kasper Boye & Petar Kehayov (eds.), *Complementizer semantics in European languages*, 809–878. Berlin/Boston: De Gruyter Mouton.

Kopitar, Jernej. 1808. *Grammatik der Slavischen Sprache in Krain, Kärnten und Steyermark.* Laibach.

Messner, Janko. 1980. Zajedalec 'naj' [The parasite 'naj']. *Jezik in Slovstvo* 7–8. 216.

Mišeska Tomić, Olga. 2012. *A grammar of Macedonian*. Indiana: Slavica.

Palmer, F.R. 2001. *Mood and modality*. Cambridge: CUP.

Pleteršnik 2010 [1894–1895]. *Pleteršnikov Slovensko-nemški slovar. Spletna izdaja* [Pleteršnik's Slovene-German dictionary. Online version]. Ljubljana 2010 (http://bos.zrc-sazu.si/pletersnik.html).

Portner, Paul 1997. The semantics of mood, complementation, and conversational force. *Natural Language Semantics* 5. 167–212.

Roeder, Carolin & Björn Hansen. 2006. Modals in contemporary Slovene. *Wiener Slavistisches Jahrbuch* 52. 153–170.

Sonnenhauser, Barbara. 2017. 'Knowing how' in Slovene: treading the other path. *Slověne* 1. 84–106.

Sonnenhauser, Barbara. 2019. Interrogative, indefinite, relative *kdo(r)*. Why Slovene is (not so) different. *Zeitschrift für Slavische Philologie* 75 (1). 151–181.
Stegovec, Adrian. 2019. Perspectival control and obviation in directive clauses. *Natural Language Semantics* 27. 47–94.
Topolińska, Zuzanna 2003. Means for grammatical accommodation of finite clauses: Slovenian between South and West Slavic. *Sprachtypologie und Universalienforschung* 56 (3). 306–322.
Uhlik, Mladen & Žele, Andreja. 2018. *Da*-predloženija pri glagolax želanija i pobuždenja v slovenskom jazyke [*Da*-clauses as complements of desiderative and manipulative verbs in Slovene]. *Voprosy jazykoznanija* 5. 87–113.
Uhlik, Mladen. 2018. O *naj* in *pust'* v slovensko-ruski sopostavitvi [On *naj* and *pust'* in Slovene and Russian]. *Slavistična revija* 66 (4). 403–419.
Weiss, Daniel. 1989. Parataxe und Hypotaxe – Versuch einer Skalierung. In Wolfgang Girke (ed.), *Slavistische Linguistik 1988*, 287–322. München: Sagner.
Widmer, Paul & Barbara Sonnenhauser. 2020. Indeed, nothing lost in the Balkans. Assessing morphosyntactic convergence in an areal context. *Balkanistica* 33. 193–131.
Wiemer, Björn. 2017. Main clause infinitival predicates and their equivalents in Slavic: Why they are not instances of insubordination. In Lukasz Jedrzejowski & Ulrike Demske (eds.), *Infinitives at the syntax-semantics interface. A diachronic perspective*, 265–338. Berlin/Boston: De Gruyter Mouton.
Zeman, Sonja. 2013. Zur Diachronie der Modalverben: 'sollen' zwischen Temporalität, Modalität und Evidentialität. In Werner Abraham & Elisabeth Leiss (eds.), *Funktionen von Modalität*, 335–366. Berlin/Boston: De Gruyter.

Sources

Gigafida: http://www.gigafida.net/.
GOS: *Korpus govorjene slovenščine* [Corpus of spoken Slovene]. http://www.korpus-gos.net/
IMP: Erjavec, Tomaž (2015). Jezikovni viri starejše slovenščine [Language sources of older Slovene]. http://nl.ijs.si/imp/.
SSKJ: *Slovar slovenskega knjižnega jezika 2016* [Dictionary of standard Slovene 2016] Ljubljana: ZRC SAZU (electronic edition: www.fran.si).

Author Bio Notes

Walter Breu has been a professor of Slavic linguistics at the University of Konstanz (Germany) since 1994. In addition to his research on verbal aspect and modality in Slavic languages and beyond, he has been working on the linguistic situation of the Albanian-speaking minorities in Calabria and Molise (Italy) since 1978 and on the grammar and lexicon of Molise Slavic in the three Slavic-speaking municipalities of Molise since 1990. He has published various articles on the morphology and syntax of Italo-Albanian, in particular, but not only, on the presumptive, on periphrastic constructions, on verbal aspect, on the forms and functions of the aorist and on linguistic variation. With regard to Molise Slavic and other Slavic micro-languages in Western and Southern Europe, he has published numerous articles in all fields of grammar as well as three monographs with commented texts. He has also organised three international conferences (2003, 2008, 2019) on the influence of Italian and German on minority varieties in situations of absolute language contact.

Hanne Eckhoff is Associate Professor of Russian Linguistics and Comparative Slavonic Philology at the University of Oxford, and Fellow and Tutor in Russian and Linguistics at Lady Margaret Hall. She has her PhD in Slavonic Linguistics from the University of Oslo, with a thesis on possessive constructions in Old Russian and Old Church Slavonic. Her research is centred on historical corpus linguistics; she has been involved in a series of historical treebank projects, and runs and maintains the Tromsø Old Russian and OCS Treebank (TOROT). She has worked primarily on morphosyntax, semantics and information structure, in particular case phenomena and verbal aspect in the history of the Slavonic languages.

Marc L. Greenberg, PhD UCLA 1990, is professor of Slavic Languages & Literatures at the University of Kansas. He focuses on comparative and historical linguistics, dialectology, and sociolinguistics. He is editor-in-chief of the *Encyclopedia of Slavic Languages and Linguistics* (Brill). In 2017 he was elected corresponding member of the Slovenian Academy of Sciences and Arts and in 2019 named Ambassador of Science of the Republic of Slovenia. In recent work he has focused on South Slavic dialect issues. His most recent book is an annotated translation from Hungarian of Avgust Pavel's *Prekmurje Slovene Grammar, Vend nyelvtan* (1942), published as vol. 47 of Studies in Slavic and General Linguistics (Brill). He has held fellowships from Fulbright, National Endowment for Humanities, International Research & Exchanges Board, and the American Philosophical Society. He serves on editorial boards of linguistics journals in Bosnia & Herzegovina, Bulgaria, Croatia, Montenegro, Russia, Slovenia, and the US.

Jasmina Grković-Major is a professor at the Department of Serbian Language and Linguistics at the University of Novi Sad (Serbia) and a member of the Serbian Academy of Sciences and Arts. Her research interests include Old Church Slavonic, the history of the Serbian language, comparative grammar of Slavic languages, and historical-comparative linguistics, with a focus on Slavic diachronic syntax and semantics in a broader Indo-European perspective. She aims for an integrative approach in order to reveal the interplay of universal and language-specific factors inducing and directing language changes, with an emphasis on their cognitive and typological motivation. Her publications include 7 books, 11 edited volumes, and a great number of articles published in Austria, Bulgaria, the Czech Republic, Germany, Greece, Japan, Serbia, Slovenia, Russia, the USA, etc. She has led several projects dealing with the history of

Serbian vernaculars and literary language. She is editor-in-chief of the journal *Zbornik Matice srpske za filologiju i lingvistiku* (Serbia) and member of the editorial boards of the journals *Slověne. International Journal of Slavic Studies* (Russia) and *Wiener Slavistisches Jahrbuch* (Austria).

Iliyana Krapova is Associate Professor in Slavic Linguistics at the University Ca' Foscari of Venice. She teaches courses in Slavic linguistics and Balkan linguistics at the BA and MA level. She has been a Fulbright scholar at University of Massachusetts, USA, Fellow of the Institute for Advanced Studies in the Humanities (Edinburgh) and of the University of Connecticut, USA. Iliyana Krapova's scientific interests include Slavic linguistics, Balkan linguistics, and comparative grammar of Bulgarian and South Slavic. On these topics, she has published articles and books, among which *The morphosyntax of verb agreement in* Bulgarian, Sofia (2014), and *Balkan Syntax and Universal Grammar,* Mouton de Gruyter, 2018 (with Brian Joseph, University of Ohio). She is in the international committee of several journal among which *Bălgarski ezik* (published by the Academy of Science of Bulgaria) and she is a member of the Commission for Balkan linguistics at the International Committee of Slavists.

Alexander Letuchiy
Alexander Letuchiy is professor at the School of Linguistics (HSE University, Moscow). He teaches Russian syntax and morphology, as well as more specialized courses in typology and theory of grammar. His Candidate degree (PhD) dissertation was on labile (ambitransitive) verbs, his Postdoctoral dissertation focuses on complement clauses in Russian. His main research interests are complementation and complex sentence typology, transitivity, voice and valency change, evidentiality, Russian morphology. In the complementation domain, he is particularly interested in TAM marking in complement clauses, triclausal constructions, and strategies of complementation.

Liljana Mitkovska is a professor of English grammar and English-Macedonian contrastive analysis at the Faculty of Foreign Languages, FON University, Macedonia. Her research interests comprise Macedonian linguistics from typological perspective, contrastive linguistics, second/foreign language acquisition and learner language analysis. She has worked on various linguistic topics, such as the reflexive constructions, expressing possession on the NP level, verb tenses, prepositions and prefixes, clausal complementation, contrasting Macedonian to English or other South Slavic languages. Her special interest in the field of SLA is the role of Macedonian as L1 in the acquisition of English as a foreign language. She has taken part in several international research projects and published in various journals and edited volumes. Prof. Mitkovska is also a co-author of two course books for Macedonian as a foreign language, the more recent one being the third edition of the course book *Macedonian, a course for beginning and intermediate students*, Wisconsin University press, 2011, with Christina E. Kramer.

Eleni Bužarovska is professor of linguistics in the English Department at the University of Cyril & Methodius (Skopje, Macedonia). Her professional interests involve investigation of the syntax, semantics and pragmatics of Balkan languages, Russian and English. Her research encompasses issues from both theoretical and applied linguistics with a special focus on the typology of Balkan languages and contact phenomena within the Balkan context. Apart from authoring a book in the field of contrastive syntax and coauthoring two textbooks, she has co-edited a book on Macedonian typological properties (Academie Verlag, Berlin). Other research areas in which Bužarovska is active are areal and contact linguistics, particularly in the domain of external and internal language changes in South Slavic languages. She has published a number of articles in international journals and edited volumes on grammaticalization and language change in Balkan languages.

Barbara Sonnenhauser holds a professorship in Slavic linguistics at the University of Zurich. She received her PhD at the University of Leipzig with a dissertation on grammatical aspect in Russian, Bulgarian and Turkish. Her research interests include language contact and linguistic variation as well as topics in diachronic syntax, in particular relativisation and complementation. She is currently involved in projects on morphosyntactic feature diffusion in the South Slavic and Balkan context, and the dynamics of heritage Albanian in Switzerland.

Björn Wiemer received his PhD in Slavic linguistics in 1996 (Hamburg University). He worked as research assistant at the chair of Slavic Languages at Constance University from 1996 to 2003. Subsequent to his postdoctoral thesis, which was devoted to grammaticalization (2002, venia for Slavic and Baltic linguistics) he continued doing research and teaching at Constance University until 2007, when he was appointed to the chair of Slavic Linguistics at Mainz University. His main topics of interest are aspect and other verbal categories, voice related phenomena, evidentiality and modality, clausal complementation, also from a diachronic perspective and in non-standard varieties, language contact and areal linguistics. He has contributed to all mentioned domains with publications both on synchronic and diachronic issues.

Language index

Albanian 3, 97, 254, 298, 318, 342–345, 347–348, 352–356, 359–360, 364, 366, 369, 376–377, 379, 452, 473
– Arvanitika 376
– Calabro-Albanian 343, 353–354, 356–357, 364, 366, 371, 373, 376–378, 380
– Geg 345, 356
– Italo-Albanian (Arbëresh, Arbrisht) 18, 342–345, 347, 352–353, 355–357, 360, 362, 366, 370–371, 373, 376, 378–379
– Molise Albanian 343, 346, 353–355, 361–364, 366, 371–372, 376–378, 380
– Tosk 345
Arbëresh, Arbrisht → Italo-Albanian

Balkan languages 13, 59, 115, 139, 212, 218, 257, 263, 278–279, 298, 327, 345
Balkan Slavic 5–7, 10, 12–14, 18, 21, 37, 41, 45, 50, 52, 59–60, 63–66, 68–69, 72, 74–77, 79–80, 84–85, 98, 100–101, 112, 115, 121, 132–134, 139–143, 144, 270–273, 274, 277–278, 280, 321–322, 325, 327, 329, 337, 451–452, 466
BC(M)S = Bosnian, Croatian, Montenegrin, Serbian 18, 318–319, 321, 323, 327–328, 338, 357, 444, 466
Bosnian 358
Bulgarian 3, 5, 7–8, 13–14, 16–18, 37, 39, 41–42, 44, 46, 52, 54, 58, 65–67, 73–76, 78, 80–81, 84–85, 92, 96–98, 103, 105, 111–112, 114, 116, 120–121, 123, 127–130, 135, 138, 143–144, 160–210, 211–269, 270–314, 321–322, 324, 430, 436

Calabro-Albanian → Albanian
Calabro-Greek → Greek
Cimbrian 380
Common Slavic 7, 60, 62, 317
Croatian 18, 56, 62, 92, 97, 105, 107–108, 123, 131, 144, 328, 342, 346–347, 357–362, 364, 367, 370, 373–374
– Old Croatian 431
Czech 3, 132, 217, 426, 444
Čakavian 7, 431

East Slav(on)ic 19, 84, 408, 426
– Old East Slav(on)ic 21, 387–389, 409–410, 412
Ekavian 346
English 78, 188, 217, 223–224, 229, 233, 241–242, 247, 259, 262, 298, 307, 348, 400

Friulian 347

Gallipoli Serbian → Serbian
Geg → Albanian
German 3, 7, 78, 106–107, 115, 132, 163, 217, 347, 432, 445, 448, 449, 465
Greek 3, 52, 71, 145, 223–224, 233, 247, 250, 254, 298, 318, 343, 376, 380, 420, 423
– Ancient Greek 387–414
– Calabro-Greek 380
Griko 380

Hungarian 3, 224, 241–243, 320, 329, 333

Ikavian 346
Italian 7, 18, 107, 215, 217, 229, 231, 233, 236, 247, 298, 342–384, 432
Italo-Albanian → Albanian

Jekavian 346

Kajkavian 5, 7, 318, 321–323, 325, 328, 338

Latin 106–107, 321, 324, 380, 389, 422, 431
– Vulgar Latin 7, 425–426

Macedonian 3, 7, 8, 13–14, 17, 29, 37, 52, 54, 56, 58, 65, 67, 71, 73–77, 81, 83, 85, 91, 94, 96–99, 102–104, 106–107, 112, 114–115, 121, 135–137, 143–144, 270–272, 274–275, 277–278, 280–284, 288–291, 293–296, 298–311, 318, 321–322, 325–326, 430, 436, 452
Molisan 346, 355–356, 360, 362, 366, 380
Molise Albanian → Albanian
Molise Slavic 18, 342–344, 346–347, 352, 355, 357–358, 360–367, 369–371, 373–380

North Slavic 6–8, 14, 63, 115, 132, 140, 142, 144, 430

Old Church Slav(on)ic (OCS) 18–19, 21, 66, 107, 321, 323, 387–389, 395–397, 400–403, 407–409, 412, 420, 423, 425

Polish 8, 46, 78, 324, 445, 448
Proto-Indo-European 319, 416, 420, 423
Proto-Slavic 326–372, 416, 419–420, 425, 429, 434

Romance 3, 49, 74, 217, 224, 252, 257, 259–261, 278, 342–343, 345–347, 355, 358, 360–363, 368–380, 415, 422, 425–426, 431
Romanian 254, 298, 318
Russian 8, 31, 36, 41, 43, 46, 78, 82, 113–114, 123, 160, 164–166, 169–170, 188, 190, 223, 277, 300, 387, 389, 409, 416, 426–427, 444–445, 447, 450, 453, 465
– Middle Russian 19, 387–389, 410–412

Serbian 3, 13–14, 19, 29, 54, 58–60, 62, 64, 68, 77, 85–86, 96–99, 108, 111, 120, 123, 129, 144–145, 307, 346, 358, 415–441

– Gallipoli Serbian 357
– Old Serbian 91, 105, 415, 418–422, 424–225, 429, 431, 434, 436
Serbian-Croatian (Serbo-Croatian) 3, 5, 7, 38, 50–51, 53–56, 59–60, 62–64, 69, 72, 74–76, 79, 82, 84–85, 95, 103–105, 108, 132, 142–143, 145, 346
Slovak 3, 318
Slovene 3, 5–7, 12, 14, 17–19, 21, 29, 53–55, 62–64, 69, 74, 80–81, 96, 101, 103–105, 107–108, 118, 126, 142–145, 168, 318–319, 321–323, 325–328, 332–333, 335, 338, 342, 347, 367, 368, 370–373, 378, 442–476
– Prekmurje Slovene 17–18, 317–341, 371
South Slavic 3–28, 29–159, 277–278, 317–319, 321–323, 326–327, 337–338, 342–386, 426, 429, 431, 435–436, 444
Štokavian 3, 5–6, 108, 143, 327–328, 338, 346

Torlak (dialects) 13, 22, 37, 740 (Timok), 108, 145
Tosk → Albanian

West Slavic 8–9, 20, 84, 318, 342, 426

Subject index

2P-clitics 70, 74, 102, 143, 145

Aboutness Topic 230
Abstand language 344, 383
AcP-construction 105
Acquaviva (Collecroce) 342, 346, 360, 370, 374, 378, 382
actional class 16, 160, 195, 205–206
action nominal 104, 122, 124, 127, 129, 274
adjective 110, 160–161, 172, 176, 183, 185, 196–197, 274
adjunct 4, 30, 34, 44, 56, 58, 61–63, 78, 95–96, 109, 116, 166, 168–170, 183, 209, 212, 310, 416, 418, 424–425, 435, 472
adverb 19, 22, 47–48, 93, 111, 134–135, 241, 243, 246, 253, 260, 262, 274, 276–277, 294–295, 326, 363–364, 380, 388, 391, 393, 397, 399–400, 405, 409, 429–430
– manner 277
– sentential 43, 47
adverbial 77, (88, 106, 111, 125–126, 129, 231, 295, 354, 399, 423, 445
affirmative 50, 215, 294–295, 297, 298, 305, 307, 309, 310, 354
agreement 19–20, 65–66, 68, 74, 136–137, 213–215, 231, 234, 250, 258, 260, 272, 387–388, 400, 402–403, 416, 473
akanye 346, 360, 369, 371
alignment 409
– semantic 416, 434
– syntactic 416, 434
alloglottic (variety, minority language, etc.) 342, 377, 379–380
anaphora 147, 185
annotation 19, 21–22, 387–389, 391, 408–409, 412–413
aorist 67, 69, 93, 100, 128, 135, 172, 174, 178, 278, 284, 291, 380, 404
argument 4, 16, 23, 30–35, 42–44, 46, 47, 58, 61, 69–70, 75, 77–79, 88, 104, 107–109, 110, 112–115, 118, 120–124, 126, 128–131, 137, 140, 149–150, 153–154, 156–158, 160–164, 166–172, 181, 183–186, 188–194, 197, 199–200, 202, 204–207, 209, 212, 217, 226–227, 231, 238, 254, 265, 267, 273, 300, 390, 393–395, 400, 402–403, 406, 412, 416, 418, 425, 443, 465, 472
article 12–13, 83, 124, 129, 163–164, 172, 176, 201–205,
aspect 7, 62, 66, 79, 93–94, 100, 105, 123–124, 127–128, 136–137, 162
imperfective 61–62, 94, 127–128, 180
– perfective 61–64, 66, 69, 105, 108, 128, 144–145, 180, 219, 320, 359
progressive 352
aspectual characteristics/properties/opposition 192, 199, 259–260, 263, 270, 272, 274, 278–279
aspectual restriction 291, 294, 307, 321, 342
assertion 8, 33, 49, 54, 214–215, 219, 221, 224, 236, 250, 264, 286, 334, 337, 442, 444, 458–459, 468–469
assertiveness 47–50, 64–66, 69, 79, 132–133, 280, 310, 444, 453, 473
asyndetic construction 287
asyndetic pattern 421, 434
attachment site 112, 391, 413
– nominal 16, 90, 109–110, 112, 115, 119
– verbal 16, 90, 109–110, 113
attitude 256, 442, 444, 455, 456–459, 472
– emotional 358, 360, 374
– epistemic (= cognitive) 40, 51, 56, 65, 81, 99
– holder 55, 64–65, 99, 454–459, 462, 468
– propositional 41, 49, 220, 253, 257, 264, 273
auxiliary 9–10, 19, 42, 59, 73, 75, 132, 145, 166, 260, 348, 391, 399–400, 404–405, 461
– modal 31, 50, 63, 135–136

Balkanism 12–14, 277, 279, 323
Balkan Sprachbund 3, 311, 318, 337, 347, 415, 422, 427, 430, 434, 436
Borrowing 52, 354, 356, 364, 366, 372–373, 378–380
– MAT (matter) 13, 342, 344, 355–356, 366, 370–371, 373, 375, 377–378

484 — Subject index

- PAT (pattern) 13, 18, 342, 344, 355–356, 366, 370–371, 374, 377–378
boundary shift 424, 426, 435
bridging construction 78

calque 364, 366, 371
- hybrid 355, 363, 375
- semantic 344
- syntactic 344, 361
causality 19, 42–43, 47, 56, 57, 131, 324, 338, 428, 435
causation → causality
causative 9, 42–43, 131, 145, 166, 416
clause V, 4, 6–10, 12, 16, 19–22, 29–37, 43–50, 55–56, 59–61, 63, 65–66, 69–72, 73, 75–77, 79, 80, 85, 87, 88, 88–91, 98, 100–102, 104–111, 113–115, 117–119, 122–124, 128–135, 137, 139–142, 144, 160, 166–171, 199, 202, 205, 211–216, 219, 221–223, 225–226, 229–230, 233–238, 240, 244, 250–251, 254, 256–257, 259–262, 264, 272–274, 277–278, 280–283, 286, 293, 295–300, 307, 309, 320, 323, 326–327, 331–332, 335, 337–338, 342, 350–353, 355–359, 361–362, 365, 369, 379, 387, 393, 399, 407–410, 412, 416, 418, 422, 429, 435, 442–445, 449–452, 454–459, 466–468, 472
- adjunct/adverbial 21, 32, 61, 64, 66, 69, 109, 169, 225, 256, 397, 399, 417, 423, 429, 454
- causal 18, 54, 362, 376, 378, 424, 426–427, 429
- comparative 356–357, 362
- complement → complement clause
- complex 233, 442–443, 454
- concessive 84, 88, 449
- conditional 55, 84, 223, 247, 348, 351, 364, 409, 412, 449
- consecutive 88, 114, 358
- če-clause 56, 232, 257, 262, 299, 304
- čtoby-clause 166
- da-clause 5, 19, 59–68, 83, 96, 108–109, 114–116, 118–119, 121, 132, 135, 140, 142–143, 145, 166–167, 170, 218, 251–252, 257–258, 260, 262, 271, 277–279, 281, 293, 296–297, 299, 305, 307–308, 310, 322, 327, 337, 388, 408, 415, 420–421, 424, 431, 434–436
- dali-clause 221-223, 247, 254, 257
- declarative 16, 62, 65–66, 104, 129, 142, 211–215, 217–220, 223, 225, 230–232, 234–235, 237, 247, 249–251, 254, 264, 276, 279, 353, 358, 367, 369–370, 428, 453
- deka-clause 305
- deontic → modal(ity), deontic
- dependent 17, 20–21, 32, 35, 38, 65–66, 86, 104–105, 110, 169, 171, 174, 212, 271, 274, 277, 279, 282–283, 286, 320–321, 388, 395–396, 400, 403, 406–408, 412
- embedded 16, 55, 80, 89, 115, 160, 166, 205, 211–212, 214–217, 219, 221, 225, 231, 233, 237–238, 240, 264, 277, 283, 298–300, 351, 443
- factual → factual
- finite → finite(ness)
- gd(j)e-clause 415, 429, 435-436
- independent → clause, main
- infinitive/infinitival 65, 108, 170, 361, 418
- interrogative 101, 219, 223, 237, 350–351, 354, 362, 364, 373
- IP-clause 213, 254
- jako-clause 406
- jer(e)-clause 415, 422, 424
- ka-clause 337
- kako/kak-clause 271, 285, 310
- main 33, 43, 63–64, 66, 69, 73, 77, 79, 85–86, 100, 104–105, 118, 122, 129, 133, 140, 142, 167, 220–221, 253, 273, 278, 327, 335, 350–351, 359–361, 399–400, 420–421, 428, 434, 444–445, 450, 452, 467, 472
- matrix 30–32, 35, 55, 64, 81, 83, 87, 89–91, 96, 108, 113, 115, 117, 120, 134, 212, 258, 273, 287, 293, 299–300, 302, 305, 454–455, 457, 460, 468
- naj-clause 87-88, 91, 117
- object 342, 350, 352–353
- purpose (= final) 6, 9, 20, 59, 63, 69, 78, 107, 115, 169–170, 225, 331–333, 336, 362, 369, 466
- quod-clause 422

Subject index — **485**

- relative 12, 18, 71, 96, 110, 116, 121, 163, 214, 235, 259, 298–299, 359, 366, 373, 387, 396, 399, 410, 412
- temporal 212, 357
- *that*-clause 235, 259

clause union 9, 19, 59, 63, 77–78, 122, 317, 322, 326, 333, 428, 467, 470

clitic 6, 13, 34, 45–46, 60, 65–66, 69–70, 72–76, 79–80, 91, 93, 96, 115, 122, 133, 140, 176, 218, 226–228, 238, 240, 244, 247, 249–250, 274, 279, 300, 302–303, 305, 336, 360

- climbing 75–76, 143
- cluster 6, 139, 143, 145, 426–427

enclitic 60, 68, 72, 74, 76, 102, 132, 140, 145, 424, 426–427, 435

- proclitic 6, 16, 60, 69, 72–76, 79–80, 85, 93, 122, 143, 145, 278

commitment → epistemic support

complement clause 16, 18, 32–36, 44, 48–49, 54, 56, 63, 66, 82, 100–101, 104, 108, 110, 115, 121, 128–129, 138, 142, 160–161, 163–165, 169–172, 175–178, 180–207, 253–254, 258, 271–274, 278–279, 282, 286, 293–294, 298–300, 302, 307–310, 348–349, 353, 360, 362, 368, 379, 387, 388, 390–394, 396–397, 400, 402–403, 407–412, 415–417, 421–424, 428–429, 432, 434–436, 454, 460

complementation 3–15, 17–19, 21–22, 29–33, 35–38, 42–43, 47, 49, 61, 66, 73, 76, 79–80, 85–90, 105–106, 108–111, 115–117, 119–120, 123, 129–131, 134–141, 143–145, 164, 166–167, 169, 180, 183–184, 186, 190, 192, 196, 199, 201, 203, 207, 225, 250, 270–273, 276–277, 309, 317, 328–330, 342, 347, 353, 370, 387, 390, 393, 395, 408–409, 412, 415–417, 421–422, 434

- device 13, 16–17, 98, 108, 420
- functional domain of 32
- marker 37–38, 43, 45–46, 50–53, 55, 80, 84, 92, 95–96, 99, 101–103, 111–112, 117, 119, 131–133, 139, 141–142, 144
- strategy 33, 115, 117, 119, 121–122, 197, 388, 415, 417, 429, 434–444

complementizer 5–9, 16–22, 29, 37–38, 40, 43–47, 50–52, 54, 56–60, 63, 69–70, 72–73, 76, 78–80, 84–87, 89–91, 94–98, 100–103, 106–107, 111–112, 117–121, 131–134, 137–144, 160, 166–168, 172–178, 181–182, 184–185, 196–198, 211–218, 220–237, 240, 243–244, 246–251, 254–255, 264, 271, 273–274, 277–279, 287, 289, 292–293, 300–301, 310, 317, 319–324, 337, 342–343, 345–371, 373–380, 388, 393–395, 400, 403, 415, 423–424, 428–430, 434–435, 442–445, 449, 451–452, 454, 458, 465, 467–468, 470, 472–474

- canonical 45, 65, 69, 111, 117, 133, 141
- default (= neutral) 7, 18, 54, 71, 84, 91, 97, 112, 134, 141–142, 144, 168
- double 45, 132–134, 140
- zero 5, 35, 131, 134, 137

complement-taking predicate (CTP) 5, 8, 16, 19–20, 22, 31–35, 38, 40–43, 46–48, 50–56, 62–64, 69, 72, 75–76, 78–81, 83–84, 86, 89, 92–94, 96–100, 103–107, 109, 111, 113–114, 120–121, 131–132, 136–139, 144–145, 165, 171, 222, 273, 293, 307, 320–321, 330–332, 334–335, 337, 339, 388, 394–396, 400, 403, 405, 415, 417, 432, 435

compound past 75

conjunction 44, 46, 59–60, 62, 70, 72, 80, 212, 277–278, 320–321, 324, 327, 334, 342, 348, 350–351, 355–356, 359, 361–362, 364–365, 369, 373, 375–376, 378, 380, 389, 400, 415, 424, 426–429, 435, 443, 445, 449–454, 458, 473

- adverbial 449–451, 473
- causal 7, 19, 351, 356, 370, 372–376, 378–379, 423–424, 426–427, 429–430, 433
- compound 354, 357, 363–364, 374, 426

connective 5–9, 16–19, 21–22, 37–38, 41, 43, 51–52, 57–59, 71–72, 76, 79, 93–95, 97, 100–101, 118, 133, 137, 140–144

consecutio temporum 94, 360

contact superposition zone 3

control 21, 40, 42, 107, 109, 252, 260, 445, 455
– object 59, 76, 107–108, 144
– subject 75–76, 107–108, 144
converb 104–107, 129
corpus linguistics V, 21–22
correlative structure 390, 394, 425, 431
creolization 13
cyclic development 472

Dachsprache 344, 347
dative + infinitive 420, 434
declarative → clause, declarative
definite(ness) 13–14, 83, 160–161, 164–165, 172, 189, 201–207, 278, 300
dependency grammar 388–391, 393, 399
depictive 300
deranking 33, 104–105, 129
diagrammar 344, 368
diaphasic 12, 14, 30, 36, 60, 64, 139, 145
diastratic 12, 14, 30, 36, 60, 64, 86, 108, 139, 145
diasystem 344
diatopic 8, 11–12, 14–15, 22, 30, 36, 60, 86, 139, 145, 319–320, 417, 434, 436, 474
differential argument marking (DAM) 46
discursively primary (vs secondary) use 35
donor language 342, 344, 346, 380
double case construction 416, 420

ellipsis 111, 300, 396
emotion predicate 19, 40, 415–426, 428–432, 434–436
enclave (linguistic) 342, 347, 357, 380
epistemic support 7–9, 40, 48–51, 54, 56, 65, 78, 81, 83–84, 92, 99, 103, 113, 137, 166, 252–253, 256–258, 274, 277, 309, 330, 334, 337, 348, 352, 357, 359–360
evaluational 34
evidential(ity) 9, 13, 34, 66–67, 97, 100, 135, 221, 224, 253, 275–276, 286, 289, 321, 442, 448
– indirect 92
– inferential 67, 92, 135
– reportive 19, 65, 67, 135, 377
exclamation 66, 296

factive 7, 19, 33–34, 40, 47–54, 56–58, 76, 80, 83, 103, 111–114, 118, 121, 142–143, 168, 182, 211–212, 220–222, 224, 232–233, 250, 274, 348, 357–358, 415, 417–419, 422, 424, 430–436, 451–453, 469
factual 7, 16, 18–19, 29, 47, 50–54, 56, 61, 76, 80–81, 83–84, 89, 98–99, 103, 112, 114, 120, 141–144, 157, 168, 214, 251, 273–277, 279–280, 286, 289, 297, 310, 320–321, 333–335, 337–338, 347–348, 352–353, 355, 357, 359–362, 365, 367–368, 370–371, 379, 444, 451–452, 466
finite(ness) 5–6, 12, 21, 62, 65–66, 68, 74–75, 79, 104–107, 111–113, 122–123, 125, 142–143, 145, 165, 170, 175, 211, 214–215, 217–219, 224, 226, 233, 235, 254, 258, 261, 263–264, 272, 277–278, 294, 322, 348–349, 352, 354, 393, 396, 443, 445, 447–448, 451, 454–456, 458, 460–462, 468
focus 17, 35, 48, 78, 102, 119, 164–165, 190, 212, 215–216, 226, 229, 232–251, 254, 264, 292, 295, 306, 320–321
– contrastive 211, 216, 226, 236–239, 241–243, 245–246, 249
– marked 78, 102, 229, 244, 255
Frascineto 342, 353–354, 356
Friuli-Venezia Giulia 343
future 7, 10, 55, 60, 65–66, 69, 72–75, 88, 93–94, 100, 108, 145, 181, 227, 253–254, 278–279, 319–320, 332–335, 337, 345, 360, 396, 417, 419, 421, 435, 464, 471
– de-obligative 353, 360, 371, 379
– in the past 353

generic 109, 160, 162, 171, 181, 192–195, 200, 205–207
gerund 75
Given Topic 227, 230
Gniva 372

habitual 48, 64, 69, 143, 181, 279, 294
head (syntactic) 16, 43–44, 46, 66, 107, 119–121, 123–124, 142, 144, 160, 164–165, 170, 175–176, 181–189, 191–197, 199, 201––207, 213–214, 216, 224–226, 231–232, 245–246, 248–249,

Subject index —— **487**

254, 258, 388, 390–396, 399, 406, 408–410, 412, 449, 451–454, 457, 459, 467–469, 471–473
historical linguistics 413
hortative 19, 66, 84, 86–87, 89, 443, 445

if-clause → clause, conditional
illocutionary force 30–31, 36, 63, 66, 79, 124, 142, 211, 214, 219–220, 224–225, 234, 273, 330, 457, 472
illocution 31, 36, 41, 46, 66, 102, 104–105, 133–134, 142
– directive 55, 88–90
imperative 66, 75, 90, 104, 214, 225, 251–253, 262, 359, 368–369, 371, 379, 405, 442–443, 445–447, 449, 450, 452, 455, 458–460, 462–465, 467–468, 470
imperfect 7, 67, 69, 84, 94, 100, 130, 135, 175, 278, 284, 348, 352–353
indirect questions 119–121, 172, 175–176, 180, 392–393, 407–410, 412–413
infinitive 5–6, 11–12, 15, 45, 59, 65, 76, 105, 107–110, 132, 143, 145, 165–166, 170, 215, 258–261, 263–264, 277, 317, 322, 326–327, 345, 348, 360–362, 369–371, 379, 390, 393–396, 407, 415, 418–423, 434, 448, 460–461, 463, 466
– embedded 76
– infinitive loss 5–6, 60, 218, 322, 326–327, 338
– short (= truncated) 74, 105, 322, 327, 338
information structure 22, 45, 70, 106, 108, 141, 236, 294
interpretive (= echoic) deontics 86, 445
intertranslatability 13
irrealis 6–7, 13–14, 16–19, 37, 40–41, 48–49, 54, 60–63, 65–66, 68–69, 71, 79–80, 83–84, 98–99, 101–102, 118, 135–136, 140–144, 167, 211, 213–214, 247, 263–264, 279, 317–321, 323, 325–326, 399–400, 415, 419–420, 434
iussive 448

juxtaposition 21, 66, 85, 416, 420–421, 434

Kosova 345

left periphery 16, 22, 211–213, 215–219, 226–227, 231, 235–238, 240, 242–243, 247, 248–251, 255, 258, 264, 458, 468, 472
loan translation 13
Luserna 380

manner 40, 43, 72, 92–94, 98–99, 104, 106, 119, 144, 277, 293
mental perception 17, 270, 274–277, 280, 284, 286, 288, 290–292, 303, 305–308, 310
metatypy 13
micro-language 342–344, 347, 357, 364, 366, 369–370, 373, 377–380
Minimalism 43
mirative 100, 104–105, 142, 216, 236
Mirror Principle 123
modal(ity) 48, 62, 132, 214–215, 218, 251–252, 254, 261, 264, 274, 323, 415, 419, 434, 444
– bouletic 40, 48
– deontic 7, 9, 40, 48, 84–85, 168, 260, 262, 353, 360, 444, 448, 459, 461, 463, 465, 468
– doxastic 38, 40, 56, 84, 256
– epistemic 7–9, 19, 34, 40, 48–51, 54–56, 66–67, 78, 81, 83–84, 86, 92, 95, 97, 99–100, 102, 109, 111, 113, 135–136, 168, 221, 224, 228, 256, 262–263, 321–322, 337, 448, 456
modal marker 218, 224, 248, 254, 261–262, 264, 442, 448, 462, 465, 470
model language 342, 344
modifier 32, 34, 48, 106, 111, 136–137, 139–140, 160, 162–163, 170–171, 180–181, 183–191, 194–195, 199–202, 204–207, 300, 450, 463
– propositional 34, 43, 67, 128–129, 135, 137–138, 141, 144
Molise 18, 342–347, 352–367, 369–380
Montecilfone 345, 353, 356
Montemitro 346, 360, 370, 374, 377, 379
mood 9–10, 16, 21, 29, 36, 46, 55, 58, 60–62, 65, 78–80, 84, 90, 101, 132–134, 140, 213–215, 219, 221, 251–258, 260, 263, 272, 278, 321, 428, 445, 447–452, 455, 457, 459, 472
– analytical mood 80

- analytical subjunctive/conditional 46, 59, 80
- indicative 139, 214, 221, 273, 278, 298
- subjunctive 167, 214, 279

NcP-construction 106
Negation 8, 47–48, 50, 55, 73, 77, 81, 98, 100–101, 169, 190, 215, 222–223, 233, 257, 270, 272–274, 279–280, 287, 293–294, 309–310, 353–354, 359–360, 391, 461
negative polarity 77
nemobilan present 62, 79
Neretva valley (Herzegovina) 346
Nominal 16, 20, 40, 47, 90, 103–104, 109–110, 112–113, 115, 118–120, 122–124, 127, 129–130, 142, 145, 161–165, 170–172, 175–176, 180, 183–184, 187–190, 193–197, 200–201, 204–206, 224, 226, 274, 302–303, 410, 416, 419–420, 471, 473
- argument-structure (= eventive) 130–131
- Complex Event 130, 161–163, 171, 181, 193–195, 199–201, 207
nominalization 31, 104, 112, 122–125, 128–129, 160–165, 167, 170–172, 175, 180, 186, 192, 194–199, 201, 205
non-finite(ness) 5–6, 15, 21, 45, 104–105, 139, 141, 214–215, 217–218, 254, 258, 261, 263–264, 298, 393, 445
non-veridical(ity) → veridical(ity)

Optative 62, 64, 66, 69, 84, 104, 142, 214, 251, 278, 327–328, 331, 359, 364–365, 368, 415, 420–421, 434–435, 443, 445, 459, 464
Oseacco 372

Parenthetical 31, 35, 131, 287
Participle 6, 104–107, 128–129, 322, 326, 345, 390, 394–396, 416, 419, 434
- *l*-participle 10, 60–63, 67–68, 73–74, 86, 449
Particle 19, 19, 22, 45, 61, 65, 79, 94–95, 132–135, 137–138, 140, 142, 191, 211, 213, 218, 226, 246–248, 254–255, 257–258, 264, 271, 274, 277, 318, 323, 326, 345, 348–350, 352–354, 359–360, 367, 371, 373, 387–388, 391–394, 397, 399–400, 403, 405–406, 420, 422–424, 434, 452–453, 463, 465, 468
- interrogative 226, 240, 244, 246–247, 350–351
- modal 17, 60, 62, 134, 211–213, 218, 226, 247, 251, 254–255, 263–264, 271, 278, 301, 323, 445, 448–449, 456, 461, 468
passive 106, 128, 290
perception 8, 17, 41, 43, 55, 81, 91–94, 96–100, 104–107, 113, 120–121, 137, 270–277, 279–280, 282–283, 287, 289–294, 296–300, 305–310, 330, 337, 395, 417, 419, 435
- immediate (=direct) 17, 43, 95–97, 107, 144, 275–277, 280, 282–285, 287, 290, 297, 303, 305–306, 308–310
- mental 17, 270, 274–277, 280, 284, 286, 288, 290–292, 303, 305–308, 310
perfect 10, 13, 67, 69, 100, 130, 135, 140, 256, 278, 282, 288, 295–296, 307, 432
permission, permissive 19, 42, 62, 84, 86, 89, 260–263, 455, 458–459, 461–463
polarity 77, 237, 239–240, 247, 249, 256
polysemy 38, 65, 342, 355–356, 365–366, 373, 374, 376, 378–379, 417
- copying 13, 18, 366, 379
predicate 4–5, 7–8, 16–17, 19–21, 29–35, 38, 40, 42–43, 45–48, 55–58, 60–61, 76, 79, 83, 86–87, 91, 96–97, 101, 104–105, 108–109, 111–113, 115, 118–121, 123, 125–126, 129, 134, 136–139, 164–165, 167–168, 171–172, 176, 196, 198, 208, 214, 220–222, 232–234, 241–242, 253, 256–257, 259–262, 264, 272–274, 277, 279–280, 290, 298–300, 309–310, 321, 348, 388, 394–396, 400, 403, 405, 415–417, 419, 421, 424–425, 428, 430, 433–435, 442–444, 449–458, 466, 468–469, 471–472
- complex 5, 9, 19, 21, 31, 41–42, 59, 69, 72–76, 84, 86, 105, 132, 140, 452, 457
- desiderative 41–42, 273, 279, 348, 419, 445, 452, 466
- dynamic 296
- manipulative 41–42, 273, 279, 455, 452, 466

- phasal 42, 273, 279
- resultative 42, 310
predicative 8, 10, 19, 31, 34, 38, 41–42, 83, 108–111, 113, 122, 125, 129, 177, 197, 261, 300, 454
predicativity 31
prepositional phrase (PP) 58, 197, 204
presupposition (logical) 8, 47, 56–57, 216, 221–223, 232, 236, 238, 242, 252
pronoun 22, 33, 76, 78, 93, 96, 113, 121, 128, 132, 164, 172, 183–185, 190, 204, 207, 303, 305–306, 323, 325–326, 355, 366, 374, 378, 400, 402–403, 420, 425, 469
- cataphoric, correlative 71, 113–115, 172
- indefinite 294, 301, 306, 388, 407–409, 412
- interrogative 18–19, 277, 350–351, 355–356, 359, 362, 364–366, 369–375, 378–380, 387–388, 393, 409
- relative 12, 21, 45, 163, 212, 356, 366, 370, 372–373, 387–388, 407, 410, 412, 466
proposition 4, 7, 9, 16, 19, 29–36, 38, 43, 47–50, 53, 55–57, 64–66, 72, 81, 83–84, 98, 112, 120, 123–124, 126–127, 135–136, 140–141, 166, 186, 214, 220–221–223, 229, 233, 239, 241, 245, 248, 252–253, 256–258, 263, 273–274, 279, 310, 317, 320, 321, 323, 330, 332, 337, 348, 357, 447, 449, 456–457, 472

question 31, 35, 119–121, 172, 175–176, 180, 213, 222–223, 238, 245, 250, 253, 256–257, 279, 296, 331, 362, 369, 376, 392–393, 407–410, 412–413, 447
- deliberative 66, 100, 102
- embedded 44, 71, 103–104, 118, 120–121, 221, 231–232, 240, 247
- particle 271, 350–351
- unselected 221, 223
- WH- 118, 120, 219, 229, 350, 359
- yes/no- 54, 221, 231, 244, 247, 351, 359, 364
quotation 31, 66
quotative 41, 387, 403, 406, 448

raising 8, 11, 21, 31, 58, 75, 77–78, 81, 123, 167, 300
- subject-to-object 44, 95, 298, 300
- subject-to-subject 95, 138

realis → irrealis
reality 12, 168, 181–182, 188, 191, 206, 276, 320, 337
reanalysis 67, 95, 135, 388, 413, 444, 467, 470, 472
relativiser 355–356, 359, 366, 369, 371–373, 378–380, 388
relativum generale 121, 423, 425, 427, 435
replica language 342, 367, 379
reported speech 62, 65, 87–89, 143, 328, 387
Resia 18, 342, 347
Role & Reference Grammar 41

San Felice (del Molise) 346, 360
San Giorgio 347, 372
Semantic Integration Hierarchy 41–43, 49, 59, 76, 78, 98, 105, 132, 142, 144
semantics 8, 22, 38, 47, 50, 56–58, 79, 83, 100, 110, 124, 126, 132, 160, 168, 186, 188, 190, 199, 205–206, 216, 222–223, 238–239, 244, 247, 253, 263–264, 270, 272–273, 284, 291, 310, 323, 326–327, 415, 419–421, 424–425, 434–435, 444, 446, 452, 455, 462
sentence 32–33, 35–36, 51, 77, 96, 101, 115, 118, 122–124, 135, 137–138, 143, 184, 186, 187, 212, 214, 222, 224, 236, 240, 252–253, 255, 263, 281, 289, 298–299, 305, 307–309, 348, 353, 357, 361
- biclausal 31, 132, 135
- complex 7, 86, 111–113, 416–417, 420, 424, 432, 434–435
- declarative 370
- embedded 235, 239
- independent 85, 105, 400, 420, 434
- indicative 281
- interrogative 350, 379
- juxtaposed 420, 435
- non-factual 359, 370, 379
similative marker 92, 118
source language 379
state of affairs (SoA) 4, 7–8, 16, 29–30, 32–34, 36, 38, 42–43, 48–50, 52–53, 71–72, 81–84, 98, 104, 112, 120, 122–123, 126–127, 135–136, 273, 321, 402, 417, 458–459, 472

Stolvizza 372
što-clauses 19, 415, 428, 431–433, 435–436
subjectification 9
subordination 21, 30, 33, 64, 66, 69, 79, 85, 105, 117, 119, 140, 224–226, 317–318, 321, 329, 337, 338, 407–409, 412, 416, 420, 424, 434–435, 469
– adverbial 73, 84, 88, 94, 106–107, 117, 143
subordinator 20, 62, 69, 90, 95, 115, 163, 224–225, 250, 317–319, 321–323, 326, 337–338, 389, 412, 430, 435
– adverbial 44, 56, 59, 88, 117
universal 423
supine 5–6, 107, 317, 322, 326–327, 332, 471
support → epistemic support

time/temporal reference 274, 276, 282
– dependent 42, 215, 219, 274, 282–283, 285, 289, 307
– independent 31, 42, 65, 223, 258, 263, 274, 283, 285, 289, 307
Tobler-Mussafia effect 75
topic 17, 44, 138, 141, 212, 215–216, 226–239, 243, 249–251, 255, 258, 264, 280
– contrastive 228–230, 238, 249, 255
– marked 70, 78, 141
topicalization 78, 227, 229, 234, 305
transitivity 19, 232, 415–416, 434–436
treebanks 19, 387–389, 395, 400, 413
triangulation 11, 18, 19, 21, 329, 343, 357

umbrella language 344, 347

valency 20, 61, 124, 451–452, 454, 469, 471, 473
validational → evaluational
verb 6, 8–10, 16–17, 19, 31, 33, 38–40, 42–43, 47, 54, 59–62, 65–66, 69–76, 79, 84–86, 90, 100–102, 105, 107–108, 110, 112–113, 118, 122–123, 125, 127–129, 131–132, 136–140, 143–145, 160–164, 166–170, 172–178, 180, 182, 188, 200, 214–215, 218–221, 232–233, 248, 250, 252–256, 258–262, 271, 274–279, 281–285, 287, 289, 291–294, 296, 298, 300, 304, 307, 309, 320–322, 328–332, 347–349, 352, 354, 358–361, 364, 377, 388–389, 391–393, 395–396, 399–400, 402–403, 405–407, 409, 412, 416, 419–420, 424, 427, 429, 435, 444–448, 450, 452, 455–463, 465–466, 468, 470–471
– illocutionary → speech act (verb)
– mental/cognitive 40, 54, 92, 435
– perception 8, 17, 33, 43, 81, 91–97, 100, 270, 272–277, 279–280, 287, 290–291, 293–294, 296–300, 305–310, 330, 335, 337, 395, 419, 435
– speech act 86, 471
veridical(ity) 8, 47, 55–56, 211, 220–223, 232–233, 247, 251–258, 264
volition(al) 40, 48, 55, 62, 83–84, 103, 114–115, 168, 330, 368, 452, 455, 458–459, 461–464

whether-clause → clause, interrogative
WH-fronting 78, 229

www.ingramcontent.com/pod-product-compliance
Lightning Source LLC
Chambersburg PA
CBHW030514230426
43665CB00010B/610